# Artificial Intelligence in Pathological Image Analysis

# Artificial Intelligence in Pathological Image Analysis

Editor

**Masayuki Tsuneki**

Basel • Beijing • Wuhan • Barcelona • Belgrade • Novi Sad • Cluj • Manchester

*Editor*
Masayuki Tsuneki
Medmain Inc., Medmain Res
Fukuoka
Japan

*Editorial Office*
MDPI AG
Grosspeteranlage 5
4052 Basel, Switzerland

This is a reprint of articles from the Special Issue published online in the open access journal *Diagnostics* (ISSN 2075-4418) (available at: https://www.mdpi.com/journal/diagnostics/special_issues/Pathological_Image).

For citation purposes, cite each article independently as indicated on the article page online and as indicated below:

Lastname, A.A.; Lastname, B.B. Article Title. *Journal Name* **Year**, *Volume Number*, Page Range.

ISBN 978-3-7258-2141-9 (Hbk)
ISBN 978-3-7258-2142-6 (PDF)
doi.org/10.3390/books978-3-7258-2142-6

© 2024 by the authors. Articles in this book are Open Access and distributed under the Creative Commons Attribution (CC BY) license. The book as a whole is distributed by MDPI under the terms and conditions of the Creative Commons Attribution-NonCommercial-NoDerivs (CC BY-NC-ND) license.

# Contents

**Masayuki Tsuneki**
Editorial on Special Issue "Artificial Intelligence in Pathological Image Analysis"
Reprinted from: *Diagnostics* 2023, 13, 828, doi:10.3390/diagnostics13050828 . . . . . . . . . . . . . 1

**Christiane Palm, Catherine E. Connolly, Regina Masser, Barbara Padberg Sgier, Eva Karamitopoulou, Quentin Simon, et al.**
Determining HER2 Status by Artificial Intelligence: An Investigation of Primary, Metastatic, and HER2 LowBreast Tumors
Reprinted from: *Diagnostics* 2023, 13, 168, doi:10.3390/diagnostics13010168 . . . . . . . . . . . . . 5

**Mohammad Faizal Ahmad Fauzi, Wan Siti Halimatul Munirah Wan Ahmad, Mohammad Fareed Jamaluddin, Jenny Tung Hiong Lee, See Yee Khor, Lai Meng Looi, et al.**
Allred Scoring of ER-IHC Stained Whole-Slide Images for Hormone Receptor Status in Breast Carcinoma
Reprinted from: *Diagnostics* 2022, 12, 3093, doi:10.3390/diagnostics12123093 . . . . . . . . . . . . 17

**Yoshimasa Kawazoe, Kiminori Shimamoto, Ryohei Yamaguchi, Issei Nakamura, Kota Yoneda, Emiko Shinohara, et al.**
Computational Pipeline for Glomerular Segmentation and Association of the Quantified Regions with Prognosis of Kidney Function in IgA Nephropathy
Reprinted from: *Diagnostics* 2022, 12, 2955, doi:10.3390/diagnostics12122955 . . . . . . . . . . . . 34

**Bennett VanBerlo, Delaney Smith, Jared Tschirhart, Blake VanBerlo, Derek Wu, Alex Ford, et al.**
Enhancing Annotation Efficiency with Machine Learning: Automated Partitioning of a Lung Ultrasound Dataset by View
Reprinted from: *Diagnostics* 2022, 12, 2351, doi:10.3390/diagnostics12102351 . . . . . . . . . . . . 54

**Gerardo Cazzato, Alessandro Massaro, Anna Colagrande, Teresa Lettini, Sebastiano Cicco, Paola Parente, et al.**
Dermatopathology of Malignant Melanoma in the Era of Artificial Intelligence: A Single Institutional Experience
Reprinted from: *Diagnostics* 2022, 12, 1972, doi:10.3390/diagnostics12081972 . . . . . . . . . . . . 72

**Maximilian Legnar, Philipp Daumke, Jürgen Hesser, Stefan Porubsky, Zoran Popovic, Jan Niklas Bindzus, et al.**
Natural Language Processing in Diagnostic Texts from Nephropathology
Reprinted from: *Diagnostics* 2022, 12, 1726, doi:10.3390/diagnostics12071726 . . . . . . . . . . . . 84

**Shima Nofallah, Beibin Li, Mojgan Mokhtari, Wenjun Wu, Stevan Knezevich, Caitlin J. May, et al.**
Improving the Diagnosis of Skin Biopsies Using Tissue Segmentation
Reprinted from: *Diagnostics* 2022, 12, 1713, doi:10.3390/diagnostics12071713 . . . . . . . . . . . . 109

**Mircea-Sebastian Șerbănescu, Raluca Maria Bungărdean, Carmen Georgiu and Maria Crișan**
Nodular and Micronodular Basal Cell Carcinoma Subtypes Are Different Tumors Based on Their Morphological Architecture and Their Interaction with the Surrounding Stroma
Reprinted from: *Diagnostics* 2022, 12, 1636, doi:10.3390/diagnostics12071636 . . . . . . . . . . . . 127

**Youngjin Park, Mujin Kim, Murtaza Ashraf, Young Sin Ko and Mun Yong Yi**
MixPatch: A New Method for Training Histopathology Image Classifiers
Reprinted from: *Diagnostics* 2022, 12, 1493, doi:10.3390/diagnostics12061493 . . . . . . . . . . . . 144

**Sabina Zurac, Cristian Mogodici, Teodor Poncu, Mihai Trăscău, Cristiana Popp, Luciana Nichita, et al.**
A New Artificial Intelligence-Based Method for Identifying Mycobacterium Tuberculosis in Ziehl–Neelsen Stain on Tissue
Reprinted from: *Diagnostics* **2022**, *12*, 1484, doi:10.3390/diagnostics12061484 . . . . . . . . . . . . . 165

**Eun Bok Baek, Ji-Hee Hwang, Heejin Park, Byoung-Seok Lee, Hwa-Young Son, Yong-Bum Kim, et al.**
Artificial Intelligence-Assisted Image Analysis of Acetaminophen-Induced Acute Hepatic Injury in Sprague-Dawley Rats
Reprinted from: *Diagnostics* **2022**, *12*, 1478, doi:10.3390/diagnostics12061478 . . . . . . . . . . . . . 193

**Kai Rakovic, Richard Colling, Lisa Browning, Monica Dolton, Margaret R. Horton, Andrew Protheroe, et al.**
The Use of Digital Pathology and Artificial Intelligence in Histopathological Diagnostic Assessment of Prostate Cancer: A Survey of Prostate Cancer UK Supporters
Reprinted from: *Diagnostics* **2022**, *12*, 1225, doi:10.3390/diagnostics12051225 . . . . . . . . . . . . . 205

**Masayuki Tsuneki, Makoto Abe, Fahdi Kanavati**
A Deep Learning Model for Prostate Adenocarcinoma Classification in Needle Biopsy Whole-Slide Images Using Transfer Learning
Reprinted from: *Diagnostics* **2022**, *12*, 768, doi:10.3390/diagnostics12030768 . . . . . . . . . . . . . . 221

**Inho Kim, Kyungmin Kang, Youngjae Song and Tae-Jung Kim**
Application of Artificial Intelligence in Pathology: Trends and Challenges
Reprinted from: *Diagnostics* **2022**, *12*, 2794, doi:10.3390/diagnostics12112794 . . . . . . . . . . . . . 238

*Editorial*

# Editorial on Special Issue "Artificial Intelligence in Pathological Image Analysis"

Masayuki Tsuneki

Medmain Research, Medmain Inc., 2-4-5-104, Akasaka, Chuo-ku, Fukuoka 810-0042, Japan; tsuneki@medmain.com; Tel.: +81-92-707-1977

The artificial intelligence (AI), especially deep learning models, is highly compatible with medical images and natural language processing and is expected to be applied to pathological image analysis and other medical fields. In routine pathological diagnosis, the histopathological and cytopathological examination of specimens is conventionally performed under a light microscope. Whole slide images (WSIs) are the digitized counterparts of the conventional glass slides obtained using specialized scanning devices. In recent years, digital pathology has been steadily introduced into clinical workflows, such as intraoperative consultations and secondary consultations. Pathology diagnosis support systems (computer-aided detection/diagnosis: CAD) using AI are useful for various classification tasks, such as histopathological subtyping, tumor grading, immunohistochemical scoring, and predictions of genetic mutation and protein expression profiles [1]. It is becoming possible to develop AI that can not only perform image classification and detection tasks, but also infer histopathological findings from images by combining pathological images with natural language. In a time of distinct paradigm shifts and novel technological innovations, it is necessary for us to establish a unified comprehension(s) of AI approaches in experimental and clinical pathology. In this Special Issue "Artificial Intelligence in Pathological Image Analysis", we collected a review and thirteen research articles in the areas of AI models in clinical and experimental pathology and computer vision in pathological image analysis. The published studies in this Special Issue provide great insights into the latest knowledge about the application of AI for pathological image analysis.

Kim et al. summarized the current trends and challenges to the application of AI in pathology [2]. In this review article, the authors described the development of computational pathology (CPATH), its applicability to AI development, and the challenges it faces, such as algorithm validation and interpretability, computing systems, reimbursement, ethics, and regulations. Further, the authors presented an overview of novel AI-based approaches that could be integrated into the pathology laboratory workflow. As the authors described, explainable AI and ethics and security issues are important topics in CPATH. To develop safe and reliable AI, the pathology community needs more clinical research and laboratory practices. This review paper provides the current research status of AI in pathology and future perspectives for successful applications.

Our research article demonstrated a deep learning model for prostate adenocarcinoma classification in core needle biopsy WSIs using transfer learning [3]. In routine clinical practice, diagnosing 12 core biopsy specimens using a microscope is time-consuming, manual process, and it is limited in terms of human resources. The authors trained deep learning models capable of classifying core needle biopsy WSIs into adenocarcinoma and benign (non-neoplastic) lesions and achieved an ROC-AUC of up to 0.978 in the core needle biopsy test sets for adenocarcinoma. Deep learning-based computational algorithms might be useful as routine histopathological diagnostic aids for prostate adenocarcinoma classification in core needle biopsy specimens.

Rakovic et al. conducted a survey of prostate cancer UK supporters for the use of digital pathology and AI in the histopathological diagnosis of prostate cancer [4]. A total

**Citation:** Tsuneki, M. Editorial on Special Issue "Artificial Intelligence in Pathological Image Analysis". *Diagnostics* **2023**, *13*, 828. https://doi.org/10.3390/diagnostics13050828

Received: 17 February 2023
Accepted: 20 February 2023
Published: 21 February 2023

**Copyright:** © 2023 by the author. Licensee MDPI, Basel, Switzerland. This article is an open access article distributed under the terms and conditions of the Creative Commons Attribution (CC BY) license (https://creativecommons.org/licenses/by/4.0/).

of 1276 responses to the online survey were analyzed. It was revealed that most of the respondents were in favor of advances in prostate cancer diagnosis by means of digital pathology and AI-assisted diagnostics as adjuncts to current clinical workflows. However, a small minority of them were not in favor of the use of AI in histopathology for reasons which are not easily addressed. Importantly, the patients are more comfortable with the overall responsibility for a histopathology report remaining with the histopathologist and relying on their decision making to use AI and integrate its findings into the final report.

Baek et al. demonstrated the AI-assisted image analysis of acetaminophen-induced acute hepatic injury in Sprague-Dawley rats [5]. The aim of this study was to apply deep learning models for the assessment of toxicological pathology in a non-clinical study. Authors trained the model for various hepatic lesions, including necrosis, inflammation, infiltration, and portal triad at the WSI level. The deep learning model achieved an overall model accuracy of 96.44%. Importantly, the model predicted lesions of portal triad, necrosis, and inflammation with high correlations with annotated lesions by toxicologic pathologists. This study suggested that the deep learning algorithm (Mask R-CNN algorithm) can be applied to implement diagnosis and prediction of hepatic lesions in toxicological pathology.

Zurac et al. developed the AI-based method for identifying mycobacterium tuberculosis in Ziehl–Neelsen-stained tissue specimen WSIs [6]. In routine histopathological diagnosis, detecting mycobacterium tuberculosis in Ziehl–Neelsen-stained slides is difficult and time consuming because of the bacillus size. The developed deep learning model achieved an ROC-AUC of 0.977, an accuracy of 98.33%, a sensitivity of 95.65%, and a specificity of 100% for identifying mycobacterium tuberculosis bacilli on WSIs, which were better than or similar to those data of a team of pathologists who manually inspected slides and WSIs. By using the developed deep learning algorithm, the pathologists saved at least one-third of the total examining time.

Park et al. proposed a new training method called MixPatch, which was designed to improve a CNN-based classifier by specifically addressing the prediction uncertainty problem and examine its effectiveness at improving the diagnosis performance in the context of histopathological image analysis [7]. MixPatch generates and uses a new subtraining dataset, which consists of mixed patches and their pre-defined ground-truth labels. Importantly, by specifically considering the mixed region variation characteristics of the histopathology images, MixPatch augments the extant mixed image methods for medical image analysis, in which the prediction uncertainty is a crucial issue. MixPatch provides a new way to systematically alleviate the overconfidence problem of CNN-based classifiers and improve their prediction accuracy, contributing toward more calibrated and reliable histopathology image analysis.

Serbanescu et al. demonstrated the morphological difference between nodular (low-risk subtype) and micronodular (high-risk subtype) basal cell carcinomas using a classical morphometric approach (a gray-level co-occurrence matrix and histogram analysis) and a deep learning semantic segmentation approach [8]. The authors identified distinct pathological patterns of the tumor component in random fields of the tumor island that did not contain peripheral palisading. They demonstrated that the most significant difference between the morphology of the two (nodular and micronodular) subtypes was represented by the peritumoral cleft component. Importantly, the deep learning semantic segmentation approach provided new insight into the morphologies of nodular and micronodular subtypes of basal cell carcinoma.

Nofallah et al. demonstrated the potential application of the semantic segmentation of clinically important tissue structures for improving the diagnosis of skin biopsy WSIs [9]. It has been revealed that including a clinically important tissue structure along with WSIs improves the learning of the model, especially in challenging diagnostic classes, such as melanoma in situ and invasive melanoma (T1a). The model showed a 6% improvement in the F-score when whole slide images were used along with epidermal nests and cancerous dermal nest segmentation masks compared to that which was achieved using WSIs alone in training and testing the diagnosis pipeline. Importantly, comparing scores with

187 pathologists' performance on the same test set showed that the model can outperform or have comparable performance in the cases with the aforementioned diagnostic classes.

Legnar et al. investigated the possibility to predict a final diagnosis based on a written neuropathological description using various natural language processing (NLP) methods [10]. Certain diagnoses or groups of diagnoses (e.g., amyloid-deposition-associated diseases) could be predicted very well; however, in several cases, the morphological description was apparently not sufficient to make accurate predictions. This is because some diagnoses are associated with one pattern, but for others, there is a complex pattern combination which makes the prediction difficult without patho-physiological knowledge. Overall, it has been revealed that the morphological description texts, used as a surrogate for image analysis, enable the correct diagnosis to be achieved for some entities.

Cazzato et al. trained the fast random forest (FRF) algorithm to be able to support the specialist to automatically highlight the anomalous pixel regions and to estimate a possible risk by quantifying the percentage of these regions with atypical morphological features starting from routine histopathological images [11]. An important tool for melanoma diagnosis is the probability image estimated by the processed FRF output image. The probability image is useful to discriminate between information about ambiguous lesions. The FRF algorithm proved to be successful, with a discordance of 17% with respect to the results of the dermatopathologist, meaning that this type of supervised algorithm to can help the dermatopathologist in achieving the challenging diagnosis of malignant melanoma.

VanBerlo et al. developed a deep learning solution for automatic lung ultrasound view annotation that effectively improves the efficiency of downstream annotation tasks, which can distinguish between parenchymal and pleural lung ultrasound views with 92.5% accuracy [12]. The automatic partitioning of a 780 clip lung ultrasound dataset by view led to a 42 min reduction of the downstream manual annotation time and resulted in the production of $55 \pm 6$ extra relevant labels per hour. This deep learning-based automated tool considerably improved the annotation efficiency, resulting in a higher throughput relevant to the annotating task at hand, which can be applied to other unannotated datasets to save considerable manual annotation time and effort.

Kawazoe et al. demonstrated an automated computational pipeline to detect glomeruli and to segment the histopathological regions inside of the glomerulus in a WSI [13]. The computational pipeline automatically detects glomeruli on PAS-stained WSIs, followed by segmenting the Bowman's space, the glomerular tuft, the crescentic, and the sclerotic region inside of the glomeruli. To predict the estimated glomerular filtration rate (eGFR) in cases of immunoglobulin A nephropathy (IgAN), it is important to quantify the sclerotic region using the developed pipeline. Importantly, the developed automated computational pipeline could aid in diagnosing renal pathology by visualizing and quantifying the histopathological feature of the glomerulus and potentially accelerate the research in order to better understand the prognosis of IgAN.

Fauzi et al. demonstrated a cell detection and classification system based on a deep learning model for use with the Allred scoring system for breast carcinoma hormone receptor status testing [14]. The computational pipeline first detects all of the cells within the specific regions and classifies them into negatively, weakly, moderately, and strongly stained ones, followed by Allred scoring for the estrogen receptor (ER) status evaluation on WSIs. The automated Allred scores matches well with pathologists' scores for both the actual Allred score and hormonal treatment cases. The proposed system can automate the exhaustive exercise to provide fast and reliable assistance to pathologists and medical personnel.

Palm et al. examined the performance of a digitalized and artificial intelligence (AI)-assisted workflow for HER2 status determination in accordance with the American Society of Clinical Oncology (ASCO)/College of Pathologists (CAP) guidelines [15]. The HER2 4B5 algorithm in the uPath enterprise software and the HER2 Dual ISH image analysis algorithm (Roche Diagnostic International, Rotkreuz, Switzerland) were used in this study. The authors demonstrated the feasibility of a combined HER2 IHC and ISH AI workflow in the primary and metastatic breast cancers, with a Cohen's κ of 0.94 when it was assessed in accordance with the ASCO/CAP recommendations.

In summary, in this Special Issue, there are wide varieties of valuable scientific papers including a review article and papers on deep learning models in pathological applications, human and toxicological pathology, and various methodologies. AI-based computational algorithms, including deep learning models, are taking digital pathology beyond mere digitization and telepathology [1]. The incorporation of AI-based computer vision and natural language processing algorithms in routine clinical workflows is on the horizon, reducing processing time and increasing the detection rate of anomalies [1]. It is necessary to continue to share the latest findings and updated methodologies in "Artificial Intelligence in Pathological Image Analysis" and continue to conduct valuable research.

**Funding:** This research received no external funding.

**Conflicts of Interest:** M.T. is the employee of Medmain Inc.

## References

1. Tsuneki, M. Deep learning models in medical image analysis. *J. Oral Biosci.* **2022**, *64*, 312–320. [CrossRef] [PubMed]
2. Kim, I.; Kang, K.; Song, Y.; Kim, T.J. Application of Artificial Intelligence in Pathology: Trends and Challenges. *Diagnostics* **2022**, *12*, 2794. [CrossRef] [PubMed]
3. Tsuneki, M.; Abe, M.; Kanavati, F. A Deep Learning Model for Prostate Adenocarcinoma Classification in Needle Biopsy Whole-Slide Images Using Transfer Learning. *Diagnostics* **2022**, *12*, 768. [CrossRef] [PubMed]
4. Rakovic, K.; Colling, R.; Browing, L.; Dolton, M.; Horton, M.R.; Protheroe, A.; Lamb, A.D.; Bryant, R.J.; Scheffer, R.; Crofts, J.; et al. The Use of Digital Pathology and Artificial Intelligence in Histopathological Diagnostic Assessment of Prostate Cancer: A Survey of Prostate Cancer UK Supporters. *Diagnostics* **2022**, *12*, 1225. [CrossRef] [PubMed]
5. Baek, E.B.; Hwang, J.H.; Park, H.; Lee, B.S.; Son, H.Y.; Kim, Y.B.; Jun, S.Y.; Her, J.; Lee, J.; Cho, J.W. Artificial Intelligence-Assisted Image Analysis of Acetaminophen-Induced Acute Hepatic Injury in Sprague-Dawley Rats. *Diagnostics* **2022**, *12*, 1478. [CrossRef] [PubMed]
6. Zurac, S.; Mogodici, C.; Poncu, T.; Trascau, M.; Popp, C.; Nichita, L.; Cioplea, M.; Ceachi, B.; Sticlaru, L.; Cioroianu, A.; et al. A New Artificial Intelligence-Based Method for Identifying Mycobacterium Tuberculosis in Ziehl–Neelsen Stain on Tissue. *Diagnostics* **2022**, *12*, 1484. [CrossRef] [PubMed]
7. Park, Y.; Kim, M.; Ashraf, M.; Ko, Y.S.; Yi, M.Y. MixPatch: A New Method for Training Histopathology Image Classifiers. *Diagnostics* **2022**, *12*, 1493. [CrossRef] [PubMed]
8. Serbanescu, M.S.; Bungardean, R.M.; Georgiu, C.; Crisan, M. Nodular and Micronodular Basal Cell Carcinoma Subtypes Are Different Tumors Based on Their Morphological Architecture and Their Interaction with the Surrounding Stroma. *Diagnostics* **2022**, *12*, 1636. [CrossRef]
9. Nofallah, S.; Li, B.; Mokhtari, M.; Wu, W.; Knezevich, S.; May, C.J.; Chang, O.H.; Elmore, J.G.; Shapiro, L.G. Improving the Diagnosis of Skin Biopsies Using Tissue Segmentation. *Diagnostics* **2022**, *12*, 1713. [CrossRef] [PubMed]
10. Legnar, M.; Daumke, P.; Hesser, J.; Porubsky, S.; Popovic, Z.; Bindzus, J.N.; Siemoneit, J.H.H.; Weis, C.A. Natural Language Processing in Diagnostic Texts from Nephropathology. *Diagnostics* **2022**, *12*, 1726. [CrossRef] [PubMed]
11. Cazzato, G.; Massaro, A.; Colagrande, A.; Lettini, T.; Cicco, S.; Parente, P.; Nacchiero, E.; Lospalluti, L.; Cascardi, E.; Giudice, G.; et al. Dermatopathology of Malignant Melanoma in the Era of Artificial Intelligence: A Single Institutional Experience. *Diagnostics* **2022**, *12*, 1972. [CrossRef] [PubMed]
12. VanBerlo, B.; Smith, D.; Tschirhart, J.; VanBerlo, B.; Wu, D.; Ford, A.; McCauley, J.; Wu, B.; Chaudhary, R.; Dave, C.; et al. Enhancing Annotation Efficiency with Machine Learning: Automated Partitioning of a Lung Ultrasound Dataset by View. *Diagnostics* **2022**, *12*, 2351. [CrossRef]
13. Kawazoe, Y.; Shimamoto, K.; Yamaguchi, R.; Nakamura, I.; Yoneda, K.; Shinohara, E.; SHintani-Domoto, Y.; Ushiku, T.; Tsukamoto, T.; Ohe, K. Computational Pipeline for Glomerular Segmentation and Association of the Quantified Regions with Prognosis of Kidney Function in IgA Nephropathy. *Diagnostics* **2022**, *12*, 2955. [CrossRef] [PubMed]
14. Fauzi, M.F.A.; Ahmad, W.S.H.M.W.; Jamaluddin, M.F.; Lee, J.T.H.; Khor, S.Y.; Looi, L.M.; Abas, F.S.; Aldahoul, N. Allred Scoring of ER-IHC Stained Whole-Slide Images for Hormone Receptor Status in Breast Carcinoma. *Diagnostics* **2022**, *12*, 3093. [CrossRef] [PubMed]
15. Palm, C.; Connolly, C.E.; Masser, R.; Sgier, B.P.; Karamitopoulou, E.; Simon, Q.; Bode, B.; Tinguely, M. Determining HER2 Status by Artificial Intelligence: An Investigation of Primary, Metastatic, and HER2 Low Breast Tumors. *Diagnostics* **2023**, *13*, 168. [CrossRef] [PubMed]

**Disclaimer/Publisher's Note:** The statements, opinions and data contained in all publications are solely those of the individual author(s) and contributor(s) and not of MDPI and/or the editor(s). MDPI and/or the editor(s) disclaim responsibility for any injury to people or property resulting from any ideas, methods, instructions or products referred to in the content.

Article

# Determining HER2 Status by Artificial Intelligence: An Investigation of Primary, Metastatic, and HER2 Low Breast Tumors

Christiane Palm [1,2], Catherine E. Connolly [1,*], Regina Masser [1], Barbara Padberg Sgier [1], Eva Karamitopoulou [1], Quentin Simon [1], Beata Bode [1,2] and Marianne Tinguely [1,2]

[1] Pathologie Institute Enge, 8005 Zurich, Switzerland
[2] Faculty of Medicine, University of Zurich, 8006 Zurich, Switzerland
* Correspondence: catherine.connolly@patho.ch

**Abstract:** The expression of human epidermal growth factor receptor 2 (HER2) protein or gene transcripts is critical for therapeutic decision making in breast cancer. We examined the performance of a digitalized and artificial intelligence (AI)-assisted workflow for HER2 status determination in accordance with the American Society of Clinical Oncology (ASCO)/College of Pathologists (CAP) guidelines. Our preliminary cohort consisted of 495 primary breast carcinomas, and our study cohort included 67 primary breast carcinomas and 30 metastatic deposits, which were evaluated for HER2 status by immunohistochemistry (IHC) and in situ hybridization (ISH). Three practicing breast pathologists independently assessed and scored slides, building the ground truth. Following a washout period, pathologists were provided with the results of the AI digital image analysis (DIA) and asked to reassess the slides. Both rounds of assessment from the pathologists were compared to the AI results and ground truth for each slide. We observed an overall HER2 positivity rate of 15% in our study cohort. *Moderate* agreement (Cohen's κ 0.59) was observed between the ground truth and AI on IHC, with most discrepancies occurring between 0 and 1+ scores. Inter-observer agreement amongst pathologists was *substantial* (Fleiss´ κ 0.77) and pathologists' agreement with AI scores was 80.6%. *Substantial* agreement of the AI with the ground truth (Cohen´s κ 0.80) was detected on ISH-stained slides, and the accuracy of AI was similar for the primary and metastatic tumors. We demonstrated the feasibility of a combined HER2 IHC and ISH AI workflow, with a Cohen's κ of 0.94 when assessed in accordance with the ASCO/CAP recommendations.

**Keywords:** HER2 immunohistochemistry; HER2 in situ hybridization; artificial intelligence; digital pathology; breast carcinoma

## 1. Introduction

Approximately 15–20% of newly diagnosed invasive breast cancers (IBC) overexpress the human epidermal growth factor receptor 2 (HER2) oncogene, which is associated with increased tumor progression and metastasis [1–3]. Since HER2 positive tumors can be targeted with medical therapies, a reliable method is necessary to determine the HER2 status on both primary and metastatic breast tumors [4,5]. The standard diagnostic workflow involves immunohistochemistry (IHC) and in situ hybridization (ISH) methods with manual assessment by pathologists. According to the 2018 American Society of Clinical Oncology (ASCO)/College of American Pathologists (CAP) guidelines, both completeness and intensity of HER2 membrane staining must be evaluated to determine the HER2 status on IHC-stained slides [6]. However, the visual assessment of stained slides is subject to inter-pathologist variability, and unusual or heterogeneous staining patterns often present diagnostic challenges [7,8]. Therefore, pathologists may strategically assess relatively more cases as score 2+, in order to defer them for ISH testing, which, although more conclusive in determining HER2 positive and negative cases in the IHC 2+ cohort, is significantly more cost- and labor-intensive [9].

Recent and emerging evidence provides a strong case for moving away from the dichotomous 'positive' or 'negative' reporting of HER2 status, in favor of identifying a category of IBC with a low HER2 status as they demonstrate a response to new anti-HER2 antibody-conjugate therapy. According to the recently published DESTINY-Breast 04 trial results, HER2 low tumors were defined as a score of 1+ on IHC or 2+ on IHC with a negative ISH result, and this cohort of patients demonstrated significantly longer progression-free and overall survival when treated with trastuzumab deruxtecan in comparison to chemotherapy [10]. Currently, the DAISY trial is now underway and seeks to further investigate the efficacy of this drug in three cohorts: HER2 overexpressing (HER2 IHC 3+ or IHC 2+ with positive ISH) vs. HER2 low-expressing (IHC 1+ or IHC 2+ with negative ISH) vs. HER2 non-expressing (IHC 0) [11]. Therefore, the ability of pathologists to accurately classify HER2 IHC scores and interpret ISH in a standardized manner, with minimal inter-observer variability, is of upmost priority.

Technological advances, specifically in the field of artificial intelligence (AI) and digital image analysis (DIA), offer the added potential to minimize inter- and intra-pathologist variability in the scoring process by offering an objective comparative value [12–19]. Several studies have analyzed the potential role of AI in determining the HER2 status and DIA has been acknowledged as a possible diagnostic modality in the current ASCO/CAP guidelines. However, to our knowledge, no research has been published on the AI-assisted assessment of HER2 status, incorporating both the IHC and ISH methods into a complete workflow. Since both IHC and ISH supplement each other in the diagnostic process of determining HER2 status, and are described in this way in the ASCO/CAP guidelines, we aimed to investigate whether an approach that incorporates algorithms for both methods could offer the chance of a more effective and objective diagnosis [6]. Additionally, no studies were identified in the literature that assesses the performance of AI on metastatic or HER2 low breast tumors. Therefore, we sought to evaluate a novel AI-assisted workflow including both IHC and ISH for determining the HER2 status of primary and metastatic breast cancer.

## 2. Materials and Methods

### 2.1. Setting and Ethics

This study was conducted at Pathologie Institut Enge AG, Switzerland, and was approved by the Ethics Committee of the Canton of Zurich (BASEC-Nr.: 2021-00210).

### 2.2. Cohort Selection, Tissue Staining and Interpretation

Core needle biopsies (CNB) of 495 newly diagnosed primary IBCs (category B5b) and 30 metastatic breast carcinomas consecutively diagnosed at our institute throughout 2020 were identified using the institutional lab informatics system (PathoWin+, Basys Data, Basel, Switzerland). Existing IHC slides for all primary breast carcinoma cases in 2020 were retrieved, digitalized, and analyzed (see the method in Section 2.3) as a preliminary cohort. For further analyses, we included all 30 metastatic tumors and their matched primaries and a further random selection of primary tumors from the preliminary cohort (total study cohort, $n$ = 97). The 2 µm (IHC) and 4 µm (ISH) sections were newly cut from routinely processed formalin-fixed paraffin embedded tissues and mounted on TOMO Adhesion Microscope Slides (Matsunami Glass, Japan). Both IHC and ISH were performed using the Ventana BenchMark ULTRA automated slide stainer with the Ultraview Detection Kit (Roche Diagnostic International, Rotkreuz, Switzerland). IHC and ISH were performed in accordance with the vendor's package insert protocols using the VENTANA anti-HER2/neu (4B5) rabbit monoclonal primary antibody and VENTANA HER2 Dual ISH DNA Probe Cocktail Assay, respectively (Roche Diagnostic International, Rotkreuz, Switzerland). ISH was performed on 55/97 samples, corresponding to all cases with an IHC HER2 score of $\geq$1+. Both IHC and ISH were interpreted according to the 2018

ASCO/CAP guidelines and HER2 low tumors were defined as IHC 1+ or IHC 2+ with negative ISH (Figure 1a) [6,10].

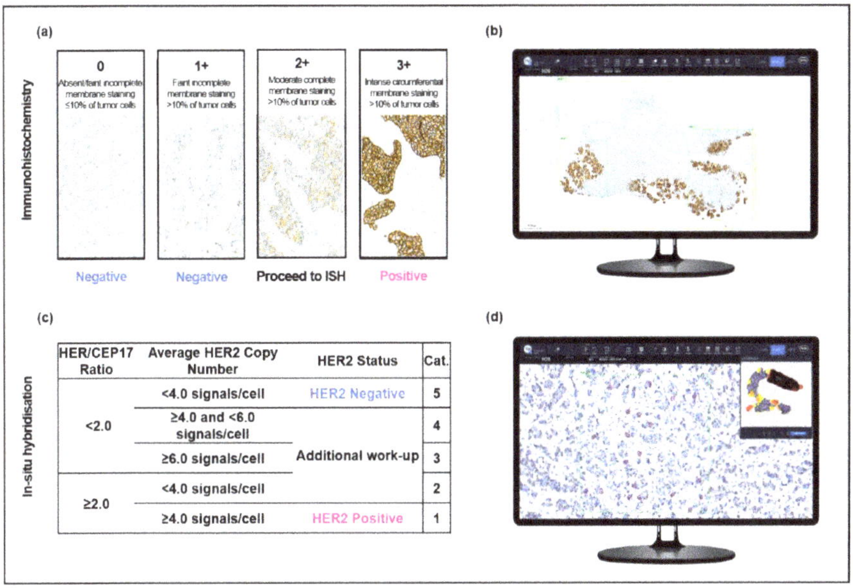

**Figure 1.** Overview of the study protocol for HER2 evaluation. Pathologists performed manual, light microscopic evaluation of HER2 (**a**) immunohistochemistry and (**c**) in situ hybridization in accordance with the 2018 ASCO/CAP guidelines. Slides were also analyzed with the support of two AI algorithms: AI-assisted immunohistochemistry analysis (**b**) was performed by placing three regions of interest (green) over tumor tissue and (**d**) AI-assisted in situ hybridization was analyzed by selecting a region of interest (green) within an area of high HER2 expression, as indicated by the heatmap (upper right). Within the region of interest, the algorithm calculated the HER2 and CEP17 signals for 20 cells (red).

*2.3. AI Analysis of Immunohistochemistry Slides*

IHC slides were digitalized using a VENTANA DP200 (Roche Diagnostic International, Rotkreuz, Switzerland) and analyzed using the HER2 4B5 algorithm in the uPath enterprise software (Roche Diagnostic International, Rotkreuz, Switzerland). Three regions of interest (ROI) were selected per slide: two smaller ROIs were placed over separate areas with at least 100 tumor cells ("area 1" and "area 2"), and a large ROI was placed over all tumor tissue on the slide ("area 3"). The mean score of these three areas was calculated and taken to represent the AI-determined HER2 IHC score (Figure 1b). This method was developed in order to minimize ROI- and user-dependent factors in the AI evaluation.

*2.4. AI Analysis of In Situ Hybridization Slides*

ISH slides were digitalized using the VENTANA DP200 and analyzed using the HER2 Dual ISH image analysis algorithm (Roche Diagnostic International, Rotkreuz, Switzerland). The algorithm enables the selection of one ROI, which is aided by a heatmap overlay highlighting areas of the slide with the highest HER2 expression (Figure 1d). Within the selected ROI, the algorithm identifies 20 cells with the highest HER2 amplification, provides HER2 and CEP17 counts for each cell, and calculates the ratio. As our aim was to understand the performance of an AI image analysis protocol for HER2 status determination, the manual correction features in both the IHC and ISH algorithms were not used.

## 2.5. Manual Assessment of Slides

To compare the pathologists' assessments to the AI results, three pathologists were asked to independently assess the IHC slides by light microscopy as they would in routine diagnostics (Group: "Pathologists"). Following a minimum washout period of 2 weeks, they were provided with the AI results and asked to re-evaluate the IHC slides per microscope (Group: "AI-assisted Pathologists"). The ground truth for the IHC results was defined as the consensus score reached by the three pathologists for each case. The ground truth for the ISH results was determined by a single pathologist counting the HER2 signals per cell and the HER2/CEP17 ratio for 20 cells. Area selection was performed following a review of the ISH slide and paired IHC slide to determine potential areas of HER2 amplification. For equivocal results, a second pathologist recounted the ISH signals of 20 cells, and diagnoses were allocated in accordance with the 2018 ASCO/CAP guidelines [6].

## 2.6. Statistical Analysis

To assess the accuracy and compare the assessments by AI and pathologists to our defined ground truth, we calculated the Cohen's κ. Inter-observer variability was measured with Fleiss' κ. The interpretation of agreement was performed according to Landis and Koch: κ-values 0.01–0.20 = slight agreement, 0.21–0.40 = fair agreement, 0.41–0.60 = moderate agreement, 0.61–0.8 = substantial agreement, 0.81–1.0 = almost perfect agreement [20]. The sensitivity and specificity values were calculated for each diagnostic step in HER2 status determination including the overall workflow and our level of significance was set at $p < 0.05$. To assess the significance of difference in kappa between observations, two-sided pairwise t-tests were performed. The Pearson Chi2 test was used to compare the agreement levels and their significance. Statistical calculations were performed using IBM software SPSS Version 27 and Microsoft Excel.

## 3. Results

### 3.1. Clinicopathological Features

During 2020, there were 495 cases of B5b IBC diagnosed at our institute, and all cases were included in our preliminary cohort (Table 1). The average age of patients was 61 years (range 29–95 years), and all but two were women. The most prevalent tumor type was invasive carcinoma of no special type (80%) and our estrogen receptor (ER), progesterone receptor (PR), and HER2 positivity rates were 85%, 75%, and 12%, respectively. The distribution of tumor grading included: 23% grade 1, 48% grade 2, and 29% grade 3. There were 97 CNBs (67 primary breast tumors, 30 metastases) included in our study cohort for further analyses. All tissue samples of this cohort were from women and the mean age of the study cohort was 60 years (range 30–80 years). The majority of primary tumors were invasive carcinoma of no special type (82%), and most tumors were classified as grade 2 (45%), followed by grade 3 (42%) and grade 1 (14%). ER was positive in 87% and PR in 78%. The reported HER2 positivity rate was 15%. At the time of original diagnosis, 20 tumors were investigated with ISH for HER2 status determination in addition to routine IHC. Metastatic sites included lymph nodes ($n = 22$) and liver ($n = 8$), and the mean size of the metastatic lymph node deposits was 4.99 mm (range 0.3–12 mm).

### 3.2. Preliminary Cohort

From our preliminary cohort of 495 cases of B5b primary invasive breast carcinoma, we retrieved a total of 475 IHC slides with adequate tissue and staining for digitalization and analysis. The remaining 20 slides were excluded as they were not suitable for further analysis. The IHC scoring distribution according to manual assessment by pathologists included 181 cases as IHC score 0 (38.1%), 156 cases as 1+ (32.8%), 87 cases as 2+ (18.3%), and 51 cases as 3+ (10.7%). In contrast, the AI-IHC algorithm identified 22 cases as 0 (4.6%), 137 cases as 1+ (28.8%), 254 cases as 2+ (53.5%), and 62 cases as 3+ (13.1%). In total, we observed only 182/475 concordant cases (38.3%) between the AI and pathologists, and the AI overestimated the number of 2+ cases in comparison to the pathologists (254 cases vs.

87 cases). In 184/475 cases (38.7%), the discordance observed in scoring would lead to significant consequences such as the inclusion or omission of HER2 ISH testing, or a change in the tumors' HER2 status. Following analysis of our preliminary cohort and discussions with the vendor, we identified deviations in our round robin tested laboratory HER2 IHC staining protocol in comparison with the vendor's recommended protocol for use with the AI software. Consequently, we made changes to our total Ultra Cell Conditioning Solution (CC1) incubation time (172 min to 56 min), antibody incubation time (24 min to 12 min), and counterstaining time (8 min to 4 min) to conform to the vendor's recommendations. New sections were prepared from the FFPE tissue for our study cohort ($n = 97$) and were stained according to the adjusted protocol, with the results shown in Sections 3.3–3.7. We observed an overall improvement in concordance between the AI and manual assessment in our study cohort primary tumors ($n = 67$), with 77.6% of cases showing full concordance, and only 4.5% showing discordance with diagnostic consequence. There were 57 cases that were part of both our preliminary and study cohorts and the comparative results using our laboratory and amended staining protocols are presented in Supplementary Table S1.

**Table 1.** Overview of the clinicopathological features for the preliminary ($n = 495$) and study ($n = 97$) cohorts. Tumor data for the study cohort pertain to the 67 primary tumors.

|  | Preliminary Cohort | Study Cohort |
| --- | --- | --- |
| No. of Cases | 495 | 97 (67 *) |
| Average Patient Age, yrs | 61 | 60 |
| Range | 29–95 | 30–80 |
| Tumor Type, No. (%) |  |  |
| Ductal | 394 (80) | 55 (82) |
| Lobular | 75 (15) | 6 (9) |
| Other | 26 (5) | 6 (9) |
| Tumor Grade, No. (%) |  |  |
| 1 | 112 (23) | 9 (14) |
| 2 | 237 (48) | 30 (45) |
| 3 | 146 (29) | 28 (42) |
| ER positive, No. (%) | 421 (85) | 58 (87) |
| PR positive, No. (%) | 371 (75) | 52 (78) |
| HER2 positive, No. (%) | 59 (12) | 10 (15) |

* 67 were primary tumors, and clinicopathological data pertains only to primaries.

### 3.3. Primary B5b IBC: Immunohistochemistry

In our study cohort, the AI-IHC algorithm had moderate concordance with the ground truth (Cohen's κ 0.59, 95% CI 0.43–0.75). When pathologists were asked to score the IHC slides with the assistance of AI, the "AI-assisted Pathologists" concordance with the ground truth was almost perfect (Cohen's κ 0.89, 95% CI 0.77–1.0), with individual concordance rates of Cohen's κ 0.71, 0.71, and 0.61. The greatest discrepancies in scoring between "Pathologists" and AI occurred on the IHC slides with a ground truth score of 0 (Figure 2). When the "Pathologists" were provided with the AI results, their overall agreement with the algorithm's findings increased by 9% (71.6% vs. 80.6%), indicating that pathologists were likely to adjust their assessment to match that of the algorithm.

We observed substantial inter-observer agreement in the assessment of the IHC slides within the groups "Pathologists" (Fleiss κ 0.77, 95% CI 0.68–0.86) and "AI-assisted Pathologists" (Fleiss κ 0.74, 95% CI 0.65–0.82). As shown in Figure 3, inter-observer agreement was highest for cases rated as score 3+ (Fleiss κ 0.89, 95% CI 0.75–1.0) and lowest for cases assessed as 1+ (Fleiss κ 0.63, 95% CI 0.50–0.77).

**Figure 2.** Heatmap representation of HER2 scoring for primary B5b invasive breast carcinomas. IHC scores (0, 1, 2, 3) are shown for Pathologists, AI-assisted Pathologists, and AI in comparison to the ground truth. ISH was designated as negative (−), positive (+), or requiring further assessment (+/−).

### 3.4. Primary B5b IBC: In Situ Hybridization

A total of 26/67 cases, corresponding to all cases with an IHC HER2 consensus score of 1+ or above, were evaluated by ISH. Concordant results were noted between AI and the ground truth HER2 status in 25/26 cases, and AI demonstrated almost perfect accuracy (Cohen's κ 0.92, 95% CI 0.77–1.0). The AI-ISH algorithm classified eight cases into categories 2, 3, or 4 (Figure 1c). As per the ASCO/CAP guidelines, seven of these would be considered negative following the inclusion of their IHC 1+ scores, and one would require a second observer to count 20 cells on the ISH slide, as the IHC score was 2+. AI-recounts were not performed, therefore, our discordant case is depicted as +/− in Figure 2. Notably, the AI-ISH algorithm occasionally assigned unexpectedly high HER2 counts of up to 74 signs/cell and HER2/CEP17 ratios of up to 15, and on average, the AI counts amounted to over three times that from the Pathologists (Figure 4). However, the tendency of AI to provide exaggerated counts did not significantly affect the outcomes, with only one negative case being upgraded by the AI, and as per the ASCO/CAP guidelines, this case would require reassessment by ISH.

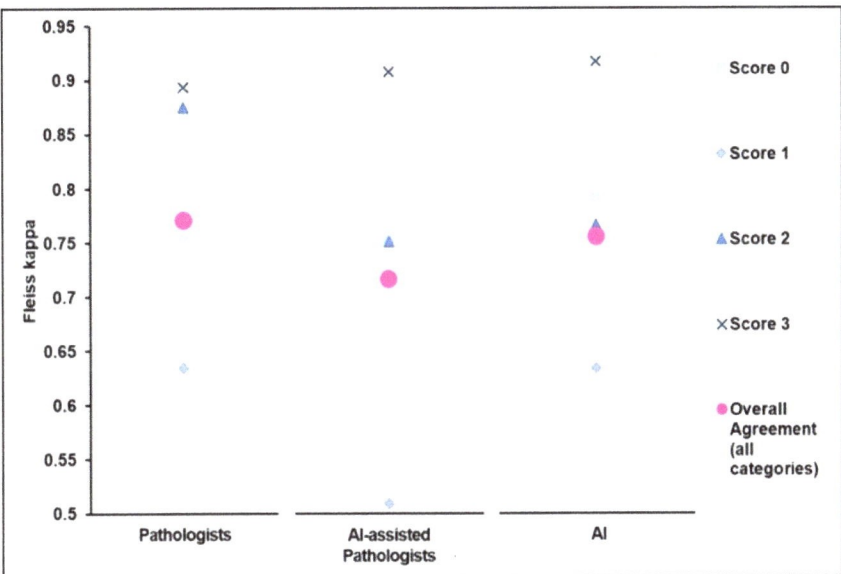

**Figure 3.** Evaluation of inter-observer agreement. Fleiss' kappa for the measurement of inter-observer agreement amongst Pathologists, AI-assisted Pathologists, and AI on the IHC-stained slides. Agreement is presented for each IHC score and combined.

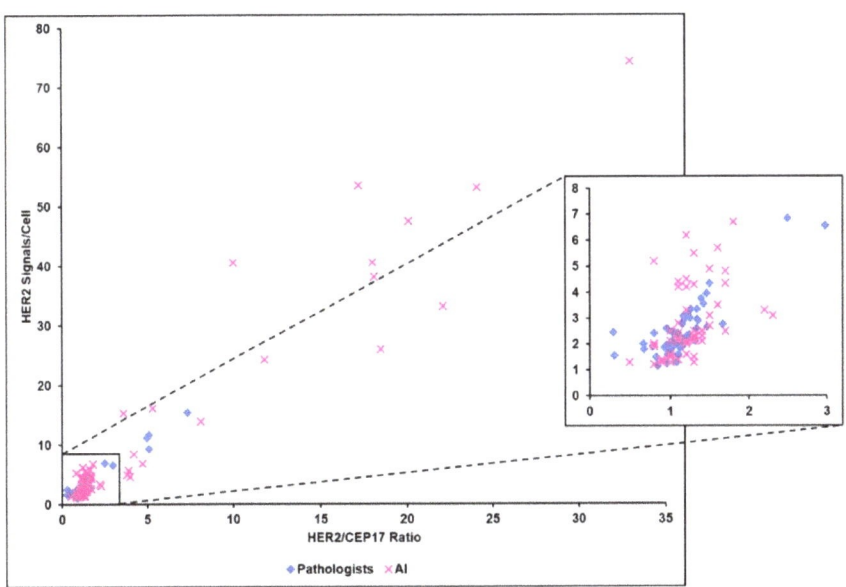

**Figure 4.** Comparison of the calculated HER2/CEP17 ratio and the HER2 signals/cell between Pathologists and AI-assisted DIA on the ISH-stained slides.

## 3.5. Primary B5b IBC: HER2 Low Tumors

According to our defined ground truth, the study cohort contained 16 HER2 low tumors. For this group, the level of concordance between the AI and the ground truth was moderate (Cohen's κ 0.54, 95% CI 0.19–0.90). However, the AI classified 20 tumors as IHC 1+ and seven tumors as IHC 2+/ISH negative, totaling 27 HER2 low tumors and increasing our proportion of HER2 low tumors by 16%. For our ground truth HER2 low tumors, we observed substantial inter-observer agreement in classification amongst Pathologists (Fleiss κ 0.78, 95% CI 0.55–1.0), which was slightly lower, but remained substantial, in the "AI-assisted Pathologists" group (Fleiss κ 0.61, 95% CI 0.40–0.81).

## 3.6. Primary B5b IBC: Metastatic Breast Cancer

For our cohort of 30 metastatic breast cancers, the accuracies of both the AI algorithms for IHC (Cohen's κ 0.43, 95% CI 0.25–0.61) and ISH (Cohen's κ 0.52, 95% CI 0.08–0.97) were moderate. The IHC algorithm performed slightly better on metastatic tumors (25/30 cases, Cohen's κ 0.48, 95% CI 0.24–0.73) compared to their matched primary tumors (20/30 cases, Cohen's κ 0.36, 95% CI 0.07–0.64) (Figure 5). Conversely, inter-observer agreement on IHC scoring between Pathologists was 4% higher on primary tumors compared to metastatic deposits (Fleiss' κ primary 0.77 vs. metastatic 0.73). Of the 25 cases that underwent ISH assessment, three were positive according to the pathologist and six were positive according to AI. A conversion of HER2 status between the primary and metastatic lesions was observed in 1/30 cases, which was confirmed by both pathologists and AI with both IHC and ISH. A significant difference in the evaluation of metastatic tissue between the liver and lymph node sites was not observed.

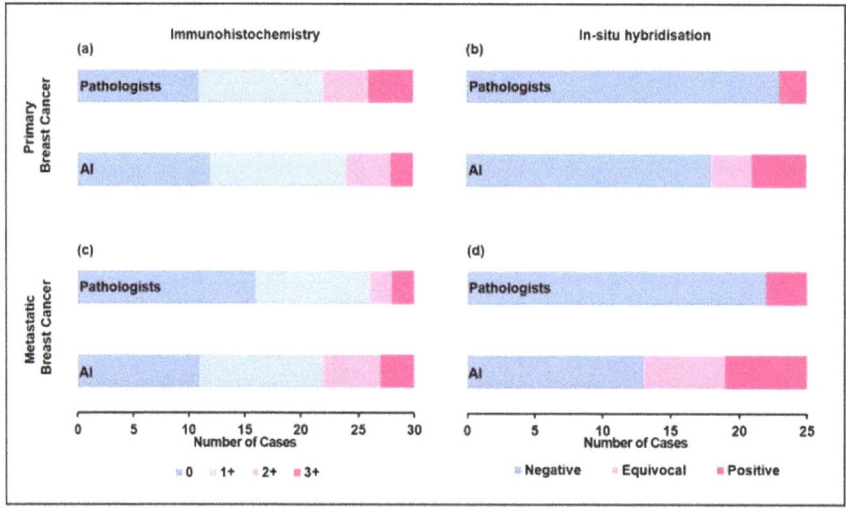

**Figure 5.** Primary breast cancer (**a**) IHC scores and (**b**) ISH status, and matched metastatic breast cancer (**c**) IHC scores and (**d**) ISH status assessed by the Pathologists versus AI. Equivocal ISH scores refer to groups 2, 3, and 4 in the 2018 ASCO/CAP guidelines.

## 3.7. Primary B5b IBC: Accuracy of AI-Assisted Digitalized Workflow

We incorporated both the HER2 IHC and ISH results in our assessment of how an AI-assisted, digitalized workflow compared to the manual assessment by pathologists. The ground truth HER2 status for all cases in our cohort was determined by consensus in the Pathologists' opinions. In accordance with the ASCO/CAP guidelines, we only considered the ISH results for cases rated as 2+ by IHC. For cases evaluated as a score 0 or 1+ on IHC, we set a final HER2 negative status, and for cases evaluated as HER2 score

3+ by IHC, we set a final HER2 positive status. In total, 15% of cases were HER2 positive. When we compared the final HER2 status for each case as determined by the AI-assisted workflow versus their respective ground truths, we observed almost perfect agreement. The sensitivity and specificity for the IHC algorithm were 93.8% and 96.1% and for the ISH algorithm, 100% and 94.7%.

## 4. Discussion

This feasibility study demonstrates almost perfect agreement between a digitalized AI-assisted workflow and routine light microscopy for the determination of HER2 IHC and ISH status in our cohort of primary and metastatic breast carcinomas and according to the 2018 ASCO/CAP guidelines. While previous studies have reported on the performance of digitalizing individual steps in the workup of HER2 status, we have demonstrated, for the first time, the successful implementation of a complete digital AI-assisted workflow [17,21,22]. The overall HER2 positivity rate in our study cohort was 15%, which is consistent with the rates reported in the literature [23,24].

When considering the performance of the IHC algorithm independently, we observed a moderate concordance rate, which was similar to other algorithms described in the literature. Several studies assessing the performance of IHC-based AI algorithms have merged the IHC scores 0 and 1+ into a single 'negative' category, which markedly improved their overall concordance rates [17,21,25]. We also observed significant improvement when merging these groups, resulting in an almost perfect concordance (Cohen's κ 0.59 vs. 0.85, $p < 0.001$ χ2 test). However, we acknowledge that the utility of this methodology is limited following the results of the DESTINY-Breast 04 trial concerning HER2 low tumors [10]. In their recent publication, Modi et al. concluded that trastuzumab deruxtecan prolongs progression-free and overall survival in patients with HER2 low tumors and called for a review of current HER2 diagnostic practices, given that "more than half of patients historically categorized as having HER2-negative breast cancer" could now exhibit improved treatment outcomes [10].

Extending upon these findings, preliminary results from the DAISY trial (due to be completed in 2025) are suggestive of antitumor activity by directed HER2 therapy in patients with an IHC HER2 score of 0 [11]. However, as observed in our study and by countless other groups, the HER2 IHC method and interpretation are plagued by low inter-rater agreement, particularly in the 0 and 1+ range [26]. Whilst the combined IHC/ISH method performed well for the detection of amplified and non-amplified HER2 tumors, it had shortcomings in the classification of HER2 low tumors. Alternative laboratory methods such as a combined protocol involving immunofluorescence and mass spectrometry may be capable of systematic and standardized quantification of drug-targetable HER2 amplification [26]. However, further studies stratifying molar HER2 quantities with response to therapy are required in order to understand if this approach is fit for purpose. In the midst of the uncertainty in defining the boundaries for the group with the best benefit–risk response profile to trastuzumab deruxtecan, it is crucial that the assessment of HER2 is as objective and standardized as possible.

The ISH-algorithm demonstrated substantial concordance with our ground truth. Whilst we noted a tendency for AI to provide higher HER2 counts and HER2/CEP17 ratios than paired manual slides, this did not have a significant impact on the overall diagnostic performance. Various reasons contributing to the higher counts included misinterpretation of the cell borders, misinterpretation of dark cytoplasmic staining secondary to cell shrinkage artefact as HER2 signals, and assigning higher counts to clusters. An advantage of the ISH algorithm is the heat-map overlay on the whole-slide image, which provides a continuous graded coloring system to delineate areas of normal and high HER2 signals/cell or HER2/CEP17 ratios, and thus aids the user in selecting an appropriate ROI. Due to the small size of HER2 and CEP17 signals, such insight is not possible through low-powered manual microscopy. The heatmap supports the user to distinguish tumor and non-tumor tissue, and may also facilitate the identification of clustered-type intratumoral heterogeneity in HER2 status [2,27]. This is important because emerging evidence suggests that different therapeutic approaches should be considered for HER2 heterogeneous breast carcinomas as they are less responsive to anti-HER2 therapies, display lower rates of pathologic complete response, and are associated with worse survival outcomes [27].

Before embarking on digitalization and incorporating artificial intelligence in diagnostic pathology, it is important to appreciate the potential impacts on pre-analytical, analytical and post-analytical procedures. For example, the IHC-algorithm used in this study was highly dependent on tight adherence to the vendor's immunostaining protocol and could not be adapted to perform with the existing local laboratory practices. Therefore, for the purpose of this study, we deviated from our routine laboratory HER2 IHC staining protocol in order to match the vendor recommendation for their digital scanner and paired AI algorithm. In our experience, vendors are reluctant to adapt AI software for end-users on the basis that this may invalidate their CE-certification status. The changes in IHC staining protocols made by laboratories should undergo internal and external validation, and be suitable for both AI and manual interpretation.

Moreover, whilst we chose to analyze the performance of the AI-assisted DIA independently, without manual correction, its intended use is as a real-time diagnostic adjunct and it would therefore necessitate that all users have access and training. Interestingly, we noted a reduction in the accuracy of our Pathologists' IHC scoring with the consensus scores after they had viewed the AI results (Cohen's κ Pathologists 0.85–0.88 vs. AI-assisted Pathologists 0.61–0.71, t = 4.921, $p < 0.05$). This observation differs to other studies, which describe an AI-enhancing effect on diagnostic accuracy [28–30]. We also noted a reduction in the inter-observer agreement for AI-assisted Pathologists compared to Pathologists, however, this observation was not statistically significant in our cohort. It would be important to review and quantify the impact of AI on the existing reporting patterns as well as consider the time and cost-effectiveness prior to implementing new workflows [29].

A limitation of our work was the small sample size of our study cohort—whilst this was sufficient to demonstrate feasibility, it limited the statistical significance of our comparisons. According to recommendations from the CAP, FDA-approved and FDA-cleared HER2 IHC quantitative image analysis systems should be validated with 20 known positive and 20 known negative cases, and should show an agreement threshold of 90% for HER2 positive and 95% for HER2 negative samples [25]. Future studies combining the results from multiple institutions, and including resection specimens in addition to CNBs, would be beneficial to understand the impact of inter-laboratory and pre-analytical specimen processing and sampling on the performance of IHC and ISH methods [31].

In conclusion, this study demonstrates the feasibility of a combined IHC and ISH digitalized AI-assisted workflow for HER2 status determination in primary and metastatic breast cancer including the newly recognized group of HER2 low tumors.

**Supplementary Materials:** The following supporting information can be downloaded at: https://www.mdpi.com/article/10.3390/diagnostics13010168/s1, Table S1: IHC scores assigned by AI of 57 primary IBCs using laboratory staining compared to amended (vendor recommended) staining protocols.

**Author Contributions:** Conceptualization, M.T.; Methodology, C.P., C.E.C. and M.T.; Formal analysis, C.P., C.E.C. and M.T.; Investigation, C.P., C.E.C., R.M., B.P.S., E.K., Q.S., B.B. and M.T.; Data curation, C.P. and C.E.C.; Writing—original draft preparation, C.P., C.E.C. and M.T.; Writing—review and editing, C.P., C.E.C., R.M., B.P.S., E.K., Q.S., B.B. and M.T.; Supervision, M.T. All authors have read and agreed to the published version of the manuscript.

**Funding:** This research received no external funding.

**Institutional Review Board Statement:** The study was conducted in accordance with the Declaration of Helsinki, and approved by the Ethics Committee of Canton Zurich (BASEC-NR.: 2021-00210).

**Informed Consent Statement:** Patient consent for the use of anonymized biological material was in accordance with Article 34 of the Human Research Act, The Federal Assembly of the Swiss Confederation.

**Data Availability Statement:** The datasets generated and analyzed during the study are available from the corresponding author on reasonable request.

**Acknowledgments:** We would like to thank our laboratory staff for their excellent technical support.

**Conflicts of Interest:** The authors declare no conflict of interest.

## References

1. Konecny, G.E.; Meng, Y.G.; Untch, M.; Wang, H.-J.; Bauerfeind, I.; Epstein, M.; Stieber, P.; Vernes, J.-M.; Gutierrez, J.; Hong, K.; et al. Association between HER-2/neu and Vascular Endothelial Growth Factor Expression Predicts Clinical Outcome in Primary Breast Cancer Patients. *Clin. Cancer Res.* **2004**, *10*, 1706–1716. [CrossRef] [PubMed]
2. Ahn, S.; Woo, J.W.; Lee, K.; Park, S.Y. HER2 status in breast cancer: Changes in guidelines and complicating factors for interpretation. *J. Pathol. Transl. Med.* **2020**, *54*, 34–44. [CrossRef] [PubMed]
3. Slamon, D.J.; Clark, G.M.; Wong, S.G.; Levin, W.J.; Ullrich, A.; McGuire, W.L. Human breast cancer: Correlation of relapse and survival with amplification of the HER-2/neu oncogene. *Science* **1987**, *235*, 177–182. [CrossRef] [PubMed]
4. Patel, A.; Unni, N.; Peng, Y. The Changing Paradigm for the Treatment of HER2-Positive Breast Cancer. *Cancers* **2020**, *12*, 2081. [CrossRef]
5. Cameron, D.; Piccart-Gebhart, M.J.; Gelber, R.D.; Procter, M.; Goldhirsch, A.; de Azambuja, E.; Castro, G., Jr.; Untch, M.; Smith, I.; Gianni, L.; et al. 11 years' follow-up of trastuzumab after adjuvant chemotherapy in HER2-positive early breast cancer: Final analysis of the HERceptin Adjuvant (HERA) trial. *Lancet* **2017**, *389*, 1195–1205. [CrossRef]
6. Wolff, A.C.; Hammond, M.E.H.; Allison, K.H.; Harvey, B.E.; Mangu, P.B.; Bartlett, J.M.S.; Bilous, M.; Ellis, I.O.; Fitzgibbons, P.; Hanna, W.; et al. Human Epidermal Growth Factor Receptor 2 Testing in Breast Cancer: American Society of Clinical Oncology/College of American Pathologists Clinical Practice Guideline Focused Update. *J. Clin. Oncol.* **2018**, *36*, 2105–2122. [CrossRef]
7. Layfield, L.J.; Frazier, S.; Esebua, M.; Schmidt, R.L. Interobserver reproducibility for HER2/neu immunohistochemistry: A comparison of reproducibility for the HercepTest™ and the 4B5 antibody clone. *Pathol. Res. Pract.* **2016**, *212*, 190–195. [CrossRef]
8. Thomson, T.A.; Hayes, M.M.; Spinelli, J.J.; Hilland, E.; Sawrenko, C.; Phillips, D.; Dupuis, B.; Parker, R.L. HER-2/neu in Breast Cancer: Interobserver Variability and Performance of Immunohistochemistry with 4 Antibodies Compared with Fluorescent In Situ Hybridization. *Mod. Pathol.* **2001**, *14*, 1079–1086. [CrossRef]
9. Moelans, C.; de Weger, R.; Van der Wall, E.; van Diest, P. Current technologies for HER2 testing in breast cancer. *Crit. Rev. Oncol.* **2011**, *80*, 380–392. [CrossRef]
10. Modi, S.; Jacot, W.; Yamashita, T.; Sohn, J.; Vidal, M.; Tokunaga, E.; Tsurutani, J.; Ueno, N.T.; Prat, A.; Chae, Y.S.; et al. Trastuzumab Deruxtecan in Previously Treated HER2-Low Advanced Breast Cancer. *N. Engl. J. Med.* **2022**, *387*, 9–20. [CrossRef]
11. Hurvitz, S.A. DESTINY-Changing Results for Advanced Breast Cancer. *N. Engl. J. Med.* **2022**, *387*, 75–76. [CrossRef] [PubMed]
12. Turashvili, G.; Leung, S.; Turbin, D.; Montgomery, K.; Gilks, B.; West, R.; Carrier, M.; Huntsman, D.; Aparicio, S. Inter-observer reproducibility of HER2 immunohistochemical assessment and concordance with fluorescent in situhybridization (FISH): Pathologist assessment compared to quantitative image analysis. *BMC Cancer* **2009**, *9*, 165. [CrossRef] [PubMed]
13. Ellis, C.M.; Dyson, M.J.; Stephenson, T.J.; Maltby, E.L. HER2 amplification status in breast cancer: A comparison between immunohistochemical staining and fluorescence in situ hybridisation using manual and automated quantitative image analysis scoring techniques. *J. Clin. Pathol.* **2005**, *58*, 710–714. [CrossRef] [PubMed]
14. Brügmann, A.; Eld, M.; Lelkaitis, G.; Nielsen, S.; Grunkin, M.; Hansen, J.D.; Foged, N.T.; Vyberg, M. Digital image analysis of membrane connectivity is a robust measure of HER2 immunostains. *Breast Cancer Res. Treat.* **2011**, *132*, 41–49. [CrossRef]
15. Masmoudi, H.; Hewitt, S.M.; Petrick, N.; Myers, K.J.; Gavrielides, M.A. Automated Quantitative Assessment of HER-2/neu Immunohistochemical Expression in Breast Cancer. *IEEE Trans. Med. Imaging* **2009**, *28*, 916–925. [CrossRef]
16. Yousif, M.; Huang, Y.; Sciallis, A.; Kleer, C.G.; Pang, J.; Smola, B.; Naik, K.; McClintock, D.S.; Zhao, L.; Kunju, L.P.; et al. Quantitative Image Analysis as an Adjunct to Manual Scoring of ER, PgR, and HER2 in Invasive Breast Carcinoma. *Am. J. Clin. Pathol.* **2021**, *157*, 899–907. [CrossRef]
17. Yue, M.; Zhang, J.; Wang, X.; Yan, K.; Cai, L.; Tian, K.; Niu, S.; Han, X.; Yu, Y.; Huang, J.; et al. Can AI-assisted microscope facilitate breast HER2 interpretation? A multi-institutional ring study. *Virchows Arch.* **2021**, *479*, 443–449. [CrossRef]
18. Shamai, G.; Binenbaum, Y.; Slossberg, R.; Duek, I.; Gil, Z.; Kimmel, R. Artificial Intelligence Algorithms to Assess Hormonal Status From Tissue Microarrays in Patients With Breast Cancer. *JAMA Netw. Open* **2019**, *2*, e197700. [CrossRef]
19. Qaiser, T.; Mukherjee, A.; Pb, C.R.; Munugoti, S.D.; Tallam, V.; Pitkäaho, T.; Lehtimäki, T.; Naughton, T.; Berseth, M.; Pedraza, A.; et al. HER2 challenge contest: A detailed assessment of automated HER2 scoring algorithms in whole slide images of breast cancer tissues. *Histopathology* **2017**, *72*, 227–238. [CrossRef]
20. Landis, J.R.; Koch, G.G. The Measurement of Observer Agreement for Categorical Data. *Biometrics* **1977**, *33*, 159–174. [CrossRef]

21. Koopman, T.; Buikema, H.J.; Hollema, H.; de Bock, G.H.; van der Vegt, B. What is the added value of digital image analysis of HER 2 immunohistochemistry in breast cancer in clinical practice? A study with multiple platforms. *Histopathology* **2018**, *74*, 917–924. [CrossRef] [PubMed]
22. Helin, H.O.; Tuominen, V.J.; Ylinen, O.; Helin, H.J.; Isola, J. Free digital image analysis software helps to resolve equivocal scores in HER2 immunohistochemistry. *Virchows Arch.* **2015**, *468*, 191–198. [CrossRef] [PubMed]
23. Rüschoff, J.; Lebeau, A.; Kreipe, H.; Sinn, P.; Gerharz, C.D.; Koch, W.; Morris, S.; Ammann, J.; Untch, M. Assessing HER2 testing quality in breast cancer: Variables that influence HER2 positivity rate from a large, multicenter, observational study in Germany. *Mod. Pathol.* **2016**, *30*, 217–226. [CrossRef] [PubMed]
24. Godoy-Ortiz, A.; Sanchez-Muñoz, A.; Parrado, M.R.C.; Álvarez, M.; Ribelles, N.; Dominguez, A.R.; Alba, E. Deciphering HER2 Breast Cancer Disease: Biological and Clinical Implications. *Front. Oncol.* **2019**, *9*, 1124. [CrossRef] [PubMed]
25. Bui, M.M.; Riben, M.W.; Allison, K.H.; Chlipala, E.; Colasacco, C.; Kahn, A.G.; Lacchetti, C.; Madabhushi, A.; Pantanowitz, L.; Salama, M.E.; et al. Quantitative Image Analysis of Human Epidermal Growth Factor Receptor 2 Immunohistochemistry for Breast Cancer: Guideline From the College of American Pathologists. *Arch. Pathol. Lab. Med.* **2018**, *143*, 1180–1195. [CrossRef] [PubMed]
26. Moutafi, M.; Robbins, C.J.; Yaghoobi, V.; Fernandez, A.I.; Martinez-Morilla, S.; Xirou, V.; Bai, Y.; Song, Y.; Gaule, P.; Krueger, J.; et al. Quantitative measurement of HER2 expression to subclassify ERBB2 unamplified breast cancer. *Lab. Investig.* **2022**, *102*, 1101–1108. [CrossRef] [PubMed]
27. Marchiò, C.; Annaratone, L.; Marques, A.; Casorzo, L.; Berrino, E.; Sapino, A. Evolving concepts in HER2 evaluation in breast cancer: Heterogeneity, HER2-low carcinomas and beyond. *Semin. Cancer Biol.* **2020**, *72*, 123–135. [CrossRef]
28. Sakamoto, T.; Furukawa, T.; Lami, K.; Pham, H.H.N.; Uegami, W.; Kuroda, K.; Kawai, M.; Sakanashi, H.; Cooper, L.A.D.; Bychkov, A.; et al. A narrative review of digital pathology and artificial intelligence: Focusing on lung cancer. *Transl. Lung Cancer Res.* **2020**, *9*, 2255–2276. [CrossRef]
29. Jahn, S.; Plass, M.; Moinfar, F. Digital Pathology: Advantages, Limitations and Emerging Perspectives. *J. Clin. Med.* **2020**, *9*, 3697. [CrossRef]
30. Ahmad, Z.; Rahim, S.; Zubair, M.; Abdul-Ghafar, J. Artificial intelligence (AI) in medicine, current applications and future role with special emphasis on its potential and promise in pathology: Present and future impact, obstacles including costs and acceptance among pathologists, practical and philosophical considerations. A comprehensive review. *Diagn. Pathol.* **2021**, *16*, 24. [CrossRef]
31. Varga, Z.; Noske, A.; Ramach, C.; Padberg, B.; Moch, H. Assessment of HER2 status in breast cancer: Overall positivity rate and accuracy by fluorescence in situ hybridization and immunohistochemistry in a single institution over 12 years: A quality control study. *BMC Cancer* **2013**, *13*, 615. [CrossRef] [PubMed]

**Disclaimer/Publisher's Note:** The statements, opinions and data contained in all publications are solely those of the individual author(s) and contributor(s) and not of MDPI and/or the editor(s). MDPI and/or the editor(s) disclaim responsibility for any injury to people or property resulting from any ideas, methods, instructions or products referred to in the content.

Article

# Allred Scoring of ER-IHC Stained Whole-Slide Images for Hormone Receptor Status in Breast Carcinoma

Mohammad Faizal Ahmad Fauzi [1,*], Wan Siti Halimatul Munirah Wan Ahmad [1], Mohammad Fareed Jamaluddin [1], Jenny Tung Hiong Lee [2], See Yee Khor [3], Lai Meng Looi [4], Fazly Salleh Abas [5] and Nouar Aldahoul [1]

1. Faculty of Engineering, Multimedia University, Cyberjaya 63100, Selangor, Malaysia
2. Department of Pathology, Sarawak General Hospital, Kuching 93586, Sarawak, Malaysia
3. Department of Pathology, Queen Elizabeth Hospital, Kota Kinabalu 88200, Sabah, Malaysia
4. Department of Pathology, University Malaya Medical Center, Kuala Lumpur 59100, Malaysia
5. Faculty of Engineering and Technology, Multimedia University, Ayer Keroh 75450, Melaka, Malaysia
* Correspondence: faizal1@mmu.edu.my

**Abstract:** Hormone receptor status is determined primarily to identify breast cancer patients who may benefit from hormonal therapy. The current clinical practice for the testing using either Allred score or H-score is still based on laborious manual counting and estimation of the amount and intensity of positively stained cancer cells in immunohistochemistry (IHC)-stained slides. This work integrates cell detection and classification workflow for breast carcinoma estrogen receptor (ER)-IHC-stained images and presents an automated evaluation system. The system first detects all cells within the specific regions and classifies them into negatively, weakly, moderately, and strongly stained, followed by Allred scoring for ER status evaluation. The generated Allred score relies heavily on accurate cell detection and classification and is compared against pathologists' manual estimation. Experiments on 40 whole-slide images show 82.5% agreement on hormonal treatment recommendation, which we believe could be further improved with an advanced learning model and enhancement to address the cases with 0% ER status. This promising system can automate the exhaustive exercise to provide fast and reliable assistance to pathologists and medical personnel. The system has the potential to improve the overall standards of prognostic reporting for cancer patients, benefiting pathologists, patients, and also the public at large.

**Keywords:** Allred scoring; estrogen receptor; hormone receptor; tumor biomarker; breast carcinoma; digital pathology

## 1. Introduction

Breast cancer is the most common cancer occurring in women and is the second leading cause of cancer-related deaths in women. The majority of breast tumors and breast cancers are first detected using either mammography, magnetic resonance imaging (MRI), or ultrasound scans. However, for better diagnosis and prognosis of breast cancer, tissue samples must be obtained, either through biopsy or surgery, for analysis by pathologists. In the case of breast cancer treatment, a crucial step is to test the tumor tissue to determine if it has estrogen receptors (ER), progesterone receptors (PR), and/or human epidermal growth factor receptor 2 (HER2). These markers provide key information about how the cancer may behave. Along with tumor grade and cancer stage, tumor marker status helps determine the best treatment options for breast cancer patients. ER, together with PR, has been recognized as a "predictive" marker for which women with breast cancer would respond to hormonal treatment.

Predictive immunohistochemistry (IHC) is commonly used in breast histopathology practice to determine the expression of hormone receptor proteins. The use of IHC to assess the ER and PR status of breast cancers in formalin-fixed, paraffin-embedded (FFPE) tissue sections of cancer samples is now a routine part of pathology practice worldwide and is

recommended to be performed in all primary invasive breast carcinomas and on recurrent or metastatic tumors. The hormone receptor status of a breast cancer helps the doctor to decide whether the patient should be offered hormonal therapy or other treatments. Hormonal therapy includes medications that either lower the amount of estrogen in the body or block estrogen from supporting the growth and function of breast cells. If the breast cancer cells have hormone receptors, then these medications could help to slow or even stop their growth. Patients with ER-positive cancers are highly receptive to endocrine therapy and have a higher chance of survival [1]. If the cancer is hormone-receptor-negative (no hormone receptors are present), then hormonal therapy is unlikely to work. In this case, other kinds of treatment should be sought.

Valid determination of ER and PR status is thus a prerequisite for establishing adequate treatment strategies for breast cancer patients, regardless of disease stage. The determination of these protein expressions, however, is currently carried out manually, which is not only tedious and time-consuming for the pathologists, but is also prone to errors and inaccuracies. In this paper, we proposed a system for automated estrogen receptor status evaluation in breast carcinoma patients which consists of four stages: cell detection, positive/negative classification, weak/moderate/strong classification, and Allred scoring. As both ER and PR share similar staining characteristics, the system can be further extended to determine PR (and possibly HER2) expression in the future with minor modifications to make for a complete hormone receptor system.

Figure 1 shows the block diagram of our proposed system. In our previous work, indicated by blue boxes and arrows, we have reported our initial work on cell detection [2], positively and negatively stained (PN) cell classification [3] and weakly, moderately, or strongly stained (WMS) cell classification [4] on their own. In this work, we integrated the three stages into a single system, experimented with each stage with the same set of images, and evaluated their performances objectively and transitively in order to observe the overall performance of the integrated system. Positively and negatively stained cells are quite distinguishable based on their color properties, i.e., negative cells are stained with a blue/purple hue, while positive cells are stained with a brown hue. Color analysis based on the weighted hue and value of the cells (from the HSV color model), which we previously used in p53 expression analysis of brain glioblastoma, can be used.

Cell detection and WMS classification on the other hand, are more challenging. For cell detection, the challenges lie in detecting the boundaries, in which some cells which are too close to each other appear as if they belong to single large cells, while some others have rather weak and unclear boundaries. For WMS classification, the differences between the weakly, moderately, and strongly stained cells are not very obvious. The moderately stained cells especially are very tricky as they can easily be classified into either the weak or strong classes. The convolutional neural network (CNN) excels in these types of challenges by learning the features end to end while avoiding the manual feature selection in traditional image classification. Because of this we decided to use a deep convolutional neural network for both the cell detection and WMS classification stages. Cell detection was carried out using CNN with regression layer in order to obtain accurate cell boundaries (hence correct cell detection), while WMS classification utilizes the CNN with the regular classification layer to classify the cells into the three staining strengths.

The detected and classified cells are then fed to the final stage of the system, indicated by the red box and arrows, for estrogen receptor status evaluation. By computing the distribution of the strong, moderate, weak, as well as negatively stained cells within the slides or regions of interest, the estrogen receptor expression for the slide is determined by computing the Allred score [5], and compared to the pathologists' manual scoring. Alternatively, the H-score [6] can also be used for assessing estrogen receptor status, but in this project we focus on Allred scoring as we have the ground truth available for evaluation. To the best of our knowledge, this is the first work of its kind in developing such a system with the scoring of whole-slide images, which would be a valuable tool for histopathologists in improving the reliability of tumor marker reporting as well as reducing manual intervention workload. There are some similar works found in the literature [7–9] working on Allred scoring of ER-IHC patches. Since we aim to replicate the pathologists' process flow in deciding the score, which is on whole-slide images, the existing work from the literature is not a fair comparison either in terms of accuracy or computational time.

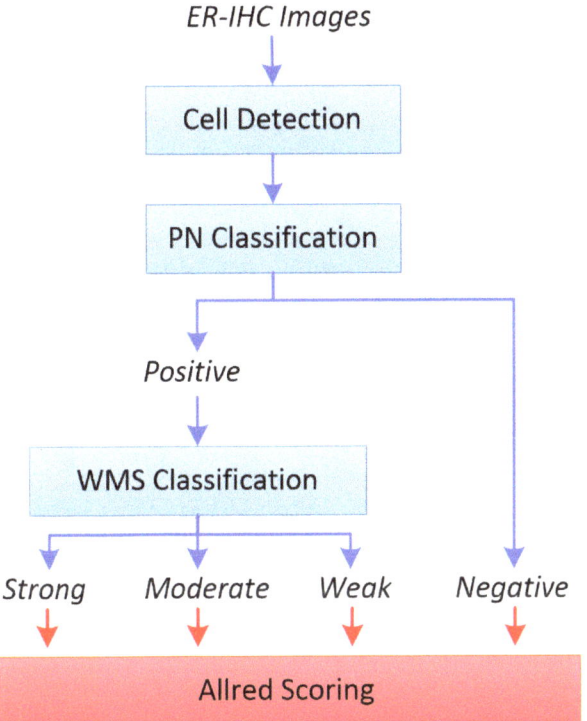

**Figure 1.** Flowchart for the overview of the system.

This paper is organized as follows. Section 2 describes all the stages involved in the proposed automated Allred scoring system in detail. Section 3 explains the experimental set-up, while Section 4 discusses the experimental observations. Finally, the conclusion and future works are presented in Section 5.

## 2. Methods

In this section, the three prior stages to the Allred scoring, which are cell detection, PN classification, and WMS classification will be described before discussing the Allred scoring methodology for hormone receptor evaluation.

*2.1. Cell Detection*

Our cell detection stage is based on the work by [10], where a score map is predicted based on the Euclidean distance transform for cell centers in a given input image. The prediction of the score map is performed using a regression method trained from cell images and ground truth cell locations, similar to the work by [11]. The idea is to train the network to fine-tune the boundary of individual cells regardless of their class, shape, color, and overlapping parts, if any. In constructing the model, we experimented with a network up to 20 layers by stacking the convolution, rectified linear units (ReLU), and max pooling (maxpool) layers, followed by the regression layer at the end. Due to the limitation of our workstation, we kept the design minimal and the footprint smaller. Figure 2 shows the proposed CNN model for our cell detection stage, together with an example of the score map.

During training, we asked our collaborating pathologists to mark each cell inside small regions of around 500 × 500 pixels as the ground truth. Each cell mark is expanded as a circle with a radius of 32 pixels, and 64 × 64 patches were extracted for use to train the network. During detection, a score map is generated for the whole image by the CNN-based regression model, and initial segmentation is obtained by thresholding the score map (a score of 0.2 and higher constitutes cells). To address the problem of closely connected cells, watershed-based boundary processing is carried out. Another thresholding is then applied to remove the non-cells region (an area greater than 240) from the final detection. As we are more interested in cell detection rather than cell segmentation, the choice of thresholds does not affect the final outcome much. The centroids of the detected cells are passed to the next stage for classification.

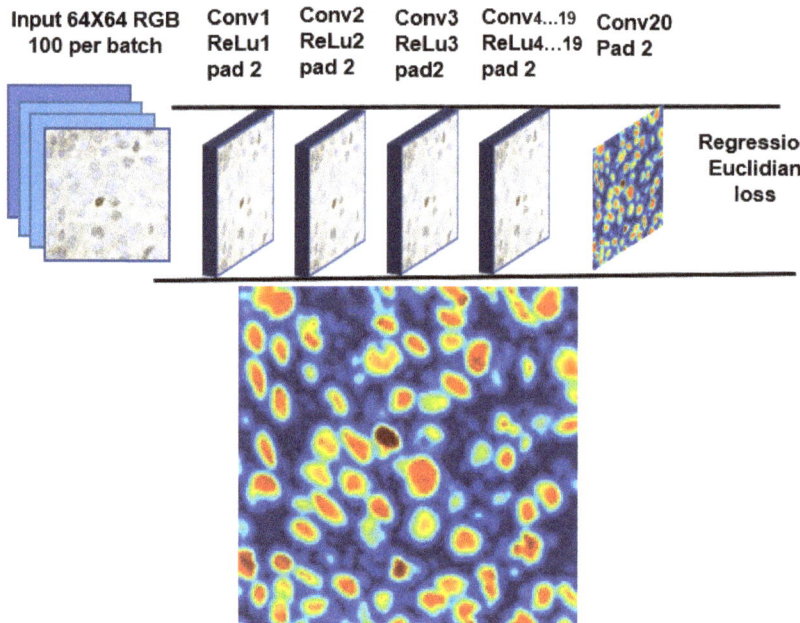

**Figure 2.** CNN model for cell detection, with regression layer at the end of the network (**top**), and the generated score map at 20× magnification (**bottom**).

## 2.2. PN Classification

The classification of cells into positively and negatively stained cells is based on our earlier work in classifying positive and negative cells in p53 expressions [3,12] of brain glioblastoma. Similar to p53 images, the positively and negatively stained cells in ER-IHC stained images are quite distinguishable based on their color. Negative cells are characterized by their blueish hue and low intensity. Positive cells, on the other hand, are characterized by their brownish hue and rather high intensity. The classification of the cells into positive or negative stains can thus be based on the intensity and color of the cells.

For each of the detected cells found in the previous stage, 32 × 32 pixel blocks are extracted around their centroid, and converted into the HSV (hue/saturation/value) color model. While most cells fit nicely into this 32 × 32 pixel block, there are some cases where the cells are too big or too small. For the former, we should still be able to obtain the color and intensity information from the part of the cells that fit into the block. For the latter, however, it is possible that some other cells may also be captured by the block, thus compromising the color and intensity information of that particular cell. To address this, we used weighted hue and weighted value instead to compute the color and intensity, respectively. The weights used are inversely proportional to the pixels' distance to the centroid, with those closer to the center of the block receiving higher weight, and those further from the center receiving less weight.

The weighted hue and value are calculated for each block and these values are used for classifying the cells. Negative ER-stained cells tend to be blue (higher hue) and less intense (higher value), while positive ER-stained cells tend to be brown (lower hue) with varying intensities. Based on these properties, we propose a two-step classification rule: (1) if the weighted value (wV) for a block is less than a particular threshold (darker), the block will be classified as containing a positive cell, regardless of its weighted hue (wH); (2) otherwise, the classification depends on weighted hue, with wH less than a particular threshold meaning that the block contains positive cells, and wH more than the threshold meaning it contains negative cells. From experiment, wH > 40 and wV < 50 were found to be suitable thresholds for our ER-IHC images. Figure 3 summarizes the proposed positive/negative cell classification process in a flowchart.

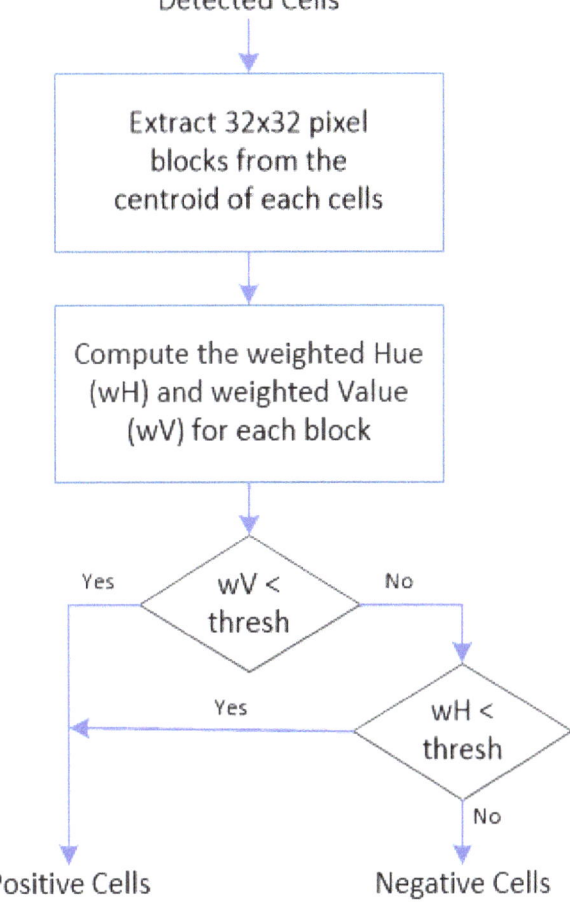

**Figure 3.** PN classification process.

### 2.3. WMS Classification

In order to get the best result in learning the features of ER-positive cells, a different CNN model is proposed, which is based on earlier CNNs such as LeNet [13], ImageNet [14], GoogLeNet [15], and a few others [10,11,16,17], and their recommendations. These include the effect of the convolutional network depth on its accuracy in large-scale image recognition settings; usage of back-to-back convolution layers with padding to maintain more pixel information in shrinking spatial information but increase model layer depth; usage of ReLu as the activation layer to reduce training time, and the addition of dropout layer to reduce overfitting in imbalance dataset. Nevertheless, similar to the model used in cell detection, the key is to be able to run an optimized CNN model with a small footprint using our limited hardware capability. Our network for this 3-class classification problem is made up of nine convolutional layers including the fully connected layer. Figure 4 shows the proposed CNN model for the WMS classification stage. The input to the network is 32 × 32 patches of positive cells from the previous classification stage, while the output is one of the strong, moderate, or weak classes.

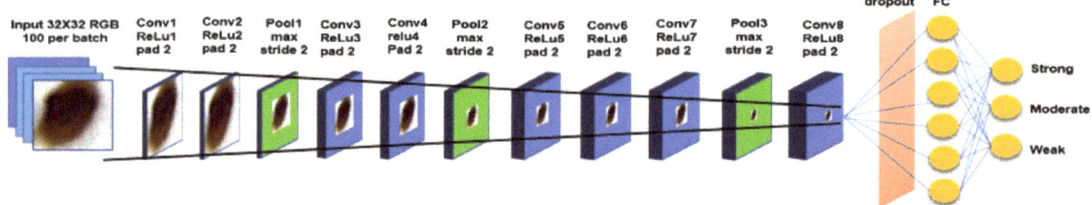

**Figure 4.** Our proposed 9-layer convolutional layer including the fully connected layer.

The same regions used for the cell detection experiment were used in generating training and testing samples and their ground truth. Data augmentation such as horizontal flipping, random cropping, and normalization is done to increase our training samples. The network is trained for 600 epochs using Matconvnet [18]. The weight of each layer is initialized by multiplying a small random number with the zero mean, sampled from Gaussian's standard deviation. Stochastic gradient descent is used to reduce the objective loss with a learning rate set in two vectors of logarithmic space: the first 10 epochs are set to 10-2 and the remaining epochs are set to 10-4 increments to improve the network convergence.

### 2.4. Allred Scoring

In this work, we used the Allred score to express ER, where the evaluation is based on the proportion of ER-positive cancer cells and the intensity of the reaction product in most of the positive cells [19]. Table 1 shows how the respective proportion and intensity scores are derived. Based on the percentage of ER-positive cells, the cancer is assigned one of six possible proportion scores (0 to 5). Based on the intensity of most of the ER-positive cancer cells, the cancer is also assigned one of four possible intensity scores (score of 0 to 3 for negative, weak, moderate, and strong, respectively). The 2 scores are then added together for a final score with 8 possible values (the Allred score). Allred scores of 0 and 2 are considered negative for ER (i.e., not actionable), while scores of 3 to 8 are considered positive (i.e., recommended for hormonal therapy). Note that a score of 1 is not a possible outcome.

Given an ER-stained whole-slide image, all the cells in the image are first detected and classified into one of 4 classes: negatively, weakly, moderately, and strongly stained cells (N, W, M, and S, respectively), as described in the previous three stages. The percentage of positively stained cells over all cells, as well as the intensity score derived from the majority class, is then used in computing the Allred score for hormone receptor status for the particular slide.

**Table 1.** Allred score * for estrogen and progestrone receptor evaluation.

| ER Status (Positive Cells %) | Proportion Score | Intensity | Intensity Score |
|---|---|---|---|
| 0 | 0 | None | 0 |
| <1 | 1 | Weak | 1 |
| 1 to 10 | 2 | Intermediate | 2 |
| 11 to 33 | 3 | Strong | 3 |
| 34 to 66 | 4 | | |
| ≥67 | 5 | | |

* Allred score = proportion score + intensity score.

## 3. Experimental Setup

Our ER-stained whole-slide images (WSI) of breast cancer are scanned using a 3DHistech scanner at 20× magnification with a resolution of 0.243 micrometer/pixel, resulting in images with a resolution of more than 80,000 by 200,000 pixels. Altogether, 40 whole-slide ER-stained images are available for use in all our experiments (refer Table 2). All 40 whole-slide images were uploaded to our in-house Linux lab server which has been installed with web interface [20] as shown in Figure 5, enabling an easy online WSI viewing and annotation for the pathologists marking the ground truth. The ground truth for the images (cell location, class, Allred score, etc.) is provided by pathologists from the Department of Pathology, University of Malaya Medical Center.

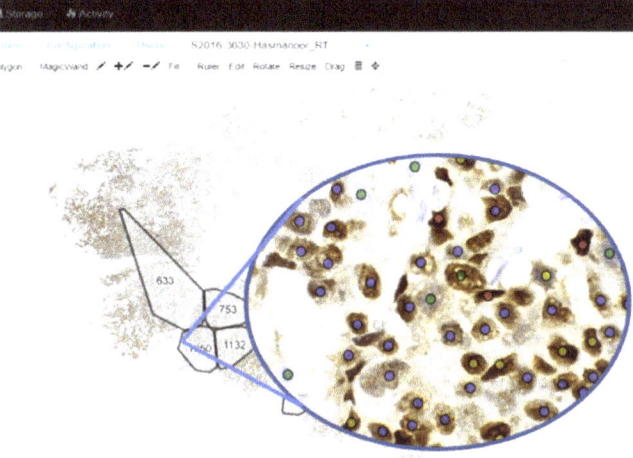

**Figure 5.** Part of the Cytomine interface, which enabled online annotation on whole-slide images and convenient working on gigabyte data of images. The different color dots show the different classes: green for negative, blue for positive-weak, yellow for positive-moderate and red for positive-strong class nuclei.

For cell detection and classification, the evaluation is based on the ability of the system to detect and classify cells. For this, comprehensive annotation by the collaborating pathologists was required. Since it is impossible to annotate all cells in the whole-slide images, the following approach is observed. For each of the 40 whole-slide images, a small region (around 500 × 500 pixels) is selected for annotation by the pathologists. However, due to time constraints, only 37 regions were eventually annotated. Thus 37 regions will be used in the detection and classification experiments: 30 regions used for training and 7 regions used for testing. For a particular region to be annotated, the pathologists were asked to identify all cells, and label them into either negatively, weakly, moderately, or strongly stained cells. Cells were annotated by marking the center of the cell, followed by annotating the cells into one of the four classes.

Table 2. Summary of the images used in the experiments.

| Image ID | GT | Exp A | Exp B |
|---|---|---|---|
| 01099 | Y | Train | Test |
| 05247 | Y | Train | Test |
| 05255 | Y | Train | Test |
| 05261 | Y | Train | Train |
| 05267 | Y | Train | Train |
| 05273 | Y | Train | Train |
| 05279 | Y | Train | Train |
| 05285 | Y | Train | Train |
| 05293 | N | NA | NA |
| 05299 | N | NA | NA |
| 05305 | Y | Train | Train |
| 05311 | Y | Train | Train |
| 05317 | N | NA | NA |
| 05323 | Y | Train | Train |
| 05329 | Y | Train | Train |
| 05337 | Y | Train | Train |
| 05343 | Y | Train | Train |
| 05349 | Y | Train | Test |
| 05355 | Y | Train | Test |
| 05361 | Y | Train | Test |
| 05367 | Y | Train | Test |
| 05373 | Y | Train | Train |
| 05379 | Y | Train | Train |
| 05385 | Y | Train | Train |
| 05391 | Y | Train | Train |
| 05397 | Y | Train | Train |
| 05403 | Y | Train | Train |
| 05409 | Y | Train | Train |
| 05415 | Y | Train | Train |
| 05421 | Y | Train | Train |
| 05427 | Y | Train | Train |
| 05435 | Y | Train | Train |
| 05441 | Y | Train | Train |
| 05447 | Y | Test | Train |
| 05453 | Y | Test | Train |
| 05459 | Y | Test | Train |
| 05465 | Y | Test | Train |
| 60537 | Y | Test | Train |
| 55522 | Y | Test | Train |
| 78990 | Y | Test | Train |

Figure 6 shows a couple of examples for the 37 regions used for this experiment, together with their annotation. A total of 3445 cells were marked by the pathologists from 37 annotated regions. Two-fold cross-validation was used, and we refer to these experiments as Experiments A and B, respectively, as detailed in Table 2. All the marked cells were later extracted as $32 \times 32$ augmented image patches. Data augmentation such as horizontal flipping, random cropping, and normalization is carried out to increase our training samples. To evaluate the performance of the system in detecting and classifying the cells, the number of true positives (TPs), false positives (FPs), true negatives (TNs), and false positives (FPs) were recorded. The performance of the proposed classification system is presented in terms of the precision and recall for each of the detection, classification, and quantification.

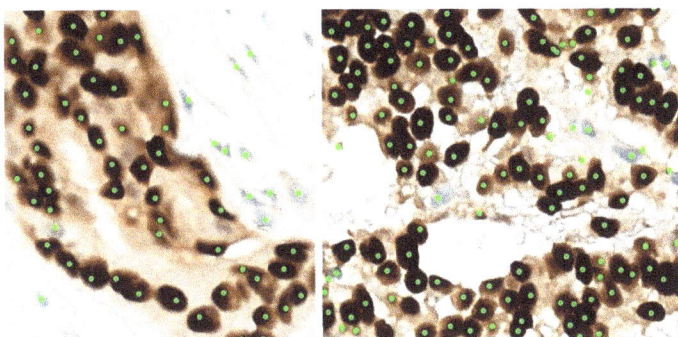

**Figure 6.** Two of the thirty-seven regions used for the cell detection and classification experiments.

For the Allred scoring experiment, the evaluation is done at the whole-slide level, i.e., to compare the Allred score automatically computed by the system to the ones estimated by the pathologists. No detailed cell-level annotation is required, instead only the Allred score from the pathologists' calculation/estimation for the 40 images is needed as the ground truth. Note that even though for 30 of the image there is some bias (since there is a region within the slides that were used in training), these regions are very small (around 500 × 500) compared to the whole slides (less than 0.01%), so the bias is very minimal, if any. To evaluate the performance of the Allred scoring, cell detection and classification are applied on each of the 40 whole-slide images (divided into non-overlapping high power field regions within the tissue area), before Allred scoring is carried out for each image and compared to the ones manually computed/estimated by the pathologists. Figure 7 shows one example of the 40 whole-slide images used in this experiment.

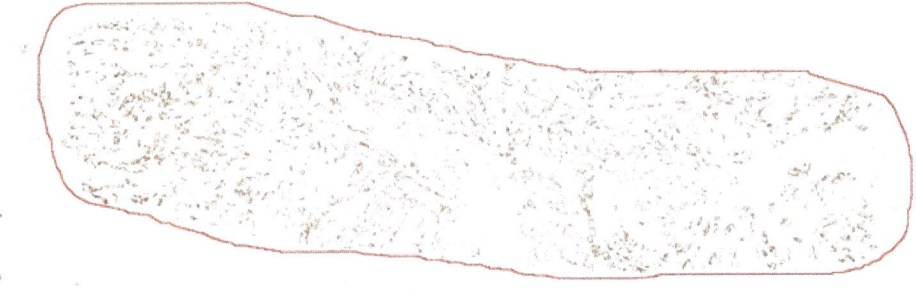

**Figure 7.** Example of the whole-slide image used in the Allred scoring experiment.

## 4. Results and Discussion

The results are presented in two subsections. In the first subsection, the performances of cell detection, PN classification, and WMS classification are evaluated at the cell level objectively and transitively. In the second subsection the performance of Allred scoring is evaluated at the slide level.

### 4.1. Cell Detection and Classification

As mentioned in the previous section, 30 regions were used for training and 7 images were used for testing. Two-fold cross-validation was carried out, named Exp A and Exp B, respectively. Table 3 shows the true positives, false positives, false negatives, recall, and precision for cell detection results for each of the 14 test images from the two-fold experiments. Overall there are 1425 cells from the 14 test images, 1328 of which were correctly detected. A total of 97 cells were missed, while 62 non-cells were detected as cells, giving a precision of 93% and recall of 96%, which shows that the proposed system is able to carry out its task reliably. Upon closer inspection, of the 62 false positive cells, 46 are non-tumor cells of the supportive stroma such as stromal cells and epithelial cells, and only 16 are actually non-cells. An improved system that can differentiate between tumor cells from stromal and epithelial cells would further improve the detection performance.

Table 4 shows the summary of the PN classification and Table 5 shows the classification of the detected cells into positive and negative cells for each of the 14 test images. The 62 false positive cases (non-tumor cells and non-cells wrongly detected in the previous stage) are also included in the classification experiment (last row of Table 3). As can be seen, only 13 cells were wrongly classified among 1328 correctly detected cells from the previous stage. The overall accuracy for all the detected cells is 95%, but if the false positive cases are removed (the error actually stemmed from the previous stage), the accuracy improved to 99%. This is also true for the true positive rate (correct classification of positive cells) and true negative rate (correct classification of negative cells). Overall, the proposed color-based classification is very reliable in classifying cells into positively and negatively stained cells.

Table 6 shows the classification of the detected positive cells into the strong, moderate, and weak classes for the 14 test images. The negative and non-tumor cells wrongly detected and classified as positive cells in the previous stages are also included in this experiment. As can be seen, most cells are classified correctly. Of the incorrect classification, 10 are from strong cells (classified as moderate), 13 are from moderate cells (6 classified as strong, and 7 as weak), and only 1 from weak cells (classified as moderate). Most of the negative and non-tumor cells that were classified as positive are classified as weak. Table 7 summarizes the overall accuracy as well as the positive prediction value (PPV) and the true positive rate (TPR) for each class. The overall accuracy of 88% is observed when including the false positive cells from prior stages, which improved to 90% if these cells were excluded.

**Table 3.** Cell detection results.

|       | Image ID | TP   | FP | FN | Recall | Precision |
|-------|----------|------|----|----|--------|-----------|
|       | 05447    | 107  | 4  | 5  | 0.96   | 0.96      |
|       | 05453    | 100  | 3  | 1  | 0.99   | 0.97      |
|       | 05459    | 43   | 7  | 4  | 0.91   | 0.86      |
| Exp A | 05465    | 73   | 0  | 3  | 0.96   | 1.00      |
|       | 60537    | 112  | 4  | 6  | 0.95   | 0.97      |
|       | 55522    | 103  | 2  | 5  | 0.95   | 0.98      |
|       | 78990    | 99   | 3  | 3  | 0.97   | 0.97      |
|       | 01099    | 84   | 13 | 13 | 0.87   | 0.87      |
|       | 05247    | 97   | 0  | 7  | 0.93   | 1.00      |
|       | 05255    | 80   | 15 | 9  | 0.90   | 0.84      |
| Exp B | 05349    | 96   | 6  | 6  | 0.94   | 0.94      |
|       | 05355    | 76   | 0  | 6  | 0.93   | 1.00      |
|       | 05361    | 128  | 0  | 13 | 0.91   | 1.00      |
|       | 05367    | 130  | 5  | 16 | 0.89   | 0.96      |
|       | Overall  | 1328 | 62 | 97 | 0.93   | 0.96      |

**Table 4.** PN classification results.

|           | Positive | Negative |
|-----------|----------|----------|
| Positive  | 238      | 12       |
| Negative  | 1        | 1077     |
| Non-Tumor | 5        | 57       |

Table 5. PN classification results for 14 test images.

| | Image ID | All Detected Cells | | | Only True Tumor Cells | | |
|---|---|---|---|---|---|---|---|
| | | Acc. | TPR | TNR | Acc. | TPR | TNR |
| Exp A | 05447 | 0.96 | NA | 0.96 | 1.00 | NA | 1.00 |
| | 05453 | 0.92 | 0.00 | 0.97 | 0.95 | 0.00 | 1.00 |
| | 05459 | 0.86 | 0.40 | 0.91 | 1.00 | 1.00 | 1.00 |
| | 05465 | 0.93 | 0.55 | 1.00 | 0.93 | 0.55 | 1.00 |
| | 60537 | 0.97 | 0.00 | 0.97 | 1.00 | NA | 1.00 |
| | 55522 | 0.97 | NA | 0.97 | 0.99 | NA | 0.99 |
| | 78990 | 0.96 | 0.00 | 0.97 | 0.99 | 0.00 | 1.00 |
| Exp B | 01099 | 0.87 | 1.00 | 0.48 | 1.00 | 1.00 | 1.00 |
| | 05247 | 1.00 | 1.00 | 1.00 | 1.00 | 1.00 | 1.00 |
| | 05255 | 0.84 | 0.99 | 0.00 | 1.00 | 1.00 | NA |
| | 05349 | 0.94 | NA | 0.94 | 1.00 | NA | 1.00 |
| | 05355 | 1.00 | 1.00 | 1.00 | 1.00 | 1.00 | 1.00 |
| | 05361 | 0.99 | 0.93 | 1.00 | 0.99 | 0.93 | 1.00 |
| | 05367 | 0.96 | NA | 0.96 | 1.00 | NA | 1.00 |
| | Overall | 0.95 | 0.93 | 0.95 | 0.99 | 0.95 | 1.00 |

The performance of the WMS classification agrees with our previous finding on 1200 extracted individual cells (400 weakly, 400 moderately, and 400 strongly stained cells). As reported in our previous article [4], 1066 out of 1200 cells have been classified correctly, which constitutes 88.8% accuracy on average and an overall AUC (area under curve) of 97.5%. The individual PPVs for the strong, moderate, and weak categories were reported as 90.5%, 88%, and 88%, respectively, which is in line with what is observed in this experiment. The results from this experiment on 14 test regions, as well as the previous experiments on 1200 individual cells (32 × 32 blocks) proved that the proposed WMS classification algorithm is reliable in classifying the positive cells into the three staining strengths. Figure 8 shows several visual examples of the final detection and classification results, while Figure 9 shows the proposed algorithms integrated into our ER-IHC breast carcinoma assessment system, for use in prognostic applications.

Table 6. WMS classification results.

| | Strong | Moderate | Weak |
|---|---|---|---|
| Strong | 48 | 10 | 0 |
| Moderate | 6 | 86 | 7 |
| Weak | 0 | 1 | 80 |
| Negative | 0 | 0 | 1 |
| Non Tumor Cells | 1 | 0 | 4 |

Table 7. Accuracy, PPV, and TPR for WMS classification.

| | All Detected Positive Cells | Only True Positive Cells |
|---|---|---|
| Accuracy | 0.88 | 0.90 |
| PPV-Strong | 0.87 | 0.89 |
| PPV-Moderate | 0.89 | 0.89 |
| PPV-Weak | 0.87 | 0.92 |
| TPR-Strong | 0.83 | NA |
| TPR-Moderate | 0.87 | NA |
| TPR-Weak | 0.99 | NA |

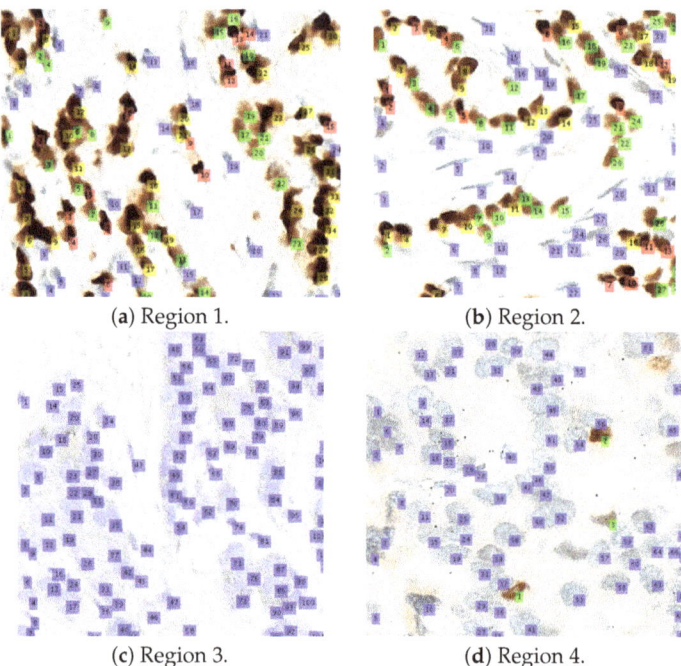

**Figure 8.** Examples of the classification results for 4 regions. Legends: blue (negative), green (weak), yellow (moderate), and red (strong).

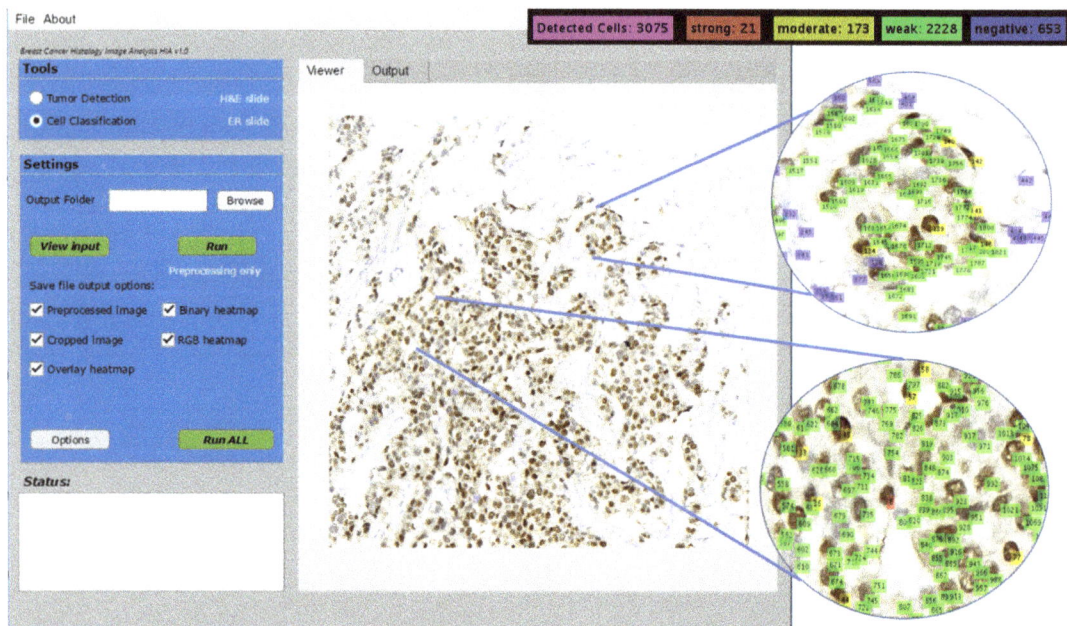

**Figure 9.** Cell detection and classification in ER-IHC breast carcinoma assessment system.

*4.2. Allred Scoring*

Table 8 shows the computer prediction of the Allred scoring for all 40 whole-slide images against the pathologist's estimation. The images were sorted according to the pathologist's estimated Allred score, from lowest to highest. As mentioned in the previous section, there are eight possible scores for each slide, with scores of 0 and 2 considered negative, while scores of 3 to 8 are considered positive (actionable for hormonal treatment). For more than half of the images (23), the computer predicted exactly the same score as the pathologist's estimation. Seven other images recorded a difference of only a single score, while another seven images recorded a difference of two scores. Only three images recorded a difference of more than two between the pathologist's estimation and the computer prediction. Figure 10 illustrates the difference better, where it can be seen that except for a few images, the computer prediction more or less follows the general pattern of the pathologist's estimation.

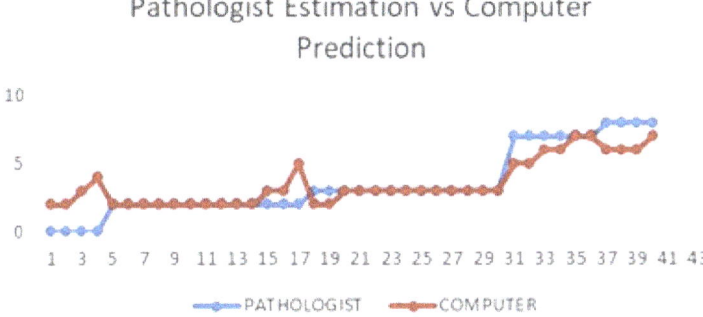

**Figure 10.** Pathologist's estimation vs. computer prediction.

**Table 8.** Allred scoring results.

| Image ID | Manual | | | | | Automated | | | | | | |
|---|---|---|---|---|---|---|---|---|---|---|---|---|
| | ER Status | Intensity | P Score | I Score | Allred Score | ER Status | S | M | W | P Score | I Score | Allred Score |
| 05349 | 0% | NONE | 0 | 0 | 0 | 0.83% | 0.01 | 0.02 | 0.8 * | 1 | 1 | 2 |
| 05367 | 0% | NONE | 0 | 0 | 0 | 0.19% | 0.16 * | 0.01 | 0.02 | 1 | 3 | 4 |
| 05305 | 0% | NONE | 0 | 0 | 0 | 1.87% | 0.02 | 0.03 | 1.83 * | 2 | 1 | 3 |
| 55522 | 0% | NONE | 0 | 0 | 0 | 0.8% | 0.01 | 0.03 | 0.77 * | 1 | 1 | 2 |
| 60537 | <1% | WEAK | 1 | 1 | 2 | 0.14% | 0.02 | 0.01 | 0.12 * | 1 | 1 | 2 |
| 05409 | <1% | WEAK | 1 | 1 | 2 | 0.11% | 0.01 | 0.01 | 0.09 * | 1 | 1 | 2 |
| 05317 | <1% | WEAK | 1 | 1 | 2 | 1.29% | 0.02 | 0.04 | 1.23 * | 2 | 1 | 3 |
| 05343 | <1% | WEAK | 1 | 1 | 2 | 0.63% | 0.02 | 0.01 | 0.6 * | 1 | 1 | 2 |
| 78990 | <1% | WEAK | 1 | 1 | 2 | 0.33% | 0.03 | 0.05 | 0.25 * | 1 | 1 | 2 |
| 05337 | <1% | WEAK | 1 | 1 | 2 | 0.80% | 0.03 | 0.04 | 0.74 * | 1 | 1 | 2 |
| 05403 | <1% | WEAK | 1 | 1 | 2 | 1.09% | 0.03 | 0.05 | 1.01 * | 2 | 1 | 3 |
| 05267 | <1% | WEAK | 1 | 1 | 2 | 0.15% | 0.02 | 0 | 0.12 * | 1 | 1 | 2 |
| 05385 | <1% | WEAK | 1 | 1 | 2 | 0.5% | 0.07 | 0.12 | 0.31 * | 1 | 1 | 2 |
| 05329 | <1% | WEAK | 1 | 1 | 2 | 0.35% | 0.01 | 0.03 | 0.32 * | 1 | 1 | 2 |
| 05447 | <1% | WEAK | 1 | 1 | 2 | 0.56% | 0.02 | 0.01 | 0.53 * | 1 | 1 | 2 |
| 05459 | <1% | WEAK | 1 | 1 | 2 | 0.56% | 0.03 | 0.1 | 2.84 * | 1 | 1 | 2 |
| 05441 | <1% | WEAK | 1 | 1 | 2 | 47.54% | 1.69 | 2.76 | 43.09 * | 4 | 1 | 5 |
| 05397 | 1–10% | WEAK | 2 | 1 | 3 | 2.54% | 0.02 | 0.08 | 2.44 * | 2 | 1 | 3 |
| 05391 | 1–10% | WEAK | 2 | 1 | 3 | 3.55% | 0.01 | 0.06 | 3.47 * | 2 | 1 | 3 |
| 05355 | 1–10% | WEAK | 2 | 1 | 3 | 1.99% | 0.02 | 0.04 | 1.93 * | 2 | 1 | 3 |
| 05421 | 1–10% | WEAK | 2 | 1 | 3 | 4.42% | 0.05 | 0.19 | 4.18 * | 2 | 1 | 3 |
| 05453 | 1–10% | WEAK | 2 | 1 | 3 | 4.61% | 0.05 | 0.07 | 4.49 * | 2 | 1 | 3 |
| 05279 | 1–10% | WEAK | 2 | 1 | 3 | 3.38% | 0.12 | 0.19 | 3.07 * | 2 | 1 | 3 |

Table 8. Cont.

| Image ID | ER Status | Manual | | | | | Automated | | | | | |
|---|---|---|---|---|---|---|---|---|---|---|---|---|
| | | Intensity | P Score | I Score | Allred Score | ER Status | S | M | W | P Score | I Score | Allred Score |
| 05379 | 1–10% | WEAK | 2 | 1 | 3 | 0.76% | 0.02 | 0.03 | 0.7 * | 1 | 1 | 2 |
| 05373 | 1–10% | WEAK | 2 | 1 | 3 | 1.31% | 0.01 | 0.02 | 1.28 * | 2 | 1 | 3 |
| 05361 | 1–10% | WEAK | 2 | 1 | 3 | 2.91% | 0.04 | 0.06 | 2.81 * | 2 | 1 | 3 |
| 05415 | 1–10% | WEAK | 2 | 1 | 3 | 3.67% | 0.03 | 0.09 | 3.55 * | 2 | 1 | 3 |
| 05285 | 1–10% | WEAK | 2 | 1 | 3 | 0.22% | 0.03 | 0.05 | 0.14 * | 1 | 1 | 2 |
| 05427 | 1–10% | WEAK | 2 | 1 | 3 | 7.89% | 0.44 | 0.25 | 7.2 * | 2 | 1 | 3 |
| 05465 | 1–10% | WEAK | 2 | 1 | 3 | 8.41% | 0.01 | 0.05 | 8.35 * | 2 | 1 | 3 |
| 05273 | >95% | STRONG | 5 | 3 | 8 | 46.39% | 9.59 | 19.65 * | 17.15 | 4 | 2 | 6 |
| 05299 | >80% | MODERATE | 5 | 2 | 7 | 47.73% | 4.97 | 26.56 * | 16.19 | 4 | 2 | 6 |
| 05435 | >95% | MODERATE | 5 | 2 | 7 | 77.44% | 12.46 | 36.19 * | 28.8 | 5 | 2 | 7 |
| 05247 | >90% | MODERATE | 5 | 2 | 7 | 49.84% | 12.36 | 17.87 * | 19.6 | 4 | 1 | 5 |
| 01099 | >95% | MODERATE | 5 | 2 | 7 | 62.63% | 7.55 | 21.58 | 33.5 * | 4 | 1 | 5 |
| 05255 | >95% | STRONG | 5 | 3 | 8 | 73.15% | 18.02 | 40.22 * | 14.91 | 5 | 2 | 7 |
| 05261 | >95% | STRONG | 5 | 3 | 8 | 49.47% | 14.65 | 23.91 * | 10.91 | 4 | 2 | 6 |
| 05311 | >95% | MODERATE | 5 | 2 | 7 | 73.5% | 22.27 | 40.96 * | 10.26 | 5 | 2 | 7 |
| 05293 | >95% | MODERATE | 5 | 2 | 7 | 43.75% | 16.66 | 19.54 | 7.54 | 4 | 2 | 6 |
| 05323 | >90% | STRONG | 5 | 3 | 8 | 48.39% | 11.65 | 22.11 | 14.63 | 4 | 2 | 6 |

* Highest positive class proportion.

It is interesting to note that for the four images considered to be 0% ER status by the pathologists (i.e., 100% of the cells were stained negatively), none of them were correctly predicted by the computer. The reason is, while the computer detection more or less agrees that the cells are almost entirely negative, it still detected a very small percentage of brownish objects, which could be either actual positive cells or other artifacts with similar characteristics to the positive cells such as noise. These images will thus automatically have a score of at least 1 for the proportional score (a score of 1 for those between 0% and 1%, and a score of 2 for those between 1% and 2%), and a score of at least 1 for the intensity score (since the intensity score is still given regardless of how small the positive proportion is). The final Allred scores for these four images are 2, 2, 3, and 4, respectively. In future work, we will work with our collaborating pathologists to suggest possible rules for a more accurate prediction for this kind of images.

It is possible that the pathologist misses some positive cells due to the sheer size of the images, so the rule may be very useful. The only other image with a score difference of more than 2 is image 05441, where the pathologists estimated an ER status of less than 1%, while the computer predicted it to be close to 50%. Upon detailed inspection, it was found that this particular image was a rather brownish in general compared to other images with similar status, which could be caused by an error during the staining process. Overall, the proposed approach managed to predict the scores similar to the pathologists, except for a few cases explained earlier.

In terms of hormonal treatment (not actionable vs. recommended for hormonal therapy), 33 out of 40 computer-predicted treatments agree with the pathologist's recommendation, giving an accuracy of 82.5%. Note that the pathologist's recommendation is based on manual computation and/or estimation from sampled regions, while the computer prediction is based on the counting throughout the whole slides. It is possible that there may be some bias in the pathologist's sampling, although this will be very hard to prove due to the large size of the images. The computer prediction, on the other hand, is free from this sampling bias, as all regions are considered. Overall this is a very promising result. Out of the seven disagreements, four are caused by the single difference between scores 2 and 3, which can be addressed with a more advanced learning model. The other three were from the 0% ER status and staining error case, as discussed previously. It is also interesting to note that five out of the seven disagreements are for the negative treatment cases, meaning the system has more difficulties predicting negative treatment cases. Further improvement to the deep learning model can help to address this problem.

The results demonstrate that the proposed system can be very useful in assisting pathologists in their predictive tumor marker reporting of breast carcinoma. It helps to reduce the bias in sampling, reduce inter- and intra-reader variability, provide more consistent reporting, and can reduce pathologists' workload significantly. Further improvement to the system will only enhance its performance.

## 5. Conclusions

We have proposed a cell detection and classification system based on a convolutional neural network model for use with the Allred scoring system for breast carcinoma hormone receptor status testing. The system classifies each cell in the ER-stained whole-slide images into negatively, weakly, moderately, and strongly stained cells, before Allred scoring is carried out to recommend hormonal treatment options. To the best of our knowledge, this is the first work of its kind in developing such a system, which would be a valuable tool for histopathologists in improving the reliability of predictive tumor marker reporting as well as reducing manual intervention workload. The cell detection and classification were applied on 40 whole-slide images before Allred scoring was carried out to recommend hormonal treatment options. Experimental result shows very promising observations for both the detection and classification processes, as well as the Allred scoring computation. The automated Allred scoring matches well with pathologists scoring, for both the actual Allred score and hormonal treatment cases. Future work will focus on further improving the accuracy of the system, extending the system on PR and possibly HER2 expression, as well as reducing the computational load in running the system on very large whole-slide breast carcinoma images. The improvement to the accuracy can be either by increasing the training samples, improving the network model, or by proposing some rules for the 0% ER status images as this proved to be the main source of error during performance evaluation.

**Author Contributions:** Conceptualization, M.F.A.F. and M.F.J.; methodology, W.S.H.M.W.A. and M.F.J.; software, W.S.H.M.W.A., M.F.J. and N.A.; validation, J.T.H.L., S.Y.K., L.M.L. and F.S.A.; formal analysis, W.S.H.M.W.A. and M.F.J.; investigation, M.F.A.F. and W.S.H.M.W.A.; resources, J.T.H.L., S.Y.K. and L.M.L.; data curation, W.S.H.M.W.A. and M.F.J.; writing—original draft preparation, M.F.A.F.; writing—review and editing, M.F.A.F. and W.S.H.M.W.A.; visualization, M.F.A.F. and W.S.H.M.W.A.; supervision, M.F.A.F.; project administration, M.F.A.F.; funding acquisition, M.F.A.F. All authors have read and agreed to the published version of the manuscript.

**Funding:** This study is supported by the Ministry of Higher Education (MOHE) Malaysia under the Research Excellence Consortium (Konsortium Kecemerlangan Pendidikan, KKP) grant, KKP-2021. This project has also supported Master's programs at both Multimedia University and the University of Malaya.

**Institutional Review Board Statement:** This study was approved by the Medical Research Ethics Committee of the University of Malaya Medical Centre (MREC ID No: 2016720-4037) on 22 December 2016.

**Informed Consent Statement:** Patient consent was waived due to the anonymity of the study.

**Data Availability Statement:** The image data used to support the findings of this study are available from the corresponding author upon request.

**Acknowledgments:** We would like to thank our collaborators for providing the image dataset and their ground truth for evaluation.

**Conflicts of Interest:** The authors declare no conflict of interest.

**Abbreviations**

The following abbreviations are used in this manuscript:

| | |
|---|---|
| ER | Estrogen receptor |
| PR | Progesterone receptor |
| HER2 | Human epidermal growth factor receptor 2 |
| IHC | Immunohistochemistry |
| PN | Positive and negative |
| WMS | Weak, moderate, strong |
| CNN | Convolutional neural network |
| WSI | Whole-slide image |
| TP | True positive |
| FP | False positive |
| TN | True negative |
| FN | False negative |
| PPV | Positive prediction value |
| TPR | True positive rate |
| AUC | Area under the curve |

## References

1. Hammond, M.E.H.; Hayes, D.F.; Dowsett, M.; Allred, D.C.; Hagerty, K.L.; Badve, S.; Fitzgibbons, P.L.; Francis, G.; Goldstein, N.S.; Hayes, M.; et al. American Society of Clinical Oncology/College of American Pathologists Guideline Recommendations for Immunohistochemical Testing of Estrogen and Progesterone Receptors in Breast Cancer. *J. Clin. Oncol.* **2010**, *28*, 2784–2795. [CrossRef] [PubMed]
2. Jamaluddin, M.F.; Fauzi, M.F.A.; Abas, F.S.; Lee, J.T.H.; Khor, S.Y.; Teoh, K.H.; Looi, L.M. Cells Detection and Segmentation in ER-IHC Stained Breast Histopathology Images. In Proceedings of the 2020 IEEE Region 10 Conference (Tencon), Osaka, Japan, 16–19 November 2020; pp. 73–76. [CrossRef]
3. Fauzi, M.F.A.; Gokozan, H.N.; Elder, B.; Puduvalli, V.K.; Pierson, C.R.; Otero, J.J.; Gurcan, M.N. A multi-resolution textural approach to diagnostic neuropathology reporting. *J. Neuro-Oncol.* **2015**, *124*, 393–402. [CrossRef] [PubMed]
4. Jamaluddin, M.F.; Fauzi, M.F.A.; Abas, F.S.; Lee, J.T.H.; Khor, S.Y.; Teoh, K.H.; Looi, L.M. Cell Classification in ER-Stained Whole Slide Breast Cancer Images Using Convolutional Neural Network. In Proceedings of the 2018 40th Annual International Conference of the IEEE Engineering in Medicine and Biology Society (EMBC), Honolulu, HI, USA, 18–21 July 2018; pp. 632–635. [CrossRef]
5. Shousha, S. Oestrogen receptor status of breast carcinoma: Allred/H score conversion table. *Histopathology* **2008**, *53*, 346–347. [CrossRef] [PubMed]
6. Fitzgibbons, P.L.; Murphy, D.A.; Hammond, M.E.H.; Allred, D.C.; Valenstein, P.N. Recommendations for Validating Estrogen and Progesterone Receptor Immunohistochemistry Assays. *Arch. Pathol. Lab. Med.* **2010**, *134*, 930–935. [CrossRef] [PubMed]
7. Mahanta, L.B.; Hussain, E.; Das, N.; Kakoti, L.; Chowdhury, M. IHC-Net: A fully convolutional neural network for automated nuclear segmentation and ensemble classification for Allred scoring in breast pathology. *Appl. Soft Comput.* **2021**, *103*, 107136. [CrossRef]
8. Mouelhi, A.; Rmili, H.; Ali, J.B.; Sayadi, M.; Doghri, R.; Mrad, K. Fast unsupervised nuclear segmentation and classification scheme for automatic allred cancer scoring in immunohistochemical breast tissue images. *Comput. Methods Programs Biomed.* **2018**, *165*, 37–51. [CrossRef] [PubMed]
9. Mungle, T.; Tewary, S.; DAS, D.; Arun, I.; Basak, B.; Agarwal, S.; Ahmed, R.; Chatterjee, S.; Chakraborty, C. MRF-ANN: A machine learning approach for automated ER scoring of breast cancer immunohistochemical images. *J. Microsc.* **2017**, *267*, 117–129. [CrossRef]
10. Kainz, P.; Urschler, M.; Schulter, S.; Wohlhart, P.; Lepetit, V. You Should Use Regression to Detect Cells. In *Medical Image Computing and Computer-Assisted Intervention— MICCAI 2015*; Springer International Publishing AG: Switzerland, 2015; Volume 9351, pp. 276–283. ._33. [CrossRef]
11. Xue, Y.; Ray, N.; Hugh, J.; Bigras, G. Cell Counting by Regression Using Convolutional Neural Network. In *Proceedings of the ECCV Workshops (1)*; Springer: Cham, Swizerland, 2016; pp. 274–290.
12. Fauzi, M.F.A.; Gokozan, H.N.; Pierson, C.R.; Otero, J.J.; Gürcan, M.N. Prognostic Reporting of p53 Expression by Image Analysis in Glioblastoma Patients: Detection and Classification. In *Proceedings of the HIS*; Springer: Cham, Swizerland, 2015.
13. Lecun, Y.; Bottou, L.; Bengio, Y.; Haffner, P. Gradient-based learning applied to document recognition. *Proc. IEEE* **1998**, *86*, 2278–2324. [CrossRef]
14. Krizhevsky, A.; Sutskever, I.; Hinton, G.E. ImageNet classification with deep convolutional neural networks. *Commun. ACM* **2017**, *60*, 84–90. [CrossRef]

15. Szegedy, C.; Liu, W.; Jia, Y.; Sermanet, P.; Reed, S.; Anguelov, D.; Erhan, D.; Vanhoucke, V.; Rabinovich, A. Going deeper with convolutions. In Proceedings of the 2015 IEEE Conference on Computer Vision and Pattern Recognition (CVPR), Boston, MA, USA, 7–12 June 2015; pp. 1–9. [CrossRef]
16. Zeiler, M.D.; Fergus, R. Visualizing and Understanding Convolutional Networks. In Proceedings of the European Conference on Computer Vision, Zurich, Switzerland, September, 6–12 September 2014; Springer: Cham, Swizerland, 2014.
17. Simonyan, K.; Zisserman, A. Very Deep Convolutional Networks for Large-Scale Image Recognition. *arXiv* **2014**, arXiv:1409.1556.
18. Vedaldi, A.; Lenc, K. MatConvNet: Convolutional Neural Networks for MATLAB. In Proceedings of the 23rd ACM International Conference on Multimedia, Brisbane, Australia, 26–30 October 2015; ACM: Brisbane, Australia, 2015; pp. 689–692. [CrossRef]
19. Fitzgibbons, P.L.; Dillon, D.A.; Alsabeh, R.; Berman, M.A.; Hayes, D.F.; Hicks, D.G.; Hughes, K.S.; Nofech-Mozes, S. Template for Reporting Results of Biomarker Testing of Specimens From Patients With Carcinoma of the Breast. *Arch. Pathol. Lab. Med.* **2014**, *138*, 595–601. [CrossRef] [PubMed]
20. Marée, R.; Rollus, L.; Stévens, B.; Hoyoux, R.; Louppe, G.; Vandaele, R.; Begon, J.M.; Kainz, P.; Geurts, P.; Wehenkel, L. Collaborative analysis of multi-gigapixel imaging data using Cytomine. *Bioinformatics* **2016**, *32*, 1395–1401. [CrossRef] [PubMed]

Article

# Computational Pipeline for Glomerular Segmentation and Association of the Quantified Regions with Prognosis of Kidney Function in IgA Nephropathy

Yoshimasa Kawazoe [1,*], Kiminori Shimamoto [1], Ryohei Yamaguchi [2], Issei Nakamura [3], Kota Yoneda [4], Emiko Shinohara [1], Yukako Shintani-Domoto [5], Tetsuo Ushiku [6], Tatsuo Tsukamoto [7] and Kazuhiko Ohe [8]

1 Artificial Intelligence in Healthcare, Graduate School of Medicine, The University of Tokyo, 7-3-1, Hongo, Bunkyo-ku, Tokyo 113-0033, Japan
2 Ohshima Memorial Kisen Hospital, 3-5-15, Misaki, Chiba 274-0812, Japan
3 NTT DOCOMO, Inc., Sanno Park Tower, 2-11-1, Nagata-cho, Chiyoda-ku, Tokyo 100-6150, Japan
4 Department of Reproductive, Developmental, and Aging Sciences, Graduate School of Medicine, The University of Tokyo, 7-3-1, Hongo, Bunkyo-ku, Tokyo 113-0033, Japan
5 Department of Diagnostic Pathology, Nippon Medical School Hospital, 1-1-5, Sendagi, Bunkyo-ku, Tokyo 113-8602, Japan
6 Department of Pathology, Graduate School of Medicine, The University of Tokyo, 7-3-1, Hongo, Bunkyo-ku, Tokyo 113-0033, Japan
7 Department of Nephrology and Dialysis, Tazuke Kofukai Medical Research Institute, Kitano Hospital, 2-4-20, Ohgimachi, Kita-ku, Osaka 530-8480, Japan
8 Department of Biomedical Informatics, Graduate School of Medicine, The University of Tokyo, 7-3-1, Hongo, Bunkyo-ku, Tokyo 113-0033, Japan
* Correspondence: kawazoe@m.u-tokyo.ac.jp; Tel.: +81-3-5800-9077

**Abstract:** The histopathological findings of the glomeruli from whole slide images (WSIs) of a renal biopsy play an important role in diagnosing and grading kidney disease. This study aimed to develop an automated computational pipeline to detect glomeruli and to segment the histopathological regions inside of the glomerulus in a WSI. In order to assess the significance of this pipeline, we conducted a multivariate regression analysis to determine whether the quantified regions were associated with the prognosis of kidney function in 46 cases of immunoglobulin A nephropathy (IgAN). The developed pipelines showed a mean intersection over union (IoU) of 0.670 and 0.693 for five classes (i.e., background, Bowman's space, glomerular tuft, crescentic, and sclerotic regions) against the WSI of its facility, and 0.678 and 0.609 against the WSI of the external facility. The multivariate analysis revealed that the predicted sclerotic regions, even those that were predicted by the external model, had a significant negative impact on the slope of the estimated glomerular filtration rate after biopsy. This is the first study to demonstrate that the quantified sclerotic regions that are predicted by an automated computational pipeline for the segmentation of the histopathological glomerular components on WSIs impact the prognosis of kidney function in patients with IgAN.

**Keywords:** computer vision; deep learning; digital pathology; whole slide imaging (WSI); object detection; segmentation; kidney disease; IgA nephropathy; glomerular sclerosis; renal prognosis

## 1. Introduction

The number of patients who are on dialysis due to end-stage renal failure is increasing worldwide, which has become a major health economic problem. According to a recent report [1], the number of patients undergoing chronic dialysis worldwide exceeded two million in 2010, and this number may double by 2030. The early detection and management of chronic kidney disease (CKD) is important in order to prevent its progression to end-stage renal failure. Immunoglobulin A nephropathy (IgAN) is the leading cause of CKD worldwide. It typically progresses to end-stage renal failure in 15–20% of patients after

10 years, and approximately 40% of patients after around 20 years [2,3]. Using evidence-based clinical practice guidelines in Japan [4], the clinical predictors for the progression of IgAN at the time of the initial renal biopsy include the following: (1) the presence of hypertension; (2) the amount of proteinuria with a usual cut-off of >1 g/day; (3) the degree of renal dysfunction; and (4) the histopathological grade, based on renal pathology. Of these predictors, histopathological findings play a key role but require observation by experts under a microscope. Patients with IgAN have varied histopathological lesions, ranging from mild mesangial proliferation, endocapillary hypercellularity, and crescentic glomerulonephritis to global and segmental sclerosis. For example, sclerosis represents the final appearance of glomerular injury that is caused by various diseases. When sclerosis occurs globally, determining the cause of the injury can be difficult.

Two histopathological grading systems are referred to in the clinical guidelines. The first system is the Oxford classification [5,6], which is based on the score of mesangial hypercellularity (M: M0, ≤0.5; M1, >0.5), endocapillary hypercellularity (E: E0, absent; E1, present), segmental sclerosis (S: S0, absent; S1, present), tubular atrophy or interstitial fibrosis (T: T0, 0–25%; T1, 26–50%; T2, >50%), and cellular or fibrocellular crescents (C: C0, absent; C1, 0–25%; C2, >25%). The second system is the Japanese histological grade classification (H-Grade) [7,8], which is based on the presence of acute lesions (i.e., cellular crescent, tuft necrosis, and fibrocellular crescent) and chronic lesions (i.e., global sclerosis, segmental sclerosis, and fibrous crescent). Detecting these complex findings among all of the glomeruli in whole slide images (WSIs) is laborious and time consuming, even for highly trained pathologists or nephrologists. Furthermore, the assessment is not always consistent [9,10]. Suppose the findings of all of the glomeruli on a WSI could be quantified with a computer, it may lead to a more thorough investigation of their impact on the prognosis of immunoglobulin A nephropathy (IgAN) and accelerate such research.

In the past decade, the number of studies aiming to develop deep learning applications for nephropathology has increased rapidly. Computational image recognition focusing on the glomerulus is generally classified into the following three types: the detection of glomeruli [11–14], the classification of the glomeruli [10,15], and the segmentation of the glomeruli [16–24]. The glomeruli that are detected in the WSI are localized by drawing bounding boxes. This approach would be a good application of automation because detecting glomeruli is simple but tedious for humans. Additionally, the development of such tools is realistic, as previously reported [13]. The classification of glomeruli, such as the presence or the absence of certain pathological findings, is more challenging because it requires the interpretation of quantitative histopathological lesions into qualitative expressions, for which expert assessment is not always consistent [9,10]. The segmentation of glomeruli localizes and quantifies every glomerulus by identifying the regions of each glomerulus in the pixels. Several studies have attempted to distinguish between the entire glomerulus and the background [16,17] or to distinguish between the normal and the sclerotic glomeruli [20,21,24]. Other studies have focused on the tubules, the blood vessels, and the interstitium, in addition to the glomerulus [19,23], or on the components inside of the glomerulus [18,22]. Segmenting the glomerulus and its components would be more helpful for a better understanding of kidney disease because it will be applied in the classification of pathological findings and to develop a prognostic model by utilizing quantified histopathological regions. Table 1 shows the previous studies for glomerular segmentation from WSI.

Table 1. Previous studies for glomerular segmentation from WSI.

| Author | Year | Object | Method | Subsequent Analysis | Extrapolation Evaluation |
|---|---|---|---|---|---|
| Kato et al. [16] | 2015 | Glomerulus | S-HOG + SVM | - | - |
| Gallego et al. [17] | 2018 | Glomerulus | CNN | - | - |
| Ginley et al. [18] | 2019 | Glomerulus and Internal components ((1) a nuclear component; (2) a PAS-positive component consisting of mesangium, glomerular basement membranes, and Bowman's capsule; (3) a luminal component consisting of Bowman's space and capillary lumina) | Deep Lab v2 | Tervaert classification and classification scheme defined by authors | - |
| Hermsen et al. [19] | 2019 | Renal structures (glomerulus, sclerotic glomerulus, empty Bowman's capsules, proximal tubule, distal tubule, atrophic tubule, undefined tubule, artery, interstitium, and capsule) | U-Net | Banff classification | Radboud University and Mayo Clinic |
| Bueno et al. [20] | 2020 | Glomerulus (normal, sclerosed) | SegNet and U-Net | - | - |
| Antini et al. [21] | 2020 | Glomerulus (normal, sclerosed) | SegNet and Deeplab v3+ | - | - |
| Zeng et al. [22] | 2020 | Glomerulus (global sclerosis, segmental sclerosis, crescent, or none of the above) and intraglomerular structures (mesangial cells, endothelial cells, and podocytes) | U-Net, DenseNet, LSTM-GCNet, and 2D V-Net | Mesangial hypercellularity score | - |
| Bouteldja et al. [23] | 2021 | Renal structures (glomerular tuft, glomerulus including Bowman's capsule, tubules, arteries, arterial lumina, and veins) | U-Net | - | - |
| Jiang et al. [24] | 2021 | Glomerulus (normal, global sclerosis, and glomerular with other lesions) | Mask R-CNN | - | - |

As the configuration of segmentation tasks varies from researcher to researcher, the high performance of a machine learning model does not necessarily indicate its usefulness for subsequent analyses. Previous studies [18,19,22] have assessed the usefulness of segmentation results in subsequent analyses, whereas other studies have only assessed the performance of machine learning models. In addition, these previous studies have only [19] evaluated the performance of machine learning models against external WSI, whereas the other studies have evaluated a single facility. Due to their high performance, deep neural networks (DNNs) tend to overfit to minute differences in the images that are used for training. Furthermore, the pathological specimens differ between facilities due to the differences in the preparation protocols. These factors have a non-negligible impact on the generalizability of studies dealing with WSI in DNNs. Therefore, in assessing the performance of the developed DNNs, an internal evaluation using only the WSIs of a single facility is not sufficient; external evaluations of the WSIs of different facilities are also important. Based on these two points, we propose an automated computational pipeline to detect the glomeruli from periodic acid-Schiff (PAS)-stained WSI and to segment the Bowman's space, the glomerular tuft, and the histopathological components of crescentic and sclerotic regions. The pipelines were developed using the WSIs of two facilities independently, and the performances across the facilities were evaluated. In order to assess the significance of the quantified histopathological regions, we conducted a multivariate regression analysis to determine whether the proportion of the sclerotic regions was significantly associated with the prognosis of kidney function in patients with IgAN.

## 2. Materials and Methods

### 2.1. Data Collection

The Institutional Review Board approved all experiments and data collection at the University of Tokyo Hospital (Tokyo, Japan; approval number: 11455) and Tazuke Kofukai Medical Research Institute, Kitano Hospital (Osaka, Japan; approval number: P17-05-004). All of the experiments were conducted following the Ethical Guidelines for Medical and Biological Research Involving Human Subjects in Japan. Informed consent was obtained from all participants through opt-out on the website. (See Figure A1 in Appendix A for an overview of the data collection and selection).

#### 2.1.1. Collection of the WSIs from Two Facilities

The University of Tokyo Hospital (facility T) collected 353 PAS-stained WSIs of renal biopsy specimens from 2010 to 2016. From Kitano Hospital (facility K), 324 PAS-stained WSIs were collected from 2005 to 2017. In both facilities, various kidney diseases were included in the WSIs, and the slide digitization was conducted using a NanoZoomer C9600-12 slide scanner (Hamamatsu Photonics, Hamamatsu City, Shizuoka, Japan) with a 40× objective at a resolution of 0.23 μm/pixel.

#### 2.1.2. Eligible IgAN Cases for the Regression Analysis

For the regression analysis for the prognosis of kidney function in IgAN cases, the data of 71 patients with IgAN, who had undergone a renal biopsy between 2010 and 2016 at facility T, were collected from their electronic health records (EHRs), which included information on their age, sex, diagnosis, blood, and urine test findings, and clinical records. Among these patients, those who met the following criteria were excluded: (1) <18 years at the time of the biopsy, (2) end-stage renal failure (e.g., maintenance hemodialysis, kidney transplantation, or estimated glomerular filtration rate (eGFR) <15 mL/min/1.73 m$^2$) at the time of biopsy, and (3) <1 year of eGFR follow-up after the biopsy. The data of 46 patients with IgAN were ultimately eligible for the regression analysis. Table 2 shows the statistical summary of the patients with IgAN.

**Table 2.** Statistical summary of the patients with IgAN.

| Facility | Case | Age (Median [IQR]) | Sex (Female:Male) | Hypertension (Absent:Present) | eGFR (Median [IQR]) | UPCR (Median [IQR]) |
|---|---|---|---|---|---|---|
| T | 46 | 42, [32, 61] | 21:25 | 18:28 | 65.15 [45.80, 83.88] | 1.18 [0.64, 2.39] |

IgAN, immunoglobulin A nephropathy; IQR, interquartile range; eGFR, estimated glomerular filtration ratio (mL/min/1.73 m$^2$); UPCR, urine protein–creatinine ratio ($g/g$).

### 2.2. Ground Truth Annotations

An assistant manually annotated the glomerular regions by bounding boxes in the 353 WSIs from facility T and the 324 WSIs from facility K using a computer-based commercial tool (RectLabel; available at https://rectlabel.com accessed on 19 November 2022) under the supervision of a nephrologist and a physician. The annotation for glomerular detection by bounding boxes requires the location of four vertex and class labels as supervised data. The average number of glomeruli in the WSI from facility T and facility K was 34 per WSI and 26 per WSI, respectively.

The annotation for segmentation requires assigning each pixel in an image to a specific class of object. We assigned each pixel of the cropped glomerular images to the following five classes: Bowman's space, glomerular tuft, crescentic region, sclerotic region, and background. The inner region surrounded by Bowman's capsule was annotated as a Bowman's space, and the area containing the glomerulocapillaries and intraglomerular mesangium region was annotated as a glomerular tuft. The crescentic and sclerotic regions were annotated using our previously developed criteria [10]. According to these criteria, there are three types of crescents, namely the "fibrous crescent," "fibrocellular crescent," and "cellular crescent." However, we did not distinguish between these crescentic regions in this study. "Sclerosis" comprises "capillary collapse," "segmental sclerosis," and "global sclerosis"; similarly, we did not distinguish between these sclerotic regions.

A nephrologist and a pathologist depicted paper-based annotation drafts in the 46 WSIs from facility T and the 43 WSIs from facility K. Two assistants also performed the annotations using a computer-based tool (labelme; available at https://github.com/wkentaro/labelme accessed on 19 November 2022). Figure 1 illustrates examples of annotation for glomerular detection and segmentation. Table 3 shows the characteristics of the dataset that was used for glomerular segmentation.

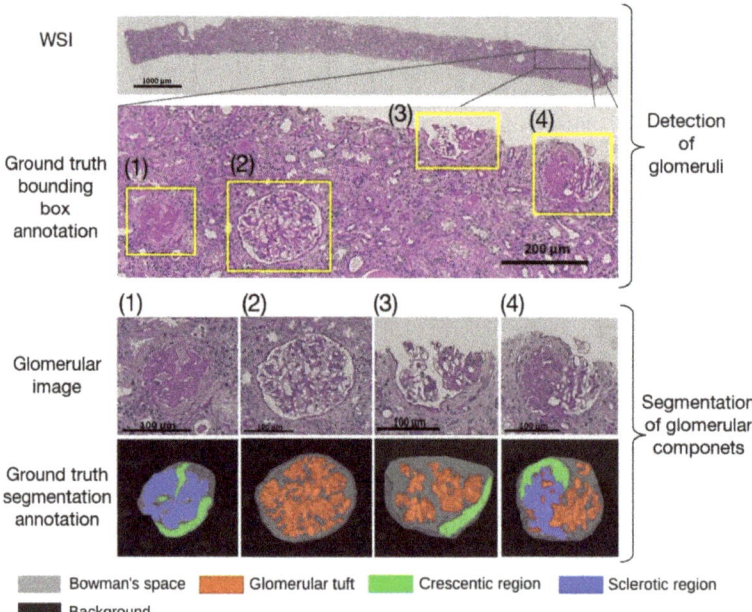

**Figure 1.** Example of a whole slide image (WSI) (**top row**). The bounding boxes of a glomerulus are shown as a rectangle with a yellow border in the second row. The glomerular images cropped by the bounding boxes are shown in the third row. The annotated images for the segmentation corresponding to the cropped glomeruli are shown in the bottom row. The examples in the (**bottom row**) (1)–(4) include cases with different percentages of sclerotic regions. (1) is an example of global sclerosis, in which there is no glomerular tuft (red). (2) and (3) are examples without sclerosis, in which there is no sclerotic region (blue). (4) is an example of segmental sclerosis, in which the glomerular tuft (red) and sclerotic region (blue) are almost equal in area.

Table 3. Characteristics of the annotated WSI for glomerular segmentation.

| Facility | WSI | Number of Glomeruli (Total; Median [IQR]) | Percentage of Crescentic Regions to Glomerulus (Median [IQR]) | Percentage of Sclerotic Regions to Glomerulus (Median [IQR]) |
|---|---|---|---|---|
| T | 46 | 1713; 27.5 [20, 39.5] | 3.46 [1.41, 6.47] | 2.57 [0.74, 6.49] |
| K | 42 | 1011; 24.0 [15, 30] | 4.78 [1.39, 10.27] | 5.37 [1.36, 9.06] |

WSI, whole slide image; IQR, interquartile range.

*2.3. Computational Pipeline*

To segment the histopathological regions inside the glomeruli from a high-resolution WSI, we developed a computational pipeline comprising the following two steps: (1) the detection of glomeruli, which draws bounding boxes surrounding the glomeruli in a WSI using Faster R-CNN, as described by Ren et al. [25], and (2) the segmentation of glomerular components, which classifies image pixels in bounding boxes into five classes (i.e., Bowman's space, glomerular tuft, crescentic region, sclerotic region, and background) using SegFormer, as described by Xie et al. [26], which is a transformer-based [27] state-of-the-art segmentation method. All of the pixels that were detected as "not glomerulus" in the first step were assigned to the background. The labels of each pixel that were calculated in step 2 were repositioned in the WSI to compose the results of the entire WSI. Figure 2 shows an overview of the computational pipeline.

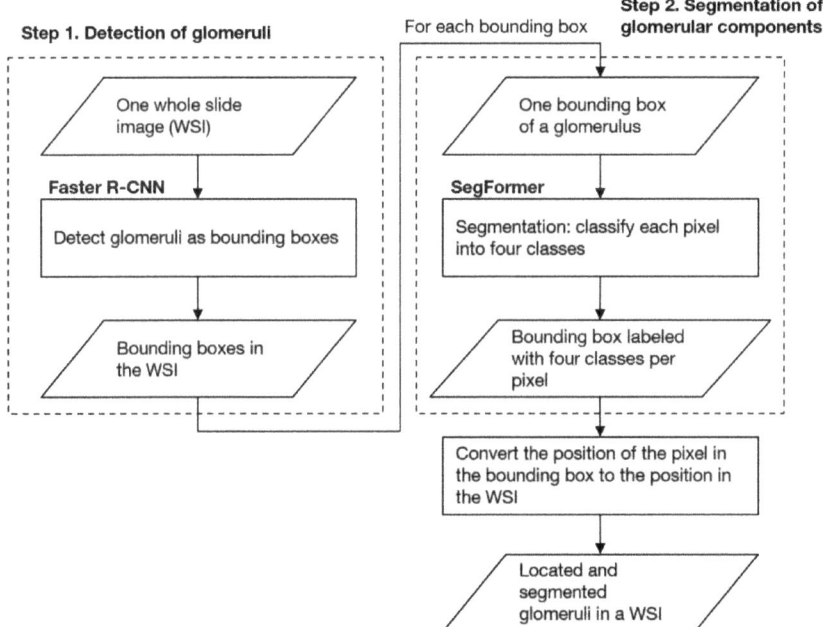

**Figure 2.** Overview of the computational pipeline. The parallelograms indicate the input or output data. The rectangles indicate the process. Faster R-CNN is described by Ren et al. [25], and SegFormer is described by Xie et al. [26].

2.3.1. Step 1: Detection of Glomeruli

Faster R-CNN with a sliding window, as presented in [13], was applied. All of the WSIs were downsampled from 40× magnification to 5× magnification to balance the detection accuracy and processing speed. To train the model, images that were cropped by 2000 μm-square windows centered on each annotated glomerulus were used. Incomplete glomerular bounding boxes at the boundaries of the windows were ignored. Data augmentation techniques (e.g., flipping, Gaussian blurring, and sharpening) were applied to train the network to improve its robustness for variations in morphology and staining. The entire WSI was scanned with a sliding window (row-by-row, left-to-right) to evaluate the model. Each image of the sliding window was fed into the model. Neighboring windows overlapped each other by 10% (i.e., 200 μm), such that all of a glomerulus could be included in a window, even if it was at the boundary of the window. When a detected glomerulus was in the overlapping region of the neighboring windows, the bounding boxes that were overlapping by 35% or more were merged into one.

2.3.2. Step 2: Segmentation of the Glomerular Components

SegFormer was used to segment the glomerular components, which classified each pixel of a glomerular image into the following five classes: Bowman's space, glomerular tuft, crescentic region, sclerotic region, and background. To train the model, manually cropped glomerular images with an added margin of 20 μm were used to facilitate the easy training of the features outside of the glomerulus. This 20 μm margin width was set to 1/10 of the 200 μm, which is the estimated diameter of a glomerulus. When evaluating the model after glomerular detection, a 20 μm margin was added to the obtained image so that it would be similar to the training image. Data augmentation techniques (e.g., flipping, scaling, cropping, changing contrast, Gaussian blurring, and sharpening) were applied. The "Method details" section in Appendix G describes the critical aspects of Faster R-CNN and SegFormer and the evaluation metrics.

*2.4. Multivariate Analysis for eGFR Prognosis in IgAN*

The WSI and clinical information of 46 eligible patients with IgAN from facility T were analyzed (see Figure A1(1)). The prognostic variables were as follows: (1) age at biopsy, (2) sex, (3) presence or absence of prebiopsy hypertension, (4) eGFR at biopsy, (5) urine protein–creatinine ratio (UPCR) at biopsy, and (6) the mean proportion of the sclerotic regions compared to the whole glomerular regions in a WSI. For the histopathological variables, we used the proportion of the area of the sclerotic regions compared to the combined area of glomerular tuft and sclerotic regions.

The whole glomerular tuft region was obtained by combining the glomerular tuft and sclerotic regions. Variables 1–5 were obtained from the EHRs, and variable 6 was obtained with the developed computational pipeline by calculating the proportion of a sclerotic region to the whole glomerular tuft for all glomeruli in a WSI. The whole glomerular tuft was calculated as the sum of the glomerular tufts and sclerotic regions in the glomerular image. For the objective variable, we used the eGFR slope that was calculated from eGFRs within 2 years after renal biopsy. The eGFR slope was the slope of the univariate linear regression model of eGFR over time. This outcome represents a more dynamic tendency, compared to measurements taken at one point [28–33]. Multivariate regression analysis was conducted to assess the impact of the prognostic factors on the eGFR slope by estimating the partial regression coefficients and their *p*-values. Multicollinearity between the prognostic variables was assessed using VIF statistics.

*2.5. Experiment Settings*

To consider the mutual applicability between the facilities, computational pipelines were developed by independently using WSIs from facility T and facility K and evaluating the performances across the facilities. The details of the cross-validation settings and evaluation across facilities are described in the Appendix G.1.7.

## 3. Results

*3.1. Performance of the Computational Pipeline*

### 3.1.1. Glomerular Detection

As for the results of the glomerular detection alone, the F1 score (standard error) of the model that was trained with the WSIs of facility T (educational university hospital) for the WSIs of facility T (i.e., T to T) was 0.919 (0.003). The F1 score of the model that was trained with the WSIs of facility K (general hospital and research center) for the WSIs of facility K (i.e., K to K) was 0.912 (0.009). No significant difference existed between these F1 scores ($p = 0.08$), indicating no difference in the model's performance against the WSI of its facility, which has been referred to as "internal performance." In contrast, the F1 scores of T to K and K to T were 0.892 (0.005) and 0.875 (0.009), respectively. Significant differences existed between the scores of T to T and T to K ($p < 0.01$) and between K to K and K to T ($p = 0.01$). These results have revealed that, in both models, the performance decreased against the external facility's WSI, which has been referred to as "external performance." Table A1 in Appendix B shows the performance of glomeruli detection. Figure A2 in Appendix C depicts an example of the results of glomerular detection on a WSI.

### 3.1.2. Glomerular Segmentation and the Pipeline

The top of Table 4 presents the segmentation performance. The mean (standard error (SE)) intersection over union (IoU) of T to T and K to K were 0.741 (0.011) and 0.764 (0.016), respectively. This finding indicated no significant difference between the internal performance of each model ($p = 0.285$). However, the external performance of the models tended to decrease. The mean IoU (SE) of K to T was 0.682 (0.002), which was lower than the mean IoU (SE) of T to T [0.741 (0.011)], and showed a significant difference ($p = 0.003$). The mean IoU of T to K was 0.737 (0.005), which was lower than the mean IoU of K to K [0.764 (0.016)], but the difference was not significant ($p = 0.164$). The bottom of Table 4 shows the segmentation performance after the detection (i.e., pipeline). The pipeline results were generally lower than those of the segmentation alone, owing to the accumulated error in the detection. As in the cases of segmentation alone, no significant difference existed in the mean IoU between T to T (0.670) and K to K (0.693), which indicated no difference in their internal performance ($p = 0.395$). In addition, the external performance of the models tended to decrease, as in the case of segmentation alone. The mean IoU of K to T was 0.609 (0.002), which was lower than the mean IoU of T to T [0.670 (0.017)], and showed a significant difference ($p = 0.015$). The mean IoU of T to K was 0.678 (0.002), which was lower than the mean IoU of K to K [0.693 (0.020)], but the difference was not significant ($p = 0.509$). Figure 3 depicts an example of the results that were obtained by the pipeline of T to T and K to T. Some examples of glomeruli with a high or low mean IoU that were obtained by the pipeline of K to T are shown in Figure 4.

**Table 4.** Performance of glomerular segmentation.

| Evaluation Scope | Model to WSI | Background | Bowman's Space | Glomerular Tuft | Crescentic Region | Sclerotic Region | Mean IoU |
|---|---|---|---|---|---|---|---|
| | T to T | 0.965 (0.001) | 0.664 (0.009) | 0.770 (0.006) | 0.596 (0.032) | 0.707 (0.021) | 0.741 (0.011) |
| | K to K | 0.973 (0.002) | 0.696 (0.013) | 0.810 (0.014) | 0.665 (0.033) | 0.674 (0.032) | 0.764 (0.016) |
| | *p* | 0.028 * | 0.094 | 0.037 * | 0.160 | 0.418 | 0.285 |
| Segmentation Alone | T to T | 0.965 (0.001) | 0.666 (0.009) | 0.770 (0.006) | 0.596 (0.032) | 0.707 (0.021) | 0.741 (0.011) |
| | K to T | 0.956 (0.000) | 0.586 (0.016) | 0.738 (0.002) | 0.523 (0.047) | 0.604 (0.006) | 0.682 (0.002) |

Table 4. Cont.

| Evaluation Scope | Model to WSI | Background | Bowman's Space | Glomerular Tuft | Crescentic Region | Sclerotic Region | Mean IoU |
|---|---|---|---|---|---|---|---|
| | p | 0.003 * | <0.001 * | 0.004 * | 0.070 | 0.004 * | 0.003 * |
| | K to K | 0.973 (0.002) | 0.696 (0.013) | 0.810 (0.014) | 0.665 (0.033) | 0.674 (0.032) | 0.764 (0.016) |
| | T to K | 0.963 (0.001) | 0.667 (0.004) | 0.789 (0.002) | 0.629 (0.005) | 0.638 (0.007) | 0.737 (0.005) |
| | p | 0.008 * | 0.077 | 0.195 | 0.326 | 0.312 | 0.164 |
| | T to T | 0.999 (0.000) | 0.594 (0.014) | 0.736 (0.015) | 0.497 (0.041) | 0.521 (0.023) | 0.670 (0.017) |
| | K to K | 0.999 (0.000) | 0.626 (0.020) | 0.768 (0.017) | 0.530 (0.039) | 0.540 (0.038) | 0.693 (0.020) |
| | p | NA | 0.230 | 0.190 | 0.568 | 0.691 | 0.395 |
| Segmentation after detection (i.e., pipeline) | T to T | 0.999 (0.000) | 0.594 (0.014) | 0.736 (0.015) | 0.497 (0.041) | 0.521 (0.023) | 0.670 (0.017) |
| | K to T | 0.999 (0.000) | 0.509 (0.005) | 0.683 (0.001) | 0.412 (0.003) | 0.442 (0.003) | 0.609 (0.002) |
| | p | NA | 0.001 * | 0.015 * | 0.094 | 0.019 * | 0.015 * |
| | K to K | 0.999 (0.000) | 0.626 (0.020) | 0.768 (0.017) | 0.530 (0.039) | 0.540 (0.038) | 0.693 (0.020) |
| | T to K | 0.999 (0.000) | 0.602 (0.002) | 0.749 (0.002) | 0.516 (0.006) | 0.527 (0.003) | 0.678 (0.002) |
| | p | NA | 0.293 | 0.323 | 0.727 | 0.748 | 0.509 |

Unless otherwise specified, the data are presented as the mean (standard error). "T to T" represents the results from the facility T model against the facility T data. "K to K" represents the results from the facility K model against the facility K data. "T to K" is the result of the facility T model against facility K data. "K to T" is the result of the facility K model against the facility T data. * indicates a statistically significant difference (i.e., $p < 0.05$). The $p$ value is based on Welch's $t$-test for the equality of the means of two samples. WSI, whole slide image; NA not available; SE standard error.

### 3.1.3. Regression Analysis for Kidney Prognosis

Table 5 shows the results of the multivariate analysis of the estimated glomerular filtration rate (eGFR) slope within two years after renal biopsy in 46 patients with IgAN. The column of the ground truth shows the results when manually annotated regions of the glomerular tuft and the sclerotic region were used. The columns of T to T and K to T show the results when each pipeline's predicted sclerotic regions were used. The coefficients of determination ($R^2$) for the ground truth, T to T, and K to T models were 0.18, 0.17, and 0.16, respectively. For multicollinearity, no variable had a variance inflation factor (VIF) value of > 3.0 in the ground truth model. In all of the models, the proportion of the sclerotic regions had a significant negative impact on the eGFR slope ($p < 0.05$). However, no other variables showed a significant impact. The results of the univariate regression analysis showed the same tendency (see Table A2 in Appendix D).

Table A3 in Appendix E presents the correlation coefficients between the ground truth regions and the predicted regions by the pipeline for the sclerotic and the semicircular regions in 46 IgAN cases. The results were high values that exceeded 0.96. The scatter plots for the sclerotic regions in the T to T and K to T models are shown in Figure A3 in Appendix F.

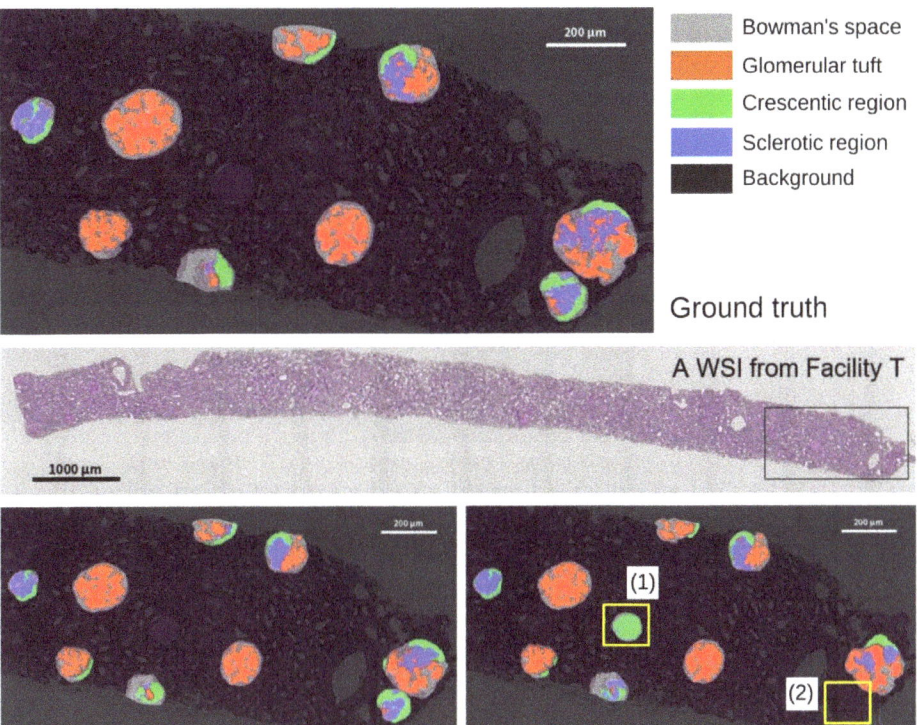

**Figure 3.** Example of the results of a whole slide image (WSI) from facility T. **Top**: manually annotated glomeruli and their components (i.e., ground truth). Middle: The WSI of the renal sample. The box is the area depicted in the top and bottom images. **Bottom left**: The predicted result obtained by model T (i.e., internal model). **Bottom right**: The predicted result obtained by model K (i.e., external model). In the example of the predicted result in the bottom right (K to T), (1) a dilated tubule filled with Tamm–Horsfall protein is incorrectly detected as glomerulus, and (2) a glomerulus is undetected, both of which are due to errors that occurred in the detection process in the first step of the computational pipeline.

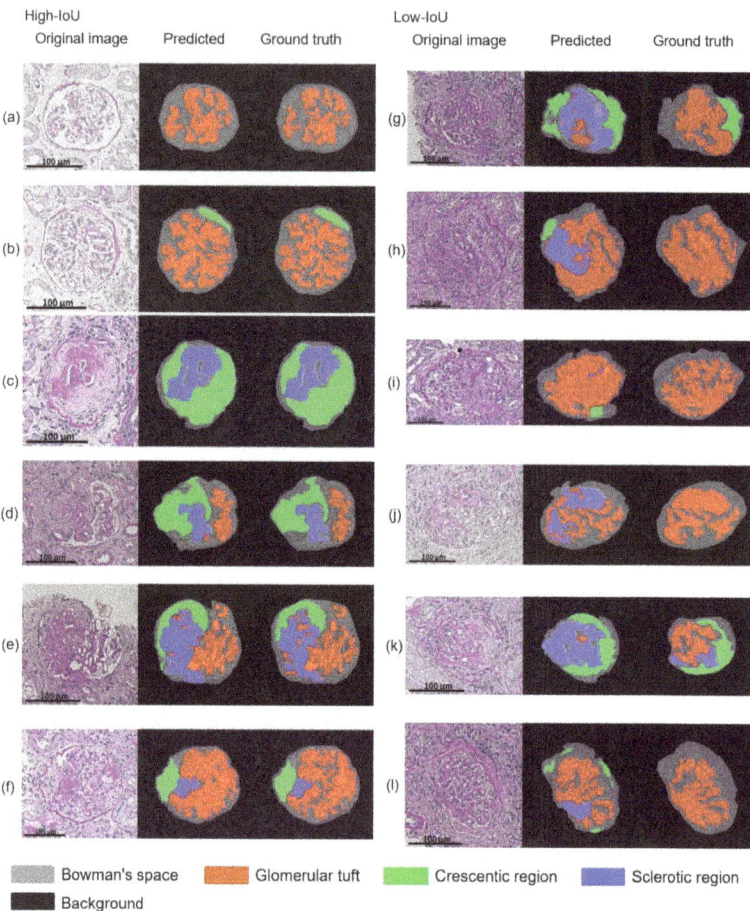

**Figure 4.** Example of the glomerular component segmentation obtained by the pipeline of K to T (predicted by the external model). The left column shows examples with higher mean intersection over union (IoU) of (**a**) 0.894, (**b**) 0.879, (**c**) 0.846, (**d**) 0.818, (**e**) 0.792, and (**f**) 0.780. The right column shows examples with lower mean IoU of (**g**) 0.377, (**h**) 0.384, (**i**) 0.412, (**j**) 0.417, (**k**) 0.438, and (**l**) 0.453. In the right column (**a**–**f**), the Bowman's space, glomerular tuft, crescentic, and sclerotic region are correctly segmented. The pairs of the proportions of the sclerotic region of ground truth that are predicted in left column are (**a**–**c**) 0.0 to 0.0, (**d**) 0.485 to 0.446, (**e**) 0.451 to 0.518, and (**f**) 0.085 to 0.101, which are generally corresponding. (**g**) Most of the glomerular tuft region is incorrectly segmented as the sclerotic region, and the left side of the Bowman's spaces are incorrectly segmented to the crescentic regions. (**h**) The left side of the glomerular tuft region is incorrectly segmented to the sclerotic region, and the upper left Bowman's space is incorrectly segmented as the crescentic region. (**i**) The Bowman's spaces in the glomerular tuft gaps are incorrectly segmented as the glomerular tuft areas, and the bottom of the glomerular tuft is incorrectly segmented as the crescentic regions. (**j**) The upper and lower left glomerular tuft areas are incorrectly segmented as the sclerotic regions. (**k**) Most of the glomerular tuft region from the upper left to the center is incorrectly segmented to the sclerotic region. (**l**) The lower left glomerular tuft region near the vascular pole is incorrectly segmented to the sclerotic region, and several small regions around the Bowman's space are incorrectly segmented to the crescentic regions. The pairs of the proportions of the sclerotic region of ground truth that are predicted in right column are (**g**) 0.0 to 0.832, (**h**) 0.0 to 0.282, (**i**) 0.0 to 0.009, (**j**) 0.0 to 0.430, (**k**) 0.247 to 0.967, and (**l**) 0.0 to 0.158. All scale bars indicate 100 mm.

Table 5. Results of the multivariate regression analysis.

| | Ground Truth ($R^2$ = 0.18) | | | T to T ($R^2$ = 0.17) | | | K to T ($R^2$ = 0.16) | | |
|---|---|---|---|---|---|---|---|---|---|
| | Beta | p Value | VIF | Beta | p Value | VIF | Beta | p Value | VIF |
| Age | −1.289 (1.369) | 0.34 | 1.9 | −1.217 (1.376) | 0.37 | 1.9 | −1.242 (1.393) | 0.36 | 1.9 |
| Sex (male = 1) | −0.604 (1.144) | 0.59 | 1.4 | −0.550 (1.149) | 0.62 | 1.3 | −0.359 (1.151) | 0.75 | 1.3 |
| Hypertension (presence = 1) | −0.926 (1.194) | 0.43 | 1.5 | −0.999 (1.199) | 0.39 | 1.5 | −1.115 (1.211) | 0.35 | 1.5 |
| eGFR at renal biopsy (mL/min/1.73 m$^2$) | −2.793 (1.554) | 0.071 | 2.5 | −2.727 (1.562) | 0.079 | 2.5 | −2.370 (1.540) | 0.12 | 2.4 |
| UPCR at renal biopsy (g/g) | 0.211 (1.169) | 0.85 | 1.4 | 0.024 (1.169) | 0.98 | 1.4 | 0.069 (1.185) | 0.95 | 1.4 |
| Proportion of sclerotic regions (%) | −2.885 (1.207) | 0.018 * | 1.5 | −2.732 (1.196) | 0.024 * | 1.5 | −2.333 (1.126) | 0.039 * | 1.3 |

The data are presented as the mean (standard error), unless otherwise specified. "T to T" is the result of the facility T model applied to facility T data. "K to T" is the result of the facility K model applied to facility T data. * indicates a statistically significant difference (i.e., $p < 0.05$). The $p$ value is based on Welch's $t$-test for the equality of the means of two samples. Beta, standardized partial regression coefficient; $R^2$, coefficient of determination; eGFR, estimated glomerular filtration rate; UPCR, urine protein–creatinine ratio; VIF, variance inflation factor.

## 4. Discussion

In this paper, we describe an automated computational pipeline that can detect glomeruli in PAS-stained WSI and segment the histopathological components inside of the glomerulus. Based on multivariate analysis, the predicted sclerotic regions, even the regions that were predicted by the external model, had a significant negative impact on the eGFR slope within two years after biopsy. We believe that this study is the first to demonstrate the usefulness of an automated computational pipeline for segmenting the histopathological glomerular components on WSIs and demonstrate that quantified sclerotic regions impact the prognosis of the kidney function in patients with IgAN.

Several studies [18–21] aiming for pixel-level semantic segmentation for WSI of renal tissue sections have set the task of distinguishing between nonsclerotic and sclerotic glomeruli. Bueno et al. [20] sequentially applied SegNet-VGG19 [34] in order to segment glomeruli and applied AlexNet to classify them as nonsclerotic or sclerotic glomeruli. The segmentation accuracies for the nonsclerotic and the sclerotic were 96.06% and 83.22%, respectively. Hermsen et al. [19] evaluated U-Net-based 11 class segmentation, as described by Ronneberger et al. [35]. The normal glomeruli, sclerotic glomeruli, empty Bowman's capsules, tubules, arteries, interstitium, and the capsules were fully annotated. The Dice coefficients of the normal and the sclerotic glomeruli were 0.95 and 0.62, respectively. Altini et al. [21] conducted SegNet-based semantic segmentation of nonsclerotic and sclerotic glomeruli; their IoUs were 0.66546 and 0.49215, respectively. Jiang et al. [24] conducted a mask region-based convolutional neural network (R-CNN)-based semantic segmentation for classifying glomeruli with a normal structure, an abnormal structure, and global sclerosis; the mean IoU for PAS-stained WSIs were 0.697, 0.544, and 0.646, respectively. The results of these previous studies could help us to quantify global glomerulosclerosis, the ratio between sclerotic glomeruli, and the overall number of glomeruli. However, because glomerular sclerosis does not always occur globally, pixel-level segmentation for partially sclerosed regions is required for detailed quantification. Such quantification should have an essential role in understanding kidney diseases.

As shown in Table 4, the performance of the segmentation alone and the pipeline showed no significant differences in the mean IoU between T to T and K to K. This finding indicated that their internal performances were comparable. This finding supports that the annotation for glomerular detection and segmentation was conducted with a constant quality. Compared to the performance of the models that were trained with internal WSIs, the performance of the models that were trained with external WSIs tended to decrease in the segmentation alone and the pipeline. One of the reasons for this finding may be due to differences in the slide preparation to the digitization process between the facilities. The differences in the staining protocols, the manufacturing processes, and the digital scanner processing between the laboratories caused minute differences in the WSIs; however, the pathological samples were stained similarly. This difference is imperceptible to the human eye, but it is sufficient to affect deep learning-based applications [36–38]. We applied color normalization in the preprocessing step and Gaussian blurring, sharpening, and contrast changes during the data augmentation. However, extended methods are required in order to compensate for the minute differences in WSIs between the facilities, which increases the robustness against external WSI. The successful adaptation of WSI in deep neural network-based applications depends on each step of high-quality pathology slide preparation, such as embedding, cutting, staining, and scanning [39,40], as well as color variations. Using precise and homogeneous WSIs is desirable; however, such a model may not necessarily be robust against external WSIs that have more diversity. Improving the interfacility applicability of the developed model is an important issue for the success of deep learning applications in digital pathology. In addition, the performance of K to T is significantly lower for both the segmentation alone and the pipeline, while the performance degradations of T to K are not significant. This may be because a small number of glomerular images (1011) were used to develop the segmentation in model K, compared to the number of glomerular images that were used to develop model T (1713). We used the same number of WSIs from both of the facilities for the segmentation task. However, the number of images differed because of the different number of glomeruli that were contained in each WSI. The relatively small number of glomerular images in the training data for model K may have resulted in less diversity, leading to the significant performance degradation of K to T.

As shown in Table 5, the manually quantified (ground truth) sclerotic regions were associated with negatively impacting the eGFR slope in the multivariate analysis. Segmental sclerosis, which is defined by the Oxford Classification [5,6], or the chronic lesions including segmental sclerosis and global sclerosis, which are defined by the H-Grade [7,8] have a negative impact on the poor prognosis of IgAN; however, the current study showed that the quantified sclerotic regions also have a negative impact on the eGFR slope within two years after biopsy. In our analysis, the effect of the post-biopsy treatment on eGFR was not adjusted because of the retrospective design, which is a limitation of this analysis. In addition, other limitations of this analysis were that the 2-year period was relatively short and the number of IgAN cases ($n$ = 46) was also limited; these may have affected the relatively low coefficients of determination (0.18 in the ground truth model).

Table 5 also shows the same tendency in the standardized partial regression coefficients among the ground truth, the T to T (i.e., internal model), and the K to T (i.e., external model) models. The correlation between the ground truth regions and the predicted regions in each WSI aids in the understanding of their impact in the regression model. In Table A3 in Appendix E, the correlation coefficient for the sclerotic regions exceeded 0.96, even when using the external model. This finding indicated that the estimation of the total amount of sclerotic and glomerular tuft regions in each WSI was approximately correct. In light of the previous results, our developed pipeline shows a certain level of robustness for quantifying the glomerular tuft and sclerotic regions from WSI, even if the model is applied to the WSI of external facilities.

Another limitation of this study is that the concordance of the ground truth labels that have been used for developing glomerular detection and segmentation was not evaluated; however, the experts provided them. Surrounding the glomeruli with bounding boxes and drawing their histopathological components required distinguishing unclear boundaries with an understanding of pathology. Such labeling could vary among experts. Well-annotated examples are important in supervised learning; the main challenge in deep neural network-based applications for digital histopathology is obtaining high-quality labels. We carefully conducted the annotation with multiple experts, including a nephrologist and a pathologist, however the possibility of errors does exist. Nonetheless, annotation errors are not specific to this research; however, they should be kept in mind in studies on supervised learning.

## 5. Conclusions

We developed an automated computational pipeline for detecting glomeruli on PAS-stained WSIs, followed by segmenting the Bowman's space, the glomerular tuft, the crescentic, and the sclerotic region inside of the glomeruli. The internal and external evaluation of the pipeline using WSIs from two facilities showed that the mean IoU of five regions, including the background, was 0.670 (T to T) and 0.693 (K to K) in the internal evaluation, and 0.609 (K to T) and 0.678 (T to K) in the external evaluation. The multivariate analysis for eGFR prognosis in cases of IgAN showed that the proportion of sclerotic regions that were quantified by the pipelines, even those that were quantified by the external model, had a significant negative impact on the eGFR slope, while five other clinical prognostic factors (i.e., age, sex, hypertension, eGFR at biopsy, and UPCR at biopsy) had no significant impact. These findings suggest the importance of quantifying the sclerotic region, as well as the usefulness and the robustness of the developed pipeline, for the purpose of predicting eGFR in cases of IgAN. The developed pipeline could aid in diagnosing renal pathology by visualizing and quantifying the histopathological feature of glomerulus. In addition, this high-throughput approach could potentially accelerate research in order to better understand the prognosis of IgAN.

**Author Contributions:** Conceptualization, Y.K., R.Y. and E.S.; Methodology, K.S., I.N. and K.Y.; Validation, R.Y. and Y.S.-D.; Resource, T.U. and T.T.; Writing—original draft, Y.K. and K.S.; Writing—review and editing, Y.K., K.S., R.Y., I.N., K.Y., E.S., Y.S.-D., T.U., T.T. and K.O.; Supervision, T.T. and K.O.; Funding acquisition, Y.K. and K.O. All authors have read and agreed to the published version of the manuscript.

**Funding:** This research was supported by the Health Labour Sciences Research Grants, Japan (JPMH28030401) and the Japan Science and Technology Agency, promoting individual research to nurture the seeds of future innovation and organize unique, innovative networks (JPMJPR1654).

**Institutional Review Board Statement:** The Institutional Review Board approved all experiments and data collection at the University of Tokyo Hospital (Tokyo, Japan; approval number: 11455) and Tazuke Kofukai Medical Research Institute, Kitano Hospital (Osaka, Japan; approval number: P17-05-004).

**Informed Consent Statement:** Informed consent was obtained from all subjects involved in the study.

**Data Availability Statement:** The datasets of the WSIs are unavailable to the public, and their use is restricted. The source code, network configurations, and trained network-derived results are available at the following URL: https://github.com/jinseikenai/glomeruli_segmentation accessed on 19 November 2022.

**Conflicts of Interest:** Y.K., K.S. and E.S. belong to the Artificial Intelligence in Healthcare, Graduate School of Medicine (University of Tokyo, Tokyo, Japan), which is an endowment department, and were supported by an unrestricted grant from I&H Co., Ltd. (Hyogo, Japan) and EM Systems Company (Osaka, Japan). However, these sponsors had no control over this work's interpretation, writing, or publication. I.N. is affiliated with NTT DOCOMO, INC. (Tokyo, Japan) and had no control over the interpretation, writing, or publication of this work. R.Y., K.Y., Y.D., T.U., T.T. and K.O. declare no competing interests.

## Appendix A.

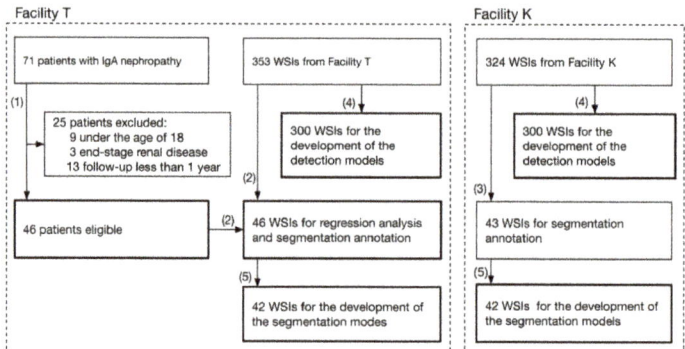

**Figure A1.** Overview of the data collection and selection procedure. (1) Eligibility criteria of immunoglobulin A nephropathy (IgAN) for regression analysis. (2) Facility T: whole slide image (WSI) selection for regression analysis and segmentation annotation. (3) Facility K: WSI selection for segmentation annotation. (4) WSI selection for the development of glomerular detection models. (5) WSI selection for the development of the glomerular segmentation models. Bold boxes indicate the data used in the experiments described below.

## Appendix B.

**Table A1.** Performance of glomerular detection.

|  | T to T | K to K | $p$ | T to T | T to K | $p$ | K to K | K to T | $p$ |
|---|---|---|---|---|---|---|---|---|---|
| F1 score | 0.919 (0.003) | 0.912 (0.009) | 0.08 | 0.919 (0.003) | 0.892 (0.005) | <0.01 * | 0.912 (0.002) | 0.875 (0.009) | 0.01 * |

F1 is the harmonic mean of precision and recall. "T to T" is the result of the facility T model against the WSIs of facility T. "K to K" is the result of the facility K model against the WSIs of facility K. "T to K" is the result of the facility T model against the WSIs of facility K. "K to T" is the result of the facility K model against the WSIs of facility T. * indicates a statistically significant difference (i.e., $p < 0.05$). The $p$-value is based on Welch's $t$-test for equality of means of two results. Note: The data are presented as the mean F1 score (standard error).

## Appendix C.

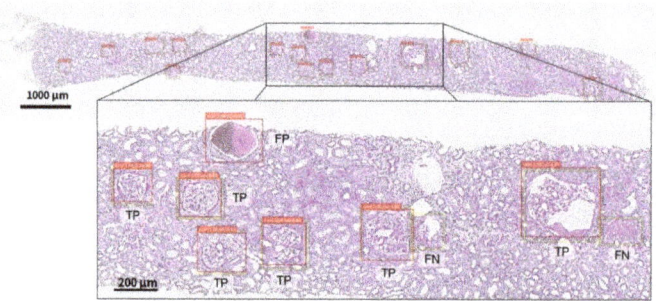

**Figure A2.** Example of glomerular detection results from a WSI. The yellow frames indicate the ground truth of the glomerular. The red frames indicate the predicted glomerular regions proposed by Faster R-CNN. The regions with overlapped yellow and red frames indicate a true positive (TP), the regions surrounded by only red frames indicate a false positive (FP), and the regions surrounded by only yellow frames indicate a false negative (FN).

## Appendix D.

Table A2. Results of the univariate regression analysis.

|  | Ground Truth | | T to T | | K to T | |
|---|---|---|---|---|---|---|
|  | Beta | p-Value | Beta | p-Value | Beta | p-Value |
| Age | −0.652 (1.014) | 0.51 | −0.652 (1.014) | 0.51 | −0.652 (1.014) | 0.51 |
| Sex (male = 1) | −0.368 (1.017) | 0.71 | −0.368 (1.017) | 0.71 | −0.368 (1.017) | 0.71 |
| Hypertension (present = 1) | −0.864 (1.010) | 0.38 | −0.864 (1.010) | 0.38 | −0.864 (1.010) | 0.38 |
| eGFR at renal biopsy (mL/min/1.73 m$^2$) | −0.167 (1.018) | 0.87 | −0.167 (1.018) | 0.87 | −0.167 (1.018) | 0.87 |
| UPCR (g/g) | −0.479 (1.016) | 0.63 | −0.479 (1.016) | 0.63 | −0.479 (1.016) | 0.63 |
| Proportion of sclerotic regions (%) | −1.865 (0.975) | 0.055 | −1.786 (0.979) | 0.067 | −1.764 (0.980) | 0.071 |

Unless otherwise specified, the data are presented as mean (standard error). "T to T" is the result of the facility T model applied to facility T data. "K to T" is the result of the facility K model applied to facility T data. The $p$-value is based on Welch's $t$-test for the equality of the means of two samples. Beta, standardized partial regression coefficient; GFR, estimated glomerular filtration rate; UPCR, urine protein–creatinine ratio.

## Appendix E.

Table A3. Correlation coefficients between the ground truth and predicted regions.

| Model to WSI | Proportion of the Sclerotic Regions to the Combined Area of Glomerular Tuft and Sclerotic Regions |
|---|---|
| T to T | 0.967 |
| K to T | 0.963 |

"T to T" is the result of the facility T model applied to facility T data. "K to T" is the result of the facility K model applied to facility T data. The correlation coefficient between T and T was derived from one of the six cross-validations. The correlation coefficient of "K to T" is the average of the six cross-validations.

## Appendix F.

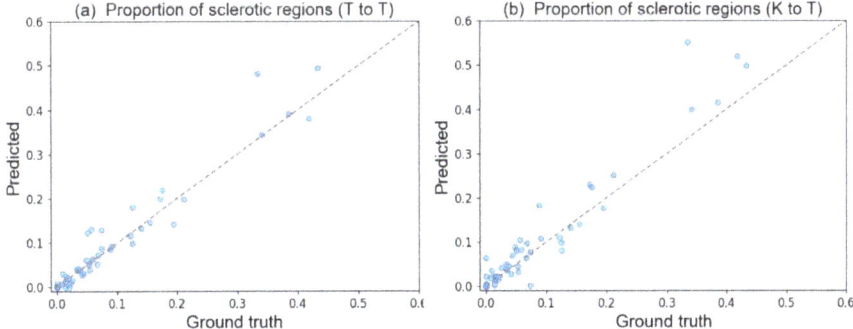

Figure A3. Scatter plots of the proportion of sclerotic regions between the ground truth and predicted regions. (a) Sclerotic regions of T to T. (b) Sclerotic regions predicted by K to T. "T to T" is the result of the facility T model for the WSIs of facility T. "K to T" is the result of the facility K model for the WSIs of facility T.

**Appendix G.**

*Appendix G.1. Method Details*

Appendix G.1.1. Faster R-CNN

A faster region-based convolutional neural network (Faster R-CNN [31]) is an object detection method that is based on convolutional neural networks (CNNs). Faster R-CNN consists of the following two modules: the region proposal network (RPN), which identifies the region of an object in an image, and a network that classifies the objects in the proposed region. Faster R-CNN first processes the input image by performing convolution and pooling layers in order to obtain feature maps and passes them to the RPN. The RPN then scans over the feature maps using a sliding window with different scales and aspect ratios and calculates two scores indicating whether each window contains an object and whether the object is a background or not. In order to solve the redundancy of the candidate regions that are obtained by the RPN, non-maximum suppression is used. The candidate regions with different sizes are converted into fixed-sized vectors through region of interest (ROI) pooling to be input into a fully connected layer. Finally, the coordinates and class information of the predicted multiple objects are output by performing fully connected layers.

Appendix G.1.2. SegFormer

SegFormer [34] is a semantic segmentation method that is based on transformers. Multiple semantic segmentation methods have been proposed. Most of them are based on CNNs, but recently, those that are based on transformers, which have been used in language models, have shown higher accuracy and are being used. SegFormer is an efficient and accurate semantic segmentation architecture among these transformer-based methods. It follows the encoder–decoder architecture. SegFormer consists of a hierarchical transformer encoder to extract coarse and fine features, and a lightweight all multi-layer perceptron (MLP) decoder. The performance of SegFormer may be slightly lower than some of the methods that require larger memory, such as Vision Transformer (ViT). However, SegFormer is significantly faster, with fewer model parameters than the other transformer-based architectures, and this feature is important for medical institutions without rich GPU resources.

Appendix G.1.3. Color Normalizations

In glomerular detection and segmentation, each RGB channel in a WSI was normalized by dividing the difference between the value of a pixel and the mean value of a pixel by the variance of the pixels. The mean and the variance were calculated from the training and validation datasets in order to train the network. The mean and the variance were calculated from the test dataset in order to test the network.

Appendix G.1.4. Evaluation Metrics

In order to evaluate the accuracy of glomerular detection, we calculated the micro average F1 score over all of the WSIs for each cross-validation trial. We used the average of these six cross-validations. If the IoU of the detected glomerulus and the ground truth were greater than 0.5, we classified the detection as a true positive (TP), and if the IoU was less than 0.5, we classified the detection as a false positive (FP). If the ground truth glomerulus had no overlapped predicted glomerulus with IoU $\geq$ 0.5, we classified the ground truth glomerulus as a false negative (FN). The equations that were used for the evaluation metrics were as follows (Equations (A1)–(A3)):

$$\text{Recall} = \frac{\text{TP}}{\text{TP} + \text{FN}} \tag{A1}$$

$$\text{Precision} = \frac{\text{TP}}{\text{TP} + \text{FP}} \tag{A2}$$

$$\text{F1 score} = \frac{2 \times \text{Recall} \times \text{Precision}}{\text{Recall} + \text{Precision}} \tag{A3}$$

In order to evaluate the accuracy of the glomerular component segmentation, we calculated the micro average IoU of each class over all of the WSIs for each trial, and we used the average of these six cross-validations. In this instance, the pixels in which the estimated label and the correct label matched are denoted as TP, the pixels with only the estimated class are denoted as FP, and the pixels with only the correct label are denoted as FN. The mean IoU was determined as the macro average of the IoU for each class (Equation (A4)) as follows:

$$\text{IoU} = \frac{\text{TP}}{\text{TP} + \text{FP} + \text{FN}} \quad (A4)$$

In evaluating the accuracy of the entire computational pipeline, we repositioned the predicted and correct segmentation labels on the entire WSI. We counted the number of TP, FP, and FN pixels over all of the WSIs that were included in the evaluation data in order to calculate the IoU (Equation (A4)). We evaluated the accuracy of the entire pipeline process using the averages of the six cross-validations.

Appendix G.1.5. Tools for Implementation

In order to develop the pipeline, we used Python, version 3.6.7 (Python Software Foundation, Wilmington, DE, USA), and the machine learning framework PyTorch version 1.7.1 (Facebook's AI Research Lab, Menlo Park, CA, USA). We also implemented a Faster R-CNN that was provided by the PyTorch project and the implementation of SegFormer was provided by Hugging Face. The statistical analysis was conducted in R version 4.1.1 (R Foundation, Vienna, Austria), using the packages stats 4.1.1, tidyverse 1.3.1, ppcor 1.1, and car 3.0.11 cross-validation settings.

We split the entire dataset into training, validation, and test sets. The validation set was used for the model selection in order to avoid excessively fitting the model to the test set, which would impair the generalization performance. The test set was used in order to evaluate the performance. For glomerular detection, 300 WSIs in each facility were divided into six subsets by stratified splitting based on the number of glomeruli in each WSI. Six-fold cross-validations were conducted using 200 WSIs for the training, 50 WSIs for the validation, and 50 were used for the test.

Glomerular detection is a binary classification task that is evaluated by whether Faster R-CNN can correctly detect the bounding boxes surrounding the glomeruli given as ground truth. The micro average of the F1 score, which is the harmonic mean of precision and recall, was employed as an evaluation metric. In order to maximize the F1 score in the validation set, the threshold to distinguish between the glomerulus and the background was set. For the glomerular segmentation, 42 WSIs from each facility were divided into six subsets via stratified splitting based on the total pixels of the crescentic and sclerotic regions. Six-fold cross-validations were conducted using 28 WSIs for the training, 7 WSIs for the validation, and 7 WSIs for the test. Glomerular segmentation is a multiclassification task that is evaluated by whether SegFormer can correctly classify the pixels in an image into the ground truth labels. Micro averages of intersection over union (IoU) were employed as the evaluation metrics.

Appendix G.1.6. Hyperparameters

In Faster R-CNN, the hyperparameters are the same as they were in previous studies by the authors [13]. The optimizer that dynamically changed the learning rate used Momentum SGD; the learning rate was 0.0003, the momentum was 0.9, and the learning rate was reduced to 0.00003 after 900,000 iterations. Data augmentation techniques were also applied in order to train the network, which used a combination of vertical and horizontal flip. The training iterations were terminated by monitoring the F-measure of the validation set when the network had been trained sufficiently.

In SegFormer, the hyperparameters inherit those of the original SegFormer; the model size of SegFormer was mit-b4 [26], which has the second largest number of parameters due to limited computing resources and computational efficiency. An implementation by

Hugging Face [41] was used. The batch size was set to 20 when training the model, and the model was selected at the epoch with the best mean IoU for the validation data, with an upper limit of 1000 epoch iterations.

Appendix G.1.7. Evaluation across Facilities

For glomerular detection and segmentation, six models that were developed using six-fold cross-validations were applied to all of the 300 or 42 WSIs of the other facilities. The average of each of the six times was assessed. For the evaluation of the computational pipelines, six pipelines consisting of six segmentation models, followed by one detection model, were applied to all 42 of the WSIs of the other facilities, and the average of the six times was assessed.

**References**

1. Liyanage, T.; Ninomiya, T.; Jha, V.; Neal, B.; Patrice, H.M.; Okpechi, I.; Zhao, M.H.; Lv, J.; Garg, A.X.; Knight, J.; et al. Worldwide access to treatment for end-stage kidney disease: A systematic review. *Lancet* **2015**, *385*, 1975–1982. [CrossRef]
2. Magistroni, R.; D'Agati, V.D.; Appel, G.B.; Kiryluk, K. New developments in the genetics, pathogenesis, and therapy of IgA nephropathy. *Kidney Int.* **2015**, *88*, 974–989. [CrossRef]
3. Wyatt, R.J.; Julian, B.A. IgA nephropathy. *N. Engl. J. Med.* **2013**, *368*, 2402–2414. [CrossRef]
4. Yuzawa, Y.; Yamamoto, R.; Takahashi, K.; Katafuchi, R.; Tomita, M.; Fujigaki, Y.; Kitamura, H.; Goto, M.; Yasuda, T.; Sato, M.; et al. Evidence-based clinical practice guidelines for IgA nephropathy 2014. *Clin. Exp. Nephrol.* **2016**, *20*, 511–535. [CrossRef]
5. Working Group of the International IgA Nephropathy Network and the Renal Pathology Society; Roberts, I.S.; Cook, H.T.; Troyanov, S.; Alpers, C.E.; Amore, A.; Barratt, J.; Berthoux, F.; Bonsib, S.; Bruijn, J.A.; et al. The Oxford classification of IgA nephropathy: Pathology definitions, correlations, and reproducibility. *Kidney Int.* **2009**, *76*, 546–556. [CrossRef]
6. Trimarchi, H.; Barratt, J.; Cattran, D.C.; Cook, H.T.; Coppo, R.; Haas, M.; Liu, Z.H.; Roberts, I.S.; Yuzawa, Y.; Zhang, H.; et al. Oxford classification of IgA nephropathy 2016: An update from the IgA Nephropathy Classification Working Group. *Kidney Int.* **2017**, *91*, 1014–1021. [CrossRef]
7. Joh, K.; McNamara, K.M. Differences of histological classification between the Japanese histological grade classification and the Oxford classification. In *Pathogenesis and Treatment in IgA Nephropathy*; Tomino, Y., Ed.; Springer: Tokyo, Japan, 2016; pp. 69–87. [CrossRef]
8. Tomino, Y. Diagnosis and treatment of patients with IgA nephropathy in Japan. *Kidney Res. Clin. Pract.* **2016**, *35*, 197–203. [CrossRef]
9. Barisoni, L.; Troost, J.P.; Nast, C.; Bagnasco, S.; Avila-Casado, C.; Hodgin, J.; Palmer, M.; Rosenberg, A.; Gasim, A.; Liensziewski, C.; et al. Reproducibility of the Neptune descriptor-based scoring system on whole-slide images and histologic and ultrastructural digital images. *Mod. Pathol.* **2016**, *29*, 671–684. [CrossRef]
10. Yamaguchi, R.; Kawazoe, Y.; Shimamoto, K.; Shinohara, E.; Tsukamoto, T.; Shintani-Domoto, Y.; Nagasu, H.; Uozaki, H.; Ushiku, T.; Nangaku, M.; et al. Glomerular classification using convolutional neural networks based on defined annotation criteria and concordance evaluation among clinicians. *Kidney Int. Rep.* **2021**, *6*, 716–726. [CrossRef]
11. Simon, O.; Yacoub, R.; Jain, S.; Tomaszewski, J.E.; Sarder, P. Multi-radial LBP features as a tool for rapid glomerular detection and assessment in whole slide histopathology images. *Sci. Rep.* **2018**, *8*, 2032. [CrossRef]
12. Marée, R.; Dallongeville, S.; Olivo-Marin, J.-C.; Meas-Yedid, V. An approach for detection of glomeruli in multisite digital pathology. In Proceedings of the 2016 IEEE 13th International Symposium on Biomedical Imaging (ISBI), Prague, Czech Republic, 13–16 April 2016; pp. 1033–1036. [CrossRef]
13. Kawazoe, Y.; Shimamoto, K.; Yamaguchi, R.; Shintani-Domoto, Y.; Uozaki, H.; Fukayama, M.; Ohe, K. Faster R-CNN-based glomerular detection in multistained human whole slide images. *J. Imaging.* **2018**, *4*, 91. [CrossRef]
14. Temerinac-Ott, M.; Forestier, G.; Schmitz, J.; Hermsen, M.; Brasen, J.H.; Feuerhake, F.; Wemmert, C. Detection of glomeruli in renal pathology by mutual comparison of multiple staining modalities. In Proceedings of the 10th International Symposium on ISPA, Ljubljana, Slovenia, 18–20 September 2017; pp. 19–24. [CrossRef]
15. Uchino, E.; Suzuki, K.; Sato, N.; Kojima, R.; Tamada, Y.; Hiragi, S.; Yokoi, H.; Yugami, N.; Minamiguchi, S.; Haga, H.; et al. Classification of glomerular pathological findings using deep learning and nephrologist-AI collective intelligence approach. *Int. J. Med. Inform.* **2020**, *141*, 104231. [CrossRef]
16. Kato, T.; Relator, R.; Ngouv, H.; Hirohashi, Y.; Takaki, O.; Kakimoto, T.; Okada, K. Segmental HOG: New descriptor for glomerulus detection in kidney microscopy image. *BMC Bioinform.* **2015**, *16*, 316. [CrossRef] [PubMed]
17. Gallego, J.; Pedraza, A.; Lopez, S.; Steiner, G.; Gonzalez, L.; Laurinavicius, A.; Bueno, G. Glomerulus classification and detection based on convolutional neural networks. *J. Imaging.* **2018**, *4*, 20. [CrossRef]
18. Ginley, B.; Lutnick, B.; Jen, K.Y.; Fogo, A.B.; Jain, S.; Rosenberg, A.; Walavalkar, V.; Wilding, G.; Tomaszewski, J.E.; Yacoub, R.; et al. Computational segmentation and classification of diabetic glomerulosclerosis. *J. Am. Soc. Nephrol.* **2019**, *30*, 1953–1967. [CrossRef]

19. Hermsen, M.; de Bel, T.; den Boer, M.; Steenbergen, E.J.; Kers, J.; Florquin, S.; Roelofs, J.J.T.H.; Stegall, M.D.; Alexander, M.P.; Smith, B.H.; et al. Deep learning-based histopathologic assessment of kidney tissue. *J. Am. Soc. Nephrol.* **2019**, *30*, 1968–1979. [CrossRef]
20. Bueno, G.; Fernandez-Carrobles, M.M.; Gonzalez-Lopez, L.; Deniz, O. Glomerulosclerosis identification in whole slide images using semantic segmentation. *Comput. Methods Programs Biomed.* **2020**, *184*, 105273. [CrossRef]
21. Altini, N.; Cascarano, G.D.; Brunetti, A.; Marino, F.; Rocchetti, M.T.; Matino, S.; Venere, U.; Rossini, M.; Pesce, F.; Gesualdo, L.; et al. Semantic segmentation framework for glomeruli detection and classification in kidney histological sections. *Electronics* **2020**, *9*, 503. [CrossRef]
22. Zeng, C.; Nan, Y.; Xu, F.; Lei, Q.; Li, F.; Chen, T.; Liang, S.; Hou, X.; Lv, B.; Liang, D.; et al. Identification of glomerular lesions and intrinsic glomerular cell types in kidney diseases via deep learning. *J. Pathol.* **2020**, *252*, 53–64. [CrossRef] [PubMed]
23. Bouteldja, N.; Klinkhammer, B.M.; Bülow, R.D.; Droste, P.; Otten, S.W.; Freifrau von Stillfried, S.; Moellmann, J.; Sheehan, S.M.; Korstanje, R.; Menzel, S.; et al. Deep learning–based segmentation and quantification in experimental kidney histopathology. *J. Am. Soc. Nephrol.* **2021**, *32*, 52–68. [CrossRef]
24. Jiang, L.; Chen, W.; Dong, B.; Mei, K.; Zhu, C.; Liu, J.; Cai, M.; Yan, Y.; Wang, G.; Zuo, L.; et al. A deep learning-based approach for glomeruli instance segmentation from multistained renal biopsy pathologic images. *Am. J. Pathol.* **2021**, *191*, 1431–1441. [CrossRef]
25. Ren, S.; He, K.; Girshick, R.; Sun, J. Faster R-CNN: Towards real-time object detection with region proposal networks. *IEEE Trans. Pattern Anal. Mach. Intell. Proc.* **2017**, *39*, 1137–1149. [CrossRef]
26. Xie, E.; Wang, W.; Yu, Z.; Anandkumar, A.; Alvarez, J.M.; Luo, P. SegFormer: Simple and efficient design for semantic segmentation with transformers. *Adv. Neural Inf. Process. Syst.* **2021**, *34*, 12077–12090. [CrossRef]
27. Vaswani, A.; Shazeer, N.; Parmar, N.; Uszkoreit, J.; Jones, L.; Gomez, A.; Kaiser, L.; Polosukhin, I. Attention is all you need. In Proceedings of the NIPS, Long Beach, CA, USA, 4–7 December 2017; pp. 5998–6008. [CrossRef]
28. Van Pottelbergh, G.; Den Elzen, W.P.; Degryse, J.; Gussekloo, J. Prediction of mortality and functional decline by changes in eGFR in the very elderly: The Leiden 85-plus study. *BMC Geriatr.* **2013**, *13*, 61. [CrossRef]
29. Turin, T.C.; Coresh, J.; Tonelli, M.; Stevens, P.E.; de Jong, P.E.; Farmer, C.K.; Matsushita, K.; Hemmelgarn, B.R. Change in the estimated glomerular filtration rate over time and risk of all-cause mortality. *Kidney Int.* **2013**, *83*, 684–691. [CrossRef]
30. Vaes, B.; Beke, E.; Truyers, C.; Elli, S.; Buntinx, F.; Verbakel, J.Y.; Goderis, G.; Van Pottelbergh, G. The correlation between blood pressure and kidney function decline in older people: A registry-based cohort study. *BMJ Open.* **2015**, *5*, e007571. [CrossRef]
31. Naimark, D.M.J.; Grams, M.E.; Matsushita, K.; Black, C.; Drion, I.; Fox, C.S.; Inker, L.A.; Ishani, A.; Jee, S.H.; Kitamura, A.; et al. Past decline versus current eGFR and subsequent mortality risk. *J. Am. Soc. Nephrol.* **2016**, *27*, 2456–2466. [CrossRef]
32. Oshima, M.; Jun, M.; Ohkuma, T.; Toyama, T.; Wada, T.; Cooper, M.E.; Hadjadj, S.; Hamet, P.; Harrap, S.; Mancia, G.; et al. The relationship between eGFR slope and subsequent risk of vascular outcomes and all-cause mortality in type 2 diabetes: The ADVANCE-ON study. *Diabetologia* **2019**, *62*, 1988–1997. [CrossRef]
33. Inker, L.A.; Heerspink, H.J.L.; Tighiouart, H.; Levey, A.S.; Coresh, J.; Gansevoort, R.T.; Simon, A.L.; Ying, J.; Beck, G.J.; Wanner, C.; et al. GFR Slope as a surrogate end point for kidney disease progression in clinical trials: A meta-analysis of treatment effects of randomized controlled trials. *J. Am. Soc. Nephrol.* **2019**, *30*, 1735–1745. [CrossRef]
34. Badrinarayanan, V.; Kendall, A.; Cipolla, R. SegNet: A deep convolutional encoder-decoder architecture for image segmentation. *IEEE Trans. Pattern Anal. Mach. Intell.* **2017**, *39*, 2481–2495. [CrossRef]
35. Ronneberger, O.; Fischer, P.; Brox, T. *U-Net: Convolutional Networks for Biomedical Image Segmentation*; Miccai, N.N., Ed.; Springer: Cham, Switzerland, 2015; pp. 234–241. [CrossRef]
36. Dimitriou, N.; Arandjelović, O.; Caie, P.D. Deep learning for whole slide image analysis: An overview. *Front. Med.* **2019**, *6*, 264. [CrossRef]
37. Khened, M.; Kori, A.; Rajkumar, H.; Krishnamurthi, G.; Srinivasan, B. A generalized deep learning framework for whole-slide image segmentation and analysis. *Sci. Rep.* **2021**, *11*, 11579. [CrossRef]
38. Bansal, R.; Raj, G.; Choudhury, T. Blur Image Detection Using Laplacian Operator and Open-CV. In Proceedings of the 2016 International Conference System Modeling & Advancement in Research Trends (SMART), Moradabad, India, 25–27 November 2016. [CrossRef]
39. Cui, M.; Zhang, D.Y. Artificial intelligence and computational pathology. *Lab. Investig.* **2021**, *101*, 412–422. [CrossRef]
40. Serag, A.; Ion-Margineanu, A.; Qureshi, H.; McMillan, R.; Saint Martin, M.J.; Diamond, J.; O'Reilly, P.; Hamilton, P. Translational AI and deep learning in diagnostic pathology. *Front. Med.* **2019**, *6*, 185. [CrossRef]
41. SegFormer. Available online: https://huggingface.co/docs/transformers/model_doc/segformer#segformer (accessed on 8 November 2022).

Article

# Enhancing Annotation Efficiency with Machine Learning: Automated Partitioning of a Lung Ultrasound Dataset by View

Bennett VanBerlo [1], Delaney Smith [2], Jared Tschirhart [3], Blake VanBerlo [2,*], Derek Wu [4], Alex Ford [5], Joseph McCauley [6], Benjamin Wu [5], Rushil Chaudhary [4], Chintan Dave [7], Jordan Ho [8], Jason Deglint [6], Brian Li [6] and Robert Arntfield [7]

[1] Faculty of Engineering, University of Western Ontario, London, ON N6A 5C1, Canada
[2] Faculty of Mathematics, University of Waterloo, Waterloo, ON N2L 3G1, Canada
[3] Schulich School of Medicine and Dentistry, Western University, London, ON N6A 5C1, Canada
[4] Department of Medicine, Western University, London, ON N6A 5C1, Canada
[5] Lawson Health Research Institute, London, ON N6C 2R5, Canada
[6] Faculty of Engineering, University of Waterloo, Waterloo, ON N2L 3G1, Canada
[7] Division of Critical Care Medicine, Western University, London, ON N6A 5C1, Canada
[8] Department of Family Medicine, Western University, London, ON N6A 5C1, Canada
* Correspondence: bvanberl@uwaterloo.ca

**Abstract:** Background: Annotating large medical imaging datasets is an arduous and expensive task, especially when the datasets in question are not organized according to deep learning goals. Here, we propose a method that exploits the hierarchical organization of annotating tasks to optimize efficiency. Methods: We trained a machine learning model to accurately distinguish between one of two classes of lung ultrasound (LUS) views using 2908 clips from a larger dataset. Partitioning the remaining dataset by view would reduce downstream labelling efforts by enabling annotators to focus on annotating pathological features specific to each view. Results: In a sample view-specific annotation task, we found that automatically partitioning a 780-clip dataset by view saved 42 min of manual annotation time and resulted in $55 \pm 6$ additional relevant labels per hour. Conclusions: Automatic partitioning of a LUS dataset by view significantly increases annotator efficiency, resulting in higher throughput relevant to the annotating task at hand. The strategy described in this work can be applied to other hierarchical annotation schemes.

**Keywords:** computer vision; machine learning; annotation; labelling; lung ultrasound; medical imaging; deep learning

## 1. Introduction

Unlike several mainstream computer vision application domains, annotators of medical imaging datasets must possess a sufficient degree of domain expertise to ensure that ground truth is clinically correct. In many cases, labels must be reviewed by clinical experts prior to being officially admitted to a dataset. Given the cost and limited availability of clinical expertise for such tasks, strategies to accurately automate the labelling of medical imaging datasets are desirable.

Lung ultrasound (LUS) is a well described, portable, inexpensive, and accurate point of care technique to assess respiratory disease at the bedside [1–7], with potential deployment in a wide variety of environments [8,9]. In comparison to the traditional methods used to image the lungs, such as a CT scan or chest X-ray, LUS displays comparable or improved diagnostic accuracy at a reduced cost [4,5]. There are two broadly categorized regions, or views, of the lung that are acquired: parenchymal (anterior and anterolateral chest) and pleural (posterolateral chest) [3,10,11]. Each of these views interrogate different anatomic areas of the lung that may contain separate and distinct disease processes [12]. For example, as seen in Figure 1, if annotating clips for a classifier that identifies A line and B line artifacts [13,14], annotators would be interested in parenchymal views only, since these artifacts are of greatest clinical importance when seen in these views. Conversely, important findings such as the curtain sign, pleural effusion, or consolidation patterns are sought in the pleural views of the lungs [15]. Additional examples of how this is reflected in a hierarchical annotation workflow are shown in Figure 1. The hierarchical nature of LUS interpretation and annotation provides an opportunity to impose high-level structure by partitioning an otherwise unstructured dataset into two clinical and radiographic groups. If the view of every clip in the dataset is known, then the entire dataset can be partitioned by view, and expert annotators need only be provided with clips for which the view is relevant to the annotating task (see Figure 1). LUS is a particularly important modality for optimizing annotation efforts due to the paucity of individuals with sufficient domain expertise to perform LUS annotation [16,17]. Thus, an approach to automated partitioning based on view represents a key opportunity to improve annotation throughput and optimize workforce allocation, while providing a model that is clinically relevant [18,19].

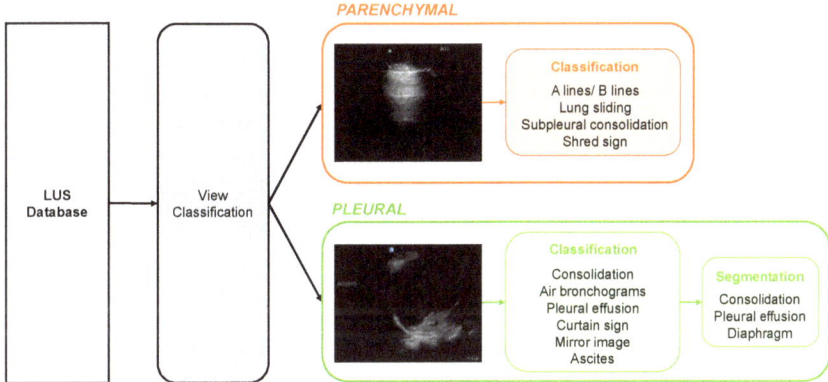

**Figure 1.** Summary of the hierarchical annotation workflow. LUS classification tasks are view-specific. Automation of the view classification step separates LUS clips. Further, segmentation tasks can subsequently be stratified by classification.

Solutions have been proposed to offset the cost of annotating medical images. Multiple studies have explored the use of active learning, a special case of machine learning where the learner can query a user to label new data points [20]. The direct incorporation of human intervention in the active learning process has been shown to improve both the annotating accuracy and efficiency [21].

The process of leveraging a small, annotated subset of a larger dataset to generate new labels that will be added to a training set has also been explored with notable success. Gu et al. [22] used an annotated training set with 20,000 examples to generate labels for a 100,000-example dataset. This study exhibited a significant improvement in model performance when 80,000 automatically generated labels were added to the human-annotated training set for the purpose of classification [22]. A similar method was used to efficiently label data in [23], where regions of interest in CT examinations were segmented and automatically annotated to circumvent annotation costs.

Deep learning approaches that have been trained for automatic annotating have rivalled the performance of domain experts [24,25]. In this case, radiology reports were used to generate chest X-ray labels. The performance of radiologists was used as a benchmark for model performance, and the margin between the resulting predictions by their deep network and the expert annotator was narrow. This evidence suggests that similar methodologies can be used to rival the annotating accuracy of medical professionals. These findings are encouraging for our work, as the benchmark for this automatic annotating method is also the annotating performance of medical experts. Success in these other domains provide justification for our current work.

The objective of this work is to develop a deep learning solution for automatic LUS view annotation that effectively improves the efficiency of downstream annotation tasks. In particular, a neural network capable of distinguishing parenchymal from pleural LUS views is developed, validated, and used to partition a sample LUS dataset by view. A downstream view-specific annotation task is then performed on both the partitioned dataset and an equally-sized non-partitioned dataset by the same annotation team to investigate whether automatic view annotation improved their efficiency and throughput. We aim for our methods to form the foundation for an improved, more cost-effective LUS annotation workflow that can be applied to other annotation schemes with a hierarchical organization.

## 2. Materials and Methods

### 2.1. Data Curation and Annotation

All data in this study were collected retrospectively from our institutional point-of-care ultrasound database (Qpath E, Port Coquitlam, BC, Canada). To generate ground truth labels, all clips were uploaded to an online platform (Labelbox, San Francisco, CA, USA), where they were annotated by a team of medical professionals trained in LUS. Project oversight, including ambiguous or difficult examples, was provided by an international expert in LUS. Annotation tasks were divided into 200 clip benchmarks for annotators and clip-level classifications were applied, including the view (parenchymal vs. pleural), findings relevant to the respective view (see Figure 1), and quality markers (inappropriate gain, depth, composition, etc.). Annotators also had the option to discard clips that did not meet diagnostic or machine learning standards. Examples include inappropriate ultrasound exams (such as an echocardiogram), user-applied text within the ultrasound image, and removal of the ultrasound probe from the patient's chest during the video clip. Lastly, annotators had a *skip* option to reserve clips for future annotation. This option was applied when the clip in question did not match the current annotation goals (e.g., a pleural clip when the goal was the annotation of parenchymal findings). The labelling platform automatically tracked the time taken to label or skip clips, which facilitated analysis of annotator efficiency.

### 2.2. View (Parenchymal vs. Pleural) Classifier

#### 2.2.1. Clip-Level Data

To train the neural network, a class-balanced dataset of 2908 LUS clips (1454 parenchymal and 1454 pleural clips) was randomly selected from data previously annotated as described in Section 2.1. By convention, parenchymal and pleural were assigned the negative and positive class, respectively. The details of our training dataset are provided in Table 1.

#### 2.2.2. Frame-Based Data

As the view of an individual LUS image (hereafter referred to as "frame") can typically be discerned by clinicians, we sought to train a frame-based classification model that could predict the view of a particular LUS frame, where the ground truth view of the frame was the view of the clip (determined by the annotator). Dividing the videos into constituent frames greatly expanded the size of the dataset to 369,832 parenchymal and 330,191 pleural frames. Clip-level predictions could subsequently be inferred from the frame-level predictions using a clip classification algorithm (see Section 2.2.5).

Table 1. Characteristics of the datasets used for view classifier training and validation.

|  | Training Data | | Holdout Data | |
| --- | --- | --- | --- | --- |
| Clip label | Parenchymal | Pleural | Parenchymal | Pleural |
| Patients | 611 | 342 | 441 | 466 |
| Number of clips | 1454 | 1454 | 457 | 488 |
| Frames | 369,832 | 330,191 | 107,205 | 100,616 |
| Average clips/patient | 2.38 | 4.25 | 1.04 | 1.05 |
| Class-patient overlap | 303/650 | | 32/875 | |
| Age (std) | 64.0 (17.2) | 64.5 (16.2) | 64.1 (18.0) | 64.4 (17.4) |
| Sex | Female: 238 (39%) Male: 347 (57%) Unknown: 26 (4%) | Female: 134 (39%) Male: 193 (56%) Unknown: 15 (4%) | Female: 156 (35%) Male: 269 (61%) Unknown: 16 (4%) | Female: 205 (44%) Male: 235 (50%) Unknown: 26 (6%) |

2.2.3. Dataset Pre-Processing

After deconstructing the clips into composite frames, all information external to the ultrasound beam (e.g., vendor logos, depth markers) was removed using ultrasound masking software (AutoMask, WaveBase Inc., Waterloo, ON, Canada). The frames were then resized to 128 × 128 pixels using bilinear interpolation and fed to the model in RGB channel format. During training, the frame dataset was augmented by applying the following transformations stochastically: random zooming inward/outward by up to 20%, horizontal flipping, brightness shifting by up to 20%, contrast shift of up to 10%, and rotation clockwise/counterclockise by up to $\frac{\pi}{4}$ radians.

2.2.4. Model Architecture

We employed the EfficientNetB0 architecture as the base model [26], with weights pre-trained on ImageNet [27]. The head of the EfficientNetB0 network was replaced with a 2D global average pooling layer, followed by dropout (with dropout rate 0.3), a 128-node fully connected layer with ReLU activation, and a 1-node fully connected output layer with sigmoid activation. The model's output was the probability $p$ that a LUS frame was a pleural view. The predicted frame-level class was taken to be *pleural view* if $p$ was at least 0.5 and *parenchymal view* otherwise.

Multiple convolutional neural network architectures were considered for the frame classification task. The weights of each architecture were initialized with pretrained ImageNet [27] weights. A variable number of the first layers in the architecture were kept frozen throughout training. We observed significant overfitting with all architectures studied other than EfficientNetB0: The other architectures achieved an area under the receiver operating curve (AUC) score of at least 0.999 on training data, but consistently obtained significantly lower accuracy on the validation set (see Appendix A). Most of these alternative architectures have more capacity than required for the present task. The EfficientNetB0 architecture, which is more compact, exhibited less overfitting. It was therefore designated as the frame classification architecture. In addition, EfficientNetB0 offers a significant boost in training and inference efficiency compared to other contemporary deep convolutional architectures [26].

2.2.5. Clip Predictions

Since the neural network performed frame-based classification, it was necessary to devise a method to convert a series of outputs into clip-level predictions. Classifying clips in this manner facilitates a direct comparison against our expert annotations and more faithfully resembles clinical, dynamic LUS interpretation. Our approach was based on the clip classification method described in [28]. In summary, the clip prediction was taken to be the positive class if there was at least $\tau \in \mathbb{N}$ consecutive frames with a prediction probability exceeding the classification threshold $t \in [0, 1]$. Such logic is also applicable to LUS view classification because some frames in pleural clips may resemble parenchymal frames due to the curtain sign artifact (created by movement of aerated lung into and out of view during inspiration and expiration), but not vice versa. To reduce noise in frame-level predictions, we smoothed the frame-level predictions by computing a moving average with a window of width $w \in \mathbb{N}$ before applying the existing clip classification method. A visual representation of the hyperparameters involved in generating a clip-level prediction from a series of constituent frame-level predictions is provided in Figure 2.

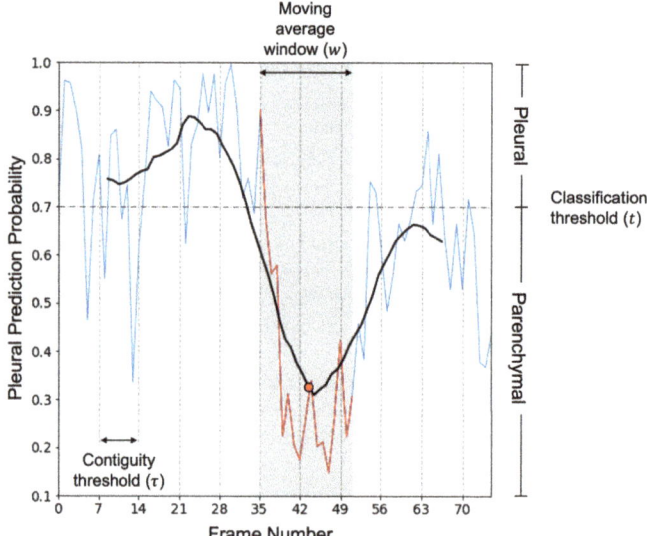

**Figure 2.** Visual representation of the clip prediction method. For each clip, the raw frame-level prediction probabilities outputted from the neural network (blue curve) are smoothed by computing a moving average (black curve): each point (red dot) on the smoothed prediction curve represents the average of a set of $w$ consecutive frame-level prediction probabilities (red curve). The clip is predicted as pleural if $\tau$ contiguous smoothed predictions meet or exceed the classification threshold $t$, and parenchymal otherwise. A true positive (pleural) clip is shown, as predicted using the optimal hyperparameter set ($\tau = 7$, $t = 0.7$, $w = 17$).

2.2.6. Validation Strategy

To verify the choice of model architecture and clip prediction hyperparameters, 10-fold cross validation was conducted with the training set. The folds were split by patient ID to prevent data leakage. Values of $\tau$, $t$, and $w$ were selected via grid search to maximize the average validation set accuracy across all folds. All 14,400 parameter combinations across $\tau, w \in \{1, 2, \ldots, 40\}$ and $t \in \{0.1, 0.2, \ldots, 0.9\}$ were considered in the analysis. We then completed a final training run with a dedicated test split to estimate how well the clip classification method would perform on unseen clips from our database.

To evaluate the clip classification method on unseen data, we sampled a disjoint holdout set of $n$ clips from the unannotated LUS database. The holdout set (described in Table 1) was annotated by the standard team as outlined in Section 2.1. To determine the size of the holdout set, we conservatively assumed that the standard annotation team would achieve 96% accuracy on unseen data when compared with the clinical expert's annotations. Given that we require 95% confidence that the accuracy on the holdout set will lie within $\pm M$ of the conservative estimate of $A$, $n$ can be calculated using Cochran's formula for sample size estimation [29].

$$n = \frac{Z_\alpha^2 A(1-A)}{M^2} \quad (1)$$

In the above, $Z_\alpha$ is the Z-value corresponding to a $\alpha$ confidence range, and $M$ is the margin of error. Applying Equation (1) with $\alpha = 95\%$, $M = 1.25\%$, and $A = 0.960$, we obtained $n = 945$ for the size of the holdout set. The accuracy of the clip classification method was compared with that of the standard annotators, where the ground truth was taken as the LUS expert's decision.

A summary of the complete view classification workflow described in Section 2.2, from pre-processing to classification and analysis, is provided in Figure 3.

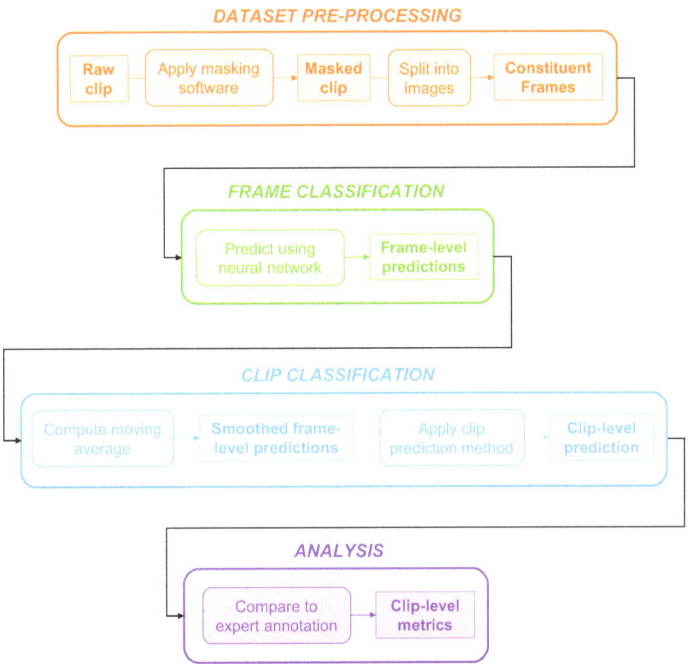

**Figure 3.** Summary of the view classification workflow. **Data pre-processing:** raw clips were masked to remove information external to the ultrasound beam, then deconstructed into constituent frames. **Frame classification:** processed frames were inputted into the neural network, which predicted the probability that the input frame was a pleural view. **Clip classification:** A moving average was computed over the series of composite frames of a given clip. The smoothed frame-level predictions were then inputted into the contiguous clip prediction method outlined in [28] to generate a whole clip-level prediction. **Analysis:** Clip-level predictions were compared to expert clinical annotations.

*2.3. Automating the View Annotation Task*

2.3.1. Partitioning a LUS Dataset by View

To investigate the utility of the view classifier as an automatic annotation tool, we deployed the model on a distinct set of 2000 clips from the unannotated LUS database and partitioned the data by view prediction. The partitioning criteria was based on the predicted clip-level class as well as the average frame-level prediction probability. In particular, parenchymal-predicted clips with an average frame-level (pleural) prediction probability less than 0.3 were selected to form a parenchymal-specific auto-partitioned dataset. An average frame-level probability of 0.3 was chosen as the threshold for partitioning given the optimal classification threshold ($t = 0.7$) that was observed on the validation set (see Section 3) as well as to minimize the number of pleural clips that would appear in the partitioned dataset. In total, 823 clips met the partitioning criteria, from which 780 were randomly selected for inclusion in the final dataset used for the downstream annotation task. Details of this dataset are available in Table 2.

**Table 2.** Data characteristics of the control and auto-partitioned datasets used for the parenchymal-specific annotation task.

| Clip Label | Control Data | | Auto-Partitioned Data | |
|---|---|---|---|---|
|  | Parenchymal | Pleural | Parenchymal | Pleural |
| Patients | 339 | 371 | 660 | 34 |
| Number of clips | 351 | 383 | 701 | 35 |
| Average clips per patient | 1.04 | 1.03 | 1.06 | 1.03 |
| Patient overlap across classes | 25/685 | | 5/689 | |
| Mean age (std) | 63.7 (18.1) | 64.0 (16.1) | 64.0 (16.6) | 63.7 (18.3) |
| Sex | Female: 117 (35%)<br>Male: 193 (57%)<br>Unknown: 29 (9%) | Female: 156 (42%)<br>Male: 201 (54%)<br>Unknown: 14 (4%) | Female: 259 (39%)<br>Male: 374 (57%)<br>Unknown: 27 (4%) | Female: 12 (35%)<br>Male: 21 (62%)<br>Unknown: 1 (3%) |

### 2.3.2. The Annotation Task

To study the effect of automatic view partitioning on annotator efficiency, a downstream parenchymal-specific annotation task was performed on the aforementioned auto-partitioned dataset. The same annotation task was also performed on a 780-clip, distinct, non-partitioned (control) dataset for comparison (for details, see Table 2). Four experienced members of our annotation team participated in the task, with each member annotating 195 clips from both the control and auto-labelled set as separate annotation tasks (sprints). Sprints were completed in a randomized order, with two members completing the control sprint first, and two completing the auto-partitioned sprint first. Annotators were asked to label all parenchymal and non-usable clips according to the workflow described in Section 2.1, while *skipping* all pleural clips. The effect of automatic view annotation on our overall annotation workflow is outlined in Figure 4.

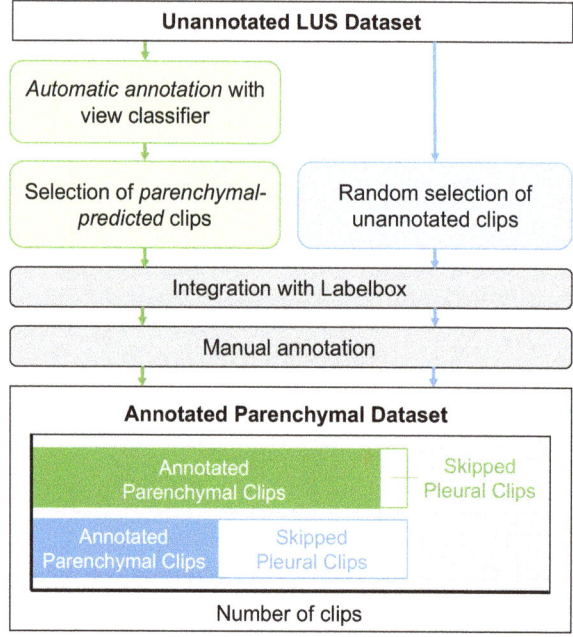

**Figure 4.** Annotation workflow with (green) and without (blue) automatic view annotation for a parenchymal-specific annotation task. Annotators need only be provided with parenchymal-predicted clips for a parenchymal-specific labelling task, resulting in more annotated parenchymal clips per labelling sprint and fewer skipped pleural clips, saving annotation time.

2.3.3. Statistical Analysis

A one-way paired Student's t-Test was used to compare control to auto-annotated for each annotation efficiency metric to test for statistical significance. All data are presented as mean ± standard deviation.

## 3. Results

*3.1. View Classifier Validation*

Table 3 details the results of the 10-fold cross validation experiment as well as the performance on the holdout set. The model was evaluated in terms of positive (pleural) and negative (parenchymal) predictive value, given the intended function as an automatic annotation tool: if partitioning for a parenchymal-specific labelling task, then we would aim to minimize the number of false negatives in our dataset (maximize the negative predictive value). If partitioning for a pleural-specific labelling task, then we would aim to minimize the number of false positives in our dataset (maximize the positive predictive value).

**Table 3.** Metrics for a 10-fold cross validation experiment and the holdout set inference.

| Dataset | Fold | Accuracy | | Negative Predictive Value | | Positive Predictive Value | | AUC |
|---|---|---|---|---|---|---|---|---|
| | | Frames | Clips | Frames | Clips | Frames | Clips | Frames |
| Training | 1 | 0.944 | 0.966 | 0.933 | 0.972 | 0.957 | 0.961 | 0.973 |
| | 2 | 0.930 | 0.947 | 0.897 | 0.938 | 0.963 | 0.954 | 0.969 |
| | 3 | 0.938 | 0.969 | 0.910 | 0.952 | 0.972 | 0.986 | 0.972 |
| | 4 | 0.913 | 0.935 | 0.895 | 0.921 | 0.940 | 0.952 | 0.941 |
| | 5 | 0.907 | 0.939 | 0.856 | 0.908 | 0.974 | 0.970 | 0.963 |
| | 6 | 0.851 | 0.872 | 0.885 | 0.855 | 0.812 | 0.893 | 0.931 |
| | 7 | 0.914 | 0.939 | 0.891 | 0.935 | 0.947 | 0.943 | 0.956 |
| | 8 | 0.922 | 0.933 | 0.916 | 0.951 | 0.932 | 0.911 | 0.971 |
| | 9 | 0.917 | 0.939 | 0.883 | 0.926 | 0.968 | 0.952 | 0.966 |
| | 10 | 0.890 | 0.919 | 0.864 | 0.891 | 0.920 | 0.951 | 0.940 |
| | Mean | 0.913 | 0.936 | 0.893 | 0.925 | 0.935 | 0.947 | 0.959 |
| | (STD) | (0.025) | (0.027) | (0.022) | (0.034) | (0.046) | (0.027) | (0.015) |
| Holdout | — | 0.912 | 0.925 | 0.869 | 0.881 | 0.969 | 0.975 | 0.966 |

### 3.1.1. Frame-Based Performance

The area under (AUC) the receiver-operator curve (ROC) of our frame-based neural network averaged 0.959 (±0.015) on our 10-fold cross validation experiment (Figure 5A) and 0.966 (Figure 5B) on our unseen holdout set. The corresponding frame-level confusion matrices indicated a low proportion of incorrect predictions (Figure 5C,D). This frame-wise performance was deemed satisfactory by clinical team members.

### 3.1.2. Clip-Based Performance

To evaluate our classifier at the clip-level, an optimal clip classification hyperparameter set was required. The parameter set $(\tau, t, w) = (7, 0.7, 17)$ was found to maximize the average validation set accuracy across each fold for each $\tau, w \in \{1, 2, \ldots, 40\}$ and $t \in \{0.1, 0.2, \ldots 0.9\}$. The clip-wise performance metrics reported in Table 3 were obtained using this designated parameter set. As shown in Figure 5, the corresponding clip level confusion matrices for both the 10-fold cross-validation experiment (Panel E) and inference on the holdout set (Panel F) showed a high percentage of correct predictions.

Using the results of the holdout set inference, we then sought to estimate how the model would perform if deployed on the remainder of our LUS database as an automatic view annotation tool. By considering the clip-level accuracy obtained on the holdout set (0.925) as a point estimate of our classifier's performance, we applied Cochran's formula

(Equation (1)) to estimate that the true accuracy on the remaining unannotated database would lie within a range of $0.925 \pm 0.017$ with 95% confidence. Therefore, we estimate that the true accuracy, applied to the entire LUS database, is within $[0.908, 0.942]$ at the clip level with 95% confidence. The accuracy of our clinical annotation team, as evaluated on the same holdout set, was 0.991.

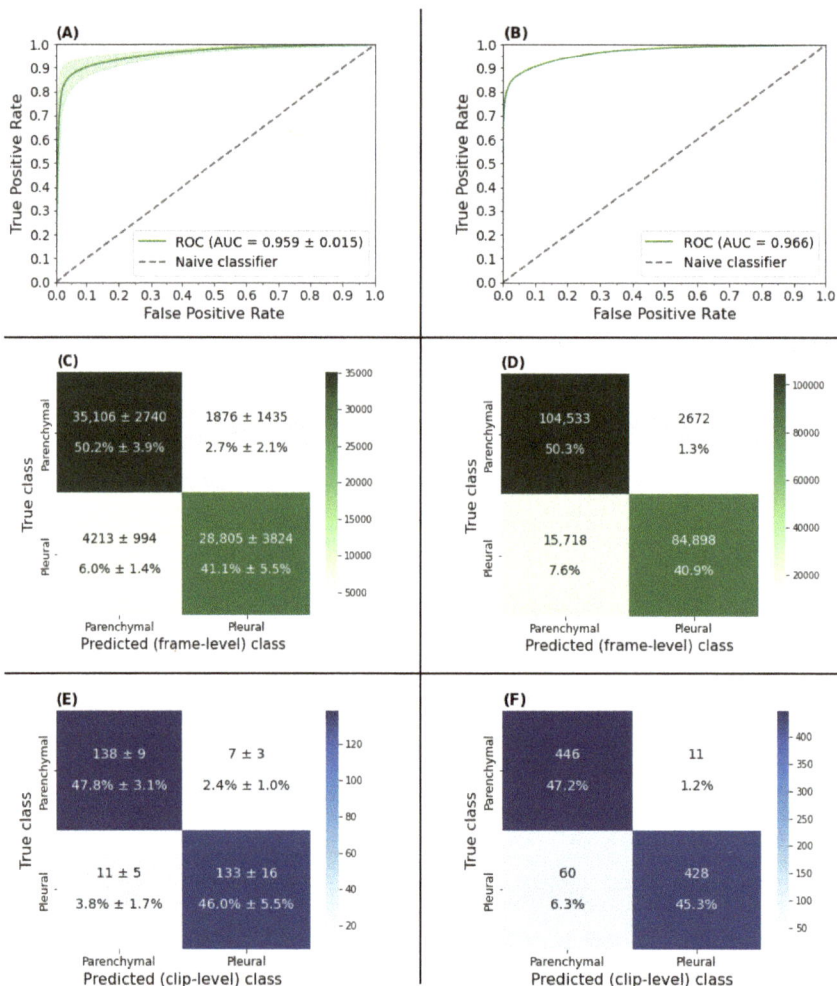

**Figure 5.** Receiver-operator characteristic curves with corresponding frame (green) and clip-based (blue) confusion matrices for the 10-fold cross validation experiment (**A,C,E**) and holdout set inference (**B,D,F**). (**A**) AUC of the 10-fold cross validation experiment averaged 0.959 ($\pm 0.015$) with the corresponding frame and clip-based confusion matrix results in (**C**) and (**E**), respectively. (**B**) Inference on the holdout set yielded an AUC of 0.966 with the corresponding frame and clip-based confusion matrix results in (**D**) and (**F**), respectively.

3.1.3. Frame-Based Explainability

To audit the neural network decisions and instill further confidence in our model at the frame-level, a series of Grad-CAM++ [30] explanations for unseen frames was manually examined by annotators. Annotators largely agreed that the heatmaps highlighted regions considered important for discerning the view of a LUS frame. Figure 6 provides some illustrative examples of correctly and incorrectly classified frames. A post hoc error analysis by clinical team members revealed that false negative predictions were most common for frames where the diaphragm was not visible or obscured. This observation further supports the model's decision-making ability, given that for a clinician, the diaphragm is a critical structure required for the sonographic landmarking of the pleural view.

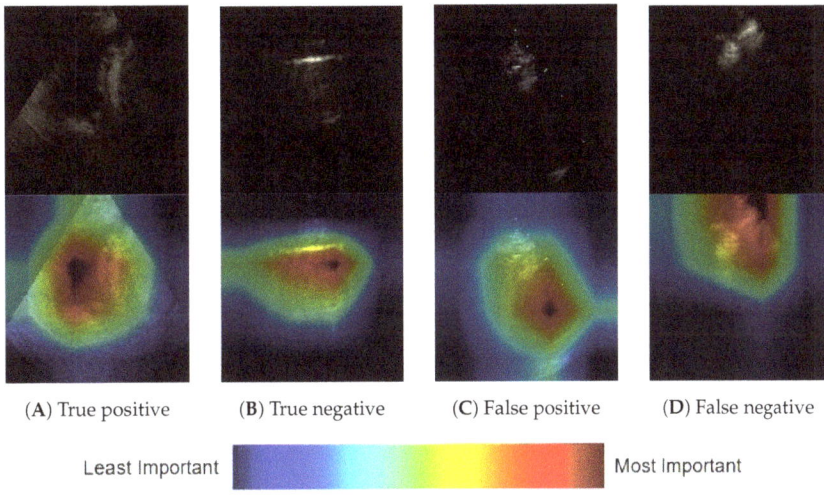

**Figure 6.** Selected Grad-CAM++ explanations for the neural network model view predictions for single LUS frames. Red regions were the most important to the prediction. The true positive (**A**) is confirmed by the heat map highlighting a pleural effusion which is only seen in the pleural view, and the true negative (**B**) highlights an A line, or reverberation, artifact seen in parenchymals views. The false positive (**C**) highlights the heart likely mistaken as an abdominal organ found in pleural views, and the false negative (**D**) highlights transient parenchymal tissue that comes into frame during inspiration.

3.1.4. Clip-Based Explainability

Although informative, many LUS artifacts cannot be fully captured by static frame-based explainability methods given the dynamic nature of clip acquisition and interpretation. Therefore, to investigate these dynamic artifacts in detail and gain further confidence in our clip-level predictions, we sought to visualize how the predicted frame-level probabilities change over the duration of a given clip. To do so, we generated prediction probability time series plots and overlaid them onto the respective masked LUS clips. A temporal indicator was then added to the graph to create an animation. Illustrative examples of these plots for correctly predicted and incorrectly predicted clips are given in Figure 7, with corresponding animations linked in the figure caption. A clinical post hoc analysis of these animations revealed that our clip-prediction method, in general, is successful in generating accurate clip-level predictions when dynamic artifacts common to LUS interpretation are observed. In particular, the majority of clips displaying the curtain sign artifact are correctly predicted as pleural (Figure 7A; Figure A2A), despite the oscillation in frame-level prediction probability that is observed (and expected). Furthermore, analysis of our incorrectly predicted clips revealed that false positives and negatives were commonly the result of poor acquisition technique. For example, there were several cases where the LUS user moved between parenchymal and pleural views during the same clip (for an example, see Figure A2G). There were also cases where structures indicative of the pleural view, such as the diaphragm or the liver, were either not visualized or were obscured by rib shadowing artifacts (Figure A2F) or aerated lung (Figure A2H).

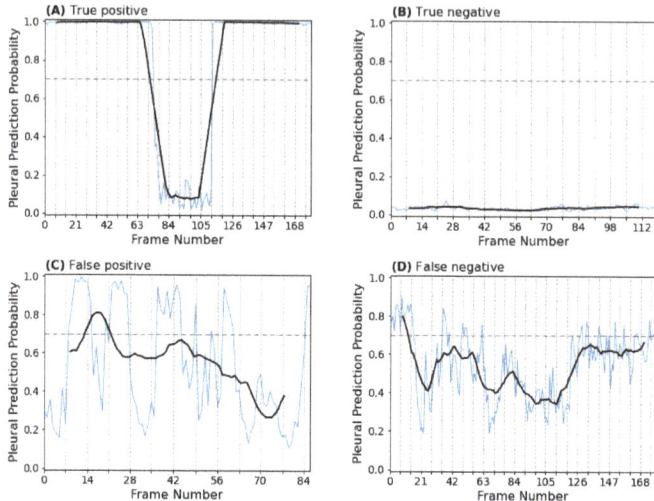

**Figure 7.** Pleural prediction probability time series for selected true positive (**A**), true negative (**B**), false positive (**C**), and false negative (**D**) clips. The true positive (**A**) clip displays the curtain sign artifact which indicates the lack of pleural pathology (consolidated lung or pleural effusion). The true negative (**B**) clip displays normal lung parenchyma (A line pattern) bordered by rib shadows. The false positive (**C**) clip contains heart tissue, which the model likely mistook for an abdominal organ usually seen in pleural views. The diaphragm is largely missing from the false negative clip (**D**), with only a sliver appearing on a few occasions that correspond to bursts in pleural prediction probability; however, the average probability does not remain above the classification threshold long enough to meet the contiguity threshold. Supplementary Videos S1–S4.

### 3.2. Automating the View Annotation Task

#### 3.2.1. Performance on an Auto-Partitioned Dataset

Of the 780 clips included in our disjoint dataset auto-partitioned by parenchymal view prediction, 701 were identified as true parenchymal views by our clinical team. Of the 79 clips remaining, 35 were misclassified as pleural views and 44 were discarded for quality control, as described in Section 2.1. Excluding the discarded clips from the analysis, our classifier achieved an accuracy of $701/736 = 0.952$ on this unseen dataset. This is equivalent to the negative predictive value, given that no pleural predictions were included in the dataset. Comparing these results to that of our holdout set and cross validation experiment, we observed a 7.1% and 2.7% improvement in negative predictive value, respectively. This increase in performance is likely the result of our partitioning criteria: By selecting clips with a pleural prediction probability less than 0.3, we reduced the number of false positives appearing in our final partitioned dataset.

#### 3.2.2. Annotation Efficiency

Automatically partitioning by view significantly increased the efficiency of a downstream parenchymal-specific annotation task—the number of relevant (parenchmal) clips included in the 780-clip datasets increased from 351 to 701, while the number of irrelevant (pleural) clips decreased from 383 to 35. The number of clips discarded for quality control was similar (44 in the auto-partitioned dataset and 46 in the control dataset). The lower prevalence of pleural clips in the auto-partitioned dataset ($-45\%$) resulted in significant time savings for annotators, as the average time required to skip a pleural clip was 8.5 s (averaged over the combined 1560-clip dataset). As shown in Figure 8A, the annotators produced more relevant parenchymal labels/hour in the auto-partitioned sprints ($176 \pm 30$) than in the control sprints ($121 \pm 24$; $p = 0.04$). The increase in parenchymal labels/hour corresponded with a decrease in the number of irrelevant pleural clips being skipped per hour (Figure 8B; 131 ± 11 (control) vs. 9 ± 4 (auto-partitioned); $p < 0.001$) and the time spent skipping pleural clips (Figure 8C; 12.6 ± 5.3 min (control) vs. 2.1 ± 0.8 min (auto-partitioned); $p = 0.02$).

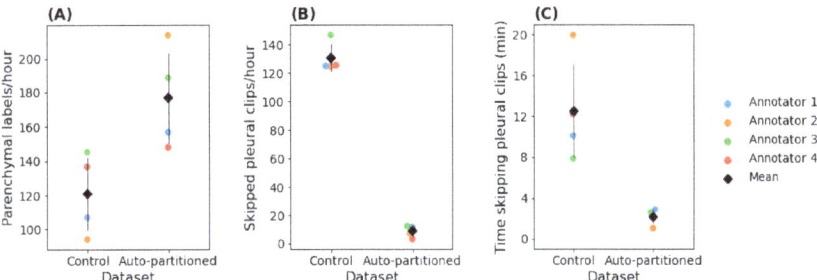

**Figure 8.** Efficiency analysis of control (non-partitioned) and auto-partitioned (parenchymal-predicted) sprints from the parenchymal-specific labelling task. Time metrics exported from the labelling platform were used to determine the rate of parenchymal labels/hour (**A**), skipped pleural clips/hour (**B**), and the time spent skipping pleural clips (**C**) for each of the four annotators. The diamond represents the mean, and error bars represent standard deviation

## 4. Discussion

In this work, a method capable of distinguishing between parenchymal and pleural LUS views with 92.5% accuracy was developed, validated, and deployed as an automated view annotation tool. The automatic partitioning of a 780-clip LUS dataset by view led to a 42 minute reduction in downstream manual annotation time and resulted in the production of 55 ± 6 extra relevant labels per hour. Our methods form the foundation for an improved annotation workflow that is more efficient, more cost-effective, and applicable to similar hierarchical labelling tasks.

The performance of our clip prediction method on unseen data (displayed in Table 3) was deemed acceptable for internal annotation purposes. Although the accuracy trailed 6.5% behind the clinical annotation team, we demonstrated that implementing an automatic annotation workflow resulted in significant time savings on a sample downstream annotation task. In particular, by not examining the extra 348 irrelevant pleural clips screened out by the view classifier in our sample 780-clip datasets, the annotation team saved 42 min. Extrapolating these results to our remaining unannotated 100,000-clip LUS database, we estimate that automatic view annotation would save the annotation team over 4 days (8.5 s × (0.49 − 0.04) × 100,000 clips × 1 day/86 400 s) when accumulating a dataset of 45,000 parenchymal clips (assuming the same false positive rate of our sample auto-partitioned dataset (0.04), pleural frequency of our sample control dataset (0.49), and average time to skip a pleural clip (8.5 s, see Section 3.2.2)). Expensive expert annotation efforts could then be reallocated to more challenging annotation tasks.

Our approach differs from other automated workflow-enhancing annotation strategies, due to the hierarchical nature of the annotation task at hand. First, we require image-level LUS data only, whereas many others [23–25] rely on the presence of additional text data from corresponding clinical reports. Secondly, unlike other methods that seek to minimize the number of annotations required for a specific supervised learning task [20,21], we sought to minimize the time required to annotate a dataset of fixed size with multiple relevant labels downstream in the hierarchy (Figure 1). The resultant annotated dataset is more versatile, since it can be used in the development of multiple classifiers. Further, a similar approach could be taken to automatically partition all parenchymal clips into sets containing either A lines or B lines [28]. Annotation tasks deeper in the hierarchy include lung sliding identification (for clips containing A lines) and B line severity classification (for clips containing B lines).

Despite the aforementioned novelties, the present study is not devoid of limitations. The frame classifier was trained on data from one healthcare institution, hindering application to datasets gathered from external institutions. For most of the downstream annotation tasks, external validation is central to the establishment of model generalizability. In future work, this could be addressed by fine-tuning our classifier on data from external healthcare institutions.

Another future investigation could focus on retraining the frame classifier with an augmented training set that includes automatically annotated LUS clips. Gu et al. [22] witnessed an improvement in model performance using the above procedure. Second, given the comparatively lower metrics for pleural views (likely due to the greater diversity of both radiographic and clinical findings compared to parenchymal views), increasing the proportion of pleural clips in the training set may improve performance.

The classifier developed in this work has utility beyond automatic view annotation. Firstly, it may form the foundation for novel classifiers capable of identifying unique temporal LUS signatures. For example, by visualizing frame prediction probabilities over time, we identified a signature oscillatory pattern that could potentially be used to identify the curtain sign pattern (for examples, see Figures 7A and A2A). In terms of clinical utility, the step-wise deployment of relevant classifiers (view, A line vs. B line, lung sliding, B line severity, etc.) could form the backbone of completely automated LUS interpretation at the bedside. View classification would act as the first step in this hierarchy, ensuring that a potentially novice user has the ultrasound probe in the correct location.

## 5. Conclusions

We describe the development of a deep learning model to accurately partition a large LUS dataset by view. To our knowledge, this is the first description of a method wherein a relatively small subset of a dataset was used to develop a classifier that can automatically partition the rest of an unannotated dataset. Our automated approach considerably improved annotation efficiency, resulting in higher throughput relevant to the annotating task at hand. We propose that this approach can be applied to other unannotated datasets to save considerable manual annotation time and effort. In the clinical environment, view classification could form the backbone of a completely automated LUS interpretation system, where clips are triaged to appropriate classifiers based on the predicted view. Future work involves automatically partitioning the remaining unannotated portion of our LUS database based on other clinical findings downstream in the hierarchy to further optimize annotation resource allocation.

**Supplementary Materials:** The following supporting information can be downloaded at https://www.mdpi.com/article/10.3390/diagnostics12102351/s1.

**Author Contributions:** Conceptualization, D.W. and R.A.; methodology, J.T., D.S., R.A. and B.V. (Blake VanBerlo); software, B.V. (Blake VanBerlo), B.V. (Bennett VanBerlo), D.W. and D.S.; validation, B.V. (Bennett VanBerlo), D.S. and J.T.; formal analysis, B.V. (Bennett VanBerlo) and D.S.; investigation, B.V. (Bennett VanBerlo), J.T. and D.S.; resources, R.A., A.F. and J.T.; data curation, J.T., R.A., A.F., C.D., R.C., J.M., B.W. and J.H.; writing—original draft preparation, B.V. (Bennett VanBerlo), D.S., B.V. (Blake VanBerlo) and J.T.; writing—review and editing, D.S., B.V. (Bennett VanBerlo), B.V. (Blake VanBerlo), J.T., R.A., D.W, C.D., J.D., B.L. and R.C.; visualization, B.V. (Bennett VanBerlo) and D.S.; supervision, R.A.; project administration, B.V. (Blake VanBerlo) and R.A. All authors have read and agreed to the published version of the manuscript.

**Funding:** This research received no external funding.

**Institutional Review Board Statement:** Our project received research ethics board approval from Western University (REB 116838) on 28 January 2021.

**Informed Consent Statement:** Given the retrospective nature of this work, informed consent was not required by the institutional review boards involved.

**Data Availability Statement:** The details of the deep learning model used in this manuscript are available in Appendix B and the implementation can be found at this project's GitHub repository: https://github.com/deepbreathe-ai/pleural-vs-parenchymal (accessed on 25 July 2022). The patient data itself is not available for open-source sharing at this time but may be able to be made available in the future.

**Acknowledgments:** We would like to thank Nathan Phelps for sharing their statistical expertise. Additionally, we wish to acknowledge Gregory Hogg, Marwan Rahman, Jaswin Hargun, Ashritha Durvasula, Claire Vanelli, Faraz Ali, and Hoseok Lee for their useful contributions to motivating discussions and critical review of the present draft.

**Conflicts of Interest:** Arntfield and Deglint declare an ownership stake in WaveBase Inc, whose masking tool was used to process the images. No other authors have any competing interests to declare.

## Abbreviations

The following abbreviations are used in this manuscript:

| | |
|---|---|
| AUC | Area under the receiver operating curve |
| Grad-CAM | Gradient-weighted Class Activation Mapping |
| LUS | Lung ultrasound |
| ReLU | Rectified linear activation function |
| ROC | Receiver operator curve |

### Appendix A. Alternative Model Architectures

Five neural network architectures were initially investigated. Initial training experiments were conducted for random subsets of the training data, with a smaller subset apportioned for validation. As shown in Table A1, highly parameterized architectures tended to overfit to the training set. EfficientNetB0 was selected due to its lightweight architecture and least observed overfitting.

**Table A1.** Performance metrics for model alternatives during initial experimentation, along with number of parameters. Highly parameterized models exhibited overfitting.

| Base | Accuracy | | AUC | | Parameters |
|---|---|---|---|---|---|
| | Train | Validation | Train | Validation | |
| Inceptionv3 [31] | 0.9996 | 0.9207 | 1.0000 | 0.9362 | $2.18 \times 10^7$ |
| ResNet14v2 [32] | 0.9976 | 0.9307 | 0.9999 | 0.9600 | $1.45 \times 10^6$ |
| ResNet50v2 [32] | 0.9995 | 0.9465 | 1.0000 | 0.9648 | $2.36 \times 10^7$ |
| EfficientNetB0 [26] | 0.9471 | 0.9021 | 0.9887 | 0.9595 | $4.21 \times 10^6$ |
| EfficientNetB7 [26] | 0.9981 | 0.9194 | 0.9999 | 0.9438 | $6.44 \times 10^7$ |

### Appendix B. Training Details

Here we provide further details regarding the training of the EffientNetB0 convolutional neural network described in Section 2.2.4.

Multiple measures were applied to combat overfitting. Dropout regularization [33] (with dropout rate 0.3) was applied prior to the penultimate fully connected layer, and L2 regularization was included in the loss (with $\lambda = 10^{-4}$). Bayesian optimization was conducted to refine the hyperparameters [34]. The hyperparameters explored and their corresponding ranges were as follows: learning rate in $[10^{-6}, 10^{-3}]$, dropout regularization rate in $[0.0, 0.6]$, $\lambda$ in $[10^{-9}, 10^{-5}]$, and the number of nodes in the second-last fully connected layer in $\{16, 32, 64, 128\}$.

The model was trained for up to 15 epochs to minimize the binary cross entropy loss function. The Adam optimizer [35] was employed with an initial learning rate of $10^{-6}$, which was halved if the loss on a validation set did not decrease for 3 consecutive epochs.

Further, early stopping was employed if the loss on a validation set did not decrease over 5 consecutive epochs.

All code was written in Python 3.8.5 and the model was implemented using TensorFlow 2.5. The hardware used for training experiments contained an Intel® Core™ i9-10900K CPU at 3.7 GHz and a NVIDIA® GeForce RTX® 3090 GPU. Using this hardware, the inference runtime of the model, averaged over 1000 trials, was 48 ms.

## Appendix C. Explainability

Here we provide extra examples of both frame-based (Grad-CAM++; Figure A1) and clip-based (pleural probability time series; Figure A2) explanations.

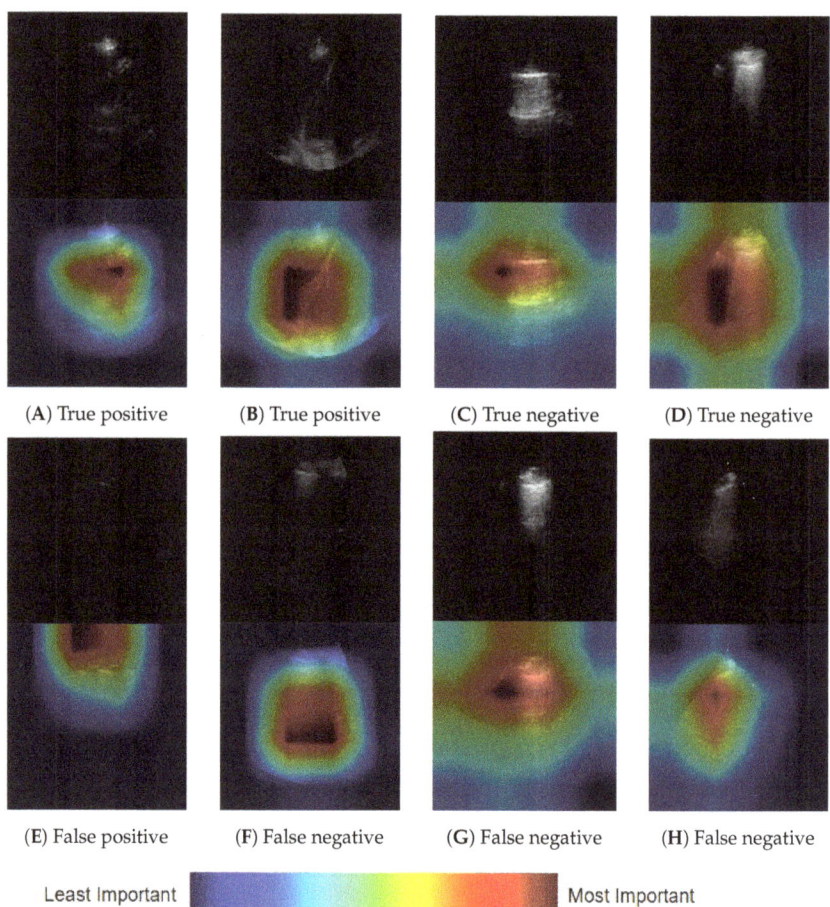

**Figure A1.** Additional Grad-CAM++ heatmaps from true positive (**A,B**), true negative (**C,D**), false positive (**E**), and false negative (**F–H**) example frames. Red regions were the most important to the prediction. True positive frames demonstrate activation on abdominal organs (**A**) and areas featuring pleural effusion, consolidation, and diaphragm (**B**). True negative frames demonstrate activation on the bat wing sign (pleural line bordered by rib shadows), A line artefacts (**C**) and B line artefacts (**D**). The false positive frame (**E**) shows activation proximal to the pleural line, likely because the clip was under-gained and lacked appreciable features of typical parenchymal clips. False negative frames showed activation in areas of aerated lung despite the presence of abdominal organs (**F,H**) and features found in parenchymal clips (pleural line and A lines) due to the probe being positioned superiorly during the first part of the acquisition (**G**).

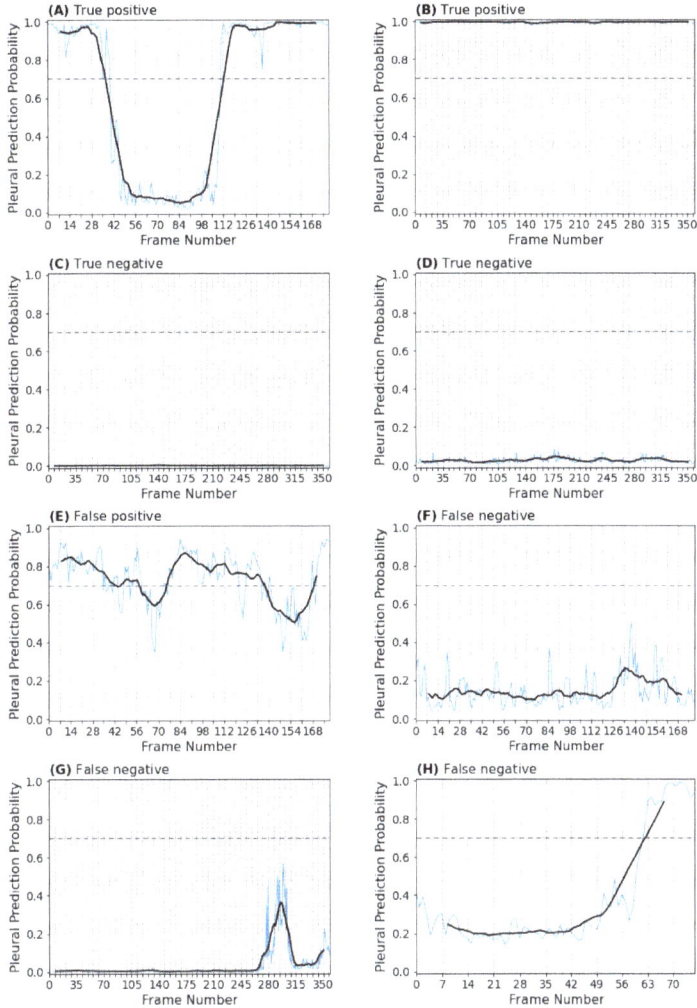

**Figure A2.** Additional Pleural predication probability time series for selected true positive (**A**,**B**), true negative (**C**,**D**), false positive (**E**), and false negative (**F**–**H**) clips. Only one additional false positive example is displayed due to the relatively low number of false positives encountered. (**A**) True positive example displaying the curtain sign, with corresponding predictions oscillating between parenchymal and pleural as expected. (**B**) True positive example with strong pleural predictions throughout, corresponding to a clip that demonstrated the diaphragm and liver on screen right, with pleural effusion and consolidated lung on screen left. (**C**,**D**) True negative examples corresponding to an A-line pattern clip with absent lung sliding (**C**) and a B-line pattern clip (**D**). (**E**) False positive example, corresponding to a clip that was under-gained and relatively deep for a parenchymal acquisition, which hindered visibility of normal parenchymal artefacts and landmarks. (**F**,**G**) False negative examples corresponding to clips where: (**F**) abdominal organs were visible, but the diaphragm was obscured by a rib shadow; (**G**) the first part of the clip was parenchymal, then the operator moved the probe inferiorly to the level of a pleural view (though the predictions still did not meet threshold for pleural classification); (**H**) abdominal contents were obscured by aerated lung, but come into view at the end of the clip, corresponding to an increase in pleural prediction probability that met the classification, but not the contiguity threshold. Supplementary Videos S5–S12.

## References

1. Long, L.; Zhao, H.T.; Zhang, Z.Y.; Wang, G.Y.; Zhao, H.L. Lung ultrasound for the diagnosis of pneumonia in adults: A meta-analysis. *Medicine* **2017**, *96*, e5713. [CrossRef] [PubMed]
2. Ma, O.J.; Mateer, J.R. Trauma ultrasound examination versus chest radiography in the detection of hemothorax. *Ann. Emerg. Med.* **1997**, *29*, 312–316. [CrossRef]
3. Lichenstein, D.; Meziere, G. Relevance of lung ultrasound in the diagnosis of acute respiratory failure. *Chest* **2008**, *134*, 117–125. [CrossRef] [PubMed]
4. Chiumello, D.; Umbrello, M.; Papa, G.F.S.; Angileri, A.; Gurgitano, M.; Formenti, P.; Coppola, S.; Froio, S.; Cammaroto, A.; Carrafiello, G. Global and regional diagnostic accuracy of lung ultrasound compared to CT in patients with acute respiratory distress syndrome. *Crit. Care Med.* **2019**, *47*, 1599–1606. [CrossRef] [PubMed]
5. Nazerian, P.; Volpicelli, G.; Vanni, S.; Gigli, C.; Betti, L.; Bartolucci, M.; Zanobetti, M.; Ermini, F.R.; Iannello, C.; Grifoni, S. Accuracy of lung ultrasound for the diagnosis of consolidations when compared to chest computed tomography. *Am. J. Emerg. Med.* **2015**, *33*, 620–625. [CrossRef]
6. Stassen, J.; Bax, J.J. How to do lung ultrasound. *Eur. Heart J.-Cardiovasc. Imaging* **2022**, *23*, 447–449. [CrossRef]
7. Ruaro, B.; Baratella, E.; Confalonieri, P.; Confalonieri, M.; Vassallo, F.G.; Wade, B.; Geri, P.; Pozzan, R.; Caforio, G.; Marrocchio, C.; et al. High-Resolution Computed Tomography and Lung Ultrasound in Patients with Systemic Sclerosis: Which One to Choose? *Diagnostics* **2021**, *11*, 2293. [CrossRef]
8. Ginsburg, A.S.; Lenahan, J.L.; Jehan, F.; Bila, R.; Lamorte, A.; Hwang, J.; Madrid, L.; Nisar, M.I.; Vitorino, P.; Kanth, N.; et al. Performance of lung ultrasound in the diagnosis of pediatric pneumonia in Mozambique and Pakistan. *Pediatr. Pulmonol.* **2021**, *56*, 551–560. [CrossRef]
9. Alsup, C.; Lipman, G.S.; Pomeranz, D.; Huang, R.W.; Burns, P.; Juul, N.; Phillips, C.; Jurkiewicz, C.; Cheffers, M.; Evans, K.; et al. Interstitial pulmonary edema assessed by lung ultrasound on ascent to high altitude and slight association with acute mountain sickness: A prospective observational study. *High Alt. Med. Biol.* **2019**, *20*, 150–156. [CrossRef]
10. Lichtenstein, D.A. Lung ultrasound in the critically ill. *Ann. Intensive Care* **2014**, *4*, 1–12. [CrossRef]
11. Lichtenstein, D.A. BLUE-protocol and FALLS-protocol: Two applications of lung ultrasound in the critically ill. *Chest* **2015**, *147*, 1659–1670. [CrossRef] [PubMed]
12. Gargani, L.; Volpicelli, G. How I do it: Lung ultrasound. *Cardiovasc. Ultrasound* **2014**, *12*, 1–10. [CrossRef] [PubMed]
13. Lichtenstein, D.A.; Mezière, G.A.; Lagoueyte, J.F.; Biderman, P.; Goldstein, I.; Gepner, A. A-lines and B-lines: Lung ultrasound as a bedside tool for predicting pulmonary artery occlusion pressure in the critically ill. *Chest* **2009**, *136*, 1014–1020. [CrossRef]
14. Lichtenstein, D.; Meziere, G.; Biderman, P.; Gepner, A.; Barre, O. The comet-tail artifact: An ultrasound sign of alveolar-interstitial syndrome. *Am. J. Respir. Crit. Care Med.* **1997**, *156*, 1640–1646. [CrossRef] [PubMed]
15. Lee, F.C.Y. The Curtain Sign in Lung Ultrasound. *J. Med. Ultrasound* **2017**, *25*, 101–104. [CrossRef]
16. Eisen, L.A.; Leung, S.; Gallagher, A.E.; Kvetan, V. Barriers to ultrasound training in critical care medicine fellowships: A survey of program directors. *Crit. Care Med.* **2010**, *38*, 1978–1983. [CrossRef]
17. Wong, J.; Montague, S.; Wallace, P.; Negishi, K.; Liteplo, A.; Ringrose, J.; Dversdal, R.; Buchanan, B.; Desy, J.; Ma, I.W. Barriers to learning and using point-of-care ultrasound: A survey of practicing internists in six North American institutions. *Ultrasound J.* **2020**, *12*, 1–7. [CrossRef]
18. Azar, A.T.; El-Metwally, S.M. Decision tree classifiers for automated medical diagnosis. *Neural Comput. Appl.* **2013**, *23*, 2387–2403. [CrossRef]
19. Wang, F.; Kaushal, R.; Khullar, D. Should health care demand interpretable artificial intelligence or accept "black box" medicine? *Ann. Intern. Med.* **2020**, *172*, 59–60. [CrossRef]
20. Rahimi, S.; Oktay, O.; Alvarez-Valle, J.; Bharadwaj, S. Addressing the Exorbitant Cost of Labeling Medical Images with Active Learning. In Proceedings of the International Conference on Machine Learning in Medical Imaging and Analysis, Singapore, 24–25 May 2021.
21. Zhang, L.; Tong, Y.; Ji, Q. Active Image Labeling and Its Application to Facial Action Labeling. In Proceedings of the Computer Vision—ECCV 2008, Marseille, France, 12–18 October 2008; Forsyth, D.; Torr, P.; Zisserman, A., Eds.; Springer: Berlin/Heidelberg, Germany, 2008; pp. 706–719.
22. Gu, Y.; Leroy, G. Mechanisms for Automatic Training Data Labeling for Machine Learning. In Proceedings of the ICIS, Munich, Germany, 15–18 December 2019.
23. Gong, T.; Li, S.; Wang, J.; Tan, C.L.; Pang, B.C.; Lim, C.C.T.; Lee, C.K.; Tian, Q.; Zhang, Z. Automatic labeling and classification of brain CT images. In Proceedings of the 2011 18th IEEE International Conference on Image Processing, Brussels, Belgium, 11–14 September 2011; pp. 1581–1584. [CrossRef]
24. Irvin, J.; Rajpurkar, P.; Ko, M.; Yu, Y.; Ciurea-Ilcus, S.; Chute, C.; Marklund, H.; Haghgoo, B.; Ball, R.; Shpanskaya, K.; et al. CheXpert: A Large Chest Radiograph Dataset with Uncertainty Labels and Expert Comparison. In Proceedings of the AAAI Conference on Artificial Intelligence, Honolulu, HI, USA, 27 January–1 February 2019. [CrossRef]
25. Smit, A.; Jain, S.; Rajpurkar, P.; Pareek, A.; Ng, A.; Lungren, M.P. CheXbert: Combining Automatic Labelers and Expert Annotations for Accurate Radiology Report Labeling Using BERT. In Proceedings of the EMNLP, Online, 16–20 November 2020. [CrossRef]

26. Tan, M.; Le, Q. Efficientnet: Rethinking model scaling for convolutional neural networks. In Proceedings of the International conference on machine learning. PMLR, Long Beach, CA, USA, 10–15 June 2019; pp. 6105–6114.
27. Deng, J.; Dong, W.; Socher, R.; Li, L.J.; Li, K.; Fei-Fei, L. Imagenet: A large-scale hierarchical image database. In Proceedings of the 2009 IEEE Conference on Computer Vision And Pattern Recognition, Miami, FL, USA, 20–25 June 2009; pp. 248–255.
28. Arntfield, R.; Wu, D.; Tschirhart, J.; VanBerlo, B.; Ford, A.; Ho, J.; McCauley, J.; Wu, B.; Deglint, J.; Chaudhary, R.; et al. Automation of Lung Ultrasound Interpretation via Deep Learning for the Classification of Normal versus Abnormal Lung Parenchyma: A Multicenter Study. *Diagnostics* **2021**, *11*, 2049. [CrossRef]
29. Heinisch, O. Cochran, W. G.: Sampling Techniques, 2. Aufl. John Wiley and Sons, New York, London 1963. Preis s. *Biom. Z.* **1965**, *7*, 203. [CrossRef]
30. Chattopadhyay, A.; Sarkar, A.; Howlader, P.; Balasubramanian, V.N. Grad-CAM++: Generalized Gradient-based Visual Explanations for Deep Convolutional Networks. In Proceedings of the 2018 IEEE Winter Conference on Applications of Computer Vision (WACV), Lake Tahoe, NV, USA, 12–15 March 2018.
31. Szegedy, C.; Vanhoucke, V.; Ioffe, S.; Shlens, J.; Wojna, Z. Rethinking the inception architecture for computer vision. In Proceedings of the IEEE conference on Computer Vision and Pattern Recognition, Las Vegas, NV, USA, 27–30 June 2016; pp. 2818–2826. [CrossRef]
32. He, K.; Zhang, X.; Ren, S.; Sun, J. Deep residual learning for image recognition. In Proceedings of the IEEE Conference on Computer Vision and Pattern Recognition, Las Vegas, NV, USA, 27–30 June 2016; pp. 770–778. [CrossRef]
33. Srivastava, N.; Hinton, G.; Krizhevsky, A.; Sutskever, I.; Salakhutdinov, R. Dropout: A Simple Way to Prevent Neural Networks from Overfitting. *J. Mach. Learn. Res.* **2014**, *15*, 1929–1958.
34. Louppe, G.; Kumar, M. Bayesian Optimization with Skopt, 2016. Available online: https://scikit-optimize.github.io/stable/auto_examples/bayesian-optimization.html (accessed on 25 July 2022).
35. Kingma, D.P.; Ba, J. Adam: A Method for Stochastic Optimization. *arXiv* **2014**, arXiv:1412.6980.

Article

# Dermatopathology of Malignant Melanoma in the Era of Artificial Intelligence: A Single Institutional Experience

Gerardo Cazzato [1,*,†], Alessandro Massaro [2,3,†], Anna Colagrande [1], Teresa Lettini [1], Sebastiano Cicco [4], Paola Parente [5], Eleonora Nacchiero [6], Lucia Lospalluti [7], Eliano Cascardi [8,9], Giuseppe Giudice [6], Giuseppe Ingravallo [1], Leonardo Resta [1], Eugenio Maiorano [1] and Angelo Vacca [4]

1. Section of Molecular Pathology, Department of Emergency and Organ Transplantation (DETO), University of Bari "Aldo Moro", 70124 Bari, Italy
2. LUM Enterprise srl, S.S. 100-Km.18, Parco il Baricentro, 70010 Bari, Italy
3. LUM—Libera Università Mediterranea "Giuseppe Degennaro", S.S. 100-Km.18, Parco il Baricentro, 70010 Bari, Italy
4. Centro Interdisciplinare Ricerca Telemedicina—CITEL-, Università degli Studi di Bari "Aldo Moro", 70124 Bari, Italy
5. Unit of Pathology, Fondazione IRCCS Ospedale Casa Sollievo della Sofferenza, 71013 San Giovanni Rotondo, Italy
6. Section of Plastic Surgery, Department of Emergency and Organ Transplantation (DETO), University of Bari "Aldo Moro", 70124 Bari, Italy
7. Section of Dermatology and Veneorology, Department of Biomedical Sciences and Human Oncology (DIMO), University of Bari "Aldo Moro", 70124 Bari, Italy
8. Department of Medical Sciences, University of Turin, 10094 Turin, Italy
9. Pathology Unit, FPO-IRCSS Candiolo Cancer Institute, Str. Provinciale 142 km 3.95, 10060 Candiolo, Italy
* Correspondence: gerardo.cazzato@uniba.it; Tel.: +39-3405203641
† These authors contributed equally to this work.

**Abstract:** The application of artificial intelligence (AI) algorithms in medicine could support diagnostic and prognostic analyses and decision making. In the field of dermatopathology, there have been various papers that have trained algorithms for the recognition of different types of skin lesions, such as basal cell carcinoma (BCC), seborrheic keratosis (SK) and dermal nevus. Furthermore, the difficulty in diagnosing particular melanocytic lesions, such as Spitz nevi and melanoma, considering the grade of interobserver variability among dermatopathologists, has led to an objective difficulty in training machine learning (ML) algorithms to a totally reliable, reportable and repeatable level. In this work we tried to train a fast random forest (FRF) algorithm, typically used for the classification of clusters of pixels in images, to highlight anomalous areas classified as melanoma "defects" following the Allen–Spitz criteria. The adopted image vision diagnostic protocol was structured in the following steps: image acquisition by selecting the best zoom level of the microscope; preliminary selection of an image with a good resolution; preliminary identification of macro-areas of defect in each preselected image; identification of a class of a defect in the selected macro-area; training of the supervised machine learning FRF algorithm by selecting the micro-defect in the macro-area; execution of the FRF algorithm to find an image vision performance indicator; and analysis of the output images by enhancing lesion defects. The precision achieved by the FRF algorithm proved to be appropriate with a discordance of 17% with respect to the dermatopathologist, allowing this type of supervised algorithm to be nominated as a help to the dermatopathologist in the challenging diagnosis of malignant melanoma.

**Keywords:** artificial intelligence; AI; malignant melanoma; skin; software; algorithms; fast random forest (FRF)

Citation: Cazzato, G.; Massaro, A.; Colagrande, A.; Lettini, T.; Cicco, S.; Parente, P.; Nacchiero, E.; Lospalluti, L.; Cascardi, E.; Giudice, G.; et al. Dermatopathology of Malignant Melanoma in the Era of Artificial Intelligence: A Single Institutional Experience. *Diagnostics* 2022, 12, 1972. https://doi.org/10.3390/diagnostics12081972

Academic Editor: Masayuki Tsuneki

Received: 20 July 2022
Accepted: 11 August 2022
Published: 15 August 2022

**Publisher's Note:** MDPI stays neutral with regard to jurisdictional claims in published maps and institutional affiliations.

**Copyright:** © 2022 by the authors. Licensee MDPI, Basel, Switzerland. This article is an open access article distributed under the terms and conditions of the Creative Commons Attribution (CC BY) license (https://creativecommons.org/licenses/by/4.0/).

## 1. Introduction

After the foundations of artificial intelligence (AI) were established, as postulated by the mathematician Alan Mathison Turing [1], the study and the analysis of AI underwent an important halt under the weight of expectations until the end of the last century; from these years, indeed, a new wave of technological development allowed the functional enhancement of computers, which became more and more powerful and complex [2]. Even today it is not clear whether a machine (computer) could be able to think, but certainly the development of increasingly complex systems, such as convolutional neural networks (CNNs) [3], has allowed a rapid increase in performance not only in fields of computer science, but also in different fields, such as medical, pathological and even subclassified dermatopathological fields [4,5].

The first attempts based on convolutional neural networks (CNNs) have already proven to be up to expectations, but the objective difficulty in reproducibility of the criteria for labeling a lesion as malignant or benign has also been reflected in the training of AI applied to differential diagnostics of atypical pigmented lesions. [3,4]. Indeed, it is not always easy to diagnose melanoma by analyzing the images with a "naked eye" approach. The problem has been known for some time and is classically defined as the "gray zone" of dermatopathology: in fact, beyond the extremes of the spectrum of benign and malignant, there is a fairly large number of atypical pigmented lesions that it is not easy to define "tout-court" as having benign or malignant biological behavior. This uncertainty is the consequence of the fact that the criteria normally used to define a lesion as malignant melanoma become conflicting and blurred in certain situations; for example, nevi with severe dysplasia, Spitz nevi with dysplastic aspects (so-called SPARK nevus) or melanocytic lesions with an uncertain potential for malignancy such as MELTUMP or SAMPUS. The loss of criteria defined and recognized by all, as well as the interpretative subjectivity, has repercussions on the reduction or, sometimes, loss of agreement between dermatopathologists, and also (as some studies have highlighted) even on intraobserver agreement over time [2–4].

In this work we tried to train the proposed fast random forest (FRF) algorithm to be able to support the specialist to highlight automatically the "anomalous pixel regions" and to estimate a possible risk by quantifying the percentage of these regions with atypical morphological features starting from routine histopathological images (digital pathology).

## 2. Materials and Methods

*2.1. Data Acquisition*

For training, validation and testing, we used a dataset of 125 photomicrographs of 63 patients suffering from malignant melanoma, originally taken at 1280 × 1080 pixels (SONY® Sensor IMX185, Tokyo, Japan) at 10× magnification, obtained from blocks of material fixed in formaldehyde and embedded in paraffin (FFPE) from 1 January 2020 to 1 January 2021. For each patient, demographic and clinical characteristics, including the Breslow thickness and other histopathological features, were recorded for routine clinical practice. Informed consent was obtained from all patients involved and the study was approved by the local ethical committee. In total, 63 specimens (mean length ± SD 1.64 ± 0.93 cm) were processed. For all specimens, hematoxylin and eosin (H&E) staining was used for histopathological analysis and, in some cases, ancillary immunohistochemical techniques were performed for a final correct diagnosis. For each of them, each individual case was analyzed and a more representative slide was chosen by two dermatopathologists with a lot of experience in skin histopathology (G.C. and A.C.). After collecting all the slides, we proceeded to identify at least 5 potential defects (hotspots) normally used in routine dermatopathological diagnostics to differentiate a dysplastic nevus from a malignant melanoma. The defects analyzed were divided into architectural (disposition of the single and aggregates of melanocytes, symmetry/asymmetry of the lesion in question) and cytological (nuclear atypia, pagetoid spreading of the melanocyte, possible necrosis) groups following the Spitz–Allen criteria [6] (Table 1).

**Table 1.** Summary of these criteria.

| Dysplastic Nevus | Malignant Melanoma |
|---|---|
| *Architectural criteria (mandatory, major)* | |
| Lentiginous or contiguous melanocytic hyperplasia | Poor circumscription of the intraepidermal melanocytic component of the lesion |
| Focal melanocytic atypia | Increased number of melanocytes, solitary and in nests, within and above the epidermal basal cell layer and within adnexal epithelia (pagetoid spreading) |
| | Marked variation in size and shape of the melanocytic nests |
| | Absence of maturation of melanocytes with descent into the dermis |
| | Melanocytes in mitosis |
| *Architectural criteria (minor, at least 2)* | |
| "Shoulder phenomenon" | Melanocytes with nuclear atypia |
| Fusion of epithelial cones | Necrosis or degeneration of melanocytes |
| Subepidermal concentric lamellar fibrosis | |

## 2.2. Fast Random Forest (FRF) Image Classification

The artificial intelligence image processing algorithm used to classify and to enhance anomalies contained in the microscope image is the fast random forest (FRF) algorithm. The algorithm was designed by using a Java-based script framework. The learning process of the algorithm is based on a preliminary classification of clusters of pixels of the same image [5] including possible melanoma areas: the preliminary identification of melanoma morphological features represents the labeling approach typical of machine learning-supervised algorithms. The FRF testing provides as output the processed image with color-enhanced melanoma pixel clusters (each class selected in the learning step is represented by a color), probabilistic maps (high probability highlighted with white to identify an anomaly in a specified image region) and algorithm performance indicators (precision, recall, and receiver operating characteristic (ROC) curves [5]). The FRF algorithm executes an ensemble of decision trees able to classify clusters of pixels constituting an image with good accuracy, low computational cost and performing a multiclass segmentation [7–12]. The classification process is addressed by labeling clusters of pixels defined by the same features (clusters of gray pixel intensities). At the beginning, decision trees randomly select clusters of pixels by splitting the features at each node. The final classification of image areas are a result of the average classification of all the trees constructed during the algorithm iterations. The method is sketched in Figure 1, where it is possible to distinguish the following phases:

- Different clusters of pixels (features) are used for the training model;
- A marked region is distinguished as the features to find in the same image to process;
- The RF is executed by finding similar features in the same image (similar features of similar clusters having a similar gray pixel intensity distribution).

The training model can be constructed by setting the following tools or procedures (algorithm parameters):

- Gaussian blur filtering, obtaining a blurred image to process;
- Sobel filtering, which is able to approximate the image by a gradient of the intensity;
- Hessian filtering, defined as:

$$H = \begin{pmatrix} h_1 & h_2 \\ h_3 & h_4 \end{pmatrix} \qquad (1)$$

where $h1$, $h2$, $h3$ and $h4$ are the elements of the Hessian matrix formed by the second-order partial derivatives stating the variation of the intensity of each pixel (derivative at the pixel point) in the x, y and xy direction (plane directions of the 2D image).

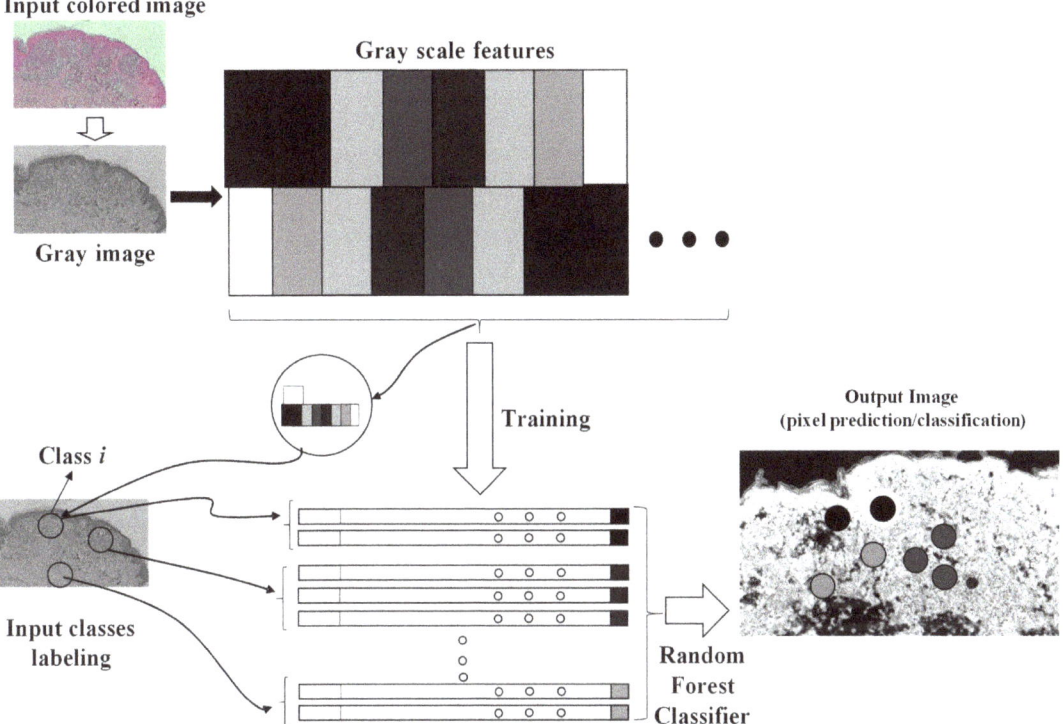

**Figure 1.** Image processing procedure based on pixel feature training and random forest classifier.

Defined by a *Trace*, a determinant (*Det*), a first eigenvalue (*Fe*), a second eigenvalue (*Se*), an orientation (*Or*; angle of the maximal second derivative), a *Gamma*, and a *Square Gamma*:

$$Trace = h_1 + h_4 \tag{2}$$

$$Det = \sqrt{h_1^2 + h_2 h_3 + h_4^2} \tag{3}$$

$$Fe = \frac{h_1 + h_4}{2} + \sqrt{\frac{4h_2^2 + (h_1 - h_4)^2}{2}} \tag{4}$$

$$Se = \frac{h_1 + h_4}{2} - \sqrt{\frac{4h_2^2 + (h_1 - h_4)^2}{2}} \tag{5}$$

$$Or = \frac{1}{2}\arccos(4h_2^2 + (h_1 - h_4)^2) \tag{6}$$

$$Gamma = t^4(h_1 - h_4)^2((h_1 - h_4)^2 + 4h_2^2) \text{ with } t = 1^{3/4} \tag{7}$$

$$Square\ Gamma = t^2((h_1 - h_4)^2 + 4h_2^2) \text{ with } t = 1^{3/4} \tag{8}$$

- Difference of Gaussian functions;
- Membrane projections due to the rotation of the original image kernel;
- Main pixel parameters (mean, minimum, maximum, etc.);
- Anisotropic diffusion filtering preserving sharp edges;

- Bilateral filtering preserving edges;
- Lipschitz filtering (preserving edges and decreasing noise);
- Gabor filtering (mainly adopted for texture analysis);
- Derivative filtering estimating high order derivatives;
- Structured filtering estimating the eigenvalues;
- Shifting of the image in different directions.

The optimized hyperparameters and filter properties applied for the image FRF processing (feature training) are: the Gaussian blur filter, Hessian matrix filter, membrane projections, membrane thickness equal to 1, membrane patch size equal to 19, minimum sigma equal to 1, and maximum sigma equal to 16.

In the proposed approach, the same image is adopted both for the training and for the testing: each image is converted into a grayscale image, and in the same image [12] the classes training the model are identified (classes of similar features including those of the Spitz nevi).

Different algorithms can be applied to calculate automatically the different areas [13]. In order to enhance classified clusters in the probabilistic image, a threshold filtering adjusting the intensities of the output grayscale image was adopted (see example of Appendix A): this setting is important to estimate with good precision the areas enclosing dermatological defects. The testing images were preliminary selected, taking into account images with certain defects in order to train the FRF algorithm efficiently.

The adopted method is summarized by the following steps:

- A preliminary selection of images focusing the attention on the characteristics of dysplastic nevi and malignant melanoma (validation of the training model focusing on this classification);
- Performing of a training of the selected images (FRF training model based on the classification of anomalous image areas embedding features of dysplastic nevi and MM, and the identification of other no-risk areas as structures of clusters of grayscale pixels);
- Setting the optimization of the FRF algorithm parameters for the best identification of classes of the testing dataset;
- Testing the execution of the FRF algorithm's detection and estimation of anomalous areas by applying, after the analysis, image threshold filters (for the calculus, all the images have the same dimension of 1000 pixels × 2000 pixels);
- Verification of the algorithm performance by estimating its precision.

## 3. Results

For five pixel clusters of the same dimensions (closest to the particular anomaly), a number of about 300 instances (computational cycles) occurs to achieve the maximum precision (equal to 1), with a computational cost of about 2 min using a processor, the Intel(R) Core(TM) i5-7200U CPU, 2.71 GHz. The minimum recall performance parameter (near to 0) is achieved in about 392 instances. The ROC curve (representing the true positive rate versus the false positive rate in the plane) is matched with the ideal curve of a perfect classifier (Figure 2). The performance indicators confirm the correct setting of the FRF hyperparameters.

Appendix B illustrates the FRF probabilistic images of some of the classified areas. The algorithm performance is estimated by the precision parameter representing the metric of the FRF score (probability of algorithm error). A maximum precision of 1 is achieved after about 250 iteration steps (see Figure 2).

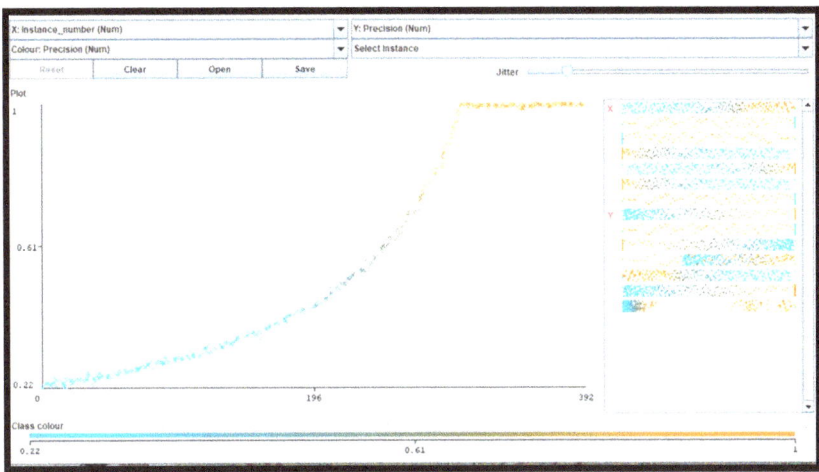

**Figure 2.** This figure illustrates the error metric (precision parameter [5]) of the adopted FRF algorithm versus iteration number (instance number) by proving that the final results are characterized by the maximum precision.

An example of image classification is illustrated in Figure 3 where C1, C3 and C4 are the four classes used to construct the learning model (areas having similar characteristics).

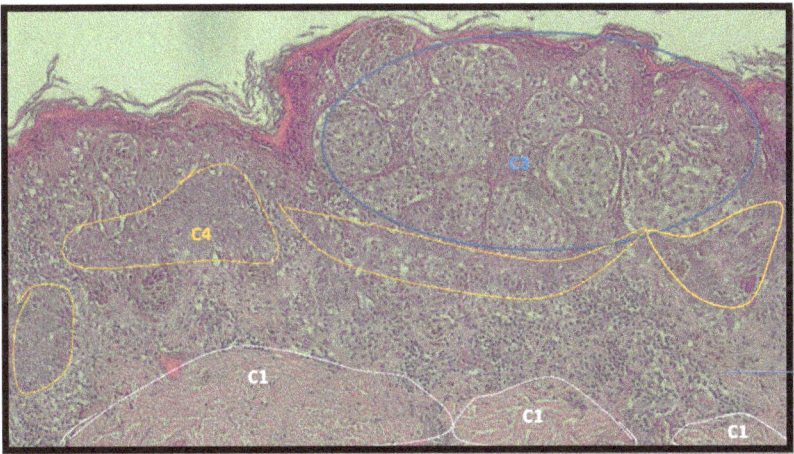

**Figure 3.** Example of analysis and selection of defects (such as architectural and cytological atypia, pagetoid spreading, possible ulceration) in the macro-area of an image of malignant melanoma. Note the different colors of the circles/ellipses used to subclassify the anomalies (defects).

In Tables 2 and 3 the FRF enhancement of possible classified defects are shown by estimating the percentage coverage in 1 mm × 2 mm images.

**Table 2.** Example of analysis of two micrographs of malignant melanoma in which some constituent elements of the Allen–Spitz criteria have been analyzed, such as: symmetrical or asymmetrical lesion, clustering of melanocytes in nests or presence of single melanocyte, and eventual pagetoid spreading.

| Original Image | Defect Type (Name) | Defect Cluster (Enhanced Probability Image) | Percentage Presence on the Whole Image | Extension [mm$^2$] |
|---|---|---|---|---|
| IMG00131 EE | // | | 5.3% | 0.106 |
| IMG00132 EE | // | | 4.1% | 0.082 |

**Table 3.** Example of two other images whose cytological characteristics were studied, including: cellular atypia, eventual pagetoid spreading, mitosis and nuclear pleomorphism.

| Original Image | Defect Type (Name) | Defect Cluster (Enhanced Probability Image) | Percentage Presence on the Whole Image | Extension [mm$^2$] |
|---|---|---|---|---|
| IMG00150 | // | | 6.6% | 0.132 |
| IMG00151 | // | | 8.8% | 0.176 |

Analyzing the discrepancy between the performance of the FRF algorithm and the diagnosis by the dermatopathologist, a value of 17% was found, which is slightly lower than that described in the interobserver variability (about 25–26%).

## 4. Discussion

Historically, the histopathological diagnosis of malignant melanoma has always fluctuated from rather simple and easy to classify cases up to very complex and difficult to interpret cases [14], considering that, in the context of human pathology, MM is defined as the "great mime" [15]. For example, in a recent 2017 paper, *Elmore G.J.* et al. [15] analyzed the diagnostic results of 187 practicing pathologists in 10 states by comparing them with each other and with a consensus diagnosis reached by a group of three experienced dermatopathologists. The authors asked the 187 pathologists to interpret the same skin lesions after a certain time range (8 months) in order to have an estimate of the intraobserver readability. The degree of accuracy was very high (about 92%) in the case of diagnosing slightly atypical pigmented lesions and reached about 72% in the case of invasive melanomas. Conversely, diagnostic accuracy became much lower in the case of lesions in the spectrum between these two extremes. For example, fewer than half of diagnoses agreed with expert consensus for cases classified as severely atypical lesions, melanoma in situ, or early stage invasive melanoma. Similarly, over time, the diagnoses of the so-called "gray zone" of dermatopathology lost intraobserver reproducibility [16].

In this context, the development of artificial intelligence methods applied to pathological anatomy [17] had the merit of offering a possibility to understand if the evaluation of a melanocytic lesion that represented a malignant melanoma could be made more "objective" compared to lesions not endowed with the potential for malignancy "tout-court".

This work is based on the definition of the steps to follow to classify malignant melanoma defects. A metric estimating the precision of the applied FRF algorithm is applied to estimate the error of the classification. The low computational cost related the image processing and the use of the same image for the algorithm training allow us to apply the FRF algorithm to new images without constructing a training model based on historical images. In this way, we used a set of images of lesions previously diagnosed by two board-certified dermatopathologists to understand how much the FRF algorithm was able to assist the pathologist in the decision-making process.

The precision achieved by the FRF algorithm proved to be appropriate, allowing this type of supervised algorithm to be nominated as a help in the dermatopathological diagnosis of MM. In particular, analyzing the discrepancy between the performance of the FRF algorithm and the diagnosis by the dermatopathologist, a value of 17% was found, which is slightly lower than that described in the interobserver variability (about 25–26%). These data are similar to that reported by *Hekler* et al. [18] who, in their paper, trained a CNN according to a binary model of classification of nevi and melanoma, and reported a discrepancy value between the trained CNN and dermatopathologist equal to 18% for melanoma, 20% for nevi and 19% overall. On the other hand, it is important to underline that any AI algorithm is trained on diagnostic criteria chosen "a priori" by the pathologist and, therefore, there can similarly be false-positive misdiagnoses: this is the case with Spitz nevi. Indeed, *Hart S.N.* et al. [19] trained a CNN for binary classification between conventional nevi and Spitz nevi. Their algorithm was tested on WSIs of Spitz nevi and conventional nevi, producing a classification accuracy of 92% overall, based on a sensitivity of 85% and specificity of 99%. In a second phase of their study, the authors demonstrated how important it was to improve the diagnostic performance values of the AI algorithm to allow a dermatopathologist to preselect the areas of interest of the entire WSI, as in the absence of this, the validation accuracy was unacceptable at only 52%.

All these data agree in allowing us to consider the inclusion of the FRF algorithm in the normal workflow of histopathological diagnostics. The framework of the FRF algorithm used in this work is based on Weka [20] libraries implemented in the Java language.

The main motivation is in the novel approach adopted for the algorithm training. Other studies use a traditional approach based on the discrimination of the training model and of the testing model, which are performed by adopting different images [21]. In the proposed approach, it adopts the same image both for the training and for the testing: each image is converted into grayscale images, and in the same image [12] the classes training the model are identified (classes of similar features, including those of the Spitz nevi). In this way the doctor can circle the areas (classes) without having a historical dataset of images. The algorithm versatility gives an idea of the anomalous distribution (enhancing anomalous groups of pixels) of malignant areas quickly by estimating the covering percentage.

Furthermore, from a clinical point of view, there have already been numerous papers published in the literature that have attempted to correlate, specifically, dermoscopic characteristics with clinical diagnosis. A very interesting contribution by Argenziano et al. [22] in 2003 evaluated the sensitivity, specificity and, therefore, diagnostic accuracy of criteria commonly used for the diagnosis of MM. In the paper, 108 melanocytic lesions were evaluated by 40 experienced dermoscopists in an attempt to evaluate the interobserver and intraobserver agreement by using four algorithms such as the pattern analysis, ABCD rule, Menzies method and 7-point checklist. Of all these, there was a good agreement except for with the dermoscopic criteria, demonstrating how important it is also in dermoscopy to adopt more "accurate" parameters.

*Limitations*

It is important to note that in our paper we used exclusively histopathological (morphological) criteria and, therefore, were subject to limitations including the different sizes of cancer cells, a concept intrinsic to tumor heterogeneity [23].

## 5. Conclusions

The FRF images were processed by following a specific image diagnostic protocol, oriented on reading and algorithm error minimization. An important tool for melanoma diagnosis is the probability image estimated by the processed FRF output image. The probability image is useful to better discriminate information about ambiguous lesions. A single probability image refers to a particular class of "defect" and enhances, by the white color, the defect distribution in the whole analyzed image. By knowing the dimension of the acquired microscope image, it is also possible to estimate the defect distribution percentage. All the adopted approaches are suitable to create a specific image vision platform for telemedicine digital pathology.

**Author Contributions:** Conceptualization, G.C., A.C., T.L., P.P., S.C., G.I., L.R., E.M. and A.V.; methodology, G.C., L.L., E.C., E.N. and A.M.; software, A.M.; validation, T.L., S.C., G.I., L.R. and E.M.; formal analysis, G.C.; investigation, G.C., A.C., T.L., S.C., G.I., L.R., E.M. and A.V.; resources, G.C.; data curation, G.C., A.C., T.L., S.C., G.I., L.R. and E.M.; writing—original draft preparation, G.C. and A.M.; writing—review and editing, G.C., A.C., T.L., S.C., G.G., G.I., L.R., E.M. and A.V.; visualization, G.C.; supervision, A.V. All authors have read and agreed to the published version of the manuscript.

**Funding:** This research received no external funding.

**Institutional Review Board Statement:** Approved by CITEL (Dipartimento di Scienze Biomediche e Oncologia Umana—Dimo U.O.C. Medicina Interna "G. Baccelli" Policlinico di Bari, number 5732).

**Informed Consent Statement:** Informed consent was recorded by all patients involved in the study.

**Data Availability Statement:** Not applicable.

**Acknowledgments:** In memory of Antonietta Cimmino (A.C.).

**Conflicts of Interest:** The authors declare no conflict of interest.

## Appendix A

The enhancement of the classified areas by the FRF algorithm can be performed by adopting different image processing filters. In Figure A1 different image filtering approaches enhancing classes and the probabilistic image are shown. The probabilistic image refers to a particular class related to a defect.

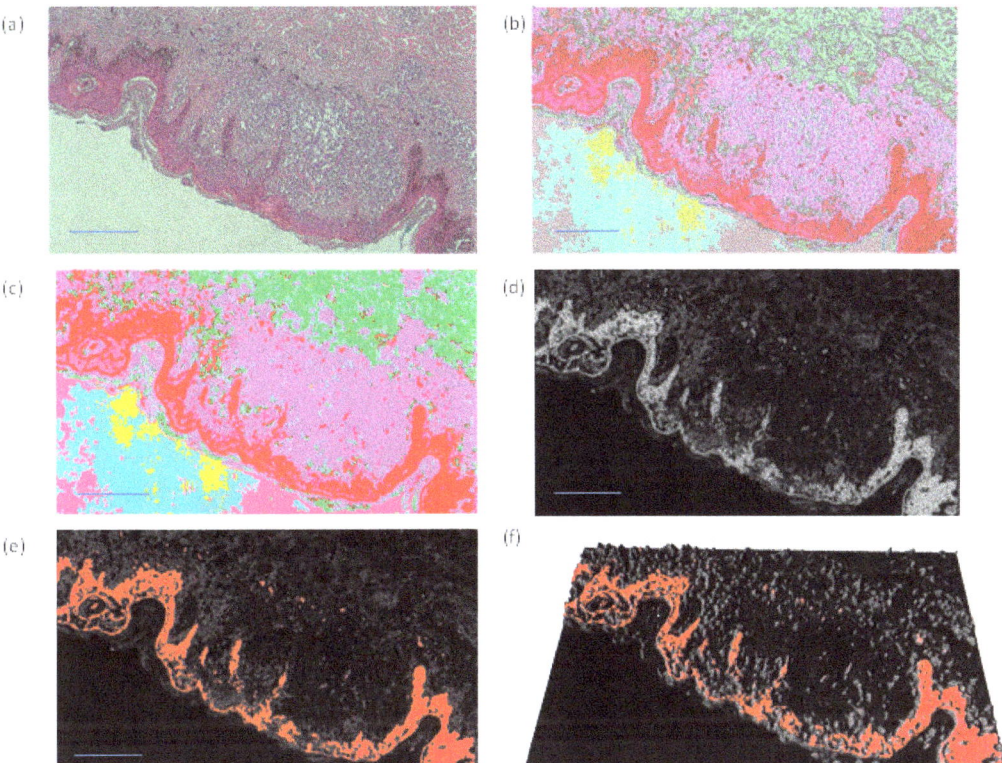

**Figure A1.** (**a**) Original image. (**b**,**c**) Images with all detected classes defined by different colors. (**d**,**e**) Probabilistic image and (**f**) related 3D reconstruction.

Figure A1 indicates possible alternative color schemes to highlight dangerous areas: the red color of the classified output image (b, c), the white color of the probabilistic images (d) and the red color of the probabilistic image in a 2D (f) and 3D scheme (g).

## Appendix B

The probabilistic images are the output of the FRF algorithm. In Figure A2 some pixel cluster classifications of the original image of Figure 3 are shown.

Figure A2 is an example that represents different classes, where each one is a probabilistic image with the white color representing the higher probability value to find specific class features. Alternatively, all classes are identified in the same image by different colors.

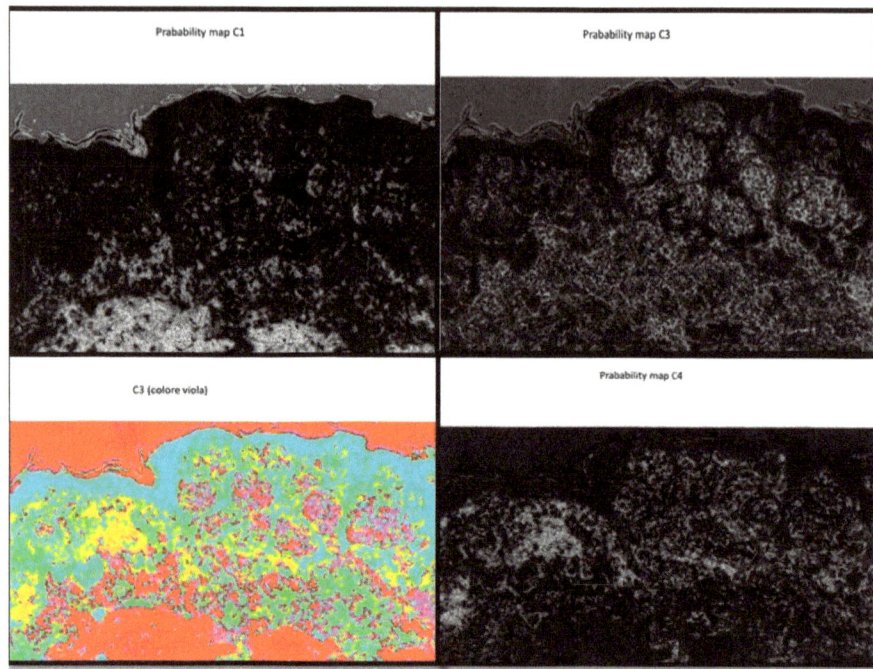

**Figure A2.** Example of distribution of the probability classes from C1 (low probability of recognition of the anomaly, black shade) to C4 (high probability of recognition of the anomaly, white shade).

## References

1. Turing, A.M. I.—Computing Machinery and Intelligence. *Mind* **1950**, *LIX*, 433–460. [CrossRef]
2. Bjola, C. AI for development: Implications for theory and practice. *Oxf. Dev. Stud.* **2022**, *50*, 78–90. [CrossRef]
3. Venerito, V.; Angelini, O.; Cazzato, G.; Lopalco, G.; Maiorano, E.; Cimmino, A.; Iannone, F. A convolutional neural network with transfer learning for automatic discrimination between low and high-grade synovitis: A pilot study. *Intern. Emerg. Med.* **2021**, *16*, 1457–1465. [CrossRef] [PubMed]
4. Onega, T.; Reisch, L.M.; Frederick, P.D.; Geller, B.M.; Nelson, H.D.; Lott, J.P.; Radick, A.C.; Elder, D.E.; Barnhill, R.L.; Piepkorn, M.W.; et al. Use of digital whole slide imaging in dermatopathology. *J. Digit. Imaging* **2016**, *29*, 243–253. [CrossRef] [PubMed]
5. Massaro, A. *Electronic in Advanced Research Industry: From Industry 4.0 to Industry 5.0 Advances*; Wiley: Hoboken, NJ, USA; IEEE: New York, NY, USA, 2021; ISBN 9781119716877.
6. Allen, A.C.; Spitz, S. Malignant melanoma; a clinicopathological analysis of the criteria for diagnosis and prognosis. *Cancer* **1953**, *6*, 1–45. [CrossRef]
7. Breiman, L. Random forests. *Mach. Learn.* **2001**, *45*, 5–32. [CrossRef]
8. Mahapatra, D. Analyzing training information from random forests for Improved image segmentation. *IEEE Trans. Image Process.* **2014**, *23*, 1504–1512. [CrossRef] [PubMed]
9. Belgiu, M.; Drăguţ, L. Random forest in remote sensing: A review of applications and future directions. *ISPRS J. Photogramm. Remote Sens.* **2016**, *114*, 24–31. [CrossRef]
10. Arganda-Carreras, I.; Kaynig, V.; Rueden, C.; Eliceiri, K.W.; Schindelin, J.; Cardona, A.; Seung, H.S. Trainable Weka segmentation: A machine learning tool for microscopy pixel classification. *Bioinformatics* **2017**, *33*, 2424–2426. [CrossRef] [PubMed]
11. Lormand, C.; Zellmer, G.F.; Németh, K.; Kilgour, G.; Measd, S.; Palmer, A.S.; Sakamoto, N.; Yurimoto, H.; Moebis, A. Weka trainable segmentation plugin in ImageJ: A semi-automatic tool applied to crystal size distributions of microlites in volcanic rocks. *Microsc. Microanal.* **2018**, *24*, 667–675. [CrossRef] [PubMed]
12. Alessandro, M. *Detection of Anomalies in Images by Machine Learning Fast Random Forest—FRF-Algorithm*; Zenodo: Geneva, Switzerland, 2022. [CrossRef]
13. Lay-Ekuakille, A.; Spano, F.; Mvemba, P.K.; Massaro, A.; Galiano, A.; Casciaro, S.; Conversano, F. Conductivity image characterization of gold nanoparticles based-device through atomic force microscopy. In Proceedings of the IEEE 2018 Nanotechnology for Instrumentation and Measurement (NANOfIM), Mexico City, Mexico, 7–8 November 2018; IEEE: Piscataway, NJ, USA, 2019.

14. Roush, G.C.; Kirkwood, J.M.; Ernstoff, M.; Somma, S.J.; Duray, P.H.; Klaus, S.N.; Stenn, K.S.; Titus, L.J.; Lerner, A.B. Reproducibility and validity in the clinical diagnosis of the nonfamilial dysplastic nevus: Work in progress. *Recent Results Cancer Res.* **1986**, *102*, 154–158. [CrossRef] [PubMed]
15. Cazzato, G.; Colagrande, A.; Cimmino, A.; Demarco, A.; Lospalluti, L.; Arezzo, F.; Resta, L.; Ingravallo, G. The Great Mime: Three Cases of Melanoma with Carcinoid-Like and Paraganglioma-Like Pattern with Emphasis on Differential Diagnosis. *Dermatopathology* **2021**, *8*, 130–134. [CrossRef] [PubMed]
16. Elmore, J.G.; Barnhill, R.L.; Elder, D.E.; Longton, G.M.; Pepe, M.S.; Reisch, L.M.; Carney, P.A.; Titus, L.J.; Nelson, H.D.; Onega, T.; et al. Pathologists' diagnosis of invasive melanoma and melanocytic proliferations: Observer accuracy and reproducibility study. *BMJ* **2017**, *357*, j2813. [CrossRef] [PubMed]
17. Harrison, J.H.; Gilbertson, J.R.; Hanna, M.G.; Olson, N.H.; Seheult, J.N.; Sorace, J.M.; Stram, M.N. Introduction to Artificial Intelligence and Machine Learning for Pathology. *Arch. Pathol. Lab. Med.* **2021**, *145*, 1228–1254. [CrossRef] [PubMed]
18. Hekler, A.; Utikal, J.S.; Enk, A.H.; Berking, C.; Klode, J.; Schadendorf, D.; Jansen, P.; Franklin, C.; Holland-Letz, T.; Krahl, D.; et al. Pathologist-level classification of histopathological melanoma images with deep neural networks. *Eur. J. Cancer* **2019**, *115*, 79–83. [CrossRef] [PubMed]
19. Hart, S.N.; Flotte, W.; Norgan, A.P.; Shah, K.K.; Buchan, Z.R.; Mounajjed, T.; Flotte, T.J. Classification of Melanocytic Lesions in Selected and Whole-Slide Images via Convolutional Neural Networks. *J. Pathol. Inform.* **2019**, *10*, 5. [CrossRef] [PubMed]
20. Witten, I.H.; Frank, E.; Hall, M.A.; Pal, C.J. *Data Mining*, 4th ed.; Morgan Kaufmann: Burlington, MA, USA, 2017; ISBN 9780128042915. [CrossRef]
21. Raza, R.; Zulfiqar, F.; Tariq, S.; Anwar, G.B.; Sargano, A.B.; Habib, Z. Melanoma Classification from Dermoscopy Images Using Ensemble of Convolutional Neural Networks. *Mathematics* **2022**, *10*, 26. [CrossRef]
22. Argenziano, G.; Soyer, H.P.; Chimenti, S.; Talamini, R.; Corona, R.; Sera, F.; Binder, M.; Cerroni, L.; De Rosa, G.; Ferrara, G.; et al. Dermoscopy of pigmented skin lesions: Results of a consensus meeting via the Internet. *J. Am. Acad. Dermatol.* **2003**, *48*, 679–693. [CrossRef] [PubMed]
23. Kłós, A.; Płonka, P.M. Growth of mixed cancer cell population—In silico the size matters. *Acta Biochim. Pol.* **2020**, *67*, 453–463. [CrossRef] [PubMed]

Article

# Natural Language Processing in Diagnostic Texts from Nephropathology

Maximilian Legnar [1,2,*,†], Philipp Daumke [3], Jürgen Hesser [2,4], Stefan Porubsky [5], Zoran Popovic [2,†], Jan Niklas Bindzus [2,†], Joern-Helge Heinrich Siemoneit [2,†] and Cleo-Aron Weis [2,6,*]

[1] Mannheim Institute for Intelligent Systems in Medicine (MIISM), Medical Faculty Mannheim, Heidelberg University, 68167 Mannheim, Germany
[2] Institute of Pathology, Medical Faculty Mannheim, Heidelberg University, 68167 Mannheim, Germany; juergen.hesser@medma.uni-heidelberg.de (J.H.); zoran.popovic@medma.uni-heidelberg.de (Z.P.); jan.bindzus@stud.uni-heidelberg.de (J.N.B.); siemoneit@stud.uni-heidelberg.de (J.-H.H.S.)
[3] Averbis GmbH, 79098 Freiburg, Germany; philipp.daumke@averbis.com
[4] Data Analysis and Modeling, MIISM, Medical School, Interdisciplinary Center for Scientific Computing (IWR), Central Institute for Computer Engineering (ZITI), CZS Heidelberg Center for Model-Based AI, Heidelberg University, 69117 Heidelberg, Germany
[5] Institute of Pathology, Medical Faculty Mainz, University Hospital Mainz, 55131 Mainz, Germany; stefan.porubsky@unimedizin-mainz.de
[6] Institute of Pathology, Medical Faculty Heidelberg, 69120 Heidelberg, Germany
* Correspondence: maximilian.legnar@medma.uni-heidelberg.de (M.L.); cleo-aron.weis@medma.uni-heidelberg.de (C.-A.W.); Tel.: +49-621-383-4072 (C.-A.W.)
† Current address: Institute of Pathology, Medical Faculty Mannheim, Heidelberg University, 69117 Heidelberg, Germany.

**Citation:** Legnar, M.; Daumke, P.; Hesser, J.; Porubsky, S.; Popovic, Z.; Bindzus, J.N.; Siemoneit, J.-H.H.; Weis, C.-A. Natural Language Processing in Diagnostic Texts from Nephropathology. *Diagnostics* **2022**, *12*, 1726. https://doi.org/10.3390/diagnostics12071726

Academic Editor: Masayuki Tsuneki

Received: 31 May 2022
Accepted: 12 July 2022
Published: 15 July 2022

**Publisher's Note:** MDPI stays neutral with regard to jurisdictional claims in published maps and institutional affiliations.

**Copyright:** © 2022 by the authors. Licensee MDPI, Basel, Switzerland. This article is an open access article distributed under the terms and conditions of the Creative Commons Attribution (CC BY) license (https://creativecommons.org/licenses/by/4.0/).

**Abstract:** Introduction: This study investigates whether it is possible to predict a final diagnosis based on a written nephropathological description—as a surrogate for image analysis—using various NLP methods. Methods: For this work, 1107 unlabelled nephropathological reports were included. (i) First, after separating each report into its microscopic description and diagnosis section, the diagnosis sections were clustered unsupervised to less than 20 diagnostic groups using different clustering techniques. (ii) Second, different text classification methods were used to predict the diagnostic group based on the microscopic description section. Results: The best clustering results (i) could be achieved with HDBSCAN, using BoW-based feature extraction methods. Based on keywords, these clusters can be mapped to certain diagnostic groups. A transformer encoder-based approach as well as an SVM worked best regarding diagnosis prediction based on the histomorphological description (ii). Certain diagnosis groups reached F1-scores of up to 0.892 while others achieved weak classification metrics. Conclusion: While textual morphological description alone enables retrieving the correct diagnosis for some entities, it does not work sufficiently for other entities. This is in accordance with a previous image analysis study on glomerular change patterns, where some diagnoses are associated with one pattern, but for others, there exists a complex pattern combination.

**Keywords:** NLP; text analysis; nephropathology; text classification; topic modelling; BERT; transformer encoder; machine learning; deep learning

## 1. Introduction

Due to complex histomorphological change patterns and diagnoses, nephropathology is a challenging sub-discipline of surgical pathology [1]. This field is hard to learn for beginners, which is reflected, among other things, in a steep learning curve. However, after such a learning process, many assessments by experts in the field show strong inter-observer agreement between results. The high-level specialization of such pathologists is achieved by long, tedious training, which makes them as rare as they are necessary [2]. One idea for assisting novices in the learning process is to utilise machine learning (ML) tools to assist in reaching plausible differential diagnoses or even the correct diagnosis [3,4].

For instance, there were several works from the field of image analysis or respectively computational pathology published by many different groups in recent years [5,6]. In this context, we have also recently published a paper on the classification of glomerular changes in histological images by means of convolutional neural networks (CNNs). Based on a defined small number of change patterns, we were able to diagnose entities defined by only a small number of patterns [7]. For instance, on the basis of images of a patients glomeruli, amyloidosis and diabetic glomerulopathy are easy to predict [1,7,8]. A diagnosis like lupus nephritis, which can show a plethora of patterns over time and space (within one biopsy), is in contrast not predicable solely based on one glomerular change pattern [1,7,8]. Demonstrating that only a part of kidney tissues (in our case glomeruli) is not enough to make a correct diagnosis is not surprising. It seems logical that at least the entire tissue needs to be taken into account; if not, disease models or pathophysiological contexts would have to be included in the diagnostic classification task.

An analysis tool for all kidney tissue compartments, e.g., by combination of a segmentation model to obtain the compartments of interest and subsequent classification, needs to be trained on larger and diverse data sets. Typically, such image data sets are very sparse or, respectively, not easy to create. The problem is not so much the preparation of a compilation of final diagnoses and images, but rather the laborious generation of correct annotations. As an example, in our recent publication, three experts spent several weeks classifying individual images in order to generate a sufficiently large data set [7]. For a segmentation task, where every part of the images needs to be labelled, the effort is significantly higher.

In contrast to this image data scarcity, there is plenty of high-quality text data in the field of nephropathology. For every kidney biopsy, there is a medical report that contains a short description of the histology. These texts are each written by a professionally trained but most likely not-always-available nephropathologist. Furthermore, as mentioned above, for many entities, there is high agreement between these experts. In summary, most image data is not very well annotated; however, the quality of most diagnosis text is presumably very high.

This leads to the idea of using the diagnosis text for analysis, in contrast to our recent work on image data [7]. In a sense, this text analysis is a surrogate for non-existent image data and image analysis tools. Analysing texts instead of images, of course, requires methods of natural language processing (NLP).

Like image analysis, NLP includes a wide range of methods for many different areas of application. In the medical field, the analysis and especially classification of surgical pathology report texts is a well-known application. For instance, there are cancer registries that rely on information extraction from pathology reports or on the classification of such reports. The manual information extraction from (bio-)medical free-text documents and especially pathology reports is very time consuming and requires the commitment of specialists. Automatic, pre-existing NLP-approaches provide a solution to overcome this obstacle. For the described cancer registry task, Schulz et al. combined several different classification techniques to extract a particularly large quantity of different information such as cancer type (by e.g., support vector machine (SVM) or tumor morphology (by e.g., convolutional neural network (CNN) with embeddings) from German texts [9]. Besides this mentioned example, there are already numerous other works for the classification of medical texts. Fabacher et al. trained an SVM as a binary text-classfier for French texts [10]. And Oleynik et al. trained an SVM to classify pathology reports according to the International Classification of Diseases for Oncology (ICD-O) code [11,12]. The aim in a recent work by Lopprich et al. [13] was to make a manual documentation process more efficient by using methods of NLP for multiclass classification of diagnostic reports to automatically document the diagnosis and status of disease of myeloma patients.

Against this background, the main aim of this work was to test if the textural description of the entire kidney tissue in (German) nephropathology reports can be used to make a diagnosis or respectively assign the report text to the correct diagnosis. For this purpose, each nephropathological report was divided into two parts, each of which belonged to each other: Part one is the microscopic description section; and part two is the corresponding diagnosis section. As for image data, manual annotation of the cases is sparse. Therefore, we use a two step approach: (i) First, the text-classification task was preceded by a topic modelling task in order to summarize the many given, each individually formulated diagnosis sections into less than 20 diagnosis clusters, where each cluster is a collection of thematically related documents, representing a certain diagnostic group. By doing so, we avoid manual labelling. (ii) Second, different text classification methods were used to predict the corresponding diagnostic group, obtained in step (i), on the basis of the given description section. This tests whether the text description (as a surrogate of the image analysis) contains all the information necessary to generate the correct diagnosis.

For the steps (i) and (ii), different text clustering- and text classification-methods were applied. Overall, we experimented with simple Bag-of-Words (BoW)-based methods (Sections 2.3.1 and 2.5.1) as well as with techniques based on distributed representations (Sections 2.3.2 and 2.5.2) to solve the given NLP problems.

## 2. Materials and Methods

### 2.1. Data Collection

Anonymized medical reports (n = 1185 from the years 2018–2021, memory size: 5 MB) were retrieved from the electronic archive of the Institute of Pathology, Medical Faculty Mannheim, Heidelberg University. Only the plain texts are used without information on patient age, gender, clinical course, etc. The data collection and all experiments were conducted in accordance with a vote of the ethics commission II of the Heidelberg University (vote 2020-847R). The total corpus consists of 152,650 words, with each report consisting of 136 words on average.

### 2.2. Overview

An overview of what has been done in the underlying work is provided by Figure 1.

We started with a corpus consisting of 1185 nephropathological reports. Each report was then divided into its diagnosis section and microscopic description section (Figure 1: data preparation). This was done based on German section tags or keywords usually placed at the beginning of a section, like "Klinische Angaben" (Engl. clinical information) for the clinical information section, "Mikroskopie" (Engl. microscopy) for the description section, and "Beurteilung" (Engl. conclusion) for the diagnosis section. The diagnosis section is later used for the text clustering task (i), and the description section is later used for the text classification task (ii).

Below is an example of a conclusion text with its associated microscopic description section:

Example of a microscopic description section (translated from German to English):
*Renal medulla and cortex with 18 glomeruli. These were inconspicuous by light microscopy, specifically without evidence of necrosis or extracapillary proliferation. Arcuate artery and interlobular artery with mild subendothelial fibrosis. Arterioles unremarkable.*
*Tubulointerstitium with only small areas of atrophic tubules and interstitial matrix proliferation. Percentage of chronically damaged tubulointerstitium: 5%.*

Example of corresponding diagnosis section (translated from German to English):
*Mild arteriosclerosis. Unremarkable chronic tubulointerstitial damage (5% of the cortex). Conventional microscopy moreover an unremarkable finding with no evidence of glomerular necrosis or extracapillary proliferation. The results of the further immunohistochemical examination will be reported afterwards.*

**UMLS!** (**UMLS!**) [14] was used for the translation (German to English) in order to use internationally standardized medical terms if possible.

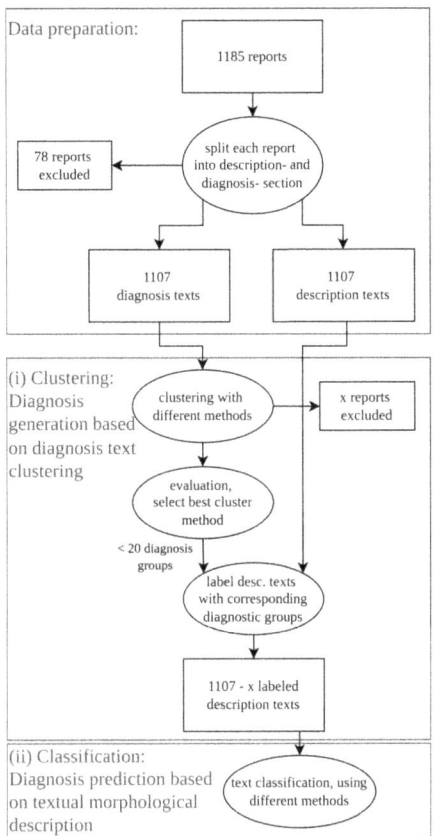

**Figure 1.** Flowchart, describing the general procedure of the project. After splitting each nephropathological report into its diagnosis and description section (data preparation), we first applied the clustering task (i) to the diagnosis texts in order to summarize them into less than 20 clusters. After labelling each cluster of diagnosis texts with a corresponding diagnostic group, we applied the classification task (ii) to the description texts in order to find out if it's possible to predict the correct diagnostic group of a given description text with NLP techniques.

Some reports (78) did not meet all requirements and could therefore not be divided into the two sections and were excluded. After that, 1107 reports are left, consisting of one diagnosis and one description text.

After data preparation, two main tasks were performed: In the *clustering task (i)*, diagnoses were assigned to the description texts. In the second step, the *classification task (ii)*, the aim was to predict the correct diagnosis for each (morphological) description text, using different text classification methods.

Here are more detailed descriptions of the two main tasks:

(i) *Clustering and topic modelling*

The diagnostic segments (example above) are clustered using different approaches (as described below in Section 2.3). The results of the various clustering methods are then compared to select the best method, which can be used for the topic modelling task of the corpus. The clusters of the winner are then analyzed in more detail to assign a suitable diagnostic group name for each cluster. After that, we obtained a labelled corpus, where each report is labelled with one diagnostic group that can be identified using the associated cluster index.

(ii) *Classification*

The classification part (Section 2.5) involves testing how accurately the labelled microscopic description texts can be classified using different text classification methods (as described below in Section 2.5). The aim is to find out whether the descriptive texts contain enough information to predict the diagnosis. For the classification task, different text classification methods were tested, to compare how they differ from each other in terms of performance.

All text processings, analyses, and evaluations performed in this thesis were conducted with German texts. In principle, the analyses shown here can be applied to reports written in any other language. More about this is mentioned in Section 4.3. Furthermore, only freely available software was used in this work. All python libraries used are referenced in the appropriate places (via hyperlink and or citation). The code for this work is available on GitLab (see section *Data Availability Statement*).

*2.3. Clustering and Topic Modeling*

We tested and compared seven different clustering approaches to cluster the diagnosis sections of the given reports. The resulting clusters were then used as labels for the classification task (ii). Here, a trade-off was necessary between too few clusters (or respectively labels or diagnostic groups) having a high intra-cluster heterogeneity and too many clusters with low intra-cluster heterogeneity but only a few cases. Too few clusters would generally be easier for a prediction model. With too many, on the other hand, the low number of cases per group would be problematic. To balance this, the amount of clusters was set to a minimum of 10 and a maximum of 20.

The used clustering methods can be divided into two main categories: BoW-based approaches (Section 2.3.1) and approaches with distributed representations (Section 2.3.2), where we make use of word embeddings and pre-trained transformer encoder models.

2.3.1. Clustering with Bag-of-Words Approaches

The clustering methods used in the underlying work, which are based on BoW representations [15], are listed here:

- *k-means*
  K-means clustering, using scikit-learn's [16] python implementation.
- *LDA*
  **LDA!** (**LDA!**) clustering, using the implementation shown in [17]
- *HDBSCAN*
  **HDBSCAN!** (**HDBSCAN!**), as shown in [18], using the supplied python library hdbscan. Before applying HDBSCAN, we first reduced the dimensionality of the document vectors as the HDBSCAN clustering algorithm handles high dimensionality poorly. We used Uniform Manifold Approximation and Projection (UMAP) [19] for the dimensionality reduction.
- *GSDPMM*
  **GSDPMM!** (**GSDPMM!**) model for text clustering [20].

For text vectorization, term frequency–inverse document frequency (tf–idf) has been used (using scikit learn's implementation). Moreover, the text has been pre-processed intensively to keep the vocabulary small, which results in smaller document vectors. We used stop word filtering, with general purpose German stop words, using the nltk.corpus [16] package (slightly customized by removing words like "no" or "none" from the predefined stop words list and adding words like "approx"), as well as lemmatization with the (German) Hanover Tagger [21]. We expanded this lemmatizer with custom word replacements, to adapt it to our specific nephropathological language. Moreover, we used a multi-word expression tokenizer (nltk.tokenize.mwe), to merge multi-word expressions, like "Lupus␣Nephritis" (Engl. lupus nephritis) or "tubulointerstitieller␣Schaden"

(Engl. tubulo-interstitial damage), into single tokens. We used an elbow-method-based approach to find the optimal number of clusters (*k*) for each cluster method. We removed numbers like dates, quantities, or report identification numbers to prevent reports from being clustered only by irrelevant numerical values. Furthermore, we used uncased texts, and we removed punctuation.

2.3.2. Clustering with Distributed Representations

Distributed representations of documents and words led to a considerable breakthrough in NLP due to their ability to capture the semantics of words or even word sequences. Word embeddings, or contextual word embeddings from transformer encoder models, can provide a certain language or textual context understanding, which is required for many NLP tasks and is also useful for clustering and topic-modelling problems [22–24].

- *top2vec*
  `top2vec` [24], uses distributed representations, obtained with `word2vec` [25] and `doc2vec` [26], to measure the semantic similarity of documents.

- *BERT-based clustering*
  Since the break through of the Bidirectional Encoder Representations from Transformers (BERT) model [27], a huge collection of pre-trained transformer encoder models have become available for various domains. Most of them are freely available on platforms such as huggingface.co [28]. We used different pre-trained transformer encoder models to embed the diagnostic texts in 512-dimensional document vectors (as shown in [29], using the supplied sentence_transformers library). After reducing the dimensionality of the document vectors (bidirectional, contextual embeddings) with UMAP [19], we clustered the documents using **HDBSCAN!** [18].
  The following BERT-based models were used in this work:

    - *German-BERT*
      There are some promising pre-trained transformer encoder models for the biomedical domain [30–32], but these models have only been trained with English texts. Since we are dealing with German bio-medical language, we used bert-base-german-cased (henceforth called *German-BERT*) which has been pre-trained with German wikipedia articles, the *OpenLegalData* dump and news articles. German-BERT comes with BERTs *WordPiece tokenizer* [27] (30,000 token vocabulary) which is able to divide unknown words into known subwords. Therefore it can be used for a wide range of domain-specific languages without getting many **OOV!** (**OOV!**) cases. Only one OOV case appeared during the tokenization of the entire corpus with German-BERT with **OOV!** token "q:".

    - *Patho-BERT*
      In order to adapt German-BERT to our specific nephropathological vocabulary, we pre-trained it with a masked language modelling) (MLM) objective, using the whole nephropathological corpus and 1607 additional nephropathological reports as training data. The resulting model was then saved as `ger-patho-bert` (henceforth called *Patho-BERT*) and used as another transformer model for further clustering attempts as well as for classification tasks in Section 2.5.

When working with distributed representations, little to no text pre-processing is usually required [33]. However, irrelevant numbers have been filtered out to prevent clustering based on numerical values only, as explained in Section 2.3.1.

2.4. Evaluation of Clustering Results

Each clustering method divides the included 1107 diagnosis texts into less than 20 clusters. In other words, each clustering method generates a set of clusters, henceforth called *cluster-set*. Now the question arises how we can evaluate the quality of such a cluster-set. For this we have taken into account the shape of the cluster-set as well as its texts contained in each cluster in order to find the most homogeneous and diagnostically meaningful clusters.

2.4.1. Clustering Metrics

There is still no perfect standard way to evaluate the quality of a cluster-set. In some publications, metrics like purity or **NMI!** (**NMI!**) are used to evaluate and compare clustering results [20,34–36]. However, a so-called *golden cluster-set* is required for such metrics, which is not available in our case. The present work generated clusters using different methods without ground truth data. This significantly limits the number of cluster metrics that can be used. The following methods were used to measure the overall clustering quality:

- *silhouette score*
  The mean silhouette coefficient of all samples, using scikit-learn's implementation. This metric is generally higher for convex clusters and is therefore not suitable for every cluster-set.

- *relative entropy*
  The entropy of the documents, relative to the clusters. It is a measure of how much the documents differ from all other documents in the same cluster (regarding term frequency). A small value means that the documents of a cluster are similar in terms of vocabulary (on average). We calculated the relative document entropy as follows:

$$\text{mean}_{j=1}^{m}(\text{mean}_{i=1}^{n}(\texttt{entropy}(\texttt{tf}(\texttt{doc}_{i,j}), \texttt{tf}(\texttt{cluster}_j))))$$

where `tf` is the term frequency (calculated with scikit learn's `CountVectorizer`) and $\texttt{entropy}(\texttt{tf}(\texttt{doc}_{i,j}), \texttt{tf}(\texttt{cluster}_j))$ is the entropy of the $i$-th document of cluster $j$, relative to all other documents of cluster $j$. The entropy was calculated with scipy's entropy function, which uses the Kullback–Leibler divergence.

- *classification accuracy (cls accuracy)*
  The idea is to test how well a simple **SVM!** (**SVM!**) can classify a given cluster-set, as it was also done in [35] to compare different topic models. The diagnosis sections of the reports are the input of the SVM and the labels to be guessed are the corresponding clusters.

2.4.2. Visual Presentation of Clustering Results

We visualized the data points of each cluster-set with **UMAP!** (**UMAP!**) [19] in order to get an impression of how well the clusters are separated from each other.

2.4.3. Keywords Extraction

In order to determine the topics of the individual clusters, the most relevant words (henceforth called *keywords*, or *topic words*) have to be extracted from the clusters. Two methodologically different approaches were used for this purpose. First, term frequency–inverse document frequency (tf–idf) as term frequency-based method was used. Here, keywords are identified based on their different frequencies in the clusters. Second, we used an "*SVM-based*" topic words extraction method, which is based on the model explainability of an **SVM!**. After training a linear SVM to predict the clusters of each diagnosis text, we applied a weight analysis to the SVM, in order to get the ten words which make the SVM most likely to predict a particular cluster (using the eli5 module). Only the documents predicted correctly by the SVM were included in the analysis.

2.4.4. Cluster Naming Based on Keywords

After keyword extraction, medical experts (JNB and CAW) then mapped proper diagnostic group names for each cluster (see Section 3.1.2).

## 2.5. Classification

In the previous section, we clustered the diagnosis sections of the reports into different cluster-sets with different clustering methods (bag of word-based and embedding-based). The hypothesis is that each cluster represents a diagnostic group (e.g., Lupus nephritis), which should hypothetically result from the associated microscopic description section of the same report.

To test this hypothesis, we tested how well these microscopic descriptions can be classified to the corresponding diagnostic group (represented by the clusters of a given cluster-set), with machine learning techniques. Therefore, we trained and tested different text classifiers which are typically used in **NLP!** (**NLP!**). These again include simple **BoW!** (**BoW!**)-based methods (Section 2.5.1) as well as more advanced techniques, based on embeddings and transformer encoder models (Section 2.5.2).

### 2.5.1. Classification with Bag-of-Words Approaches

First, the description texts are pre-processed and tokenized with the same techniques, as for the **BoW!**-based clustering in Section 2.3.1. The tf–idf-vectorized description-texts are then passed to one of four different classifiers for the final prediction:

- *SGD-classifier*
  **SVM!** (**SVM!**) with **SGD!** (**SGD!**) learning.
- *MLP-lassifier*
  **MLP!** (**MLP!**) classifier with Adam optimization.
- *Logistic Regression*
  Logistic regression (aka logit, MaxEnt) classifier with regularization and multinomial loss fit.
- *Multinomial NB*
  Multinomial **NB!** (**NB!**) classifier.

All **BoW!**-based classifiers are implemented with scikit-learn [16].

### 2.5.2. Classification with Distributed Representations

In addition to **BoW!**-based classification, we also made use of classification methods, which are based on distributed representations. Bidirectional recurrent neural networks and convolutional neural networks with word embeddings, as well as BERT-based transformer encoder models were tested:

- *RNN + embeddings:*
  **RNN!** (**RNN!**), consisting of a bidirectional **LSTM!** (**LSTM!**) layer, trained together with word2vec word embeddings as input.
- *CNN + embeddings:*
  **CNN!** (**CNN!**), trained together with word2vec word embeddings as input, as shown in [37]. The 1D convolution layer has been trained with 32 kernels with a size of 3, followed by a max pooling layer and two fully connected layers to get one final prediction value for each class. We used the **ReLU!** (**ReLU!**) activation function for the convolution layer, as well as for the first dense layer. For the last dense layer, we used a *softmax* activation function.
- *German-BERT:*
  The transformer model bert-base-german-cased, fine-tuned with our text classification problem.
- *Patho-BERT:*
  Our pre-trained Patho-BERT transformer, as introduced in Section 2.3.2.

Both, the **RNN!**- and the **CNN!**-approaches are implemented with tensorflow [38]. We used the transformers package from huggingface [28] for the implementation of all transformer-based methods and trained the models with the included pytorch [39] Trainer API, which uses an adam optimizer with weight decay regularization as introduced in [40].

The texts were pre-processed using the same techniques, as mentioned in Section 2.3.2.

### 2.6. Evaluation of Classification Results

To evaluate and compare different classifiers with one another, we measured various metrics such as accuracy, precision, recall, F1-score (the harmonic mean of precision and recall), and the cohen's kappa coefficient [41]. Each metric value was determined using ten-fold cross-validation. In order to examine the classification ability of a classifier in more detail, confusion matrices were plotted and analyzed.

## 3. Results

### 3.1. Topic Moelling Based on Text Clustering on the Diagnosis Section of Nephropathological Reports (Ad Task I)

Before documents can be classified, the number of possible classes should be reduced. To accomplish this, the text-classification task was preceded by a topic modelling task (task i). This was done by testing different text-clustering approaches to find the one resulting in the most homogeneous and diagnostically meaningful clusters.

#### 3.1.1. What Are the Differences of the Tested Clustering Methods?

In the present work, **BoW!**-based approaches and embedding-based approaches were used to cluster the given diagnosis texts into several diagnostic groups. As a metric for the clustering quality, we used the **s-score!** (s-score!), relative entropy, and the classification accuracy. The silhouette-score assumes convex cluster shapes and is therefore not well-suited for clusters of other shapes. To be independent of the cluster shape, the **SVM!**-classification-based **cls accuracy!** (cls accuracy!) (as described in Section 2.4 above) is used as additional clustering metric. Table 1 shows the measured metric values for each clustering approach and Figure 2 shows the UMAP-representations of the respective cluster-sets.

**Table 1.** Metrics of different cluster-sets.

| Cluster Method | s-Score | cls Accuracy | rel Entropy | Clusters | Corpus Size |
|---|---|---|---|---|---|
| HDBSCAN | 0.587 | 0.951 | 0.588 | 16 | 906 |
| German-BERT | 0.576 | 0.856 | 0.618 | 13 | 759 |
| top2vec | 0.545 | 0.372 | 0.780 | 18 | 1026 |
| Patho-BERT | 0.536 | 0.848 | 0.531 | 17 | 757 |
| LDA | 0.517 | 0.581 | 0.611 | 7 | 1107 |
| k-means | 0.038 | 0.905 | 0.612 | 10 | 1107 |
| GSDPMM | 0.033 | 0.805 | 0.675 | 14 | 1107 |

We used the silhouette score (s-score), relative entropy (rel entropy) and the **SVM!** (SVM!)-based classification performance (cls accuracy) to evaluate and compare different cluster-sets, generated with different cluster methods (far left column). The entry clusters indicate how many clusters were generated by which method. Corpus size indicates how many reports remained after clustering, since several reports were identified as outliers and sorted out. **HDBSCAN!** (HDBSCAN!) has the best silhouette score as well as the best cls accuracy score. Although top2vec has an acceptable silhouette score, it is notable for its very poor predictability (cls accuracy: 0.372). Although k-means and **GSDPMM!** (GSDPMM!) have low silhouette scores, they are well predictable.

Compared by visual inspection to all other tested clustering methods, the clusters of k-means (Figure 2g) and **GSDPMM!** (Figure 2h) seem to be much more poorly separated, which is also reflected in their low silhouette scores in Table 1. Interestingly, **HDBSCAN!**, a **BoW!**-approach, achieved the highest silhouette-score, the highest cls accuracy and the second best entropy value. Moreover, it turned out that a reasonably shaped cluster-set is not necessarily easier to predict with a support vector machine: Although top2vec has achieved a good silhouette-score (s-score: 0.545) and shows well separated clusters in its **UMAP!**-representation (Figure 2d), an **SVM!** can't predict the clusters very well (cls accuracy: 0.372). Top2vec has with 0.780 the highest relative entropy value, which hints to a low intra-cluster heterogeneity. This heterogeneity could be one reason why top2vec-clusters are so difficult to predict. On the other hand, k-means and GSDPMM achieved the lowest silhouette-scores, but are quite well predictable with a cls-accuracy of 0.905 (k-means) and respectively of 0.805 (GSDPMM). Both methods also have lower entropy values with 0.612 and respectively 0.675 than top2vec.

For LDA, k-means and GSDPMM, no outlier detection has been implemented. Contrary, outliers can be detected for the other clustering techniques and subsequently be removed from the further analysis. Especially in the case of Patho-BERT and German-BERT, several documents were identified as outliers, which reduced the amount of left documents-the *corpus size*-noticeably from 1107 documents to less than 760.

A fairly imbalanced cluster distribution can be found in almost every cluster-set. However, such uneven distributions of cases is nothing unusual in this domain, as some diseases occur much less frequently than others.

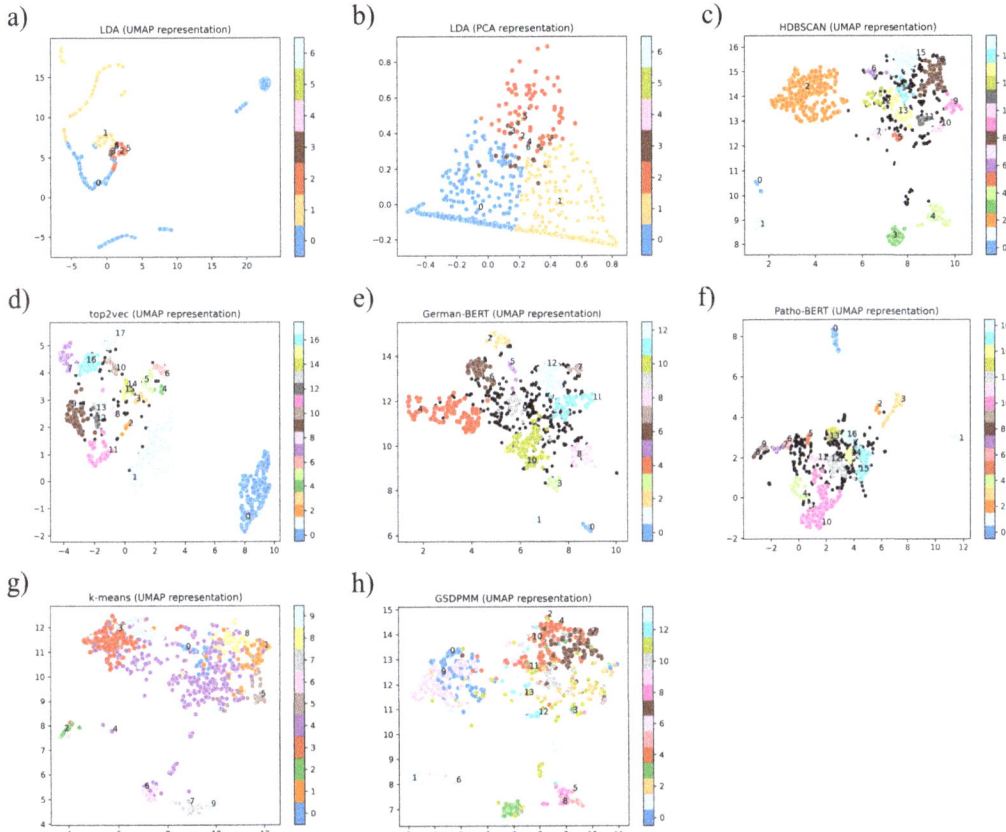

**Figure 2.** UMAP! (UMAP!) and PCA! (PCA!) of different cluster-sets. UMAP representations of the cluster-sets generated with (**a**) **LDA!** (**LDA!**), (**c**) **HDBSCAN!** (**HDBSCAN!**), (**d**) top2vec, (**e**) German-BERT, (**f**) Patho-BERT, (**g**) k-means and (**h**) **GSDPMM!** (**GSDPMM!**). The **LDA!** cluster-set is also shown as **PCA!** (**PCA!**) in (**b**). Each data point represents a diagnosis section of a report. The data points are coloured according to the respective clusters. Black points represent outliers that were not assigned to any cluster. Above all, the clusters of top2vec and **HDBSCAN!** appear particularly tidy and separated. The clusters of k-means and **GSDPMM!** appear less well separated, which is probably also due to the fact that no data points are sorted out here.

### 3.1.2. Can the Clusters Be Named on Basis of Keywords?

All cluster metrics used so far have the disadvantage that one cannot derive diagnostically comprehensible clusters from them. These methods only give a metric for the intra-cluster homogeneity.

To give the produced clusters meaningful names, we first used different keyword extraction methods (described in Section 2.4.3 above). The extracted topic words of the HDBSCAN cluster-set (translated from German to English) can be found in Tables 2 and 3. The original (German) topic word tables can be found in Appendix A and the extracted topic words of all other cluster-sets can be found at https://doi.org/10.11588/data/KS5W0H (accessed date 14 July 2022). As explained in Section 2.4, the ten (by each keyword extraction approach identified) most relevant words per cluster are shown in these topic word tables.

Second, two medical experts (JNB as medical student and CAW as board-examined pathologist) analyzed these tables to find out how well the topic words of each cluster fit together and whether the topic words of a cluster fit to a certain diagnostic or topic group (henceforth called *cluster name*).

The medical experts annotated the topic word tables as follows: If a suitable name was found for a cluster, the cluster name can be found next to the corresponding cluster index (see Table 2, left column). A particularly large number of topic words strongly refer to cluster names highlighted in green (*strong cluster names*). In the case of cluster names marked in orange, only a few topic words indicated the specified cluster name (*weak cluster name*). The same applies to the colour-coded topic words: topic words that strongly indicate a cluster name are highlighted in green (*strong topic words*). Orange highlighted topic words only weakly indicate a cluster name (*weak topic words*).

Especially in the case of **HDBSCAN!**, for many clusters the extracted keywords fit thematically well together. In this case, diagnostically meaningful and comprehensible cluster names based on the keywords could be assigned to 14 out of 16 detected clusters (as shown in Tables 2 and 3). For instance, keywords like "lupus nephritis" or "chronicity index" are characteristic for documents in the cluster "systemic lupus erythematosus". Or for "IgA-nephritis" words like "oxford" or "IgA" are typical.

### 3.1.3. Do the Authors of the Nephropathological Reports Have an Impact on the Clustering?

With only three authors (CAW, SP and ZVP) writing in different combinations the included reports, we wondered if the clustering is influenced by the different authors. It is conceivable, for example, that one of the authors is an expert in a particular diagnosis and at the same time has a characteristic wording. In this case, the clustering methods would possibly be influenced by the wording.

To look for the authors, Figure A1 (see Appendix B) shows the same **UMAP!** plots as Figure 2, but coloured according to the authors who wrote the respective reports. Some of the reports were written by multiple authors, these are represented by black points. When examining these figures, especially **HDBSCAN!**, k-means and **GSDPMM!** tend to form a group for author 1 (orange dots) and author 2 (green dots) that is separate from author 0 (blue dots). This group is always located in the upper left area. Based on this, the question arises whether these separations are due to the different writing styles of some authors or whether the authors worked on different subject areas. In the manual cluster word analysis, some clusters could be identified, which were probably mainly grouped according to the language style of author 1, e.g., cluster 2 of the HDBSCAN cluster-set. The topic words of this cluster refer only weakly to the topic *tubulo-interstitial nephritis* (see Tables 2 and 3).

**Table 2.** Annotated topic words (translated from German to English), extracted from the **HDBSCAN!** (**HDBSCAN!**) cluster-set, using the tf–idf based extraction method. A particularly large number of topic words strongly refer to cluster names (left column) highlighted in green (strong cluster names). In the case of cluster names marked in orange, only a few topic words indicated the specified cluster name (weak cluster name). The same applies to the colour-coded topic words: topic words that strongly indicate a cluster name are highlighted in green (strong topic words). Orange highlighted topic words only weakly indicate a cluster name (weak topic words).

| Cluster Index-Cluster Name | Keywords According to tf–idf |
|---|---|
| 0-systemic lupus erythematosus | scale, chronicity_index, class, activity_index, nih, lupus_nephritis, iv, who, glomerular, iii |
| 1-rapid progressive glomerulonephritis | quantity, glomeruli, scarred, necrosis, fresh, proliferating_glomerulonephritis, approx, segmental_necrotizing, extracapillary, concerning |
| 2-tubulo-interstitial nephritis | approx, concerning, cortex, minor, immunostaining, damage, included, moderate, chronic, supplementary |
| 3-pauci immune glomerulonephritis | of_this, glomeruli, total_amount, intact, extracapillary, scarred, global, necrosis, proliferating_glomerulonephritis, tubulointerstitial_damage |
| 4-IgA nephritis | oxford, m1, e0, s1, t0, c0, classification, iga, glomerulonephritis, cell_count |
| 5-FSGN | fsg, primary, distinction, focal, secondary, collapsing, chronic, glomerulosclerosis, take_place, hint |
| 6-thrombotic microangiopathy | microangiopathy, thrombotic, active, reparation, preglomerular, glomerular, located, chronic, tubulointerstitial_damage, hypertension |
| 7-multiple myeloma | nephropathy, kappa, cast, amyloidosis, myeloma_kidney, lcdd, a_notice, chronic, no, tubulointerstitial_damage |
| 8-kidney transplant | rejection, routinely, chronic, success, immunohistochemical, examination, toxicity, hint, nephrosclerosis, mild |
| 9-unremarkable finding | renal_parenchyma, unremarkable, left_over, mainly, normal, special, acute, tubular_damage, histological, glomerulonephritis |
| 10 | cut_level, hardly, noteworthy, chronic, tubulointerstitial_damage, deep, so_far, processing, nephrosclerosis, mild |
| 11 | microscopy, conventional, requirement, result, renal_parenchyma, foresee, chronic, nephrosclerosis, mild, examination |
| 12 - membranous glomerulonephritis | pla2r, membranous, honorable, glomerulonephritis, stage, churg, chronic, tubulointerstitial_damage, positive, nephrosclerosis |
| 13-diabetic glomerulosclerosis | diabetic_glomerulosclerosis, chronic, tubulointerstitial_damage, nodular, light_microscopic, picture, nephrosclerosis, difficult, examination, consist |
| 14-glomerulosclerosis | glomerulosclerosis, global, tubulointerstitial_damage, chronic, nephrosclerosis, focal_segmental, focal, moderate, take_place, secondary |
| 15-tubulo-interstitial nephritis | a_mild, tubular_damage, acute, chronic, nephrosclerosis, tubulointerstitial_damage, mild, a_moderate, moderate, potentially_reversible |

**Table 3.** Annotated topic words (translated from German to English), extracted from the **HDBSCAN!** (HDBSCAN!) cluster-set, using the **SVM!** (SVM!) based extraction method. A particularly large number of topic words strongly refer to cluster names (left column) highlighted in green (strong cluster names). In the case of cluster names marked in orange, only a few topic words indicated the specified cluster name (weak cluster name). The same applies to the colour-coded topic words: topic words that strongly indicate a cluster name are highlighted in green (strong topic words). Orange highlighted topic words only weakly indicate a cluster name (weak topic words).

| Cluster Index-Cluster Name | Keywords According to SVM |
|---|---|
| 0-systemic lupus erythematosus | scale, chronicity_index, activity_index, class, -nih, iv, lupus_nephritis, component, iii, who |
| 1-rapid progressive glomerulonephritis | quantity, sclerosing, glomeruli, scarred, glomerulus, fresh, of_which1, proliferating_glomerulonephritis, necrosis, sclerosed |
| 2-tubulo-interstitial nephritis | tubular_epithelial_damage, moderate, minor, damage, none, completion, fibrosis, finally, known, tubulointerstitial |
| 3-pauci immune glomerulonephritis | of_this, total_amount, intact, pauci_immune_glomerulonephritis, necrotizing, glomeruli, scarred, *, remaining, extracapillary |
| 4-IgA nephritis | oxford_classification, e0, s1, m1, t0, c0, iga_glomerulonephritis, s0, applicable, e1 |
| 5-FSGN | fsg, primary, distinction, look_together, secondary, segmental_glomerulosclerosis, collapsing, at_most, continuing, patient |
| 6-thrombotic microangiopathy | microangiopathy, thrombotic, reparation, preglomerular, glomerular, located, active, glomerular_thrombotic, hypertension, overwhelmingly |
| 7-multiple myeloma | cast_nephropathy, myeloma_kidney, lcdd, lambda, kappa, amyloidosis, followed_by, light_chains, al-amyloidosis, light_chain_nephropathy |
| 8-kidney transplant | rejection, routinely, success, examination, calcineurin_inhibitor_toxicity, ascending, humorous, bacterial, urinary_tract_infection, follow-up_report |
| 9-unremarkable finding | renal_parenchyma, unremarkable, normal, largely, left_over, for_now, furthermore, special, iga-, pathological |
| 10 | hardly, cut_level, noteworthy, deep, so_far, processing, using, congo_red_coloring, to_exclusion, cellularor |
| 11 | microscopy, conventional, requirement, foresee, mild, membranous, early, cell_proliferation, result, g |
| 12 - membranous glomerulonephritis | membranous, proteinuria, as_a_result, glomerulonephritis, pla2r, stage, churg, honorable, electron_microscopy, pla2r_positive |
| 13-diabetic glomerulosclerosis | diabetic_glomerulosclerosis, consist, immune_complex_glomerulonephritis, nodular, picture, light_microscopic, partly, arteriolohyalinosis, diabetic_glomerulosclerosis, additionally |
| 14-glomerulosclerosis | global, focal_segmental, segmental_glomerulosclerosis, glomerulosclerosis, focal_global, diffusesegmental, incl, focal, tubulointerstitial_damage, scarring |
| 15-tubulo-interstitial nephritis | tubular_damage, a_mild, mild, tubulointerstitial_damage, change, a_moderate, mild, constantly, acute, malignancy |

### 3.1.4. Which Clustering Method Is the Best?

Since the **HDBSCAN!**-clustered data set has a good clustering accuracy according to the applied metrics (compare Section 2.4), since it has less outliers than German-BERT or Patho-BERT, and, since it achieved decent results in the manual topic word analysis (compare Section 2.4.3), it has been rated as the best clustering approach. Therefore, it, or rather its cluster-set, has been used as the target for the classification task described in the next section.

*3.2. Assignment of Nephropathological Description Sections to Specific Diagnostic Groups (Ad Task Ii)*

The second task is mapping the histomorphological descriptions to the diagnosis sections or, more specifically, to the previously defined topics (task ii). Based on Section 3.1.1, **HDBSCAN!** was selected as the preferred clustering method on which basis different classifications methods were tested.

3.2.1. Which Methods Can Be Used to Map Descriptive Sections to the Correct Diagnostic Groups?

In summary, eight different text classification methods were used. Four of the classification methods (here abbreviated called SGD-classifier, **MLP!**-classifier, logistic regression and multinomial **NB!**) are bag-of-words approaches (compare Section 2.5.1). The other four classification methods (here abbreviated as RNN + embeddings, CNN + embeddings, German-BERT and Patho-BERT) are in contrast based on distributed representations (compare Section 2.3.2).

In Table 4 the performance of the different approaches for mapping the description sections to the HDBSCAN clustered data set is shown. The performance is quantified by calculating the F1-score and the Cohen's kappa coefficient with ten-fold cross-validation, as mentioned in Section 2.6.

**Table 4.** Performance of different classification models, trained with the HDBSCAN cluster-set.

| Classifier | F1-Score | Cohen's Kappa Coefficient |
|---|---|---|
| Patho-BERT | 0.667 | 0.631 |
| SGD-classifier | 0.644 | 0.598 |
| MLP-classifier | 0.639 | 0.599 |
| German-BERT | 0.610 | 0.572 |
| Logistic Regression | 0.589 | 0.567 |
| CNN + embeddings | 0.523 | 0.450 |
| RNN + embeddings | 0.464 | 0.394 |
| Multinomial NB | 0.442 | 0.370 |

F1-score and Cohen's kappa coefficient of the tested classification methods, which were trained to predict the **HDBSCAN!** clustered data set. Each score is determined with ten-fold cross-validation. The transformer based model Patho-BERT and the **SVM!** (**SVM!**)-based SGD-classifier performed best.

Interestingly, according to the different metrics used, there is no clear winner when comparing embedding-based approaches to **BoW!**-based approaches. There are poorly-performing and better-performing models on both sides. Patho-BERT performed higher (best F1-score and Cohen's kappa coefficient) compared to the other classifiers. So the time-consuming pre-training of a BERT model with **MLM!** (**MLM!**) seems to be worthwhile in this case. But surprisingly, the SGD-classifier, a BoW-based classifier, achieved a significantly better F1-score than German-BERT. In return, German-BERT achieved a better Cohen's kappa coefficient.

3.2.2. Can Certain Diagnoses Be Better Predicted than Others? And If So, What Are the Reasons?

Besides the overall classification performance, as shown above, the performance with view to the single classes was of interest. To visualize this, in Figure 3 the confusion matrices of the four best classification methods are shown. In addition, the F1-scores per cluster can be read in Table 5, which were achieved using Patho-BERT as classifier.

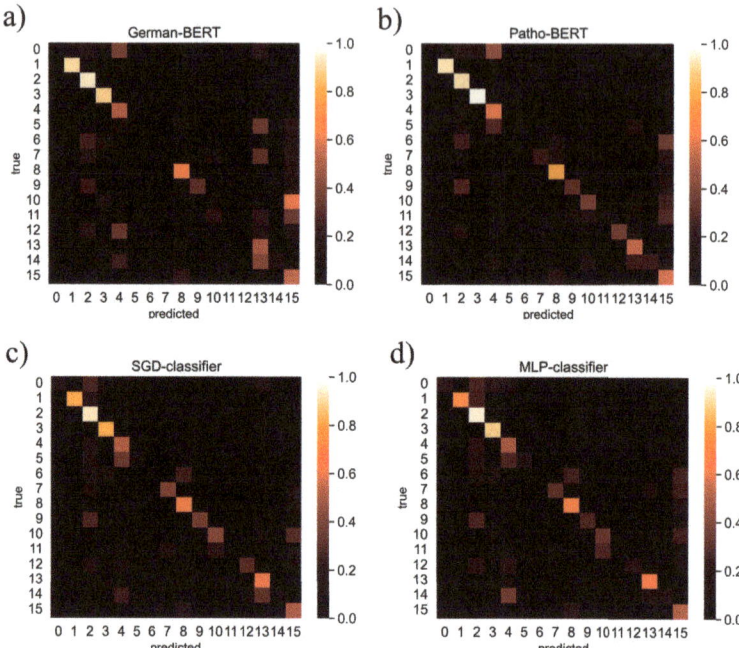

**Figure 3.** Confusion matrices of the classification models. (**a**) German-BERT, (**b**) Patho-BERT, (**c**) the **SVM!** (**SVM!**)-based SGD-classifier, and (**d**) the **MLP!** (**MLP!**)-classifier. The brightness of a cell indicates how many times the class on the x-axis was predicted by the classifier. The true class is indicated by the index of the y-axis. Interestingly, there are classes that could be recognized well by all classifiers, including the weaker ones, e.g., class 1 (*rapid progressive glomerulonephritis*), 2 (*tubulo-interstitial nephritis*) and 3 (*pauci immune glomerulonephritis*). Although the transformer-based classifiers (**a**,**b**) generally performed better, the **BoW!**-based methods were able to detect class 0 (*systemic lupus erythematosus*) or 5 (*fsgn*) better (**c**,**d**).

First, it can be observed that the **HDBSCAN!** cluster-set contains some clusters that can be recognized well by all classifiers, even the weaker ones. Especially the clusters 1 (*systemic lupus erythematosus*), 2 (*tubulo-interstitial nephritis*), and 3 (*pauci immune glomerulonephritis*) could be recognized well by all classifiers, according to the confusion matrices (Figure 3). The Patho-BERT model was able to achieve F1-scores of over 0.8 for these three diagnostic groups, with group 3 (*pauci immune glomerulonephritis*) performing best with an F1-score of 0.892 (see Table 5). The clusters 4 (*iga nephritis*), 8 (*kidney transplant*), 13 (*diabetic glomerulosclerosis*) and 15 (*tubulo-interstitial nephritis*) could be recognized moderately good, with F1-scores of over 0.5. Interestingly, although Patho-BERT has the best overall F1-score (Table 1), the **BoW!**-based methods were able to detect class 0 (*systemic lupus erythematosus*) and 5 (*FSGN*) better, according to the confusion matrices (Figure 3). Table 5 also lists the *support* of each cluster. The support indicates how many documents (microscopic description texts) were available for a cluster (or a diagnostic group). Cluster 2 in particular is significantly more supported than all other clusters, while there are some particularly small clusters consisting of less than 20 documents. Such imbalanced datasets can lead classification algorithms to ignore the minority class entirely, as seems to be the case for clusters 0, 5, and 6 in Table 5. Table 5 shows clearly that the lower the support, the more difficult it is to recognize the cluster. Presumably, these diagnostic groups could have been recognized better if more training data had been available or if each cluster had been large enough, respectively.

Table 5. Classification performance of the Patho-BERT-classifier, predicting the HDBSCAN cluster-set.

| Cluster/Diagnostic Group | F1-Score | Support |
| --- | --- | --- |
| 3  | 0.892 | 72  |
| 2  | 0.880 | 324 |
| 1  | 0.847 | 51  |
| 8  | 0.728 | 76  |
| 4  | 0.601 | 71  |
| 15 | 0.545 | 78  |
| 13 | 0.529 | 56  |
| 12 | 0.417 | 26  |
| 10 | 0.367 | 23  |
| 9  | 0.364 | 31  |
| 7  | 0.333 | 19  |
| 14 | 0.312 | 19  |
| 11 | 0.160 | 17  |
| 0  | 0.000 | 18  |
| 5  | 0.000 | 14  |
| 6  | 0.000 | 11  |

Cluster-Predictability of the **HDBSCAN!** cluster-set, using Patho-BERT as classifier. The cluster predictability was determined with the F1-score and the table is sorted by descending F1-scores. Each F1-score is the result of a 10 fold cross validation (average of 10 test measurements). Cluster 3 has the highest F1-score. Cluster 2 has a particularly strong support, which means this cluster is particularly large (324 documents) and was therefore often seen during training. The support specifies how many documents a cluster consists of. It can be observed that especially the smaller clusters could be recognized with difficulty or not at all.

3.2.3. Which Classification Approach Is the Best?

Overall, the best classification results were obtained using our custom BERT model (Patho-BERT) as well as using a simple **SVM!** (SGD-classifier). However, the description sections of the **HDBSCAN!**-clustered reports could not be classified passably: An F1-score of more than 0.7 could not be achieved, even with our custom pre-trained **BERT!** (**BERT!**) model (Patho-BERT). In many other medical text classification problems, significantly higher F1-scores could be achieved [9,11,13]. Nevertheless, the problem presented here can hardly be compared with such classification problems, due to the fact that no human-labelled data was available. Instead, we clustered the diagnosis sections to label the data. During development it could be observed that the classification performance was strongly related to the quality of the cluster-set. Moreover, not much training data was available, which resulted in several small clusters consisting of only 10 to 20 documents. In particular, predicting small clusters was hard to accomplish in most cases. Nevertheless, certain clusters are well distinguishable, as mentioned earlier.

4. Discussion

Digital medical reports can be found in many different medical sub-disciplines. They usually represent a condensate of one or a combination of the many different, complex, available medical data types such as radiological images, molecular profiles, clinical examination findings, etc. On the one hand, it is of great research interest to obtain usable information for further analyses from medical reports, which are often written in a non-standardized way. On the other hand, the relationship between the underlying data (e.g., histological images) and the text is also of great interest. Against this background, we examined diagnostic texts from the field of nephropathology by means of natural language processing (**NLP!**). In this sub-field of pathology, among others, we were able to show in a recent publication that images of glomeruli can be mapped by means of machine learning to some diagnoses (such as amyloidosis), whereas for other diagnoses (such as lupus nephritis) prediction based on glomerular changes alone does not work well. To test without extensive image processing efforts, if the morphological information in the entire kidney tissue is enough for diagnosis prediction, we examined nephropathological reports. By doing so, we were able to show the following points: (i) First, we could show that long-known **NLP!**-tools like bag-of-word-based techniques and newer embedding techniques likes BERT can be applied to different parts of histological reports written in German (see Section 4.1 below). (ii) Second, we could demonstrate that different text parts like the description or the diagnosis section can be clustered without supervision to diagnostic groups (see Section 3.1.1 above and Section 4.1 below). In contrast to the unsupervised clustering of images, this is much easier and numerous methods are known here from various other fields (see Section 4.1 below). (iii) Third, we could show that these diagnostic groups can be predicted by machine learning models based on the description section (see Section 3.2 above and Section 4.1 below).

*4.1. Natural Language Processing and Image Processing Techniques in Nephrology and Nephropathology*

In this work, we applied a wide range of different **NLP!**-techniques to the histological reports from the field of nephropathology. These medical reports are composed of several sections, with the descriptive and diagnostic sections being particularly relevant for us. We can show that there is a correlation between the morphological description and the final diagnosis by predicting the diagnosis on basis of the description with our custom Patho-BERT transformer encoder model or even with less complex support vector machines (Section 3.2). After a previous work on glomerular change patterns in histological images [7], we used the morphological description by nephropathological experts as surrogate for image analysis. This would have the advantage of eliminating the need to establish a reliable image analysis. For such image analysis, the amount of large, properly annotated datasets is a common bottleneck that we tried to avoid by using textual data [42–44].

Of course, textual data must also be prepared or annotated for analysis. We have reduced this workload here in part by using unsupervised clustering methods Section 3.1.1. These clusters or diagnostic groups can then be predicted by a classifier like a support vector machine or with a domain specific pre-trained **BERT!**-based model. Furthermore, by examining the keywords relevant for the respective clusters, one can establish a relationship to diagnostic groups and give the clusters umbrella names such as those in standard nephropathology textbooks [1,8]. The establishment of a relationship between the results of an unsupervised approach and the real-world labels is also a common issue in image analysis. There, the main solution is also to have names assigned to the labels by human experts. For other, also machine-learning-based approaches, such as extending models with a re-mapping block, we were recently unable to show any benefit for lung carcinoma [45].

Our previous focus on image analysis fits quite well into the overall context. In nephropathology, machine learning seems to be mainly used in the form of image analysis [3,4,46,47], but rarely in the form of **NLP!**, although **NLP!** is recognized as a topic of interest [48,49]. This is indeed surprising, since nephropathology seems to be predestined for text analysis due to various standardization efforts. There are, for instance, well written and extensive recommendations on how to write and structure a report [50–53]; albeit somehow controversial and not followed by everyone. There are also efforts on creating common ontologies, taxonomies, or at least vocabularies for nephropathology [53,54]. The clustering of diagnosis texts or the reduction of different diagnoses to diagnostic groups, which we show here (Figure 2), can be seen in the context of stratification procedures. Since we have not investigated the relationships between clusters here (no ontological approach), nor have we investigated hierarchical relationships (no taxomic approach), our work can be seen as the automatic generation of a vocabulary. In the works dealing with stratification or unification approaches, common vocabularies are described as the basis for more complex tasks like creating a taxonomy or ontology [53,54].

*4.2. How Do Our Results Fit into the Big Picture?*

Even though the method of the present work differs significantly from our previous work, and even though, in contrast to our previous work, the entire kidney tissue or its descriptor was included in the study, the results fit together surprisingly well [7]. Again, certain diagnoses or groups of diagnoses can be predicted very well. For example, amyloid-deposition-associated diseases are again among the best predicted diagnoses. This is not very surprising, since in images it is characterized by typical, amorphous deposits, and in texts it is characterized by the word "amyloid". In the same way, the IgA nephropathies, for example, are characterized by the description of the typical finding of granular IgA deposits in the mesangium. Since in the previous work only glomeruli without additional staining were analyzed, text analysis is significantly better for diagnoses that are defined by certain, specific findings.

Nevertheless, in several cases the morphological description is apparently not sufficient to make accurate predictions. The combination of image analysis and text analysis as well as the additional integration of patient data or other clinical features could help to identify more correlations and improve the prediction accuracy. Moreover, such diagnosis prediction models could also be used to select and revise potentially incorrect diagnoses.

*4.3. Other Languages*

All text analyses shown in this work have been applied to German reports only. In principle, all methods shown can be applied to documents written in other languages without much additional effort. For the shown **BoW!**-based analyses, some (keyword-based) text pre-processing steps would have to be adapted to the used language. For example, a different stop word list, as well as a different lemmatizer would have to be used. Especially for all transformer encoder based approaches (BERT-classification and BERT-clustering), other pre-trained transformer models would have to be used. Depending on the language, more or less suitable models are freely available. For example, there are many large transformer models for the English medical domain [30–32].

*4.4. Technical Weaknesses and Possible Improvements*

One drawback of this work is that the cluster naming (Section 3.1.2) could almost not be evaluated and refined. For this, not enough experts were available. Moreover, only experts trained by the same instructors were available. Therefore, no detailed inter-observer variability studies could be performed to measure the reliability of the cluster topics. For this we would need to recruit more experts from different institutions for future projects.

Moreover, the examined dataset was unfortunately too small to find enough text data for each diagnosis group. This resulted in some particularly small clusters that could hardly or not at all be predicted by any of the tested classification approaches. Resampling-based solutions for imbalanced data (e.g., **SMOTE!** (**SMOTE!**) [55]) could not be successfully implemented in this work because of the text complexity and the different text vectorization methods used. Another possibility to improve the classification results could be the use of optimization methods for imbalanced classification problems, such as using the dice loss as done in [56]. However, it is also questionable whether this would be effective for the smallest clusters.

In this work we used German-BERT's word-piece tokenizer for our BERT-based models, since it fits well for German languages and is able to divide unknown medical terms into several known subwords, resulting in very less **OOV!** cases. Although this worked out in principle, using a custom tokenizer, which is specialized to the German nephropathological vocabulary might produce even better classification and or clustering results.

## 5. Conclusions

Overall, it can be said that the morphological description texts, as surrogate for image analysis, enable the correct diagnosis to be achieved for some entities. For other entities, this associative approach does not work adequately. As in our previous image analysis-based study on glomerular change patterns [7], it can be said here that some diagnoses are associated with one pattern, and for others, there is a complex pattern combination which makes the prediction difficult without patho-physiological knowledge. This raises the consideration of including disease models in the analysis to improve accuracy. However, methods such as semantic graphs should perhaps be tested beforehand, as they are much easier to implement.

Besides the only associative approach here, one major issue of this work was the inadequate amount of labelled training data, which is why we performed a time-consuming topic-modelling task first. In general, with more, manually-labelled, balanced data, better text classification results could have been possible. In addition, the classification performance depends on the properties of the given data and on the text pre-processing methods used. These influences were not examined in detail.

The combination of text-based and image-based analysis could be worthwhile in order to be able to take into account additional features regarding the whole tissue in addition to the glomerular changes, which is mainly extracted in the image analysis.

The use of **VL-PTMs!** *(VL-PTMs!)* [57], e.g., *ViLBERT* [58] or *Unicoder-VL* [59], could be a good opportunity to combine image analysis with text analysis in nephropathology. Therefore, sufficient image-text data pairs would be needed. The benefit would be that time-consuming image-labelling would not be necessary.

**Author Contributions:** Conceptualization, methodology, programming and writing M.L. and C.-A.W.; methodology, conceptualization, methodology and writing P.D. and J.H.; conceptualization, data curation, nephropathological expertise and writing S.P. and Z.P.; conceptualization, data curation, medical expertise and writing J.N.B. and J.-H.H.S. All authors have read and agreed to the published version of the manuscript.

**Funding:** This research was funded by ZIM ("Zentrales Innovationsprogramm Mittelstand") by the German Federal Ministry for Economic Affairs and Climate Action (ZIM-grant KK5256201LU1).

**Institutional Review Board Statement:** The data collection, the experiments, and the data publication were conducted in accordance with a vote (vote 2020-847R) and an associated amendment (2020-847_1-AF 11) of the ethics commission II of the Heidelberg University.

**Informed Consent Statement:** Not applicable, as only completely anonymized report texts were used here in a retrospective evaluation. No experiments were performed directly on the patient.

**Data Availability Statement:** The code for this work is available on GitLab: http://gitlab.medma.uni-heidelberg.de/mlegnar/nlp-in-diagnostic-texts-from-nephropathology (14 July 2022). Furthermore, the vectorized or embedded text documents are available on HeiData: https://doi.org/10.11588/data/KS5W0H (14 July 2022). The raw texts (i.e., descriptive and diagnostic sections) are explicitly not made available, since it cannot be ruled out here that it is possible to infer the patient or the person making the report. This is in accordance with our local ethics committee.

**Acknowledgments:** We thank our project partners Averbis AG for the collaboration in this project. Furthermore, the authors express their gratitude to the data storage service SDS@hd supported by the Ministry of Science, Research and the Arts Baden-Württemberg (MWK) and the German Research Foundation (DFG) through grant INST 35/1314-1 FUGG and INST 35/1503-1 FUGG. The authors also thank the IT department staff of Medical Faculty Mannheim and especially Bohne-Lang for supervising the computer administration and infrastructure.

**Conflicts of Interest:** The authors declare no conflict of interest. The above-described funding had no role regarding the design of the study; the collection, analyses or interpretation of data; the writing of the manuscript; or the decision to publish the results.

## Abbreviations

The following abbreviations are used in this manuscript:

| | |
|---|---|
| BoW | Bag-of-Words |
| SVM | support vector machine |
| NLP | natural language processing |
| OOV | out of vocabulary |
| MLM | masked language modeling |
| LSTM | long short-term memory |
| ICD-O | International Classification of Diseases for Oncology |
| CNN | convolutional neural network |
| RNN | Recurrent Neural Network |
| BERT | Bidirectional Encoder Representations from Transformers |
| UMAP | Uniform Manifold Approximation and Projection |
| HDBSCAN | Hierarchical Density-Based Spatial Clustering of Applications with Noise |
| GSDPMM | Gibbs Sampling algorithm for the Dirichlet Process Multinomial Mixture |
| SGD | Stochastic Gradient Descent |
| PCA | Principal Component Analysis |
| tf-idf | term frequency–inverse document frequency |
| NMI | normalized mutual information |
| ReLU | rectified linear unit |
| VL-PTMs | Vision-Language Pre-Trained Models |
| s-score | silhouette score |
| cls accuracy | classification accuracy |
| ML | machine learning |
| LDA | Latent Dirichlet Allocation |
| NB | naive bayes |
| MLP | multilayer perceptron |
| UMLS | Unified Medical Language System |
| SMOTE | synthetic minority over-sampling technique |

## Appendix A. Additional Annotated Topic Word Tables

**Table A1.** Annotated German topic words, extracted from the **HDBSCAN!** (**HDBSCAN!**) cluster-set, using the tf–idf based extraction method. A particularly large number of topic words strongly refer to cluster names (left column) highlighted in green (strong cluster names). In the case of cluster names marked in orange, only a few topic words indicated the specified cluster name (weak cluster name). The same applies to the colour-coded topic words: topic words that strongly indicate a cluster name are highlighted in green (strong topic words). Orange highlighted topic words only weakly indicate a cluster name (weak topic words).

| Cluster Index-Cluster Name | Keywords according to tf-idf |
|---|---|
| 0-Systemischer Lupus erythematodes | skala, chronizitätsindex, klasse, aktivitätsindex, nih, lupus_nephritis, iv, who, glomerulärer, iii |
| 1-Rapid progressive Glomerulonephritis | anzahl, glomeruli, vernarbten, nekrosen, frisch, proliferierende_glomerulonephritis, ca, segmental_nekrotisierend, extrakapillär, betreffend |
| 2-Tubulo-interstitielle Nephritis | ca, betreffend, cortex, leicht, immunfärbung, schädigung, miterfasst, mäßig, chronisch, ergänzend |
| 3-Pauci-Immun-Glomerulonephritis | hiervon, glomeruli, gesamtzahl, intakt, extrakapillär, vernarbt, global, nekrosen, proliferierende_glomerulonephritis, tubulointerstitieller_schaden |
| 4-Ig A Nephritis | oxford, m1, e0, s1, t0, c0, klassifikation, iga, glomerulonephritis, zellzahl |
| 5-FSGN | fsg, primär, unterscheidung, fokal, sekundär, kollabierend, chronisch, glomerulosklerose, erfolgen, hinweis |
| 6-Thrombotic microangiopathy | mikroangiopathie, thrombotisch, floride, reparation, präglomerulär, glomeruläre, befindlich, chronisch, tubulointerstitieller_schaden, hypertonie |
| 7-Multiples Myelom | nephropathie, kappa, cast, amyloidose, myelomniere, lcdd, hinweis, chronisch, kein, tubulointerstitieller_schaden |
| 8-Nierentransplantat | abstoßung, routinemäßig, chronisch, erfolg, immunhistochemisch, untersuchung, toxizität, hinweis, nephrosklerose, leichtgradig |
| 9-Unauffälliger Befund | nierenparenchym, unauffällig, übrig, weitgehend, normal, speziell, akut, tubulusschaden, histologisch, glomerulonephritis |
| 10 | schnittstufe, kaum, nennenswert, chronisch, tubulointerstitieller_schaden, tief, bislang, aufarbeitung, nephrosklerose, leichtgradig |
| 11 | mikroskopie, konventionell, maßgabe, ergeben, nierenparenchym, absehen, chronisch, nephrosklerose, leichtgradigen, untersuchung |
| 12- Membranöse Glomerulonephritis | pla2r, membranöse, ehrenreich, glomerulonephritis, stadium, churg, chronisch, tubulointerstitieller_schaden, positiv, nephrosklerose |
| 13- Diabetische Glomerulosklerose | diabetische_glomerulosklerose, chronisch, tubulointerstitieller_schaden, nodulär, lichtmikroskopisch, bild, nephrosklerose, schwer, untersuchung, bestehen |
| 14-Glomerulosklerose | glomerulosklerose, global, tubulointerstitieller_schaden, chronisch, nephrosklerose, fokal_segmental, fokal, mäßiggradig, erfolgen, sekundär |
| 15-Tubulo-interstitielle Nephritis | leichtgradiger, tubulusschaden, akut, chronisch, nephrosklerose, tubulointerstitieller_schaden, leichtgradig, mäßiggradiger, mäßiggradig, potentiell_reversibel |

**Table A2.** Annotated German topic words, extracted from the **HDBSCAN!** (**HDBSCAN!**) cluster-set, using the **SVM!** (**SVM!**) based extraction method. A particularly large number of topic words strongly refer to cluster names (left column) highlighted in green (strong cluster names). In the case of cluster names marked in orange, only a few topic words indicated the specified cluster name (weak cluster name). The same applies to the colour-coded topic words: topic words that strongly indicate a cluster name are highlighted in green (strong topic words). Orange highlighted topic words only weakly indicate a cluster name (weak topic words).

| Cluster Index-Cluster Name | Keywords according to SVM |
|---|---|
| 0-Systemischer Lupus erythematodes | skala, chronizitätsindex, aktivitätsindex, klasse, -nih, iv, lupus_nephritis, komponente, iii, who |
| 1-Rapid progressive Glomerulonephritis | anzahl, sklerosieren, glomeruli, vernarbten, glomerulus, frisch, davon1, proliferierende_glomerulonephritis, nekrosen, sklerosierten |
| 2-Tubulo-interstitielle Nephritis | tubulusepithelschaden, mäßig, leicht, schädigung, keine, komplettierung, fibrose, abschließend, bekannt, tubulointerstitiell |
| 3-Pauci-Immun-Glomerulonephritis | hiervon, gesamtzahl, intakt, pauci-immun-glomerulonephritis, nekrotisierend, glomeruli, vernarbt, *, restlich, extrakapillär |
| 4-Ig A Nephritis | oxford-klassifikation, e0, s1, m1, t0, c0, iga-glomerulonephritis, s0, anwendbar, e1 |
| 5-FSGN | fsg, primär, unterscheidung, zusammenschau, sekundär, segmentale_glomerulosklerose, kollabierend, allenfalls, weiterführend, patient |
| 6-Thrombotic microangiopathy | mikroangiopathie, thrombotisch, reparation, präglomerulär, glomeruläre, befindlich, floride, glomerulärethrombotisch, hypertonie, überwiegend |
| 7-Multiples Myelom | cast-nephropathie, myelomniere, lcdd, lambda, kappa, amyloidose, anschließen, leichtketten, al-amyloidose, leichtkettennephropathie |
| 8-Nierentransplantat | abstoßung, routinemäßig, erfolg, untersuchung, calcineurininhibitor-toxizität, aufsteigend, humorale, bakteriell, harnwegsinfekt, nachbericht |
| 9-Unauffälliger Befund | nierenparenchym, unauffällig, normal, weitgehend, übrig, vorbehaltlich, imübrigen, speziell, iga-, pathologisch |
| 10 | kaum, schnittstufe, nennenswert, tief, bislang, aufarbeitung, mittels, kongorot-färbung, zumausschluss, zelluläreoder |
| 11 | mikroskopie, konventionell, maßgabe, absehen, leichtgradigen, membranösen, früh, zellvermehrung, ergeben, g |
| 12-Membranöse Glomerulonephritis | membranöse, proteinurie, infolge, glomerulonephritis, pla2r, stadium, churg, ehrenreich, elektronenmikroskopie, pla2r-positiv |
| 13-Diabetische Glomerulosklerose | diabetische_glomerulosklerose, bestehen, immunkomplexglomerulonephritis, nodulär, bild, lichtmikroskopisch, teils, arteriolohyalinose, diabetische_glomeruloskleros, zusätzlich |
| 14-Glomerulosklerose | global, fokal_segmental, segmentaleglomerulosklerose, glomerulosklerose, fokalglobale, diffussegmental, einschl, fokal, tubulointerstitieller_schaden, vernarbung |
| 15-Tubulo-interstitielle Nephritis | tubulusschaden, leichtgradiger, leichtgradig, tubulointerstitieller_schaden, veränderung, mäßiggradiger, leichtgradige, andauernd, akut, malignität |

## Appendix B. UMAP Representations of the Cluster-Sets, Colored According to the Authors

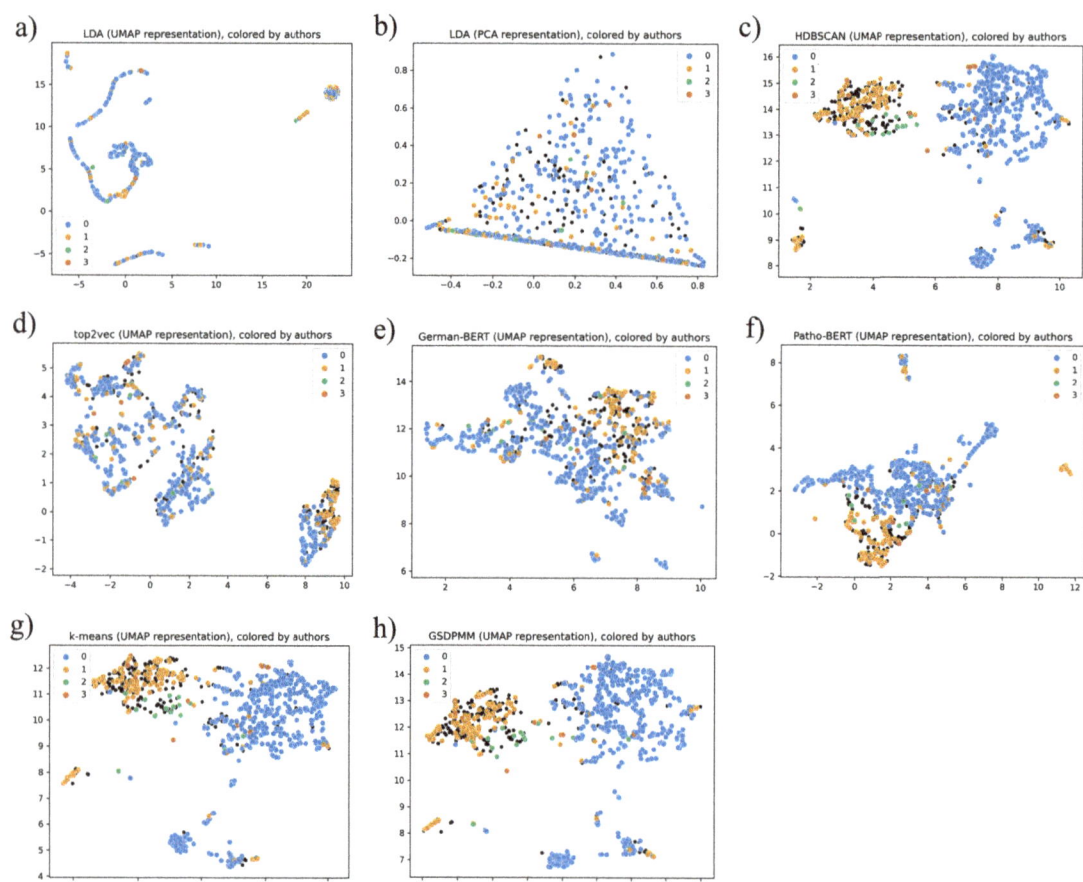

Figure A1. UMAP! (UMAP!) of the cluster-sets generated with (a) LDA! (LDA!), (c) HDBSCAN! (HDBSCAN!), (d) top2vec, (e) German-BERT, (f) Patho-BERT, (g) k-means and (h) GSDPMM! (GSDPMM!). The LDA! (LDA!) cluster-set is also shown as PCA! (PCA!) in (b). Each dot colour represents a different author. The authors of the reports marked in black are unknown (e.g. because multiple authors were involved).

## References

1. Colvin, R.B.; Chang, A. *Diagnostic Pathology: Kidney Diseases E-Book*; Elsevier Health Sciences: Amsterdam, The Netherlands, 2019.
2. Martul, E.V.; Praga, M. Nephropathology and nephrology. The need for a change. *Nefrología* **2018**, *38*, 247–249. [CrossRef]
3. Barisoni, L.; Lafata, K.J.; Hewitt, S.M.; Madabhushi, A.; Balis, U.G. Digital pathology and computational image analysis in nephropathology. *Nat. Rev. Nephrol.* **2020**, *16*, 669–685. [CrossRef] [PubMed]
4. Becker, J.U.; Mayerich, D.; Padmanabhan, M.; Barratt, J.; Ernst, A.; Boor, P.; Cicalese, P.A.; Mohan, C.; Nguyen, H.V.; Roysam, B. Artificial intelligence and machine learning in nephropathology. *Kidney Int.* **2020**, *98*, 65–75. [CrossRef]
5. Bukowy, J.D.; Dayton, A.; Cloutier, D.; Manis, A.D.; Staruschenko, A.; Lombard, J.H.; Woods, L.C.S.; Beard, D.A.; Cowley, A.W. Region-based convolutional neural nets for localization of glomeruli in trichrome-stained whole kidney sections. *J. Am. Soc. Nephrol.* **2018**, *29*, 2081–2088. [CrossRef]
6. Hermsen, M.; de Bel, T.; Den Boer, M.; Steenbergen, E.J.; Kers, J.; Florquin, S.; Roelofs, J.J.; Stegall, M.D.; Alexander, M.P.; Smith, B.H.; et al. Deep learning–based histopathologic assessment of kidney tissue. *J. Am. Soc. Nephrol.* **2019**, *30*, 1968–1979. [CrossRef]

7. Weis, C.A.; Bindzus, J.N.; Voigt, J.; Runz, M.; Hertjens, S.; Gaida, M.M.; Popovic, Z.V.; Porubsky, S. Assessment of glomerular morphological patterns by deep learning algorithms. *J. Nephrol.* **2022**, 1–11. [CrossRef]
8. Fogo, A.B.; Cohen, A.H.; Colvin, R.B.; Jennette, J.C.; Alpers, C.E. *Fundamentals of Renal Pathology*; Springer: Berlin/Heidelberg, Germany, 2014.
9. Schulz, S.; Fix, S.; Klügl, P.; Bachmayer, T.; Hartz, T.; Richter, M.; Herm-Stapelberg, N.; Daumke, P. Comparative evaluation of automated information extraction from pathology reports in three German cancer registries. *GMS Med. Inform. Biom. Epidemiol.* **2021**, *17*, Doc01. [CrossRef]
10. Fabacher, T.; Godet, J.; Klein, D. Machine learning application for incident prostate adenocarcinomas automatic registration in a French regional cancer registry. *Int. J. Med. Inform.* **2020**, *139*, 5. [CrossRef]
11. Oleynik, M.; Patrão, D.; Finger, M. Automated Classification of Semi-Structured Pathology Reports into ICD-O Using SVM in Portuguese. *Stud. Health Technol. Inform.* **2017**, *32*, 1–10. [CrossRef]
12. World Health Organization. *International Classification of Diseases for Oncology (ICD-O)*, 3rd ed.; 1st Revision Ed.; World Health Organization: Geneva, Switzerland, 2013.
13. Löpprich, M.; Krauss, F.; Ganzinger, M.; Senghas, K.; Riezler, S.; Knaup, P. Automated Classification of Selected Data Elements from Free-text Diagnostic Reports for Clinical Research. *Methods Inf. Med.* **2016**, *55*, 373–380. [CrossRef]
14. Bodenreider, O. The Unified Medical Language System (UMLS): Integrating biomedical terminology. *Nucleic Acids Res.* **2004**, *32*, 267D–270D. [CrossRef] [PubMed]
15. Juluru, K.; Shih, H.H.; Keshava Murthy, K.N.; Elnajjar, P. Bag-of-Words Technique in Natural Language Processing: A Primer for Radiologists. *RadioGraphics* **2021**, *41*, 1420–1426. [CrossRef]
16. Bird, S.; Klein, E.; Loper, E. *Natural Language Processing with Python: Analyzing Text with the Natural Language Toolkit*; O'Reilly Media, Inc.: Sebastopol, CA, USA, 2009.
17. Rehurek, R.; Sojka, P. *Gensim–Python Framework for Vector Space Modelling*; NLP Centre, Faculty of Informatics, Masaryk University: Brno, Czech Republic, 2011; Volume 3.
18. McInnes, L.; Healy, J.; Astels, S. hdbscan: Hierarchical density based clustering. *J. Open Source Softw.* **2017**, *2*, 223–228. [CrossRef]
19. McInnes, L.; Healy, J.; Melville, J. UMAP: Uniform Manifold Approximation and Projection for Dimension Reduction. *arXiv* **2020**, arXiv:1802.03426.
20. Yin, J.; Wang, J. A model-based approach for text clustering with outlier detection. In Proceedings of the 2016 IEEE 32nd International Conference on Data Engineering (ICDE), Helsinki, Finland, 16–20 May 2016; pp. 625–636. [CrossRef]
21. Wartena, C. A Probabilistic Morphology Model for German Lemmatization. In Proceedings of the 15th Conference on Natural Language Processing (KONVENS 2019), Erlangen-Nürnberg, Germany, 9–11 October 2019; pp. 40–49. [CrossRef]
22. Dieng, A.B.; Ruiz, F.J.R.; Blei, D.M. Topic Modeling in Embedding Spaces. *Trans. Assoc. Comput. Linguist.* **2020**, *8*, 439–453. [CrossRef]
23. Rangarajan Sridhar, V.K. Unsupervised Topic Modeling for Short Texts Using Distributed Representations of Words. In *Proceedings of the 1st Workshop on Vector Space Modeling for Natural Language Processing*; Association for Computational Linguistics: Denver, CO, USA, 2015; pp. 192–200. [CrossRef]
24. Angelov, D. Top2Vec: Distributed Representations of Topics. *arXiv* **2020**, arXiv:2008.09470. Available online: http://arxiv.org/abs/2008.09470 (accessed on 27 May 2022).
25. Mikolov, T.; Chen, K.; Corrado, G.; Dean, J. Efficient Estimation of Word Representations in Vector Space. *arXiv* **2013**, arXiv:1301.3781.
26. Le, Q.V.; Mikolov, T. Distributed Representations of Sentences and Documents. *arXiv* **2014**, arXiv:1405.4053. Available online: https://arxiv.org/abs/1405.4053 (accessed on 27 May 2022).
27. Devlin, J.; Chang, M.; Lee, K.; Toutanova, K. BERT: Pre-training of Deep Bidirectional Transformers for Language Understanding. *arXiv* **2018**, arXiv:1810.04805. Available online: https://arxiv.org/abs/1810.04805 (accessed on 27 May 2022).
28. Wolf, T.; Debut, L.; Sanh, V.; Chaumond, J.; Delangue, C.; Moi, A.; Cistac, P.; Rault, T.; Louf, R.; Funtowicz, M.; et al. HuggingFace's Transformers: State-of-the-art Natural Language Processing. *arXiv* **2020**, arXiv:1910.03771.
29. Reimers, N.; Gurevych, I. Sentence-BERT: Sentence Embeddings using Siamese BERT-Networks. *arXiv* **2019**, arXiv:1908.10084.
30. Lee, J.; Yoon, W.; Kim, S.; Kim, D.; Kim, S.; So, C.H.; Kang, J. BioBERT: A pre-trained biomedical language representation model for biomedical text mining. *arXiv* **2019**, arXiv:1901.08746. Available online: https://arxiv.org/abs/1901.08746 (accessed on 27 May 2022).
31. Alsentzer, E.; Murphy, J.R.; Boag, W.; Weng, W.; Jin, D.; Naumann, T.; McDermott, M.B.A. Publicly Available Clinical BERT Embeddings. *arXiv* **2019**, arXiv:1904.03323. Available online: https://arxiv.org/abs/1904.03323 (accessed on 27 May 2022).
32. Chakraborty, S.; Bisong, E.; Bhatt, S.; Wagner, T.; Elliott, R.; Mosconi, F. *BioMedBERT: A Pre-Trained Biomedical Language Model for QA and IR*; International Committee on Computational Linguistics: Praha, Czech Republic, 2020; pp. 669–679. [CrossRef]
33. Brownlee, J. *Deep Learning for Natural Language Processing*; Machine Learning Mastery: Melbourne, Australia, 2019.
34. Pugachev, L.; Burtsev, M. Short Text Clustering with Transformers. *arXiv* **2021**, arXiv:2102.00541.
35. Qiang, J.; Qian, Z.; Li, Y.; Yuan, Y.; Wu, X. Short Text Topic Modeling Techniques, Applications, and Performance: A Survey. *IEEE Trans. Knowl. Data Eng.* **2020**, *14*, 17. [CrossRef]
36. Christopher, D.M.; Prabhakar, R.; Hinrich, S. *Introduction to Information Retrieval*; Cambridge University Press: Cambridge, UK, 2008.

37. Kim, Y. Convolutional Neural Networks for Sentence Classification. *CoRR* **2014**. Available online: https://arxiv.org/abs/1408.5882 (accessed on 27 May 2022).
38. Abadi, M.; Agarwal, A.; Barham, P.; Brevdo, E.; Chen, Z.; Citro, C.; Corrado, G.S.; Davis, A.; Dean, J.; Devin, M.; et al. TensorFlow: Large-Scale Machine Learning on Heterogeneous Distributed Systems. *arXiv* **2016**, arXiv:1603.04467.
39. Paszke, A.; Gross, S.; Massa, F.; Lerer, A.; Bradbury, J.; Chanan, G.; Killeen, T.; Lin, Z.; Gimelshein, N.; Antiga, L.; et al. PyTorch: An Imperative Style, High-Performance Deep Learning Library. In *Proceedings of the Advances in Neural Information Processing Systems*; Wallach, H., Larochelle, H., Beygelzimer, A., Alché-Buc, F.D., Fox, E., Garnett, R., Eds.; Curran Associates, Inc.: New York, NY, USA, 2019; Volume 32.
40. Loshchilov, I.; Hutter, F. Decoupled Weight Decay Regularization. *arXiv* **2019**, arXiv:1711.05101.
41. Cohen, J. A Coefficient of Agreement for Nominal Scales. *Educ. Psychol. Meas.* **1960**, *20*, 37–46. [CrossRef]
42. Tizhoosh, H.R.; Pantanowitz, L. Artificial intelligence and digital pathology: Challenges and opportunities. *J. Pathol. Inform.* **2018**, *9*, 6. [CrossRef]
43. Abels, E.; Pantanowitz, L.; Aeffner, F.; Zarella, M.D.; van der Laak, J.; Bui, M.M.; Vemuri, V.N.; Parwani, A.V.; Gibbs, J.; Agosto-Arroyo, E. Computational pathology definitions, best practices, and recommendations for regulatory guidance: A white paper from the Digital Pathology Association. *J. Pathol.* **2019**, *249*, 286–294. [CrossRef]
44. Ravì, D.; Wong, C.; Deligianni, F.; Berthelot, M.; Andreu-Perez, J.; Lo, B.; Yang, G.Z. Deep learning for health informatics. *IEEE J. Biomed. Health Inform.* **2016**, *21*, 4–21. [CrossRef] [PubMed]
45. Weis, C.A.; Weihrauch, K.R.; Kriegsmann, K.; Kriegsmann, M. Unsupervised Segmentation in NSCLC: How to Map the Output of Unsupervised Segmentation to Meaningful Histological Labels by Linear Combination? *Appl. Sci.* **2022**, *12*, 3718. [CrossRef]
46. Noriaki, S.; Eiichiro, U.; Yasushi, O. Artificial Intelligence in Kidney Pathology. In *Artificial Intelligence in Medicine*; Springer: Berlin/Heidelberg, Germany, 2021; pp. 1–11.
47. Chan, L.; Vaid, A.; Nadkarni, G.N. Applications of machine learning methods in kidney disease: Hope or hype? *Curr. Opin. Nephrol. Hypertens.* **2020**, *29*, 319–326. [CrossRef] [PubMed]
48. Burger, G.; Abu-Hanna, A.; de Keizer, N.; Cornet, R. Natural language processing in pathology: A scoping review. *J. Clin. Pathol.* **2016**, *69*, 949–955. [CrossRef] [PubMed]
49. Schena, F.P.; Magistroni, R.; Narducci, F.; Abbrescia, D.I.; Anelli, V.W.; Di Noia, T. Artificial intelligence in glomerular diseases. *Pediatr. Nephrol.* **2022**, *6*, 13. [CrossRef]
50. Haas, M.; Seshan, S.V.; Barisoni, L.; Amann, K.; Bajema, I.M.; Becker, J.U.; Joh, K.; Ljubanovic, D.; Roberts, I.S.; Roelofs, J.J.; et al. Consensus definitions for glomerular lesions by light and electron microscopy: Recommendations from a working group of the Renal Pathology Society. *Kidney Int.* **2020**, *98*, 1120–1134. [CrossRef]
51. Chang, A.; Gibson, I.W.; Cohen, A.H.; Weening, J.W.; Jennette, J.C.; Fogo, A.B. A position paper on standardizing the nonneoplastic kidney biopsy report. *Hum. Pathol.* **2012**, *43*, 1192–1196. [CrossRef]
52. Sethi, S.; Haas, M.; Markowitz, G.S.; D'Agati, V.D.; Rennke, H.G.; Jennette, J.C.; Bajema, I.M.; Alpers, C.E.; Chang, A.; Cornell, L.D.; et al. Mayo clinic/renal pathology society consensus report on pathologic classification, diagnosis, and reporting of GN. *J. Am. Soc. Nephrol.* **2016**, *27*, 1278–1287. [CrossRef]
53. Leh, S.; Dendooven, A. Systematic reporting of medical kidney biopsies. *Clin. Kidney J.* **2022**, *15*, 21–30. [CrossRef]
54. Ong, E.; Wang, L.L.; Schaub, J.; O'Toole, J.F.; Steck, B.; Rosenberg, A.Z.; Dowd, F.; Hansen, J.; Barisoni, L.; Jain, S.; et al. Modelling kidney disease using ontology: Insights from the Kidney Precision Medicine Project. *Nat. Rev. Nephrol.* **2020**, *16*, 686–696. [CrossRef]
55. Chawla, N.V.; Bowyer, K.W.; Hall, L.O.; Kegelmeyer, W.P. SMOTE: Synthetic Minority Over-sampling Technique. *J. Artif. Intell. Res.* **2002**, *16*, 321–357. [CrossRef]
56. Li, Xiaoya; Sun, Xiaofei; Meng, Yuxian; Liang, Junjun; Wu, Fei Li, Jiwei Dice Loss for Data-imbalanced NLP Tasks. *arXiv* **2020**, arXiv:1911.02855 .
57. Du, Yifan; Liu, Zikang; Li, Junyi; Zhao, Wayne Xin A Survey of Vision-Language Pre-Trained Models. *arXiv* **2022**, arXiv:2202.10936.
58. Lu, J.; Batra, D.; Parikh, D.; Lee, S. ViLBERT: Pretraining Task-Agnostic Visiolinguistic Representations for Vision-and-Language Tasks. *arXiv* **2019**, arXiv:1908.02265.
59. Li, G.; Duan, N.; Fang, Y.; Gong, M.; Jiang, D. Unicoder-VL: A Universal Encoder for Vision and Language by Cross-Modal Pre-Training. *Proc. AAAI Conf. Artif. Intell.* **2020**, *34*, 11336–11344. [CrossRef]

Article

# Improving the Diagnosis of Skin Biopsies Using Tissue Segmentation

Shima Nofallah [1,*], Beibin Li [2], Mojgan Mokhtari [3], Wenjun Wu [4], Stevan Knezevich [5], Caitlin J. May [6], Oliver H. Chang [7], Joann G. Elmore [8,†] and Linda G. Shapiro [1,2,4,†]

1. Department of Electrical and Computer Engineering, University of Washington, Seattle, WA 98195, USA; shapiro@cs.washington.edu
2. Paul G. Allen School of Computer Science and Engineering, University of Washington, Seattle, WA 98195, USA; beibin@uw.edu
3. Pathology Department, Isfahan University of Medical Sciences, Isfahan 8174673461, Iran; mokhtari.ptlgy@gmail.com
4. Department of Biomedical Informatics and Medical Education, University of Washington, Seattle, WA 98195, USA; wenjunw@uw.edu
5. Pathology Associates, Clovis, CA 983611, USA; stevanrk@gmail.com
6. Dermatopathology Northwest, Bellevue, WA 98005, USA; campbell.cait@gmail.com
7. Department of Pathology, University of Washington, Seattle, WA 98195, USA; ochang@uw.edu
8. David Geffen School of Medicine, UCLA, Los Angeles, CA 90024, USA; jelmore@mednet.ucla.edu
* Correspondence: shimz@uw.edu
† These authors contributed equally to this work.

**Abstract:** Invasive melanoma, a common type of skin cancer, is considered one of the deadliest. Pathologists routinely evaluate melanocytic lesions to determine the amount of atypia, and if the lesion represents an invasive melanoma, its stage. However, due to the complicated nature of these assessments, inter- and intra-observer variability among pathologists in their interpretation are very common. Machine-learning techniques have shown impressive and robust performance on various tasks including healthcare. In this work, we study the potential of including semantic segmentation of clinically important tissue structure in improving the diagnosis of skin biopsy images. Our experimental results show a 6% improvement in F-score when using whole slide images along with epidermal nests and cancerous dermal nest segmentation masks compared to using whole-slide images alone in training and testing the diagnosis pipeline.

**Keywords:** whole slide imaging; skin biopsy; melanoma diagnosis; machine learning; semantic segmentation; transformers; accuracy

## 1. Introduction

Melanoma is one of the deadliest types of skin cancer, and its incidence has been increasing faster than any other cancer [1–3]. If Melanoma is caught in its earlier stages, it is highly curable; however, because of the complexity of skin biopsies and the subjectivity of visual interpretation, there is significant uncertainty in the accuracy of pathology reports. Studies have shown that pathologists' diagnoses of moderately dysplastic nevi to thin invasive melanomas are neither accurate nor reproducible in some cases [4]. These reports raise concerns about appropriate treatment and the consequences of both under- and over-diagnosis. Deep learning has shown excellent performance on various tasks, and healthcare is not an exception [5–8]. Using deep-learning techniques to provide prognostic and diagnostic information for pathologists during screening and treatment stages can be an aid in clinical care.

Deep learning and artificial intelligence (AI) have achieved unparalleled success in various tasks such as classification, segmentation, detection, etc. However, though the state-of-the-art approaches in this field show fast and accurate performance, they face

challenges in dealing with medical datasets. Medical datasets usually are small in sample size, have large images, and do not have many examples of perfect annotations. As the field of AI in healthcare has grown significantly in recent years, more robust methods in this area have emerged.

In addition, demand for diagnostic models and classification tools based on histopathological images has increased due to inter- and intra-observer variability in pathology and the potential solution that AI methods can produce. Providing prognostic and diagnostic information at the time of cancer diagnosis has important implications on patient outcomes, as automated machine-learning methods on whole-slide images provide a promising way forward for efficient and robust pathology analysis.

Various studies have introduced diagnosis models based on whole slide images (WSIs). In [9], the authors introduced a CNN-based deep feature extraction framework to build slide-level feature representations via weighted aggregation of the patch representations and overcome the challenge of working with variable-sized regions of interest. Li et al. [10] extracted relevant patch representation using self-supervised contrastive learning and introduced a dual-stream architecture with trainable distance measurement to train an MIL model called the dual-stream multiple instance learning network (DSMIL). Chikontwe et al. [11] proposed a multiple instance learning (MIL) method based on a transformer that first selects the top-k patches, and then used these patches for instance-learning and bag-representation learning. In addition, this method uses a center loss that maps embeddings of instances from the same bag to a single centroid and reduces intra-class variations for final diagnosis.

Segmentation-based methods are another approach that has been studied in the field of histopathology image analysis, as different tissues and entities in these images might play an important role in the diagnosis of the case. Several works with this approach first generate semantic segmentation masks on WSIs, and using the extracted information from those masks, produce an image-level diagnosis [12–14]. While this approach is a valuable study direction, the challenge of dealing with imperfect annotation or lack of annotation is not addressed in such studies.

In our prior AI-based diagnosis work in pathology, our studies utilize regions of interest (ROI) rather than the larger whole slide images (WSI) [9,13,15]. There are two main reasons we used the full WSI for the current study. First, Mercan et al. [16], in the effort to find diagnostically relevant ROIs on breast biopsy WSI, reported that 74% of the output probability map overlapped with the actual ROIs from pathologist viewing behavior, while 26% did not. If such early probability maps are utilized for diagnosis tasks, there is a chance that important diagnostic information is missed or misused. The second reason behind our approach using WSI relates to the interpretive process used by pathologists as they view, assess, and interpret WSI of skin biopsies using current published definitions for clinical classification. The pathologists' clinical process and classification systems vary by tissue type—for breast biopsy cases, a single ROI of an area within a duct might suffice to allow the pathologists to come to a diagnosis. However, the process used by pathologists of reviewing skin biopsy image data and the information within skin biopsies used to determine a diagnosis is different—information on the image from larger structural data in addition to image data within small clusters of cells is important to both rule in and rule out different diagnoses. Thus, for a diagnosis of melanoma and its precursors, reviewing information from the larger WSI is required in current clinical practice by pathologists before they can provide a diagnosis.

In this work, we therefore incorporate tissue segmentation masks that were generated based on sparse and coarse annotations of the full skin biopsy WSIs. The goal is to investigate the potential of providing this information in the process of skin biopsy diagnosis using WSI. Our experimental results show that including a clinically certain important tissue structure along with WSIs improves the learning of the model, especially in challenging diagnostic classes such as melanoma in situ (MIS) and invasive melanoma (T1a). Examples of tissue structures that show the highest improvements are Epidermal Nests and melanoma dermal nests (cancerous). These tissues are considered clinically important in the decision-making process by human pathologists. Comparing our results with 187 pathologists' performance on the same test set shows that our model can outperform or have comparable performance on the cases with the aforementioned diagnostic classes.

## 2. Materials and Methods

### 2.1. M-Path Dataset

Our dataset comes from the M-Path study [4] that was approved by the Institutional Review Board at the University of Washington (protocol number STUDY00008506) and was conducted by a Bellevue, Washington dermatopathology laboratory. Two-hundred-and-forty hematoxylin and eosin (H&E)-stained slides of digitized skin biopsy images from this study are included in our project and can be classified into five different MPATH-Dx (melanocytic pathology assessment tool and hierarchy for diagnosis) simplified categories based on presumed risk of the lesion and suggested treatment recommendations [17]. Example diagnostic terms for each MPATH-Dx class are as follows: (I) mildly dysplastic nevi, (II) moderately dysplastic nevi, (III) melanoma in situ and severely dysplastic nevi, (IV) invasive melanoma stage T1a, and (V) invasive melanoma stage $\geq$ T1b. Table 1 shows the distribution of the diagnostic categories of the M-path dataset. Figure 1 shows examples of three different WSIs in the M-Path dataset.

**Table 1.** Distribution of diagnostic categories in M-Path data.

| Diagnostic Category | Number of Cases |
|---|---|
| Class I (e.g., Mildly Dysplastic Nevi) | 25 |
| Class II (e.g., Moderately Dysplastic Nevi) | 36 |
| Class III (e.g., Melanoma in Situ) | 60 |
| Class IV (e.g., Invasive Melanoma Stage T1a) | 72 |
| Class V (e.g., Invasive Melanoma Stage $\geq$ T1b) | 47 |
| Total | 240 |

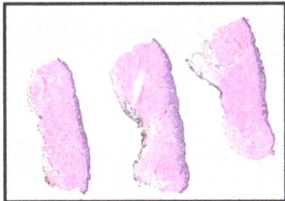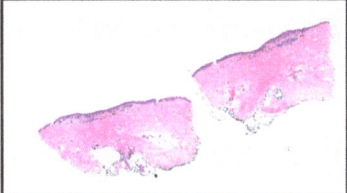

**Figure 1.** Three examples of WSIs in the M-Path dataset. The left image is a case with class IV diagnosis (invasive melanoma stage T1a), the middle image is a case with class V diagnosis (invasive melanoma stage $\geq$ T1b), and the right image is a case with class IV diagnosis (invasive melanoma stage T1a).

Using the MPATH-Dx classification tool [18] that is described above, a consensus panel of three dermatopathologists with internationally recognized expertise made a consensus diagnosis for all cases. Following these meetings, the expert panel, as well as an additional dermatopathologist (S. Knezevich), assigned one rectangular area as a region of interest (ROI) per case. These ROIs represent an important area of the WSI for diagnosis. Since there was a limitation of one ROI per case, there might have been other diagnostically important regions on WSIs that are not included in the final ROI. However, assigned regions have valuable information that can be used for various purposes. These variable-sized ROIs (Figure 2) can be extracted using their coordinates.

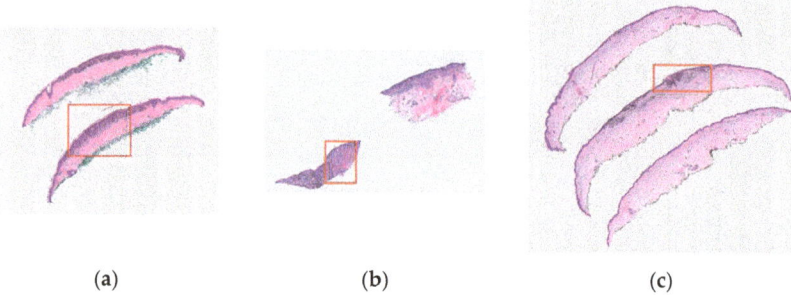

**Figure 2.** Examples of variable-sized region of interests (ROI) assigned by pathologists that contain important diagnostic information are shown in red boxes: (**a**) a case with class II diagnosis (moderately dysplastic nevus), (**b**) a case with class V diagnosis (invasive melanoma stage ≥ T1b), (**c**) a case with class IV diagnosis (invasive melanoma stage T1a).

To reduce the input image size and eliminate the unnecessary information from the slides' orientation (since this information is not relevant to the diagnosis of a case), we used extracted slices from the WSIs. An example of a WSI and its corresponding extracted slices is shown in Figure 3.

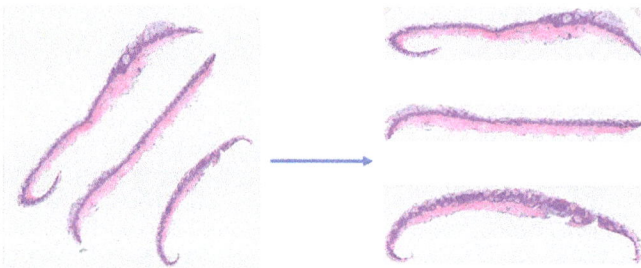

**Figure 3.** An example of a WSI (**left**) and its corresponding slice extraction (**right**).

2.1.1. Segmentation Masks

In a previous study [19], using coarse and sparse annotations, we trained a two-stage segmentation pipeline that generates tissue segmentation masks on whole slide images of skin biopsies. The segmentation masks include epidermis (EP), dermis (DE), stratum corneum (COR), epidermal nests (EPN), dermal nests (DMN), and background (BG). In the first stage, using a U-Net model, a model is trained that is able to segment large entities such as dermis, epidermis, stratum corneum, and background. In the second stage, two models are trained on the smaller tissue structures of the skin biopsy images. This stage includes two branches that are trained separately: (1) stage 2-dermis, which uses a U-Net to train a model on the dermis portion of the image (i.e., DMN); (2) stage 2-epidermis, which trains a U-Net on the epidermis portion of the image (i.e., EPN).

Using this pipeline, we were able to generate segmentation masks for both large entities (i.e., dermis, epidermis) and smaller entities (dermal nests, epidermal nests) with high-quality performance. However, since the annotations of DMN and EPN were coarse, we observed over-labeling of these entities in segmentation results as well. Figure 4 shows some examples of segmentation masks generated from WSIs.

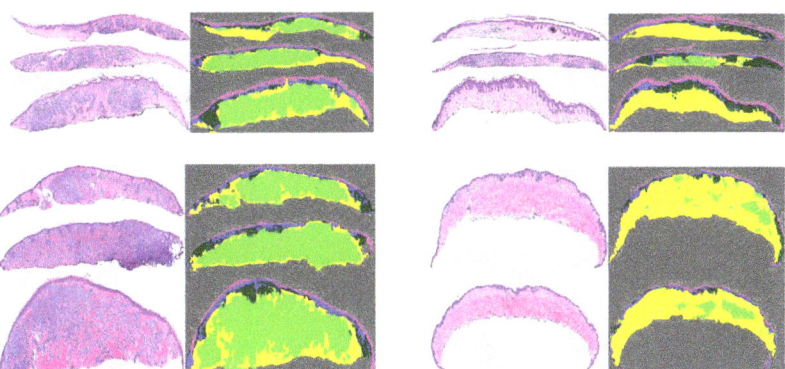

**Figure 4.** Examples of original WSIs and their corresponding segmentation mask. The segmentation images contain the dermis, epidermis, stratum corneum, background, dermal, and epidermal nests. The model was trained on coarse and sparse annotations.

*2.2. Dermal Nest Classification*

Pathologists investigate structural entities in digitized whole-slide images of melanocytic skin lesions and assign a diagnosis class to the case based on the various factors, including morphological characteristics of the cells present in the biopsy images. Assessment of the architecture and cytomorphology of junctional (epidermal) melanocytes and dermal melanocytes is necessary to classify and risk-stratify melanocytic lesions.

The evaluation of dermal nests is key in distinguishing a melanocytic nevus from invasive melanoma. It can also represent one of the most challenging tasks for a pathologist, especially in the absence of additional lab testing. Generally, dermal nests are categorized into the two sub-groups of nevus nests and melanoma nests. Dysplastic melanocytic nevi and severely dysplastic nevi may contain benign dermal melanocytic nests, but only invasive melanoma contains malignant dermal melanocytic nests.

In [19], we proposed a two-stage segmentation pipeline in which epidermal nests (EPN) and dermal nests (DMN) were segmented in its second stage. However, since not enough examples of nevus dermal nests (DMN-N) were available, especially compared to other entities such as melanoma dermal nests (DMN-M) and epidermal nests (EPN), we decided to combine nevus dermal nests (DMN-N) and melanoma dermal nests (DMN-M) into one class of dermal nests (DMN) in that project. In this paper, we propose an additional step to the output of our segmentation model that allows us to classify segmented DMNs into two sub-categories of nevus or melanoma. We train a CNN model that is able to segment dermal nest into melanoma dermal nest and nevus dermal nest. The classes of epidermal nests, melanoma dermal nests, and nevus dermal Nests can now be used in our experimental pipeline.

2.2.1. Dermal Nest Dataset

To train a dermal nest classifier, some ground truth on different categories of dermal nests is required. The ground-truth annotations in this project are a subset of the coarse and sparse annotations that were introduced in Section 2.1.1. The original set contained a small number of examples of nevus dermal nests on ROIs with the diagnostic classes of I, II, and III, while there was a relatively larger number of examples of melanoma dermal nests on ROIs belonging to cases with diagnostic classes IV and V. The main challenges in working with these annotations were two-fold: (1) There was a huge gap between the sample size of nevus dermal nests and melanoma dermal nests in which melanoma dermal nests contained ~400 M pixels, which is eight times the size of nevus dermal nests with ~50 M pixels and (2) no examples of nevus dermal nests on any invasive melanoma cases were annotated. The only examples of dermal Nest annotation in these classes belonged to melanoma dermal nests, while in reality, both types of nests can be present in one invasive melanoma case. Hence, in the segmentation model of [19], all dermal nest annotations were combined into a single class of dermal nests (DMN). Figure 5 shows example annotations of nevus dermal nests (DMN-M) (Figure 5b) and melanoma dermal nests (DMN-M) (Figure 5e) and their conversion to dermal nests (DMN) ((Figure 5c) and (Figure 5f)), which were used for the dataset of [19].

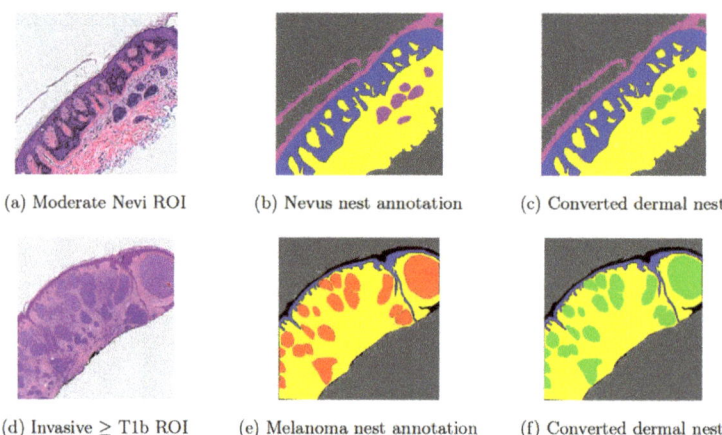

(a) Moderate Nevi ROI  (b) Nevus nest annotation  (c) Converted dermal nest

(d) Invasive ≥ T1b ROI  (e) Melanoma nest annotation  (f) Converted dermal nest

**Figure 5.** Examples of input ROI images and their corresponding annotations. (**a**) shows a moderate Nevi ROI image, (**b**) shows the original Nevus dermal nest annotation in purple, (**c**) is the converted version of (**b**) in which purple annotations of nevus dermal nests (DMN-N) are converted to green markings of dermal nest (DMN), (**d**) shows an invasive melanoma stage ≥ T1b ROI image, (**e**) shows the original melanoma nests annotation in red, (**f**) is the converted version of (**e**) in which red annotation of melanoma dermal nests (DMN-M) are converted to green markings of dermal nest (DMN).

In this paper, instead of combining the two types of dermal nests, we kept them separate and extracted them into two categories of nevus dermal nests (DMN-M) (Figure 5b) and melanoma dermal nests (DMN-M) (Figure 5e). For the nest extraction step, after masking out everything other than dermal nests in the ROIs, we sampled the nests into two classes of "nevus" and "melanoma". The sampling window size is $100 \times 100$. As expected, there was a noticeable imbalance in the final dataset between the two classes of "nevus" and "melanoma" nests. The number of extracted nevus nests was 604 samples, while the number of extracted melanoma nests was 5732 samples. To solve this imbalanced dataset issue, we used the result of our previous segmentation model as explained in Section 2.2.2.

2.2.2. Solving Nest Sample Imbalance in the Training Dataset

After acquiring the segmentation model output, the opportunity of overcoming the annotation imbalance in dermal nests arises. It is known that cases with a diagnosis class of I, II, and III only contain nevus dermal nests, while both nevus dermal nests and melanoma dermal nests can appear in a case with diagnostic class IV or V. Although the segmentation model of [19] does not distinguish between nevus dermal nests and melanoma dermal nests, we know that all the nests on class I, class II, and class III cases are nevus dermal nests. The reason is that if there is any appearance of a melanoma dermal nest on a case, that case will move to one of the invasive melanoma diagnostic categories. Figure 6a shows an example of segmented dermal nests on a class II case in which we assume all nests are of nevus type based on the diagnosis of the case. Figure 6b shows an example of segmented dermal nests on a class V case. Such a case would not be usable for training in this project since it is not specified which parts of the segmented dermal nests are nevus and which parts are melanoma.

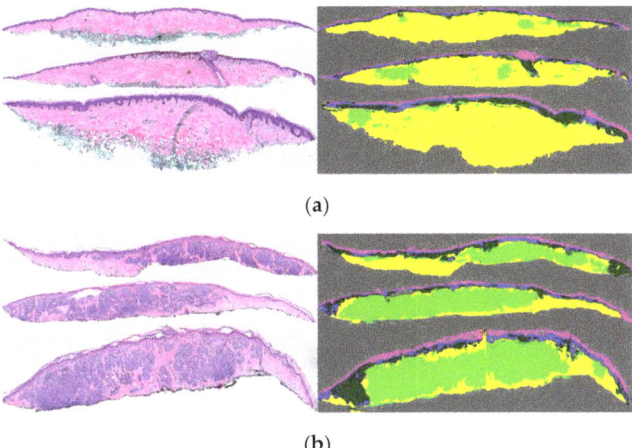

**Figure 6.** Example of dermal nest segmentation (in light green) on WSI: (**a**) a moderate nevi case; all the dermal nests are nevi type. (**b**) An invasive melanoma stage $\geq$ T1b case; the segmented dermal nests might contain both nevi and melanoma dermal nests.

Since the training and testing split of the dataset is consistent throughout all the projects, in addition to the fact that all the dermal nests in cases with diagnosis classes of I, II, and III must be nevus dermal nests, it is only logical to apply the trained segmentation model from [19] to WSI of cases I, II, and III to detect dermal nests (DMN); extract them; and re-label them as nevus dermal nests. Using the new nevus dermal nests, we can randomly extract DMN-N samples and add them to the nest classification training set to reach a balanced number of samples for both classes of DMN-N and DMN-M in the training set.

2.2.3. Dermal Nest Classifier

Since convolutional neural networks (CNNs) have shown good performance in various computer vision and machine-learning tasks, we used this approach in training our dermal nest classifier. We trained three different architectures, using PyTorch torchvision [20] pre-trained CNN models, trained on the ImageNet dataset [21]:

- DenseNet: Huang, G., et al. [22], introduced a densely connected convolutional neural network that improves the flow of information between different stacked convolutional layers. In our experiments, we used a pre-trained torchvision *densenet161* architecture as a nest classifier model.
- ShuffleNet: ShuffleNet [23] is a convolutional neural network that utilized two new operations, point-wise group convolution, and channel shuffle, to reduce computation cost while maintaining accuracy. We used a pre-trained torchvison *shufflenet_v2* for our experiments.
- ResNet: A residual neural network [24] is a CNN that utilizes skip connections to jump over some layers. We used a pre-trained torchvison *resnet18* for two of our experiments with different training datasets.

In the preprocessing step, we included random cropping, random rotation, horizontal flip, and normalization in the Dataloader function. All the models were trained for 20 epochs with cross-entropy [25] as a loss function, and Adam optimizer [26] with a learning rate of 0.001. After the training, we evaluated each model's performance on the same testing dataset and compared the results.

*2.3. WSI Diagnosis Using Tissue Segmentation*

In this section, we study the impact of adding each tissue mask to the WSIs in the classification of our dataset into diagnostic categories. The M-path dataset described in

Section 2.1 with five diagnostic classes of (1) Class I: mild dysplastic nevi, (2) class II: moderate dysplastic nevi, (3) Class III: (e.g., melanoma in situ and severely dysplastic nevi), (4) Class IV: invasive melanoma stage T1a, and (5) Class V: invasive melanoma stage $\geq$ T1b. The only difference is that since the clinical risk for progression of both Class I and Class II is extremely low, and we have a limited sample size in the aforementioned classes, we regrouped the five classes to four diagnostic classes by combining samples from class I and II into one class. The final four classes will be (1) Class I–II: mild and moderate dysplastic nevi (MMD), (2) Class III: (e.g., melanoma in situ, severely dysplastic nevi) (MIS), (3) Class IV: invasive melanoma stage T1a (T1a), and (4) Class V: invasive melanoma stage $\geq$ T1b (T1b).

As mentioned in Section 2.1, we used extracted slices to train and evaluate our diagnosis models. The main resolution that we used to extract individual slices was 20×. Using this resolution, we extracted lower resolutions of 7.5×, 10×, and 12.5×, which we later used for our experimental studies.

2.3.1. Binarized Segmentation Masks

The segmentation masks generated by the proposed pipeline in Section 2.1.1 were used in the current project. Each tissue mask from that project (epidermis (EP), dermis (DE), epidermal nest (EPN), and dermal nest (DMN)) was separated into a single binary mask in order to have more control over tissue combination in our experimental studies on the diagnosis accuracy. In addition to the aforementioned tissue masks, we included the two types of dermal masks from 2.2 as two separate binary masks of nevus dermal nest (DMN-N) and melanoma dermal nest (DMN-M). Figure 7 shows examples of binary masks for two classes of mild and moderate nevi (MMD) and invasive melanoma stage $\geq$ T1b (T1b). Note that the moderate nevi (MMD) case does not include any DMN-M; hence, the corresponding mask is all zeros.

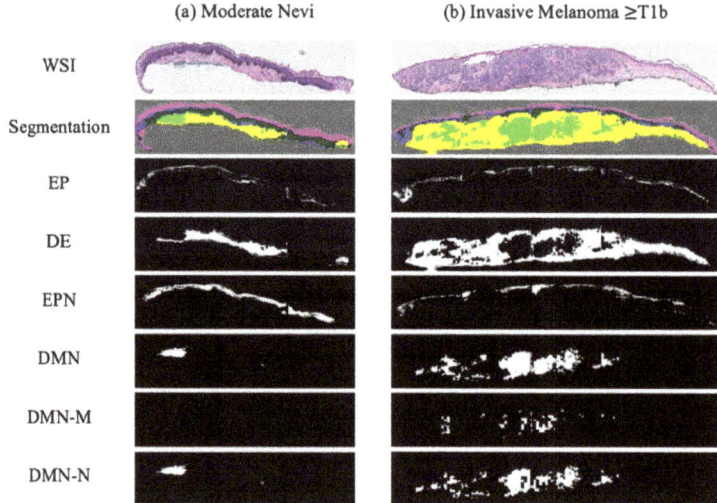

**Figure 7.** Examples of binarized segmentation masks: (**a**) a moderate nevi case; (**b**) an invasive melanoma stage $\geq$ T1b. From top to bottom, one extracted slice from a WSI, all segmentation masks in one mask (containing EP, DE, EPN, and DMN), binary Epidermis (EP) mask, binary dermis (DE) mask, binary epidermal nest (EPN) mask, binary dermal nest (DMN) mask, binary melanoma dermal nest (DMN-M), and binary nevus dermal nest (DMN-N) mask are shown.

2.3.2. Dataset Split

The dataset of WSIs before the extraction of slices was divided in half, conserving the original set's diagnostic class distribution over both subsets. One-half of the dataset was used for training and validation subsets, and the other half of the dataset was kept unseen from the model during the training and solely used for the final evaluation of the trained model. This split was kept fixed over all the experiments. After splitting the dataset, the extraction step that is explained in Section 2.1 was applied to all the WSIs in the training, validation, and testing subsets.

2.3.3. Soft Labels

Usually, each WSI has multiple slices from the same skin biopsy; however, not all the slices contain related information to the assigned diagnostic class of the case. In clinical practice, if a pathologist detects invasive melanoma in just one or two slices on one case, the overall biopsy is diagnosed as invasive melanoma to guide clinical care and treatment. In our dataset, the ROIs (some examples in Figure 2) that helped pathologists in diagnosis belong to one or two tissue slices, while the other tissue slices may correspond to other diagnostic categories. If all the extracted slices from a WSI are assigned to one diagnostic class, there is the risk of false representation of that diagnostic class, which can interfere with the learning process of a model. To handle this issue, we used a method that was previously developed by our group in which, using a singular-value decomposition (SVD), soft labels are assigned to the slices that do not have an ROI on them. For more information about the details of this method, refer to [27].

2.3.4. Combining WSI and Segmentation Masks

We tried various methods to combine the information from WSIs and corresponding segmentation masks. The final method that we chose to implement and run our experiments is as follows: Each WSI has three channels of RGB: red (R), green (G), and blue (B). In order to add segmentation mask information to our data, we concatenate each mask as a new channel to the image. For example, if we add a DMN channel to the WSI, we will have a new input with four channels: R, G, B, and DMN. This approach gives the flexibility of investigating any combination of tissue masks that are of interest. In addition, the feature extractor obtains the information of appended tissue masks along with the original WSI, which might result in a more representative feature set.

2.3.5. Feature Extraction

We used MobileNetv2 [28] pre-trained on the ImageNet dataset [21] as a feature extractor on our extracted patches. MobileNetv2 outputs 1280-dimensional patch-wise features after global average pooling. Since the pre-trained network on the ImageNet dataset is essentially a network with three input channels of RGB, we modified the first layer of the network by replacing it with a *Conv2d* layer that has input channels equal to the number of input image channels. The number is not fixed since, as explained in Section 2.3.4, the number of input image channels depends on the tissue mask combination in a specific experiment. Changing the first layer of the network, which is not pre-trained on any image, has the potential of negatively impacting the feature extraction step; however, as we will see in the next sections, the results do not show any clear effect of such. The reason might be the nature of CNNs in which the first few layers are focused on low-level features, while the middle layers mainly extract high-level and fine detailed features.

2.3.6. Scale-Aware Transformer Network (ScATNet)

In previous work, Wu et al. [27] proposed scale-aware transformer network (ScATNet) for diagnosing melanocytic lesions using WSIs. ScATNet uses local and global representations from various scales. In this architecture, the first step is to learn local patch-level embeddings on each scale using a pre-trained CNN. Then, using a transformer, the model learns the contextualized patch embeddings for each scale. In the last step, scale-aware embeddings across various scales are trained to the model [27].

ScATNet projects extracted patch-wise features explained in Section 2.3.5 linearly to a 128-dimensional space. In the second and third steps of the ScATNet pipeline, a stack of two transformer units is used. Each transformer unit has four heads in the self-attention layer with a feed-forward dimension of 512.

2.3.7. Experimental Studies

In order to investigate the impact of different tissue types, we designed several experiments with various combinations of tissue segmentation masks, using ScATNet as the basic model. In each experiment, we included specific segmentation masks along with the WSI; extracted the features as explained in Section 2.3.5; and using the extracted features, we trained and tested a diagnosis model. We ran the experiments with various resolution scales (7.5×, 10×, 12.5×, combination of two scales, and all three scales), with different hyperparameters, and after finding the best setting, we ran all the experiments with different random seeds.

Figure 8 shows an overview of our approach.

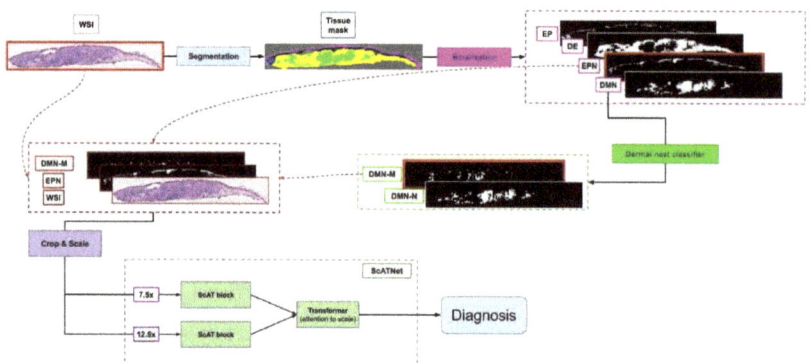

**Figure 8.** Overview of our diagnosis pipeline. The WSI goes to the segmentation pipeline to generate a tissue segmentation mask. Then, four clinically important tissue structures: epidermis (EP), dermis (DE), epidermal nest (EPN), and dermal nest (DMN) will be extracted into four corresponding binary masks. Extracted Dermal Nests will go through a dermal nests classification step to generate two sub-categories of melanoma dermal nest (DMN-M) and nevus dermal nest (DMN-N). Then, the selected tissue masks based on the experiment will be concatenated to the RGB channels of the WSI image. Each image will be cropped into smaller patches afterward. The patches go through the ScATNet pipeline that extracts patch embeddings, then, using contextualized patch-embedding and scale-aware embedding across available scales, chooses the diagnostic class of the case from mild and moderate dysplastic nevi (MMD), melanoma in situ and severely dysplastic nevi (MIS), invasive melanoma T1a (T1a) and melanoma invasive $\geq$ T1b (T1b). Note that the concatenated masks to the WSI (DMN-M and EPN) and ScATNet scales (7.5× and 12.5×) shown in this figure are just one example of our multiple experimental studies.

2.3.8. Hyperparameters

ScATNet was trained for 200 epochs in an end-to-end fashion using the ADAM optimizer with a linear learning rate warm-up strategy and step learning rate decay. The best result in our experimental studies was achieved using a single scale of 7.5×.

## 3. Results

*3.1. Dermal Nest Classification Results*

All the models from both approaches were evaluated by a testing set of ROI images that was kept unseen from the model during the training process. Note that in the testing dataset, no nest samples from the segmentation model are included. The testing dataset only contains extracted nests from ROIs in which we had a pathologist's annotation as ground-truth to compare model prediction against them. Using the model with the best performance on ROI images, we generate DMN-M and DMN-N on extracted slices of the WSI.

3.1.1. Quantitative Results on ROIs

All the trained models were evaluated on the same ROI testing set. Each nest classifier's performance was measured using these metrics: F-score, precision, sensitivity (recall), and specificity. The results of this evaluation are summarized in Table 2.

**Table 2.** Quantitative nest classification results on ROIs-CNN models.

| Method | F-Score | Precision | Sensitivity | Specificity |
|---|---|---|---|---|
| DenseNet | 0.88 | 0.87 | 0.89 | 0.82 |
| ShuffleNet | 0.78 | 0.80 | 0.76 | 0.74 |
| ResNet | 0.96 | 0.95 | 0.97 | 0.93 |

As a model selection step after training each experiment for 200 epochs, and to improve the model's robustness against stochastic noise, we averaged the best five model checkpoints within a single training process inspired by [29]. Then we evaluated all our experiments over the same testing set. A WSI might contain multiple tissue slices, which were extracted into single slices, and each of these slices might have a different diagnostic class prediction. To decide on the final diagnosis of a specific WSI, we used max-voting, which means if one of the tissue slices in a WSI is invasive melanoma, then the entire WSI corresponds to invasive melanoma and cannot be MMD or MIS. This approach was inspired by how pathologists make their diagnosis decision on skin biopsy images.

3.1.2. Qualitative Results on WSIs

After acquiring our best nest classifier (ResNet), we ran the model on all the dermal nests (DMN) extracted from the previous segmentation mask of invasive melanoma stage T1a and $\geq$ T1b WSIs to generate melanoma dermal nests (DMN-M). Any segmented DMN samples in these classes that were not classified as a DMN-M by the nest classifier model are assigned to nevus dermal nest (DMN-N). Figure 9 shows examples of an extracted slice of invasive melanoma WSI, corresponding dermal nest mask generated by our previous segmentation model, melanoma dermal nest (DMN-M) portion of the dermal nest (DMN) as a result of nest classifier output, and nevus dermal nest (DMN-N) portion of dermal nest (DMN) as a result of the complement of DMN-M on DMN.

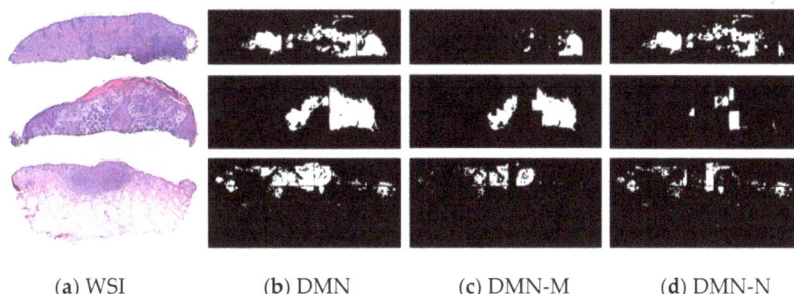

(a) WSI  (b) DMN  (c) DMN-M  (d) DMN-N

**Figure 9.** Examples of our best nest classifier, ResNet's results on WSI: (**a**) extracted slices of invasive melanoma WSIs; (**b**) dermal nest results of segmentation model; (**c**) melanoma dermal nest (DMN-M) portion of DMN; (**d**) nevus dermal nest (DMN-N) portion of DMN.

3.2. Diagnosis Experiment Results

We evaluated all the models based on micro F-score, sensitivity (recall), and specificity. Note that in dealing with a multi-class classification, where every test datum should belong to only 1 class and not multi-label, we cannot use the same F-score as in binary class classification (i.e., macro F-score in multi-class classification). The correct way to report an F-score in multi-class classification is to calculate the micro-averaged F-score (AKA micro F-score) based on micro-precision and micro-recall. Micro-precision measures the precision of the aggregated contributions of all classes, and micro-recall measures the recall of the aggregated contributions of all classes.

- Micro_precision = $TP_{sum}/(TP_{sum} + FP_{sum})$
- Micro_recall = $TP_{sum}/(TP_{sum} + FN_{sum})$
- Micro F-score = $2 \times$ (micro_precision $\times$ micro_recall)/(micro_precision + micro_recall)
- Sensitivity (recall) = $TP_{sum}/(TP_{sum} + FN_{sum})$
- Specificity = $TN_{sum}/(TN_{sum} + FP_{sum})$

### 3.2.1. Experimental Results

The summary of the results is shown in Table 3. The F-score of each experiment is reported based on 10 different random seeds, along with average sensitivity and specificity over the 10 random seeds per experiment. In our experiments, the (average, max) F-scores were (0.54, 0.58) for the raw WSI with no segmentation masks, which improved to a high of (0.60, 0.62) for the raw WSI plus the epidermis mask and the dermal melanoma mask (i.e., the cancerous nests in the dermis). The addition of the dermal melanoma mask was important as it gave a significant gain over just providing dermal nests. Note that we started with a rather low F-score for the raw WSI and fixed those parameters to achieve stability, so it is possible that even higher values [27] can be achieved by starting with a different set of parameters for the WSI run. However, we favored stability, and the (0.54, 0.58) scores were stable, in that they could be achieved repeatably.

**Table 3.** Experimental results of WSI diagnosis along with segmentation masks.

| Experiments | F-Score * | | | | Sensitivity ** | Specificity ** |
|---|---|---|---|---|---|---|
| | Average | Min | Max | Median | | |
| **WSI + EPN + DMN-M** | 0.60 | 0.58 | 0.63 | 0.59 | 0.60 | 0.87 |
| WSI + EPN + DMN | 0.57 | 0.54 | 0.61 | 0.56 | 0.57 | 0.85 |
| WSI + EPN + DMN-M + DMN-N | 0.56 | 0.53 | 0.60 | 0.55 | 0.56 | 0.85 |
| WSI + EP + DE + EPN + DMN | 0.55 | 0.53 | 0.59 | 0.54 | 0.55 | 0.85 |
| WSI | 0.54 | 0.53 | 0.58 | 0.54 | 0.54 | 0.85 |
| WSI + EPN | 0.54 | 0.52 | 0.58 | 0.53 | 0.54 | 0.85 |
| WSI + DMN | 0.54 | 0.51 | 0.56 | 0.54 | 0.54 | 0.85 |
| WSI + DMN-M + DMN-N | 0.54 | 0.52 | 0.55 | 0.54 | 0.54 | 0.86 |
| WSI + DMN-M | 0.52 | 0.50 | 0.55 | 0.51 | 0.52 | 0.84 |

* F-score is reported for 10 random seeds; ** sensitivity and specificity are average scores over 10 random seeds per experiment.

### 3.2.2. Comparison of Confusion Matrices

Table 4 shows a comparison of two experiments' confusion matrices. Table 4a is an example of a multi-class confusion matrix of experiments that only contain RGB channels of the WSI in the dataset, while Table 4b shows an example of an experiment in which we had R, G, and B channels of the WSI along with two extra channels of epidermal nest (EPN) binary segmentation mask and melanoma dermal nest (DMN-M) binary segmentation mask (a total of five channels per image).

As shown in the tables, the number of true positives (TP) of classes MIS, T1a, and T1b increased in the experiment in which we included segmentation masks along with WSI. Another important finding is that the misclassified cases of MIS when we have EPN and DMN-M information are mostly on T1b. In the real world, MIS is a challenging case for pathologists to make a definite diagnosis. The comparison of confusion matrices in Table 4 and tissue experiments' results in Table 4b shows that the model is able to learn more information when segmentation masks are introduced along with the WSI, which can be an assistance to pathologists in challenging cases.

**Table 4.** Comparison of two confusion matrices. Rows are defined by expert consensus and columns are by model predictions. (**a**) An example experiment with only WSI and no segmentation mask. (**b**) An example experiment of WSI + EPN + DMN-M.

|  | MMD | MIS | T1a | T1b |  | MMD | MIS | T1a | T1b |
|---|---|---|---|---|---|---|---|---|---|
| MMD | **17** | 8 | 4 | 0 | MMD | **17** | 9 | 3 | 0 |
| MIS | 7 | **12** | 9 | 2 | MIS | 3 | **16** | 10 | 1 |
| T1a | 0 | 9 | **18** | 4 | T1a | 5 | 2 | **18** | 4 |
| T1b | 0 | 2 | 9 | **12** | T1b | 0 | 0 | 8 | **15** |
|  | (a) WSI |  |  |  |  | (b) WSI + EPN + DMN-M |  |  |  |

### 3.2.3. Single-Scale vs. Multi-Scale

In our experiments, we ran each setting of tissue experiments with single scale, two scales, and three scales. A summary of results for one example tissue experiment (WSI + EPN + DMN-M) in comparison with a raw WSI, which has the exact same parameters and scales, are summarized in Table 5. These results suggest that having segmentation masks does not improve the performance when ScATNet is trained on multiple scales, and the gain of improvement is lower when the higher resolution of WSI along with segmentation masks is used.

**Table 5.** Comparison of F-score results of raw WSI and tissue experiment (WSI + EPN + DMN-M) on single-scale experiments and multi-scale experiments.

| Scale | WSI | WSI + EPN + DMN-M |
|---|---|---|
| 7.5× | 0.54 | 0.60 |
| 12.5× | 0.56 | 0.57 |
| 7.5× & 12.5× | 0.57 | 0.56 |
| 7.5× & 10× & 12.5× | 0.57 | 0.55 |

This behavior can be explained by the specific strategy of ScATNet in patching input images on different scales. For example, images in 7.5× resolution are divided into 5 × 5 = 25 crops while 12.5× images are divided into 9 × 9 = 81 crops. In addition, the transformer unit in the ScATNet architecture includes a self-attention module that learns to pay more attention (i.e., assign higher weight) to specific patches in an image. When we introduce a WSI along with its corresponding dermal nests and epidermal nests, the model learns during the training process that these structures are important in decision making. Hence, when these tissue structures appear in a testing case's segmentation mask, the model assigns higher weights to the patches that contain those structures. If a segmentation mask of a testing case is inaccurate, especially when some important structures are over-labeled, it can negatively impact the model's decision-making and lead to a false prediction. The possibility of such an impact could be higher in higher resolutions since there will be more patches with inaccurate tissue labels; hence, higher weights on irrelevant patches. Figure 10 shows an example of a test set WSI and corresponding segmentation mask (Figure 10a) that includes dermis, epidermis, melanoma dermal nest, epidermal nest, corneum, and background. The segmentation of epidermal nests is inaccurate and over-labeled, and potentially led to a wrong prediction on resolution 12.5× (Figure 10c), since the number of patches with noise at that resolution is more than at resolution 7.5× (Figure 10b).

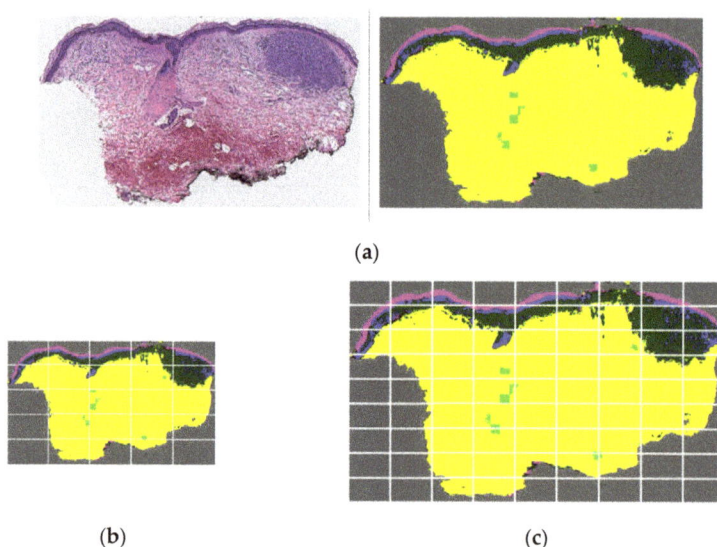

(a)

(b)          (c)

**Figure 10.** Low-resolution vs. high-resolution patching when there is an inaccurate segmentation mask in the testing case. (**a**) A WSI and corresponding segmentation mask that includes dermis, epidermis, melanoma dermal nest, epidermal nest, corneum, and background. In this example case, epidermal nests are inaccurately segmented and over-labeled. (**b**) The segmentation mask in 7.5× scale divided into 25 crops as input patches for ScATNet. (**c**) The segmentation mask in 12.5× scale divided into 81 crops as input patches for ScATNet. There is a higher number of patches with inaccurate and noisy segmentation on the 12.5× scale compared to the 7.5× scale, which possibly led to a false prediction on the 12.5× scale using ScATNet.

3.2.4. Comparison to US Pathologists

We have access to the interpretation of 187 US pathologists on the same testing set that we used in our experimental studies. Table 6 shows the comparison of the F-score, sensitivity, and specificity of pathologists' performance and our best model (WSI + EPN + DMN-M) performance. We observe that our model either outperforms the pathologists' results on the challenging classes of MIS and T1a or has a comparable performance. This finding shows the potential that providing an assistant tool can have in the time of cancer diagnosis and treatment.

**Table 6.** Comparison of class-based F-score, sensitivity, and specificity of 187 US pathologists and our best model (WSI + EPN + DMN-M) on the same testing set.

| Class | F-Score | | Sensitivity | | Specificity | |
|---|---|---|---|---|---|---|
| | Pathologists | Ours | Pathologists | Ours | Pathologists | Ours |
| MMD | 0.71 | 0.67 | 0.92 | 0.76 | 0.76 | 0.81 |
| MIS | 0.49 | 0.50 | 0.46 | 0.44 | 0.85 | 0.89 |
| T1a | 0.62 | 0.57 | 0.51 | 0.64 | 0.95 | 0.79 |
| T1b | 0.72 | 0.67 | 0.78 | 0.57 | 0.97 | 0.96 |

3.2.5. Comparison to Other Baselines

We compared our results with several other methods developed to make a diagnosis based on histopathology images.

- Weighted Feature Aggregation: Deep Feature Representations for Variable-Sized Regions of Interest was introduced by [9]. In this method, a CNN-based deep feature extraction framework builds slide-level feature representations via weighted aggre-

gation of the patch representations. In this pipeline, the patch-wise feature will be extracted by a VGG16 pre-trained CNN, then using two different approaches of either penultimate layer features (penultimate-weighted) or hypercolumn features (hypercolumn-weighted), the features are concatenated in a weighted manner. As the last step, using average pooling, a slide-level representation is generated, which is later used for training and testing the diagnosis CNN model.
- Dual-stream Multiple Instance Learning Network (DSMIL): In this work, Li et al. [10] used self-supervised contrastive learning to extract good representations from patches and using an aggregator that models the relations of the instances in a dual-stream architecture with trainable distance measurement, trained a MIL model.
- Multiple Instance Learning with Center Embeddings (ChikonMIL): [11] proposed a multiple instance learning (MIL) method that first selects the top-k patches, and then uses these patches for instance-learning and bag-representation learning. In addition, this method uses a center loss that maps embeddings of instances from the same bag to a single centroid and reduces intra-class variations for the final diagnosis.

The results of all the baseline methods and their comparison with our best model are summarized in Table 7. Our model using the epidermal nests and dermal melanoma nests is able to beat all of them.

**Table 7.** Comparison of baseline methods with our best model (WSI + EPN + DMN-M).

| Method | F-Score | Sensitivity | Specificity |
| --- | --- | --- | --- |
| penultimate-weighted [9] | 0.44 | 0.44 | 0.81 |
| hypercolumn-weighted [9] | 0.43 | 0.43 | 0.81 |
| DSMIL [10] | 0.50 | 0.50 | 0.83 |
| ChikonMIL [11] | 0.56 | 0.56 | 0.85 |
| Ours * | 0.60 | 0.60 | 0.87 |

* Our model is the tissue experiment with (WSI + EPN + DMN-M).

## 4. Discussion

The rapidly growing number of melanoma cases along with inter- and intra-observer variability of diagnosis by human pathologists is of concern in this field. On the other hand, advances in machine learning and artificial intelligence methods have presented the potential to provide assistant tools for the pathologists to analyze whole-slide images (WSIs) for diagnosis and prognosis objectives.

In recent years, interest in artificial intelligence research in various fields including healthcare has been increasing rapidly. Deep-learning methods have shown impressive and robust performance on various tasks and hold promise for providing assistant tools in healthcare research including pathology. Dermatopathology research is not an exception in benefiting from the advancement of artificial intelligence [30–32]. In the time of cancer monitoring and treatment, AI-developed tools have the potential to assist dermatopathologists especially with challenging cases. In addition, the educational and research aspects of AI-developed methods in tutoring practicing pathologists introduce new prospects for reducing the diagnostic errors in clinical care.

In recent years, deep-learning methods have proven to have excellent performance in different tasks such as image classification. However, most of the state-of-the-art methods either require a fairly large dataset to train a model or a large amount of pixel-level annotation. Both of these requirements are a challenge in dealing with medical datasets as these datasets are usually small, especially compared to general datasets such as ImageNet [21], and obtaining fine manual annotation on them is not a time or cost-effective task.

In this work, we proposed an approach that uses the segmentation masks that we previously obtained using sparse and coarse annotation [19], and adds information to WSI from a dataset of skin biopsy images. In this work, we first designed a dermal nest classifier that can classify segmented dermal nests (DMN) into two sub-categories of nevus dermal nests (DMN-N) and melanoma dermal nests (DMN-M). Using the previous and new masks, the goal was to investigate the potential of each important tissue mask in skin biopsy images to improve the results of a multi-class diagnosis model.

Our experiments showed that including certain segmentation masks along with WSIs yields a better diagnosis output with one scale. One of the foremost tissue types in skin biopsy images are nests that contain various types such as epidermal nests (EPN), nevus dermal nests (DMN-N), and melanoma dermal nest (DMN-M). We observed significant improvement when including EPN and DMN-M (which is considered the cancerous type of dermal nests) along with the corresponding WSI, compared to the experiments that do not include any segmentation masks. Further analysis showed that including the aforementioned entities improved the learning of the model on invasive melanoma and melanoma in situ, which are challenging classes on which to make a consensus decision. Improvement in the challenging classes proves the potential AI has in healthcare and pathology.

As mentioned in Section 2, each WSI in the M-path dataset has an expert-assigned ROI that carries either important diagnostic or prognostic information. However, since (1) experts were limited to one ROI per case, and (2) the diagnosis of some skin biopsies requires review of the full whole slide image, we designed our diagnosis pipeline to utilize full WSIs rather than a single ROI per case. One might wonder if multiple ROIs would be sufficient in place of the WSI, and perhaps more efficient. For example, if multiple ROIs were generated by an AI program for use in diagnosis, these may actually slow down the diagnosis process if provided to human pathologists who are used to their own way of examining slides. If multiple ROIs were identified by expert pathologists and were provided to a computer program classifier, it would not know which (if any) were more important, and thus, looking at the WSI is still the best course for the computer diagnosis for skin biopsy specimens.

Certain limitations need to be considered. The dataset that we used in this project is small and of melanocytic skin lesions, and while the cases included were carefully selected to represent the full spectrum of cases in clinical practices in the US, we are not certain how well the method would perform on the full spectrum of skin biopsies (e.g., including non-melanocytic lesions). In addition, the sparse annotations for the segmentation project were provided on ROIs on the WSI, which means there was prior knowledge of which part of the WSI contained valuable information. Not all medical datasets benefit from having ROI assigned to each case.

The unique strengths of this work include the ability to compare our results to the diagnostic interpretations given to the cases by actively practicing U.S. pathologists. This comparison showed that our model could outperform or have comparable performance to pathologists in some challenging classes. Ours is the first deep-learning model to add segmentation data of the clinically important tissue structure to the raw images to improve melanoma diagnosis. Since our segmentation model was trained on a sparse and coarse annotation set, providing a diagnosis pipeline that improves the outcome by leveraging the imperfect segmentation masks highlights the potential of AI approaches in dealing with challenges and shows a promising future for AI in healthcare.

**Author Contributions:** Conceptualization, S.N.; Funding acquisition, J.G.E. and L.G.S.; Investigation, S.N.; Methodology, S.N. and B.L.; Resources, M.M., S.K., C.J.M., O.H.C. and J.G.E.; Software, S.N. and W.W.; Supervision, J.G.E. and L.G.S.; Validation, S.N.; Writing—original draft, S.N.; Writing—review & editing, L.G.S. All authors have read and agreed to the published version of the manuscript.

**Funding:** The research reported in this study was supported by grants R01CA151306, R01CA200690, and U01CA231782 from the National Cancer Institute of the National Institutes of Health, 622600 from the Melanoma Research Alliance, and W81XWH-20-1-0797 and W81XWH-20-1-0798 from the US Department of Defense. The funders had no role in the design and conduct of the study; collection; management; analysis; and interpretation of the data, preparation, review, or approval of the manuscript, nor the decision to submit the manuscript for publication.

**Informed Consent Statement:** This work involved human subjects in its research. Approval of all ethical and experimental procedures and protocols was granted by the University of Washington under Application STUDY00008506.

**Data Availability Statement:** The dataset that has been used in this research is a private dataset. Contact J Elmore if you would like to discuss using the dataset.

**Acknowledgments:** We would like to thank Lisa Reisch, Raul Moreno, and Megan Eguchi for providing the resources we needed to organize and perform our research.

**Conflicts of Interest:** The authors declare no conflict of interest.

# References

1. Rigel, D.S.; Carucci, J.A. Malignant melanoma: Prevention, early detection, and treatment in the 21st century. *CA A Cancer J. Clin.* **2000**, *50*, 215–236. [CrossRef] [PubMed]
2. Kosary, C.L.; Altekruse, S.F.; Ruhl, J.; Lee, R.; Dickie, L. Clinical and prognostic factors for melanoma of the skin using SEER registries: Collaborative stage data collection system, version 1 and version 2. *Cancer* **2014**, *120*, 3807–3814. [CrossRef] [PubMed]
3. Guy Jr, G.P.; Thomas, C.C.; Thompson, T.; Watson, M.; Massetti, G.M.; Richardson, L.C. Vital signs: Melanoma incidence and mortality trends and projections—United States, 1982–2030. *MMWR. Morb. Mortal. Wkly. Rep.* **2015**, *64*, 591.
4. Elmore, J.G.; Barnhill, R.L.; Elder, D.E.; Longton, G.M.; Pepe, M.S.; Reisch, L.M.; Carney, P.A.; Titus, L.J.; Nelson, H.D.; Onega, T. Pathologists' diagnosis of invasive melanoma and melanocytic proliferations: Observer accuracy and reproducibility study. *Bmj* **2017**, *357*, j2813. [CrossRef] [PubMed]
5. Tsuneki, M.; Abe, M.; Kanavati, F. A Deep Learning Model for Prostate Adenocarcinoma Classification in Needle Biopsy Whole-Slide Images Using Transfer Learning. *Diagnostics* **2022**, *12*, 768. [CrossRef] [PubMed]
6. Dwivedi, C.; Nofallah, S.; Pouryahya, M.; Iyer, J.; Leidal, K.; Chung, T.; Watkins, T.; Billin, A.; Myers, R.; Abel, J. Multi stain graph fusion for multimodal integration in pathology. In Proceedings of the IEEE/CVF Conference on Computer Vision and Pattern Recognition, Los Alamitos, CA, USA, 1 July 2022; pp. 1835–1845.
7. Al-Waisy, A.; Mohammed, M.A.; Al-Fahdawi, S.; Maashi, M.; Garcia-Zapirain, B.; Abdulkareem, K.H.; Mostafa, S.; Kumar, N.M.; Le, D.N. COVID-DeepNet: Hybrid multimodal deep learning system for improving COVID-19 pneumonia detection in chest X-ray images. *Comput. Mater. Contin.* **2021**, *67*, 2409–2429. [CrossRef]
8. Afshar, P.; Mohammadi, A.; Plataniotis, K.N. Brain tumor type classification via capsule networks. In Proceedings of the 2018 25th IEEE International Conference on Image Processing (ICIP), Athens, Greece, 7–10 October 2018; IEEE: Manhattan, NY, USA, 2018; pp. 3129–3133.
9. Mercan, C.; Aygunes, B.; Aksoy, S.; Mercan, E.; Shapiro, L.G.; Weaver, D.L.; Elmore, J.G. Deep feature representations for variable-sized regions of interest in breast histopathology. *IEEE J. Biomed. Health Inform.* **2020**, *25*, 2041–2049. [CrossRef] [PubMed]
10. Li, B.; Li, Y.; Eliceiri, K.W. Dual-stream multiple instance learning network for whole slide image classification with self-supervised contrastive learning. In Proceedings of the IEEE/CVF Conference on Computer Vision and Pattern Recognition, Nashville, TN, USA, 20–25 June 2021; pp. 14318–14328.
11. Chikontwe, P.; Kim, M.; Nam, S.J.; Go, H.; Park, S.H. Multiple instance learning with center embeddings for histopathology classification. In Proceedings of the International Conference on Medical Image Computing and Computer-Assisted Intervention, Strasbourg, France, 27 September–1 October 2020; Springer: Berlin/Heidelberg, Germany, 2020; pp. 519–528.
12. Xu, H.; Lu, C.; Berendt, R.; Jha, N.; Mandal, M. Automated analysis and classification of melanocytic tumor on skin whole slide images. *Comput. Med. Imaging Graph.* **2018**, *66*, 124–134. [CrossRef] [PubMed]
13. Mercan, E.; Mehta, S.; Bartlett, J.; Shapiro, L.G.; Weaver, D.L.; Elmore, J.G. Assessment of machine learning of breast pathology structures for automated differentiation of breast cancer and high-risk proliferative lesions. *JAMA Netw. Open* **2019**, *2*, e198777. [CrossRef] [PubMed]
14. Ni, H.; Liu, H.; Wang, K.; Wang, X.; Zhou, X.; Qian, Y. WSI-Net: Branch-Based and Hierarchy-Aware Network for Segmentation and Classification of Breast Histopathological Whole-Slide Images; Springer: Berlin/Heidelberg, Germany, 2019; pp. 36–44.
15. Mercan, E.; Mehta, S.; Bartlett, J.; Weaver, D.L.; Elmore, J.G.; Shapiro, L.G. Automated Diagnosis of Breast Cancer and Pre-Invasive Lesions on Digital Whole Slide Images. In Proceedings of the 7th International Conference on Pattern Recognition Applications and Methods, Madeira, Portugal, 16–18 January 2018. [CrossRef]
16. Mercan, E.; Aksoy, S.; Shapiro, L.G.; Weaver, D.L.; Brunyé, T.T.; Elmore, J.G. Localization of Diagnostically Relevant Regions of Interest in Whole Slide Images: A Comparative Study. *J. Digit. Imaging* **2016**, *29*, 496–506. [CrossRef] [PubMed]
17. Piepkorn, M.W.; Barnhill, R.L.; Elder, D.E.; Knezevich, S.R.; Carney, P.A.; Reisch, L.M.; Elmore, J.G. The MPATH-Dx reporting schema for melanocytic proliferations and melanoma. *J. Am. Acad. Dermatol.* **2014**, *70*, 131–141. [CrossRef] [PubMed]
18. Carney, P.A.; Reisch, L.M.; Piepkorn, M.W.; Barnhill, R.L.; Elder, D.E.; Knezevich, S.; Geller, B.M.; Longton, G.; Elmore, J.G. Achieving consensus for the histopathologic diagnosis of melanocytic lesions: Use of the modified Delphi method. *J. Cutan. Pathol.* **2016**, *43*, 830–837. [CrossRef] [PubMed]

19. Nofallah, S.; Mokhtari, M.; Wu, W.; Mehta, S.; Knezevich, S.; May, C.J.; Chang, O.H.; Lee, A.C.; Elmore, J.G.; Shapiro, L.G. Segmenting Skin Biopsy Images with Coarse and Sparse Annotations using U-Net. *J. Digit. Imaging* **2022**, 1–12. [CrossRef] [PubMed]
20. Marcel, S.; Rodriguez, Y. Torchvision the machine-vision package of torch. In Proceedings of the 18th ACM International Conference on Multimedia, Firenze, Italy, 25–29 October 2010; pp. 1485–1488.
21. Deng, J.; Dong, W.; Socher, R.; Li, L.-J.; Li, K.; Fei-Fei, L. Imagenet: A large-scale hierarchical image database. In Proceedings of the 2009 IEEE Conference on Computer Vision and Pattern Recognition, Miami, Florida, USA, 20–25 June 2009; IEEE: Manhattan, NY, USA, 2009; pp. 248–255.
22. Huang, G.; Liu, Z.; Van Der Maaten, L.; Weinberger, K.Q. Densely connected convolutional networks. In Proceedings of the IEEE Conference on Computer Vision and Pattern Recognition, Honolulu, HI, USA, 21–26 July 2017; pp. 4700–4708.
23. Zhang, X.; Zhou, X.; Lin, M.; Sun, J. Shufflenet: An extremely efficient convolutional neural network for mobile devices. In Proceedings of the IEEE Conference on Computer Vision and Pattern Recognition, Salt Lake City, UT, USA, 18–23 June 2018; pp. 6848–6856.
24. He, K.; Zhang, X.; Ren, S.; Sun, J. Deep residual learning for image recognition. In Proceedings of the IEEE Conference on Computer Vision and Pattern Recognition, Las Vegas, NV, USA, 27–30 June 2016; pp. 770–778.
25. De Boer, P.-T.; Kroese, D.P.; Mannor, S.; Rubinstein, R.Y. A tutorial on the cross-entropy method. *Ann. Oper. Res.* **2005**, *134*, 19–67. [CrossRef]
26. Kingma, D.P.; Ba, J. Adam: A method for stochastic optimization. *arXiv* **2014**, arXiv:1412.6980.
27. Wu, W.; Mehta, S.; Nofallah, S.; Knezevich, S.; May, C.J.; Chang, O.H.; Elmore, J.G.; Shapiro, L.G. Scale-Aware Transformers for Diagnosing Melanocytic Lesions. *IEEE Access* **2021**, *9*, 163526–163541. [CrossRef] [PubMed]
28. Sandler, M.; Howard, A.; Zhu, M.; Zhmoginov, A.; Chen, L.-C. Mobilenetv2: Inverted residuals and linear bottlenecks. In Proceedings of the IEEE Conference on Computer Vision and Pattern Recognition, Salt Lake City, UT, USA, 18–23 June 2018; pp. 4510–4520.
29. Chen, H.; Lundberg, S.; Lee, S.-I. Checkpoint ensembles: Ensemble methods from a single training process. *arXiv* **2017**, arXiv:1710.03282.
30. Chen, S.B.; Novoa, R.A. Artificial intelligence for dermatopathology: Current trends and the road ahead. In *Seminars in Diagnostic Pathology*; Elsevier: Amsterdam, The Netherlands, 2022.
31. Wells, A.; Patel, S.; Lee, J.B.; Motaparthi, K. Artificial intelligence in dermatopathology: Diagnosis, education, and research. *J. Cutan. Pathol.* **2021**, *48*, 1061–1068. [CrossRef] [PubMed]
32. Cazzato, G.; Colagrande, A.; Cimmino, A.; Arezzo, F.; Loizzi, V.; Caporusso, C.; Marangio, M.; Foti, C.; Romita, P.; Lospalluti, L. Artificial intelligence in dermatopathology: New insights and perspectives. *Dermatopathology* **2021**, *8*, 418–425. [CrossRef] [PubMed]

Article

# Nodular and Micronodular Basal Cell Carcinoma Subtypes Are Different Tumors Based on Their Morphological Architecture and Their Interaction with the Surrounding Stroma

Mircea-Sebastian Șerbănescu [1,†], Raluca Maria Bungărdean [2,\*,†], Carmen Georgiu [2] and Maria Crișan [3]

[1] Department of Medical Informatics and Biostatistics, University of Medicine and Pharmacy of Craiova, 200349 Craiova, Romania; mircea_serbanescu@yahoo.com
[2] Department of Pathology, Iuliu Hațieganu University of Medicine and Pharmacy, 400012 Cluj-Napoca, Romania; carmen.georgiu@elearn.umfcluj.ro
[3] Department of Histology, Iuliu Hațieganu University of Medicine and Pharmacy, 400012 Cluj-Napoca, Romania; maria.crisan@elearn.umfcluj.ro
\* Correspondence: maria.bungardean@yahoo.com
† These authors contributed equally to this work.

**Abstract:** Basal cell carcinoma (BCC) is the most frequent cancer of the skin and comprises low-risk and high-risk subtypes. We selected a low-risk subtype, namely, nodular (N), and a high-risk subtype, namely, micronodular (MN), with the aim to identify differences between them using a classical morphometric approach through a gray-level co-occurrence matrix and histogram analysis, as well as an approach based on deep learning semantic segmentation. From whole-slide images, pathologists selected 216 N and 201 MN BCC images. The two groups were then manually segmented and compared based on four morphological areas: center of the BCC islands (tumor, T), peripheral palisading of the BCC islands (touching tumor, TT), peritumoral cleft (PC) and surrounding stroma (S). We found that the TT pattern varied the least, while the PC pattern varied the most between the two subtypes. The combination of two distinct analysis approaches yielded fresh insights into the characterization of BCC, and thus, we were able to describe two different morphological patterns for the T component of the two subtypes.

**Keywords:** basal cell carcinoma; Haralick texture features; histogram moments; semantic segmentation; peritumoral cleft

## 1. Introduction

Basal cell carcinoma (BCC) is the most frequent type of skin cancer in humans [1,2]. Histopathology is considered the "gold standard" in the diagnosis of oncological skin pathology [3–5]. The origin of BCC cells is currently believed to be the basal cells located in the interfollicular epidermis or the follicular bulges [5,6]. Although BCC histology has a wide range of morphological characteristics, constant features are the islands and nests with peripheral palisading basaloid cells with scant cytoplasm and hyperchromatic nuclei, often with stromal retraction and fibromyxoid stroma [6].

The latest version of the WHO Classification of Skin Tumors recognizes 10 different subtypes of BCC and divides them into lower- and higher-risk groups based on recurrence [6]. However, some studies showed poor inter-observer reproducibility when classifying these subtypes, emphasizing the practical challenges pathologists face in everyday practice when using the present criteria [7,8]. A study by Nedved et al. showed fair agreement (k 0.301, $p < 0.001$) in BCC subtyping by six dermatopathologists, but substantial agreement (k 0.699, $p < 0.001$) in dividing them into low- and high-risk groups [8].

Pathologists usually report BCC by subtype, and afterward, clinicians decide the patient management [8]. Thus, in the context of significant inter-observer reproducibility amongst pathologists [7,8] and frequent admixture of multiple subtypes within a single tumor [9,10], confusion may arise.

However, according to some authors, the most problematic definition is that of the micronodular subtype because the definition does not take into consideration the tangential sections of other subtypes or irregularity near the margin of large nodules, which can also mimic micronodules [11,12]. Moreover, because the previous definition of micronodules states that they should be smaller than 0.15 mm but did not offer a minimal number of those small nodules in order for the tumor to be classified as micronodular, some authors implied that the presence of a single solitary micronodule in a typical nodular subtype can warrant classification as micronodular BCC [7] or a mixed-type tumor. However, the definition of the micronodular subtype improved in the fourth edition of the WHO Classification of Skin Tumors, where alongside the required size of micronodules (less than 0.15 mm in diameter), it also states that they should make up to more than 50% of the tumor [13].

This study focused on the most common low-risk subtype, namely, nodular BCC, and a high-risk subtype, namely, micronodular BCC. Deep learning showed promising results in image comprehension, reconstruction and reasoning, and particular convolutional neural network techniques were widely used for classification and segmentation tasks across a wide range of applications [14–16], allowing for better visualization of histology images, sometimes finer than the human eye [17]; therefore, digital pathology has advantages in terms of time savings and performance [18] and can improve diagnostic efficiency and accuracy [19].

Various aspects were studied in BCC diagnosis via deep learning methods using several network architectures as follows. By using U-Net for pixel segmentation and a proprietary algorithm for classification, van Zon et al. aimed to distinguish normal tissue from BCC for margin control in Mohs surgery and obtained an area under the curve (AUC) of 90% [20]. Campanella et al. also distinguished between normal and BCC tissue using a different deep learning convolutional network architecture, namely, ResNet34, and obtained high sensitivity, correctly identifying all sections with BCC and a lower specificity of 94% with four false-positive results [21]. Using GoogLeNet Inception v3, Jiang et al. studied BCC detection from images captured using using smartphones from microscope ocular lens and attained a similar performance to those captured from slides and even from whole-slide images [22]. Using the VGG11 network architecture, Kimeswenger et al. offered an artificial neural network that can identify and classify BCC on whole-slide images by comparing the network results with the eye movements of pathologists and concluded that software can improve the diagnostic quality of the human eye [23]. They also recognized BCC with a specificity and sensitivity of 95% [23]. In a previous study, the present group of authors designed a deep learning convolution-based software using transfer learning from three general-purpose image classification networks: AlexNet, GoogLeNet and ResNet-18. This software was able to classify subtypes of BCC, such as superficial, nodular (with adenoid, nodulo-cystic and keratotic variants), pigmented, with adnexal differentiation, micronodular and infiltrating [24].

To our knowledge, there are no studies in the literature that compared nodular and micronodular subtypes of BCC using deep learning techniques.

The two subtypes can be characterized using histological aspects, such as the tumor stroma, stromal retraction, peripheral palisading cells and tumor island without palisading cells. Therefore, in the following paragraphs, we consider the current literature on these aspects.

*1.1. Tumor Stroma*

In the process of tumorigenesis, not only cancer cells play an essential role, but also the tumor microenvironment [25], thus creating a habitat that protects the tumor from the immune system [26].

The vast majority of BCC have a fibro-myxoid stroma [6], which is composed of glycosaminoglycan-based ground substance with a complex network of collagen, elastin and fibronectin [27], along with inflammatory cells and fibroblasts that interact with tumor cells via growth factors or extracellular matrix proteins secretion, thus influencing tumor growth and progression, as well as angiogenesis or metastasis [28–30]. In the inflammatory infiltrate of BCC, stroma lymphocytes are dominant, having both a pro- and an anti-tumoral effect, though the anti-tumoral effect prevails, where some studies showed an increase in IL-4 and IL-10 Th2 cytokines in BCC stroma involved in tumor proliferation [31,32]. Fibroblasts present in the stroma have a particular phenotype and markers [33], thus participating in the promotion of tumor growth [34] and progression [33,35] through the production of cytokines and extracellular matrix components [34]; the presence of these fibroblasts was demonstrated in both the tumor and peritumoral stroma of BCC [36].

Nonetheless, when the high-risk and low-risk subtypes were compared, changes in the stroma component were observed. Immunoreactivity to beta-catenin, which is a protein involved in the expression of membrane type-matrix 1 metalloproteinase (MT1-MMP) [37,38], is increased at the invasion front of the micronodular versus nodular subtype [39]. In terms of the amount of inflammatory infiltrate, high-risk subtypes were found to have a more abundant infiltrate [40]. Furthermore, Th1 and Th2 are more abundant in high-risk subtypes [41].

Although the functional role of the peritumoral stroma is not clearly elucidated in BCC, it was observed that there are qualitative and quantitative differences between subtypes [28,42]. In a comparison between micronodular and nodular subtypes, a difference in the presence of actin was found. Actin was present in most cases of the micronodular subtype and was absent in the nodular subtype [43], which could explain the aggressiveness of the invasion of the micronodular subtype compared with the nodular one since the microfilaments responsible for cell motility are mainly composed of actin [44]. In terms of the histological appearance of the stroma, high-risk subtypes show more intense hyalinization, while a more fibrous stroma is associated with low-risk subtypes of BCC [45,46]. In the micronodular subtype, some researchers report a loss of stromal response [47], while others show the presence of a fibromyxoid stroma [40]. Therefore, there are some different opinions in the literature on the micronodular stroma subtype, which we aimed to study using different methods than those studied so far, namely, by using artificial intelligence.

*1.2. Tumor Island (Including Peripherally Palisaded Basaloid Cells)*

According to an X-chromosome inactivation study, BCC is a monoclonal neoplastic development of basaloid epithelial cells embedded in a polyclonal connective tissue stroma [48]. As previously mentioned, BCCs originate in the basal cells of the interfollicular epidermis or follicular bulges [5,6], and therefore, will have properties specific to this origin, such as cell adhesion specific to epithelial tissues. Although matrix metalloproteinases (MMPs) are involved in modulating the tumor microenvironment, they are also engaged in activating cell adhesion molecules [49], one of which is E-cadherin [50,51], which is essential in the cell-to-cell adhesion of epithelial tissues. Moreover, together with beta-catenin, it creates a protein complex that is involved in the mesenchymal–epithelial transition, and thus, the two are directly involved in tumor progression [52]. The presence of beta-catenin, especially in the membrane of tumor cells of the micronodular subtype of BCC, suggests another mechanism involved in this subtype [53].

Although there are common characteristics of all BCC subtypes, such as originating from the same cell type, these subtypes have different histological morphologies and biological behaviors [54,55]. Low-risk BCC types have a slow and indolent growth pattern with high bcl-2 protein labeling, while those with an aggressive subtype, either mixed or pure, display heterogeneous bcl-2 labeling [56].

Given the differences in bcl-2 protein expression, beta-catenin and MMP-1 expression in tumor islands between the nodular and micronodular subtypes, we believe that an evaluation via deep learning methods using transfer learning could provide additional information that is not visible to the human eye or available using immunohistochemical staining.

*1.3. Peritumoral Cleft*

The presence of peritumoral clefts or retraction spaces at the periphery of BCC tumor islands is frequent and can be a diagnostic clue when present [6,57]. The exact mechanism by which these peritumoral clefts form remains unknown; however, various hypotheses were proposed. Although in the past, it was stipulated that these retractions are actually a processing artifact due to fixation and dehydration [57], this was refuted by the studies of several authors that demonstrated the involvement of the tumor microenvironment. Levin et al. and Ghita et al. demonstrated the presence of in vivo peritumoral clefts using reflectance confocal microscopy. Ghita et al. observed dark spaces that surrounded tumor islets [58,59]. These findings were corroborated by Ulrich et al.'s research, which went even further to state that in the peritumoral clefts, there are mucin deposits [60]. Another study concluded that the origin of these spaces comes from the extracellular matrix degradation that occurs during tumor growth [61].

Another theory is that peritumoral retraction is caused by epithelial membrane disintegration. Some studies demonstrated the lack of laminin-5 in the area surrounding tumor nests and suggested an improper structure or an absence of the hemidesmosome-anchoring filament complex in BCC, which leads to cleavage of the basal membrane [62,63]. Breakdown of the basal membrane was also demonstrated using staining for Ep-CAM and cytokeratins by Rios-Martin et al. [57]. However, not all authors agree with this result, with some suggesting that laminin does not play a substantial part is cleft formation [64].

More recent studies reflected on the effects of MMPs, such as MMP-2 and MMP-9, and stated that extracellular matrix remodeling plays a significant part alongside a decreased expression of adhesion molecules [65], although other metalloproteinases, such as stromelysin-3, were believed to be involved in tumor invasion via degradation of the matrix of the stroma [66]. Some researchers demonstrated an increased expression of MMP-2 in the stroma of high-risk compared to low-risk BCC subtypes, suggesting a role in tumor invasiveness [67]; however, when the presence of MMP-2 and MMP-9 was studied in the peritumoral space, no statistically significant correlations were observed between these and the space [65].

Peritumoral clefts are common in nodular BCC [6], but some studies stated that they are uncommon in the micronodular subtype [68–70].

Hence, there are several theories regarding why and how these peritumoral clefts exist and whether they are present or not in the micronodular BCC subtype. These differences of opinion in the literature prompted us to study these spaces using deep learning methods.

Through this study, we aimed to identify the morphological differences that occur in these two subtypes, using, on one hand, the classical morphometric approach with gray-level co-occurrence matrix features and histogram moments, and, on the other, an approach based on deep learning segmentation.

## 2. Materials and Methods

*2.1. Materials*

The dataset included consecutive cases of N (n = 46), MN (n = 12) and mixed (n = 31) subtypes of BCC that were presented at the Cluj-Napoca Clinical Municipal Hospital in Romania between 2019 and 2021.

Prior to data collection, approval from the Research Ethical Committee (approval no. 7749/21 September 2021) was obtained.

The surgically removed tissue was histologically treated, and the slides were stained with standard hematoxylin and eosin staining. All the slides were scanned using the 20× objective of the Pannoramic SCAN II, 3DHISTECH (Budapest, Hungary), resulting in whole-slide images (WSI).

Representative BCC images with 1920 × 1017 pixels in 32-bit RGB (red, green, blue) color space, representing 0.038 square microns per pixel, were extracted from WSIs by pathologists with experience in dermatopathology. From the total of 417 images, 201 images were labeled as the micronodular subtype, while the remaining 216 images were labeled as the nodular subtype. Even in mixed-subtype WSIs, the images that were selected presented one of the specified subtypes exclusively.

*2.2. Methods*

2.2.1. Dataset Preparation

Pathologists labeled images as either nodular (N) or micronodular (MN) based on the definitions from the 4th edition of WHO Classification of Skin Tumors [6]. When assessing the micronodular subtype, the invasive character in the deeper part of the tumor was also taken into consideration.

In our assertion, the BCC interaction with the surrounding tissue creates four distinct morphological components (patterns):

- Tumor (T)—representing the center of the BCC islands, where interactions with the surrounding stroma are limited (Section 1.2);
- Touching tumor (TT)—representing the peripherally palisaded part of the tumor where the interactions with the surrounding stroma are maximal (Section 1.2);
- Peritumoral cleft (PC)—representing the peritumoral clefts where the interactions with the tumor are maximal (Section 1.3);
- Stroma (S)—representing the surrounding stroma where interactions with the tumor are limited (Section 1.1).

Each image was manually segmented by a trained pathologist with regard to the four components introduced in the first section (T, TT, PC, S). Using the segmentation mask, four different images were generated that contained only the selected component's pixels. A sample of two-subtype segmentation, with the resulting segmented images, is presented in Figure 1.

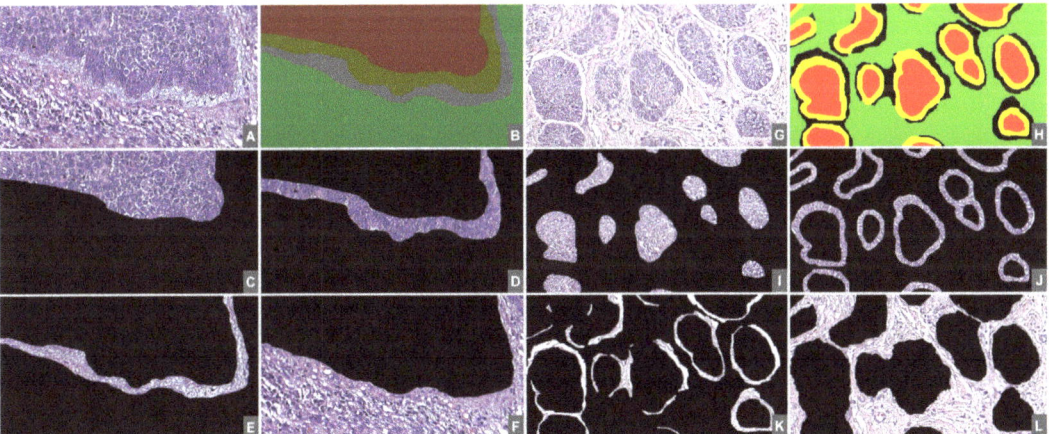

**Figure 1.** Proposed image segmentation. From (**A**–**F**)—N subtype; from (**G**–**L**)—MN subtype; (**A**,**G**)—original image; (**B**,**H**)—segmentation mask; (**C**,**I**)—T; (**D**,**J**)—TT; (**E**,**K**)—PC; (**F**,**L**)—S.

After preparing the dataset, the analysis was split into two different components: (1) a classical morphometric approach with Haralick texture features and histogram moments and (2) a semantic segmentation approach with deep learning. Both approaches aimed to quantify whether there were any textural differences between the two subtypes.

2.2.2. Morphometric Analysis

A common approach for texture analysis is to use the gray-level co-occurrence matrix (GLCM).

The GLCM counts how many times the value $i$ occurs horizontally adjacent to a pixel with the value $j$ [71]. The offset (distance between the pixel of interest and its neighbor) was set to 1 and no symmetry was considered [71].

For the GLCM computation, the four segmented images were converted to their grayscale (8-bit) version. The number of levels in GLCM was empirically set to 9. Due to the fact that the background was represented as black in the segmented images, the first line and row of the resulting GLCM were removed, thus obtaining an $8 \times 8$ GLC matrix.

The following Haralick [72,73] texture features were computed for each image of the segmented dataset: angular second moment (energy), contrast, correlation, variance, inverse difference moment (homogeneity), sum average, sum variance, sum entropy, entropy, difference variance, difference entropy, information measure of correlation I, information measure of correlation II and maximal correlation coefficient.

The resulting values were grouped by image segment and BCC subtype. Using Student's $t$-test, the (statistically) different values of each segment were compared and are presented in Table 1.

Another approach for texture analysis is using the histogram moments [74,75]. The formula for computing moments is given by

$$m_k = \sum_{i=1}^{n} \frac{(x_i - m)^k}{n} \qquad (1)$$

where $m_k$ is the computed moment value, $x_i$ is the value of pixel $i$, $m$ is the average pixel value of the image and $n$ is the number of pixels in the image.

Considering the histogram as a distribution, the first moment is the expected value (k = 1), the second moment is the variance (k = 2), and the third and fourth moments are the skewness (k = 3) and the kurtosis (k = 4), respectively. The variance, skewness, and kurtosis were computed for each image of the segmented dataset.

Similar to the analyzed Haralick texture features, the average moment values of each segment were compared using Student's $t$-test.

### 2.2.3. Semantic Segmentation Analysis

Semantic segmentation is the concept of grouping parts of an image that belong to the same object class. A semantic segmentation classifier labels all the pixels in an image, thus obtaining an image that is segmented by class. Many semantic segmentation techniques were described [76], with the best performing ones being convolution-based [16].

For our experiment, a DeepLab v3+ segmentation network [77] with weights initialized from a pre-trained ResNet-18 [78] network was used. For this, several layers from a ResNet-18 network trained on ImageNet were transferred (both architecture and weights) in the DeepLab v3+ network. Only the classification layer of the network was replaced to match the new number of output classes. The network was initialized using the MATLAB (Mathworks, Natick, MA 01760-2098, Portola Valley, CA, USA) built-in function [79].

Several of the default training parameters used for training the network were changed. Thus, the learning rate schedule (LearnRateSchedule) was set to "piecewis", the learning rate drop period (LearnRateDropPeriod) to 10, the learning rate drop factor to 3 (LearnRateDropFactor to 0.3), the momentum (Momentum) to 0.9, the initial learning rate (InitialLearnRate) to 0.001 and the L2 regularization (L2Regularization) to 0.005. All the parameters were set with the aim to accelerate the network's convergence without a premature convergence. The training was set to perform a maximum of 30 epochs, with a mini batch size of 4 and a validation patience of 10. Parameters left unchanged were initialized with their default (Mathworks-proposed) values.

Due to their stochastic characteristic, DL algorithms must be independently run several times with different input data and the evaluation result must be presented as a mean and SD. For this, the segmentation algorithm was run 100 times, where at each step, the dataset was split into subsamples of 70% training, 15% validation and 15% testing.

The network's performance was assessed in terms of accuracy, intersection over union (IoU), and F1 score. Considering a binary choice and a two-class intersection, a classified object could fall in one of four classes: true positive (TP), true negative (TN), false positive (FP) and false negative (FN).

Accuracy is defined as

$$\text{Accuracy} = (TP + TN)/(TP + TN + FP + FN) \tag{2}$$

IoU is defined as

$$\text{IoU score} = TP/(TP + FP + FN) \tag{3}$$

In order to compute the F1 score, the precision and recall are first defined as:

$$\text{Precision} = TP/(TP + FP) \tag{4}$$

$$\text{Recall} = TP/(TP + FN) \tag{5}$$

Based on Equations (4) and (5), the F1 score is defined as:

$$\text{F1 score} = (2\times \text{Precision} \times \text{Recall})/(\text{Precision} + \text{Recall}) \tag{6}$$

The average results for the semantic segmentation are presented in Table 2.

The best performing network was selected and used for further assessment. Thus, the whole dataset was tested and the resulting confusion matrix is presented in Table 3.

2.2.4. WSI Automatic Segmentation

Using PMA.start's API, which is free software offered by pathomation.com (accessed on 30 May 2022) [80], WSI images were brought into the MATLAB workspace and were segmented using the best performing network obtained in Section 2.2.3. The average time for segmenting a WSI was about 6 minutes on an Intel In(R) Silver 4216 CPU @ 2.10 GHz processor with 128 GB RAM and a Quadro RTX 6000 video adapter. A sample of two segmented WSIs is present in Figure 2.

## 3. Results

The results of the morphometric analysis assessment in terms of the Haralick texture features are presented in Table 1. The more the features were significantly different between the two subtypes, the more different their texture was.

All computed histogram moments showed statistically different values for all the components (T, TT, PC, S), except for the variance (second moment) of the S component.

Table 1. Number of Haralick texture features with statistically different averages between subtypes.

| Segment Component | Number of Statistically Different Features [1] |
|---|---|
| T | 4 |
| TT | 2 |
| PC | 12 |
| S | 5 |

[1] The theoretical maximum was 14, representing all the computed texture features.

The results of the semantic segmentation assessment are presented in Table 2. As seen in Table 2, the best accuracy score was for the S-MN component, which also had the best IoU score with 0.92, while the best F1 score was for PC-N. The lowest performance regarding accuracy was for the T-N component, regarding IoU for TT-N, and regarding the F1 score for PC-MN.

Table 2 refers to the average performance of 100 network runs, while Table 3 refers to the best performing network applied to the whole dataset. The same network was used for the WSI segmentation, with an example shown in Figure 2.

Looking at the confusion matrix in Table 3, we note that the highest confusion rate for the network was between the classes T-N and TT-N, and also for the classes S-N and PC-N, while the lowest confusion was for the S-MN class.

When comparing the patterns of the N and MN subtypes, we discovered that the PCs were quite different (12/14 Haralick texture features), while the TTs were rather similar (2/14 Haralick texture features). However, all the computed histogram moments showed statistically different values for the two subtypes on both the PC and TT components.

The WSI image with a zoomed-in detail focusing on a mixed zone containing both nodular and micronodular subtypes is presented in Figure 2.

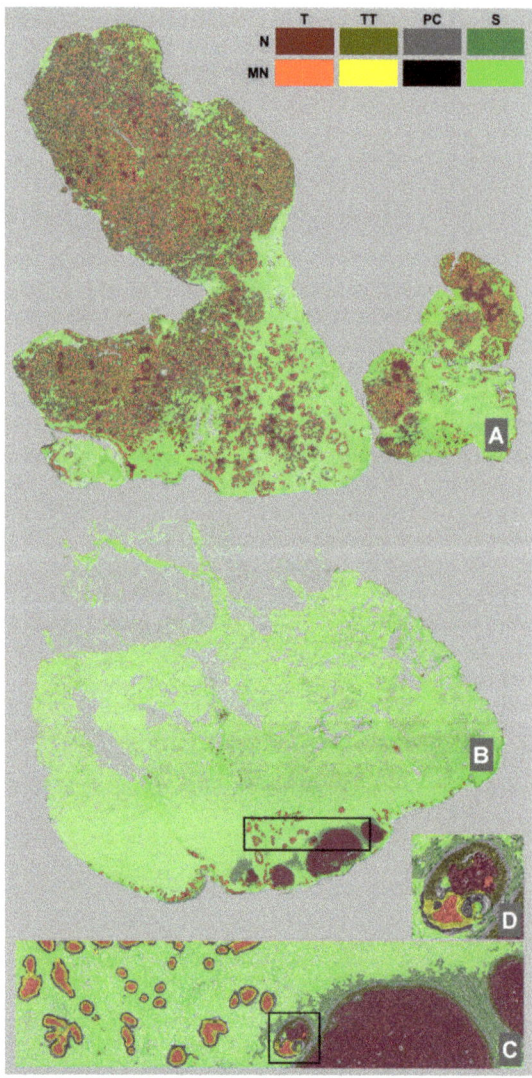

**Figure 2.** WSI segmentation using the best performing network. (**A**)—WSI with MN subtype, (**B**)—WSI with both N and MN subtypes, (**C**)—detail of the selection from (**B**,**D**)—detail of the selection from (**C**). Color labels for the segmented objects are available in the top-right corner.

**Table 2.** Semantic segmentation performance.

| Segment Component | Accuracy | IoU | F1 Score |
|---|---|---|---|
| T-N | 0.75 | 0.70 | 0.56 |
| TT-N | 0.79 | 0.47 | 0.63 |
| PC-N | 0.76 | 0.61 | 0.76 |
| S-N | 0.85 | 0.75 | 0.66 |
| T-MN | 0.88 | 0.81 | 0.64 |
| TT-MN | 0.83 | 0.34 | 0.39 |
| PC-MN | 0.86 | 0.59 | 0.54 |
| S-MN | 0.94 | 0.92 | 0.69 |
| AVERAGE | 0.83 | 0.65 | 0.61 |

**Table 3.** Normalized confusion matrix of the best performing semantic segmentation network on the whole dataset.

| | | T-N | TT-N | PC-N | S-N | T-MN | TT-MN | PC-MN | S-MN |
|---|---|---|---|---|---|---|---|---|---|
| | T-N | 0.75 | 0.12 | 0.01 | 0.00 | 0.10 | 0.00 | 0.00 | 0.00 |
| | TT-N | 0.09 | 0.79 | 0.08 | 0.00 | 0.00 | 0.03 | 0.00 | 0.00 |
| | PC-N | 0.01 | 0.10 | 0.76 | 0.10 | 0.00 | 0.00 | 0.03 | 0.00 |
| Target | S-N | 0.00 | 0.00 | 0.12 | 0.85 | 0.00 | 0.00 | 0.01 | 0.01 |
| Classes | T-MN | 0.04 | 0.00 | 0.00 | 0.00 | 0.88 | 0.05 | 0.01 | 0.00 |
| | TT-MN | 0.00 | 0.01 | 0.00 | 0.00 | 0.06 | 0.83 | 0.09 | 0.00 |
| | PC-MN | 0.00 | 0.00 | 0.01 | 0.00 | 0.00 | 0.06 | 0.86 | 0.07 |
| | S-MN | 0.00 | 0.00 | 0.00 | 0.00 | 0.00 | 0.00 | 0.05 | 0.94 |
| | | | | | Predicted Classes | | | | |

## 4. Discussion

*4.1. Results Analysis—General Remarks*

After running the experiment, we ended up with two types of measurements. The first type of measurement fell into the "descriptive concept" category, as it showed how many of the Haralick texture features were different between the two BBC subtypes and the four defined classes (Table 1). The second type of measurement fell into the "inferential concept" category, as the resulting segmentation networks decided which pixel fell into which class based on the information learned in the training phase. The aim of training a segmentation network that was capable of segmenting four different components of two BCC subtypes was not to obtain an accurate segmentation (though an average accuracy of 83% is good), but to assess the inter-class performances as markers for similitude between patterns.

The classical morphometric analysis produced a lot of information. The numbers of Haralick texture features that differed for T and TT were 4/14 and 2/14, respectively. This showed a high similitude between the classes, and the fact that TT had the lowest value could indicate that the palisading had a similar function/mechanism. Twelve out of the fourteen Haralick texture features had statistically different values on the PC classes of the two subtypes. The value was more than double those found for T and TT. This could indicate that the possible difference between the output of the two malignancies could have its origin in the cleft formation. Last but not least, S had five significant different Haralick texture features (5/14). This fell in line with our expectation, as the normal tissue that is far enough from the tumor is actually similar (the same) between the subtypes, as any kind of signaling is unlikely.

The semantic segmentation analysis produced a lot more information that was partly in line with the morphometric analysis.

The first observation of the performance assessments (Table 2) showed that MN outperformed N in the matter of accuracy and IoU and had opposite results for the F1 score. This could be explained in part by a lower in-class variation of the MN subtype and a larger pixel representation for the N one.

The T component has a similar behavior for accuracy and IoU, with values above 0.7 for N and above 0.8 for MN (Table 2). This would translate to relatively high inter-class differentiation. From the confusion matrix (Table 3), we can observe that it was more likely that T was mistakenly classified as TT than that the two subtypes were misclassified with one another: (T-N vs. TT-N = 0.12) vs. (T-N vs. T-MN = 0.10) and (T-MN vs. TT-MN = 0.05) vs. (T-MN vs. T-N = 0.04).

The TT component had better accuracy in both subtypes than T but showed a lower performance in the matter of IoU (Table 2). Corroborating the information with the data from the confusion matrix (Table 3), it stands out that the TT is being misclassified as T and PC, and the confusion between the two BBC subtypes (TT-M and TT-MN) was relatively low. Nevertheless, in the matter of IoU, TT fell under T, in agreement with the classical morphological analysis (Table 1).

On one hand, the PC component had a similar behavior with the TT in regard to confusing nearby patterns in both subtypes; thus misclassifications were made with PC and S. On the other hand, inter-subtype confusion was more present, e.g., PC-N was misclassified as PC-NM 3% of the time while PC-MN was misclassified as PC-N 1% of the time (Table 3). The performance values, though smaller, were comparable with the ones from the TT, which was in opposition with the findings on the classic morphometric approach where the differences were large, i.e., 14 vs. 5 statistically different Haralick texture features.

### 4.2. Results Analysis of Tumor Stromas

The S component had the best performance for both the accuracy and IoU metrics (Table 2). Following Table 3, we observed that the common misclassification on both subtypes was with PC. For some reason, the classifier rarely mistook the S subtype; this was in opposition to classical morphometric assessment. When assessing the number of Haralick texture features with statistically different averages between the two subtypes, we found 5 out of 14 distinctive features, while the only similar moment (the variance) was on the S component, meaning that in our data set, the stromas were relatively similar between the two subtypes. However, the literature states that an intensely hyalinized stroma is associated with high-risk BCC and a fibrous stroma with low-risk BCC [45,46]. In our analysis, the distance of the surrounding stroma to the tumor was not taken in consideration; thus, normal tissue probably made up most of the analyzed area, resulting in a similar pattern [45,46]. In our research, in the analyzed images, we did not differently label the non-tumoral stroma from the tumor stroma; therefore, the software analyzed everything surrounding the tumor in the image. Given this, we do not consider it appropriate that our results should be considered for any literature comparison.

In the WSI analysis, the stromal inflammatory infiltrate between the N and MN subtype were different: we found scattered inflammatory infiltrate in the stroma closely surrounding the MN subtype, while for the N subtype, the infiltrate was abundant, but it was not as close to the tumor island as the one surrounding the MN islands. This is consistent with other studies in literature, such as the one done by Kaur et al., where they described a loss of inflammation in micronodular growth pattern (r = 0.2/0.5, $p \leq 0.001$) and the mean inflammatory infiltrate was lower in high-risk groups but with more abundant plasma cell and lymphoid follicle formation when compared with the low-risk group [47]. On the other hand, Dunham et al. studied the immune response in various BCC subtypes and observed a dense peritumoral inflammatory infiltrate in the majority of the high-risk subtypes (including micronodular) and a mild one in the low-risk ones [40]. In regard to the type of inflammatory response, Lefrançois et al. demonstrated a difference in the type of inflammatory cells depending on the risk group, where a macrophage-rich inflammatory infiltrate was more representative of the high-risk group and a predominantly lymphocytic infiltrate was more representative of the low-risk group [41].

*4.3. Results Analysis of Tumor Islands (Including Peripheral Palisaded Basaloid Cells)—T and TT*

Looking at Figure 2C, we can see the network produced a good performance when segmenting the image and that it correctly identified the two different BCC subtypes that were present on the same WSI. This led us to the idea that pathologists should also be able to find textural differences between the tumors and, in particular, within the T component. To support our theory, we selected 100 × 100-pixel patches from all the images in the dataset where the network uniformly segmented the area with only the correct label. A random sample of the resulting patches is presented in Figure 3.

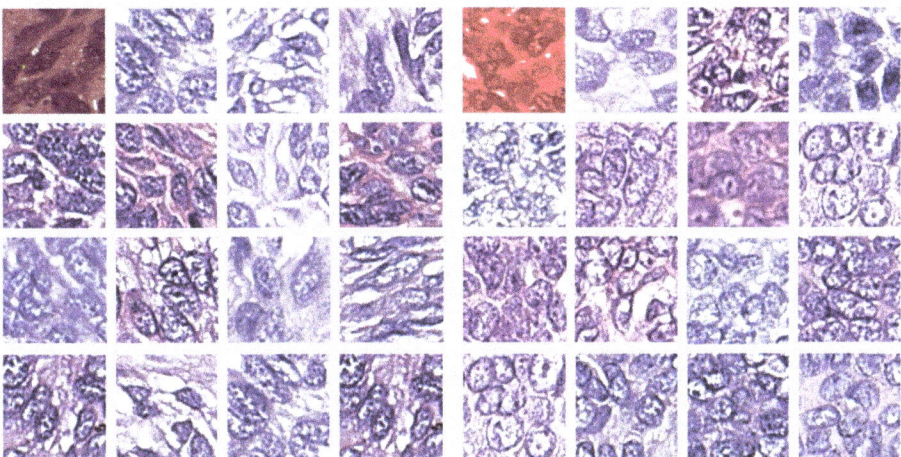

**Figure 3.** Randomly selected crops from the T component dataset, where the network uniformly segmented the area with only the correct label. The left group represents the N subtype and the right group represents the MN subtype. The first image of each group with overlaid labels represents samples from the nodule in Figure 2D.

Looking at the pictures in Figure 3, pattern differences between the two groups of images can be observed. In the left group (representing cells from the tumor island of the N type), the cells were more elongated and the intercellular matrix was better represented, i.e., the cells were more separated from each other. The right group, representing cells from the tumor island of the MN type, had more round or polygonal cells and the intercellular matrix appeared to be sparse. It was previously noted that in other malignancies, different intercellular differences within different patterns of the same tumor were present [81,82]. Furthermore, the elongated cells from the left group appeared to be oriented in one direction and were positioned one after another, while those from the right group had no clear orientation. These observations are important given that the images were from outside the TT zone, and thus, the influence of the surrounding stroma was improbable.

Another interesting observation can be made regarding Figure 2C,D, where a single BCC nodule was highlighted from a mixed tumor containing both N and MN subtypes. According to the definition of nodule size (an MN nodule is required to be smaller than 0.15 mm), the pathologists labeled the nodule as being part of the N subtype, but the software labeled the same nodule as part MN and part N. Without the information provided by the segmentation network, this nodule would only have been labeled as N. Going further into the details from Image 2D, we note that the network correctly predicted the TT, TS and S surrounding the islands of different types within the same nodule.

In addition to these morphological distinctions, authors such as Oh et al. also observed discrepancies in beta-catenin expression, which is increased in the micronodular subtype relative to the nodular subtype [39]. In the same study, they raised questions about a dysregulation mechanism of the beta-catenin E-cadherin complex in this MN BCC because of the nuclear location of the beta-catenin expression in this subtype [39]. Although the results were not statistically significant, beta-catenin was more expressed in the peripheral palisading portion of tumor islets than in the center of tumor islands [39]. In regard to MT1-MMP, Oh et al. found the same expression in both the peripheral palisading part of BCC tumor islets and in the central part of BCC tumor islands [39]. However, Son et al. observed that marked expression of MMP-1 in the tumor stroma also causes structural changes at the periphery of the tumor through a loss of peripheral palisading, which in turn leads to a poorly differentiated histological appearance that is correlated with a poor prognosis [83]; this finding has a particular significance in our study regarding the MN subtype.

*4.4. Results Analysis of Peritumoral Clefts*

Researchers have attempted to find an explanation of peritumoral clefts for years, and even in the 1990s, researchers such as Crowson, Sexton and Hendrix saw a difference in peritumoral clefts of the micronodular subtypes, stating that they are an uncommon finding in this subtype [68–70].

The texture analysis showed that the most significant differences between the two subtypes were in terms of the peritumoral cleft (Table 1). We find it important to note that the differences observed were primarily qualitative. Thus, we showed that, when present, these clefts were qualitatively different in the nodular and micronodular subtypes. Using Alcian blue stain, Ulrich et al. demonstrated the presence of mucin deposits in the PC in some subtypes of BCC, such as the nodular subtype [60]. However, in their study, they did not have cases of MN BCCs. Sahu et al. described the presence of mucin and amyloid deposits in less-aggressive nodular BCCs; however, they also did not study any MN BCCs [84]. Another hypothesis is that epithelial membrane breakdown causes peritumoral retraction, with laminin-5 perhaps playing a role [62,63]. On the other hand, other researchers disagree [64]. Newer studies, such as the one by Mentzel et al., showed that the extracellular matrix breakdown that happens during tumor growth is the source of such clefts [61].

In regard to quantity, out of the 201 MN images, 191 showed partial, focal or all-around peritumoral clefts. Although as previously stated, even though PCs are a common characteristic of BCC [6,57], they are usually uncommon in MN BCC [68,70]. A possible explanation for their abundance in our dataset was the fact that the majority of micronodular images from our cases were obtained from mixed tumors with both nodular and micronodular patterns. In our practice, we often find mixed patterns in BCC, and the most common mixed pattern we find is nodular combined with micronodular. Of course, in this situation, it is of great importance to consider tangential sectioning and irregular margins of large nodules, as researchers such as LeBoit et al. and the Australian Cancer Network also suggest [6,12]. However, the mixture of a micronodular pattern with nodular pattern is quite common, as stated in the latest edition of the WHO Classification of Skin Tumors [13].

From the confusion matrix in Table 3, we see that PC-MN was rarely confused with PC-N, but it was confused with TT-MN and S-MN. The same went for PC-N, which was confused with TT-N and S-N. This could, in part, be explained by the imperfect pathologist's annotation used for model training, where similar pixels were classified into different classes.

*4.5. Future Work*

As we demonstrated that the two variants were different cancers with regard to their morphologies, the next step is to uncover the possible epigenetic modifications that are responsible for these differences. Laser capture microdissection (LCM) is a technology that uses a laser to cut and extract portions of tissue at a microscopic level that can be later used for further analysis. LCM can be applied to almost all fields of molecular investigation, including proteomics and transcriptomics [85]. A review of epigenetic modifications in skin [86] highlighted possible uses of LCM in skin tumors and identified some specific diseases where the results are promising, such as in melanoma [87] and cutaneous T-cell lymphoma [88], but did not identify any relevant BCC study.

Furthermore, the resulting specimens from the LCM could also be transferred to a mass analyzer [89], thus obtaining mass spectra profiles for the selected cancer samples. A step forward was made in this direction and the separation of normal vs. BCC tissue was done with high accuracy with an aim toward real-time margin assessment during BCC surgery [90].

Analyzing the two tumor variants with respect to the four components (T, TT, PC and S) taken into consideration in our study by using these new approaches could produce new information that can be used to further identify the differences.

*4.6. Brief Summary*

In order to evaluate the similarities and differences between patterns of the four components (T, TT, PC, S) amongst the two subtypes of BCC (N and MN), two measurements were used: a descriptive one (Haralick texture features and histogram moments) and an inferential one (which pixels fell into which class based on the semantic segmentation).

Tumor stroma analysis revealed that both accuracy and IoU metrics performed well for S. The Haralick texture features and histogram variance indicated that the stromas in our data set were generally similar across the two subtypes. Although studies have described differences in stromas between N and MN subtypes, since we did not distinguish between the non-tumoral and tumoral stroma, normal tissue most likely made up the majority of the examined area, resulting in a similar pattern. With this being the case, we do not believe it is proper to compare the outcomes. On the other hand, the WSI analysis showed distinct stromal inflammatory infiltrate between the two subtypes, with scattered inflammatory infiltrate in the stroma intimately enclosing the MN subtype and was abundant, although it was not as close to the tumor island inflammation in the N subtype.

The results analysis of the tumor islands (including peripheral palisaded basaloid cells) showed similarities between TT components, suggesting a similar mechanism and some dissimilarities between the T components. Randomly selected crops from the T component presented morphological differences in the cell shape, orientation and intercellular matrix between N and MN BCCs. The N subtype cells were more elongated, had a similar orientation and had a more abundant intercellular matrix when compared with the rounder and unorganized MN cells. Furthermore, the semantic segmentation network was able to highlight the MN subtype within a tumor island that was labeled as N by the pathologists (Figure 2C,D).

Out of the four analyzed components, the most significant difference between the morphology of the two subtypes was represented by the PC component. We found that these clefts, when present, were fundamentally distinct in the N and MN subtypes. These differences were mostly qualitative and need further study to highlight the exact origin of those morphological differences.

## 5. Conclusions

The coupling of the standard morphometric approach with Haralick texture features and histogram moments and the semantic segmentation with deep learning analysis of BCC MN and N subtypes provided new insights into the characterization of these two subtypes. PC's pattern varied the most between the two subtypes, while the tumor cells in the palisading zone (TT) had the most similar pattern of the two groups.

We identified distinct pathological patterns of the T component in random fields of the tumor island that did not contain peripheral palisading. The N subtype had more elongated nuclei that followed the same directions and were positioned one after the other as opposed to the MN subtype, which has rounded nuclei with no visible alignment. Moreover, the intercellular matrix was more abundant in the N subtype T component as opposed to the MN subtype.

Deep learning techniques brought new insight into the morphologies of nodular and micronodular subtypes of BCC.

**Author Contributions:** R.M.B. and M.-S.Ș. contributed equally to this study regarding conceptualization, methodology and validation, and are considered the first authors. M.-S.Ș. designed and implemented the software. C.G. and M.C. contributed to data interpretation and writing. All authors have read and agreed to the published version of the manuscript.

**Funding:** This research was funded by the University of Medicine and Pharmacy of Craiova, grant number 26/24c/13.07.2021.

**Institutional Review Board Statement:** The study was conducted in accordance with the Declaration of Helsinki, and approved by the Research Ethical Committee of Cluj-Napoca Clinical Municipal Hospital (approval no. 7749/21 September 2021).

**Informed Consent Statement:** Informed consent was obtained from all subjects involved in the study and the research was approved (no. 7749/21 September 2021) by the Research Ethical Committee of the Cluj-Napoca Clinical Municipal Hospital, Romania.

**Data Availability Statement:** Data used in the present study can be shared upon reasonable request.

**Acknowledgments:** We are grateful to Cătălina Bungărdean and Diana Zamfirescu from the Cluj-Napoca Clinical Municipal Hospital for their support on image labeling.

**Conflicts of Interest:** The authors declare no conflict of interest.

# References

1. Lomas, A.; Leonardi-Bee, J.; Bath-Hextall, F. A Systematic Review of Worldwide Incidence of Nonmelanoma Skin Cancer. *Br. J. Dermatol.* **2012**, *166*, 1069–1080. [CrossRef] [PubMed]
2. Rubin, A.I.; Chen, E.H.; Ratner, D. Basal-Cell Carcinoma. *N. Engl. J. Med.* **2005**, *353*, 2262–2269. [CrossRef] [PubMed]
3. Peris, K.; Fargnoli, M.C.; Garbe, C.; Kaufmann, R.; Bastholt, L.; Seguin, N.B.; Bataille, V.; del Marmol, V.; Dummer, R.; Harwood, C.A.; et al. Diagnosis and Treatment of Basal Cell Carcinoma: European Consensusebased Interdisciplinary Guidelines. *Eur. J. Cancer* **2019**, *118*, 10–34. [CrossRef] [PubMed]
4. Trakatelli, M.; Morton, C.; Nagore, E.; Ulrich, C.; del Marmol, V.; Peris, K.; Basset-Seguin, N. Update of the European Guidelines for Basal Cell Carcinoma Management. *Eur. J. Dermatol.* **2019**, *24*, 312–329. [CrossRef]
5. Marzuka, A.G.; Book, S.E. Basal Cell Carcinoma: Pathogenesis, Epidemiology, Clinical Features, Diagnosis, Histopathology, and Management. *Yale J. Biol. Med.* **2015**, *88*, 167–179. [PubMed]
6. Elder, D.E.; Massi, D.; Scolyer, R.W.R. WHO Classification of Skin Tumours. In *Skin Tumours. Pathology and Genetics*; IARC Press: Lyon, France, 2018; Volume 11.
7. McKenzie, C.A.; Chen, A.C.; Choy, B.; Fernández-Peñas, P.; Damian, D.L.; Scolyer, R.A. Classification of High Risk Basal Cell Carcinoma Subtypes: Experience of the ONTRAC Study with Proposed Definitions and Guidelines for Pathological Reporting. *Pathology* **2016**, *48*, 395–397. [CrossRef] [PubMed]
8. Nedved, D.; Tonkovic-Capin, V.; Hunt, E.; Zaidi, N.; Kucenic, M.J.; Graves, J.J.; Fraga, G.R. Diagnostic Concordance Rates in the Subtyping of Basal Cell Carcinoma by Different Dermatopathologists. *J. Cutan. Pathol.* **2014**, *41*, 9–13. [CrossRef]
9. Cohen, P.R.; Schulze, K.E.; Nelson, B.R. Basal Cell Carcinoma with Mixed Histology: A Possible Pathogenesis for Recurrent Skin Cancer. *Derm. Surg.* **2006**, *32*, 542–551. [CrossRef]
10. Nilsson, K.D.; Neittaanmäki, N.; Zaar, O.; Angerer, T.B.; Paoli, J.; Fletcher, J.S. TOF-SIMS Imaging Reveals Tumor Heterogeneity and Inflammatory Response Markers in the Microenvironment of Basal Cell Carcinoma. *Biointerphases* **2020**, *15*, 041012. [CrossRef]
11. IARC Publications Website—Pathology and Genetics of Skin Tumours. Available online: https://publications.iarc.fr/Book-And-Report-Series/Who-Classification-Of-Tumours/Pathology-And-Genetics-Of-Skin-Tumours-2005 (accessed on 31 May 2022).
12. Clinical Practice Guide: Basal Cell Carcinoma, Squamous Cell Carcinoma (and Related Lesions): A Gu | National Library of Australia. Available online: https://catalogue.nla.gov.au/Record/4580606 (accessed on 31 May 2022).
13. Scolyer, R.A. Keratinocytic/Epidermal Tumours. In *WHO Classification of Skin Tumours*; Elder, D.E., Massi, D., Scolyer, R.A., Willemze, R., Eds.; IACR Publications: Lyon, France, 2019; Volume 11, pp. 23–63, ISBN 978-92-832-2440-2.
14. Litjens, G.; Kooi, T.; Bejnordi, B.E.; Setio, A.A.A.; Ciompi, F.; Ghafoorian, M.; van der Laak, J.A.W.M.; van Ginneken, B.; Sánchez, C.I. A Survey on Deep Learning in Medical Image Analysis. *Med. Image. Anal.* **2017**, *42*, 60–88. [CrossRef]
15. Chen, L.C.; Papandreou, G.; Kokkinos, I.; Murphy, K.; Yuille, A.L. DeepLab: Semantic Image Segmentation with Deep Convolutional Nets, Atrous Convolution, and Fully Connected CRFs. *IEEE Trans. Pattern Anal. Mach. Intell.* **2018**, *40*, 834–848. [CrossRef] [PubMed]
16. Minaee, S.; Boykov, Y.Y.; Porikli, F.; Plaza, A.J.; Kehtarnavaz, N.; Terzopoulos, D. Image Segmentation Using Deep Learning: A Survey. *IEEE Trans. Pattern Anal. Mach. Intell.* **2020**, *7*, 3523–3542. [CrossRef] [PubMed]

17. Echle, A.; Rindtorff, N.T.; Brinker, T.J.; Luedde, T.; Pearson, A.T.; Kather, J.N. Deep Learning in Cancer Pathology: A New Generation of Clinical Biomarkers. *Br. J. Cancer* **2020**, *124*, 686–696. [CrossRef] [PubMed]
18. Retamero, J.A.; Aneiros-Fernandez, J.; del Moral, R.G. Complete Digital Pathology for Routine Histopathology Diagnosis in a Multicenter Hospital Network. *Arch. Pathol. Lab. Med.* **2020**, *144*, 221–228. [CrossRef] [PubMed]
19. Steiner, D.F.; Macdonald, R.; Liu, Y.; Truszkowski, P.; Hipp, J.D.; Gammage, C.; Thng, F.; Peng, L.; Stumpe, M.C. Impact of Deep Learning Assistance on the Histopathologic Review of Lymph Nodes for Metastatic Breast Cancer. *Am. J. Surg. Pathol.* **2018**, *42*, 1636–1646. [CrossRef] [PubMed]
20. van Zon, M.C.M.; van der Waa, J.D.; Veta, M.; Krekels, G.A.M. Whole-Slide Margin Control through Deep Learning in Mohs Micrographic Surgery for Basal Cell Carcinoma. *Exp. Derm.* **2021**, *30*, 733–738. [CrossRef]
21. Campanella, G.; Hanna, M.G.; Geneslaw, L.; Miraflor, A.; Werneck Krauss Silva, V.; Busam, K.J.; Brogi, E.; Reuter, V.E.; Klimstra, D.S.; Fuchs, T.J. Clinical-Grade Computational Pathology Using Weakly Supervised Deep Learning on Whole Slide Images. *Nat. Med.* **2019**, *25*, 1301–1309. [CrossRef]
22. Jiang, Y.Q.; Xiong, J.H.; Li, H.Y.; Yang, X.H.; Yu, W.T.; Gao, M.; Zhao, X.; Ma, Y.P.; Zhang, W.; Guan, Y.F.; et al. Recognizing Basal Cell Carcinoma on Smartphone-Captured Digital Histopathology Images with a Deep Neural Network. *Br. J. Derm.* **2020**, *182*, 754–762. [CrossRef]
23. Kimeswenger, S.; Tschandl, P.; Noack, P.; Hofmarcher, M.; Rumetshofer, E.; Kindermann, H.; Silye, R.; Hochreiter, S.; Kaltenbrunner, M.; Guenova, E.; et al. Artificial Neural Networks and Pathologists Recognize Basal Cell Carcinomas Based on Different Histological Patterns. *Mod. Pathol.* **2021**, *34*, 895–903. [CrossRef]
24. Bungărdean, R.M.; Șerbănescu, M.-S.; Streba, C.T.; Crișan, M. Deep Learning with Transfer Learning in Pathology. Case Study: Classification of Basal Cell Carcinoma. *Rom. J. Morphol. Embryol.* **2021**, *62*, 1017–1028. [CrossRef]
25. Leef, G.; Thomas, S.M. Molecular Communication between Tumor-Associated Fibroblasts and Head and Neck Squamous Cell Carcinoma. *Oral Oncol.* **2013**, *49*, 381–386. [CrossRef] [PubMed]
26. Bertheim, U.; Hofer, P.Å.; Engström-Laurent, A.; Hellström, S. The Stromal Reaction in Basal Cell Carcinomas. A Prerequisite for Tumour Progression and Treatment Strategy. *Br. J. Plast. Surg.* **2004**, *57*, 429–439. [CrossRef] [PubMed]
27. Moy, R.L.; Potter, T.S.; Uitto, J. Increased Glycosaminoglycans Production in Sclerosing Basal Cell Carcinoma-Derived Fibroblasts and Stimulation of Normal Skin Fibroblast Glycosaminoglycans Production by a Cytokine-Derived from Sclerosing Basal Cell Carcinoma. *Derm. Surg.* **2000**, *26*, 1029–1036. [CrossRef]
28. Lesack, K.; Naugler, C. Morphometric Characteristics of Basal Cell Carcinoma Peritumoral Stroma Varies among Basal Cell Carcinoma Subtypes. *BMC Derm.* **2012**, *12*, 1. [CrossRef] [PubMed]
29. Reuter, J.A.; Ortiz-Urda, S.; Kretz, M.; Garcia, J.; Scholl, F.A.; Pasmooij, A.M.G.; Cassarino, D.; Chang, H.Y.; Khavari, P.A. Modeling Inducible Human Tissue Neoplasia Identifies an Extracellular Matrix Interaction Network Involved in Cancer Progression. *Cancer Cell* **2009**, *15*, 477–488. [CrossRef]
30. Parrott, J.A.; Nilsson, E.; Mosher, R.; Magrane, G.; Albertson, D.; Pinkel, D.; Gray, J.W.; Skinner, M.K. Stromal-Epithelial Interactions in the Progression of Ovarian Cancer: Influence and Source of Tumor Stromal Cells. *Mol. Cell Endocrinol.* **2001**, *175*, 29–39. [CrossRef]
31. Mantovani, A. B Cells and Macrophages in Cancer: Yin and Yang. *Nat. Med.* **2011**, *17*, 285–286. [CrossRef]
32. Kaporis, H.G.; Guttman-Yassky, E.; Lowes, M.A.; Haider, A.S.; Fuentes-Duculan, J.; Darabi, K.; Whynot-Ertelt, J.; Khatcherian, A.; Cardinale, I.; Novitskaya, I.; et al. Human Basal Cell Carcinoma Is Associated with Foxp3+ T Cells in a Th2 Dominant Microenvironment. *J. Investig. Derm.* **2007**, *127*, 2391–2398. [CrossRef]
33. Kalluri, R.; Zeisberg, M. Fibroblasts in Cancer. *Nat. Rev. Cancer* **2006**, *6*, 392–401. [CrossRef]
34. Orimo, A.; Gupta, P.B.; Sgroi, D.C.; Arenzana-Seisdedos, F.; Delaunay, T.; Naeem, R.; Carey, V.J.; Richardson, A.L.; Weinberg, R.A. Stromal Fibroblasts Present in Invasive Human Breast Carcinomas Promote Tumor Growth and Angiogenesis through Elevated SDF-1/CXCL12 Secretion. *Cell* **2005**, *121*, 335–348. [CrossRef]
35. Al-Rakan, M.A.; Colak, D.; Hendrayani, S.F.; Al-Bakheet, A.; Al-Mohanna, F.H.; Kaya, N.; Al-Malik, O.; Aboussekhra, A. Breast Stromal Fibroblasts from Histologically Normal Surgical Margins Are Pro-Carcinogenic. *J. Pathol.* **2013**, *231*, 457–465. [CrossRef] [PubMed]
36. Omland, S.H.; Wettergren, E.E.; Mourier, T.; Hansen, A.J.; Asplund, M.; Mollerup, S.; Robert, R. Cancer Associated Fibroblasts (CAFs) Are Activated in Cutaneous Basal Cell Carcinoma and in the Peritumoural Skin. *BMC Cancer* **2017**, *17*, 675. [CrossRef]
37. Takahashi, M.; Tsunoda, T.; Seiki, M.; Nakamura, Y.; Furukawa, Y. Identification of Membrane-Type Matrix Metalloproteinase-1 as a Target of the Beta-Catenin/Tcf4 Complex in Human Colorectal Cancers. *Oncogene* **2002**, *21*, 5861–5867. [CrossRef] [PubMed]
38. Liu, P.; Yang, J.; Pei, J.; Pei, D.; Wilson, M.J. Regulation of MT1-MMP Activity by β-Catenin in MDCK Non-Cancer and HT1080 Cancer Cells. *J. Cell Physiol.* **2010**, *225*, 810–821. [CrossRef] [PubMed]
39. Oh, S.T.; Kim, H.S.; Yoo, N.J.; Lee, W.S.; Cho, B.K.; Reichrath, J. Increased Immunoreactivity of Membrane Type-1 Matrix Metalloproteinase (MT1-MMP) and β-Catenin in High-Risk Basal Cell Carcinoma. *Br. J. Derm.* **2011**, *165*, 1197–1204. [CrossRef] [PubMed]
40. Duman, N.; Korkmaz, N.Ş.; Erol, Z. Host Immune Responses and Peritumoral Stromal Reactions in Different Basal Cell Carcinoma Subtypes: Histopathological Comparison of Basosquamous Carcinoma and High-Risk and Low-Risk Basal Cell Carcinoma Subtypes. *Turk. J. Med. Sci.* **2016**, *46*, 28–34. [CrossRef]

41. Lefrançois, P.; Xie, P.; Gunn, S.; Gantchev, J.; Villarreal, A.M.; Sasseville, D.; Litvinov, I.V. In Silico Analyses of the Tumor Microenvironment Highlight Tumoral Inflammation, a Th2 Cytokine Shift and a Mesenchymal Stem Cell-like Phenotype in Advanced in Basal Cell Carcinomas. *J. Cell Commun. Signal.* **2020**, *14*, 245–254. [CrossRef]
42. Tlsty, T.D.; Coussens, L.M. Tumor Stroma and Regulation of Cancer Development. *Annu. Rev. Pathol.* **2006**, *1*, 119–150. [CrossRef]
43. Christian, M.M.; Moy, R.L.; Wagner, R.F.; Yen-Moore, A. A Correlation of Alpha-Smooth Muscle Actin and Invasion in Micronodular Basal Cell Carcinoma. *Derm. Surg.* **2001**, *27*, 441–445. [CrossRef]
44. Etienne-Manneville, S. Actin and Microtubules in Cell Motility: Which One Is in Control? *Traffic* **2004**, *5*, 470–477. [CrossRef]
45. Dixon, A.Y.; Lee, S.H.; McGregor, D.H. Factors Predictive of Recurrence of Basal Cell Carcinoma. *Am. J. Derm.* **1989**, *11*, 222–232. [CrossRef] [PubMed]
46. Jacobs, G.H.; Rippey, J.J.; Altini, M. Prediction of Aggressive Behavior in Basal Cell Carcinoma. *Cancer* **1982**, *49*, 533–537. [CrossRef]
47. Kaur, P.; Mulvaney, M.; Andrew Carlson, J. Basal Cell Carcinoma Progression Correlates with Host Immune Response and Stromal Alterations: A Histologic Analysis. *Am. J. Derm.* **2006**, *28*, 293–307. [CrossRef]
48. Asplund, A.; Sivertsson, Å.; Bäckvall, H.; Ahmadian, A.; Lundeberg, J.; Ponten, F. Genetic Mosaicism in Basal Cell Carcinoma. *Exp. Derm.* **2005**, *14*, 593–600. [CrossRef] [PubMed]
49. Egeblad, M.; Werb, Z. New Functions for the Matrix Metalloproteinases in Cancer Progression. *Nat. Rev. Cancer* **2002**, *2*, 161–174. [CrossRef] [PubMed]
50. Philips, N.; Auler, S.; Hugo, R.; Gonzalez, S. Beneficial Regulation of Matrix Metalloproteinases for Skin Health. *Enzym. Res.* **2011**, *2011*, 427285. [CrossRef] [PubMed]
51. Strongin, A.Y. Mislocalization and Unconventional Functions of Cellular MMPs in Cancer. *Cancer Metastasis Rev.* **2006**, *25*, 87–98. [CrossRef] [PubMed]
52. Tian, X.; Liu, Z.; Niu, B.; Zhang, J.; Tan, T.K.; Lee, S.R.; Zhao, Y.; Harris, D.C.H.; Zheng, G. E-Cadherin/β-Catenin Complex and the Epithelial Barrier. *J. Biomed. Biotechnol.* **2011**, *2011*, 567305. [CrossRef] [PubMed]
53. El-Bahrawy, M.; El-Masry, N.; Alison, M.; Poulsom, R.; Fallowfield, M. Expression of Beta-Catenin in Basal Cell Carcinoma. *Br. J. Derm.* **2003**, *148*, 964–970. [CrossRef]
54. Wong, C.S.M.; Strange, R.C.; Lear, J.T. Basal Cell Carcinoma. *BMJ* **2003**, *327*, 794–798. [CrossRef]
55. Kim, D.P.; Kus, K.J.B.; Ruiz, E. Basal Cell Carcinoma Review. *Hematol. Oncol. Clin. North Am.* **2019**, *33*, 13–24. [CrossRef] [PubMed]
56. Ramdial, P.K.; Madaree, A.; Reddy, R.; Chetty, R. Bcl-2 Protein Expression in Aggressive and Non-Aggressive Basal Cell Carcinomas. *J. Cutan. Pathol.* **2000**, *27*, 283–291. [CrossRef] [PubMed]
57. Ríos-Martín, J.J.; Moreno-Ramírez, D.; González-Cámpora, R. What Is the Cause of Retraction Spaces Associated with Basal Cell Carcinoma? *J. Cutan. Pathol.* **2012**, *39*, 729–730. [CrossRef] [PubMed]
58. Hansen, T.; Nardone, B. Characterizing Peritumoral Clefts in Basal Cell Carcinoma with Histologic Staining and Reflectance Confocal Microscopy. *J. Am. Acad. Derm.* **2013**, *68*, AB6. [CrossRef]
59. Ghita, M.A.; Caruntu, C.; Rosca, A.E.; Kaleshi, H.; Caruntu, A.; Moraru, L.; Docea, A.O.; Zurac, S.; Boda, D.; Neagu, M.; et al. Reflectance Confocal Microscopy and Dermoscopy for in Vivo, Non-Invasive Skin Imaging of Superficial Basal Cell Carcinoma. *Oncol. Lett.* **2016**, *11*, 3019–3024. [CrossRef]
60. Ulrich, M.; Roewert-Huber, J.; González, S.; Rius-Diaz, F.; Stockfleth, E.; Kanitakis, J. Peritumoral Clefting in Basal Cell Carcinoma: Correlation of in Vivo Reflectance Confocal Microscopy and Routine Histology. *J. Cutan. Pathol.* **2011**, *38*, 190–195. [CrossRef]
61. Mentzel, J.; Anderegg, U.; Paasch, U.; Simon, J.C.; Grupp, M.; Grunewald, S. "Retraction Artefacts" in Basal Cell Carcinomas Do Not Result from Fixation but Likely Arise by Degradation of Extracellular Matrix during Tumour Growth. *J. Eur. Acad. Derm. Venereol.* **2022**, *36*, e244–e247. [CrossRef]
62. Bahadoran, P.; Perrin, C.; Aberdam, D.; Spadafora-Pisani, A.; Meneguzzi, G.; Ortonne, J.-P. Altered Expression of the Hemidesmosome-Anchoring Filament Complex Proteins in Basal Cell Carcinoma: Possible Role in the Origin of Peritumoral Lacunae. *Br. J. Dermatol.* **1997**, *136*, 35–42. [CrossRef]
63. Drewniok, C.; Wienrich, B.G.; Schön, M.; Ulrich, J.; Zen, Q.; Telen, M.J.; Hartig, R.J.; Wieland, I.; Gollnick, H.; Schön, M.P. Molecular Interactions of B-CAM (Basal-Cell Adhesion Molecule) and Laminin in Epithelial Skin Cancer. *Arch. Derm. Res.* **2004**, *296*, 59–66. [CrossRef]
64. Mostafa, W.Z.; Mahfouz, S.M.; Bosseila, M.; Sobhi, R.M.; El-Nabarawy, E. An Immunohistochemical Study of Laminin in Basal Cell Carcinoma. *J. Cutan. Pathol.* **2010**, *37*, 68–74. [CrossRef]
65. Manola, I.; Mataic, A.; Drvar, D.L.; Pezelj, I.; Dzombeta, T.R.; Kruslin, B. Peritumoral Clefting and Expression of MMP-2 and MMP-9 in Basal Cell Carcinoma of the Skin. *In Vivo* **2020**, *34*, 1271–1275. [CrossRef] [PubMed]
66. Undén, A.B.; Sandstedt, B.; Bruce, K.; Hedblad, M.A.; Ståhle-Bäckdahl, M. Stromelysin-3 MRNA Associated with Myofibroblasts Is Overexpressed in Aggressive Basal Cell Carcinoma and in Dermatofibroma but Not in Dermatofibrosarcoma. *J. Investig. Derm.* **1996**, *107*, 147–153. [CrossRef] [PubMed]
67. Poswar, F.O.; Fraga, C.A.C.; Farias, L.C.; Feltenberger, J.D.; Cruz, V.P.D.; Santos, S.H.S.; Silveira, C.M.; de Paula, A.M.B.; Guimarães, A.L.S. Immunohistochemical Analysis of TIMP-3 and MMP-9 in Actinic Keratosis, Squamous Cell Carcinoma of the Skin, and Basal Cell Carcinoma. *Pathol. Res. Pract.* **2013**, *209*, 705–709. [CrossRef]
68. Crowson, A.N.; Magro, C.M.; Kadin, M.E.; Stranc, M. Differential Expression of the Bcl-2 Oncogene in Human Basal Cell Carcinoma. *Hum. Pathol.* **1996**, *27*, 355–359. [CrossRef]

69. Sexton, M.; Jones, D.B.; Maloney, M.E. Histologic Pattern Analysis of Basal Cell Carcinoma. Study of a Series of 1039 Consecutive Neoplasms. *J. Am. Acad. Derm.* **1990**, *23*, 1118–1126. [CrossRef]
70. Hendrix, J.D.; Parlette, H.L. Micronodular Basal Cell Carcinoma. A Deceptive Histologic Subtype with Frequent Clinically Undetected Tumor Extension. *Arch. Derm.* **1996**, *132*, 295–298. [CrossRef]
71. Co-Occurrence Matrix—Wikipedia. Available online: https://en.wikipedia.org/wiki/Co-occurrence_matrix (accessed on 31 May 2022).
72. HaralickTextureFeatures—File Exchange—MATLAB Central. Available online: https://www.mathworks.com/matlabcentral/fileexchange/58769-haralicktexturefeatures (accessed on 31 May 2022).
73. Haralick, R.M.; Dinstein, I.; Shanmugam, K. Textural Features for Image Classification. *IEEE Trans. Syst. Man Cybern.* **1973**, *SMC-3*, 610–621. [CrossRef]
74. Moment (Mathematics)—Wikipedia. Available online: https://en.wikipedia.org/wiki/Moment_(mathematics) (accessed on 28 June 2022).
75. Tan, Y.Y.; Sim, K.S.; Tso, C.P. A Study on Central Moments of the Histograms from Scanning Electron Microscope Charging Images. *Scanning* **2007**, *29*, 211–218. [CrossRef]
76. Thoma, M. A Survey of Semantic Segmentation. *arXiv* **2016**, arXiv:1602.06541.
77. Chen, L.C.; Zhu, Y.; Papandreou, G.; Schroff, F.; Adam, H. Encoder-Decoder with Atrous Separable Convolution for Semantic Image Segmentation. *arXiv* **2018**, arXiv:1802.02611.
78. He, K.; Zhang, X.; Ren, S.; Sun, J. Deep Residual Learning for Image Recognition. In Proceedings of the 2016 IEEE Conference on Computer Vision and Pattern Recognition (CVPR), Las Vegas, NV, USA, 27–30 June 2016; pp. 770–778. [CrossRef]
79. Create DeepLab V3+ Convolutional Neural Network for Semantic Image Segmentation—MATLAB Deeplabv3plusLayers. Available online: https://www.mathworks.com/help/vision/ref/deeplabv3pluslayers.html (accessed on 31 May 2022).
80. PMA.Start—Pathomation. Available online: https://www.pathomation.com/pma-start/ (accessed on 31 May 2022).
81. Pleșea, I.E.; Stoiculescu, A.; Șerbănescu, M.; Alexandru, D.O.; Man, M.; Pop, O.T.; Pleșea, R.M. Correlations between Intratumoral Vascular Network and Tumoral Architecture in Prostatic Adenocarcinoma. *Rom. J. Morphol. Embryol.* **2013**, *54*, 299–308. [PubMed]
82. Pleșea, R.M.; Șerbănescu, M.S.; Alexandru, D.O.; Ciovică, V.; Stoiculescu, A.; Pop, O.T.; Simionescu, C.; Pleșea, I.E. Correlations Between Intratumoral Interstitial Fibrillary Network and Vascular Network in Gleason Patterns of Prostate Adenocarcinoma. *Curr. Health Sci. J.* **2015**, *41*, 345–355. [CrossRef] [PubMed]
83. Kyung, D.S.; Kim, T.J.; Youn, S.L.; Gyeong, S.P.; Ki, T.H.; Jin, S.L.; Chang, S.K. Comparative Analysis of Immunohistochemical Markers with Invasiveness and Histologic Differentiation in Squamous Cell Carcinoma and Basal Cell Carcinoma of the Skin. *J. Surg. Oncol.* **2008**, *97*, 615–620. [CrossRef]
84. Sahu, A.; Cordova, M.; Gill, M.; Alessi-Fox, C.; Navarrete-Dechent, C.; González, S.; Iftimia, N.; Rajadhyaksha, M.; Marghoob, A.A.; Chen, C.S.J. In Vivo Identification of Amyloid and Mucin in Basal Cell Carcinoma with Combined Reflectance Confocal Microscopy-Optical Coherence Tomography Device and Direct Histopathologic Correlation. *J. Am. Acad. Derm.* **2020**, *83*, 619–622. [CrossRef] [PubMed]
85. von Eggeling, F.; Hoffmann, F. Microdissection-An Essential Prerequisite for Spatial Cancer Omics. *Proteomics* **2020**, *20*, 2000077. [CrossRef] [PubMed]
86. Bhamidipati, T.; Sinha, M.; Sen, C.K.; Singh, K. Laser Capture Microdissection in the Spatial Analysis of Epigenetic Modifications in Skin: A Comprehensive Review. *Oxid. Med. Cell Longev.* **2022**, *2022*, 4127238. [CrossRef]
87. Sigalotti, L.; Fratta, E.; Parisi, G.; Coral, S.; Maio, M. Epigenetic Markers of Prognosis in Melanoma. *Methods Mol. Biol.* **2014**, *1102*, 481–499. [CrossRef]
88. Wu, J.; Salva, K.A.; Stutz, N.; Longley, B.J.; Spiegelman, V.S.; Wood, G.S. Quantitative Gene Analysis of Methylation and Expression (Q-GAME) in Fresh or Fixed Cells and Tissues. *Exp. Derm.* **2014**, *23*, 304–309. [CrossRef]
89. Zhang, H.; Zhao, L.; Jiang, J.; Zheng, J.; Yang, L.; Li, Y.; Zhou, J.; Liu, T.; Xu, J.; Lou, W.; et al. Multiplexed Nanomaterial-Assisted Laser Desorption/Ionization for Pan-Cancer Diagnosis and Classification. *Nat. Commun.* **2022**, *13*, 617. [CrossRef]
90. Akbarifar, F.; Jamzad, A.; Santilli, A.; Kauffman, M.; Janssen, N.; Connolly, L.; Ren, K.Y.M.; Vanderbeck, K.; Wang, A.; Mckay, D.; et al. Graph-Based Analysis of Mass Spectrometry Data for Tissue Characterization with Application in Basal Cell Carcinoma Surgery. *SPIE* **2021**, *11598*, 279–285. [CrossRef]

*Article*

# MixPatch: A New Method for Training Histopathology Image Classifiers

Youngjin Park [1], Mujin Kim [1], Murtaza Ashraf [1], Young Sin Ko [2] and Mun Yong Yi [1,*]

[1] Department of Industrial & Systems Engineering, Korea Advanced Institute of Science and Technology, Daejeon 34141, Korea; youngjpark@kaist.ac.kr (Y.P.); mujinkm@kaist.ac.kr (M.K.); murtaza@kaist.ac.kr (M.A.)
[2] Pathology Center, Seegene Medical Foundation, Seoul 04805, Korea; noteasy@mf.seegene.com
* Correspondence: munyi@kaist.ac.kr

**Abstract:** CNN-based image processing has been actively applied to histopathological analysis to detect and classify cancerous tumors automatically. However, CNN-based classifiers generally predict a label with overconfidence, which becomes a serious problem in the medical domain. The objective of this study is to propose a new training method, called MixPatch, designed to improve a CNN-based classifier by specifically addressing the prediction uncertainty problem and examine its effectiveness in improving diagnosis performance in the context of histopathological image analysis. MixPatch generates and uses a new sub-training dataset, which consists of mixed-patches and their predefined ground-truth labels, for every single mini-batch. Mixed-patches are generated using a small size of clean patches confirmed by pathologists while their ground-truth labels are defined using a proportion-based soft labeling method. Our results obtained using a large histopathological image dataset shows that the proposed method performs better and alleviates overconfidence more effectively than any other method examined in the study. More specifically, our model showed 97.06% accuracy, an increase of 1.6% to 12.18%, while achieving 0.76% of expected calibration error, a decrease of 0.6% to 6.3%, over the other models. By specifically considering the mixed-region variation characteristics of histopathology images, MixPatch augments the extant mixed image methods for medical image analysis in which prediction uncertainty is a crucial issue. The proposed method provides a new way to systematically alleviate the overconfidence problem of CNN-based classifiers and improve their prediction accuracy, contributing toward more calibrated and reliable histopathology image analysis.

**Keywords:** histopathology image analysis; deep learning; prediction uncertainty; confidence calibration

**Citation:** Park, Y.; Kim, M.; Ashraf, M.; Ko, Y.S.; Yi, M.Y. MixPatch: A New Method for Training Histopathology Image Classifiers. *Diagnostics* **2022**, *12*, 1493. https://doi.org/10.3390/diagnostics12061493

**Academic Editor:** Masayuki Tsuneki

Received: 3 May 2022
Accepted: 14 June 2022
Published: 18 June 2022

**Publisher's Note:** MDPI stays neutral with regard to jurisdictional claims in published maps and institutional affiliations.

**Copyright:** © 2022 by the authors. Licensee MDPI, Basel, Switzerland. This article is an open access article distributed under the terms and conditions of the Creative Commons Attribution (CC BY) license (https://creativecommons.org/licenses/by/4.0/).

## 1. Introduction

For the past decade, deep learning (DL) has been widely applied in computer vision tasks and achieved impressive performance, primarily due to the rapid development of convolutional neural network (CNN) techniques. The automatic diagnosis of heterogeneous diseases that can lead to loss of life is a challenging application for DL techniques. Cancer is a highly heterogeneous disease and one of the leading causes of death, ranking second in deaths per year in the world [1]. To diagnose the presence of cancer, pathologists usually examine whole-slide images (WSIs) to identify abnormal cells. The growth in the number of yearly cancer cases has led to expert pathologists working long hours, thereby increasing the chance of human errors, which has been found to be approximately 3% to 9% in anatomical pathology [2]. To alleviate this problem, DL-based frameworks for WSI analysis have been developed to assist pathologists [3–6].

DL-based WSI analysis involves the handling of large WSIs [6,7], each of which consists of many gigapixels (typically 50,000 × 50,000 pixels). Given such a large size, it is difficult to input a WSI into a CNN model due to computational constraints. Additionally, reducing the resolution of a WSI for CNN model training can negatively affect model performance because the WSI information is distorted [8]. To overcome this challenge, researchers have proposed patch-based frameworks for WSI analysis using DL [9–12]. Such frameworks commonly consist of three phases for WSI analysis: (1) splitting the target WSI into patches, (2) extracting features from these patches using a patch-level classifier, and (3) identifying abnormalities in the WSI by aggregating the extracted features of patches [13]. Prior research on patch-based analysis focused on how to design an overall framework. In particular, previous studies concentrated on how to aggregate the extracted features of patches to identify abnormalities in WSIs. However, in addition to the proper design of an overall framework, the effective training of a patch-level classifier is of critical importance because the performance of the patch-level classifier is the foundation of an overall framework.

To extract the features of patches, patch-level classifiers have been trained based on transfer learning, with little attention given to the characteristics of patches [3–5,14–17]. Additionally, to improve the performance of a CNN model as a patch-level classifier, prior studies employed image modification techniques such as data augmentation [18,19], color transformation [20,21], and stain normalization [22–24]. The goals of image modification techniques are to amplify the number of patch images, extract the morphological features, and reduce the deviations across WSI scan devices. Despite these diverse efforts, prediction uncertainty has not received much attention in patch-based analysis even though it is a serious issue, particularly in the medical domain. In this study, we propose a novel method, called MixPatch, that actively considers prediction uncertainty associated with histopathology patches.

Prediction uncertainty is largely indicated by the confidence level of the prediction output from a CNN model. A critical issue in the current baseline approach is that the confidence level is given on a binary scale of 0 or 1, thus creating overconfidence problems [25,26]. More specifically, most abnormal histopathology patches are mixed with benign regions and nonbenign regions [27]. Extracted patches are labeled by pathologists to build a training dataset for patch-level classifiers. In this process, if an extracted patch includes various class regions, the extracted patch is labeled according to the most serious diagnosis by a pathologist. However, most of the abnormal patches are mixed with benign regions and nonbenign regions to varying degrees. This *mixed-region variation* property is difficult for patch-level classifiers properly to consider. For example, if a small area of a patch is nonbenign, the prediction uncertainty of the case should be high, as most of the cell is benign. However, because of the overconfident nature of CNN, a patch-level classifier trained with a traditional method will produce a confidence value of 1 or very close to 1, even for this highly uncertain case. To alleviate this overconfidence problem, a patch classifier needs to be trained by properly incorporating the mixed-region variations in histopathology images. If prediction uncertainty information for mixed regions could be properly applied in the training process, the parameters of the CNN model would be more effectively trained, effectively enriching the extracted features of patch-based information and ultimately contributing to enhanced overall performance of the framework.

The objective of this study is to propose a new training method, called MixPatch, to improve patch-level classifiers by specifically addressing the prediction uncertainty problem and to examine its effectiveness in improving diagnosis performance in the context of histopathological image analysis. The central objective of the proposed MixPatch method is to build a new subtraining dataset that has a predefined mix of benign vs. nonbenign patches in certain ratios and the associated ground-truth labels. MixPatch is designed to explicitly consider the mixed-region variations in histopathological patch images. The dataset is generated using a small size of confirmed, clean (benign and nonbenign) histopathological patches. To define a new ground-truth label, proportion-based soft labeling [28] is used. MixPatch is a novel method applicable to the training of CNN models in the domain of digital pathology. As described in Figure 1, MixPatch prevents or limits the overconfidence problem by explicitly addressing the high level of prediction uncertainty associated with highly mixed-region cases in histopathological images.

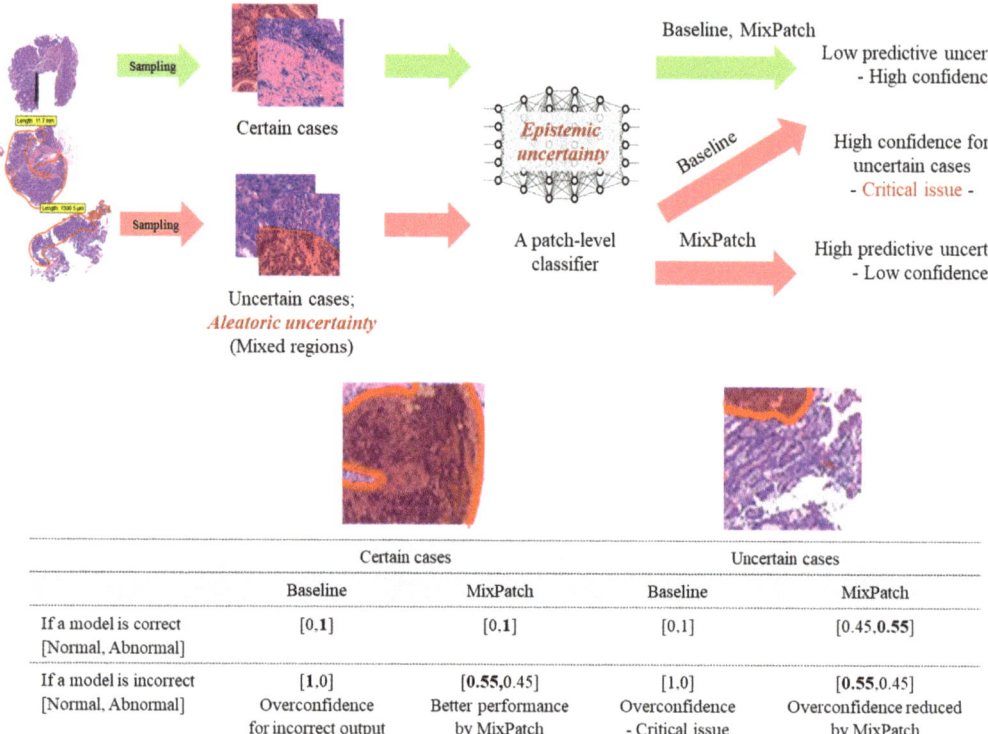

**Figure 1.** Baseline vs. MixPatch. A single WSI generates multiple patches. The process of tiling creates certain case patches and uncertain case patches. Most parts of a certain patch are covered by a single label, but those of an uncertain patch are mixed. The baseline methods are overconfident, even for uncertain patches and incorrect outputs. The proposed method, MixPatch, overcomes these problems by explicitly incorporating the mixed-region variations in histopathological images into the training process.

The major contributions of this paper are as follows:

- We propose a new method designed to train a CNN-based histopathology patch-level classifier. The method is applicable to many medical domains in which patch-based images are used.
- The proposed method estimates prediction uncertainty to varying degrees to enrich the extracted features of patch-based information and improve the overall performance of the framework for WSI analysis.
- The proposed method is tested based on histopathology stomach datasets to assess the performance improvements achieved in comparison with other state-of-the-art methods at the patch level and slide level.

## 2. Literature Review

### 2.1. Patch-Based WSI Analysis

Participation in grand challenges for digital pathology (https://grand-challenge.org/, accessed on 13 June 2022) has led to remarkable developments in automatic diagnosis. In particular, WSI classification has received extensive attention from research communities. Most researchers have relied on patch-based classification approaches due to the computational limitations of directly applying CNN models for WSI analysis. In each competition, patch-based approaches have been among the best performers.

The existing patch-based digital pathology frameworks consist of patch-level classifiers and WSI-level classifiers. A patch-level classifier is responsible for classifying each patch based on a respective class label. In contrast, the WSI-level classifier considers various information, such as the features extracted from patches, the locations of patches, and the number of patches in aggregation, to obtain a final decision with regard to the slide in question. Thus, given the complexity of this approach, the current frameworks are primarily concerned with the design of the WSI-level classifier. For example, a study focused on developing a framework that enabled CNNs to efficiently analyze WSIs by incorporating multiple instance learning was proposed [29]. Additionally, a top-performing team in the grand challenge proposed a binary classification framework in which 11 types of features were first extracted based on the available morphological and geometrical information, and then these features were used for classification with a random forest classifier [30]. Although their study relied on traditional machine learning approaches for classification modeling, recent studies have predominantly proposed frameworks using DL. Wang et al. [13] proposed a DL-based WSI multiclassification framework that first selects discriminative patches, extracts features for each class using a patch-level classifier, and then utilizes the extracted features to diagnose diseases using a multi-instance deep learning network. Dov et al. [31] proposed weakly supervised instance learning for whole-slide cytopathology images with unique slide structures. Duran-Lopez et al. [32] proposed a novel aggregated CNN model for slide-level classification using the patch-level classes obtained from a CNN. Li et al. [33] proposed a multiresolution multi-instance learning model to detect suspicious regions for fine-scale grade prediction.

The design of an overall framework is an important issue, and the tiling process (i.e., creating patches from a WSI) and patch-level classification are the fundamental building blocks of these frameworks. To implement the tiling process, the extant frameworks employed image modification methods [6,30]. The goals of such methods are to increase the amount of data using rotation, to extract morphological features using different color scales, and to reduce the variation in dyeing or scanning. Additionally, most existing studies trained patch-level classifiers by applying transfer learning, metric learning, and fine-tuning methods based on existing CNN architectures such as ResNet, VGG, and DenseNet [33–38]. These studies focused on improving the performance of patch-level classifiers in different ways, but did not pay attention to the issue of prediction uncertainty. It is important to address prediction uncertainty because a patch-level classifier is utilized as a feature extractor. Properly incorporating prediction uncertainty into the training process can substantially enrich the extracted features of patch-based information, thereby positively influencing the performance of the applied WSI analysis framework.

*2.2. Uncertainty in Deep Learning*

CNN models have displayed state-of-the-art performances in many image classification tasks [39–42]. Although CNN-based approaches have achieved superior performance in various applications over the past decade, CNN models tend to predict labels with overconfidence [43,44]. For example, CNN models often produce a high confidence probability of 91%, even for ambiguous cases and public datasets [45]. Incorrect predictions with overconfidence can be harmful. It is essential for the probability of the predicted label to reflect the corresponding likelihood of ground-truth correctness. This consideration is especially important when a CNN model is applied to a medical dataset [26].

As a remedy to this problem, two approaches have been proposed: uncertainty quantification and confidence calibration. The first approach estimates uncertainty based on a probability density over all outcomes. Bayesian probabilistic deep learning [43] and MC (Monte Carlo) dropout with ensembles [44] are two common uncertainty quantification approaches. However, such methods have not been widely adopted due to implementation challenges and long training times [46]. The second approach measures prediction uncertainty with values of confidence. The confidence level is the highest value from a probability distribution that can be extracted from the softmax layer. Methods based on the second approach can provide appropriately calibrated confidence information to limit the overconfidence issue. The second approach, the confidence-based uncertainty measurement approach (also called the confidence calibration approach), is more suitable for medical applications than is the first approach. In general, the classification of labels for medical applications are associated with the N-stage in pathology. Although the first approach separately produces a predicted label and the corresponding uncertainty, the second approach tries to produce a confidence probability for each stage and selects the predicted label with the highest confidence probability. The confidence probability for each label is helpful for computer-aided diagnosis. Additionally, the second approach is more straightforward than the first approach, and some methods that rely on the second approach, such as excessive dropout, do not use intentional random noise. Thus, robust CNN models can be established.

Noise distributions are commonly used in confidence calibration [28,47,48]. However, applying intentional random noise can cause problems for histopathological patch classification. Taking a different approach without intentional random noise, several methods utilize an additional subtraining dataset to increase variability in the training process [49]. The basic objective of this approach is to build a new subtraining dataset that consists of mixed images and their new ground-truth labels. Specifically, a new mixed image is a combination of two or more images, and the corresponding ground-truth label is defined using a label smoothing method based on the mix combination. For example, if images A and B are mixed at the same ratio, the ground-true label is based on a weight of 0.5 for both categories of A and B. Multiple methods have been proposed to mix images, including MixUp [50], CutMix [51], and RICAP [52]. MixUp combines two images by overlaying them and redefining a new ground-truth label to create a new subtraining dataset. CutMix replaces part of an image with a cropped patch from another training image and redefines a new ground truth label based on the proportions of the respective image areas. RICAP combines four images randomly cropped according to boundary positions and redefines a new ground-truth label with the same image area proportions.

The performance of these image mixing methods has been evaluated using public image datasets such as MNIST [53], CIFAR10 [54], and ImageNet [55]. In public image datasets, the main target is placed over the center of the image so that most of the main target exists during the cropping process [56]. However, these methods have the potential to cause problems when applied to histopathological images. Specifically, the cropping process can easily produce mislabeled data if nonbenign areas are all cropped from an uncertain abnormal patch. This paper proposes a novel method that produces improved performance in handling prediction uncertainty by considering the mixed-region variation in histopathological patches. The new method builds and uses an additional subtraining dataset as a patch-level classifier. The dataset consists of mixed patches, each of which is a set of mixed small images, and no cropping is required; additionally, the corresponding ground-truth labels are determined based on the mixing ratio.

## 3. Method

The primary goal of the proposed method is to address the problem of prediction uncertainty by utilizing a prearranged set of mixed patches. This method generates a new subtraining dataset consisting of randomly drawn mixed patches and their ground-truth labels and applies them to the model training process, which is further illustrated in Figure 2.

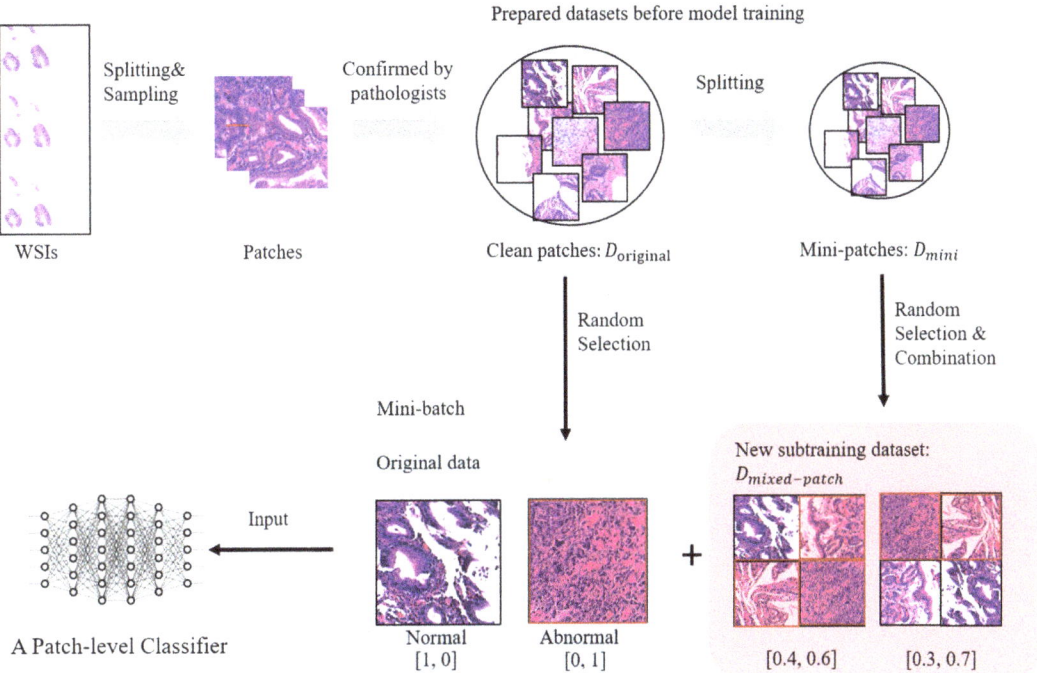

**Figure 2.** The overall process of the proposed method. In the existing methods, the patch-level classifier is trained using a CNN model and a cleaned patch dataset, $D_{original}$, which pathologists previously confirmed. The proposed method, MixPatch, additionally uses a new subtraining dataset, which consists of image $x_{mixed}$ and label $y_{mixed}$. $x_{mixed}$ is built by combining randomly selected images from the minipatch dataset. $y_{mixed}$ is defined according to the ratio of abnormal mini-patches. In the figure, a minibatch is a randomly built mix of samples from $D_{original}$ and samples from $D_{mixed-patch}$.

### 3.1. A New Subtraining Dataset: Mixed Patches and Their Ground-Truth Labels

The essential component of the proposed method is a new subtraining dataset. The dataset consists of mixed patches and their ground-truth labels. The generation process for the mixed patches and their ground truth labels is as follows. Let $(x, y) \in D_{original}$, $(x_{mixed}, y_{mixed}) \in D_{mixed-patch}$, and $(x_{mini}, y_{mini}) \in D_{mini}$ denote the original dataset, a new subtraining dataset, and a minipatch dataset, respectively. To build a new subtraining image $x_{mixed}$, minipatches $x_{mini}$ are concatenated. We use $D_{mini}$ to eliminate the cropping process and build a new mixed patch because the cropping process is not appropriate for histopathological images; this approach reduces the probability that noise affects the dataset. We initialize the number of minipatch images $k$ to build a single $x_{mixed}$. The sizes of $x_{mini}$ and $x_{mixed}$ can be adjusted according to the parameter $k$. The number of cases for a single $x_{mixed}$ is $_{|Dmin|}P_k = |D_{mini}|!/(|D_{mini}|-k)!$, indicating that an enormous number of $x_{mixed}$ values can be generated. Thus, a data augmentation effect is achieved.

After generating a new subtraining image $x_{mixed}$, we define a new ground-truth label $y_{mixed}$. As demonstrated by several existing methods [50–52], new ground-truth labels play an important role in achieving high performance and producing high calibration confidence. In prior work, new ground-truth labels were defined based on the proportions of the regions of the images. For example, prior studies defined a new ground label with a weight of 0.5 for each class if a mixed image included cats and dogs in the same proportion. However, histopathological images differ from the images found in public datasets. Histopathological images have to be diagnosed as abnormal if any proportion of the mixed image contains abnormalities. Additionally, even if a mixed image is diagnosed as abnormal, the confidence should not be fixed at 1, because the underlying composition of the classes in the image is diverse, reflecting the mixed-region variation property. Thus, to overcome the overconfidence problem, for any abnormal mixed patch, the value of abnormality in a new ground-true label needs to be defined from 0.5 to 1 according to the proportions of normal and abnormal minipatches in a mixed patch.

### 3.2. Training Process

The subtraining dataset generated from the above process is used to train a patch-level classifier. Many existing methods for confidence calibration generate new subtraining datasets, divide the data into multiple minibatches, and periodically insert selected minibatches into the training process (e.g., [51]). However, given the context of medical image analysis, our method takes a more cautious, conservative approach of mixing the newly generated subtraining dataset with the original dataset (as opposed to using only the newly generated subtraining dataset) for every minibatch. Specifically, our approach builds a set of minibatches, each of which is based on a combination of the randomly sampled original dataset and the newly generated subtraining dataset in a certain prefixed proportion according to the parameter $\gamma (0 \leq \gamma \leq 1)$. Additionally, the combined minibatches are used throughout the whole training process. Furthermore, we define loss functions as follows:

$$\mathcal{L}_{original} = \sum_{i=1}^{|\mathcal{B}| \times (1-\gamma)} D_{KL}(f(x_i)||y_i) \tag{1}$$

$$\mathcal{L}_{Mixed-Patch} = \sum_{i=1}^{|\mathcal{B}| \times \gamma} D_{KL}(f\left(x_i^{Mixed-Patch}\right)||y_i^{Mixed-Patch}) \tag{2}$$

$$\mathcal{L}_{Total} = w\mathcal{L}_{original} + (1-w)\mathcal{L}_{Mixed-Patch} \tag{3}$$

where $|\mathcal{B}|$ is the size of the minibatch; $f$ is a classifier; $D_{KL}$ is the Kullback–Leibler divergence function; $(x_i, y_i) \in D_{original}$ is the original training dataset; and $w$ $(0 \leq w \leq 1)$ is the weight for the loss of the raw training data.

### 3.3. Data Rebalancing

A new ground-truth label for a mixed patch is defined as abnormal even if a single abnormal minipatch is included. When four minipatches are used to form a single mixed patch, the probability of the new ground-truth label being defined as normal is one in sixteen ($2^4$) because all four minipatches must be normal, meaning that most of the mixed patches are likely to be designated as abnormal, resulting in a data imbalance problem. Techniques for solving data imbalance problems have been presented in various studies [57]. In this study, we employ a data resampling technique to solve the data imbalance problem. This method involves creating a balanced minibatch based on the probability of extracting an individual class from an existing dataset.

## 4. Experiment

### 4.1. Dataset

We constructed a new large histopathology dataset extracted from stomach WSIs obtained at Seegene Medical Foundation, which is one of the largest diagnosis and pathology institutions in South Korea. These slides were stained with hematoxylin and eosin and scanned by a Panoramic Flash250 III scanner at 200× magnification. The data were collected by the Seegene Medical Foundation, and their use for research was approved by the Institutional Review Board (SMF-IRB-2020-007) of the organization as well as by the Institutional Review Board (KAIST-IRB-20-379) of the Korea Advanced Institute of Science and Technology (KAIST), the university that collaborated with the medical foundation. Informed consent to use their tissue samples for clinical purposes was obtained from the medical foundation's designated collection centers. All experiments were performed in accordance with the relevant guidelines and regulations provided by the two review boards. All patient records were completely anonymized, and all the images were kept and analyzed only on the company server.

For an original training dataset, we collected 486 WSIs from different patients, and the images consisted of 204 normal and 282 abnormal slides that were classified and independently confirmed by two pathologists (Table 1). The extracted patch dataset consisted of 32,063 normal and 38,492 abnormal patches. For a minipatch dataset, we used the same WSIs used for the original training dataset, but the tiling size was one-quarter. The minipatch dataset consisted of 3500 randomly selected normal and 3500 abnormal minipatches. For a test dataset, we collected 98 WSIs from different patients, and the images included 48 normal and 50 abnormal slides. The test dataset consisted of 3733 normal and 3780 abnormal patches.

**Table 1.** Compositions of datasets.

| Class | Original Training Dataset (256 × 256) | | Minipatch Dataset (128 × 128) | | Test Dataset (256 × 256) | |
|---|---|---|---|---|---|---|
| | Normal | Abnormal | Normal | Abnormal | Normal | Abnormal |
| WSIs | 204 | 282 | 204 | 282 | 48 | 50 |
| Patches | 32,063 | 38,492 | 3500 | 3500 | 3733 | 3780 |

### 4.2. Implementation Details

The proposed method was implemented in Python with the PyTorch library on a server equipped with 2 NVIDIA RTX 2080 TI GPUs. We used ResNet-18 as the backbone CNN architecture. The primary goal of this study was to analyze the impact of the proposed methodology, not to produce the highest performance. Thus, we thought it would be better to compare the effects of the proposed methodology by adopting a contemporary, light CNN architecture. The CNN classifier was trained with the Adam optimizer [58] and $\beta_1$, $\beta_2$, and the decay coefficient were set to 0.9, 0.999, and 0.001. We trained models with 2 GPUs and set the minibatch size to 128. The models were trained for 60 epochs and used an initial learning rate of 0.1, which was divided by 10 at 20 and 40 epochs.

### 4.3. Comparison of Methods

To assess the effectiveness of the proposed method, we compared five models, each of which was trained using a different method (Table 2): Baseline, Label Smoothing (LS), Cutout, CutMix, and MixPatch (proposed method). Table 2 provides a summary of key differences of these methods, each of which is further detailed below.

**Table 2.** Summary of the compared methods.

| | Baseline | LS | Cutout | CutMix | MixPatch |
|---|---|---|---|---|---|
| Data augmentation | X | X | O | O | O |
| Soft labeling | X | O | X | O | O |
| Ratio reflection | X | X | X | O | O |
| All correct labeling | O | O | X | X | O |
| Image | | | | | |
| Label | Normal 1.0 | Normal 0.9 Abnormal 0.1 | Abnormal 1.0 | Normal 0.8 Abnormal 0.2 | Normal 0.4 Abnormal 0.6 |
| Actual label | Normal | Normal | Abnormal | Abnormal | Abnormal |

*Baseline:* The baseline method uses transfer learning and fine-tuning, which are commonly utilized by patch-level classifiers. The baseline method trains a model using hard labeling with a one-hot-encoded label vector, for which the ground-truth label value is specified as 1 and other labels are 0; thus, the model is designed to predict a label with 100% certainty [59]. For this reason, a model trained with the baseline method has the possibility of experiencing overconfidence issues. No data augmentation is employed in this method.

*Label smoothing (LS)* is a simple regularization method designed to alleviate the overconfidence problem. The LS method assigns the highest value of confidence (lower than 1) to the ground-truth class and low values from noise distributions (higher than 0) to all of the classes with a parameter $\alpha$, as shown below:

$$y_k^{ls} = y_k(1 - \alpha) + \alpha/K$$

where $k$ is the $k$th class, $K$ is the total number of classes, and $\alpha$ is the smoothing parameter.

For evaluation, $\alpha$ was set to 0.2 in this study. As in the baseline method, no data augmentation is employed in this method.

*Cutout* is a region dropout-based regularization method. Cutout randomly masks square regions of an image during training. This training method exhibited excellent robustness and performance [60]. However, Cutout may remove informative regions from training images. Thus, this method may generate mislabeled data. Cutout must define the size of pixels that are removed from an input image. This study defined the pixel size as a quarter of the image size based on the setting used in a previous study [60].

*CutMix* has been used as a state-of-the-art method for region dropout. CutMix performs data augmentation for improved accuracy and implements soft labeling for confidence calibration. CutMix builds a new training image by attaching a cropped portion of another image to a region of image that is removed and uses the soft labeling technique in consideration of the mix proportion of the new training image. Based on the labeling rules in histopathology, CutMix may generate mislabeled data. For example, as shown in Table 2, an image with small abnormal regions is attached to a base normal image, and it will be predicted as normal when the true label is abnormal.

*MixPatch* is the proposed method. MixPatch achieves a data augmentation effect similar to that of other region dropout methods, and ratio-based soft labeling is employed for confidence calibration. However, MixPatch will not accidently produce mislabeled training data, which is a strength when compared with other region dropout methods. MixPatch incorporates a soft labeling technique for confidence calibration and considers unique image combinations and labeling rules, which are specifically established for histopathological images. In our experiment, the value of abnormality for a new ground-truth label is defined as a constant that increases from 0.6 to 0.9 according to the abnormal patch ratio in a mixed patch (Table 3). Weighted random sampling, a data resampling technique, is employed for data rebalancing. We set the parameter $\gamma$ to 0.3. There is no difference between the weights of the original data and the weights of the new subtraining data used to calculate the loss value, meaning that the parameter $w$ was set to 0.5.

**Table 3.** Labeling strategy for a mixed patch.

| Abnormal Patch Ratio in a Mixed Patch | New Ground-Truth Label for a Mixed Patch |
|---|---|
| 0/4 | [0.9, 0.1] |
| 1/4 | [0.4, 0.6] |
| 2/4 | [0.3, 0.7] |
| 3/4 | [0.2, 0.8] |
| 4/4 | [0.1, 0.9] |

*4.4. Evaluation Metrics*

For evaluation, this study uses accuracy, sensitivity, specificity, area under a receiver operating characteristic curve (AUROC), and expected calibration error (ECE). Accuracy is the main metric for the performance of image classifiers, but it is not informative enough for medical systems. AUROC is a metric for binary classification in consideration of sensitivity and specificity. This study defined confidence value as the variable for AUROC analysis, as in prior research [61]. AUROC is a vital evaluation criterion for understanding the performance of models for automatic diagnosis systems as it shows how good the diagnostic model is at distinguishing between positive and negative classes by considering net benefit (sensitivity) over diagnostic cost (1-specificity). ECE has been used as the primary empirical metric to measure confidence calibration. ECE is a metric of how much confidence in predictions reflects actual model accuracy and a small value of ECE indicates a small difference between output confidence and model accuracy—small degree of miscalibration.

True positive (*TP*) is the correct classification of the positive class (Table 4). For example, the model classifies the patch as abnormal if a patch contains cancerous cells. True negative (*TN*) is the correct classification of the negative class. For example, when there is no cancerous cell present in the patch, the model predicts the patch as normal. False positive (*FP*) is the incorrect prediction of the positives. For example, the patch does have cancerous cells, but the model classifies the patch as abnormal. False negative (*FN*) is the incorrect prediction of the negatives. For example, there are cancerous cells present in the patch, and the model predicts the patch as normal.

**Table 4.** The confusion matrix for outcome of predictions.

|  |  | Actual | |
|---|---|---|---|
|  |  | Abnormal (Positive) | Normal (Negative) |
| Prediction | Abnormal (Positive) | True positive (*TP*) | False positive (*FP*) |
|  | Normal (Negative) | False negative (*FN*) | True negative (*TN*) |

**Accuracy**

It is the rate of correct identification of all items:

$$\text{Accuracy} = \frac{TP + TN}{TP + TN + FP + FN}$$

**Specificity**

It is the rate of correct identification of negative items:

$$\text{Specificity} = \frac{TN}{TN + FP}$$

**Sensitivity**

It is the rate of correct identification of positive items:

$$\text{Sensitivity} = \frac{TP}{TP + FN}$$

**Receiver Operating Characteristic Curve (ROC-Curve)**

The receiver operating characteristic curve (ROC-curve) represents the performance of the proposed model based on a threshold. In this study, we defined the confidence score of positive defined as the threshold. It is the graph of True Positive Rate (TPR) vs. False Positive Rate (FPR).

$$\text{TPR} = \frac{TP}{TP + FN}$$

$$\text{FPR} = \frac{FP}{FP + TN}$$

**Area Under the ROC Curve (AUROC)**

AUROC provides the area under the ROC-curve integrated from (0, 0) to (1, 1). It measures performance based on all classification thresholds. AUROC has a range from 0 to 1.

**Expected Calibration Error (ECE)**

ECE is approximated through partitioning predictions into equally spaced bins $B$ and taking a weighted average of the bins' accuracy vs. confidence difference. More precisely,

$$\text{ECE} = \sum_{m=1}^{M} \frac{|B_m|}{n} |accuracy(B_m) - confidence(B_m)|$$

where $n$ is the number of samples, and $M$ is the number of bins, $B_m$ is the set of samples whose prediction confidence falls into the interval $I_m = \left(\frac{m-1}{M}, \frac{m}{M}\right]$.

## 5. Results

The performances of the training methods were assessed by analyzing the mean and standard deviation of accuracy, sensitivity, specificity, AUROC, and ECE obtained from the five models trained in each method. The performance results for the trained models are shown in Table 5, ROC curve is shown in Figure 3, and detailed information on the ECE is shown in Figure 4.

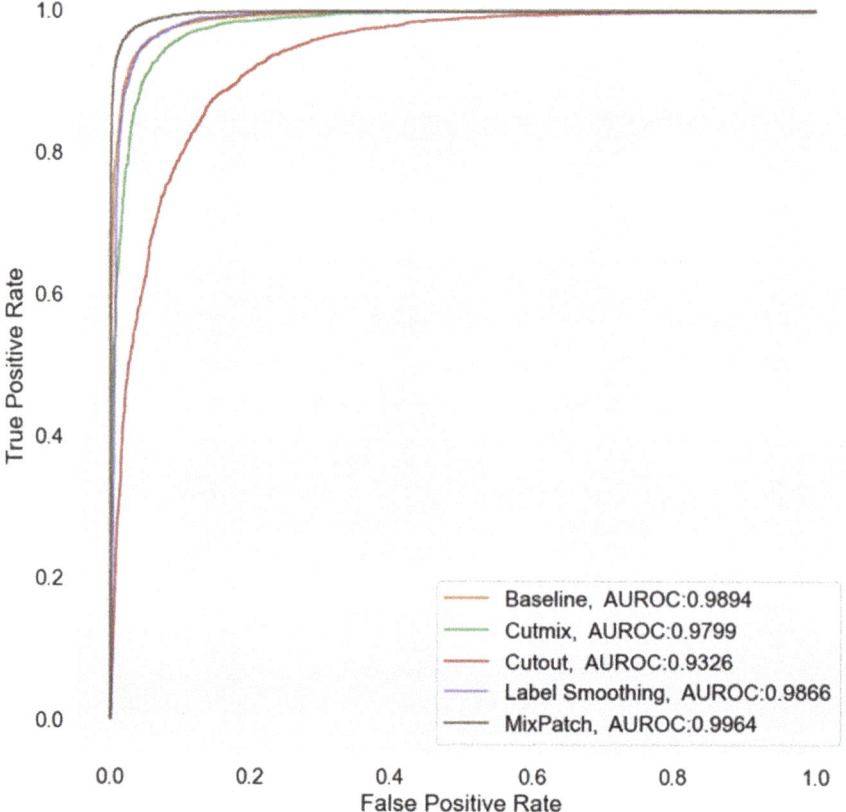

**Figure 3.** ROC curve for the different methods.

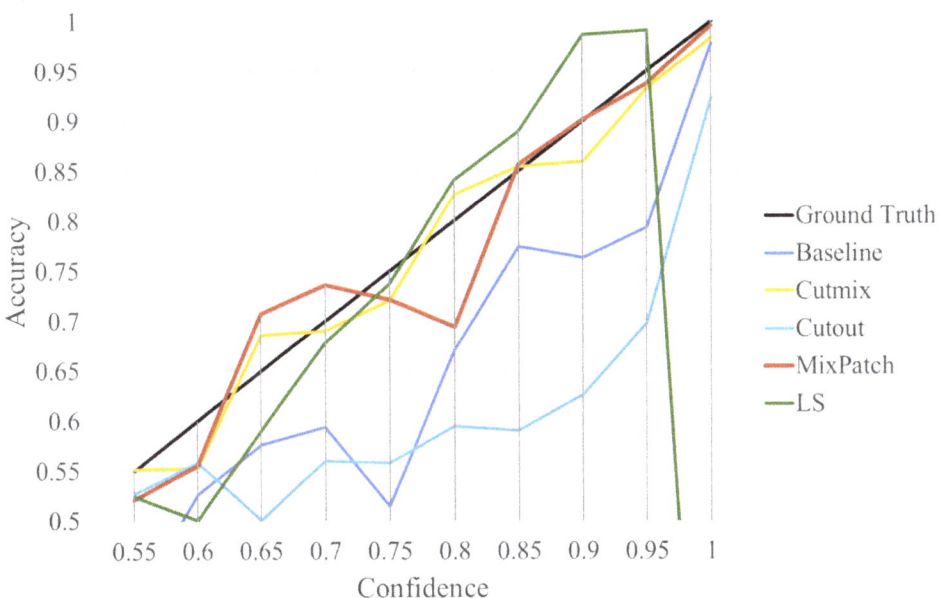

**Figure 4.** Integrated reliability diagram for patch-level classifiers trained using each method.

**Table 5.** Performance comparison of the alternative methods.

| Training Methods | Accuracy ↑ (In Percent) | Sensitivity ↑ (In Percent) | Specificity ↑ (In Percent) | AUROC ↑ | ECE ↓ (In Percent) |
|---|---|---|---|---|---|
| Baseline | 95.46 ± 0.79 | 96.96 ± 1.15 | 93.95 ± 0.71 | 0.9914 ± 0.0027 | 1.83 ± 0.43 |
| LS | 94.76 ± 0.94 | 96.15 ± 1.43 | 93.35 ± 0.51 | 0.9861 ± 0.0038 | 6.62 ± 0.34 |
| Cutout | 84.88 ± 0.47 | 82.33 ± 0.86 | 87.46 ± 0.31 | 0.9289 ± 0.0027 | 7.06 ± 0.28 |
| CutMix | 93.70 ± 0.91 | 94.30 ± 1.19 | 93.11 ± 0.92 | 0.9826 ± 0.0041 | 1.36 ± 0.22 |
| MixPatch | 97.06 ± 0.27 | 97.65 ± 0.23 | 96.46 ± 0.48 | 0.9958 ± 0.0006 | 0.76 ± 0.18 |

As shown in Table 5, the proposed method, MixPatch, yields the best performance in accuracy, sensitivity, specificity, AUROC, and ECE among the five models examined. The LS method does not show any advantage compared to the baseline method. The LS method attempts to fit training cases with a 0.9 confidence level, thus producing many test cases distributed in the bin of 0.85–0.95 (Table 6); the results suggest that the model is 90% sure about the results of most cases, even for cases that are very clear. This phenomenon is not suitable from the perspective of confidence calibration, so it is understandable that ECE performance deteriorates. The Cutout method uses one-hot encoding, similar to the baseline method. Cutout exhibits a higher ECE than the baseline approach because the Cutout method does not use a confidence calibration method, although the accuracy of this approach is comparatively low. The CutMix method yields a slightly higher ECE result than the baseline method, probably because of the influence of ratio-based soft labeling; however, the accuracy and AUROC decrease slightly because of the possibility of mislabeling. The proposed method, MixPatch, shows increased classification performances and decreased ECE, which are both desirable. Thus, applying soft labeling combined with the mix ratio of the images according to the MixPath labeling rules makes a positive contribution to both classification performance and confidence calibration.

**Table 6.** Confidence distributions of each method.

Furthermore, we illustrate the specific ECE results of the compared methods with a reliability diagram. In Figure 4, ground truth represents the ideal scores for the confidence calibration methods. The confidence value of a prediction should reflect its accuracy. Among the compared methods, CutMix and MixPatch yield similar values that are closest to the ground truth, indicating that ratio-based soft labeling methods are effective for confidence calibration.

In addition to the quantitative analysis using the ECE metric, we examine confidence distributions by quantifying true and false predictions for test cases to determine how well the proposed method considers prediction uncertainty (Table 6). A skew to a high confidence value is desired for the confidence distribution in the cases of true predictions. In contrast, a skew to a low confidence value is desired for the confidence distribution in the cases of false predictions. We need to carefully examine confidence distributions for cases with false predictions to understand the effects of the proposed methods in terms of prediction uncertainty.

The models trained with the baseline and Cutout methods exhibit an overconfidence issue (see red bins in Table 6). The two models produce high confidence values, even for false predictions. Thus, these methods should not be used when the confidence value is used as a threshold for decision making and are not suitable as patch-level classifiers, particularly in the context of histopathological image analysis. The model trained using LS or CutMix yields a flatter distribution than the baseline model for false predictions, indicating that this method better alleviates overconfidence and produces lower confidence values for uncertain cases. The model trained using MixPatch produces a flat distribution that is similar to the distribution obtained with LS or CutMix, indicating that the proposed method can effectively deal with overconfidence issues. Additionally, the proposed method, MixPatch, exhibits better performance than the other methods, confirming that the method is more suitable than the other methods for building histopathology patch-level classifiers.

For further analysis of the effect of applying confidence calibration, we construct confusion matrices according to the relevant threshold values (Table 7). We define the confidence value for abnormalities as an indicator. The baseline classification threshold is 0.5 because binary classification is used. Typical methods for WSI classification are based on counting the labels of patch-level predictions. For this method, a threshold for a patch-level classifier plays an important role in WSI classification. For example, if a low threshold is applied, a WSI classification framework will be very sensitive to positive results.

For all of the compared methods, the lower the threshold is, the lower the false-negative ratio, and the higher the false-positive ratio, with some notable differences in accuracy. For example, in the MixPatch model, if 0.1 is defined as the threshold value, the WSI classification framework is very sensitive to positive (i.e., abnormal) values while maintaining high accuracy. Conversely, in the LS model, if the threshold is defined as 0.1, it is sensitive to positive values, but the model predicts most of the results as abnormal, resulting in low accuracy.

For qualitative analysis, we applied Grad-CAM to uncertain patch images. In the first case (see Figure 5), it seems that all models can find the abnormal locations and predict them correctly. Overall, the activation map of other methods other than the baseline method is dispersed widely. However, in the case of MixPatch, the size of the activation map does not increase, which we believe is due to the confidence calibration effect. As MixPatch uses an image that combined normal and abnormal patches, it seems that MixPatch method wants to train a model more clearly to distinguish between normal regions and abnormal regions. Therefore, the activation map appears to be smaller than other methods.

**Table 7.** Confusion matrix for each method with a threshold approach (X = prediction, Y = true).

| Model | Threshold (If Cofindence$_{AB}$ ≥ Threshold, Then Prediction = Abnormal) | | | | |
|---|---|---|---|---|---|
| | 0.5 (Baseline) | 0.4 | 0.3 | 0.2 | 0.1 |
| Baseline | 3481 / 252<br>130 / 3650 | 3396 / 337<br>91 / 3689 | 3396 / 337<br>91 / 3689 | 3330 / 403<br>77 / 3703 | 3227 / 506<br>53 / 3727 |
| LS | 3472 / 261<br>129 / 3651 | 3406 / 327<br>93 / 3687 | 3322 / 411<br>64 / 3716 | 3322 / 411<br>64 / 3716 | 663 / 3070<br>2 / 3778 |
| CutMix | 3227 / 506<br>53 / 3727 | 3443 / 290<br>207 / 3573 | 3362 / 371<br>151 / 3629 | 3257 / 476<br>104 / 3676 | 3059 / 674<br>59 / 3721 |
| Cutout | 3278 / 455<br>641 / 3139 | 3237 / 496<br>568 / 3212 | 3186 / 547<br>476 / 3304 | 3083 / 650<br>401 / 3379 | 2938 / 795<br>287 / 3493 |
| MixPatch | 3601 / 132<br>90 / 3690 | 3567 / 166<br>75 / 3705 | 3540 / 193<br>62 / 3718 | 3492 / 241<br>49 / 3731 | 3394 / 339<br>26 / 3754 |

The second case is more difficult than the first case. All models except MixPatch have activations on both of the normal and abnormal regions. Especially difficult regions in the second case are the second and third quadrants. The second quadrants contain the dark and cellular areas, mimicking poorly differentiated carcinoma; however, it is lymphoid aggregates. The third quadrant shows a very small part of suspicious glandular epithelium, and slightly distorted normal parietal cells. All models predict this patch as abnormal. However, in the activation map, such difficult regions made the comparison models all confused about separating abnormal regions from normal regions. On the other hand, the MixPatch model shows noticeable improvement in clearly distinguishing abnormal regions from normal regions.

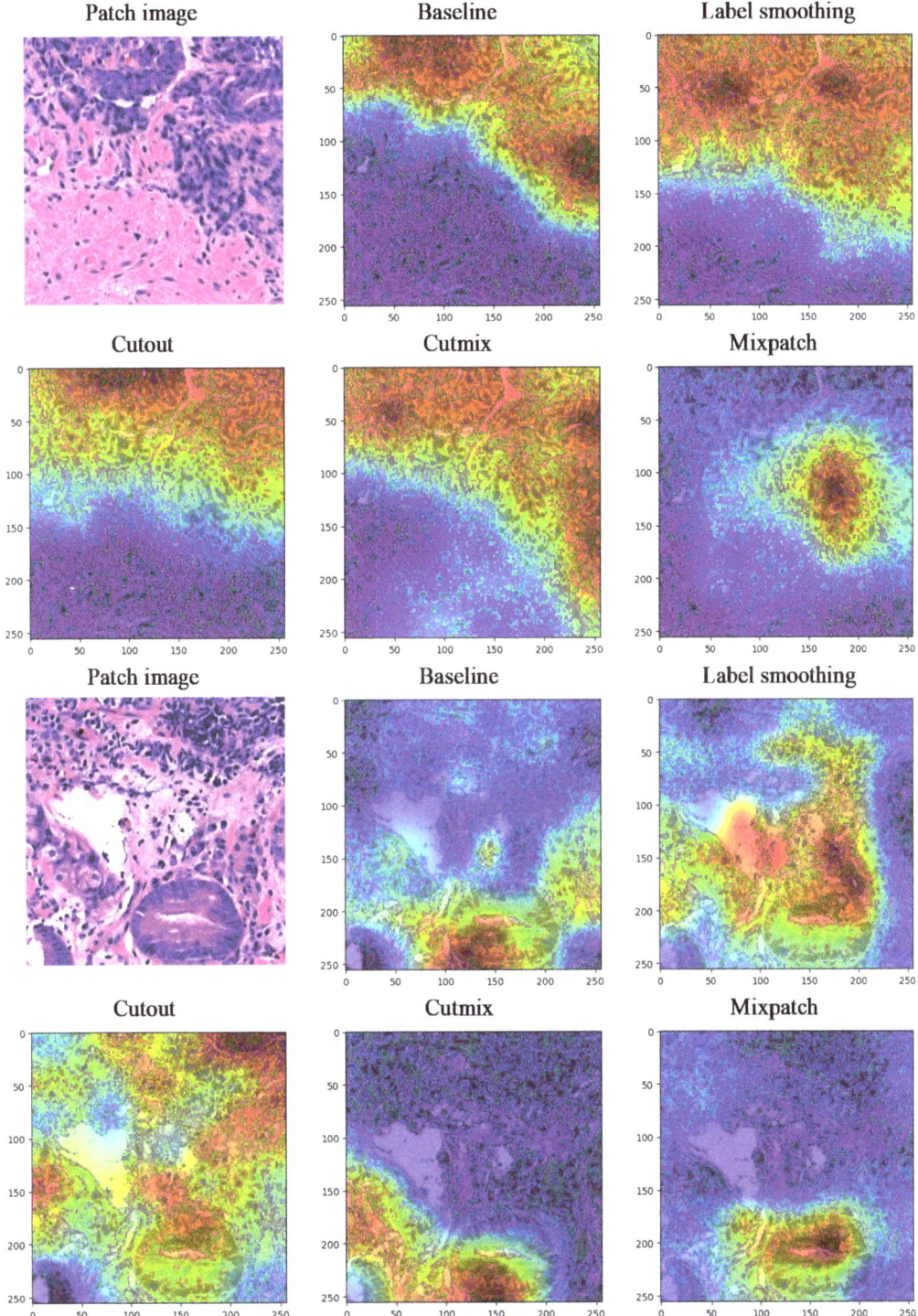

**Figure 5.** The Grad-Cam [62] visualization examples for uncertain patch images.

The objective of the patch-level classifier is to extract important information from patches for WSI classification. MixPatch not only increases the performance of patch-level prediction, but also produces appropriate prediction uncertainty values through confidence calibration. Therefore, for WSI classification, we applied an existing method [63] that uses confidence values rather than a simple method of counting patch-level predictions. This method uses a CNN model and a feature cube. A feature cube is generated using the predicted confidence scores of each label from patches. A CNN model is used as a slide-level classifier, and feature cubes are used as inputs for the slide-level classifier. In this study, we trained five CNN models under the same conditions as considered for the patch-level classifier, and Resnet-18 was used in each approach. Slides used to train patch-level classifiers were also used to train slide-level classifiers. Additionally, to analyze the performance of the slide-level classifiers using an independent set of slides at a large scale, we used separately collected, annotated test slides, including 459 normal and 604 abnormal slides.

As presented in Table 8, MixPatch produced a 1.5% performance improvement compared to the baseline at the slide level. The difference of 1.5% is notable when this approach is practically applied in the medical domain. LS yields a higher ECE than the baseline, but its WSI classification performance is similar to that of the baseline. The reason why LS yields a high ECE value is that many cases are assigned a high confidence value close to 0.9, which is the maximum confidence level for the LS slide-level classifier. Further, as shown in Table 6, LS generates more alleviated confidence scores for uncertain cases (false predictions). Thus, despite the increased ECE, it seems that the WSI classification performance of LS did not deteriorate much compared to that of the baseline, due to the more effective control of overconfidence. For CutMix, the accuracy of the patch-level classifier is lower than that of the baseline, but the slide-level classification performance is higher, probably due to better handling of overconfidence. Consistent with the study results obtained at the patch level, MixPatch exhibits the best performance at the slide level among the five classification methods considered.

**Table 8.** Performance in WSI classification.

| WSI Classifiers | WSI-Level Accuracy ↑ (In Percent) |
|---|---|
| Baseline | 97.06 ± 0.29 |
| LS | 97.15 ± 0.18 |
| Cutout | 95.82 ± 0.57 |
| CutMix | 97.46 ± 0.18 |
| MixPatch | 98.53 ± 0.16 |

## 6. Discussion

The objective of this study was to explore the possibility of improving the performance of a patch-level classifier by developing a new DL training approach called MixPatch, which employs a set of mixed patches in predefined mixing ratios and their associated labels, within the context of histopathological image analysis. The study results confirm the superiority of the proposed approach when compared to the existing approaches, not only at the patch level but also at the slide level. Prior studies have proposed two-step frameworks, each of which consists of a patch-level classifier and a slide-level classifier. The performance of a patch-level classifier is the foundation of those frameworks. However, such frameworks utilize transfer learning and well-known CNN architectures for patch-level classifiers without considering the specific characteristics of patches or the corresponding prediction uncertainty. In this study, we propose a new method for training a patch-level classifier specifically designed to address the mixed-region variation inherent in histopathological images and the derived patches.

A significant factor that underlies the performance of MixPatch is the effect of performing data augmentation without mislabeled data. A small number of minipatches can be used to build a vast number of single mixed patches, resulting in numerous different mixed patches. In general, deep learning models perform better as the amount of available data increases. Furthermore, the proposed method can solve the overconfidence issue related to prediction uncertainty when a patch-level classifier is trained. Addressing the prediction uncertainty of patch-level classification should be an important part of WSI classification frameworks. The WSI-level classifier determines whether to trust each patch's prediction based on its estimation of prediction uncertainty. Therefore, a patch-level classifier that appropriately handles prediction uncertainty should be used in a WSI classification framework to help it make more calibrated decisions.

The method proposed in this study has some limitations and boundary conditions that need to be noted. To build a single mixed patch, we utilized $128 \times 128$ pixel minipatches; this size is the minimum required for pathologists to make diagnosis decisions at the patch level. Additionally, we utilized four minipatches to build a single mixed patch. In future studies, a sensitivity analysis could be conducted using various subtraining datasets that consist of mixed patches with 9 or 16 minipatches or different pixel sizes. To define new ground-truth labels, we considered a constant increase in labels from 0.6 to 0.9 based on the proportion of abnormal minipatches in a mixed patch. However, labels could be defined differently by employing a different labeling scheme, such as an exponential scheme. In this study, we defined the proportion of the new subtraining dataset in the minibatch to be 0.25. In future studies, this percentage could be adjusted, and a sensitivity analysis could be performed to find the optimal value.

## 7. Conclusions

In this study, we have proposed a new method, MixPatch, designed to train a CNN-based histopathological patch-level classifier. The proposed method is the first that considers confidence calibration for prediction uncertainty when training a patch-level classifier. Given that the performance of the patch-level classifier is the foundation of overall framework performance, the proposed method should be used to improve the performance of existing frameworks. Moreover, it should be noted that the proposed method improves the performance of the patch-level classifier by addressing prediction uncertainty, which is particularly important in the domain of medical image analysis, where prediction uncertainty is a crucial issue. The proposed approach provides a new way to systematically alleviate overconfidence problems without a performance degradation, compared with the extant methods. The confidence calibration method proposed in this study is an important step toward securing a completely reliable diagnose performance of histopathological image analysis.

**Author Contributions:** Y.P.: Conceptualization, investigation, analysis, methodology, data curation, software, visualization, validation, writing—original draft. M.K.: Conceptualization, data curation, writing—review and editing. M.A.: Software, data curation, writing—review and editing. Y.S.K.: Resources, data curation, validation, writing—review and editing, pathologist. M.Y.Y.: Supervision, conceptualization, project administration, funding acquisition, writing—review and editing. All authors have read and agreed to the published version of the manuscript.

**Funding:** This research was supported by the Seegene Medical Foundation, South Korea under the project "Research on Developing a Next Generation Medical Diagnosis System Using Deep Learning" (Grant Number: G01180115).

**Institutional Review Board Statement:** The data were collected by the Seegene Medical Foundation, and their use for research was approved by the Institutional Review Board (SMF-IRB-2020-007) of the organization as well as by the Institutional Review Board (KAIST-IRB-20-379) of the Korea Advanced Institute of Science and Technology (KAIST), the university that collaborated with the medical foundation. All experiments were performed in accordance with the relevant guidelines and regulations provided by the two review boards.

**Informed Consent Statement:** Informed consent to use their tissue samples for clinical purposes was obtained from the medical foundation's designated collection centers. All patient records were completely anonymized, and all the images were kept and analyzed only on the company server.

**Conflicts of Interest:** The authors declare no conflict of interest.

## References

1. Siegel, L.R.; Miller, K.D.; Fuchs, H.E.; Jemal, A. Cancer statistics, 2021. *CA Cancer J. Clin.* **2021**, *71*, 7–33. [CrossRef] [PubMed]
2. Peck, M.; Moffatt, D.; Latham, B.; Badrick, T. Review of diagnostic error in anatomical pathology and the role and value of second opinions in error prevention. *J. Clin. Pathol.* **2018**, *71*, 995–1000. [CrossRef] [PubMed]
3. Aresta, G.; Araújo, T.; Kwok, S.; Chennamsetty, S.S.; Safwan, M.; Alex, V.; Marami, B.; Prastawa, M.; Chan, M.; Donovan, M.; et al. BACH: Grand challenge on breast cancer histology images. *Med. Image Anal.* **2019**, *56*, 122–139. [CrossRef]
4. Litjens, G.; Kooi, T.; Bejnordi, B.E.; Setio, A.A.A.; Ciompi, F.; Ghafoorian, M.; van der Laak, J.A.W.M.; van Ginneken, B.; Sánchez, C.I. A survey on deep learning in medical image analysis. *Med. Image Anal.* **2017**, *42*, 60–88. [CrossRef] [PubMed]
5. Bandi, P.; Geessink, O.; Manson, Q.; Van Dijk, M.; Balkenhol, M.; Hermsen, M.; Bejnordi, B.E.; Lee, B.; Paeng, K.; Zhong, A.; et al. From Detection of Individual Metastases to Classification of Lymph Node Status at the Patient Level: The CAMELYON17 Challenge. *IEEE Trans. Med. Imaging* **2018**, *38*, 550–560. [CrossRef]
6. Hou, L.; Samaras, D.; Kurc, T.M.; Gao, Y.; Davis, J.E.; Saltz, J.H. Patch-Based Convolutional Neural Network for Whole Slide Tissue Image Classification. In Proceedings of the 2016 IEEE Conference on Computer Vision and Pattern Recognition (CVPR), Las Vegas, NV, USA, 27–30 June 2016.
7. Paeng, K.; Hwang, S.; Park, S.; Kim, M. A unified framework for tumor proliferation score prediction in breast histopathology. In *Deep Learning in Medical Image Analysis and Multimodal Learning for Clinical Decision Support*; Springer: Berlin/Heidelberg, Germany, 2017; pp. 231–239.
8. Takahama, S.; Kurose, Y.; Mukuta, Y.; Abe, H.; Fukayama, M.; Yoshizawa, A.; Kitagawa, M.; Harada, T. Multi-Stage Pathological Image Classification using Semantic Segmentation. In Proceedings of the IEEE/CVF International Conference on Computer Vision, Seoul, Korea, 27 October–2 November 2019.
9. Cruz-Roa, A.; Basavanhally, A.; González, F.; Gilmore, H.; Feldman, M.; Ganesan, S.; Shih, N.; Tomaszewski, J.; Madabhushi, A. Automatic detection of invasive ductal carcinoma in whole slide images with convolutional neural networks. In *Medical Imaging 2014: Digital Pathology*; International Society for Optics and Photonics: Bellingham, WA, USA, 2014.
10. Xu, Y.; Jia, Z.; Ai, Y.; Zhang, F.; Lai, M.; Chang, E.I.-C. Deep convolutional activation features for large scale Brain Tumor histopathology image classification and segmentation. In Proceedings of the 2015 IEEE International Conference on Acoustics, Speech and Signal Processing (ICASSP), South Brisbane, Australia, 19–24 April 2015.
11. Chang, H.; Zhou, Y.; Borowsky, A.; Barner, K.; Spellman, P.; Parvin, B. Stacked Predictive Sparse Decomposition for Classification of Histology Sections. *Int. J. Comput. Vis.* **2014**, *113*, 3–18. [CrossRef]
12. Wahab, N.; Khan, A.; Lee, Y.S. Two-phase deep convolutional neural network for reducing class skewness in histopathological images based breast cancer detection. *Comput. Biol. Med.* **2017**, *85*, 86–97. [CrossRef]
13. Wang, S.; Zhu, Y.; Yu, L.; Chen, H.; Lin, H.; Wan, X.; Fan, X.; Heng, P.-A. RMDL: Recalibrated multi-instance deep learning for whole slide gastric image classification. *Med. Image Anal.* **2019**, *58*, 101549. [CrossRef]
14. Murthy, V.; Hou, L.; Samaras, D.; Kurc, T.M.; Saltz, J.H. Center-focusing multi-task CNN with injected features for classification of glioma nuclear images. In Proceedings of the 2017 IEEE Winter Conference on Applications of Computer Vision (WACV), Santa Rosa, CA, USA, 24–31 March 2017.
15. Huang, Y.; Zheng, H.; Liu, C.; Ding, X.; Rohde, G.K. Epithelium-Stroma Classification via Convolutional Neural Networks and Unsupervised Domain Adaptation in Histopathological Images. *IEEE J. Biomed. Health Inform.* **2017**, *21*, 1625–1632. [CrossRef]
16. Spanhol, F.A.; Oliveira, L.S.; Cavalin, P.R.; Petitjean, C.; Heutte, L. Deep features for breast cancer histopathological image classification. In Proceedings of the 2017 IEEE International Conference on Systems, Man, and Cybernetics (SMC), Banff, AB, Canada, 5–8 October 2017.
17. Gomes, J.; Kong, J.; Kurc, T.; Melo, A.C.; Ferreira, R.; Saltz, J.H.; Teodoro, G. Building robust pathology image analyses with uncertainty quantification. *Comput. Methods Programs Biomed.* **2021**, *208*, 106291. [CrossRef]
18. Shin, S.J.; You, S.C.; Jeon, H.; Jung, J.W.; An, M.H.; Park, R.W.; Roh, J. Style transfer strategy for developing a generalizable deep learning application in digital pathology. *Comput. Methods Programs Biomed.* **2020**, *198*, 105815. [CrossRef] [PubMed]
19. Nadeem, S.; Hollmann, T.; Tannenbaum, A. Multimarginal wasserstein barycenter for stain normalization and augmentation. In Proceedings of the International Conference on Medical Image Computing and Computer-Assisted Intervention, Lima, Peru, 4–8 October 2020.
20. Pérez-Bueno, F.; Vega, M.; Sales, M.A.; Aneiros-Fernández, J.; Naranjo, V.; Molina, R.; Katsaggelos, A.K. Blind color deconvolution, normalization, and classification of histological images using general super Gaussian priors and Bayesian inference. *Comput. Methods Programs Biomed.* **2021**, *211*, 106453. [CrossRef] [PubMed]
21. Zheng, Y.; Jiang, Z.; Zhang, H.; Xie, F.; Shi, J.; Xue, C. Adaptive color deconvolution for histological WSI normalization. *Comput. Methods Programs Biomed.* **2019**, *170*, 107–120. [CrossRef] [PubMed]

22. Janowczyk, A.; Basavanhally, A.; Madabhushi, A. Stain Normalization using Sparse AutoEncoders (StaNoSA): Application to digital pathology. *Comput. Med. Imaging Graph.* **2016**, *57*, 50–61. [CrossRef]
23. Salvi, M.; Michielli, N.; Molinari, F. Stain Color Adaptive Normalization (SCAN) algorithm: Separation and standardization of histological stains in digital pathology. *Comput. Methods Programs Biomed.* **2020**, *193*, 105506. [CrossRef] [PubMed]
24. Hoque, M.Z.; Keskinarkaus, A.; Nyberg, P.; Seppänen, T. Retinex model based stain normalization technique for whole slide image analysis. *Comput. Med. Imaging Graph.* **2021**, *90*, 101901. [CrossRef]
25. Pereyra, G.; Tucker, G.; Chorowski, J.; Kaiser, Ł.; Hinton, G. Regularizing neural networks by penalizing confident output distributions. *arXiv* **2017**, arXiv:1701.06548.
26. Guo, C.; Pleiss, G.; Sun, Y.; Weinberger, K.Q. On calibration of modern neural networks. In Proceedings of the 34th International Conference on Machine Learning, Sydney, Australia, 6–11 August 2017.
27. Hashimoto, N.; Fukushima, D.; Koga, R.; Takagi, Y.; Ko, K.; Kohno, K.; Nakaguro, M.; Nakamura, S.; Hontani, H.; Takeuchi, I. Multi-scale Domain-adversarial Multiple-instance CNN for Cancer Subtype Classification with Unannotated Histopathological Images. In Proceedings of the IEEE/CVF Conference on Computer Vision and Pattern Recognition, Seattle, WA, USA, 14–19 June 2020.
28. Müller, R.; Kornblith, S.; Hinton, G. When Does Label Smoothing Help? In *Advances in Neural Information Processing Systems 32, Proceedings of the Annual Conference on Neural Information Processing Systems 2019, NeurIPS 2019, Vancouver, BC, Canada, 8–14 December 2019*; Neural Information Processing Systems Foundation, Inc. (NeurIPS): La Jolla, CA, USA, 2019.
29. Kraus, O.Z.; Ba, J.L.; Frey, B.J. Classifying and segmenting microscopy images with deep multiple instance learning. *Bioinformatics* **2016**, *32*, i52–i59. [CrossRef]
30. Lee, B.; Paeng, K. A robust and effective approach towards accurate metastasis detection and pn-stage classification in breast cancer. In Proceedings of the International Conference on Medical Image Computing and Computer-Assisted Intervention, Granada, Spain, 16–20 September 2018.
31. Dov, D.; Kovalsky, S.; Assaad, S.; Cohen, J.; Range, D.E.; Pendse, A.A.; Henao, R.; Carin, L. Weakly supervised instance learning for thyroid malignancy prediction from whole slide cytopathology images. *Med. Image Anal.* **2020**, *67*, 101814. [CrossRef]
32. Duran-Lopez, L.; Dominguez-Morales, J.P.; Gutierrez-Galan, D.; Rios-Navarro, A.; Jimenez-Fernandez, A.; Vicente-Diaz, S.; Linares-Barranco, A. Wide & Deep neural network model for patch aggregation in CNN-based prostate cancer detection systems. *arXiv* **2021**, arXiv:2105.09974.
33. Li, J.; Li, W.; Sisk, A.; Ye, H.; Wallace, W.D.; Speier, W.; Arnold, C.W. A multi-resolution model for histopathology image classification and localization with multiple instance learning. *Comput. Biol. Med.* **2021**, *131*, 104253. [CrossRef] [PubMed]
34. Riasatian, A.; Babaie, M.; Maleki, D.; Kalra, S.; Valipour, M.; Hemati, S.; Zaveri, M.; Safarpoor, A.; Shafiei, S.; Afshari, M.; et al. Fine-Tuning and training of densenet for histopathology image representation using TCGA diagnostic slides. *Med. Image Anal.* **2021**, *70*, 102032. [CrossRef] [PubMed]
35. Srinidhi, C.L.; Ciga, O.; Martel, A.L. Deep neural network models for computational histopathology: A survey. *Med. Image Anal.* **2020**, *67*, 101813. [CrossRef]
36. Teh, E.W.; Taylor, G.W. Metric learning for patch classification in digital pathology. In Proceedings of the 2nd International Conference on Medical Imaging with Deep Learning, London, UK, 8–10 July 2019.
37. Shi, X.; Su, H.; Xing, F.; Liang, Y.; Qu, G.; Yang, L. Graph temporal ensembling based semi-supervised convolutional neural network with noisy labels for histopathology image analysis. *Med. Image Anal.* **2020**, *60*, 101624. [CrossRef] [PubMed]
38. George, K.; Faziludeen, S.; Sankaran, P. Breast cancer detection from biopsy images using nucleus guided transfer learning and belief based fusion. *Comput. Biol. Med.* **2020**, *124*, 103954. [CrossRef] [PubMed]
39. Shahi, T.B.; Sitaula, C.; Neupane, A.; Guo, W. Fruit classification using attention-based MobileNetV2 for industrial applications. *PLoS ONE* **2022**, *17*, e0264586. [CrossRef]
40. Sitaula, C.; Shahi, T.B.; Aryal, S.; Marzbanrad, F. Fusion of multi-scale bag of deep visual words features of chest X-ray images to detect COVID-19 infection. *Sci. Rep.* **2021**, *11*, 23914. [CrossRef]
41. Tan, M.; Le, Q. Efficientnetv2: Smaller models and faster training. In Proceedings of the International Conference on Machine Learning, Virtual Event, 18–24 July 2021.
42. Kabir, H.M.; Abdar, M.; Jalali, S.M.J.; Khosravi, A.; Atiya, A.F.; Nahavandi, S.; Srinivasan, D. Spinalnet: Deep neural network with gradual input. *arXiv* **2020**, arXiv:2007.03347.
43. Gal, Y.; Ghahramani, Z. Dropout as a bayesian approximation: Representing model uncertainty in deep learning. In Proceedings of the International Conference on Machine Learning, New York, NY, USA, 20–22 June 2016.
44. Lakshminarayanan, B.; Pritzel, A.; Blundell, C. Simple and scalable predictive uncertainty estimation using deep ensembles. In *Advances in Neural Information Processing Systems 30, Proceedings of the Annual Conference on Neural Information Processing Systems 2017, NeurIPS 2017, Long Beach, CA, USA, 4–9 December 2017*; Neural Information Processing Systems Foundation, Inc. (NeurIPS): La Jolla, CA, USA, 2017.
45. Hendrycks, D.; Gimpel, K. A baseline for detecting misclassified and out-of-distribution examples in neural networks. *arXiv* **2016**, arXiv:1610.02136.
46. Lee, K.; Lee, H.; Lee, K.; Shin, J. Training confidence-calibrated classifiers for detecting out-of-distribution samples. *arXiv* **2018**, arXiv:1711.09325.

47. Lee, K.; Lee, H.; Lee, K.; Shin, J. A simple unified framework for detecting out-of-distribution samples and adversarial attacks. In *Advances in Neural Information Processing Systems 31, Proceedings of the Annual Conference on Neural Information Processing Systems 2018, NeurIPS 2018, Montréal, QC, Canada, 3–8 December 2018*; Neural Information Processing Systems Foundation, Inc. (NeurIPS): La Jolla, CA, USA, 2018.
48. DeVries, T.; Taylor, G.W. Learning confidence for out-of-distribution detection in neural networks. *arXiv* **2018**, arXiv:1802.04865.
49. Shorten, C.; Khoshgoftaar, T.M. A survey on Image Data Augmentation for Deep Learning. *J. Big Data* **2019**, *6*, 60. [CrossRef]
50. Zhang, H.; Cisse, M.; Dauphin, Y.N.; Lopez-Paz, D. mixup: Beyond empirical risk minimization. *arXiv* **2018**, arXiv:1710.09412.
51. Yun, S.; Han, D.; Oh, S.J.; Chun, S.; Choe, J.; Yoo, Y. Cutmix: Regularization strategy to train strong classifiers with localizable features. In Proceedings of the IEEE/CVF International Conference on Computer Vision, Seoul, Korea, 27–28 October 2019.
52. Takahashi, R.; Matsubara, T.; Uehara, K. RICAP: Random Image Cropping and Patching Data Augmentation for Deep CNNs. In Proceedings of the Asian Conference on Machine Learning, Beijing, China, 14–16 November 2018.
53. Lecun, Y.; Bottou, L.; Bengio, Y.; Haffner, P. Gradient-based learning applied to document recognition. *Proc. IEEE* **1998**, *86*, 2278–2324. [CrossRef]
54. Krizhevsky, A.; Hinton, G. *Learning Multiple Layers of Features from Tiny Images*; Technical Report; University of Toronto: Toronto, ON, Canada, 2009.
55. Russakovsky, O.; Deng, J.; Su, H.; Krause, J.; Satheesh, S.; Ma, S.; Huang, Z.; Karpathy, A.; Khosla, A.; Bernstein, M.; et al. Imagenet large scale visual recognition challenge. *Int. J. Comput. Vis.* **2015**, *115*, 211–252. [CrossRef]
56. Zhong, Z.; Zheng, L.; Kang, G.; Li, S.; Yang, Y. Random Erasing Data Augmentation. In Proceedings of the AAAI Conference on Artificial Intelligence, New York, NY, USA, 7–12 February 2020.
57. Japkowicz, N.; Stephen, S. The class imbalance problem: A systematic study. *Intell. Data Anal.* **2002**, *6*, 429–449. [CrossRef]
58. Kingma, D.P.; Ba, J. Adam: A method for stochastic optimization. *arXiv* **2014**, arXiv:1412.6980.
59. Hinton, G.; Vinyals, O.; Dean, J. Distilling the knowledge in a neural network. *arXiv* **2015**, arXiv:1503.02531.
60. DeVries, T.; Taylor, G.W. Improved regularization of convolutional neural networks with cutout. *arXiv* **2017**, arXiv:1708.04552.
61. De Fauw, J.; Ledsam, J.R.; Romera-Paredes, B.; Nikolov, S.; Tomasev, N.; Blackwell, S.; Askham, H.; Glorot, X.; O'Donoghue, B.; Visentin, D.; et al. Clinically applicable deep learning for diagnosis and referral in retinal disease. *Nat. Med.* **2018**, *24*, 1342–1350. [CrossRef]
62. Selvaraju, R.R.; Cogswell, M.; Das, A.; Vedantam, R.; Parikh, D.; Batra, D. Grad-cam: Visual explanations from deep networks via gradient-based localization. In Proceedings of the IEEE International Conference on Computer Vision, Venice, Italy, 22–29 October 2017.
63. Shaban, M.; Awan, R.; Fraz, M.M.; Azam, A.; Tsang, Y.-W.; Snead, D.; Rajpoot, N.M. Context-Aware Convolutional Neural Network for Grading of Colorectal Cancer Histology Images. *IEEE Trans. Med. Imaging* **2020**, *39*, 2395–2405. [CrossRef] [PubMed]

Article

# A New Artificial Intelligence-Based Method for Identifying Mycobacterium Tuberculosis in Ziehl–Neelsen Stain on Tissue

Sabina Zurac [1,2,3,†], Cristian Mogodici [2,†], Teodor Poncu [2,4,†], Mihai Trăscău [2,4,\*], Cristiana Popp [1,2,\*], Luciana Nichita [1,2,3], Mirela Cioplea [1,2], Bogdan Ceachi [2,4], Liana Sticlaru [1,2], Alexandra Cioroianu [1,2], Mihai Busca [1,2], Oana Stefan [1], Irina Tudor [1], Andrei Voicu [2], Daliana Stanescu [2], Petronel Mustatea [2,5], Carmen Dumitru [1] and Alexandra Bastian [1,3]

1. Department of Pathology, Colentina University Hospital, 21 Stefan Cel Mare Str., Sector 2, 020125 Bucharest, Romania; sabina_zurac@yahoo.com (S.Z.); luciana.nichita@umfcd.ro (L.N.); mirelacioplea@yahoo.com (M.C.); liana_ro2004@yahoo.com (L.S.); dragusin_alexandra88@yahoo.com (A.C.); thanatogenesis@gmail.com (M.B.); oana.stefan93@yahoo.com (O.S.); irinafrincu@yahoo.com (I.T.); carmendumitru2004@yahoo.com (C.D.); alexandra.bastian@umfcd.ro (A.B.)
2. Zaya Artificial Intelligence, 9A Stefan Cel Mare Str., 077190 Voluntari, Romania; cristian.mogodici@zaya.ai (C.M.); teodor.poncu@zaya.ai (T.P.); bogdan.ceachi@zaya.ai (B.C.); andrei.voicu@zaya.ai (A.V.); daliana.stanescu@zaya.ai (D.S.); petronel.mustatea@umfcd.ro (P.M.)
3. Department of Pathology, Faculty of Dental Medicine, University of Medicine and Pharmacy Carol Davila, 37 Dionisie Lupu Str., Sector 1, 020021 Bucharest, Romania
4. Department of Computer Science, Faculty of Automatic Control and Computers, University Politehnica of Bucharest, 313 Splaiul Independenței, Sector 6, 060042 Bucharest, Romania
5. Department of Surgery, Faculty of Medicine, University of Medicine and Pharmacy Carol Davila, 37 Dionisie Lupu Str., Sector 1, 020021 Bucharest, Romania
\* Correspondence: mihai.trascau@zaya.ai (M.T.); brigaela@yahoo.com (C.P.)
† These authors contributed equally to this work.

**Abstract:** Mycobacteria identification is crucial to diagnose tuberculosis. Since the bacillus is very small, finding it in Ziehl–Neelsen (ZN)-stained slides is a long task requiring significant pathologist's effort. We developed an automated (AI-based) method of identification of mycobacteria. We prepared a training dataset of over 260,000 positive and over 700,000,000 negative patches annotated on scans of 510 whole slide images (WSI) of ZN-stained slides (110 positive and 400 negative). Several image augmentation techniques coupled with different custom computer vision architectures were used. WSIs automatic analysis was followed by a report indicating areas more likely to present mycobacteria. Our model performs AI-based diagnosis (the final decision of the diagnosis of WSI belongs to the pathologist). The results were validated internally on a dataset of 286,000 patches and tested in pathology laboratory settings on 60 ZN slides (23 positive and 37 negative). We compared the pathologists' results obtained by separately evaluating slides and WSIs with the results given by a pathologist aided by automatic analysis of WSIs. Our architecture showed 0.977 area under the receiver operating characteristic curve. The clinical test presented 98.33% accuracy, 95.65% sensitivity, and 100% specificity for the AI-assisted method, outperforming any other AI-based proposed methods for AFB detection.

**Keywords:** artificial intelligence; tuberculosis; Mycobacterium tuberculosis; Ziehl–Neelsen

## 1. Introduction

Tuberculosis ("consumption", "phthisis", or "white plague") is one of the ancient infectious diseases of humankind. It is produced by Mycobacterium tuberculosis, several other species of mycobacteria are pathogenic in humans (Mycobacterium bovis, Mycobacterium avium intracellulare, Mycobacterium leprae and, in special circumstances, a few others). In 2020, 10 million people had tuberculosis (TB) worldwide, with a yearly death rate of approximately 1.5 million people, thus it is in the top 13 causes of death and second cause of death by an infectious disease after COVID-19 [1].

## 1.1. Rationale for Automatic Detection of Mycobacteria

Diagnosis of TB relies on several methods; mycobacteria identification is one of the most important. In histopathology, identification of mycobacteria requires specific acid-fast stains; the most common one is the Ziehl–Neelsen (ZN) stain, the bacillus appearing red on a blue background. Fluorescent tests such as auramine (golden bacilli on black background) may be also performed but they are more expensive and more difficult to use than ZN [2]. The main problem is that Mycobacterium tuberculosis is a tiny bacillus (length 2–4/width 0.2–0.5 microns) and it must be searched for in a 2 × 3 cm fragment of tissue (6,000,000,000,000 square microns) by thoroughly examining hundreds or thousands of microscopic fields 0.5 mm in diameter.

A pathologist will experience fatigue, diminished attention, and may end by postponing examination. In fact, a pathologist will not examine the whole slide but those areas with lesions more suspicious to present bacilli (necrotic areas and epithelioid granulomatous inflammatory infiltrate with or without Langhans multinucleated giant cells), in order to reduce the time of examination. Attempts of automatic detection of mycobacteria represent the logical answer to this problem.

## 1.2. Literature Review

The first method of artificial intelligence (AI) detection of AFB was developed by Veropoulos et al., in 1999 on smears stained with auramine [3]. Several other studies proposing methods of automated detection of AFB on ZN stains evaluated smears. Other than delCarpio et al., and Law et al. (who evaluated scans of slides containing the whole section present on the slide whole slide images (WSIs)) [4,5], all the other studies evaluated images captured with cameras (small parts of slides) [6–14]. The specificity and sensibility varied from study to study as shown in Table 1.

**Table 1.** Studies of automated detection of AFB on ZN stains on smears.

| Studies on Smears | Year | Precision | Sensitivity | Specificity |
|---|---|---|---|---|
| Ayas et al. [6] | 2014 | N/A * | 89.34 | 96.97 |
| delCarpio et al. [4] | 2019 | N/A | 93.67 | 89.23 |
| Costa et al. [5] | 2008 | N/A | 76.65 | N/A |
| Costa Filho et al. [7] | 2015 | N/A | 96.8 | N/A |
| El-Melegy et al. [8] | 2019 | 82.6 | 98.3 | N/A |
| Khutlang et al. [9] | 2010 | N/A | 97.77 | N/A |
| Kuok et al. [10] | 2019 | N/A | 98.06 | 91.65 |
| Law et al. [11] | 2018 | N/A | 70.4 | 76.6 |
| Panicker et al. [12] | 2018 | 78.40 | 97.13 | N/A |
| Vaid et al. [13] | 2020 | 88.4 | 92.1 | N/A |
| Veropoulos et al. [3] | 1999 | N/A | 94.1 | 97.4 |
| Zhai et al. [14] | 2010 | N/A | 89.34 | 96.97 |

* N/A—not available.

There are other studies published on automatic AFB detection on tissue using WSIs [15–19]. Analyzing tissue is more difficult than analyzing smears. No matter how small a bacillus is, by the mere sectioning of paraffin blocks the bacillus will be cut in different incidences, in various relationships with the adjacent cells/structures. Additionally, artifacts created by sectioning are more complex with a special emphasis on conglomerated red blood cells—the membranes of adjacent red blood cells compressed one on top of the other is a very close mimic of AFB in a ZN stain.

Xiong et al. (2018) developed a convolutional neural network (CNN) model pretrained on the CIFAR-10 dataset [15]. They used a training set of 45 slides (30 positive and 15 negative) digitalized as WSIs with a KF-PRO-005 Digital Section Scanner (Ningbo Jiangfeng Bio-information Technology Co., Ltd., Ningbo, China). Annotations were made with ASAP software, the dataset consisting of 96,530 positive and 2,510,307 negative 32 × 32 pixels patches. Several augmentation techniques were used, extending the positive dataset to 578,191 patches. The test set consisted of 201 slides (108 positive and 93 negative). The test slides were divided into 32 × 32 pixels patches that were then fed to the algorithm. The model analyzed patches from slides and labeled them as positive when the probability score was over 0.5. Only one positive patch is necessary to label the entire WSI as positive. Xiong's et al., method of diagnosis is completely automated—the classification of WSIs is performed by the algorithm and does not involve a human examiner. The test was performed twice. After the first run, the false positive and false negative cases (labeled as such based on human evaluation) were reevaluated by two pathologists; seven cases were primarily missed by pathologists and six cases were not suitable for analysis due to the poor quality of the scans. In the end, the performance metrics of the model are 97.94% for sensitivity and 83.65% for specificity. Based on the data available in their paper, the accuracy of Xiong et al.'s model is 90.55%. The model has a very good sensitivity, catching most of the bacilli but the specificity is too low to give many false positive results. The dataset includes a relatively small number of cases possibly restricting the color variability of the input space that is modeled.

Yang et al. (2020) [16] constructed a pipeline that consists of combining a CNN model (Inception-V3) for tile-based classification and a logistic regression (LR) model for WSI classification. The CNN model was trained to identify tiles (patches) with AFB initially using a dataset of patches of 256 × 256 pixels originating from 14 WSIs (6 positive and 8 negative slides digitized with an Aperio AT Turbo scanner (LeicaBiosystems, Vista, CA, USA)). Then, the model was retrained using a semi-supervised active learning framework that employed the initial dataset completed with new patches originating from 19 negative WSIs. The models were validated on a separate validation set of patches with F1 scores of 99.03% and 98.75%. Then, the retrained CNN model was used to classify patches (in positive and negative) from a set of 134 WSIs (46 positive and 88 negative), the results being used by the LR model to classify the digitized slides. Yang et al., developed an AI-assisted diagnostic method. Their pipeline of analysis creating a score heatmap of AFB probability tiles overlaid onto the WSI. The pathologist examines the areas within the heatmap and confirms the positivity of the WSI. The WSI-level metrics of the pipeline were above 80%: sensitivity 87.13%, specificity 87.62%, and F1 80.18%. The analysis produces a score heat map overlaid on the WSI, guiding the pathologist in the analysis of the probable positive tiles. However, the low specificity (87.62%) indicates that the model identifies numerous patches as false negatives and forces the pathologist to examine thousands of patches suggested as positive. The model yields approximately 4,500 tiles false positive in a $1 \times 1$ cm$^2$ section of tissue. In the end, the time and energy spent analyzing the results might end up more than in the classical ("manual") microscopic examination. Additionally, the diversity of the dataset is limited. The patches are selected from 14 cases (only 6 positive) with a further addition of 19 negative ones.

Lo et al. (2020) [17] developed a CNN model to detect mycobacteria based on a dataset of 1815 patches (blocks) of 20 × 20 pixels (613 positive and 1202 negative) out of which 80% were randomly selected for training, the remaining 20% being kept for validation. Additionally, another 1383 negative patches mimicking AFB (mast cells, background stain, etc.) were selected. The annotations were performed on nine positive slides digitized with the help of a ScanScope XT whole-slide scanner (Aperio, Vista, CA, USA). The model used in the process was a pretrained CNN—AlexNet [20] of five convolution layers. The final three layers were fine-tuned for the target tasks and the blocks from the dataset were resized to 227 × 227 pixels to match the AlexNet architecture. The level of cut-off was established at 0.5. The performance metrics of Lo et al.'s model were 95.3% accuracy, 93.5% sensitivity, and 96.3% specificity. The dataset is significantly smaller than the one we used and was extracted from only nine slides. The results on the validation set are reported at patch level; no WSI analysis is provided.

Pantanowitz et al. (2021) [18] developed an algorithm based on a dataset created from 441 slides scanned with two types of scanners: Aperio AT2 (Leica Biosystems) and Hamamatsu Nanozoomer XR. The dataset included 1,117,586 patches (5678 positive and

1,111,918 negative) selected from 441 WSIs (62 positive and 379 negative) and was separated in three groups: the dataset used for training consisting of 1,054,395 patches (4629 positive and 1,049,766 negative) selected from 418 slides (47 positive and 371 negative); the dataset used for analytical validation (40,957 patches (449 positive and 40,508 negative) selected from 12 WSIs (9 positive and 3 negative)); and the dataset used for testing (22,244 patches (600 positive and 21,644 negative) selected from 11 WSIs (6 positive and 5 negative)). The annotations were made using the aetherSlide application. Two deep CNNs were used in the process, one with high sensitivity and the other with high specificity. The model with the highest accuracy (0.960 at the image patch level—calculated as area under the receiver operating characteristic (ROC) curve (AUC)) in the validation test was selected and used in further clinical validation. Pantanowitz et al., developed an AI-assisted screening method. Their tool displays a gallery of patches with their corresponding probability scores and the WSI to give the possibility of examining the suspicious patches in context. The clinical validation was performed on 138 slides. It consisted of a blind evaluation performed by two pathologists with different levels of expertise by classical "manual" microscopic evaluation of the slides, evaluation of the WSIs, and algorithm-assisted evaluation versus a gold standard represented by the signed-out assessment. The performance metrics of Pantanowitz et al.'s model were 84.6% accuracy, 64.8% sensitivity, and 95.1% specificity.

Zaizen et al. (2022) [19] developed an algorithm to detect AFB using a pre-trained HALO AI CNN. The dataset consisted of 506 AFB annotated on two autopsy cases with TB; the negative ones including two types of artifacts (nuclei of type I epithelial cells as well as fibrin and hyaline membrane) originating from 40 negative biopsies. The slides were digitized using a Motic EasyScan scanner (Motic, Hong Kong, China) and the annotations were performed using the HALO platform (version 3.0; Indica Lab, Albuquerque, NM, USA). Zaizen et al., also developed an AI-supported diagnosing method. Each patch identified as probably positive by the algorithm was evaluated by six pathologists by consensus. The clinical test included 42 cases, the 16 positive ones were either patients diagnosed with mycobacteriosis by bacteriological tests performed on material harvested during bronchoscopy, or patients who developed mycobacteriosis during the follow-up. The performance metrics of Zaizen et al.'s model were 86% sensitivity and 100% specificity.

There is another study presenting an algorithm of automated AFB detection on tissue, but it was developed on pictures (24-bit RGB images at a resolution of 800 × 600 pixels acquired using a digital camera) and not on WSIs. The accuracy obtained was 77.25% [21].

*1.3. Novelty of Our Method*

We propose an automatic method of identifying AFB using deep neural networks. These will be trained to process WSIs and indicate the AFB location. The pathologist analyzes the patches suggested as positive and decides if the slide is positive or not (AI-assisted diagnosis).

Our algorithm has several advantages compared to previous works. Our dataset is much larger, more diverse, and more carefully selected than the other datasets.

1.3.1. Dimension

Its positive component is almost 3 times bigger than the next largest one (263,000 positive patches in ours vs. 96,530 in Xiong et al.'s dataset [15]), which is 429 times bigger than the smallest ones (506 in Zaizen et al.'s set [20]). Our negative patches are 7 times more numerous than the second largest one of Pantanowitz et al. [18] (7,000,000 vs. 1,111,918). Further applied augmentation techniques (both as position—rotations, shifts, crops, etc.—and in image properties—brightness, contrast, saturation, etc.) expanded our positive group of patches to more than 2,500,000.

1.3.2. Diversity

Our dataset resulted from annotation of a total of 510 WSIs; 110 WSIs were positive. The other datasets were constructed based on 2 up to 47 positive WSIs, the variability of the positive images being much lower. Additional consideration of the variability in tinctoriality of ZN staining shows that the diversity of our dataset is significantly increased. We included bacilli in more numerous and diverse backgrounds and in a greater variety of ZN stains.

1.3.3. Model and Augmentations

We used a large set of composable augmentations from which we generated both hard-labeled and soft-labeled training samples. We proposed specific modifications to the original RegNet-X architecture that was adapted such that it better models the domain task.

1.3.4. Case Selection

Our dataset was built after a strict confirmation of positive cases. Additionally, to prevent the situations when the human examiner is not able to identify few bacilli in a paucibacillar TB, cases with specific TB morphology but with negative ZN stains were excluded. One author had to reclassify several cases [15] and another reported a very high number of cases identified as positive after AI-assisted examination (seven newly identified cases out of a total of nine positive ones) [19].

## 2. Materials and Methods

We started by selecting ZN-stained slides originating from positive and negative cases. (Section 2.1). The ZN-stained slides were scanned and annotated, in the end more than 260,000 positive and more than 7,000,000 negative patches of 64 × 64 pixels were selected. (Section 2.2). The dataset was further expanded by different augmentation techniques. (Section 2.3). We identified and customized a deep learning architecture suitable for our task. (Section 2.4). The model was validated on a validation dataset consisting of 286,000 patches (validation set) different from the dataset used for training. (Section 2.5). The model configuration with the best results in validation was further tested in clinical trials. (Section 2.6). In this phase, the scanned image of the ZN-stained slide was uploaded on a platform, divided in 64 × 64 pixels patches, and each patch was analyzed by the algorithm. The algorithm returned a score for each patch and the pathologist received a list of patches sorted in descending order by their corresponding score. The pathologist analyzed the patches, both separately and in context on the slide and decided if the patch was positive or not. Based on this evaluation, the pathologist decided if the slide was positive (one single positive patch is sufficient to diagnose the slide as positive) or not (AI-assisted diagnosis).

The pipeline's performance was measured twice:

- First evaluation ("validation") was performed using patches from pre-selected regions on the slides. On the one hand, the validation gave us the possibility to evaluate the performance of several architectures and allowed us to choose the best model for further use. On the other hand, the results obtained on other pre-selected patches (from slide areas used for active learning) were analyzed one by one by pathologists in order to establish errors (positive patches labeled as negative and vice versa; negative ones falsely labeled as positive). The mislabeled patches were correctly re-labeled and used for re-training and finetuning the model, thus improving its performance.
- Second evaluation ("clinical testing") was performed using WSIs. Each WSI was segmented in 64 × 64 pixels patches and all patches were fed to our model for analysis. The model examined each patch and gave a score of probability (0 to 1)—the probability of the patch to belong to the positive group of patches used for training = to present mycobacteria. The results were displayed as a column of patches with their class score, arranged in descending order of the score (i.e., the patch with the maximum score was listed first). A threshold must be established for a patch to be considered positive; the obvious choice should be 0.5. However, in our testing data we noticed that almost all patches with scores between 0.5 and 0.7 were negative. Our model was not classifying the WSI as positive or negative, instead it revealed

to the pathologist the patches that are more probable to harbor bacilli, leaving the final decision of the diagnosis of WSI to the human examiner. (This is considered AI-assisted diagnosis).

*2.1. Case Selection*

We analyzed the archives of the Department of Pathology of Colentina University Hospital from 2010 to 2022. We selected 2187 cases with ZN stains mentioned in the histopathology report. Consultation cases were excluded.

All the cases were re-evaluated both on H&E and ZN stains available in the archive by SZ (a senior pathologist with 23 years of expertise). Cases with discordances between the initial histopathological report and SZ's re-evaluation were excluded.

- Positive cases group: cases reported as diagnosed with TB with ZN-stain slides positive and reconfirmed as such by microscopic reevaluation.
- Negative cases group: cases without AFB bacilli in ZN stain (both primary—at the moment of diagnosis) and confirmed diagnosis of other illnesses than tuberculosis. Cases with histopathologic appearance highly suggestive of tuberculosis (epithelioid granulomatous inflammatory infiltrate with multinucleated giant cells and coagulative necrosis conserving reticulin network in Gömöri stain—specific morphological aspect of caseating necrosis) and negative ZN stain were NOT included.

All the cases were tissue fragments (either biopsies or surgical specimens) received by our department as fresh or formalin-fixed tissue. After the macroscopic examination (grossing), the fragments were immersed in 10% buffered formalin until the next day (18–24 h), routinely processed to paraffin (automatic tissue processors Leica ASP 200S (see Table S1 Supplementary Material) and Leica Peloris 3 (see Table S2 Supplementary Material) were used), embedded in paraffin blocks (embedding stations ThermoFisher Microm EC 1150 H, Leica EG 1150H, Sakura Tissue Tek and Leica Arcadia), sectioned at 3 microns thick (semi-automated Rotary Microtome Leica RM2255 and RM2265) and stained with ZN staining kit (Ziehl–Neelsen for mycobacteria—microbiology, BioOptica Italy) (see Table S3 Supplementary Material).

H&E slides were used only for analyzing the morphologic lesions, to confirm the diagnosis in positive cases, and to exclude from the negative group the cases with high-morphology suggestive of TB but without AFB in the ZN stain. For our study we use only the ZN-stained slides classified as positive and negative as previously described.

ZN-stained slides were scanned using both manual and automatic scanners, each slide being entirely scanned as whole slide image (WSI) in ".svs" format. The manual scanner was provided by Microvisioneer, Esslingen am Neckar, Germany, and consisted of a Camera Basler Ace 3.2 MP (acA2040-55uc) with Sony IMX265 Sensor and Microvisioneer manual WSI Software Professional Edition. The automatic scanner was a Leica Aperio GT450.

Finally, we obtained 570 WSIs: 133 positive and 437 negative; 510 WSIs—group A (110 positive WSIs and 400 negative WSIs)—were used for training purposes while the remaining 60 WSIs—group B (23 positive WSIs and 37 negative WSIs)—were used for testing (Table 2).

**Table 2.** Structure of the study group.

| Group | Positive | Negative | Total |
| --- | --- | --- | --- |
| A (training) | 110 | 400 | 510 |
| B (testing) | 23 | 37 | 60 |
| Total | 133 | 437 | 570 |

*2.2. Annotation Process*

The WSIs from group A were annotated by 7 pathologists with various experience (Table S4 Supplementary Material) using an in-house platform for annotation and Cytomine application (Cytomine Corporation SA, Liège). Positive areas were identified either as patches (less than 64 × 64 px) in our in-house annotation platform or point-like annotations of the bacillus in Cytomine platform. Negative samples were drawn either from WSIs labeled as negative or from manually annotated negative areas inside WSIs labeled as positive. Patches selection from negative WSIs was performed in two steps: firstly, the WSI area was filtered to contain a sufficient amount of tissue (versus background); secondly, a 64 × 64 patch was sampled via a uniform distribution from this area. In the end, we obtained a pool of negative samples containing more than 700 million patches before applying any augmentations. Examples of positive and negative areas are depicted in Figures S1–S6 (Supplementary Material).

*2.3. Image Augmentation Techniques*

Even though the dataset obtained via the annotation process contains more than 260,000 positive examples, there is a large diversity that the staining process induces to the color space of both positive and negative WSIs. In order to mitigate this, we have employed extensive augmentation techniques to cover a wider variety in WSIs. The augmentation transformations were applied to all training patches. These included random rotations in the range of 0 to 90 degrees (clockwise and counterclockwise); random shifts; random crops; and random brightness, contrast and saturation changes. In addition to these specific transformations, we also extracted positive patches around the annotated AFBs by shifting a maximum of 24 pixels in any of the two axes. Since all transformations were applied in a chain, specific to sample interpolation techniques, we considered that training examples have diversified by at least one order of magnitude.

*2.4. Deep Learning Model Development and Training*

Our patch-based classifier for AFB detection is based on RegNetX4 architecture. This deep convolutional neural network manages to yield state-of-the-art performance while preserving simplicity and speed. It has the advantage of requiring less hyperparameter tuning, which is an important consideration when dealing with the large amount of data and data manipulation techniques used in our setting. In order to better fit the task at hand, we have adapted the architecture through various custom modifications:

- We reduced the kernel size in the stem layer (plausible morphology of bacillus can be constrained in a 3 × 3 convolution filter or 5 × 5 convolution filter);
- We reduced the number of strided convolutions, as an overall larger receptive field in the final stages is not necessarily helpful due to the low spatial size of the target class;
- We employed parallel dilated convolutions (i.e., selective kernel convolutions [22], atrous convolutions [23]) in order to accommodate morphologies that are not necessarily captured in a 3 × 3 filter while still keeping a reasonable amount of trainable parameters;
- We opted for reflection padding instead of zero padding in all padded convolution layers to reduce locality bias learned by the network in order to be more robust to bacillus positioning inside boxes served at inference or testing time.

The network variant we used contains less than 160 million learnable parameters, allowing for adequate inference speed even when not using high-end hardware, without any degradation of the performance metrics.

We trained our model in a distributed fashion using parameter replicas for each Graphics Processing Unit (GPU) and gradient averaging before broadcasting parameter updates. We used a batch size of about 2048 per GPU with positive and negative examples roughly evenly split in order to mitigate the severe class imbalance. We experimented with various proportions (positive vs. negative) starting from 25–75% up to 75–25% using 5% increments. We limited our learning procedure to a maximum of 100 million samples seen (including augmented patches). The optimizer used was AdaBound where the step size $\alpha$ is provided by a linear warm-up cosine scheduler with periodic restarts [24]. Inference is performed only on the parts of the WSI containing a relevant amount of tissue. Filtering the WSI was performed using the same method as for filtering the training areas used for extracting patches. Depending on the WSI size and CPU threads used for WSI patch area extraction our baseline processing pipeline (i.e., 1 CPU thread) manages to process a WSI in 5 to 15 min.

*2.5. Model Validation*

We constructed a set of validation patches by annotating several areas collected from 37 WSIs; obviously, none of the areas selected for validation were previously used for training. The areas thus collected have been divided in non-overlapping patches of $64 \times 64$ pixels, which were subsequently annotated by the team of pathologists as either positive or negative. We have obtained 286,000 validation patches of which 15,000 are positive and 271,000 negatives. The class imbalance is intentional, as it is much more likely for the model to generate false positives than false negatives and this data distribution is much closer to real conditions than a balanced one.

*2.6. Testing Process*

For the testing process four teams of two pathologists each were involved; each team included pathologists of similar experience (Table S5 Supplementary Material). We compared three types of results: B1—results obtained by examining slides with a bright-field light microscope; B2—results obtained by examining the WSIs scanned with a Leica Aperio GT450 automated scanner; and B3—results obtained by algorithm-aided WSIs evaluation. A wash-out period of 2 weeks between each type of evaluation was respected. For each case, in each scenario (B1, B2, and B3), the pathologist registered the status (positive or negative) and the time required to reach the diagnosis. No time limit was established for examination of either slides or WSIs. All the results were compared with the "gold standard"—the original histopathological report reconfirmed by H&E and ZN stains reexamination (see Section 2.1).

*2.7. Statistical Analysis*

Model validation was performed using the validation set that the team of pathologists had produced. A receiver operating characteristic (ROC) curve was plotted to describe the diagnostic ability of the model to classify patches as containing AFB or not. The imbalance we have imposed between the number of positive and negative patches in the validation dataset has led us to select the Precision–Recall curve as a useful measure to compute the area under the receiver operating characteristic curve (AUC) for (AUPR). Due to the same reason, we also computed the F1 score and Matthew's correlation coefficient (MCC). All metrics were computed using Python libraries scikit-learn and matplotlib.

The performance metrics used to evaluate our proposed method in clinical tests are listed in Table S6 (Supplemental Material).

Statistical significance of the difference between two groups was analyzed using the $\chi^2$ test, where applicable. Statistical significance was defined as $p < 0.05$, and all statistical analyses were performed using the EXCEL program.

## 3. Results

*3.1. Internal Validation*

We have evaluated the model on the validation set. Accurately validating on entire WSIs would require slides that are completely annotated (to have each AFB indicated by an expert). The cost of obtaining such data is prohibitive and requires compromising on staining diversity, tissue morphology, and artifact types, as opposed to performing validation on selected interest areas from multiple WSI.

The evaluation of the configurations has been performed on the best checkpoint identified during the training process. We have obtained an AUC for the ROC curve (Figure 1) of 0.977 and an AUPR for the Precision-Recall curve of 0.843 (Figure 2). The sensitivity, specificity, F1-score and MCC curves are described in Figure 2. It is important to note that the AUC value the model obtained for the ROC curve is considered to be excellent for models used in medical testing [25–27]. By setting an arbitrary value of 0.5 for the decision threshold during validation (patches over the threshold are considered positive while under the threshold they are negative) we obtained an accuracy of 0.969, a sensitivity of 0.877, a specificity of 0.974, an F1-score of 0.923, and MCC of 0.745 (Figure 3).

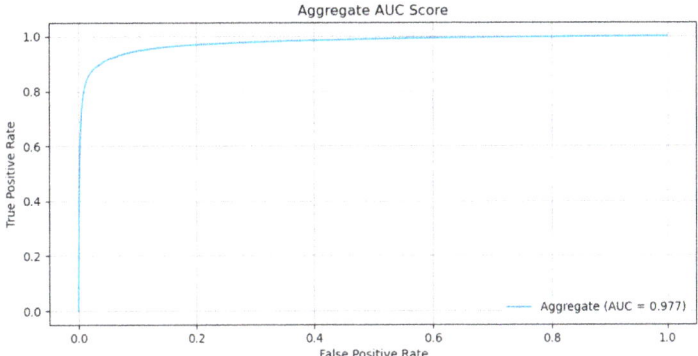

**Figure 1.** ROC curve obtained by the model on the validation set.

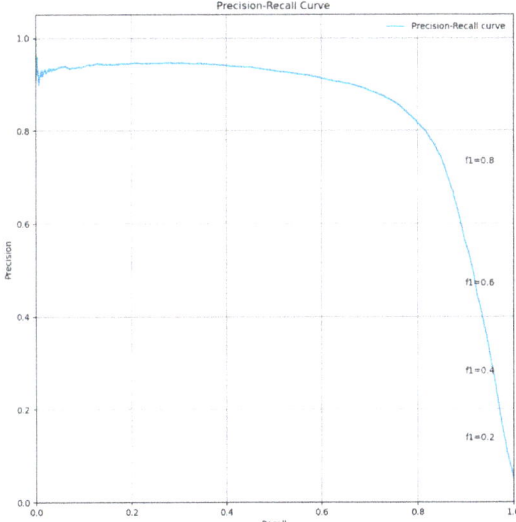

**Figure 2.** Precision-recall curve obtained by the model on the validation set.

Most frequent false positive findings during validation (at patch level) were given by red blood cells, mast cells, and fibrotic septa. Parts of red blood cells mimic AFB (Figure 4). In fact, even in classical microscopic examination of ZN stained slides, the pathologist has difficulties in differentiating between bacilli and the periphery of red blood cells, especially in case of congestion (when several red blood cells are compressed within a narrow capillary). In addition, since ZN stain has quite important variation, the level of acid–alcohol discoloration can be low, thus preserving a more intense coloration of red blood cells (red or bright pink instead of pale pink)—the internal control for a proper ZN stain is a pale-pink color of red blood cells.

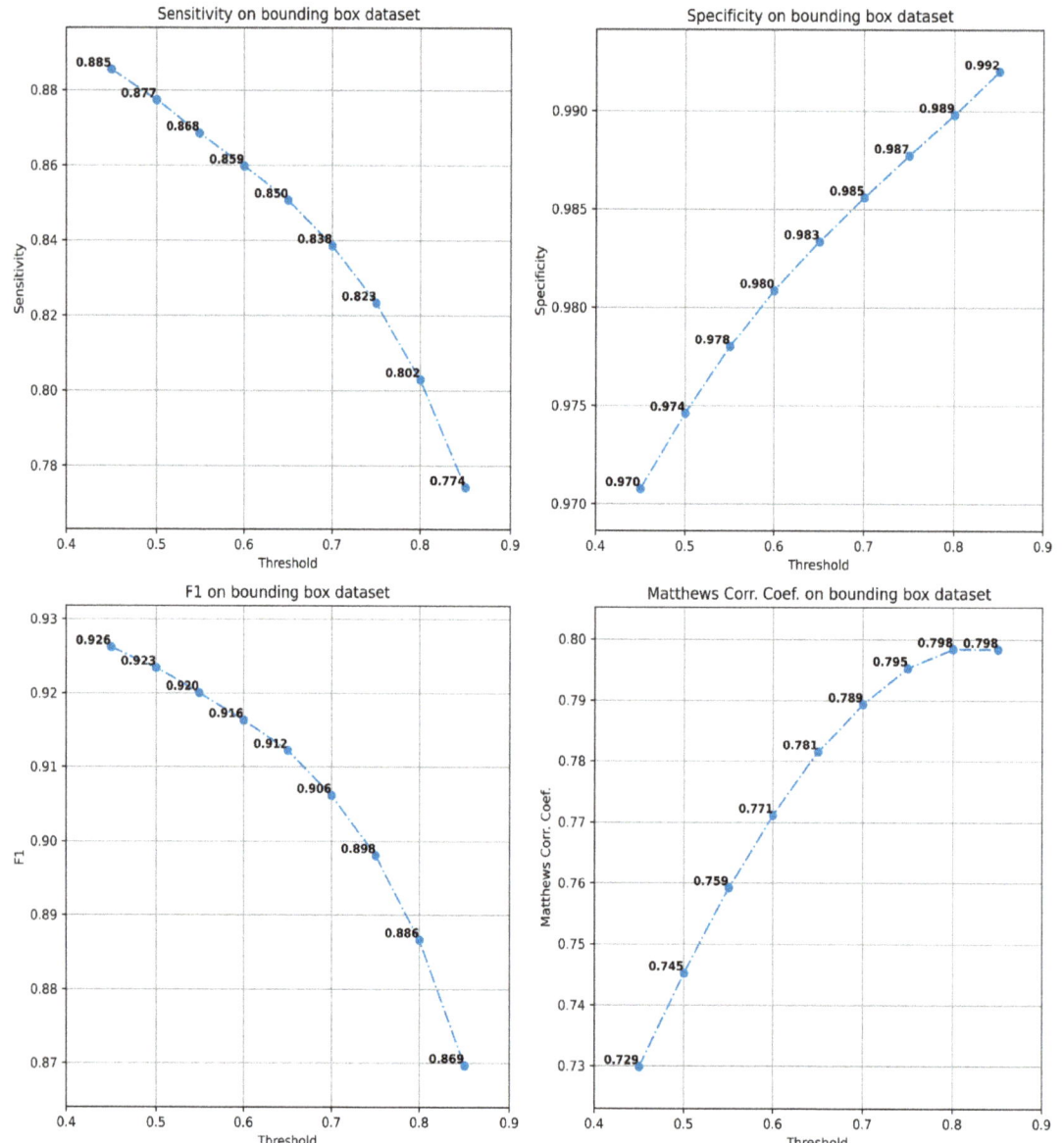

**Figure 3.** Sensitivity, specificity, F1-score, and MCC of the model computed for various thresholds.

Granules from the cytoplasm of mast cells are colored in purple in ZN by methylene blue that is used for staining the background (see Table S3 Supplementary Material for the protocol of ZN stain). Additionally, parts of a mast cell cytoplasm can be confused for an AFB when the patch includes a very small part of the cell (Figure 5).

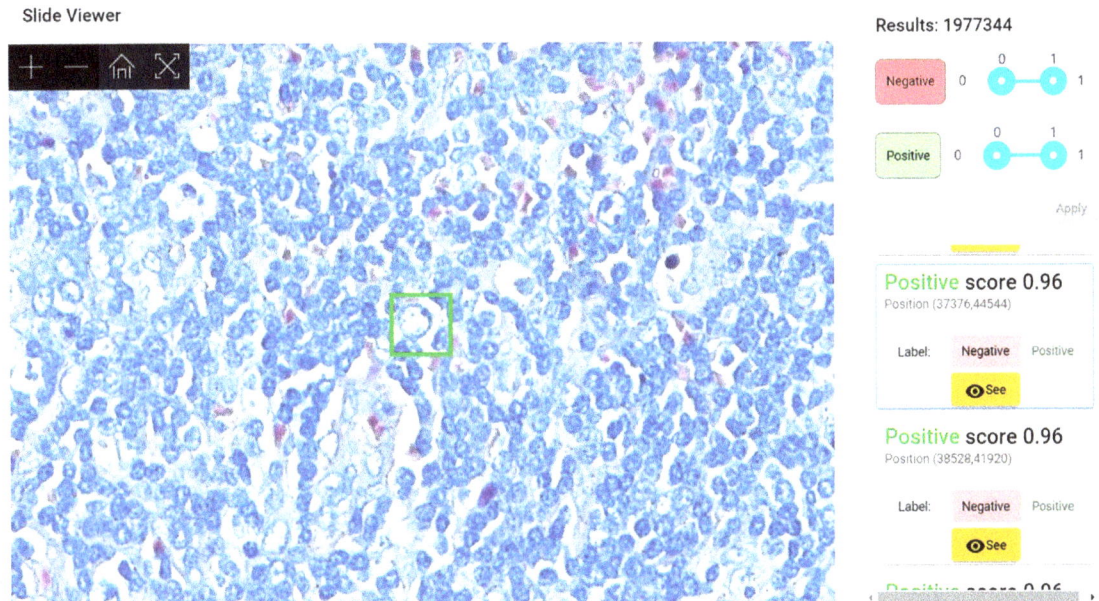

**Figure 4.** Patch of 64 × 64 pixels (in green) with a positive score (probability of similarity with positive dataset used for training) of 0.96 due to the presence in the upper left margin of the green square of a red blood cell. Lymph node with toxoplasmosis ZN × 400.

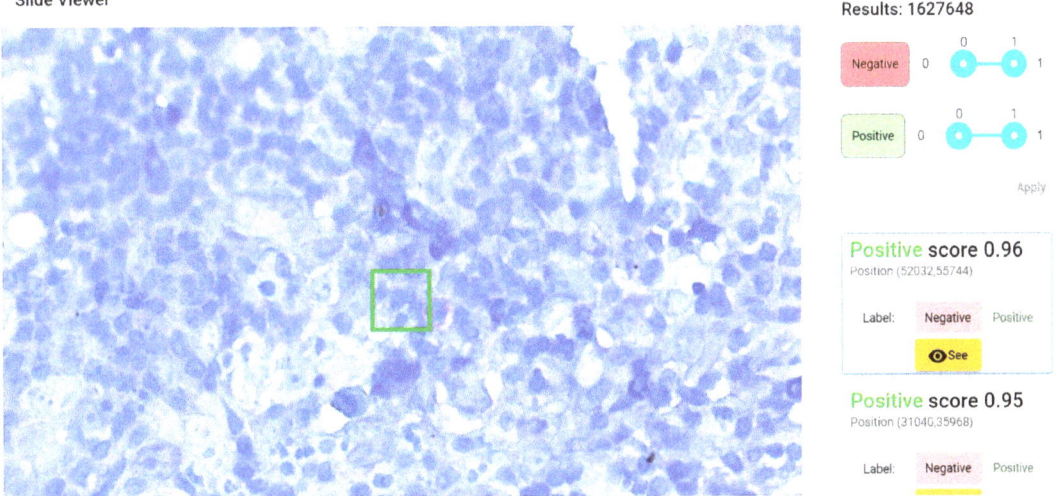

**Figure 5.** Patch of 64 × 64 pixels (in green) with a positive score of 0.96 due to the presence in the inferior right margin of the green square of several purple mast cell granules with linear arrangement mimicking an acid-fast bacillus. Hodgkin's lymphoma, nodular sclerosis variant. ZN × 400.

All patches with scores over 0.7—either positive or negative—were re-evaluated by pathologists. This analysis revealed that very few patches with a negative score over 0.7 (i.e., "more likely similar with negative training data set") were a false negative. Several patches with a positive score over 0.7 (i.e., "more likely similar with positive training data set") were erroneously labeled as such. We employed an active learning strategy for training and fine-tuning the model. To this end, we selected a fine-tuning holdout set consisting of several areas from the training WSIs that were non-overlapping with the annotations (either positive or negative). First, the model was trained from scratch with the available data. Then, inference was performed on the validation set, and the validation metrics were assessed (e.g., sensitivity, specificity, F1-score, etc.). The model then was used to classify the areas in the holdout set (which contain both positive and negative patches). The results obtained for the holdout set classification were analyzed by the pathologist team, and the mislabeled patches are correctly relabeled as negative or positive. In the end, the model was retrained for fine-tuning with these new patches. Performance was further improved by performing several iterations of this active learning cycle for the data. Given this process, as described in Figure 6, the model can be easily adapted to new conditions and variations when we obtain new WSIs.

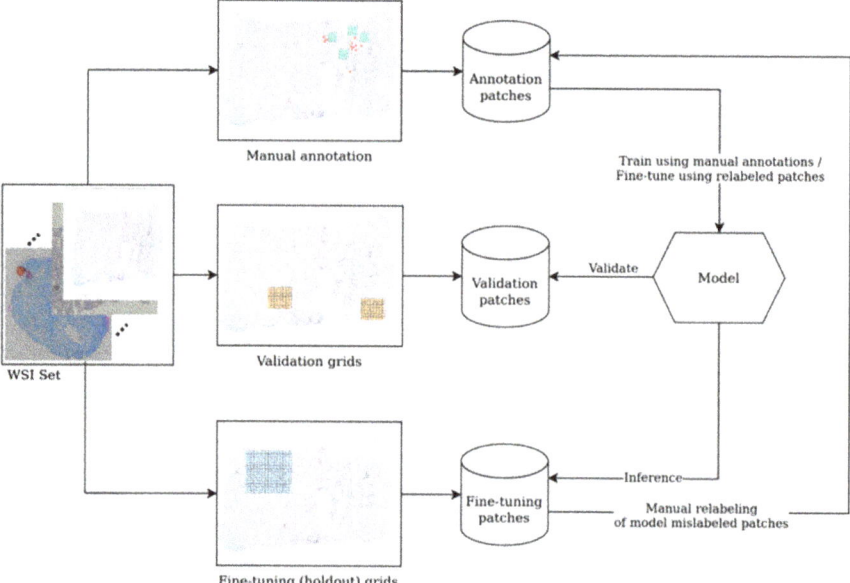

**Figure 6.** Active learning process for iteratively improving the model performance.

*3.2. Clinical Testing*

Our test group included 37 males (61.67%) and 23 females (38.33%) with a median age of 42.25 years (the youngest patient was 1 year old and the oldest was 80 years old). The specimens were represented by: lymph nodes—35 cases (58.33%), lung—10 cases (16.67%), skin—7 cases (11.67%), striated muscle—5 cases (8.33%), and intestine—3 cases (5.00%). A total of 23 cases were diagnosed as tuberculosis (38.33%) while 37 cases (61.67%) were inflammation other than tuberculosis or cancer (Figure 7): cat scratch disease 5.00%, sarcoidosis 6.67%, unspecific granulomatous inflammation 8.33%, Kikuchi 3.33%, toxoplasmosis 1.67%, unspecific inflammation 8.33%, reactive lymphadenitis 10.00%, non-Hodgkin's lymphoma 6.67%, Hodgkin's lymphoma 6.67%, and carcinoma 5.00%. All the cases of tuberculosis had AFB present in ZN stain; obviously, no AFB were present on ZN stain in the other cases. In order to avoid a possible bias in evaluating AFB presence due to correct identification of the lesion (i.e., diagnosing other disease than TB based on morphology alone), all the negative cases were selected to present either necrotizing granulomatous inflammation (cat scratch disease or unspecific granulomatous inflammation), granulomas (sarcoidosis), epithelioid histiocytes (toxoplasmosis), necrosis (Kikuchi, unspecific inflammation, lymphomas, or carcinomas), or florid histiocytosis (reactive lymphadenitis, or unspecific inflammation). No clinical data were available to the pathologists when examining either slides or WSIs.

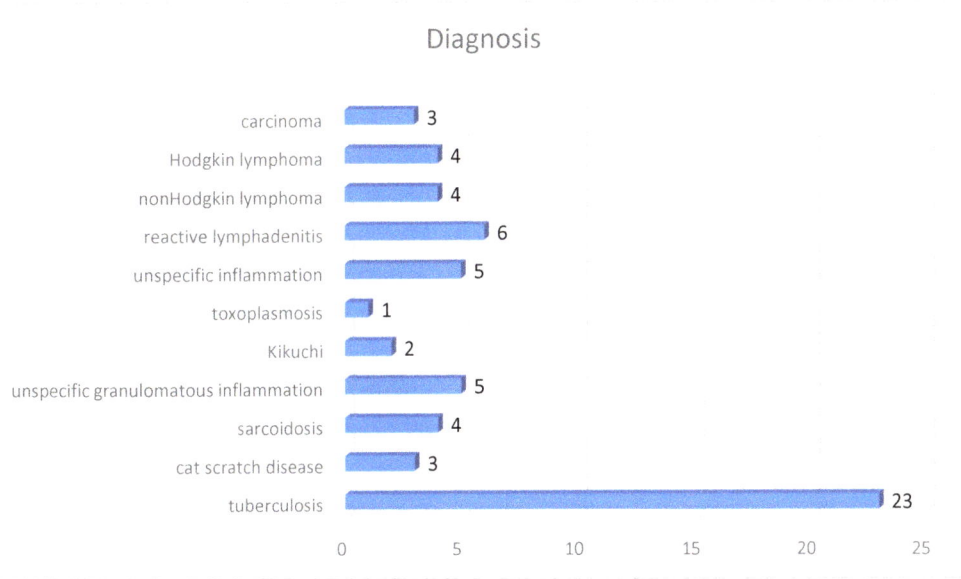

Figure 7. Repartition of the test group according to diagnosis.

3.2.1. WSIs Analysis

The results of analyzing WSIs by pathologists showed interesting results (Table 3). Accuracy (capacity to identify closer to the true value) was, with one exception, higher than 0.8333 (varied from 0.6167 to 0.9333). Sensitivity (capacity to identify true positives) varied from 0.3913 to 0.9565 and specificity (capacity to identify true negatives) varied from 0.7567 to 0.9459.

Table 3. Statistical measures of the pathologists' performance on whole slide images.

|  | Senior Pathologist 1A | Senior Pathologist 1B | Senior Pathologist 2A | Senior Pathologist 2B | Pathologist A | Pathologist B | Resident A | Resident B | Our model |
|---|---|---|---|---|---|---|---|---|---|
| Sensitivity | 0.8261 | 0.8261 | 0.9565 | 1 | 0.4782 | 1 | 0.5652 | 0.3913 | 0.9565 |
| Specificity | 0.9459 | 0.9730 | 0.9189 | 0.8648 | 1 | 0.8378 | 1 | 0.7567 | 1 |
| Precision | 0.9048 | 0.9500 | 0.8800 | 0.8214 | 1 | 0.7931 | 1 | 0.5000 | 1 |
| Negative predictive value | 0.8974 | 0.9000 | 0.9714 | 1 | 0.7551 | 1 | 0.7872 | 0.6667 | 0.9737 |
| False negative rate | 0.1739 | 0.1739 | 0.0435 | 0 | 0.5217 | 0 | 0.4348 | 0.6087 | 0.0435 |
| False positive rate | 0.0541 | 0.0270 | 0.0811 | 0.1351 | 0 | 0.1622 | 0 | 0.2432 | 0 |
| Accuracy | 0.9000 | 0.9167 | 0.9333 | 0.9167 | 0.8000 | 0.9000 | 0.8333 | 0.6167 | 0.9833 |
| F1 | 0.8636 | 0.8837 | 0.9167 | 0.9019 | 0.6471 | 0.8846 | 0.7222 | 0.4390 | 0.9778 |
| Exposure to WSI (years) | 1.5 | 1.5 | 1.5 | 1 | 0.25 | 0.5 | 0 | 0 | - |
| Experience (decades) | 1.2 | 1.4 | 0.7 | 0.9 | 0.4 | 0.4 | 0 | 0 | - |

The accuracy ($p = 0.1$), precision ($p = 0.09$), and specificity ($p = 0.06$) had a general tendency to increase as the experience of the pathologist increases, but there was no uniformity towards an increase in the sensitivity with experience ($p = 0.25$) (Figure 8a–d).

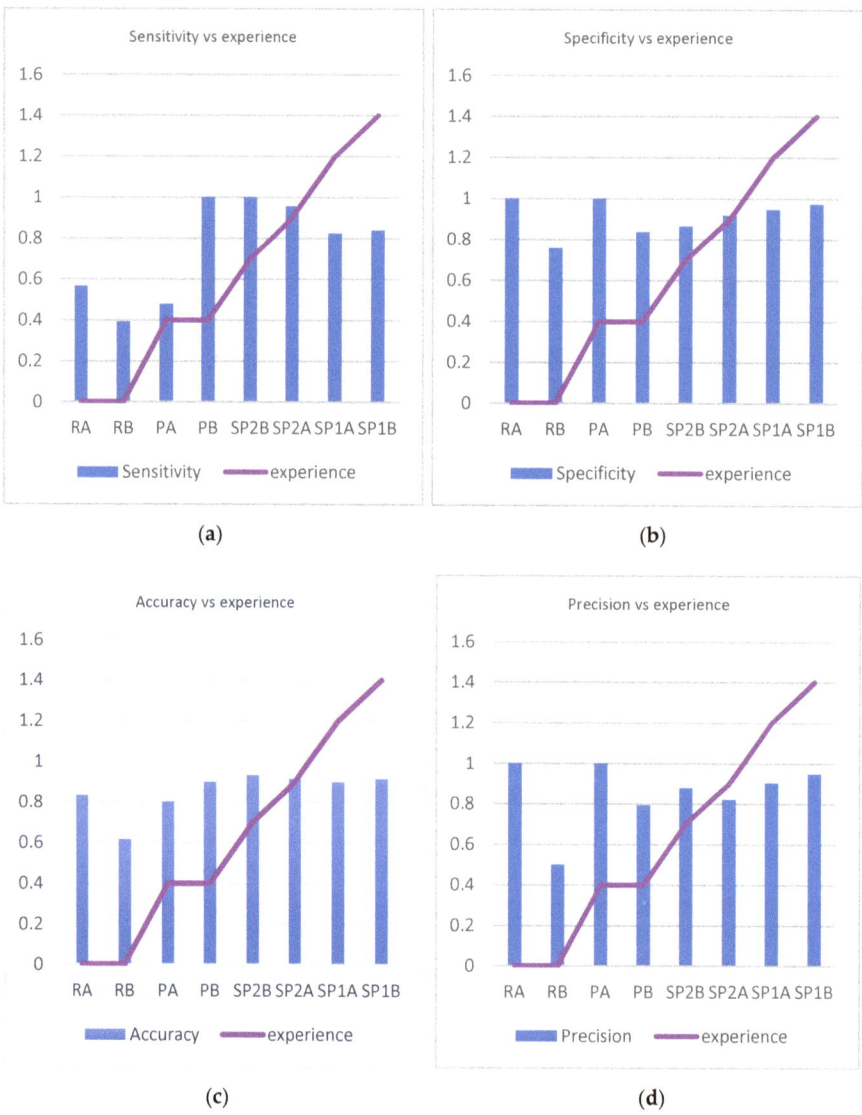

**Figure 8.** Variation of sensitivity, specificity, accuracy, and precision in correlation to pathologists' experience. (**a**) Variation of sensitivity in correlation to pathologists' experience. (**b**) Variation of specificity in correlation to pathologists' experience. (**c**) Variation of accuracy in correlation to pathologists' experience. (**d**) Variation of precision in correlation to pathologists' experience.

When looking at sensitivity, specificity, precision, and accuracy in correlation with experience in analyzing WSI (exposure to WSI) we identify a statistically significant association for specificity (P chi test 0.004), precision (P chi test 0.008), and accuracy (P chi test 0.012), but not for sensitivity (P chi test 0.06) (Figure 9a–d).

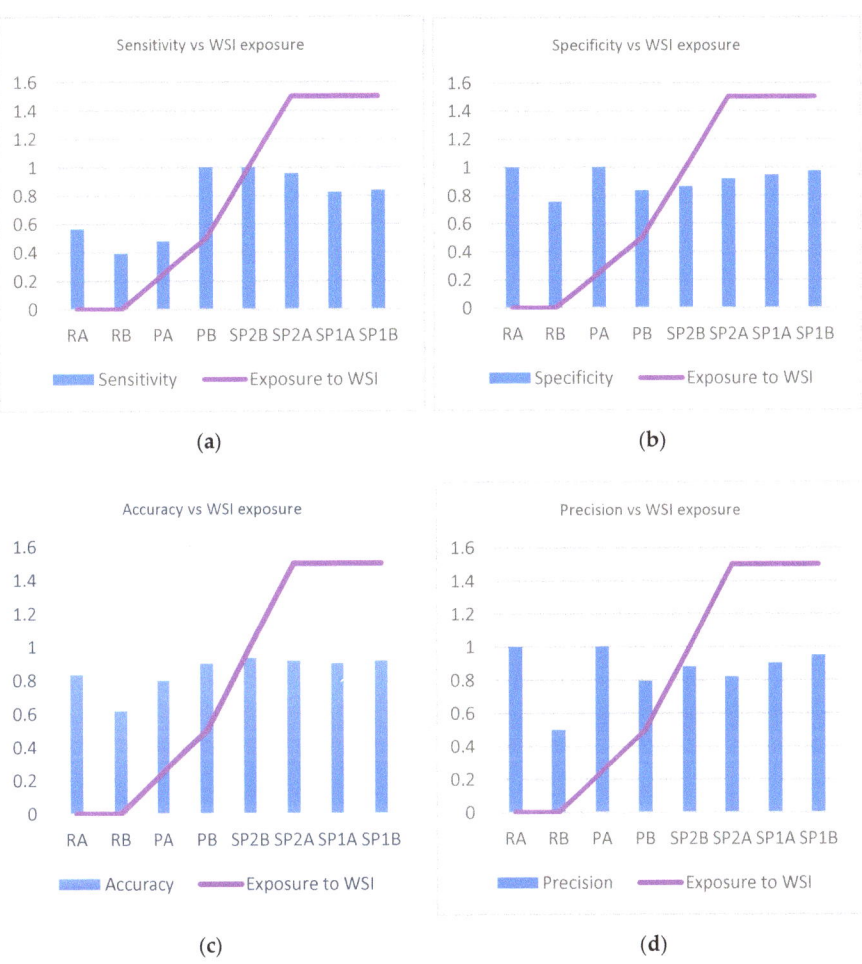

**Figure 9.** Variation of sensitivity, specificity, accuracy and precision in correlation to pathologists' experience of examining whole slide images. (**a**) Variation of sensitivity in correlation to pathologists' experience of examining WSIs. (**b**) Variation of specificity in correlation to pathologists' experience of examining WSIs. (**c**) Variation of accuracy in correlation to pathologists' experience of examining WSIs. (**d**) Variation of precision in correlation to pathologists' experience of examining WSIs.

3.2.2. Slide Analysis

Slide analysis (microscopic examination) revealed much better results than those obtained on WSIs (Table 4). The senior pathologists had one to three errors per person (senior pathologist 1A—2 errors, senior pathologist 1B—3 errors, senior pathologist 2A—3 errors, senior pathologist 2B—one error; all but one error were false negative); the pathologists had more errors—pathologist A—12 errors, pathologist B—4 errors; 4 of them were false positive and 12 false negative) while residents had 29 errors (resident A 12 errors, all false negative, resident B—17 errors, 2 false positive, 15 false negative). The results were much better than those obtained by evaluating WSIs but algorithm-assisted evaluation had better results than human evaluation either on WSIs or slides. In fact, our model results (AI-assisted evaluation) were better or similar to pathologists examining slides. Senior pathologist 2B was identical, with only one false negative result, for the same case. The resulting accuracy for our model was 98.33% with only one false negative result—sensibility of 95.65% and no false positives—specificity of 100%.

Table 4. Statistical measures of the pathologists' performance on glass slides.

| | Senior Pathologist 1A | Senior Pathologist 1B | Senior Pathologist 2A | Senior Pathologist 2B | Pathologist A | Pathologist B | Resident A | Resident B | Our model |
|---|---|---|---|---|---|---|---|---|---|
| Sensitivity | 0.9130 | 0.8695 | 0.9130 | 0.9565 | 0.5217 | 0.9565 | 0.4782 | 0.3478 | 0.9565 |
| Specificity | 1 | 1 | 0.9729 | 1 | 0.9729 | 0.9189 | 1 | 0.9459 | 1 |
| Precision | 1 | 1 | 0.9545 | 1 | 0.9230 | 0.88 | 1 | 0.8 | 1 |
| Negative predictive value | 0.9487 | 0.925 | 0.9473 | 0.9736 | 0.7659 | 0.9714 | 0.7551 | 0.7 | 0.9737 |
| False negative rate | 0.0869 | 0.1304 | 0.0869 | 0.0434 | 0.4782 | 0.0435 | 0.5217 | 0.6521 | 0.0435 |
| False positive rate | 0 | 0 | 0.0270 | 0 | 0.0270 | 0.0811 | 0 | 0.0540 | 0 |
| Accuracy | 0.9667 | 0.95 | 0.95 | 0.9833 | 0.8 | 0.9333 | 0.8 | 0.7166 | 0.9833 |
| F1 | 0.9545 | 0.9302 | 0.9333 | 0.9778 | 0.6667 | 0.9167 | 0.6471 | 0.4848 | 0.9778 |
| Experience (decades) | 1.2 | 1.4 | 0.7 | 0.9 | 0.4 | 0.4 | 0 | 0 | - |

### 3.2.3. Time Analysis

Time dedicated for WSI examination varied from 10 s to 80 min with an average time of 11.43 min per WSI. The average time of examination varied between examiners from 5.48 min to 17.06 min with shorter times for positive slides and longer for negative ones (either true or false negatives). In fact, for every pathologist, the longest time of examination was recorded for negative cases (true negative for seven examiners and false negative for the remaining one) and the shortest for true positive ones (Table 5). No relation with experience or prior exposure to WSI was identified.

Table 5. Time used by pathologists when examining whole slide images.

| Time of Examination (min) | Senior Pathologist 1A | Senior Pathologist 1B | Senior Pathologist 2A | Senior Pathologist 2B | Pathologist A | Pathologist B | Resident A | Resident B |
|---|---|---|---|---|---|---|---|---|
| All WSIs | 1–45 | 1–35 | 0.08–20 | 0.16–26 | 0.5–80 | 0.33–35 | 9.5–35 | 0.1–28 |
| Average all WSIs | 17.07 | 12.38 | 5.48 | 5.78 | 14.04 | 13.58 | 14.95 | 8.16 |
| True positive | 1–18 | 1–18 | 0.08–15 | 0.16–8 | 0.5–25 | 0.33–21 | 0.5–32 | 0.1–13 |
| Average true positive | 7.26 | 6.54 | 4.28 | 2.47 | 5.59 | 7.64 | 12.54 | 3.51 |
| False positive | 9–14 | 27 | 4–15 | 0.16–8 | - | 4–30 | - | 3–21 |
| Average false positive | 11.50 | 27.00 | 11.33 | 4.43 | - | 10.67 | - | 7.33 |
| True negative | 8–45 | 2–35 | 1–20 | 1–26 | 0.5–80 | 7–35 | 3–35 | 2–20 |
| Average true negative | 21.37 | 11.56 | 5.88 | 8.38 | 12.38 | 18.55 | 14.14 | 7.25 |
| False negative | 15-36 | 5–32 | 1 | - | 2-52 | - | 7-29 | 5-28 |
| Average false negative | 28.75 | 21.50 | 1.00 | - | 26.92 | - | 21.10 | 13.50 |

When examining slides, the pathologists spent less time than for WSIs. The overall interval varied from 3 s to 49 min with an average of 5.25 min (Table 6).

Table 6. Time used by pathologists when examining slides by microscope.

| Time of Examination (min) | Senior Pathologist 1A | Senior Pathologist 1B | Senior Pathologist 2A | Senior Pathologist 2B | Pathologist A | Pathologist B | Resident A | Resident B |
|---|---|---|---|---|---|---|---|---|
| All slides | 1–20 | 1–49 | 0.05–10 | 0.16–26 | 0.5–38 | 0.33–16 | 0.5–22 | 0.5–19 |
| Average all slides | 6.13 | 7.08 | 2.84 | 4.25 | 5.44 | 5.06 | 6.15 | 5.09 |
| True positive | 1–19 | 1–32 | 0.05–10 | 0.16–8 | 0.5–10 | 0.16–15 | 0.5–18 | 0.5–11 |
| Average true positive | 3.71 | 11.2 | 3.21 | 3.42 | 3.04 | 5.46 | 0.92 | 2.75 |
| False positive | | | 8 | | 0.5 | 3–16 | | 1–3 |
| Average false positive | - | - | 8 | - | 0.5 | 11.33 | - | 2 |
| True negative | 1–20 | 1–16 | 0.05–10 | 1–26 | 0.5–38 | 0.33–11 | 0.5–12 | 1–11 |
| Average true negative | 7.46 | 3.45 | 2.52 | 4.76 | 4.77 | 3.98 | 4.42 | 4.1 |
| False negative | 5–9 | 2–49 | 1–4 | 4 | 1.5–25 | 13 | 1–22 | 2–19 |
| Average false negative | 7 | 24.33 | 2.5 | 4 | 10.68 | 13 | 8.15 | 9.06 |

Time used by pathologists in AI-assisted examination varied from 9 s to 2.002 min for positive slides (average 0.61 min). In most of the cases, the AFB were present in the first or the second patch in the list. In one case the pathologist examined 25 patches to find a convincing AFB.

We exemplify two cases that required pathologists 32–33 min for examination (an average of 12–13 min for classic microscopic examination) (Figures 10 and 11). In negative cases, a maximum of 4–5 min weas necessary for confirmation of negativity. Average time needed for AI-assisted examination was 1.85 (1 min 51 s).

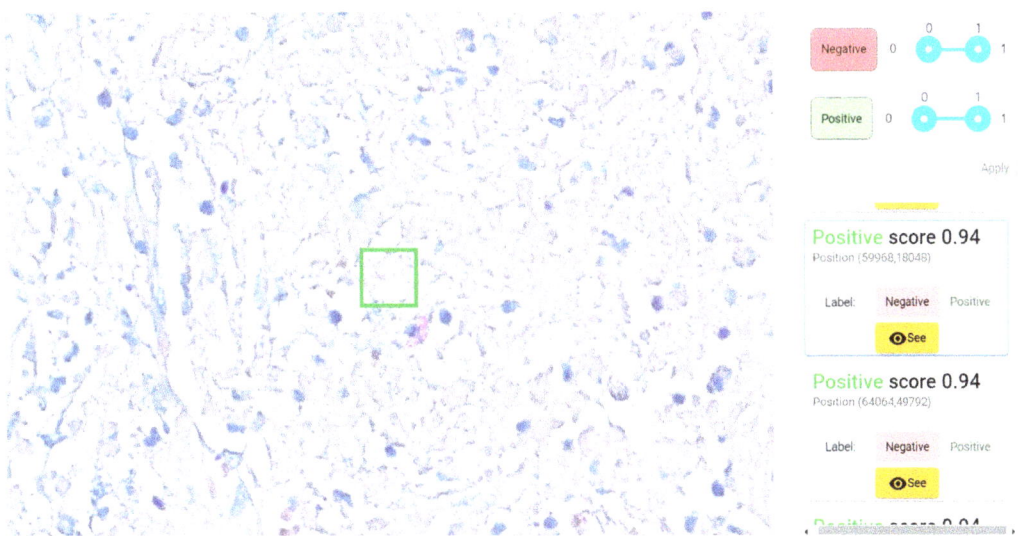

**Figure 10.** Paucibacillary lesion identified as positive by 5 of 8 pathologists in 1–32 min (medium of 13.75 min); the time of AI-assisted examination was 15 s (the convincing positive patch—the green square—was the second one).

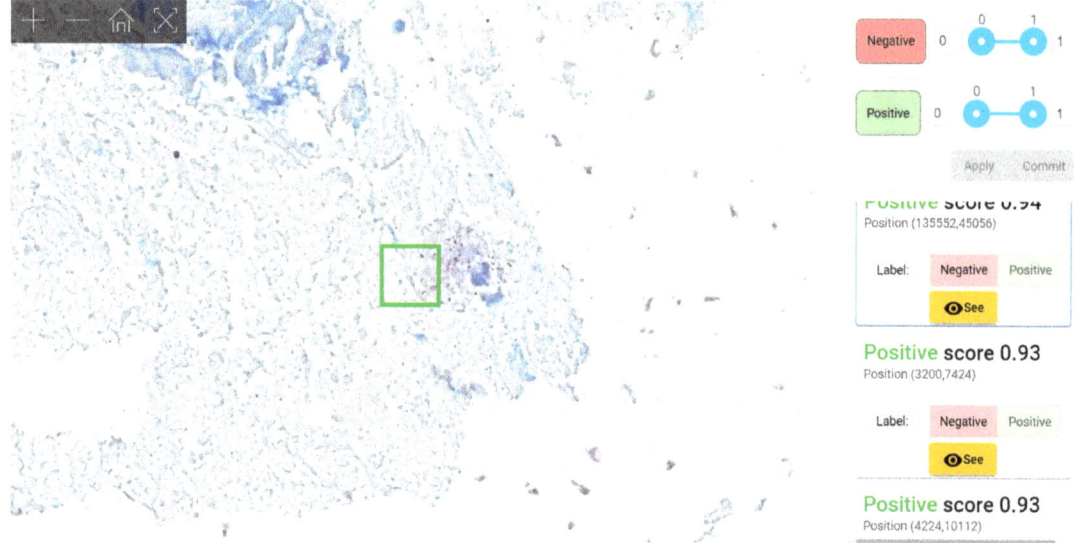

**Figure 11.** Paucibacillary lesion identified as positive by 6 of 8 pathologists in 1–33 min (medium of 12.25 min); the time of AI-assisted examination was 9 s (first patch—green square—was convincingly positive).

3.2.4. Error Analysis

We analyzed the errors made by pathologists when evaluating WSIs. To our surprise, human examination of WSIs results in an amazing proportion of 31 WSIs of a total of 60 cases that were erroneously interpreted (51.67%) with a total of 71 misinterpretations of 480 evaluations (Table 7, Figure 12a). Even when residents were excluded, errors occurred for 21 WSIs (35%)—more than one third of the cases (Table S7 Supplemental Material, Figure 12b).

**Table 7.** Errors in WSIs evaluation for qualified pathologists and residents.

| | Qualified Pathologists and Residents (8 Persons × 60 WSI) | | | |
|---|---|---|---|---|
| | | Negative Cases | Positive Cases | Total |
| | 0 | 23 | 6 | 29 |
| | 1 | 9 | 3 | 12 |
| | 2 | 1 | 5 | 6 |
| No of errors per WSI | 3 | 3 | 5 | 8 |
| | 4 | 0 | 3 | 3 |
| | 5 | 1 | 0 | 1 |
| | 6 | 0 | 1 | 1 |
| Cases with errors (of 60 WSIs) | | 14 | 17 | 31 |
| % | | 37.84% | 73.91% | 51.67% |
| No of errors (of 480 examinations) | | 25 | 46 | 71 |
| % | | 8.45% | 25.00% | 14.79% |

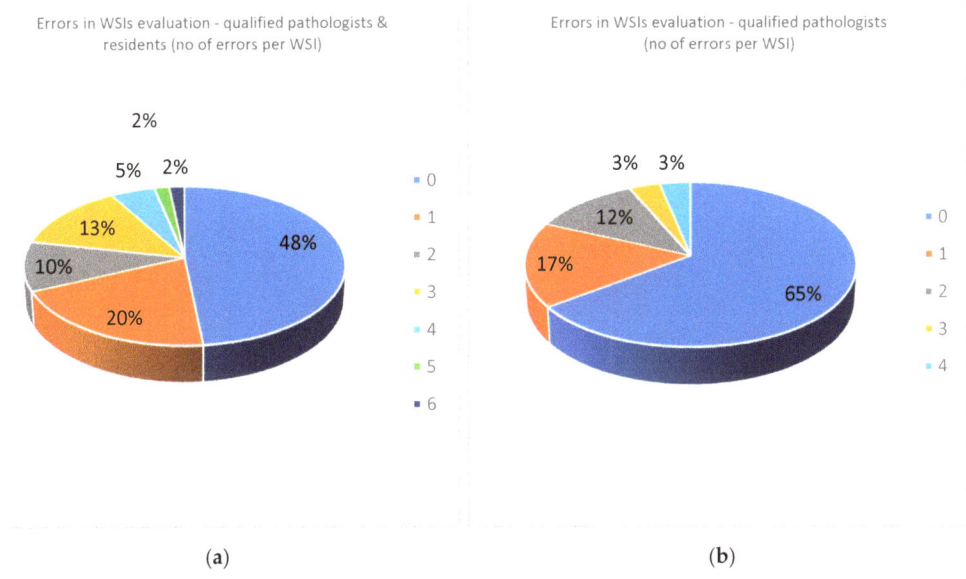

**Figure 12.** (**a**) Errors in WSIs evaluation for all the team (qualified pathologists and residents). (**b**) Errors in WSIs evaluation for qualified pathologists.

## 4. Discussion

Diagnosis of TB can be difficult. A complex interpretation of clinical and radiological images supported by immunological, bacteriological, histopathological, and molecular tests is needed. Paucibacillary lesions are particularly difficult to diagnose. Sputum and/or tissue examination often fail to identify AFB. Bacteriological tests are more successful in identifying mycobacteria than pathology (up to 50–80% more sensitivity for bacteriology compared with histopathology) [28] but the main drawback of the method is the time required by cultures—average of 14–21 days but it is not unusual to take up to 6–8 weeks [29]. PCR and bacteriological tests may also offer divergent results [30]. Immunohistochemistry for mycobacteria is expensive and due to the small dimensions of the bacillus, can be difficult to interpret in paucibacillary lesions.

Histopathologically identification of AFB in the appropriate morphological milieu represents the most precise diagnosis of TB possible because it corroborates the presence of specific lesions with the presence of the bacteria. TB is a form of "specific chronic inflammation", i.e., inflammation with microscopic lesions so characteristic that, by their presence alone, one can affirm with certitude that the culprit provoking the morphologic alterations is a species of Mycobacterium. The lesions consists of confluent epithelioid granulomas with centrally located Langhans multinucleated giant cells and caseating necrosis. In these cases, the diagnosis requires only a routine H&E stain. However, in different circumstances (early lesions, associated illnesses such as cancers, immunosuppression or (auto)immune diseases, simultaneous infection with other microorganisms, etc.), this typical morphological picture is altered and several special stains are needed for diagnosis: Gömöri staining for reticulin and van Gieson Weighert for elastic fibers (to prove the preservation of reticulin and elastic fibers in necrotic area); ZN or auramine (to identify AFBs); some other special stains (Giemsa, Gram, Grochott, Warthin Starry, etc.) to exclude the presence of other microorganisms; in some cases immunohistochemical tests for mycobacteria; and/or polymerase chain reaction (PCR) for Mycobacterium tuberculosis are performed. Moreover, clinical, blood tests (QuantiFERON-TB), and imaging data are corroborated in order to establish a diagnosis of TB [31,32].

Understanding the details of the histopathologic diagnosis of TB is mandatory in order to explain the strict inclusion and exclusion criteria one has to use for constructing the dataset. A paucibacillary lesion may include very few bacilli easy to miss even by an experienced pathologist. This is why we excluded from the negative cases group the slides with morphological appearance highly suggestive of tuberculosis even if the ZN-stained slides did not reveal any bacilli no matter how thoroughly was the examination both at the moment of diagnosis and at reexamination. Additionally, in the B group, in the negative set of cases used for testing, cases with morphology similar to TB but with a clear diagnosis of diseases other than TB were included. This was conducted in order to avoid an involuntary bias created when the pathologist examines a ZN-stained slide that he/she is convinced that the diagnosis is not TB and obviously no bacilli may be present: "it does not look as TB, for sure no AFB are present; no careful scrutiny is needed"; "it looks as TB, maybe there are AFP present; and let's look for them carefully".

Xiong et al., describe reevaluation of the cases during the process of developing the algorithm. They reclassified seven cases initially labeled as negative [15].

Zaizen et al., have an interesting approach when constructing the testing group: the positive cases were those with proven mycobacteriosis either when the biopsy was performed or during follow-up; based on this perspective, AI-supported pathological diagnosis identified 11 positive cases versus 2 positive cases in classical pathological diagnosis, without AI support [19]. It is unusual for a pathologist to miss 9 cases from a total of 42 (12.5% sensitivity). The algorithm was able to identify 11 positive cases (2 cases identified as positive by human examiner and 9 more cases) and "missed" 5 cases. Due to the design of the testing process, these "missed" cases could be real negative ones at the moment of examination (if a patient is developing an illness in the future he or she is not mandatory presenting the microorganism months in advance) or, due to the scarcity and the not uniform distribution of the mycobacteria within the tissue it is possible that the tissue examined by algorithm did not contain bacilli in the moment of investigation.

Another important advantage of our dataset is represented by the number of the cases selected for annotation and the number of positive patches. We annotated 110 positive WSIs obtaining 263,000 positive patches. As it is shown in Table 8, this is the biggest and most diverse AI training dataset for mycobacteria to date. The number of negative cases is also important; at first glance, few negative WSIs are necessary for obtaining a large number of negative patches (one slide with 1 $cm^2$ of tissue can be cut in more than 800,000 patches of $64 \times 64$ pixels). It is important, however, to have different types of tissue with different types of lesions to ensure a sufficient variability of the patches in both structure and color. The absolute number of negative WSIs of our training group is also the biggest, comparable with Pantanowitz et al., dataset but with several orders of magnitude higher than the others. The high number of ZN-stained slides is important due to the fact that it offers a higher diversity of images. ZN stain is a manual stain with high variability from lab to lab, being almost impossible to standardize. A "good" ZN stain is one that reveals mycobacteria from light pink to deep red or even purple rods on a light blue to dark blue background. In fact, its variability is so high that one technician cannot obtain two identical ZN stains on the same tissue block. This can be "a blessing in disguise" since the algorithm trained on a sufficiently large dataset (originating from a sufficiently numerous different WSIs), supplementary extended by augmentation techniques altering color, contrast, brightness, saturation, etc. will be able to properly recognize ZN-stained WSIs provided by labs worldwide.

Table 8. Studies of automated detection of AFB on ZN stains on tissue.

| Studies on Tissue | Year | Training Set Positive WSIs | Training Set Total WSIs | Patches Positive | Patches Negative | Patches (Pixels) | Test Set | Accuracy % | Sensitivity (Recall) % | Specificity % |
|---|---|---|---|---|---|---|---|---|---|---|
| Xiong et al. [15] | 2018 | 30 | 45 | 96,530 | 2,510,307 | 32 × 32 | 201 WSIs | 90.55 * | 97.94 | 83.65 |
| Yang et al. [16] | 2020 | 6 | 33 | 18,246 | 18,246 | 256 × 256 | 134 WSIs | 87 * | 87.13 | 87.62 |
| Lo et al. [17] | 2020 | 9 | 9 | 613 | 1202 | 20 × 20 | patches | 95.30 | 93.5 | 96.3 |
| Pantanowitz et al. [18] | 2021 | 47 | 418 | 5678 | 1,111,918 | 32 × 32 | 138 WSIs | 84.6 | 64.8 | 95.1 |
| Zaizen et al. [19] | 2022 | 2 | 42 | 506 | N/A | N/A | 42 WSIs | N/A | 86 | 100 |
| Our study | 2022 | 110 | 510 | 263,000 | 700,000,000 | 64 × 64 | 60 WSIs | 98.33 | 95.65 | 100 |

* calculated based on the data provided in the paper.

In the five methods of automatic identification of mycobacteria in ZN-stained slides described in the literature, one study (Lo et al. [17]) does not evaluate WSI. Its validation is solely made on patches. Xiong et al. [15] present a completely automated method of diagnosis while Yang et al. [16], Pantanowitz et al. [18], and Zaizen et al. [19] developed AI-assisted diagnostic methods as a tool in the hands (and eyes) of pathologists. In Yang et al.'s method, the pathologist evaluates a score heatmap superposed on the WSI. In Pantanowitz et al.'s method, the pathologists evaluated a gallery of patches displayed in reverse order of the probability score in relation with WSI. Both methods allow for the pathologist to evaluate the suspicious areas in the context of the specific histopathological lesion. Zaizen et al., do not describe precisely how the pathologist uses the platform for diagnosis. Instead, they specify that each probably positive patch was examined by six pathologists.

Our method is an AI-assisted diagnostic method with a similar approach to Pantanowitz's et al.'s design of the platform (analyzing a list of patches displayed in reverse order of the probability score). However, our solution employs a much larger dataset (about two orders of magnitude larger) and an active learning approach that further increases the performance metrics, especially for difficult cases (i.e., artifacts) or WSIs with peculiar staining.

Our algorithm obtained very good results compared with previous studies. Our testing method compared the AI-assisted diagnosis with the pathologist's diagnosis either on slides (by microscopic examination) or WSIs. Our test set included 60 cases based on general recommendation for the minimal size required for digital pathology validation [33]. As expected, there is a definite improvement of AFB identification by pathologists when examining slides other than WSIs. It is known that pathologists are not very keen to change from conventional microscopy to remote WSI examination as a routine. The diagnostic concordance between WSI and slide examination varies from 63% to 100% in different studies [34].

Moreover, pathologist's experience in examining WSIs affected the accuracy of finding AFB—the longer the period of exposure to WSIs, the better the pathologist's results. The accuracy of the diagnosis when our algorithm was used was higher than the accuracy of every pathologist, even when slides were examined. The algorithm was able to pick more bacilli than the human examiner alone, thus almost eliminating the false negatives. When examining slides, pathologists missed a total of 47 cases of TB (false negatives), in average almost 6 cases per person. Our algorithm helped pathologists improve Mycobacterium identification on WSIs, but the results were also better with AI-assisted evaluation than those where pathologists examined slides by microscope. In real life, a pathologist examining a slide may identify lesions suspicious of TB—epithelioid granulomas with giant cells and/or coagulative necrosis with reticuline preservation (caseum). When one suspect TB, he/she will ask for a ZN special stain in order to identify bacilli. AFB presence confirms the diagnosis of TB without biunivocal relation (i.e., AFB absence does not exclude TB diagnosis). In other words, when a pathologist fails to identify AFB, he/she will not necessarily miss TB but the positive diagnosis that will finally be obtained in most of the cases will be obtained with supplementary efforts (several costly techniques) and with some delays in significant cases. Altogether, both the patients and the medical system will benefit from implementation of such an algorithm in routine pathology.

Another issue for discussion is the debate about what metric should be preferred: specificity or sensitivity? A diagnostic method is preferable to be specific while a screening test is better to be more sensitive. We decided to use a higher specificity (fewer false positive cases) with the risk of missing some positive cases (false negative). The algorithm selects patches that are more probable to contain AFB and shows them to the pathologist. If the algorithm is picks up too many structures, the pathologist will be forced to look to a myriad of artifacts and he/she will lose a lot of time sorting through them.; In the end, it is more profitable to examine the slide without AI support.

Last but not least, when discussing our algorithm capabilities in comparison with human results, we should not forget that our team of pathologists are familiar with ZN stains and AFB identification on slides; we expect that a pathologist not used to examining ZN-stained slides would have poorer results with more numerous false negatives, especially in paucibacillary lesions.

When looking at the errors in analyzing both WSIs and slides, there are huge differences between qualified pathologists and residents. The residents were in their final year of residency and are very good and hard-working people. However, we showed that no exposure to WSIs prior to this test poorly influenced the outcome.

We have a closer look at the cases with the most numerous errors in interpretation. One negative case had five errors with eight examiners and four errors from six qualified pathologists (cat scratch disease—suppurative necrotizing granulomatous lymphadenitis). Some structures looked like AFB, but the overall quality of the stain was poor (slightly pink–pale red blood cells). In some areas, structures could be mistaken as AFB but the suspicious structures were not clear-cut bacillar structures (Figures 13 and 14).

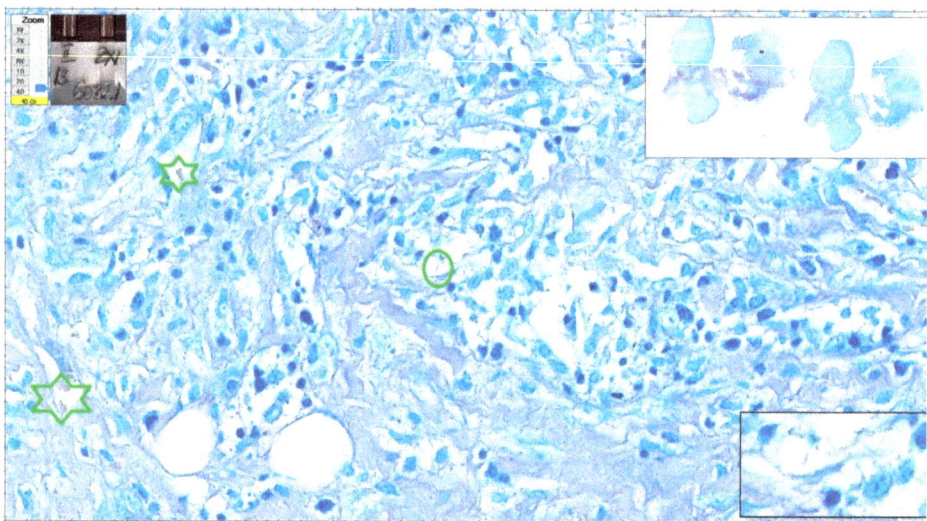

**Figure 13.** Cat scratch disease. Centrally, one structure reminiscent of AFB but pale blue in color (green oval); however, the color of red blood cells is not appropriate (green stars). Paler than regular in a good Ziehl–Neelsen stain. ZN × 400 as offered by Aperio ImageScope platform; WSI scanned with Aperio GT450, 40× magnification.

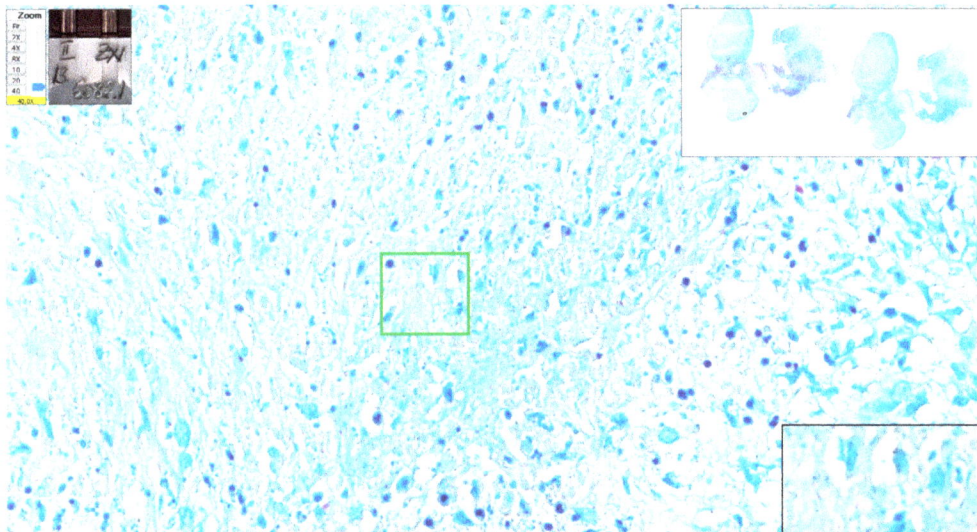

**Figure 14.** Cat scratch disease. Centrally, several structures look like AFB but pale blue in color (green rectangular area); however, enhancement of the image—black contour window in the lower right corner of the picture (digital magnification offered by Aperio ImageScope software)—shows improper format of the pink structures. ZN × 400 as offered by Aperio ImageScope platform; WSI scanned with Aperio GT450, 40× magnification.

A case of tuberculosis in striated muscle had four errors from eight examiners. There were many fragments of tissue and almost 5 cm$^2$ of tissue with very few bacilli, which were easily missed by examiners (Figure 15).

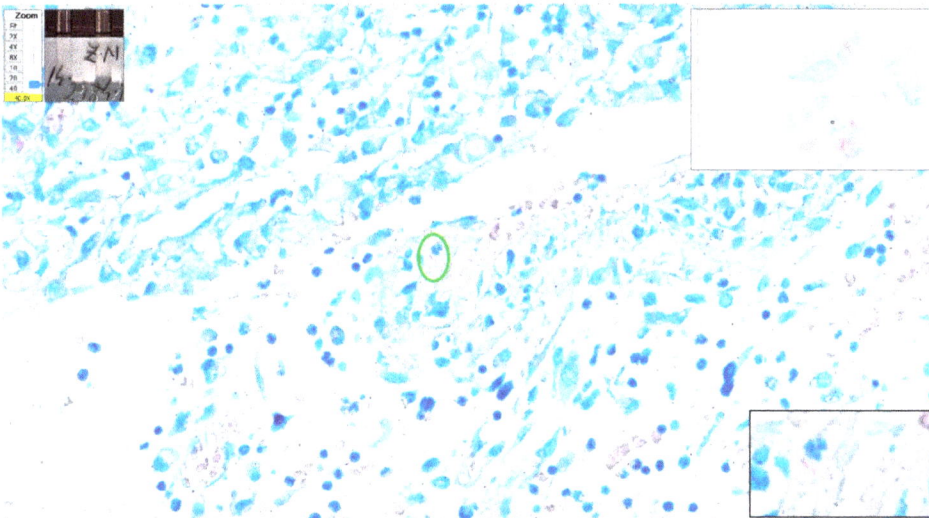

**Figure 15.** Tuberculosis. Centrally, two AFBs present (green oval); please note the good quality of the Ziehl–Neelsen stain certified by the pink color of red blood cells. ZN × 400 as offered by Aperio ImageScope platform; WSI scanned with Aperio GT450, 40× magnification.

The case with most errors in interpretation was a tuberculous epithelioid granulomatous lymphadenitis with extensive caseation with very few bacilli present in ZN stain—one to four AFB present in each section. Due to the minute dimensions of Mycobacterium tuberculosis (one micron thick), a bacillus will be completely enclosed in one section of tissue and serial sections reveal different bacilli. The slide examined in this test included two sections of tissue with very few bacilli, one in one section (Figure 16) and two on the other section. Considering the paucity of the bacilli, it is no wonder that the examiners missed them on WSIs. Interestingly, this was the case the algorithm was not able to identify bacilli. For this case, the algorithm identified 3 patches with positive scores over 0.7 and 145 patches with positive scores between 0.5 and 0.69. None of them presented convincing AFBs.

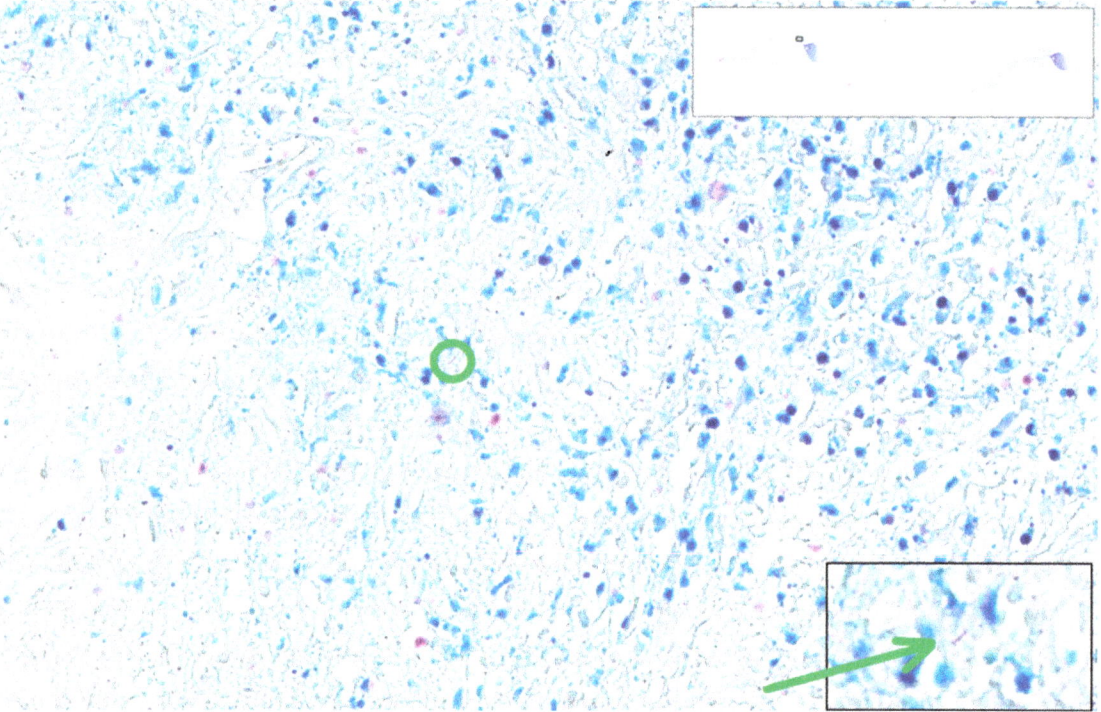

**Figure 16.** Tuberculous epithelioid granulomatous lymphadenitis with extensive caseation. One AFB is present within the center (green circle). Higher resolution is in the right inferior rectangular area (detail: green arrow). ZN × 400 as offered by Aperio ImageScope platform; WSI scanned with Aperio GT450, 40× magnification.

In fact, in order to avoid the examiner being biased by the overall picture of the lesion, the testing set was designed to include lesions with similar appearance to tuberculosis such as granulomatous inflammation, most of them with necrosis. The cases with reactive lymphadenitis, unspecific inflammation, or malignancies were not erroneously evaluated by any examiner.

The most impressive benefit of using the AI-assisted algorithm for AFB identification is saving time. AI-assisted evaluation was 2.84 times faster than human evaluation. We have to be aware that the pathologists involved in our clinical test had impressive experience in diagnosing tuberculosis and analyzing ZN stains. Our department has expertise in infectious diseases diagnosis. ZN stain is routine for lymph nodes and bronchial biopsies and, moreover, the pathologists were recently exposed to numerous positive and negative

ZN-stained WSIs during the annotation period. A "regular" pathologist likely does not have the same level of exposure, so the time required for a thorough examination of a ZN-stained slide is usually much longer. We can estimate that our algorithm saves at least one-third of the pathologist's time that can be spent on other more complex tasks.

Moreover, considering the inherent bias induced by the level of expertise of our team of pathologists, the results of our model argue in favor of an overall increase in the quality of AI-assisted diagnosis. In other words, if the model was able to reach the best performance of one of our most experienced pathologists (identifying convincing positive patches in all but one cases), for a less experienced pathologist the algorithm will certainly improve their performance. It is true that the final labeling of the status of the patch (positive versus negative) is established by the pathologist. The fact that the model is identifying highly suggestive areas helps the human examiner to make a final decision.

Situations when AI algorithms performed better than pathologists were reported during clinical testing for automatic identification of prostate cancer. One case previously missed by pathologists was suggested as malignant by the algorithm and confirmed as such by experts [35]. Additionally, algorithms for Mycobacterium tuberculosis detection identified positive cases with subsequent expert's confirmation [15,19].

Our algorithm is able to identify bacilli even in cases with a very low density of AFB and in cases that were missed by pathologists, even when considering experienced pathologists (AI-assisted diagnosis based on our method has a specificity 100% and sensibility 95.65%). The impact of this achievement is significant. Our automatic method being used to assist pathologists in identifying AFB is saving time and money that is otherwise required by other investigations. Therefore, it shortens the interval between the biopsy and the start of the treatment with major benefits, both for the patient (better results and faster improvement of health) and for society (faster decrease in the patient's infectiousness, diminishing the medical costs for expensive investigations or, longer treatments required for old lesions, diminishing the social security costs by fewer days of medical leave, etc.).

There are many limitations for our technique. The main important limitations concern the dimensions and diversity of the dataset and our method of clinical testing.

Our dataset is the largest and most diverse of the datasets for mycobacteria presented in the literature. It is also the most "correct" one, due to our method selecting cases. Unfortunately, it is not a "perfect" dataset; to reach this goal, the dataset should include all the positive slides from all over the world. This is virtually impossible. We applied several techniques of augmentation to minimize this drawback, but we are aware of this impossible to overcome drawback.

Our method of clinical testing is also flawed because of the simple fact that the team of researchers who developed the algorithm also validated it. This forced manner of designing the test of the algorithm thus biases the validation of all AI-models developed in medicine. We tried to diminish this risk by separating the people who designed and selected the test group of cases from the people who actually performed the test. Our most experienced pathologist tried to further minimize the risk by including in the test group positive paucibacillary cases and negative cases with similar microscopic appearance to TB (see the discussions above). We are aware that the bias is not completely overcome due to the simple fact that the pathologists belong to the same school of pathology with similar methods of evaluation and routines. The only answer for this limitation is for independent validation to be performed by pathologists from completely different institutions and from as many countries as possible, ideally on international cohorts of patients. Overcoming this problem represents the key towards clinical implementation of the algorithm [36].

## 5. Conclusions

We developed a model for AI-assisted detection of AFB on WSIs that is able to identify bacilli with an accuracy of 98.33%, sensitivity of 95.65%, and specificity of 100%. The results were better than or, for one case, similar to those of a team of pathologists of variable expertise when examining slides and WSIs, thus reducing human error form fatigue and loss of focus. By using our algorithm, pathologists saved at least one-third of the total examining time.

We intend to annotate the positive WSIs used for clinical testing and retrain our algorithm with the resulting supplementary patches, thus making use of our active learning setup. The new product iteration will be further tested in different hospitals to test the robustness of the algorithm when exposed with different types of ZN stains and to diminish the inherent subjectivity of the validation.

**Supplementary Materials:** The following supporting information can be downloaded at: https://www.mdpi.com/article/10.3390/diagnostics12061484/s1, Figures S1–S6; Tables S1–S7.

**Author Contributions:** Conceptualization, S.Z., C.M., T.P., M.T. and C.P.; data curation, S.Z., C.M., T.P., M.T., C.P., L.N., M.C., B.C., L.S., A.C., M.B., O.S., I.T., A.V., D.S., P.M., C.D. and A.B.; formal analysis, C.M., T.P., M.T., B.C., A.V. and D.S.; funding acquisition, S.Z., C.M., M.T., C.P. and P.M.; investigation, S.Z., C.P., L.N., M.C., L.S., A.C., M.B., O.S., I.T. and C.D.; methodology, S.Z., C.M., M.T. and C.P.; project administration, C.M.; resources, S.Z., C.P., C.D. and A.B.; software, T.P., M.T., B.C., A.V. and D.S.; supervision, S.Z., C.M., T.P., M.T. and C.P.; validation, T.P., M.T., B.C., A.V. and D.S.; visualization, S.Z., C.M., T.P., M.T., C.P. and P.M.; writing—original draft, S.Z., C.M., M.T., C.P. and P.M.; writing—review and editing, S.Z., C.M., T.P., M.T. and C.P. All authors have read and agreed to the published version of the manuscript.

**Funding:** This work was supported by a grant of the Ministry of Research, Innovation and Digitization, CNCS—UEFISCDI, project number PN-III-P4-PCE-2021-0546, within PNCDI III (no. PCE 109/2022).

**Institutional Review Board Statement:** The study was conducted in accordance with the Declaration of Helsinki, and approved by the Institutional Ethics Committee of Colentina University Hospital (protocol code 13 from 17 of November 2021).

**Informed Consent Statement:** Patient consent for the use of their harvested biological products in medical studies was granted by each patient when the biopsy was performed according to Government Decision no 451/2004.

**Data Availability Statement:** Not applicable.

**Conflicts of Interest:** The authors declare no conflict of interest.

## Abbreviations

| | |
|---|---|
| AFB | Acid-fast bacilli |
| AUC | Area under the receiver operating characteristic curve |
| AUPR | Area under the Precision–Recall curve |
| AI | Artificial intelligence |
| CNN | Convolutional neural network |
| DCNN | Deep convolutional neural network |
| GPU | Graphics processing unit |
| H&E | Hematoxylin and Eosin |
| LR | Logistic regression |
| MCC | Matthews correlation coefficient |
| ROC | Receiver operating characteristic |
| TB | Tuberculosis |
| WSI | Whole slide image |
| ZN | Ziehl–Neelsen |

## References

1. WHO. Tuberculosis. Available online: https://www.who.int/news-room/fact-sheets/detail/tuberculosis (accessed on 19 May 2022).
2. Ulukanligil, M.; Aslan, G.; Taşçi, S. A comparative study on the different staining methods and number of specimens for the detection of acid fast bacilli. *Memórias Inst. Oswaldo Cruz* **2000**, *95*, 855–858. [CrossRef]
3. Veropoulos, K.; Learmonth, G.; Campbell, C.; Knight, B.; Simpson, J. Automated identification of tubercle bacilli in sputum. A preliminary investigation. *Anal. Quant. Cytol. Histol.* **1999**, *21*, 277–282.

4. del Carpio, C.; Dianderas, E.; Zimic, M.; Sheen, P.; Coronel, J.; Lavarello, R.; Kemper, G. An algorithm for detection of tuberculosis bacilli in Ziehl-Neelsen sputum smear images. *Int. J. Electr. Comput. Eng. (IJECE)* **2019**, *9*, 2968. [CrossRef]
5. Law, Y.N.; Jian, H.; Lo, N.W.S.; Ip, M.; Chan, M.M.Y.; Kam, K.M.; Wu, X. Low cost automated whole smear microscopy screening system for detection of acid fast bacilli. *PLoS ONE* **2018**, *13*, e0190988. [CrossRef] [PubMed]
6. Ayas, S.; Ekinci, M. Random forest-based tuberculosis bacteria classification in images of ZN-stained sputum smear samples. *Signal Image Video Process.* **2014**, *8*, 49–61. [CrossRef]
7. Del Costa, M.G.F.; Costa Filho, C.F.F.; Sena, J.F.; Salem, J.; Lima, M.L. Automatic identification of mycobacterium tuberculosis with conventional light microscopy. In Proceedings of the 2008 30th Annual International Conference of the IEEE Engineering in Medicine and Biology Society, Vancouver, BC, Canada, 20–25 August 2008; pp. 382–385. [CrossRef]
8. Costa Filho, C.F.F.; Levy, P.C.; Matos Xavier, C.; Fujimoto, L.M.B.; Costa, M.G.F. Automatic identification of tuberculosis mycobacterium. *Res. Biomed. Eng.* **2015**, *31*, 33–43. [CrossRef]
9. El-Melegy, M.; Mohamed, D.; ElMelegy, T. Automatic Detection of Tuberculosis Bacilli from Microscopic Sputum Smear Images Using Faster R-CNN, Transfer Learning and Augmentation. In *Pattern Recognition and Image Analysis: 9th Iberian Conference*; Springer: Cham, Switzerland, 2019; pp. 270–278. [CrossRef]
10. Khutlang, R.; Krishnan, S.; Dendere, R.; Whitelaw, A.; Veropoulos, K.; Learmonth, G.; Douglas, T.S. Classification of Mycobacterium tuberculosis in images of ZN-stained sputum smears. *IEEE Trans. Inf. Technol Biomed.* **2010**, *14*, 949–957. [CrossRef]
11. Kuok, C.P.; Horng, M.H.; Liao, Y.M.; Chow, N.H.; Sun, Y.N. An effective and accurate identification system of Mycobacterium tuberculosis using convolution neural networks. *Microsc. Res. Tech.* **2019**, *82*, 709–719. [CrossRef] [PubMed]
12. Panicker, R.O.; Kalmady, K.S.; Rajan, J.; Sabu, M.K. Automatic detection of tuberculosis bacilli from microscopic sputum smear images using deep learning methods. *Biocybern. Biomed. Eng.* **2018**, *38*, 691–699. [CrossRef]
13. Vaid, A.; Patil, C.; Sanghariyat, A.; Rane, R.; Visani, A.; Mukherjee, S.; Joseph, A.; Ranjan, M.; Augustine, S.; Sooraj, K.P.; et al. Emerging Advanced Technologies Developed by IPR for Bio Medical Applications—A Review. *Neurol. India* **2020**, *68*, 26–34. [CrossRef]
14. Zhai, Y.; Liu, Y.; Zhou, D.; Liu, S. Automatic identification of mycobacterium tuberculosis from ZN-stained sputum smear: Algorithm and system design. In Proceedings of the 2010 IEEE International Conference on Robotics and Biomimetics, Tianjin, China, 14–18 December 2010; pp. 41–46. [CrossRef]
15. Xiong, Y.; Ba, X.; Hou, A.; Zhang, K.; Chen, L.; Li, T. Automatic detection of mycobacterium tuberculosis using artificial intelligence. *J. Thorac. Dis.* **2018**, *10*, 1936–1940. [CrossRef] [PubMed]
16. Yang, M.; Nurzynska, K.; Walts, A.E.; Gertych, A. A CNN-based active learning framework to identify mycobacteria in digitized Ziehl-Neelsen stained human tissues. *Comput. Med. Imaging Graph.* **2020**, *84*, 101752. [CrossRef]
17. Lo, C.M.; Wu, Y.H.; Li, Y.C.; Lee, C.C. Computer-Aided Bacillus Detection in Whole-Slide Pathological Images Using a Deep Convolutional Neural Network. *Appl. Sci.* **2020**, *10*, 4059. [CrossRef]
18. Pantanowitz, L.; Wu, U.; Seigh, L.; LoPresti, E.; Yeh, F.C.; Salgia, P.; Michelow, P.; Hazelhurst, S.; Chen, W.Y.; Hartman, D.; et al. Artificial Intelligence-Based Screening for Mycobacteria in Whole-Slide Images of Tissue Samples. *Am. J. Clin. Pathol.* **2021**, *156*, 117–128. [CrossRef] [PubMed]
19. Zaizen, Y.; Kanahori, Y.; Ishijima, S.; Kitamura, Y.; Yoon, H.S.; Ozasa, M.; Mukae, H.; Bychkov, A.; Hoshino, T.; Fukuoka, J. Deep-Learning-Aided Detection of Mycobacteria in Pathology Specimens Increases the Sensitivity in Early Diagnosis of Pulmonary Tuberculosis Compared with Bacteriology Tests. *Diagnostics* **2022**, *12*, 709. [CrossRef]
20. Krizhevsky, A.; Sutskever, I.; Hinton, G.E. ImageNet classification with deep convolutional neural networks. In Proceedings of the 25th International Conference on Neural Information Processing Systems—Volume 1 (NIPS'12), Lake Tahoe, NV, USA, 3–6 December 2012; Curran Associates Inc.: Red Hook, NY, USA, 2012; pp. 1097–1105. [CrossRef]
21. Osman, M.K.; Mashor, M.Y.; Jaafar, H. Tuberculosis bacilli detection in Ziehl-Neelsen-stained tissue using affine moment invariants and Extreme Learning Machine. In Proceedings of the 2011 IEEE 7th International Colloquium on Signal Processing and its Applications, Penang, Malaysia, 4–6 March 2011; pp. 232–236. [CrossRef]
22. Li, X.; Wang, W.; Hu, X.; Yang, J. Selective kernel networks. In Proceedings of the IEEE/CVF Conference on Computer Vision and Pattern Recognition, Long Beach, CA, USA, 15–20 June 2019; pp. 510–519. [CrossRef]
23. Chen, L.C.; Papandreou, G.; Kokkinos, I.; Murphy, K.; Yuille, A.L. Deeplab: Semantic image segmentation with deep convolutional nets, atrous convolution, and fully connected crfs. *IEEE Trans. Pattern Anal. Mach. Intell.* **2017**, *40*, 834–848. [CrossRef]
24. Luo, L.; Xiong, Y.; Liu, Y.; Sun, X. Adaptive gradient methods with dynamic bound of learning rate. In Proceedings of the Seventh International Conference on Learning Representations, New Orleans, LA, USA, 26 February 2019.
25. El Khouli, R.H.; Macura, K.J.; Barker, P.B.; Habba, M.R.; Jacobs, M.A.; Bluemke, D.A. Relationship of temporal resolution to diagnostic performance for dynamic contrast enhanced MRI of the breast. *J. Magn. Reson. Imaging* **2009**, *30*, 999–1004. [CrossRef] [PubMed]
26. Obuchowski, N.A. Receiver operating characteristic curves and their use in radiology. *Radiology* **2003**, *229*, 3–8. [CrossRef] [PubMed]
27. Metz, C.E. Basic principles of ROC analysis. *Semin. Nucl. Med.* **1978**, *8*, 283–298. [CrossRef]
28. Lewinsohn, D.M.; Leonard, M.K.; LoBue, P.A.; Cohn, D.L.; Daley, C.L.; Desmond, E.; Keane, J.; Lewinsohn, D.A.; Loeffler, A.M.; Mazurek, G.H.; et al. Official American Thoracic Society/Infectious Diseases Society of America/Centers for Disease Control and Prevention Clinical Practice Guidelines: Diagnosis of tuberculosis in adults and children. *Clin. Infect. Dis.* **2017**, *64*, 111–115. [CrossRef]

29. Pfyffer, G.E.; Wittwer, F. Incubation Time of Mycobacterial Cultures: How Long Is Long Enough To Issue a Final Negative Report to the Clinician? *J. Clin. Microbiol.* **2012**, *50*, 4188–4189. [CrossRef] [PubMed]
30. Sevilla, I.A.; Molina, E.; Tello, M.; Elguezabal, N.; Juste, R.A.; Garrido, J.M. Detection of Mycobacteria by Culture and DNA-Based Methods in Animal-Derived Food Products Purchased at Spanish Supermarkets. *Front. Microbiol.* **2017**, *8*, 1030. [CrossRef] [PubMed]
31. Barss, L.; Connors, W.J.A.; Fisher, D. Chapter 7: Extra-pulmonary tuberculosis. *Can. J. Respir. Crit. Care Sleep Med.* **2022**, *6* (suppl. 1), 87–108. [CrossRef]
32. Ionescu, S.; Nicolescu, A.C.; Madge, O.L.; Marincas, M.; Radu, M.; Simion, L. Differential Diagnosis of Abdominal Tuberculosis in the Adult—Literature Review. *Diagnostics* **2021**, *11*, 2362. [CrossRef] [PubMed]
33. Cross, S.; Furness, P.; Igali, L.; Snead, D.; Treanor, D. Best Practice Recommendations for Implementing Digital Pathology. The Royal College of Pathologists. 2018. Available online: https://tinyurl.com/reabrchx (accessed on 18 May 2022).
34. Goacher, E.; Randell, R.; Williams, B.; Treanor, D. The Diagnostic Concordance of Whole Slide Imaging and Light Microscopy: A Systematic Review. *Arch. Pathol. Lab. Med.* **2017**, *141*, 151–161. [CrossRef]
35. Pantanowitz, L.; Quiroga-Garza, G.M.; Bien, L.; Heled, R.; Laifenfeld, D.; Linhart, C.; Sandbank, J.; Albrecht Shach, A.; Shalev, V.; Vecsler, M.; et al. An artificial intelligence algorithm for prostate cancer diagnosis in whole slide images of core needle biopsies: A blinded clinical validation and deployment study. *Lancet Digit Health* **2020**, *2*, e407–e416. [CrossRef]
36. Bulten, W.; Kartasalo, K.; Chen, P.H.C.; Ström, P.; Pinckaers, H.; Nagpal, K.; Cai, Y.; Steiner, D.F.; van Boven, H.; Vink, R.; et al. Artificial intelligence for diagnosis and Gleason grading of prostate cancer: The PANDA challenge. *Nat. Med.* **2022**, *28*, 154–163. [CrossRef] [PubMed]

Article

# Artificial Intelligence-Assisted Image Analysis of Acetaminophen-Induced Acute Hepatic Injury in Sprague-Dawley Rats

Eun Bok Baek [1,†], Ji-Hee Hwang [2,†], Heejin Park [2], Byoung-Seok Lee [2], Hwa-Young Son [1], Yong-Bum Kim [3], Sang-Yeop Jun [4], Jun Her [4], Jaeku Lee [4] and Jae-Woo Cho [2,*]

1 College of Veterinary Medicine, Chungnam National University, Daejeon 34134, Korea; baekeunbok@hanmail.net (E.B.B.); hyson@cnu.ac.kr (H.-Y.S.)
2 Toxicologic Pathology Research Group, Department of Advanced Toxicology Research, Korea Institute of Toxicology, Daejeon 34114, Korea; jihee.hwang@kitox.re.kr (J.-H.H.); hpark@kitox.re.kr (H.P.); bslee@kitox.re.kr (B.-S.L.)
3 Department of Advanced Toxicology Research, Korea Institute of Toxicology, Daejeon 34114, Korea; ybkim@kitox.re.kr
4 Research & Development Team, LAC Inc., Seoul 07620, Korea; syjun@lacin.co.kr (S.-Y.J.); hjun@lacin.co.kr (J.H.); jklee@lacin.co.kr (J.L.)
* Correspondence: cjwoo@kitox.re.kr; Tel.: +82-42-610-8023
† These authors contributed equally to this work.

**Abstract:** Although drug-induced liver injury (DILI) is a major target of the pharmaceutical industry, we currently lack an efficient model for evaluating liver toxicity in the early stage of its development. Recent progress in artificial intelligence-based deep learning technology promises to improve the accuracy and robustness of current toxicity prediction models. Mask region-based CNN (Mask R-CNN) is a detection-based segmentation model that has been used for developing algorithms. In the present study, we applied a Mask R-CNN algorithm to detect and predict acute hepatic injury lesions induced by acetaminophen (APAP) in Sprague-Dawley rats. To accomplish this, we trained, validated, and tested the model for various hepatic lesions, including necrosis, inflammation, infiltration, and portal triad. We confirmed the model performance at the whole-slide image (WSI) level. The training, validating, and testing processes, which were performed using tile images, yielded an overall model accuracy of 96.44%. For confirmation, we compared the model's predictions for 25 WSIs at 20× magnification with annotated lesion areas determined by an accredited toxicologic pathologist. In individual WSIs, the expert-annotated lesion areas of necrosis, inflammation, and infiltration tended to be comparable with the values predicted by the algorithm. The overall predictions showed a high correlation with the annotated area. The R square values were 0.9953, 0.9610, and 0.9445 for necrosis, inflammation plus infiltration, and portal triad, respectively. The present study shows that the Mask R-CNN algorithm is a useful tool for detecting and predicting hepatic lesions in non-clinical studies. This new algorithm might be widely useful for predicting liver lesions in non-clinical and clinical settings.

**Keywords:** drug-induced liver injury; acute hepatic injury; deep neural network; mask region-based convolutional neural network; artificial intelligence; deep learning

## 1. Introduction

In recent years, artificial intelligence (AI)-assisted digital pathology has made rapid progress owing to the success of deep learning [1,2]. Some trials have applied deep-learning techniques in clinical and non-clinical fields of digital pathology, as they may be used to accomplish tasks that could not be automated using classical imaging analysis methods [3,4]. Deep-learning-based techniques are being increasingly applied in many routine contexts [5]; in research, they have been used in toxicological pathology and good laboratory practice (GLP) settings [6].

For digital pathology, convolutional neural networks (CNNs) are applied to build decision-making workflows [7]. When provided with plentiful data on annotated training images, CNNs can derive complex histological patterns by deconvoluting the image content into thousands of salient features, selecting/aggregating the most meaningful features, and then moving on to recognize the identified patterns in novel images [7]. Mask region-based CNN (Mask R-CNN), which was developed from Faster R-CNN, is one of the best-known detection-based segmentation models [8,9]. In Mask R-CNN, region of interest (ROI) alignment is used to increase the number of anchors and mask branches to achieve instance segmentation. Mask R-CNN has a faster detection speed and greater accuracy than Faster R-CNN [10]. To date, Mask R-CNN-based approaches have been used to analyze multiple organs, such as for heart, right-lung, and left-lung segmentation [9].

Acute hepatic injury can be caused by viral infection, alcohol, and/or drugs. The latter injury is termed drug-induced liver injury (DILI) [11–13]. DILI is a major concern for drug developers, regulatory authorities, and clinicians. However, we currently lack an adequate model system for assessing drug-associated DILI risk in humans [14]. The observable morphological patterns of acute hepatocellular injury include acute hepatitis, necrosis, and resolving hepatitis. Acute hepatitis is characterized by portal and parenchymal inflammation, hepatocellular injury, and/or necrosis, in the absence of fibrosis. The necrosis can be spotty or confluent; in some cases, such as that induced by acetaminophen (APAP), it can be zonal [15]. The pathological findings characteristic of APAP overdose, which include acute hepatitis with apparent centrilobular hepatic necrosis, have been targeted to develop therapeutic pharmaceuticals [16]. Several published reports have used deep learning models to predict liver injury or toxicity [17–21]. However, no previous study has applied deep learning to detect acute hepatic injury for toxicological diagnosis in a non-clinical study.

Here, we applied a deep-learning algorithm in developing a more efficient diagnostic tool for toxicity screening, based on the pathological characteristics of APAP-induced acute hepatic injury. We applied a Mask R-CNN segmentation network to detect the lesions of acute hepatitis, with a particular focus on lymphocyte/histiocyte infiltration and necrosis. We evaluated model performance by comparing the whole-slide image (WSI)-level detection of lesions by the model versus the annotation results generated by an accredited toxicologic pathologist.

## 2. Materials and Methods

### 2.1. Animal Experiments

Sprague-Dawley (SD) rats (Crl:CD; 9 weeks of age, both males and females) were obtained from Orient Bio, Inc. (Republic of Korea) and allowed to acclimate for 2 days prior to the beginning of the study. Throughout the experiments, the rats were maintained under controlled conditions (23 ± 3 °C, 30–70% relative humidity, 12 h light/12 h dark cycle of 150–300 lux, 10–20 cycles/h ventilation). A standard rat pellet diet (gamma-ray irradiated; 5053 PMI Nutrition International, San Francisco, CA, USA) was provided ad libitum. The animals had free access to municipal tap water that had been filtered and UV-irradiated. This water was analyzed for specific contaminants every 6 months by the Daejeon Regional Institute of Health and Environment (407, Daehak-ro, Yuseong-gu, Daejeon, Korea). The experiment was approved by the Assessment and Accreditation of Laboratory Animal Care International (AAALAC) and Institutional Animal Care and Use Committee (IACUC).

Animals were randomly assigned into the following three groups (n = 10 per group, 5 males and 5 females): (1) control group; (2) single dose APAP (2500 mg/kg) group; (3) repeated dose APAP group (1000 mg/kg) group. Liver from each animal was divided into 5~6 different pieces, and they were paraffin-embedded. In total, about 200 liver sections were H&E-stained and digitalized into whole-slide images (WSIs) by slide scanner. For dataset establishment, images of necrosis, inflammation, infiltration, and portal triad were cropped and labeled from 7, 16, 30, and 132 whole-slide images. Thirty-two WSIs, which were not used for model training, were left to check the performance of the trained AI model.

Acetaminophen (APAP; A7085, 99.0% purity; Sigma-Aldrich, MO, USA) was administered orally to induce acute liver injury in 10-week-old SD rats using two dosing systems: a single dose of 2500 mg/kg or a 6-day repeated dose of 1000 mg/kg. Doses of APAP were chosen from previously published reports [22,23]. Immediately prior to administration, 2500 mg or 1000 mg of APAP was dissolved in 10 mL of sterile distilled water. Administration was performed at 10 mL/kg per dose. Sterile distilled water was administered as a vehicle control. The day of the starting dose was regarded as Day 1. Single-dosing animals and six-day repeated animals were sacrificed on Day 3 and Day 7, respectively. Liver tissues were collected in 10% formaldehyde. Hematoxylin and eosin (H&E) staining was performed as previously described [24].

*2.2. Data Preparation*

Whole-slide images (WSIs) of liver sections were scanned using a Panoramic 250 Flash III (3DHistech, Hungary) with a 20× objective and bright-field illumination. The scan resolution was 0.24 μm per pixel, and the images were saved as TIFF stripes with JPEG2000 image compression. The data preparation for segmentation of portal triad, necrosis, infiltration, and inflammation was performed as previously described [8]. Briefly, the 20×-magnified WSIs were cropped into 448 × 448 pixels of tile images, and all lesions were labeled using a VGG image annotator 2.0.1.0 (Visual Geometry Group, Oxford University, Oxford, UK). The annotated lesions were confirmed by an accredited toxicologic pathologist before the algorithm training was initiated. A total of 8,291 image tiles were obtained from 201 WSIs. The lesions identified on these images were labeled and used to train and test the Mask R-CNN algorithm. The train_test split function embedded in the scikit-learn package was used to split the annotated image tiles into the training, validation, and test data sets (ratio, 7:2:1, respectively). Data augmentation was conducted to improve the training dataset; this was performed eight times using a combination of image-augmenting techniques (reverse, rotation, and brightness). A total of 46,312 images were used for training, while 1659 and 843 images were used for validation and testing, respectively (Supplementary Material Table S1).

*2.3. Generation of the Mask R-CNN Algorithm*

All procedures related to algorithm training, including the data distribution, were performed as previously described in detail [8]. Briefly, the training was performed using an open-source framework for machine learning (Tensorflow 2.1.0 with a Keras 2.4.3 backend) powered by an NVIDIA RTX 3090 24G GPU. The Matterport Mask R-CNN 2.1 package (Sunnyvale, CA, USA) was used for training. The Mask R-CNN algorithm consisted of two stages: (1) the region proposal network (RPN), which proposed candidate object-bounding boxes; and (2) RoIAlign, which was used to extract features for the prediction of pixel-accurate masks. RoIAlign uses bi-linear interpolation to compute the exact values of the input features at four regularly sampled locations in each RoI bin and aggregates the results using max pooling. A schematic of the procedure is shown in Figure 1.

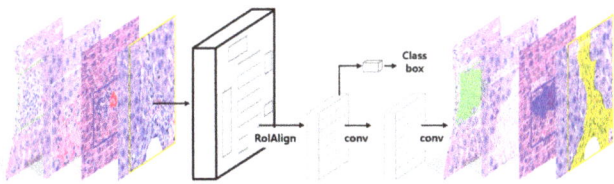

**Figure 1.** Schematic of the procedures for Mask R-CNN and segmentation of hepatic lesions.

## 2.4. Model Training, Validation, and Testing for Acute Hepatocellular Injury

### 2.4.1. Hyperparameters

A total of 48,814 images were used to train, validate, and test the model on lesions of acute hepatic injury in SD rats. The hyperparameters used during the training are described in Table 1. All configurations were set as the defaults defined by the Matterport package with the exception of the five parameters that were customized to fit the hepatic injury dataset. Four images were simultaneously analyzed using IMAGE_PER_GPU, and four GPUs were used during the training. The image size was determined as 448 × 448 by IMAGE_MAX_DIM and IMAGE_MIN_DIM according to the tile image size. The threshold of instance classification accuracy, DETECTION_MIN_CONFIDENCE, was adjusted to 0.5. Stochastic Gradient Descent (SGD) was selected as the optimizer.

**Table 1.** Hyperparameters used in Mask R-CNN training.

| Hyperparameter | Value |
| --- | --- |
| IMAGES_PER_GPU | 4 |
| GPU_COUNT | 4 |
| STEPS_PER_EPOCH | 10 |
| IMAGE_MAX_DIM | 448 |
| IMAGE_MIN_DIM | 448 |
| LAYER_1 | 60 |
| LAYER_2 | 120 |
| LAYER_3 | 200 |
| DETECTION_MIN_CONFIDENCE | 0.9 |
| LEARNING_RATE | 0.001 |
| LEARNING_MOMENTUM | 0.9 |
| WEIGHT_DECAY | 0.0001 |
| DETECTION_MAX_INSTANCES | 100 |

### 2.4.2. Loss

To calculate the training losses, the class (label), mask, and bounding box (bbox) losses observed during the training were serialized using the tf. Summary module and visualized using a tensorboard. To calculate class loss, we used the multi-class cross-entropy loss. Since the mask network uses the sigmoid to predict whether a given pixel belongs to the class, the mask loss was determined by binary cross-entropy. For the bounding box loss, we used a smooth L1 loss, which calculated the error between the prediction and ground truth. Finally, to determine the Mask R-CNN loss (total loss), we calculated the sum of the losses (i.e., the sparse softmax cross-entropy loss for the label, the smooth L1 loss for the bounding box, and the binary cross-entropy loss for the mask).

### 2.4.3. Metrics for Model Performance

To verify model performance, we calculated the mean average precision (mAP), which is derived from the intersection of the union (IoU), precision, and recall values. The IoU value was calculated as previously described [8], and generally reflected the ratio of the area overlaid by the union of the predictions and the ground truth. The mAP value reflects the accuracy of the model; here, we used the transformed mAP, which takes on a value of 0 when an image is found to contain any misprediction. We used this transformation to perform a more detailed analysis of the error cases, investigate the causes of correct and incorrect predictions, and more strictly evaluate the model performance.

## 2.5. Model Performance Confirmation at the WSI Level

Thirty-two WSIs that were not used during the training were applied as the confirmation set. All WSIs were obtained from APAP-treated animals. These WSIs were scanned using a 20× objective and bright-field illumination. Before confirmation, the hepatic lesion (including the connective tissue) of each WSI was annotated by an accredited toxicologic pathologist as the ground truth to be compared with the prediction of the algorithm. After annotation, the area of the annotated region was calculated and transformed into a percentage of the liver-section area. WSI annotation and the annotated area calculation were conducted using Aperio Image Scope version 12.4.0 (Leica Biosystems, Richmond, IL, USA) and 20× magnification-scale images. Each magnified WSI was divided into 448 × 448 pixels of tile images, and each hepatic lesion was inferred by the trained algorithm. Following the prediction, the prediction mask-bearing cropped images were merged into a WSI. The prediction mask areas were calculated and compared to the annotated lesion by linear regression

## 3. Results

*3.1. Training and Validation of the Mask R-CNN Algorithm for Acute Hepatic Injury Lesions*

To train the Mask R-CNN network for identification of acute hepatic injury lesion, a total of 46,312 annotated tile images, including the augmented samples, were used. Three hepatic lesion types, namely necrosis, inflammation, and infiltration, were trained for the identification of hepatic lesions. To improve the performance of the trained model, we also annotated portal triad, which we found could be confused with infiltration of mononuclear cell and histiocytes. Total losses, including class, mask, and bbox losses, decreased steadily during the training (Supplementary Material Figure S1). As shown in the right panels of Figure 2, the algorithm successfully distinguished between all trained lesions and normal liver cells in the image tiles. Moreover, the predicted hepatic lesions overlapped well with the labeled lesions, as shown in the middle and right panels of Figure 2.

During training and validation, we found that some of the detection results did not match the corresponding annotated lesion. Further assessment revealed that inflammatory findings in the annotation were incorrectly recognized as infiltration findings in the algorithm-based prediction (Supplementary Material Figure S2).

After training, we tested the model performance by generating mAP values for a total of 843 image tiles. The overall mAP was 96.44%, and the results obtained for portal triad, necrosis, inflammation, and infiltration were 95.10%, 100%, 96.35%, and 94.29%, respectively (Table 2). This model performance was considered to be outstanding, despite the confusion between inflammation- and infiltration-related lesions.

Table 2. Mean average precision (mAP) in Mask R-CNN training.

|  | Portal Triad | Necrosis | Inflammation | Infiltration | Total |
| --- | --- | --- | --- | --- | --- |
| mAP | 95.10% | 100% | 96.35% | 94.29% | **96.44%** |

*3.2. Model Performance Confirmation Using WSI*

To test the performance of our trained algorithm in a real-world setting, we tested its ability to predict hepatic lesions from 32 WSIs. The test was operated at 20× magnification. Portal triad (blue), necrosis (white), inflammation (yellow), and infiltration (green) were presented in different colors, as shown in Figure 3. The true annotated lesion was reported by the square micrometer ($\mu m^2$), and the algorithm-estimated pixels were converted to the same units ($\mu m^2$). Our results showed that the lesions annotated for portal triad, necrosis, inflammation, and infiltration were comparable to the images predicted by the model (Figure 3A). Using magnified WSI images, the AI algorithm successfully identified each lesion of necrosis, inflammation, and infiltration, as compared to the annotated lesions (Figure 3B).

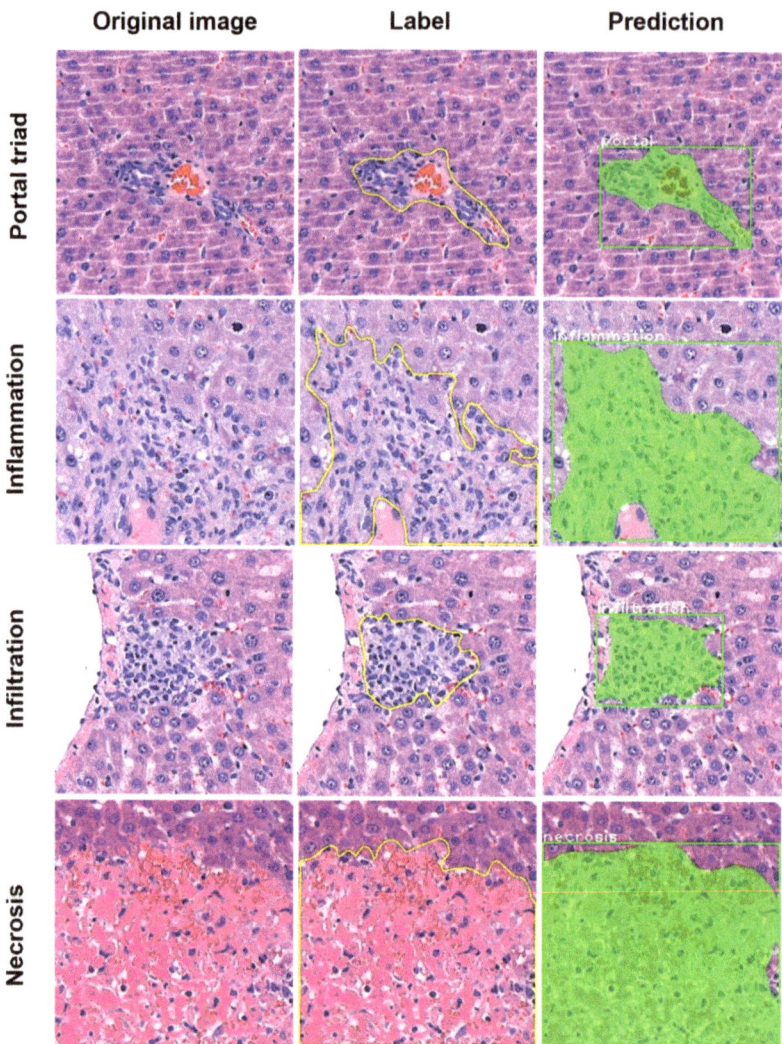

**Figure 2.** Representative segmentation for training and testing of hepatic lesions. The left panels show the original image tiles before labeling; the middle panels show labeled images for training of portal triad, necrosis, inflammation, and infiltration; the right panels show the predicted area for each lesion, as determined by Mask R-CNN.

In individual WSIs, the annotated lesion areas of necrosis, inflammation, and infiltration tended to be comparable to (albeit slightly larger than) those determined by the accredited toxicologic pathologist (Figure 4). Our combined evaluation revealed that the inflammation-plus-infiltration findings tended to show greater agreement with the annotated images, compared to either alone (Figure 4B,D,E). Correlations between the annotated and predicted lesions are shown in Figure 5. The predicted areas of portal triad and hepatic lesions showed very high correlations with the annotated dimensions; all $R^2$ values were above 0.9, with the exception of that of infiltration (Figure 5).

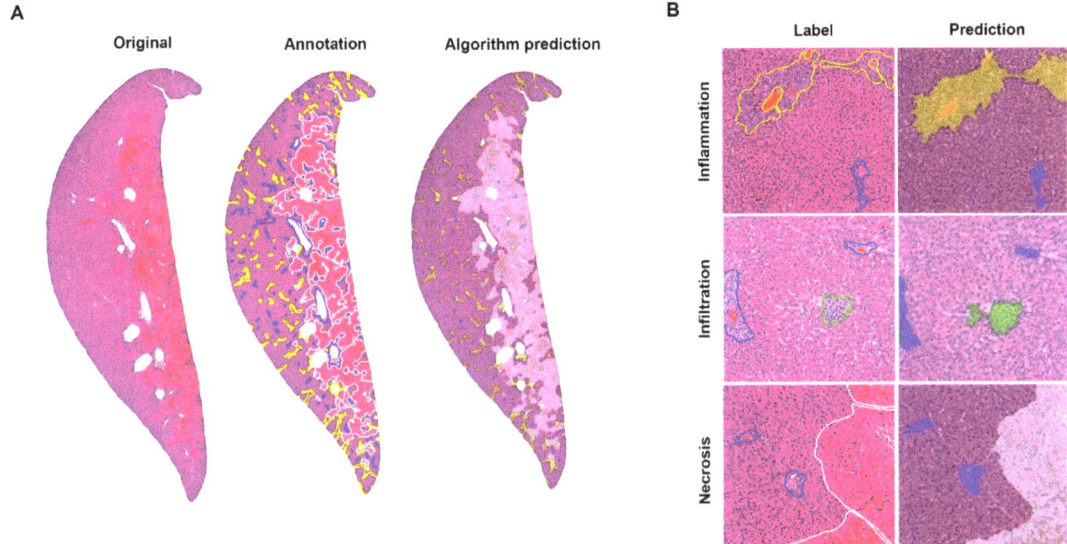

**Figure 3.** Comparison of the original image, annotated image, and algorithm-predicted image at the WSI level. (**A**) Original WSI, annotated result obtained from an accredited toxicologic pathologist, and algorithm detection results for hepatic lesion at 20× magnification. (**B**) Magnified WSI images including necrosis, inflammation, and infiltration lesions. Portal triad (blue), inflammation (yellow), infiltration (green), and necrosis (white) are shown as different colors.

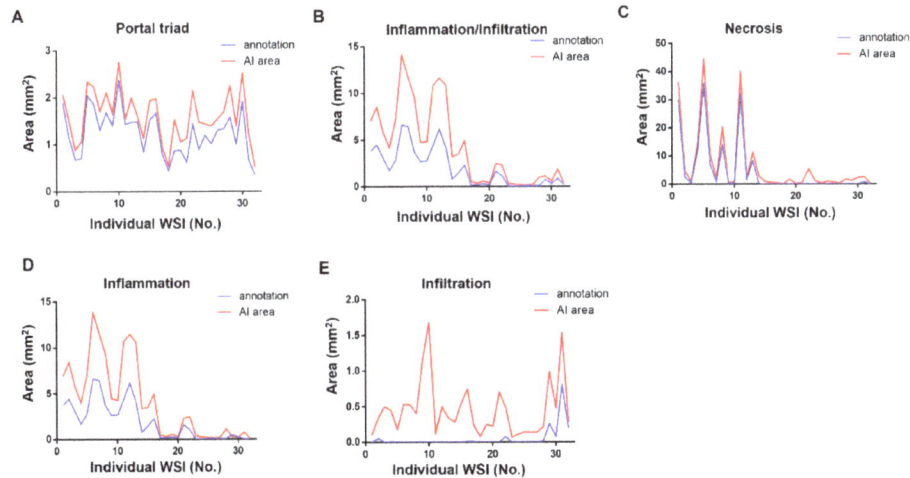

**Figure 4.** Comparison of the annotated and algorithm-predicted areas at the individual WSI level. Blue lines represent annotated area and red lines show algorithm-predicted area for portal triad (**A**), inflammation and infiltration together (**B**), necrosis (**C**), inflammation (**D**), and infiltration (**E**).

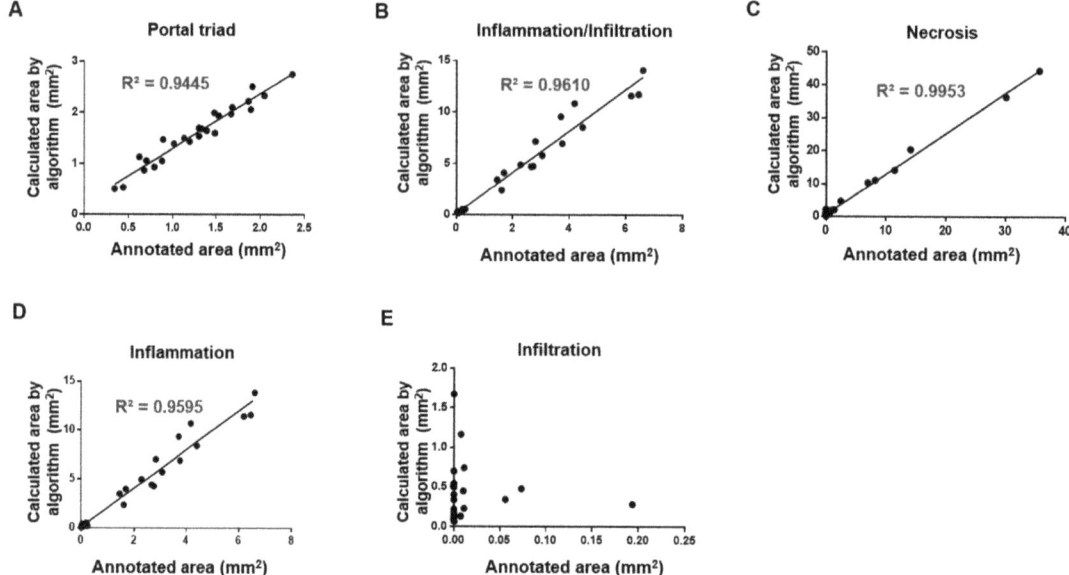

**Figure 5.** Correlations between annotated area and algorithm-predicted area. The areas annotated by an accredited toxicologic pathologist were compared by linear regression with those predicted by the established algorithm for portal triad (**A**), inflammation and infiltration together (**B**), necrosis (**C**), inflammation (**D**), and infiltration (**E**). The prediction was performed using 20× magnification-scale images.

## 4. Discussion

The development and integration of digital pathology and AI-based approaches to identify lesions from slide images can offer substantial advantages over traditional methods, such as by enabling spatial analysis while generating highly precise, unbiased, and consistent readouts that can be accessed remotely by pathologists [25]. In pre-clinical studies, CNN has been used to achieve quantitative and rapid assessment of pathological findings during drug discovery and development.

In the present study, we sought to use deep learning to implement an AI algorithm for the assessment of toxicological pathology in a non-clinical study. The model was built through training and validation for several hepatic lesions and used to predict one lesion. Going forward, training and testing with different hepatic lesions could be used to allow this algorithm to efficiently differentiate multiple hepatic lesions. The trained algorithm exhibited a total mAP of 96.44%, which is an outstanding result compared to those obtained in previous efforts to detect hepatic lesions [26,27]. Finally, we compared the annotation results assigned by an accredited toxicologic pathologist with the model prediction to evaluate model performance. The predicted lesions of portal triad, necrosis, and inflammation showed high correlations with the annotated lesions.

In several previous studies, deep-learning CNN-based algorithms were developed for detecting hepatic lesions. Heinemann et al. reported that automated deep-learning-based scores obtained using CNNs showed good agreement with the findings of a human pathologist [28]. In the CCl4- or CDAA-induced rodent models of non-alcoholic steatohepatitis (NASH), four histological features were scored (i.e., ballooning, inflammation, steatosis, and fibrosis). In another published report, a deep learning-based algorithm using CNN enabled the construction of a fully automated and accurate prediction model for scoring the stages of liver fibrosis [29]. However, although these previous studies evaluated the use of deep-learning algorithms for lesion scoring, this is the first work to use such an algorithm to predict the areas of hepatic lesions in an APAP-induced acute hepatic rat model.

APAP is widely used as an analgesic and antipyretic drug in the United States [30]. APAP-induced liver toxicity has been reported, and APAP is regarded as one of the most common pharmaceutical products capable of causing DILI. The mortality rate in APAP overdose patients is ~0.4%, which translates to 300 deaths annually in the United States [31]. New efforts to detect biomarkers of injured and necrotic hepatocytes seem promising, as it is important to identify APAP-induced acute liver injury patients at an early stage when lifesaving medical and surgical therapies can be provided. Going forward, AI approaches to predicting DILI could improve our understanding of the underlying mechanisms and our ability to anticipate hepatotoxicity for clinical applications [32].

We encountered several issues when developing our model to identify hepatic lesions. In the early stage of model establishment, portal triad was not included in the training process. However, our early results revealed that portal triad was often mistaken for inflammation or infiltration (Supplementary Material Figure S3). In the three-class model, the algorithm was trained in inflammation, infiltration, and necrosis. In this model, before training on the portal triad, confusion with the portal triad was observed with inflammatory or infiltration findings. This prompted us to include portal triad in further training, with the goal of increasing lesion recognition. Indeed, this addition, called the four-class model, improved the accuracy of lesion recognition (Supplementary Material Figure S3). We also found that some regions annotated as inflammation lesions were incorrectly predicted by the algorithm as infiltration lesions. This could lead the algorithm to over-estimate infiltration lesions relative to those identified by the accredited toxicologic pathologist. That said, there was a relatively low incidence of infiltration lesions in the studied model, so this error is not expected to significantly affect the overall prediction result. Indeed, our combined evaluation of the inflammatory and infiltration findings showed a greater agreement with the annotated findings. Simple mononuclear cell infiltration has been typically reported as inflammatory in the hepatic parenchymal tissues of normal rats [33]. It was slightly different from APAP-induced inflammation, which was characterized by histiocyte infiltration of an activated form with fluent cytoplasm around necrosis (Figure 2). A dataset of two different categories was prepared to prove whether two histological findings can be distinguished through the AI model. The dataset was divided into training, validation, and test set for model training and accuracy testing. The test result of the AI model for the infiltration was good and showed about 94% accuracy under the dataset environment. However, its test result in the WSI was not good and the correlation determinant (Figure 5E) was very low between the annotation and the result analyzed by AI model under the WSI, real world environment. The figures of infiltration and inflammation seemed confused because they have shared similar cellular components to some extent [34], and more diverse and complex figures would exist in the real world than in a dataset environment [35]. This categorization of infiltration and inflammation did not seem advisable in this study. The two findings are commonly inflammatory and were not confused with the other findings such as necrosis or portal triad. Therefore, it is thought to be more desirable to merge the values of infiltration and inflammation to evaluate the degree of inflammatory changes (Figure 5B). Finally, in WSI, connective tissue was often recognized as necrosis (Supplementary Material Figure S4). Since connective tissue was not included in our training for model establishment, WSIs including connective tissue were excluded from our evaluation of the model's performance. Careful consideration and further study will be needed before this model algorithm can be translated to real-world use.

As result of prediction using WSIs, liver injury including trained lesions might be identified. However, due to the limitations of artificial intelligence, untrained patterns or images could not be accurately distinguished. If there are untrained lesion patterns, additional dataset training will be required to identify the lesion efficiently. The presented AI algorithm efficiently predicted trained lesions, such as inflammation/infiltration, necrosis and portal triad in acute hepatic injury of rats. Further analysis of patient samples will be required to validate for human application.

Modern advancements in digital pathology mean that large quantities of quality digitized data are available for algorithm developers, scientists, and pathologists worldwide. Collaborations across the fields of digital pathology, machine learning, and big data acquisition are paving the way to revolutionize medical pathology [36,37]. Within this setting, novel approaches have been employed for image analysis in digital pathology; an example of such an approach is deep learning, which involves multi-layered neural network architectures. Some deep-learning algorithms involve a slow and hierarchical process of learning data abstractions and representations between layers and can become computationally expensive when dealing with high-dimensional image data. This can be addressed by the use of convolutional neural networks (CNNs), which effectively scale up high-dimensional data [38]. In the present study, we applied the Mask R-CNN algorithm to evaluate hepatic lesions in an APAP-induced acute hepatic injury rat model. The study results suggested that this algorithm can be used to implement diagnosis and prediction of hepatic lesions. In the future, this strategy could potentially be deployed in clinical practice.

**Supplementary Materials:** The following supporting information can be downloaded at: https://www.mdpi.com/article/10.3390/diagnostics12061478/s1. Supplementary Material Table S1. Number of cropped tile images used for the model training, validation, and testing. Supplementary Material Figure S1. Training loss during model establish-ment. Supplementary Material Figure S2. Discrepancy in inflammation detection between annota-tion and algorithm prediction. Supplementary Material Figure S3. Comparison of portal triad de-tection between 3 class model and 4 class model. Supplementary Material Figure S4. Discrepancy in connective tissue detection between annotation and algorithm prediction.

**Author Contributions:** Conceptualization, J.-W.C. and H.-Y.S.; methodology, J.-W.C., J.-H.H. and J.H.; software, Y.-B.K., S.-Y.J., J.H. and J.L.; validation and analysis, J.-H.H., E.B.B., H.P. and B.-S.L.; writing—original draft preparation, E.B.B.; writing—review and editing, E.B.B., J.L. and J.-W.C.; supervision, H.-Y.S. and J.-W.C. All authors have read and agreed to the published version of the manuscript.

**Funding:** The authors disclosed receipt of the following financial support for the research, authorship, and/or publication of this article: This research was supported by a grant (20183MFDS411) from the Ministry of Food and Drug Safety in 2022.

**Institutional Review Board Statement:** The animal experiment was approved by the Assessment and Accreditation of Laboratory Animal Care International (AAALAC) and Institutional Animal Care and Use Committee (IACUC). Approval ID: 2008-0265. Approval date: 25 August 2020.

**Informed Consent Statement:** Not applicable.

**Data Availability Statement:** Not applicable.

**Conflicts of Interest:** The authors declare no conflict of interest.

## References

1. Wang, S.; Yang, D.M.; Rong, R.; Zhan, X.; Xiao, G. Pathology Image Analysis Using Segmentation Deep Learning Algorithms. *Am. J. Pathol.* **2019**, *189*, 1686–1698. [CrossRef] [PubMed]
2. Cui, M.; Zhang, D.Y. Artificial intelligence and computational pathology. *Lab. Investig.* **2021**, *101*, 412–422. [CrossRef] [PubMed]
3. Abels, E.; Pantanowitz, L.; Aeffner, F.; Zarella, M.D.; van der Laak, J.; Bui, M.M.; Vemuri, V.N.; Parwani, A.V.; Gibbs, J.; Agosto-Arroyo, E.; et al. Computational pathology definitions, best practices, and recommendations for regulatory guidance: A white paper from the Digital Pathology Association. *J. Pathol.* **2019**, *249*, 286–294. [CrossRef] [PubMed]
4. Bertram, C.A.; Klopfleisch, R. The Pathologist 2.0: An Update on Digital Pathology in Veterinary Medicine. *Vet. Pathol.* **2017**, *54*, 756–766. [CrossRef] [PubMed]
5. Aeffner, F.; Adissu, H.A.; Boyle, M.C.; Cardiff, R.D.; Hagendorn, E.; Hoenerhoff, M.J.; Klopfleisch, R.; Newbigging, S.; Schaudien, D.; Turner, O.; et al. Digital Microscopy, Image Analysis, and Virtual Slide Repository. *ILAR J.* **2018**, *59*, 66–79. [CrossRef]
6. Carboni, E.; Marxfeld, H.; Tuoken, H.; Klukas, C.; Eggers, T.; Groters, S.; van Ravenzwaay, B. A Workflow for the Performance of the Differential Ovarian Follicle Count Using Deep Neuronal Networks. *Toxicol. Pathol.* **2021**, *49*, 843–850. [CrossRef]
7. Gertych, A.; Swiderska-Chadaj, Z.; Ma, Z.X.; Ing, N.; Markiewicz, T.; Cierniak, S.; Salemi, H.; Guzman, S.; Walts, A.E.; Knudsen, B.S. Convolutional neural networks can accurately distinguish four histologic growth patterns of lung adenocarcinoma in digital slides. *Sci. Rep.* **2019**, *9*, 1483. [CrossRef]

8. Hwang, J.H.; Kim, H.J.; Park, H.; Lee, B.S.; Son, H.Y.; Kim, Y.B.; Jun, S.Y.; Park, J.H.; Lee, J.; Cho, J.W. Implementation and Practice of Deep Learning-Based Instance Segmentation Algorithm for Quantification of Hepatic Fibrosis at Whole Slide Level in Sprague-Dawley Rats. *Toxicol. Pathol.* **2022**, *50*, 186–196. [CrossRef]
9. Shu, J.H.; Nian, F.D.; Yu, M.H.; Li, X. An Improved Mask R-CNN Model for Multiorgan Segmentation. *Math. Probl. Eng.* **2020**, *2020*, 8351725. [CrossRef]
10. Hsia, C.H.; Chang, T.H.W.; Chiang, C.Y.; Chan, H.T. Mask R-CNN with New Data Augmentation Features for Smart Detection of Retail Products. *Appl. Sci.* **2022**, *12*, 2902. [CrossRef]
11. Shammout, R.; Alhassoun, T.; Rayya, F. Acute Liver Failure due to Hepatitis A Virus. *Case Rep. Gastroenterol.* **2021**, *15*, 927–932. [CrossRef] [PubMed]
12. Hayashi, M.; Kanda, T.; Nakamura, M.; Miyamura, T.; Yasui, S.; Nakamoto, S.; Wu, S.; Arai, M.; Imazeki, F.; Yokosuka, O. Acute liver injury in a patient with alcohol dependence: A case resembling autoimmune hepatitis or drug-induced liver injury. *Case Rep. Gastroenterol.* **2014**, *8*, 129–133. [CrossRef] [PubMed]
13. David, S.; Hamilton, J.P. Drug-induced Liver Injury. *US Gastroenterol. Hepatol. Rev.* **2010**, *6*, 73–80. [PubMed]
14. Kang, M.G.; Kang, N.S. Predictive Model for Drug-Induced Liver Injury Using Deep Neural Networks Based on Substructure Space. *Molecules* **2021**, *26*, 7548. [CrossRef] [PubMed]
15. Ramachandran, R.; Kakar, S. Histological patterns in drug-induced liver disease. *J. Clin. Pathol.* **2009**, *62*, 481–492. [CrossRef]
16. Papackova, Z.; Heczkova, M.; Dankova, H.; Sticova, E.; Lodererova, A.; Bartonova, L.; Poruba, M.; Cahova, M. Silymarin prevents acetaminophen-induced hepatotoxicity in mice. *PLoS ONE* **2018**, *13*, e0191353. [CrossRef]
17. Wang, H.; Liu, R.; Schyman, P.; Wallqvist, A. Deep Neural Network Models for Predicting Chemically Induced Liver Toxicity Endpoints From Transcriptomic Responses. *Front. Pharmacol.* **2019**, *10*, 42. [CrossRef]
18. Xu, Y.; Dai, Z.; Chen, F.; Gao, S.; Pei, J.; Lai, L. Deep Learning for Drug-Induced Liver Injury. *J. Chem. Inf. Model.* **2015**, *55*, 2085–2093. [CrossRef]
19. Zhou, L.Q.; Wang, J.Y.; Yu, S.Y.; Wu, G.G.; Wei, Q.; Deng, Y.B.; Wu, X.L.; Cui, X.W.; Dietrich, C.F. Artificial intelligence in medical imaging of the liver. *World J. Gastroenterol.* **2019**, *25*, 672–682. [CrossRef]
20. Decharatanachart, P.; Chaiteerakij, R.; Tiyarattanachai, T.; Treeprasertsuk, S. Application of artificial intelligence in chronic liver diseases: A systematic review and meta-analysis. *BMC Gastroenterol.* **2021**, *21*, 10. [CrossRef]
21. Li, Y.; Wang, X.; Zhang, J.; Zhang, S.; Jiao, J. Applications of artificial intelligence (AI) in researches on non-alcoholic fatty liver disease (NAFLD): A systematic review. *Rev. Endocr. Metab. Disord.* **2022**, *23*, 387–400. [CrossRef] [PubMed]
22. Abdel-Zaher, A.O.; Abdel-Hady, R.H.; Mahmoud, M.M.; Farrag, M.M. The potential protective role of alpha-lipoic acid against acetaminophen-induced hepatic and renal damage. *Toxicology* **2008**, *243*, 261–270. [CrossRef] [PubMed]
23. Yousef, M.I.; Omar, S.A.; El-Guendi, M.I.; Abdelmegid, L.A. Potential protective effects of quercetin and curcumin on paracetamol-induced histological changes, oxidative stress, impaired liver and kidney functions and haematotoxicity in rat. *Food Chem. Toxicol.* **2010**, *48*, 3246–3261. [CrossRef] [PubMed]
24. Baek, E.B.; Rho, J.H.; Jung, E.; Seo, C.S.; Kim, J.H.; Kwun, H.J. Protective effect of Palmijihwanghwan in a mouse model of cigarette smoke and lipopolysaccharide-induced chronic obstructive pulmonary disease. *BMC Complement. Med. Ther.* **2021**, *21*, 281. [CrossRef] [PubMed]
25. Baxi, V.; Edwards, R.; Montalto, M.; Saha, S. Digital pathology and artificial intelligence in translational medicine and clinical practice. *Mod. Pathol.* **2022**, *35*, 23–32. [CrossRef] [PubMed]
26. Nam, D.; Chapiro, J.; Paradis, V.; Seraphin, T.P.; Kather, J.N. Artificial intelligence in liver diseases: Improving diagnostics, prognostics and response prediction. *JHEP Rep.* **2022**, *4*, 100443. [CrossRef]
27. Dong, X.; Zhou, Y.Z.; Wang, L.T.; Peng, J.F.; Lou, Y.B.; Fan, Y.Q. Liver Cancer Detection Using Hybridized Fully Convolutional Neural Network Based on Deep Learning Framework. *IEEE Access* **2020**, *8*, 129889–129898. [CrossRef]
28. Heinemann, F.; Birk, G.; Stierstorfer, B. Deep learning enables pathologist-like scoring of NASH models. *Sci. Rep.* **2019**, *9*, 18454. [CrossRef]
29. Yu, Y.; Wang, J.; Ng, C.W.; Ma, Y.; Mo, S.; Fong, E.L.S.; Xing, J.; Song, Z.; Xie, Y.; Si, K.; et al. Deep learning enables automated scoring of liver fibrosis stages. *Sci. Rep.* **2018**, *8*, 16016. [CrossRef]
30. Herndon, C.M.; Dankenbring, D.M. Patient perception and knowledge of acetaminophen in a large family medicine service. *J. Pain Palliat. Care Pharmacother.* **2014**, *28*, 109–116. [CrossRef]
31. Yoon, E.; Babar, A.; Choudhary, M.; Kutner, M.; Pyrsopoulos, N. Acetaminophen-Induced Hepatotoxicity: A Comprehensive Update. *J. Clin. Transl. Hepatol.* **2016**, *4*, 131–142. [CrossRef] [PubMed]
32. Vall, A.; Sabnis, Y.; Shi, J.; Class, R.; Hochreiter, S.; Klambauer, G. The Promise of AI for DILI Prediction. *Front. Artif. Intell.* **2021**, *4*, 638410. [CrossRef] [PubMed]
33. Sahota, P.S.; Popp, J.A.; Hardisty, J.F.; Gopinath, C. (Eds.) *Toxicologic Pathology: Nonclinical Safety Assessment*; CRC Press: Boca Raton, FL, USA, 2013; p. 210.
34. Thoolen, B.; Maronpot, R.R.; Harada, T.; Nyska, A.; Rousseaux, C.; Nolte, T.; Malarkey, D.E.; Kaufmann, W.; Kuttler, K.; Deschl, U.; et al. Proliferative and nonproliferative lesions of the rat and mouse hepatobiliary system. *Toxicol. Pathol.* **2010**, *38*, 5S–81S. [CrossRef] [PubMed]
35. Norori, N.; Hu, Q.; Aellen, F.M.; Faraci, F.D.; Tzovara, A. Addressing bias in big data and AI for health care: A call for open science. *Patterns* **2021**, *2*, 100347. [CrossRef]

36. Hanna, M.G.; Ardon, O.; Reuter, V.E.; England, C.; Klimstra, D.S.; Hameed, M.R. Integrating digital pathology into clinical practice (Oct, 10.1038/s41379-021-00929-0, 2021). *Mod. Pathol.* **2022**, *35*, 287. [CrossRef]
37. Parwani, A.V. Next generation diagnostic pathology: Use of digital pathology and artificial intelligence tools to augment a pathological diagnosis. *Diagn. Pathol.* **2019**, *14*, 138. [CrossRef]
38. Najafabadi, M.M.; Villanustre, F.; Khoshgoftaar, T.M.; Seliya, N.; Wald, R.; Muharemagic, E. Deep learning applications and challenges in big data analytics. *J. Big Data* **2015**, *2*, 1. [CrossRef]

*Article*

# The Use of Digital Pathology and Artificial Intelligence in Histopathological Diagnostic Assessment of Prostate Cancer: A Survey of Prostate Cancer UK Supporters

Kai Rakovic [1,2,*], Richard Colling [3,4], Lisa Browning [3,5], Monica Dolton [4], Margaret R. Horton [6], Andrew Protheroe [7,8], Alastair D. Lamb [4,9], Richard J. Bryant [4,9], Richard Scheffer [4], James Crofts [4], Ewart Stanislaus [4] and Clare Verrill [3,4,5]

1. Institute of Cancer Sciences, University of Glasgow, Switchback Road, Glasgow G61 1QH, UK
2. Department of Pathology, Queen Elizabeth University Hospital, Govan Road, Glasgow G51 4TF, UK
3. Department of Cellular Pathology, Oxford University Hospitals NHS Foundation Trust, John Radcliffe Hospital, Headley Way, Oxford OX3 9DU, UK; richard.colling@pmb.ox.ac.uk (R.C.); lisa.browning@ouh.nhs.uk (L.B.); clare.verrill@ouh.nhs.uk (C.V.)
4. Nuffield Department of Surgical Sciences, University of Oxford, John Radcliffe Hospital, Headley Way, Oxford OX3 9DU, UK; monica.dolton@nds.ox.ac.uk (M.D.); alastair.lamb@nds.ox.ac.uk (A.D.L.); richard.bryant@nds.ox.ac.uk (R.J.B.); richard.scheffer@btinternet.com (R.S.); croftsj@hotmail.com (J.C.); ewartbs@hotmail.com (E.S.)
5. NIHR Oxford Biomedical Research Centre, Oxford University Hospitals NHS Foundation Trust, John Radcliffe Hospital, Headley Way, Oxford OX3 9DU, UK
6. Paige AI, 11 Times Sq, Fl 37, New York, NY 10036, USA; margaret.horton@paige.ai
7. Department of Oncology, University of Oxford, Roosevelt Drive, Oxford OX3 7DQ, UK; andrew.protheroe@oncology.ox.ac.uk
8. Oxford Cancer & Haematology Centre, Oxford University Hospitals NHS Foundation Trust, Churchill Hospital, Old Road, Oxford OX3 7LE, UK
9. Department of Urology, Oxford University Hospitals NHS Foundation Trust, Churchill Hospital, Old Road, Oxford OX3 7LE, UK
* Correspondence: kai.rakovic@glasgow.ac.uk; Tel.: +44-(0)-141-354-9474

**Abstract:** There has been particular interest in the deployment of digital pathology (DP) and artificial intelligence (AI) in the diagnosis of prostate cancer, but little is known about the views of the public on their use. Prostate Cancer UK supporters were invited to an online survey which included quantitative and qualitative questions exploring views on the use of DP and AI in histopathological assessment. A total of 1276 responses to the survey were analysed (response rate 12.5%). Most respondents were supportive of DP (87%, 1113/1276) and of testing AI in clinical practice as a diagnostic adjunct (83%, 1058/1276). Respondents saw DP as potentially increasing workflow efficiency, facilitating research, education/training and fostering clinical discussions between clinician and patient. Some respondents raised concerns regarding data security, reliability and the need for human oversight. Among those who were unsure about AI, information was requested regarding its performance and others wanted to defer the decision to use it to an expert. Although most are in favour of its use, some are unsure, and their concerns could be addressed with more information or better communication. A small minority (<1%) are not in favour of the testing of the use of AI in histopathology for reasons which are not easily addressed.

**Keywords:** prostate cancer; digital pathology; artificial intelligence

## 1. Introduction

The role of the histopathologist (cellular pathologist) in clinical care is poorly understood by patients and the wider public [1] despite the histopathology contribution being integral for the diagnosis and management of conditions such as cancer. The practice of histopathology has rapidly evolved over the last 10 years, with now well-established

advances in molecular diagnostics and more recently the introduction of digital pathology (DP). With the impending roll out of artificial intelligence (AI), it is important to understand what level of detail the public wish to know about these advances, the role they play in diagnostic processes, what level of acceptance of such changes is likely (and why) and how we communicate these advances.

The basic techniques used in histopathology emerged in the 19th century and have not fundamentally changed to the present day [2]. They centre on the examination of stained sections of formalin-fixed paraffin-embedded tissue using light microscopy. Over the last 50 years, however, there has been an exponential growth in the complexity of tumour classification with the advent of immunohistochemistry and, in recent decades, the integration of genetic and molecular methods into diagnostics. There have been further advances in the last decade with the adoption of DP. With DP, the glass slide is scanned and the digital whole slide image is examined on a computer screen instead of a microscope. DP is gaining traction as a primary reporting modality in many cellular pathology centres in the United Kingdom (UK) [3] and is likely to become mainstream in the histopathology workflow in the coming years [4]. A survey conducted in 2017 [5] reported that 60% of pathology centres in the UK had access to DP equipment and 58.5% considered the development of DP infrastructure to be a priority.

The adoption of DP may bring improvements to the diagnostic workflow, allowing streamlined prioritisation, greater flexibility in remote working, potential financial savings [6] and ease of research collaboration [7]. Education of histopathology trainees traditionally relies on face-to-face case review with a consultant trainer on a multi-header microscope. DP allows these interactions to take place remotely, facilitating training across multiple geographical sites [8]. These benefits have particularly been demonstrated in recent years due to the COVID-19 pandemic [3]. The majority of histopathology trainees polled in a 2019 survey saw the introduction of DP into their training as a positive step [9]. Furthermore, there is potential to develop supraregional networks, streamlining the process where certain cases require external review [10].

Digitisation of histopathological images brings the potential for implementation of novel diagnostic adjuncts such as AI-assisted diagnostics. These may provide diagnostic assistance to histopathologists in assessing current standard of care features and may provide novel insights into disease biology not otherwise possible with a human observer. Examples include automation of tasks such as quantification of mitotic index [11,12] or hormone receptor scores in breast cancer [11]. Furthermore, there is evidence emerging of the potential application of deep learning in AI-assisted diagnostics to gain novel insights into morpho-molecular associations. For instance, the ability to predict aspects of the molecular profiles of malignant tumours, such as EGFR in non-small cell lung [13] cancer and microsatellite instability in gastrointestinal cancers [14], from whole slide images has been demonstrated.

One area of pathology where there has been intense interest in AI is in prostate cancer (PCa). There is potential for improved diagnostic accuracy, improved efficiency and standardisation of prognostic features such as Gleason grading and tumour quantification. The mainstay of diagnosis in PCa is core biopsy and the determination of the grade is by assessment of the morphological features by a histopathologist. These features are then assigned a grade according to the Gleason grading system (Grade Group System), which remains pivotal in prognostication and influences downstream patient management. In cases where the morphological features fall short of a definitive diagnosis of malignancy, such as in limited foci of potential tumour, ancillary studies, including immunohistochemistry to demonstrate loss of basal markers, are requested to aid the reporting histopathologist in their decision. Specific AI applications exist as adjuncts to the reporting of prostate core biopsies, such as suggestion of diagnosis and attribution of Gleason Score [15] and the pre-emptive requesting of immunohistochemistry in morphologically equivocal cases [16]. Some of these algorithms have been cleared with CE marking or FDA clearance for in vitro diagnostics and these are the first such regulatory clearances in the field [15,17]. With approximately 45,000 new diagnoses of PCa per annum in England and Wales, the benefits to the workflow are considerable [18].

The potential to use AI in histopathology practice is a potential paradigm shift in the way histopathologists work and marks a significant step forward beyond traditional light microscopy; however, the adoption of this is currently occasionally being used in specific diagnostic settings [19]. While we seek to accelerate adoption and unlock benefits of this technology, we need to be mindful of any public scepticism and concern regarding the use of technology and AI in modern life, including in healthcare. Although not specific to healthcare, a large-scale international survey of over 150,000 respondents demonstrated mixed opinion regarding implementation of AI in decision making [20]. Differences in acceptance were observed among individuals from certain demographic groups. Higher rates of acceptance were observed in those residing in Asian countries compared to western countries, and in executives and professionals versus manual and service workers.

Few studies exist exploring public perceptions about the deployment of these technological advances to patient care and there are none specific to histopathology. The view towards AI in medicine more broadly appears somewhat split. Public comments on social media in China [21] include broad support for AI in healthcare with many comments suggesting AI could replace doctors entirely. Women undergoing breast screening mammography in Scotland were found to be supportive of AI as an adjunct to diagnosis but were sceptical of fully autonomous AI [22].

Our study aims to analyse the views of a group of the public, specifically supporters of a UK-based prostate cancer charity who have previously undergone prostate biopsy. Our particular objectives were: (1) to explore the current understanding of how biopsies are reported; (2) to assess views on digitisation of histopathology; and (3) to determine whether patients would support the use of AI-assisted diagnostics as an adjunct to the routine reporting of prostate biopsies and histopathological specimens more broadly.

## 2. Materials and Methods

### 2.1. Survey Design

This study collected anonymous, non-NHS data which could not be traced back to an individual. The questions had been developed with the health information team at Prostate Cancer UK (PCUK). Given the possibility that the target population may have had limited familiarity with histopathology, questions were carefully worded to ensure comprehension. The survey was drafted with the biopsy pathway in mind, with internal review to ensure it met the needs of the study along with the needs of the charity and its users. The survey included 11 questions, and follow up questions enabled respondents to make further free text comments. The survey was developed following discussions with a small number of volunteer PCUK supporters. The survey was circulated to PCUK supporters through a mailing list for newsletters etc maintained by PCUK, focussing on men > 50 years old as this is the group who were most likely to meet the inclusion criteria (see below). The online survey was hosted on the Toluna platform (an end-to-end consumer intelligence platform where surveys can be designed and distributed to PCUK supporters); no personal data was collected, and individual respondents could not be traced. The survey was circulated on 21 May 2021 and closed in June 2021. In total, 1307 responses were obtained following circulation to 10,465 PCUK supporters (12.5% response rate).

### 2.2. Survey Composition

The survey is included as supplementary material. Briefly, limited demographic data were available (country of the respondent and, if UK-based, the region—divided into North and Scotland/Northern Ireland/Midlands and Wales/South. Respondents were questioned regarding their baseline knowledge of histopathology and the role of histopathologists in PCa diagnosis. As histopathology services adopt DP and look towards AI for diagnostic support, respondents' attitudes to the use of these technologies were explored. We specifically explored whether respondents would consider it useful to be able to view digital images of their prostate biopsy enabled by digital pathology, to aid understanding. We explored support for AI, and where there was uncertainty or negativity, we sought to explore the qualitative comments to understand these hesitations.

The survey included an introductory statement (please see online supplementary material). Completion of the survey was taken as consent to participate. There was an explicit statement about publication in an academic journal.

The only inclusion criterion was having had a prostate biopsy at any point (please see online supplementary material, Question S1). Not having had a prostate biopsy, or being unsure, was an exclusion criterion as we were aiming to capture experiences of those who had had a prostate biopsy which required histopathological assessment. A response of "no" or "did not know" to a prostate biopsy in the past resulted in the end of the survey.

*2.3. Statistical Analysis*

Descriptive statistics with graphical outputs were used to characterise survey results. Responses for free text questions were analysed, pertinent themes extracted and categorised according to said themes. Ambiguous or unclear comments were not included.

## 3. Results

*3.1. Response*

In total, 1307 responses were received, of which 87.2% were UK-based; 1276 men responded 'yes' to a history of previous prostate biopsy. The remaining respondents were excluded from further questioning.

*3.2. Understanding of the Role of Histopathology*

The majority (69.1%, 882/1276) stated that they understood the role of the histopathologist (please see online supplementary material, Questions S3–S6, and Figure 1). A further 10% (126/1276) stated they were aware of the term but unclear about the exact nature of the work carried out by histopathologists. A small proportion (39.2%, 500/1276) said that they understand the overall role of a histopathology department.

When asked whether they would wish to know more about the work of histopathologists or of cellular pathology departments, a third responded positively (30.4%, 388/1276), with a small number stating they had no opinion (16.2%, 207/1276). Around half stated they did not wish to know more (53.4%, 681/1276).

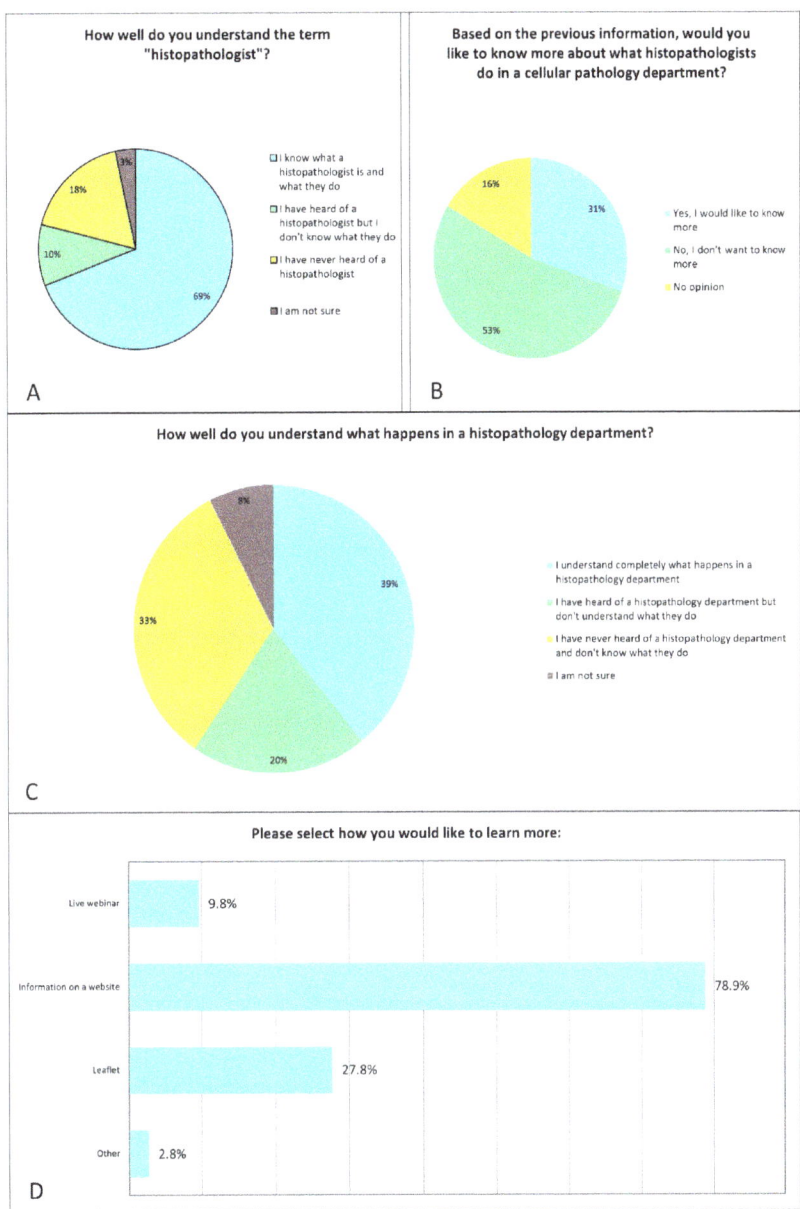

**Figure 1.** Breakdown of responses on patient understanding of histopathology (**A–C**). Those who indicated they wished to know more (388 respondents) shown in (**D**).

*3.3. Views on Digitisation of Pathology*

Most men viewed the digitisation of histopathological slides as either positive or very positive (87.2%, 1113/1276; please see online supplementary material, Question S7, and Figure 2 and Table 1). Review of free text responses revealed five broad themes: a perception of increased efficiency of turnaround time, record permanence, ease of sharing information, facilitating research and education and the potential for the development of novel technologies such as AI.

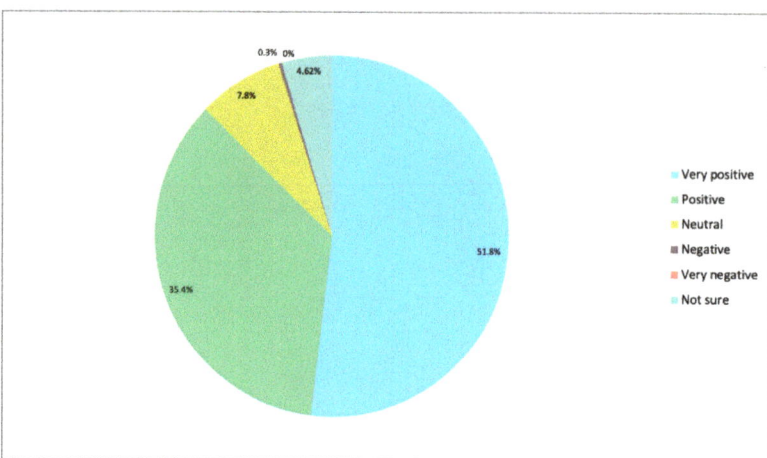

**Figure 2.** Responses to the question "Some histopathology departments are now going 'digital'. Slides containing prostate biopsy tissue can now be scanned and viewed digitally on a screen rather than through a microscope. This makes a permanent digital record of the biopsy which reduces the chances of any issues with viewing slides. This also allows histopathologists to easily get a second opinion on a diagnosis. Do you see this change in diagnosing prostate cancer as a positive or negative?" (Please see online supplementary material, Question S7).

**Table 1.** Example free text quotations from respondents on their views regarding the introduction of DP into routine practice.

| Theme | Example Quotations |
|---|---|
| (a) Efficiency and technical aspects | Having had prostate cancer anything that speeds up and increases the accuracy of diagnosis has to be good.<br>I am no expert but anything that makes viewing samples easier should make the doctors work easier and perhaps more accurate. I have done microscope work before, and it can be tiring and challenging especially if you are trying to count occurrences over an area.<br>Digital leaves less room for human error.<br>It sounds positive but without lots more information I could not say very positive, how secure will this data be, how reliable is the digital screening, is it at least as reliable . . . as a human? |
| (b) Record permanence | As a digital record, it can be transferred between departments enabling specialists to discuss it. More importantly, it can't be lost easily.<br>A permanent record would provide a baseline assessment in case of need for further biopsies.<br>A digital record could be kept for MDT meetings.<br>I approve of the positive digital record, but the sample(s) should not be discarded before a conclusive diagnosis (higher magnification may be needed than the digital images).<br>Any use of more modern technology cannot be a negative as long as the control over data is maintained properly/adequately. I suppose I wouldn't like my digital records getting into the wrong hands!! |

Table 1. Cont.

| Theme | Example Quotations |
|---|---|
| (c) Sharing of images | A digital record is easily stored and can be easily shared with appropriate people. If requested, it could be shared with the patient to aid understanding of the result. Ability to share between experts, and ability to share/show the patient. There is a digital record of the sample(s) which can easily be recalled as a basis for comparison if there is/are ever repeat tests. Also, the record will be an element in a database of all biopsies which might be valuable for statistical or other test purposes. Having an electronic library enables medical staff and researchers to have better access. I had three biopsies in all . . . I trusted the histopathologists to produce the necessary reports, which were then used to decide the way ahead. The first biopsy was abroad, and I actually brought the original slides back to UK with the report; that would, of course, have been easier had they been digital. As a patient I have no particular view on digital vs. analogue slides, except that digital probably eases record-keeping and referral. I would have been very interested to have seen the samples and had their significance explained to me. Makes the data/information available for study/research/analysis to many more specialists instantly. My consultant explained in detail what the outcome was from the histology, but I did not see a digital scan of the biopsies. I think that would be helpful. Opportunity for referring back to the images. Allows teams to see the images and comment. Other centres able to easily review the histopathology ensuring uniformity in research, etc. This should enable retrospective scanning back over images if something useful is discovered in the future, where historic biopsy data, perhaps combined with progression/survival data, would be useful. However, it's important the biological samples are retained too, so they can be used for things like genomic sequencing. |
| (d) AI | AI is infallible if programmed correctly As long as a person who checks the results is experienced in reading them and the digital image is not a just compared to a digital library. Digital images can be stored to compare at a later date, it should be a positive move. Assuming the quality of image is as good, and the data is properly managed, the added availability should help diagnosis. It may also assist machine learning for analysis and more accurate diagnosis. It seems to make sense to digitize records. It should speed their transfer from one party to another and will make it easier for more than one professional to examine them. It might also facilitate the use of ai to review them. Provided the "library" of samples was large quantities and good enough quality, using automated digital imaging can cover more areas of the "slide" and present the targeted cells for review by qualified human to maximise efficiency and throughput. AI technology can help and be taught to find needles in haystacks . . . Can machines interpret as well as humans in this situation, I don't know the answer to this question? |
| (e) Reservations towards DP | The important factor for me as a potential cancer sufferer was to know that every process was being done to the best level possible. I did not want or need to know the details of the process itself but trusted that I was getting the best. As techniques advance, I think I would have the same attitude. Trust that the people know what they are doing and using the best technology. Either cancer is present or its not, how you record it is immaterial. I am only interested in the results. As a patient I am just interested in the results regardless of how they have been arrived at. I would think that an expert examining the sample would always be more reliable than a computer, but maybe there is a role for both approaches if there is time and money available Is it necessary to keep digital records? Once you know the result, a record is kept. So what? How is this going to help me? |

Footnote: please also see online supplementary material—Question S7.

### 3.3.1. Increased Efficiency and Technical Aspects

There was a strong perception that adoption of a digital workflow would reduce turnaround time, thus reducing patient anxiety. Some men felt that reviewing digital images would lead to greater diagnostic accuracy, if images were to be of sufficient resolution and viewed on large digital displays.

### 3.3.2. Formation of a Permanent Record

Points were raised regarding the ability to easily archive and retrieve digital images compared to physical glass slides. Many perceived this to be of benefit if multiple biopsies were carried out on the same patient, thereby allowing the comparison of images. A proportion also saw utility in comparison of biopsy findings and post-operative histopathology.

### 3.3.3. Sharing of Digital Images

The ability to share images among members of the multidisciplinary team was seen as a strong benefit, and for streamlined referral across teams who may be based in geographically distanced centres. In addition to sharing among healthcare professionals, many saw a positive opportunity for images to be shared with them as patients in the clinic setting. Opportunities were seen for the distribution of images for education of trainee histopathologists. Finally, digitisation of images was seen to allow the generation of a bank of data which would be drawn upon for research purposes paving the way for future advances in the diagnosis and treatment of PCa.

When specifically asked whether they would have been interested in viewing their histopathological images (please see online supplementary material, Question S8, and Figure 3), most men (82.1%, 1048/1276) responded that this would be desirable. More specifically, in terms of the format of this, of those who responded positively, most would prefer this to be in a clinic rather than on a secure online platform.

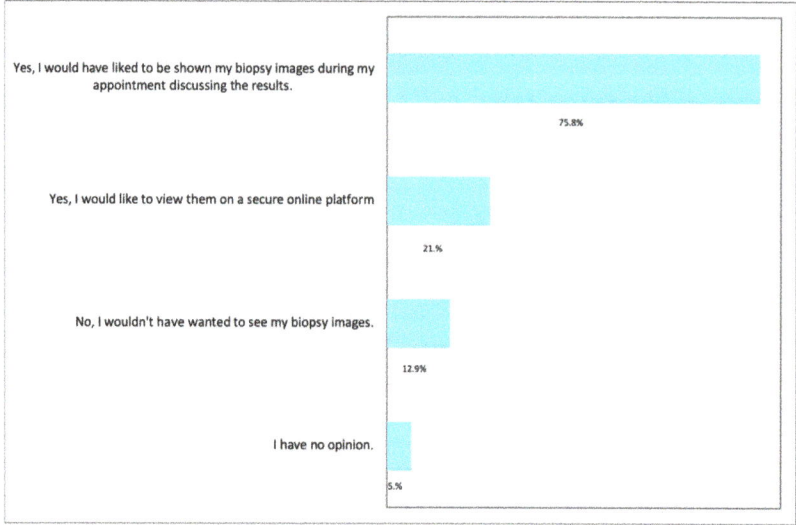

**Figure 3.** Respondents' views on viewing digital biopsy images (please see online supplementary material, Question S8). Respondents were able to choose more than one option.

### 3.3.4. Deployment of AI Techniques

Many respondents acknowledged the possibility of human error and fatigue in manual reporting of histopathological slides, thus raising the potential advantage of AI as an adjunct to reduce such errors.

Neutral responses suggested indifference to the methods of producing a histopathological report, as long as the report was produced in a timely and accurate manner. Some responses suggested indifference due to personal limitations of knowledge and understanding of possible benefits of the technology.

3.3.5. Reservations towards DP

Few responders were against the adoption of DP were relatively few, but important ideas were raised. Participants discussed the need for digital images and associated data to be held on a secure server, well protected from illicit access and accidental loss. Others felt a greater sense of trust in reports generated purely by a human without any computational intervention or distrust in computer systems.

*3.4. On the Introduction of AI in the Reporting of Histopathology*

Although most men (1058/1276, 83%) considered the testing of AI as an adjunct to histopathological reporting (please see online supplementary material, Question S9, and Figure 4) to be a positive advance, some were unsure (203/1276, 16%) and a few (15/1276, 1%) were not in favour.

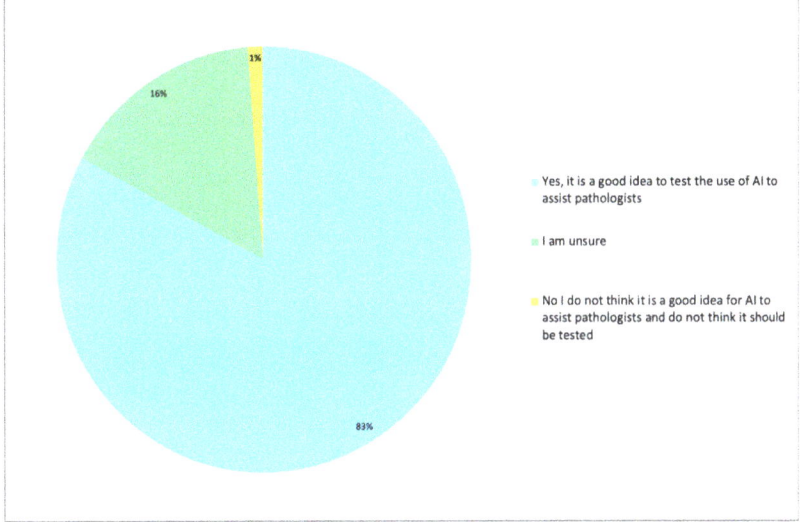

**Figure 4.** Digital developments could allow Artificial intelligence (AI) to be used in histopathology. Pathology AI means that a computer programme can potentially assist with the diagnosis of prostate cancer by double checking results. To find out for certain, more testing is being carried out. What do you think about research that will test whether pathologists can be assisted by AI when diagnosing prostate cancer?

A range of views were observed regarding whether patients wished to learn more about the use of AI in the diagnosis of PCa (please see online supplemental material, Question S10, and Figure 5). In total, 39% (498/1276) of respondents wished to learn more, 41% (524/1276) did not and 20% (254/1276) had no opinion. Of the 498 who desired further information, the majority preferred for this to be in website format (85%, 425/498) rather than a leaflet (20%, 100/498) or live webinar (15%, 75/498), and 1% (6/498) were open to receiving information by email.

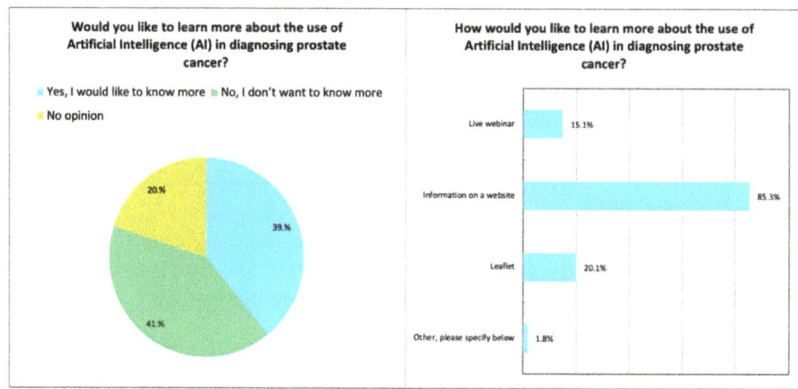

**Figure 5.** Visual representation of respondents' views on whether they would like to be further informed about AI in the diagnosis in prostate cancer and the preferred format (please see online supplementary material, Question S10).

Most comments were positive (examples in Table 2). Free comments offered by men who were ambivalent or against the use of AI were categorised into two main themes: (1) technical performance; and (2) preference for human review with a greater sense of personal trust versus the output of an algorithm. The 5/15 who were not in favour provided additional free text explanations. Two related to general mistrust of AI, two referred to wanting human input in decision making and one was uncertain about the accuracy. A summary of the free text comments for those who were unsure related to having insufficient knowledge, concerns around accuracy or performance ($n = 30$), wanting human input or double checking by a human ($n = 18$), those who were generally unsure or sceptical ($n = 9$) and those who would defer the decision to use the technology to an expert (histopathologist) ($n = 6$). Others included ensuring resources were not diverted from elsewhere ($n = 1$), no comment ($n = 1$) and not enough knowledge of histopathology to comment ($n = 1$). One respondent made two comments, so these are indicated as two comments, all others made one comment.

### 3.4.1. Technical Performance

Comments discussed the wish for a reliable result, and concerns raised regarding possible misdiagnosis although some noted that apprehension would be alleviated if more data were available for reassurance regarding the performance of the algorithms.

### 3.4.2. Preference for Human Review

Respondents expressed reassurance from involvement of a trained professional in the generation of a histopathological report. The expertise of an experienced histopathologist was felt to be preferable to AI in terms of patient confidence in the result. Some in this group stated they would be reassured if the performance of an AI algorithm be verified by a histopathologist rather than function autonomously.

**Table 2.** Example free text quotations from respondents on their views regarding the introduction of AI into routine histopathology reporting.

| Theme | Example Quotations |
|---|---|
| (a) Support for AI | AI might pick up things a tired histopathologist missed, so having them confirm each other's work would be good. I think evidence shows that the same histopathologist analysing the same slide sometime later does sometimes give a different grade. Getting the grading right is important for picking the right treatment.<br>As long as AI does not become the primary decision maker but takes the strain on some of the more mundane elements of the process, I wouldn't have a problem. Assuming that AI can meet (maybe exceed) the levels of accuracy of a human this could free up the experts' time for other uses.<br>Clearly research should be carried out to see whether AI could help. But it should only be pursued if rigorous checking indicates there are benefits over and above what a pathologist can do.<br>I think AI makes sense as long as its role is to assist and not to take over from a trained pathologist. I wouldn't be comfortable with the latter at this stage, but I see value in perhaps helping to increase the speed of diagnoses, add a degree of consistency in diagnoses which can sometimes be difficult for a pathologist to achieve all the time, and possibly to help detect patterns across a number of patients leading to potential future research and treatment areas.<br>I think it is a good idea; however, a senior pathologist needs to verify the results. Possibly the most important element to modern AI/pattern recognition methodologies is a good reliable data set and to not over train the network. It is essential, therefore, to ensure the quality of the 'AI' and also to ensure that if samples are not confirmed by human examination, then the system produces zero false negatives. Also, it is essential to be very cautious of using some 'AI' companies as partners as they are nothing short of charlatans.<br>AI has a great potential to speed up diagnosis, a benefit to patients. Quality control would be essential, checking that known true positives are picked up, and regular sampling so a histopathologist can check for false positives and false negatives. My only concern is that it may eventually lead to fewer pathologists being employed and by them becoming "de-skilled". |
| (b) Concerns regarding technical performance | I understand that AI is cost effective and probably can get through a greater workload quicker. My concern, again, is that will something be missed if the programming or the technical quality of the ai is compromised.<br>Good idea but the usual checks and balances need to be good and regularly tested—see post office debacle re their post masters and mistresses. |
| (c) Preference for human review | I'm all for the advancement of technology, but for the use of diagnostic purpose I would prefer the opinion of a doctor. You can't program experience and a "hunch". As long as AI is used alongside pathologist looking at the data, all will be good but should not replace a pathologist.<br>AI may be something that a younger generation accept without question but for an old dinosaur like me AI Is far from second nature. This does not mean that it couldn't be useful, it just means that I need convincing.<br>As a lay person, I would have thought it would assist professionals, but I would not want it to be totally replacing an expert. |

Footnote: please also see the online supplementary material—Question S9.

## 4. Discussion

The insights gained from this study demonstrate that the majority of men undergoing a prostate biopsy are supportive of the use of technology in the form of digital pathology or AI for diagnostic assistance in assessing their prostate biopsy.

An advantage of digital pathology is that it offers the ability to make histopathology images more accessible, and a recurring theme amongst the free text comments was around image sharing in various guises: for expert opinion, for teaching and education for clinicians (pathologists) and for patient information. Indeed, the survey has shown that there is an apparent patient desire to review their images alongside a healthcare professional in clinic, which may not be intuitive. Although this practice is commonplace for radiology, surgeons and oncologists are less familiar with histopathology, and this is an obstacle in the adoption of this form of clinical practice. In a recent survey setting in a testicular tumour network, oncologists potentially felt that viewing digital pathology images may complicate discussions, especially if a pathology-related question was asked [10]. There may be a role for AI-annotated images to assist the clinician in highlighting pertinent features to the patient in clinic without the need for a histopathologist to be present. We perhaps need to find ways to facilitate this, for example with histopathologists adding user friendly annotations or labels to images to aid non-histopathologists, but this has time and resource implications in a speciality in which 97% of histopathology laboratories in the UK already report too few staff to meet clinical demand [23].

Examples of conversations which could potentially be enhanced by viewing images include small foci of Gleason Grade Group 1 PCa where patients are often recommended to receive active surveillance (AS). A proportion of men commencing AS may subsequently receive treatment for "non-biological" reasons such as patient anxiety and uncertainty, with rates of 8–23% across different studies [24]. Although untested, if patients could see for themselves that their cancer is small and low grade then this might provide reassurance that it could be managed by AS. Other discussions that may be informative include different Gleason grades that are present or demonstrating that immunohistochemistry has been performed to confirm small areas of cancer for reassurance that the diagnosis is correct. Although highly relevant, a detailed discussion on conveying if and how AI results were used in formulating the histopathologist's diagnosis to a patient during assessment is beyond the scope of this paper and the experience of the authors to date will form the basis of further studies.

The outputs of this study provide useful insight for anyone looking to deploy AI outside of a retrospective, research setting and into a live clinical diagnostic workflow. We have demonstrated that the majority of men are in favour of testing AI for diagnostic assistance and potential benefits of improving diagnostic accuracy, increasing capacity within histopathology departments and standardising subjective assessments such as Gleason grading, which can be reassuring. We reiterate that the intended utility for AI systems in histopathology is as an adjunct to review by a histopathologist—there is opportunity to better and more clearly communicate this point to the general public. It could be a criticism of this study that in order to avoid overly complex medical terminology the neutrality of the overall tone of some questions may have appeared more in favour of the benefits of DP/AI.

It remains important to explore the views of those who are unsure or do not think this is a good idea to allay concerns where possible. The respondents who were unsure or not in favour of AI assistance had concerns that could potentially be addressed with more information or better communication. For example, in the 'not in favour' group, only 2/5 were genuinely distrustful of AI. In the 'not sure' group, most comments related to wanting human input, wanting more information about the relative performance of the tool or deferral of the ultimate decision whether to use the technology to an expert (histopathologist). We take away from this that in providing information to patients about AI and histopathology, the key messages that need to be conveyed are that currently these tools are an assist to histopathologists, with those same clinical experts still retaining oversight and responsibility for the diagnostic report. If AI is considered part of clinical care, there will likely be institutional opt out processes for certain parts of clinical care which those with a very strong objection can invoke.

It is important to understand that the adoption of machine-assistance in healthcare is not limited to histopathology. In surgical practice, the robotic-assisted radical prostatectomy was introduced in 2001 [25] and has been associated with favourable outcomes over traditional radical prostatectomy [26]. Men who had experienced such surgery were generally satisfied with their experience, although there was a lack of understanding in some regarding the precise role of the surgeon and the robot in such circumstances [27].

Another more general British study [28] gauged differing viewpoints of male and female patients when faced with robot-assisted surgery. Male participants were generally found to be less concerned about the adoption of the technology although female participants found the use of a robot to be dehumanising. Similar opinions were raised by some respondents in our study although given our focus on PCa patients, our cohort is exclusively male.

Within the diagnostic specialties, perhaps ahead of pathology in the adoption of AI-assisted diagnosis is radiology. A group in the Netherlands [29] explored viewpoints of patients undergoing radiological studies regarding the implementation of AI in reporting radiology. In summary, patients expressed distrust towards AI reporting, wished for preservation of human interaction and were generally ambivalent towards potential workflow efficiency gains. The domains discussed were similar to those in this study; however, a considerable difference is observed regarding the results, with many radiology patients being more reserved regarding the adoption of AI. The reasons for these reservations were comparable those expressed by our cohort of respondents.

Respondents to our survey voiced concerns over data governance relating to digital images, which has recently been identified as a source of concern amongst the histopathology community [30]. Issues regarding data retention, storage, security and use for secondary purposes such as for education and research have been raised [30,31]; however, these issues relate to glass slides also. It is believed that, currently, no specific guidance is in place to govern the application of whole slide images to the research setting in the UK. Guidance on the validation of DP for diagnosis has been issued by the Royal College of Pathologists (RCPath), although issues of data governance currently fall outside the scope of the document. Although not yet formally adopted in the UK, such guidance has been produced by the Canadian Association of Pathologists [32].

Some respondents considered the retention of data within the UK a necessity and voiced concerns against foreign interference. With regard to storage of DP data for clinical purposes, these would be governed by existing principles of patient confidentiality as set out by UK legislation and General Medical Council policy. These would then be normally kept within the UK. Regarding cross-border transfer of information, a framework set out by the Organisation for Economic Co-operation and Development [33] would be the principle by which privacy is maintained.

The adoption of DP and AI into routine practice raises the question of where ultimate responsibility will lie in the event of a clinical error and this has been the subject of some debate [34]. Due to the relative infancy of the technology and its, thus far, limited real-life use, there is no current precedent for this. It may be that, with time and further scrutiny by regulatory bodies, this becomes clearer. Our results demonstrate that patients are more comfortable with the overall responsibility for a histopathology report remaining with the histopathologist and relying on their decision making to use AI and integrate its findings into the final report.

In summary, we have found that most respondents are supportive of advances in PCa diagnosis by means of DP and AI-assisted diagnostics as adjuncts to current workflows. A potential confounder of the responses we have observed is that these have originated from supporters of a prostate cancer charity and may, therefore, reflect a more engaged patient population. There is, however, a small population with reservations for whom trust must be maintained. Patient reassurance that these methods serve to enhance the diagnostic method, rather than replace it, may be the means by which to achieve this. While the results of this study can provide general insight into patient perception of the testing of AI in histopathology, our cohort is limited to men and PCa in the UK. Further work may, then, be of utility exploring the views of other populations. These may include a more global cohort, women or those with other cancers such as breast cancer.

**Supplementary Materials:** The following supporting information can be downloaded at: https://www.mdpi.com/article/10.3390/diagnostics12051225/s1. Please see Survey Questions.

**Author Contributions:** Conceptualization, C.V.; Data curation, K.R.; Formal analysis, K.R.; Funding acquisition, M.R.H. and C.V.; Investigation, R.C., L.B., A.P., A.D.L., R.J.B. and C.V.; Methodology, L.B., M.R.H., A.P., A.D.L., R.J.B., R.S., J.C., E.S. and C.V.; Project administration, M.D.; Supervision, C.V.; Writing—original draft, K.R. and R.C.; Writing—review & editing, K.R., R.C., L.B., M.D., M.R.H., A.P., A.D.L., R.J.B., R.S., J.C., E.S. and C.V. All authors have read and agreed to the published version of the manuscript.

**Funding:** This report is independent research funded by the NHSX Artificial Intelligence in Health and Care Award: Driving system-wide improvements with real-world economics evidence and subspecialist-led adoption guidelines for full workflow implementation of AI with Paige Prostate cancer detection (Paige AI 2020, New York), grading and quantification tool in histopathology departments. (AI_AWARD02269). The views expressed in this publication are those of the author(s) and not necessarily those of the NHS, NHSX or the Department of Health and Social Care. This paper is supported by the PathLAKE Centre of Excellence for digital pathology and artificial intelligence which is funded from the Data to Early Diagnosis and Precision Medicine strand of the government's Industrial Strategy Challenge Fund, managed and delivered by Innovate UK on behalf of UK Research and Innovation (UKRI). Grant ref: File Ref 104689/application number 18181. C.V., L.B. and RTC, through their institutions, are members of the PathLAKE consortium. C.V. and L.B. receive research support from the National Institute for Health Research (NIHR) Oxford Biomedical Research Centre (BRC) Molecular Diagnostics Theme.

**Institutional Review Board Statement:** Not applicable.

**Informed Consent Statement:** Not applicable.

**Data Availability Statement:** Raw data available on request.

**Acknowledgments:** The authors would like to acknowledge the whole PathLAKE team and the Departments of Cellular Pathology and Urology at Oxford University Hospitals NHS FT (OUHT). The authors would like to acknowledge and thank Prostate Cancer UK (PCUK) and the members who completed this survey. RS, JC and ES are Articulate Pro Study Patient and Public Involvement and Engagement Representatives under the auspices of the Nuffield Department of Surgical Sciences, for which CV is the principal investigator. The views expressed here are those of the authors alone and not necessarily those of PathLAKE, PCUK, UKRI, the NIHR/BRC, OUHT or the University of Oxford.

**Conflicts of Interest:** PathLAKE is one of the UK Government's five AI Centres of Excellence and has received in kind industry investment from Philips. OU and OUHFT are part of the consortium. CV and LB receive research support from the National Institute for Health Research (NIHR) Oxford Biomedical Research Centre (BRC) Molecular Diagnostics Theme. MH is employed by Paige AI (also see funding statement above). CV is the principal investigator of the NHSX study (see funding statement above).

## References

1. Fischer, G.; Anderson, L.; Ranson, M.; Sellen, D.; McArthur, E. Public perceptions on pathology: A fundamental change is required. *J. Clin. Pathol.* **2021**, *74*, 812–815. [CrossRef] [PubMed]
2. Titford, M. A short history of histopathology technique. *J. Histotechnol.* **2006**, *29*, 99–110. [CrossRef]
3. Browning, L.; Fryer, E.; Roskell, D.; White, K.; Colling, R.; Rittscher, J.; Verrill, C. Role of digital pathology in diagnostic histopathology in the response to COVID-19: Results from a survey of experience in a UK tertiary referral hospital. *J. Clin. Pathol.* **2021**, *74*, 129–132. [CrossRef] [PubMed]
4. Salto-Tellez, M.; Maxwell, P.; Hamilton, P. Artificial intelligence-the third revolution in pathology. *Histopathology* **2019**, *74*, 372–376. [CrossRef]
5. Williams, B.J.; Lee, J.; Oien, K.A.; Treanor, D. Digital pathology access and usage in the UK: Results from a national survey on behalf of the National Cancer Research Institute's CM-Path initiative. *J. Clin. Pathol.* **2018**, *71*, 463–466. [CrossRef]
6. Williams, B.J.; Bottoms, D.; Treanor, D. Future-proofing pathology: The case for clinical adoption of digital pathology. *J. Clin. Pathol.* **2017**, *70*, 1010–1018. [CrossRef]
7. Pell, R.; Oien, K.; Robinson, M.; Pitman, H.; Rajpoot, N.; Rittscher, J.; Snead, D.; Verrill, C.; Driskell, O.J.; Hall, A.; et al. The use of digital pathology and image analysis in clinical trials. *J. Pathol. Clin. Res.* **2019**, *5*, 81–90. [CrossRef]
8. Hamilton, P.W.; Wang, Y.; McCullough, S.J. Virtual microscopy and digital pathology in training and education. *APMIS* **2012**, *120*, 305–315. [CrossRef]

9. Browning, L.; Colling, R.; Rittscher, J.; Winter, L.; McEntyre, N.; Verrill, C. Implementation of digital pathology into diagnostic practice: Perceptions and opinions of histopathology trainees and implications for training. *J. Clin. Pathol.* **2020**, *73*, 223–227. [CrossRef]
10. Colling, R.; Protheroe, A.; Sullivan, M.; Macpherson, R.; Tuthill, M.; Redgwell, J.; Traill, Z.; Molyneux, A.; Johnson, E.; Abdullah, N.; et al. Digital Pathology Transformation in a Supraregional Germ Cell Tumour Network. *Diagnostics* **2021**, *11*, 2191. [CrossRef]
11. Bankhead, P.; Fernández, J.A.; McArt, D.G.; Boyle, D.P.; Li, G.; Loughrey, M.B.; Irwin, G.W.; Harkin, D.P.; James, J.A.; McQuaid, S.; et al. Integrated tumor identification and automated scoring minimizes pathologist involvement and provides new insights to key biomarkers in breast cancer. *Lab. Investig.* **2018**, *98*, 15–26. [CrossRef] [PubMed]
12. Saha, M.; Chakraborty, C.; Arun, I.; Ahmed, R.; Chatterjee, S. An Advanced Deep Learning Approach for Ki-67 Stained Hotspot Detection and Proliferation Rate Scoring for Prognostic Evaluation of Breast Cancer. *Sci. Rep.* **2017**, *7*, 3213. [CrossRef] [PubMed]
13. Coudray, N.; Ocampo, P.S.; Sakellaropoulos, T.; Narula, N.; Snuderl, M.; Fenyö, D.; Moreira, A.L.; Razavian, N.; Tsirigos, A. Classification and mutation prediction from non-small cell lung cancer histopathology images using deep learning. *Nat. Med.* **2018**, *24*, 1559–1567. [CrossRef] [PubMed]
14. Kather, J.N.; Pearson, A.T.; Halama, N.; Jäger, D.; Krause, J.; Loosen, S.H.; Marx, A.; Boor, P.; Tacke, F.; Neumann, U.P.; et al. Deep learning can predict microsatellite instability directly from histology in gastrointestinal cancer. *Nat. Med.* **2019**, *25*, 1054–1056. [CrossRef]
15. Raciti, P.; Sue, J.; Ceballos, R.; Godrich, R.; Kunz, J.D.; Kapur, S.; Reuter, V.; Grady, L.; Kanan, C.; Klimstra, D.S.; et al. Novel artificial intelligence system increases the detection of prostate cancer in whole slide images of core needle biopsies. *Mod. Pathol.* **2020**, *33*, 2058–2066. [CrossRef]
16. Chatrian, A.; Colling, R.T.; Browning, L.; Alham, N.K.; Sirinukunwattana, K.; Malacrino, S.; Haghighat, M.; Aberdeen, A.; Monks, A.; Moxley-Wyles, B.; et al. Artificial intelligence for advance requesting of immunohistochemistry in diagnostically uncertain prostate biopsies. *Mod. Pathol.* **2021**, *34*, 1780–1794. [CrossRef]
17. Food and Drug Administration. FDA Authorizes Software That Can Help Identify Prostate Cancer. Available online: https://www.fda.gov/news-events/press-announcements/fda-authorizes-software-can-help-identify-prostate-cancer (accessed on 25 April 2022).
18. National Prostate Cancer Audit. Annual Report 2021. Available online: https://www.npca.org.uk/content/uploads/2022/01/NPCA-Annual-Report-2021_Final_13.01.22-1.pdf (accessed on 14 November 2021).
19. Betsi Cadwaladr University Health Board. 'We Are Pioneers' Says Betsi Consultant Using Artificial Intelligence to Improve Prostate Cancer Diagnosis. Available online: https://bcuhb.nhs.wales/news/health-board-news/we-are-pioneers-says-betsi-consultant-using-artificial-intelligence-to-improve-prostate-cancer-diagnosis (accessed on 15 December 2021).
20. Neudert, L.M.; Knuutila, A.; Howard, P. Global Attitudes Towards AI, Machine Learning and Automated Decision Making—Implications for Involving Artificial Intelligence in Public Service and Good Governance. Available online: https://oxcaigg.oii.ox.ac.uk/publications/global-attitudes-towards-ai-machine-learning-automated-decision-making-2/ (accessed on 14 November 2021).
21. Gao, S.; He, L.; Chen, Y.; Li, D.; Lai, K. Public Perception of Artificial Intelligence in Medical Care: Content Analysis of Social Media. *J. Med. Internet Res.* **2020**, *22*, e16649. [CrossRef]
22. de Vries, C.F.; Morrissey, B.E.; Duggan, D.; Staff, R.T.; Lip, G. Screening participants' attitudes to the introduction of artificial intelligence in breast screening. *J. Med. Screen.* **2021**, *28*, 221–222. [CrossRef]
23. Royal College of Pathologists. Meeting Pathology Demand: Histopathology Workplace Census (2017/18). Available online: https://www.rcpath.org/uploads/assets/952a934d-2ec3-48c9-a8e6e00fcdca700f/Meeting-Pathology-Demand-Histopathology-Workforce-Census-2018.pdf (accessed on 15 December 2021).
24. Nickel, B.; Moynihan, R.; Barratt, A.; Brito, J.P.; McCaffery, K. Renaming low risk conditions labelled as cancer. *BMJ* **2018**, *362*, k3322. [CrossRef]
25. Badani, K.K.; Kaul, S.; Menon, M. Evolution of robotic radical prostatectomy: Assessment after 2766 procedures. *Cancer* **2007**, *110*, 1951–1958. [CrossRef]
26. Berryhill, R., Jr.; Jhaveri, J.; Yadav, R.; Leung, R.; Rao, S.; El-Hakim, A.; Tewari, A. Robotic prostatectomy: A review of outcomes compared with laparoscopic and open approaches. *Urology* **2008**, *72*, 15–23. [CrossRef] [PubMed]
27. Reynolds, B.R.; Bulsara, C.; Zeps, N.; Codde, J.; Lawrentschuk, N.; Bolton, D.; Vivian, J. Exploring pathways towards improving patient experience of robot-assisted radical prostatectomy (RARP): Assessing patient satisfaction and attitudes. *BJU Int.* **2018**, *121* (Suppl. S3), 33–39. [CrossRef] [PubMed]
28. McDermott, H.; Choudhury, N.; Lewin-Runacres, M.; Aemn, I.; Moss, E. Gender differences in understanding and acceptance of robot-assisted surgery. *J. Robot. Surg.* **2020**, *14*, 227–232. [CrossRef]
29. Ongena, Y.P.; Haan, M.; Yakar, D.; Kwee, T.C. Patients' views on the implementation of artificial intelligence in radiology: Development and validation of a standardized questionnaire. *Eur. Radiol.* **2020**, *30*, 1033–1040. [CrossRef] [PubMed]
30. Coulter, C.; McKay, F.; Hallowell, N.; Browning, L.; Colling, R.; Macklin, P.; Sorell, T.; Aslam, M.; Bryson, G.; Treanor, D.; et al. Understanding the ethical and legal considerations of Digital Pathology. *J. Pathol. Clin. Res.* **2022**, *8*, 101–115. [CrossRef] [PubMed]
31. Sorell, T.; Rajpoot, N.; Verrill, C. Ethical issues in computational pathology. *J. Med. Ethics* **2022**, *48*, 278–284. [CrossRef]
32. Canadian Association of Pathologists. Code of Ethics for Storage and Transmission of Electronic Laboratory Data. Available online: https://cap-acp.org/code_ethics_storage_electronic_lab_data.php (accessed on 22 October 2021).

33. Organisation for Economic Cooperation and Development (OECD). Guidelines Governing the Protection of Privacy and Transborder Flows of Personal Data. Available online: https://www.oecd.org/sti/ieconomy/oecd_privacy_framework.pdf (accessed on 22 October 2021).
34. Colling, R.; Pitman, H.; Oien, K.; Rajpoot, N.; Macklin, P.; CM-Path AI in Histopathology Working Group; Snead, D.; Sackville, T.; Verrill, C. Artificial intelligence in digital pathology: A roadmap to routine use in clinical practice. *J. Pathol.* **2019**, *249*, 143–150. [CrossRef]

Article

# A Deep Learning Model for Prostate Adenocarcinoma Classification in Needle Biopsy Whole-Slide Images Using Transfer Learning

Masayuki Tsuneki [1,*], Makoto Abe [2] and Fahdi Kanavati [1]

1. Medmain Research, Medmain Inc., Fukuoka 810-0042, Fukuoka, Japan; fkanavati@medmain.com
2. Department of Pathology, Tochigi Cancer Center, 4-9-13 Yohnan, Utsunomiya 320-0834, Tochigi, Japan; makotabe@tochigi-cc.jp
* Correspondence: tsuneki@medmain.com; Tel.: +81-92-707-1977

**Abstract:** The histopathological diagnosis of prostate adenocarcinoma in needle biopsy specimens is of pivotal importance for determining optimum prostate cancer treatment. Since diagnosing a large number of cases containing 12 core biopsy specimens by pathologists using a microscope is time-consuming manual system and limited in terms of human resources, it is necessary to develop new techniques that can rapidly and accurately screen large numbers of histopathological prostate needle biopsy specimens. Computational pathology applications that can assist pathologists in detecting and classifying prostate adenocarcinoma from whole-slide images (WSIs) would be of great benefit for routine pathological practice. In this paper, we trained deep learning models capable of classifying needle biopsy WSIs into adenocarcinoma and benign (non-neoplastic) lesions. We evaluated the models on needle biopsy, transurethral resection of the prostate (TUR-P), and The Cancer Genome Atlas (TCGA) public dataset test sets, achieving an ROC-AUC up to 0.978 in needle biopsy test sets and up to 0.9873 in TCGA test sets for adenocarcinoma.

**Keywords:** deep learning; adenocarcinoma; prostate; biopsy; whole-slide image; transfer learning

## 1. Introduction

According to the Global Cancer Statistics 2020, prostate cancer was the second-most-frequent cancer and the fifth leading cause of cancer death among men in 2020 with an estimated 1,414,259 new cases and 375,304 deaths worldwide, which is the most frequently diagnosed cancer in men in over one-half (112 of 185) of the countries [1].

Serum prostate-specific antigen (PSA) is the most important and clinically useful biochemical marker in prostate [2]. PSA has contributed to an increase in the early detection rate of prostate cancer and is now advocated for routine use for screening in men [2]. Serum PSA is also an important tool in the management of prostate cancer. Elevation of PSA correlates with cancer recurrence and progression after treatment. Thus, PSA is a sensitive marker for tumor recurrence after treatment and is useful for the early detection of metastases. However, n elevated serum PSA concentration is seen not only in patients with adenocarcinoma, but also in patients with aging, prostatitis, benign prostatic hyperplasia, and transiently following biopsy [3–5]. Although PSA elevations might indicate the presence of prostate disease (e.g., prostate cancer, benign prostatic hyperplasia, and prostatitis), not all men with prostate disease have elevated PSA levels, and PSA elevations are not specific for prostate cancer. Therefore, it is necessary to perform definitive diagnosis of the presence of prostate adenocarcinoma by needle biopsy for cancer treatment.

As for needle biopsy, in the past, the standard approach was to take six cores (sextant biopsies) [6]. However, based on a systematic review [7], it has been shown that cancer yield was significantly associated with increasing number of cores, more so in the case of laterally directed cores than centrally directed cores. This is based on the finding that schemes

with 12 laterally directed cores detected 31% more cancers than the six cores. Schemes with further cores (18 to 24) showed no further gains in cancer detection. Hence, a 12-core systematic biopsy that incorporates apical and far-lateral cores in the template distribution allows maximal cancer detection, avoids repeat biopsy, and provides information adequate for identifying men who need cancer treatment [8]. However, diagnosing a large number of cases containing 12 core biopsy specimens is a time-consuming manual system for pathologists in routine practice.

Adenocarcinoma is by far the most common malignant tumor of the prostate gland. Adenocarcinoma tends to be multifocal with a predilection for the peripheral zone. Histopathologically, the majority of prostate adenocarcinomas are not difficult to diagnose. However, the separation of well-differentiated adenocarcinoma from the vast number of benign prostatic hyperplasia or atypical gland proliferation, the detection of small adenocarcinoma foci, and the differentiation of poorly differentiated adenocarcinoma from inflammatory cell infiltration are sometimes very challenging in routine diagnoses.

Therefore, all these factors mentioned above highlight the benefit of establishing a histopathological screening system based on needle biopsy specimens for prostate adenocarcinoma patients. Conventional morphological diagnosis by human pathologists has limitations, and it is necessary to construct a new diagnostic strategy based on the analysis of a large number of cases in the future.

Deep learning has been widely applied in computational histopathology, with applications such as cancer classification in whole-slide images (WSIs), cell detection and segmentation, and the stratification of patient outcomes [9–22]. For prostate histopathology in particular, deep learning has been applied for the classification of cancer in WSIs [21,23–30].

In this study, we trained a WSI prostate adenocarcinoma classification model using transfer learning and weakly supervised learning. We evaluated the models on needle biopsy, transurethral resection of the prostate (TUR-P), and TCGA public dataset test sets to confirm application of the algorithm in different types of specimens, achieving an ROC-AUC up to 0.978 in needle biopsy test sets and up to 0.9873 in The Cancer Genome Atlas (TCGA) test sets for adenocarcinoma. We also evaluated on the needle biopsy test sets, without fine-tuning, models that had been previously trained on other organs for the classification of adenocarcinomas [22,31–37]. These findings suggest that computational algorithms might be useful as routine histopathological diagnostic aids for prostate adenocarcinoma classification.

## 2. Materials and Methods

### 2.1. Clinical Cases and Pathological Records

This was a retrospective study. A total of 2926 hematoxylin and eosin (H&E)-stained histopathological specimens of human prostate adenocarcinoma and benign lesions—1682 needle biopsy and 1244 TUR-P—were collected from the surgical pathology files of five hospitals: Shinyukuhashi, Wajiro, Shinkuki, Shinkomonji, and Shinmizumaki hospitals (Kamachi Group Hospitals, Fukuoka, Japan), after histopathological review of those specimens by surgical pathologists. The cases were selected randomly so as to reflect a real clinical scenario as much as possible. The pathologists excluded cases that had poor scan quality. Each WSI diagnosis was observed by at least two pathologists, with the final checking and verification performed by a senior pathologist. All WSIs were scanned at a magnification of 20× using the same Leica Aperio AT2 scanner and were saved in the SVS file format with JPEG2000 compression.

### 2.2. Dataset

Tables 1 and 2 break down the distribution of the dataset into training, validation, and test sets. The training and validation sets consisted of needle biopsy WSIs (Table 1). The test sets consisted of needle biopsy, TUR-P, and TCGA public dataset WSIs (Table 2). The regions of the prostate sampled by TUR-P and needle biopsy tend to be different. TUR-P specimens usually consist of tissues from the transition zone, urethra, periurethral area, bladder neck, anterior fibromuscular stroma, and occasionally, small portions of seminal vesicles. In contrast, most needle biopsy specimens consist mainly of tissue from the peripheral zone. The split was carried out randomly taking into account the proportion of each label in the dataset. Hospitals that provided histopathological cases were anonymized (e.g., Hospital A, Hospital B). The patients' pathological records were used to extract the WSIs' pathological diagnoses and to assign WSI labels. Training set WSIs were not annotated, and the training algorithm only used the WSI diagnosis labels, meaning that the only information available for the training was whether the WSI contained adenocarcinoma or was benign (non-neoplastic), but no information about the location of the cancerous tissue lesions.

Table 1. Distribution of the WSIs in the training and validation sets.

|  |  | Adenocarcinoma | Benign | Total |
|---|---|---|---|---|
| Training set | Hospital A | 144 | 260 | 404 |
|  | Hospital B | 100 | 75 | 175 |
|  | Hospital C | 115 | 159 | 274 |
|  | Hospital D | 56 | 118 | 174 |
|  | Hospital E | 23 | 72 | 95 |
|  | Total | 438 | 684 | 1122 |
| Validation set | Hospital A | 6 | 6 | 12 |
|  | Hospital B | 6 | 6 | 12 |
|  | Hospital C | 6 | 6 | 12 |
|  | Hospital D | 6 | 6 | 12 |
|  | Hospital E | 6 | 6 | 12 |
|  | Total | 30 | 30 | 60 |

Table 2. Distribution of the WSIs in the test sets.

|  |  | Adenocarcinoma | Benign | Total |
|---|---|---|---|---|
| Biopsy | Hospitals A–C | 250 | 250 | 500 |
|  | Hospital A | 100 | 100 | 200 |
|  | Hospital B | 100 | 100 | 200 |
|  | Hospital C | 50 | 50 | 100 |
| TUR-P | Hospitals A–B | 162 | 1082 | 1244 |
|  | Hospital A | 109 | 352 | 461 |
|  | Hospital B | 53 | 730 | 783 |
| Public dataset | TCGA | 733 | 34 | 768 |

### 2.3. Deep Learning Models

We trained the models using the partial fine-tuning approach [38]. It consisted of using the weights of an existing pre-trained model and only fine-tuning the affine parameters of the batch normalization layers and the final classification layer. We used the EfficientNetB1 [39] model starting with pre-trained weights on ImageNet. Figure 1 shows an overview of the training method.

The training method that we used in this study was exactly the same as reported in a previous study [34]. For completeness, we repeat the method here. To apply the CNN on the WSIs, we performed slide tiling by extracting square tiles from tissue regions. On a given WSI, we detected the tissue regions and eliminated most of the white background by performing a thresholding on a grayscale version of the WSI using Otsu's method [40]. During prediction, we performed the tiling in a sliding window fashion, using a fixed-size stride, to obtain predictions for all the tissue regions. During training, we initially performed random balanced sampling of tiles from the tissue regions, where we tried to maintain an equal balance of each label in the training batch. To do so, we placed the WSIs in a shuffled queue such that we looped over the labels in succession (i.e., we alternated between picking a WSI with a positive label and a negative label). Once a WSI was selected, we randomly sampled $\frac{\text{batch size}}{\text{num labels}}$ tiles from each WSI to form a balanced batch. To maintain the balance on the WSI, we oversampled from the WSIs to ensure the model trained on tiles from all of the WSIs in each epoch. We then switched to the hard mining of tiles once there was no longer any improvement on the validation set after two epochs. To perform the hard mining, we alternated between training and inference. During inference, the CNN was applied in a sliding window fashion on all of the tissue regions in the WSI, and we then selected the $k$ tiles with the highest probability for being positive if the WSI was negative and the $k$ tiles with the lowest probability for being positive if the WSI was positive. This step effectively selected the hard examples with which the model was struggling. The selected tiles were placed in a training subset, and once that subset contained $N$ tiles, the training was run. We used $k = 8$, $N = 256$, and a batch size of 32.

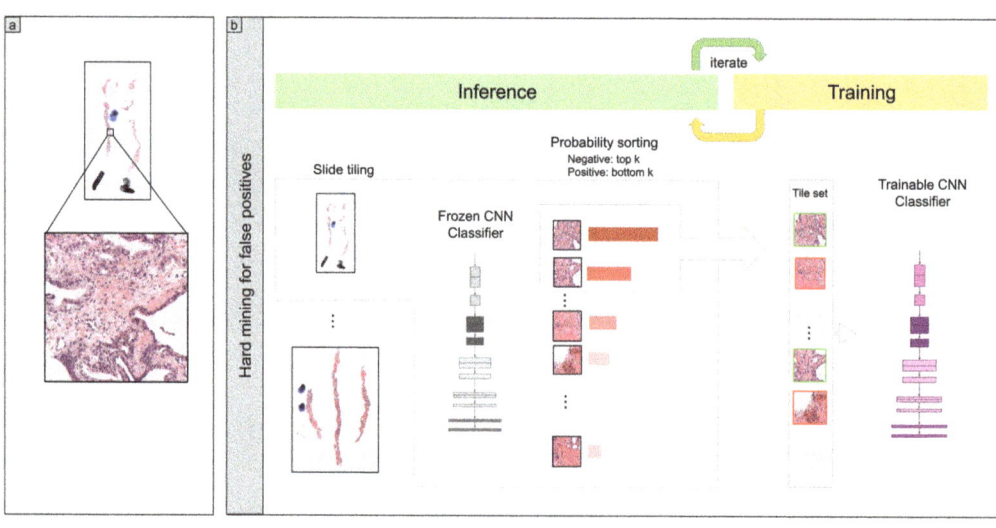

**Figure 1.** (**a**) shows a zoomed-in example of a tile in a WSI. (**b**) During training, we iteratively alternated between inference and training steps. The model weights were frozen during the inference step, and this was applied in a sliding window fashion on the entire tissue regions of each WSI. The top k tiles with the highest probabilities were then selected from each WSI and placed into a queue. During training, the selected tiles from multiple WSIs formed a training batch and were used to train the model.

To obtain a prediction on a WSI, the model was applied in a sliding window fashion, generating a prediction per tile. The WSI prediction was then obtained by taking the maximum from all of the tiles.

We trained the models with the Adam optimization algorithm [41] with the following parameters: $beta_1 = 0.9$, $beta_2 = 0.999$, and a batch size of 32. We used a learning rate of 0.001 when fine-tuning. We applied a learning rate decay of 0.95 every 2 epochs. We used the binary cross-entropy loss function. We used early stopping by tracking the performance of the model on a validation set, and training was stopped automatically when there was no further improvement on the validation loss for 10 epochs. The model with the lowest validation loss was chosen as the final model.

*2.4. Software and Statistical Analysis*

The deep learning models were implemented and trained using TensorFlow [42]. AUCs were calculated in Python using the scikit-learn package [43] and plotted using matplotlib [44]. The 95% CIs of the AUCs were estimated using the bootstrap method [45] with 1000 iterations.

The true positive rate ($TPR$) was computed as:

$$TPR = \frac{TP}{TP + FN} \quad (1)$$

and the false positive rate ($FPR$) was computed as:

$$FPR = \frac{FP}{FP + TN} \quad (2)$$

where $TP$, $FP$, and $TN$ represent true positive, false positive, and true negative, respectively. The ROC curve was computed by varying the probability threshold from 0.0 to 1.0 and computing both the $TPR$ and $FPR$ at the given threshold.

*2.5. Code Availability*

To train the classification model in this study, we used the publicly available Tensor-Flow training script available at https://github.com/tensorflow/models/tree/master/official/vision/image_classification, accessed on 23 March 2021.

## 3. Results

*3.1. High AUC Performance of the WSI Evaluation of Prostate Adenocarcinoma Histopathology Images in the Needle Biopsy, TUR-P, and TCGA Test Sets*

The aim of this retrospective study was to train deep learning models for the classification of prostate adenocarcinoma in WSIs of prostate needle biopsy specimens. We had a total of 1122 needle biopsy WSIs (438 adenocarcinoma and 684 benign WSIs) for the training set and a total of 60 WSIs (30 adenocarcinoma and 30 benign WSIs) for the validation set from five sources (Hospitals A, B, C, D, and E) (Table 1). We used a transfer learning (TL) approach based on partial fine-tuning [38] to train the models. We refer to the trained models as TL <magnification> <tile size> <model size>, based on the different configurations. As we had at our disposal ten models that had been trained specifically on specimens from different organs (breast, colon, stomach, pancreas, and lung) [22,31–37], we evaluated these models without fine-tuning on the biopsy test sets (Hospitals A–C) (Table 2) to investigate whether morphological cancer similarities transferred across organs without additional training. Table 3 breaks down the values of ROC-AUC and log loss in the biopsy test set (Hospitals A–C) and shows that the colon poorly differentiated adenocarcinoma model (colon poorly ADC-2 (20×, 512)) [36] exhibited the highest ROC-AUC (0.8172, CI: 0.7815–0.855) and the lowest log loss (0.5216, CI: 0.4748–0.5695), indicating its capability as a base model for the transfer learning approach.

Overall, we trained three different models: (1) a transfer learning model (TL-colon poorly ADC-2 (20×, 512)) using the existing colon poorly differentiated adenocarcinoma model (colon poorly ADC-2 (20×, 512)) [36] at a magnification 20× and a tile size of 512 px × 512 px; (2) a model (EfficientNetB1 (20×, 512)) using the EfficientNetB1 at magnification 20× and a tile size of 512 px × 512 px, starting with pre-trained weights from ImageNet; (3) a model (EfficientNetB1 (10×, 224)) using the EfficientNetB1 at magnification 10× and a tile size of 224 px × 224 px, starting with pre-trained weights from ImageNet.

We evaluated the trained models on the needle biopsy, TUR-P, and TCGA test sets (Table 2). We confirmed that the surgical pathologists were able to diagnose these cases from visual inspection of the H&E-stained slides alone prior to the test sets' evaluation. The distribution of the number of WSIs in each test set is summarized in Table 2. For each test set, we computed the ROC-AUC, log loss, accuracy, sensitivity, and specificity, and we summarize the results in Tables 4 and 5 and Figure 2. In Table 4, we compare the results of the ROC-AUC and log loss among three models (TL-colon poorly ADC-2 (20×, 512), EfficientNetB1 (20×, 512), and EfficientNetB1 (10×, 224)) we trained.

**Table 3.** ROC-AUC and log loss results for the various existing models on the prostate biopsy test sets.

| Existing Models | ROC-AUC | Log Loss |
|---|---|---|
| Breast IDC (10×, 512) | 0.704 [0.659–0.751] | 0.947 [0.816–1.064] |
| Breast IDC, DCIS (10×, 224) | 0.692 [0.644–0.735] | 1.413 [1.282–1.566] |
| Colon ADC, AD (10×, 512) | 0.553 [0.507–0.611] | 1.525 [1.350–1.711] |
| Colon poorly ADC-1 (20×, 512) | 0.795 [0.756–0.835] | 0.572 [0.513–0.637] |
| Colon poorly ADC-2 (20×, 512) | 0.817 [0.782–0.855] | 0.522 [0.475–0.569] |
| Stomach ADC, AD (10×, 512) | 0.706 [0.662–0.753] | 1.391 [1.248–1.569] |
| Stomach poorly ADC (20×, 224) | 0.724 [0.681–0.767] | 0.598 [0.565–0.629] |
| Stomach SRCC (10×, 224) | 0.804 [0.763–0.839] | 0.998 [0.894–1.114] |
| Pancreas EUS-FNA ADC (10×, 224) | 0.774 [0.735–0.817] | 0.587 [0.544–0.629] |
| Lung carcinoma (10×, 512) | 0.702 [0.659–0.751] | 1.398 [1.2560–1.546] |

**Table 4.** ROC-AUC and log loss results of the three different models for prostate adenocarcinoma on the biopsy, TUR-P, and TCGA test sets.

| | | TL-Colon Poorly ADC-2 (20×, 512) | |
|---|---|---|---|
| | | ROC-AUC | Log-Loss |
| Biopsy | Hospitals A–C | 0.967 [0.955–0.982] | 0.288 [0.210–0.354] |
| | Hospital A | 0.978 [0.966–0.995] | 0.209 [0.117–0.276] |
| | Hospital B | 0.972 [0.948–0.988] | 0.378 [0.276–0.536] |
| | Hospital C | 0.967 [0.922–0.993] | 0.265 [0.117–0.512] |
| TUR-P | Hospitals A–B | 0.845 [0.806–0.883] | 4.152 [4.047–4.253] |
| | Hospital A | 0.909 [0.865–0.947] | 3.269 [3.089–3.451] |
| | Hospital B | 0.737 [0.657–0.810] | 4.672 [4.559–4.798] |
| Public dataset | TCGA | 0.987 [0.977–0.995] | 0.074 [0.055–0.095] |
| | | EfficientNetB1 (20×, 512) | |
| | | ROC-AUC | Log-Loss |
| Biopsy | Hospitals A–C | 0.971 [0.955–0.982] | 0.256 [0.188–0.349] |
| | Hospital A | 0.979 [0.962–0.993] | 0.209 [0.110–0.322] |
| | Hospital B | 0.978 [0.963–0.992] | 0.279 [0.167–0.398] |
| | Hospital C | 0.977 [0.959–1.000] | 0.306 [0.037–0.406] |
| TUR-P | Hospitals A–B | 0.803 [0.765–0.848] | 5.113 [4.976–5.252] |
| | Hospital A | 0.875 [0.834–0.923] | 4.308 [4.059–4.550] |
| | Hospital B | 0.670 [0.597–0.753] | 5.588 [5.411–5.729] |
| Public dataset | TCGA | 0.945 [0.912–0.973] | 0.101 [0.067–0.147] |
| | | EfficientNetB1 (10×, 224) | |
| | | ROC-AUC | Log-Loss |
| Biopsy | Hospitals A–C | 0.739 [0.691–0.783] | 0.631 [0.545–0.724] |
| | Hospital A | 0.751 [0.668–0.810] | 0.605 [0.511–0.744] |
| | Hospital B | 0.929 [0.885–0.970] | 0.335 [0.223–0.427] |
| | Hospital C | 0.472 [0.348–0.572] | 1.278 [0.979–1.501] |
| TUR-P | Hospitals A–B | 0.804 [0.760–0.847] | 0.392 [0.369–0.417] |
| | Hospital A | 0.771 [0.705–0.820] | 0.424 [0.384–0.474] |
| | Hospital B | 0.928 [0.859–0.980] | 0.373 [0.347–0.408] |
| Public dataset | TCGA | 0.578 [0.497–0.661] | 1.575 [1.481–1.657] |

Table 5. Accuracy, sensitivity, specificity, and F1-score results of the transfer learning model (TL-colon poorly ADC-2 (20×, 512)) from the existing colon poorly differentiated adenocarcinoma model for prostate adenocarcinoma on the biopsy, TUR-P, and TCGA test sets.

|  |  | Accuracy | Sensitivity | Specificity | F1-Score |
|---|---|---|---|---|---|
| Biopsy | Hospitals A–C | 0.918 [0.894–0.942] | 0.912 [0.878–0.946] | 0.924 [0.888–0.955] | 0.918 [0.889–0.941] |
|  | Hospital A | 0.945 [0.920–0.980] | 0.930 [0.897–0.989] | 0.960 [0.915–0.991] | 0.944 [0.920–0.981] |
|  | Hospital B | 0.925 [0.885–0.955] | 0.890 [0.824–0.944] | 0.960 [0.912–0.991] | 0.922 [0.878–0.955] |
|  | Hospital C | 0.940 [0.880–0.980] | 0.900 [0.796–0.964] | 0.980 [0.921–1.000] | 0.938 [0.870–0.978] |
| TUR-P | Hospitals A–B | 0.894 [0.866–0.922] | 0.700 [0.603–0.813] | 0.926 [0.896–0.950] | 0.618 [0.561–0.675] |
|  | Hospital A | 0.918 [0.889–0.939] | 0.798 [0.712–0.867] | 0.955 [0.930–0.975] | 0.821 [0.749–0.871] |
|  | Hospital B | 0.890 [0.867–0.909] | 0.415 [0.265–0.529] | 0.925 [0.906–0.940] | 0.339 [0.212–0.424] |
| Public dataset | TCGA | 0.949 [0.934–0.965] | 0.948 [0.932–0.965] | 0.971 [0.906–1.000] | 0.973 [0.964–0.981] |

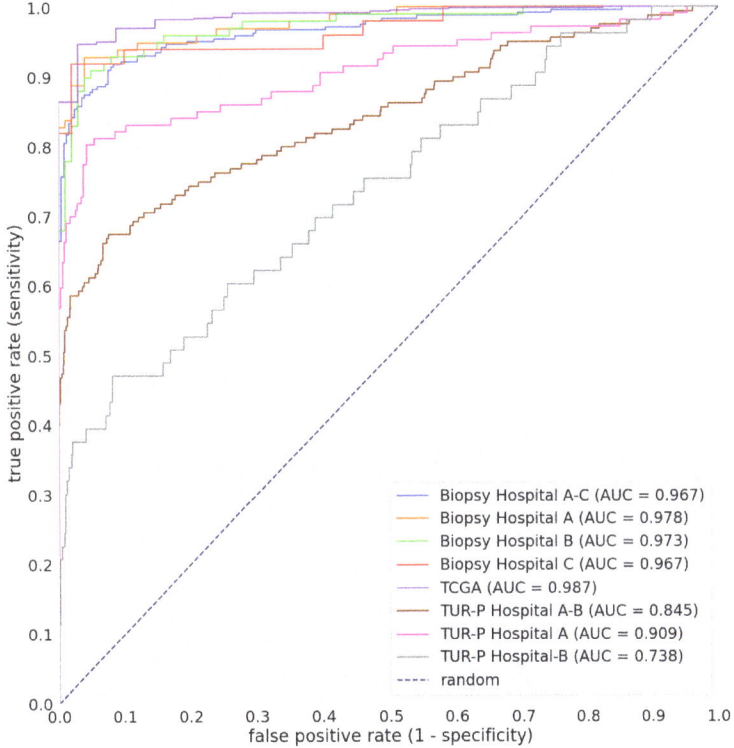

Figure 2. ROC curves on the biopsy (Hospitals A, B, C, and A–C), TUR-P (Hospitals A, B, and A and B), and TCGA test sets of the TL-colon poorly ADC-2 (20×, 512) model.

The model (TL-colon poorly ADC-2 (20×, 512)) achieved the highest ROC-AUCs of 0.9873 (CI: 0.9881-0.995) and the lowest log loss of 0.0742 (CI: 0.0551–0.0959) for prostate adenocarcinoma on the TCGA test set (Table 4). On the needle biopsy test set, the model (TL-colon poorly ADC-2 (20×, 512)) also achieved very high ROC-AUCs (0.967–0.978) with low values of the log loss (0.2094–0.3788) (Table 4). In contrast, ROC-AUCs on the TUR-P test set were lower than the biopsy test set, and the log loss on the TUR-P test set was higher than the biopsy test set (Table 4). In addition, accuracy, sensitivity, and specificity results on the model (TL-colon poorly ADC-2 (20×, 512)) on the biopsy, TUR-P, and TCGA test sets are given in Table 5. The model (TL-colon poorly ADC-2 (20×, 512)) achieved very high accuracy (0.918–0.949), sensitivity (0.89–0.948), and specificity (0.924–0.98) on the biopsy and TCGA test sets (Table 5). On the TUR-P test sets, the model (TL-colon poorly ADC-2 (20×, 512)) achieved high accuracy (0.8902–0.9176) and specificity (0.9247–0.9545), but low sensitivity (0.4151–0.7982) (Table 5). As shown in Figure 2, the model (TL-colon poorly ADC-2 (20×, 512)) is fully applicable for prostate adenocarcinoma classification on the needle biopsy WSIs, as well as the TCGA public WSI dataset, but not on the TUR-P WSIs.

Figures 3–7 show representative cases of true positives (biopsy and TUR-P), false positives (biopsy and TUR-P), and false negatives (biopsy), respectively, using the model (TL-colon poorly ADC-2 (20×, 512)).

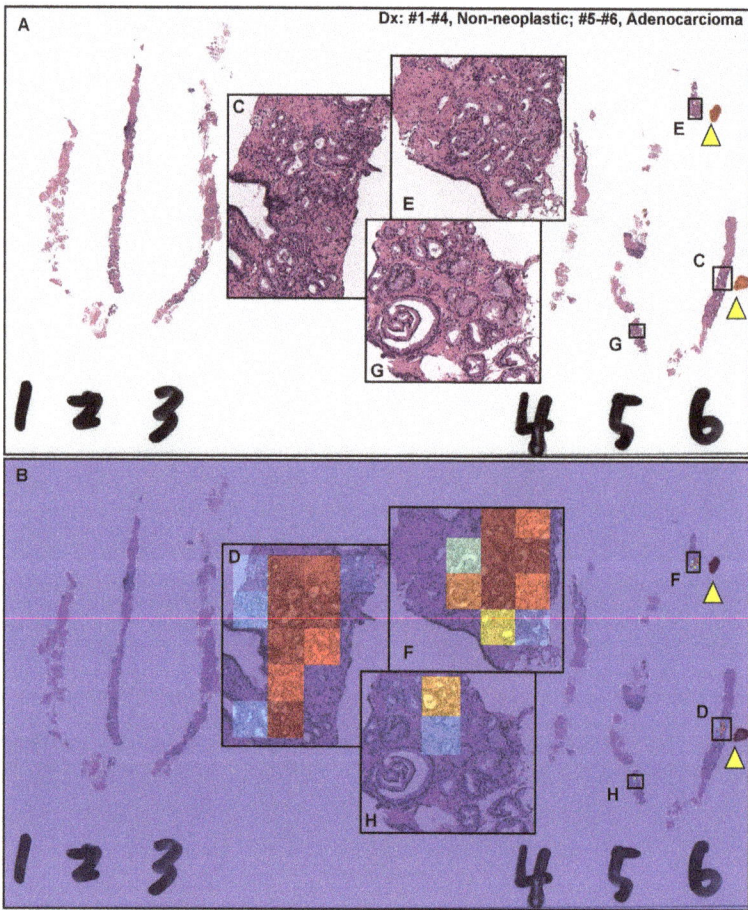

**Figure 3.** Representative true positive prostate adenocarcinoma from the biopsy test sets. On the prostate needle biopsy whole-slide image (**A**), Specimens #1–#4 are benign (non-neoplastic), and there are adenocarcinoma cell infiltration foci (**C,E,G**) in Specimens #5 and #6 based on the pathological diagnostic report, which the pathologists marked as red ink dots (yellow triangles) on the glass slides. The heat map image (**B**) shows the true positive prediction of adenocarcinoma cells (**D,F,H**) using transfer learning from the colon poorly differentiated adenocarcinoma model (TL-colon poorly ADC-2 (20×, 512)), which corresponds respectively to the H&E histopathology (**C,E,G**). The heat map uses the jet color map where blue indicates low probability and red indicates high probability.

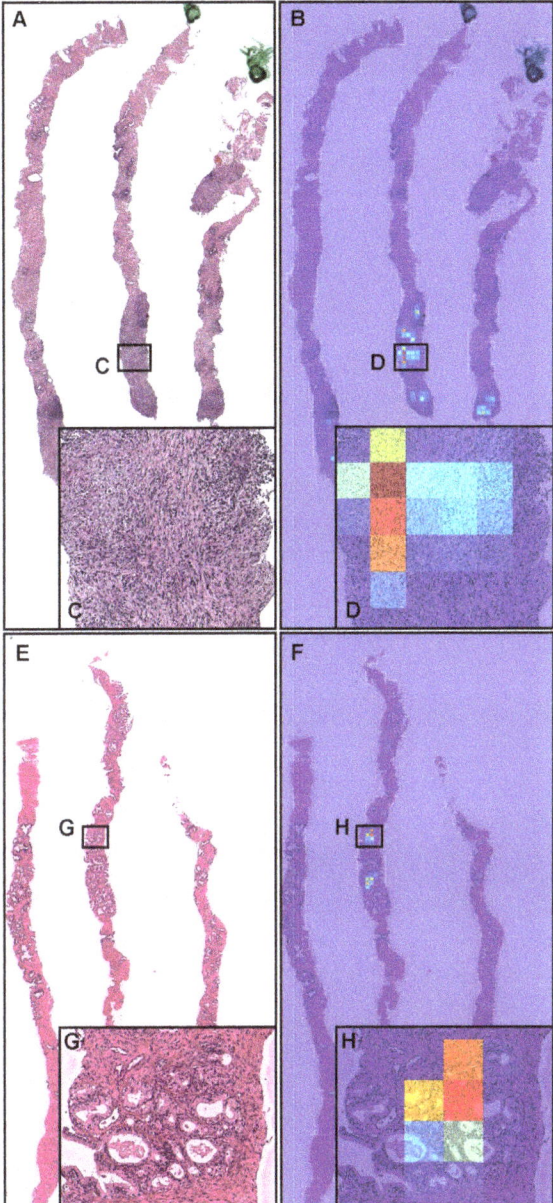

**Figure 4.** Representative examples of prostate adenocarcinoma false positive prediction outputs on cases from the needle biopsy test sets. Histopathologically, (**A**,**E**) are benign (non-neoplastic) lesions. The heat map images (**B**,**F**) exhibit false positive predictions of adenocarcinoma (**D**,**H**) using transfer learning from the colon poorly differentiated adenocarcinoma model (TL-colon poorly ADC-2 (20×, 512)). Infiltration of chronic inflammatory cells including histiocytes, lymphocytes, and plasma cells (**C**) would be the primary cause of the false positives due to a morphology analogous to adenocarcinoma cells' infiltration (**D**). Areas where prostatic hyperplasia (**G**) would be the primary cause of false positives (**H**). The heat map uses the jet color map where blue indicates low probability and red indicates high probability.

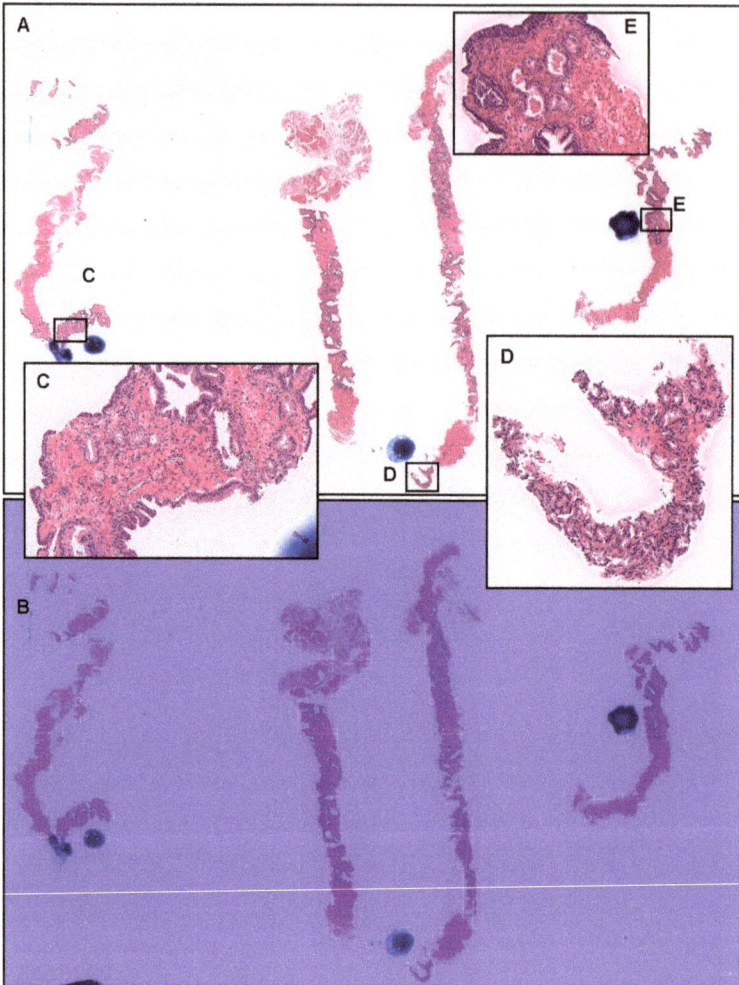

**Figure 5.** Representative false negative prostate adenocarcinoma from the needle biopsy test sets. According to the histopathological report, there were four needle biopsy specimens in the WSI, and three of them had adenocarcinomas (**A**). The pathologists marked the adenocarcinoma areas in blue dots (**A**). High-power view showing that there were adenocarcinoma foci (**C–E**). The heat map image (**B**) shows no true positive predictions of adenocarcinoma using transfer learning from the colon poorly differentiated adenocarcinoma model (TL-colon poorly ADC-2 (20×, 512)).

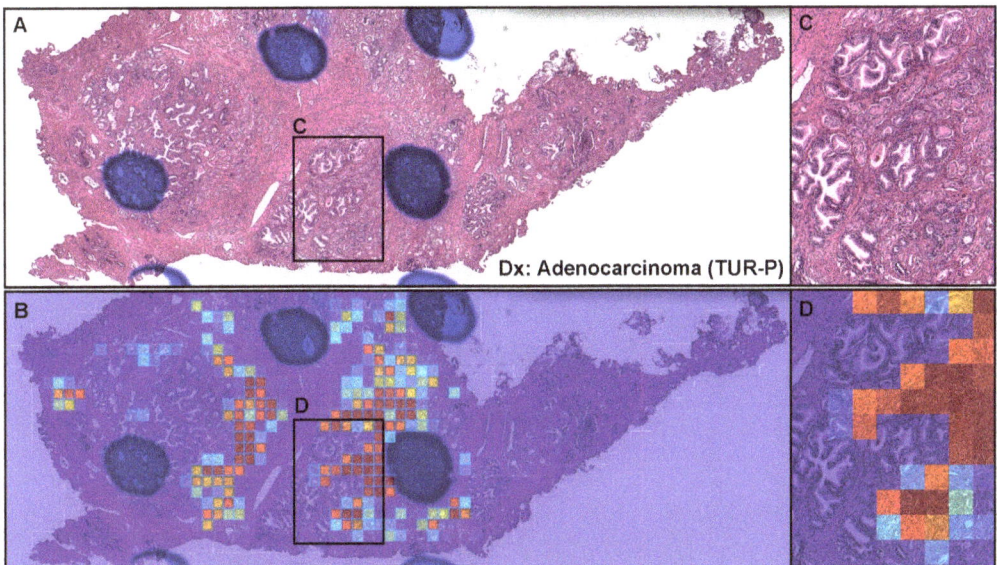

**Figure 6.** Representative true positive prostate adenocarcinoma from the transurethral resection of the prostate (TUR-P) test sets. In the TUR-P specimen (**A**), there are adenocarcinoma cell infiltration foci (**C**) based on the histopathological report. The heat map image (**B**) shows the true positive prediction of adenocarcinoma cells (**D**) using transfer learning from the colon poorly differentiated adenocarcinoma model (TL-colon poorly ADC-2 (20×, 512)). The heat map uses the jet color map where blue indicates low probability and red indicates high probability.

### 3.2. True Positive Prediction on Needle Biopsy Specimens

Our model (TL-colon poorly ADC-2 (20×, 512)) satisfactorily predicted prostate adenocarcinoma on needle biopsy specimens (Figure 3A). According to the pathological diagnostic report, there were adenocarcinoma foci in two of six needle biopsy cores (#5 and #6), which the pathologists marked as red ink dots (yellow triangles) on the glass slides. The heat map image shows true positive predictions (Figure 3B,D,F,H) of adenocarcinoma cell infiltrating areas (Figure 3C,E,G). In Figure 3G, the pathologists did not mark when they performed the diagnosis; however, the heat map image show true positive predictions of adenocarcinoma foci, which were reviewed and verified as adenocarcinoma by other pathologists (Figure 3H). In contrast, the heat map image does not show true positive predictions on glomeruloid glands precisely, which were assigned a Gleason Pattern 4 [46,47] (Figure 3G,H). Importantly, the heat map images also exhibit a perfect true negative prediction of needle biopsy cores (#1–#4) on the same WSI (Figure 3B).

### 3.3. False Positive Prediction on Needle Biopsy Specimens

Inflammatory tissues (Figure 4A) and prostatic hyperplasia (Figure 4E) were false positively predicted for prostate adenocarcinoma (Figure 4B,F) using the transfer learning model (TL-colon poorly ADC-2 (20×, 512)). In the inflammatory tissue (Figure 4A), the infiltration of chronic inflammatory cells including histiocytes, lymphocytes, and plasma cells (Figure 4C) was the primary cause of the false positive prediction (Figure 4D) due to a morphology analogous to adenocarcinoma cells. Prostatic hyperplasia (Figure 4E) with irregularly shaped and diverse sizes of tubular structures (Figure 4G) was the primary cause of the false positive prediction (Figure 4H).

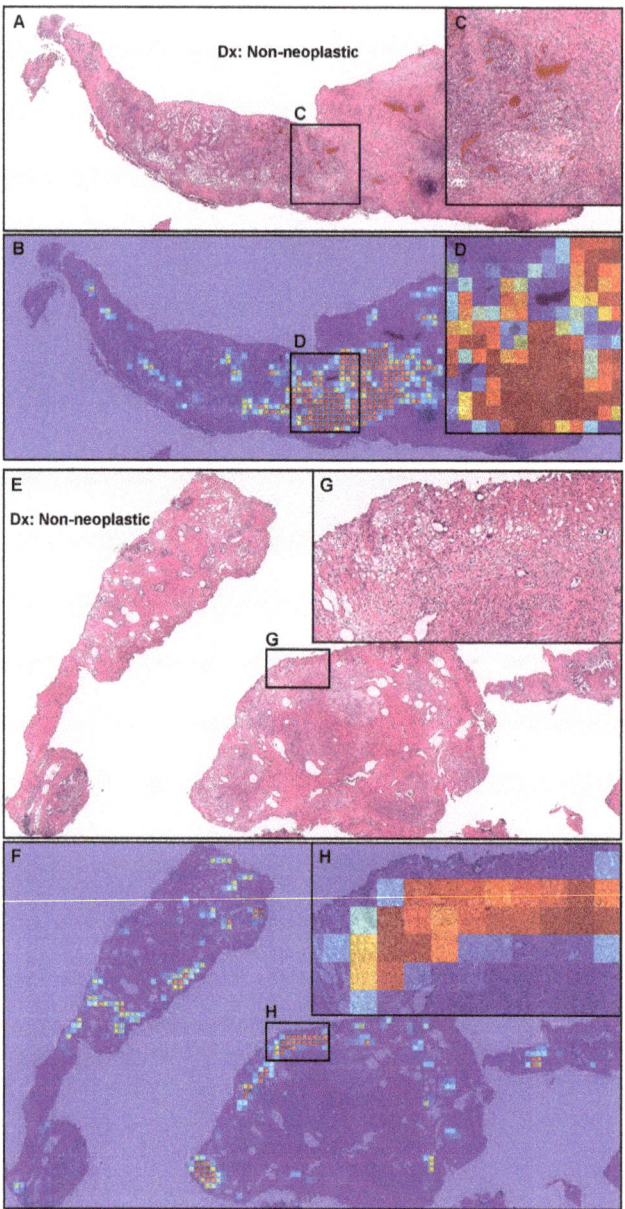

**Figure 7.** Representative examples of prostate adenocarcinoma false positive prediction outputs on cases from the transurethral resection of the prostate (TUR-P) test sets. Histopathologically, (**A**,**E**) are benign (non-neoplastic) lesions. The heat map images (**B**,**F**) exhibit false positive predictions of adenocarcinoma (**D**,**H**) using transfer learning from the colon poorly differentiated adenocarcinoma model (TL-colon poorly ADC-2 (20×, 512)). Inflammation with infiltration of inflammatory cells including foam cells (**C**) would be the primary cause of the false positives due to a morphology analogous to adenocarcinoma cells' infiltration (**D**). The cauterized area of the marginal zone of the specimen (**G**) would be the primary cause of the false positives (**H**). The heat map uses the jet color map where blue indicates low probability and red indicates high probability.

*3.4. False Negative Prediction on the Needle Biopsy Specimens*

In a representative false negative case (Figure 5A), histopathologically, there were adenocarcinoma foci (Figure 5C–E) in three out of four needle biopsy specimens, which the pathologists marked with blue dots when they performed the pathological diagnoses. However, the heat map image exhibits no true positive predictions (Figure 5B).

*3.5. True Positive Prediction on the TUR-P Specimens*

Although not as accurate as the biopsy specimens (Table 4), there were many cases in which prostate adenocarcinoma could be classified precisely on the TUR-P specimens. In a representative true positive TUR-P case (Figure 6A), the transfer learning model (TL-colon poorly ADC-2 (20×, 512)) satisfactorily predicted prostate the adenocarcinoma-invading area (Figure 6B). The heat map image shows the true positive predictions of adenocarcinoma cell infiltration (Figure 6C,D) with the true negative prediction of prostatic hyperplasia (Figure 6A,B).

*3.6. False Positive Prediction on TUR-P Specimens*

By the transfer learning model (TL-colon poorly ADC-2 (20×, 512)), false positives on the TUR-P specimens were not only due to prostatic hyperplasia, as observed for the needle biopsy specimens (Figure 4E–H), but also due to inflammation (Figure 7A–D) and false positives coinciding with areas of tissue degeneration caused by thermal ablation at the specimen margins (Figure 7E–H) because in TUR-P, the endoscope is inserted into the prostate through the urethra and the tissue is harvested with an electrocautery, resulting in marginal degeneration of the specimen due to thermal cauterization.

## 4. Discussion

In this study, we trained deep learning models for the classification of prostate adenocarcinoma in needle biopsy WSIs. Of the three models we trained (Table 4), the best model (TL-colon poorly ADC-2 (20×, 512)) achieved ROC-AUCs in the range of 0.967–0.978 on the needle biopsy, in the range of 0.7377–0.9098 on the TUR-P, and 0.9873 on the TCGA public datasets. The other two models were trained using the EfficientNetB1 [39] model starting with pre-rained weights on ImageNet at different magnifications (10×, 20×) and tile sizes (224 × 224, 512 × 512). The model based on EfficientNetB1 (EfficientNetB1 (20×, 512)) achieved high ROC-AUCs in close proximity to the values of, but lower than, the best model (TL-colon poorly ADC-2 (20×, 512)). The best model (TL-colon poorly ADC-2 (20×, 512)) was trained by the transfer learning approach based on our existing colon poorly differentiated adenocarcinoma classification model [36]. To train the models, we used only 1122 needle biopsy WSIs (adenocarcinoma: 438 WSIs, benign: 684 WSIs) without manual annotations by the pathologists [22,37], as compared to the previous study (about 8400 needle biopsy WSIs for training) [21]. However, we needed to train the models for TUR-P WSIs separately in the next step because TUR-P WSIs were not applicable to be predicted precisely by the best model (TL-colon poorly ADC-2 (20×, 512)).

The best model (TL-colon poorly ADC-2 (20×, 512)) achieved similar values of the ROC-AUC, log loss, accuracy, sensitivity, and specificity among three independent medical institutes (Hospitals A, B, C) and the TCGA public dataset test sets (Tables 4 and 5), meaning that the best model has general versatility in prostate needle biopsy WSIs.

Various benign (non-neoplastic) lesions can mimic adenocarcinoma on needle biopsy specimens, which include glandular lesions such as adenosis, atrophy, verumontanum mucosal gland hyperplasia, atypical adenomatous hyperplasia, nephrogenic metaplasia, hyperplasia of mesonephric remnants, and basal cell hyperplasia [48]. Inflammation (acute and chronic or granulomatous prostatitis) and prostatic hyperplasia are often present in needle biopsy specimens, and they may become problematic to differentiate between benign and adenocarcinoma if their histopathological features are similar to adenocarcinoma in routine diagnosis. Similar to human pathologists, the major causes for false positives predicted by the best model (TL-colon poorly ADC-2 (20×, 512)) were inflammatory cell infiltration, especially histiocytes, lymphocytes, and plasma cells, which morphologically mimic adenocarcinoma cells and prostatic hyperplasia with irregularly shaped and different sizes of tubular structures (Figure 4). In addition, normal benign prostate tissues including seminal vesicles, paraganglia, and ganglion cells may also be confused histopathologically with adenocarcinoma in needle biopsy specimens [48], which were also predicted as adenocarcinoma at the tile level in the small areas of false positively predicted WSIs in this study. Moreover, in routine clinical practice, prostate adenocarcinoma with atrophic features is easily confused with benign acinar atrophy [49], which may cause false negative prediction by deep learning models. It may be necessary to add controversial prostate adenocarcinoma and benign WSIs, which are more likely to cause false positives and false negatives, to attempt to further improve the model's performance on such cases. Interestingly, false positive predictions in cauterized areas of the marginal zone of the specimens were characteristic of TUR-P WSIs (Figure 7). The lower observed results on TUR-P were potentially due to the presence of prostate hyperplasia, which morphologically mimics prostate adenocarcinoma. This indicates that to further improve performance on TUR-P cases, we would require a training set that would specifically account for such cases so as to aid the model in reducing false positives.

A greater number of prostate biopsies (usually 12-core systemic biopsy) are performed currently, and more biopsy cores are submitted to surgical pathology than ever before, resulting in a huge interpretive burden for pathologists. Indeed, many patients undergo biopsy for elevated serum PSA with no other clinical evidence of cancer, resulting in an enormous number of biopsies performed even if numerous diagnostic pitfalls (e.g., fatigue, time-consuming workflow) and mimics of prostate cancer have been described. Thus, the ultimate goal of prostate adenocarcinoma detection, as well as the prediction of the outcome for the individual patient should be augmented by deep-learning-based software applications. The deep learning models established in the present study achieved very high ROC-AUC performances (Figure 2 and Table 4) on prostate needle biopsy WSIs; they offer promising results that indicate they could be beneficial as a screening aid for pathologists prior to observing histopathology on glass slides or WSIs. At the same time, it can be used as a double-check to reduce the risk of missed cancer foci. The major advantage of using an automated tool is that it can systematically handle large amounts of WSIs without potential bias due to the fatigue commonly experienced by pathologists, which could drastically alleviate the heavy clinical burden of practical pathology diagnosis using conventional microscopes. While the results are promising, further clinical validation studies are required in order to further evaluate the robustness of the models in a potential clinical setting before they can actually be used in clinical practice. If such models are deemed viable after rigorous clinical validation, they can transform the future of healthcare and precision oncology.

**Author Contributions:** M.T., M.A. and F.K. contributed equally to this study; M.T. and F.K. designed the studies; M.T., M.A. and F.K. performed the experiments and analyzed the data; M.A. performed the pathological diagnoses and reviewed the cases; M.T. and F.K. performed the computational studies; M.T., M.A. and F.K. wrote the manuscript; M.T. supervised the project. All authors reviewed and approved the final manuscript.

**Funding:** This research received no external funding.

**Institutional Review Board Statement:** The experimental protocol (Code 173) was approved by the Ethical Board of the Kamachi Group Hospitals on 8 April 2020. All research activities complied with all relevant ethical regulations and were performed in accordance with relevant guidelines and regulations in the all hospitals mentioned above.

**Informed Consent Statement:** Informed consent to use histopathological samples and pathological diagnostic reports for research purposes had previously been obtained from all patients prior to the surgical procedures at all hospitals, and the opportunity for refusal to participate in the research had been guaranteed in an opt-out manner.

**Data Availability Statement:** The datasets generated during and/or analyzed during the current study are not publicly available due to specific institutional requirements governing privacy protection, but are available from the corresponding author upon reasonable request. The datasets that support the findings of this study are available from Shinyukuhashi, Wajiro, Shinkuki, Shinkomonji, and Shinmizumaki hospitals (Kamachi Group Hospitals, Fukuoka, Japan), but restrictions apply to the availability of these data, which were used under a data use agreement that was made according to the Ethical Guidelines for Medical and Health Research Involving Human Subjects as set by the Japanese Ministry of Health, Labour and Welfare, and so are not publicly available. However, the data are available from the authors upon reasonable request for private viewing and with permission from the corresponding medical institutions within the terms of the data use agreement and if compliant with the ethical and legal requirements as stipulated by the Japanese Ministry of Health, Labour and Welfare. The external prostate TCGA datasets are publicly available through the Genomic Data Commons (GDC) Data Portal (https://portal.gdc.cancer.gov/ accessed on 1 April 2020).

**Acknowledgments:** We are grateful for the support provided by Shin Ichihara at Department of Surgical Pathology, Sapporo Kosei General Hospital. We thank the pathologists who were engaged in reviewing cases for this study.

**Conflicts of Interest:** M.T. and F.K. are employees of Medmain Inc. All authors declare no competing interest.

# References

1. Sung, H.; Ferlay, J.; Siegel, R.L.; Laversanne, M.; Soerjomataram, I.; Jemal, A.; Bray, F. Global cancer statistics 2020: GLOBOCAN estimates of incidence and mortality worldwide for 36 cancers in 185 countries. *CA Cancer J. Clin.* **2021**, *71*, 209–249. [CrossRef] [PubMed]
2. Montironi, R.; Mazzucchelli, R.; Algaba, F.; Bostwick, D.G.; Krongrad, A. Prostate-specific antigen as a marker of prostate disease. *Virchows Arch.* **2000**, *436*, 297–304. [CrossRef] [PubMed]
3. Sershon, P.D.; Barry, M.J.; Oesterling, J.E. Serum prostate-specific antigen discriminates weakly between men with benign prostatic hyperplasia and patients with organ-confined prostate cancer. *Eur. Urol.* **1994**, *25*, 281–287. [CrossRef] [PubMed]
4. Nadler, R.B.; Humphrey, P.A.; Smith, D.S.; Catalona, W.J.; Ratliff, T.L. Effect of inflammation and benign prostatic hyperplasia on elevated serum prostate specific antigen levels. *J. Urol.* **1995**, *154*, 407–413. [CrossRef]
5. Oesterling, J.E.; Jacobsen, S.J.; Chute, C.G.; Guess, H.A.; Girman, C.J.; Panser, L.A.; Lieber, M.M. Serum prostate-specific antigen in a community-based population of healthy men: Establishment of age-specific reference ranges. *JAMA* **1993**, *270*, 860–864. [CrossRef]
6. Peller, P.A.; Young, D.C.; Marmaduke, D.P.; Marsh, W.L.; Badalament, R.A. Sextant prostate biopsies. A histopathologic correlation with radical prostatectomy specimens. *Cancer* **1995**, *75*, 530–538. [CrossRef]
7. Eichler, K.; Hempel, S.; Wilby, J.; Myers, L.; Bachmann, L.M.; Kleijnen, J. Diagnostic value of systematic biopsy methods in the investigation of prostate cancer: A systematic review. *J. Urol.* **2006**, *175*, 1605–1612. [CrossRef]
8. Bjurlin, M.A.; Carter, H.B.; Schellhammer, P.; Cookson, M.S.; Gomella, L.G.; Troyer, D.; Wheeler, T.M.; Schlossberg, S.; Penson, D.F.; Taneja, S.S. Optimization of initial prostate biopsy in clinical practice: Sampling, labeling and specimen processing. *J. Urol.* **2013**, *189*, 2039–2046. [CrossRef]
9. Yu, K.H.; Zhang, C.; Berry, G.J.; Altman, R.B.; Ré, C.; Rubin, D.L.; Snyder, M. Predicting non-small cell lung cancer prognosis by fully automated microscopic pathology image features. *Nat. Commun.* **2016**, *7*, 12474. [CrossRef]
10. Hou, L.; Samaras, D.; Kurc, T.M.; Gao, Y.; Davis, J.E.; Saltz, J.H. Patch-based convolutional neural network for whole slide tissue image classification. In Proceedings of the IEEE Conference on Computer Vision and Pattern Recognition, Las Vegas, NV, USA, 26 June–1 July 2016; pp. 2424–2433.
11. Madabhushi, A.; Lee, G. Image analysis and machine learning in digital pathology: Challenges and opportunities. *Med. Image Anal.* **2016**, *33*, 170–175. [CrossRef]
12. Litjens, G.; Sánchez, C.I.; Timofeeva, N.; Hermsen, M.; Nagtegaal, I.; Kovacs, I.; Hulsbergen-Van De Kaa, C.; Bult, P.; Van Ginneken, B.; Van Der Laak, J. Deep learning as a tool for increased accuracy and efficiency of histopathological diagnosis. *Sci. Rep.* **2016**, *6*, 26286. [CrossRef] [PubMed]
13. Kraus, O.Z.; Ba, J.L.; Frey, B.J. Classifying and segmenting microscopy images with deep multiple instance learning. *Bioinformatics* **2016**, *32*, i52–i59. [CrossRef] [PubMed]
14. Korbar, B.; Olofson, A.M.; Miraflor, A.P.; Nicka, C.M.; Suriawinata, M.A.; Torresani, L.; Suriawinata, A.A.; Hassanpour, S. Deep learning for classification of colorectal polyps on whole-slide images. *J. Pathol. Inform.* **2017**, *8*, 30. [PubMed]
15. Luo, X.; Zang, X.; Yang, L.; Huang, J.; Liang, F.; Rodriguez-Canales, J.; Wistuba, I.I.; Gazdar, A.; Xie, Y.; Xiao, G. Comprehensive computational pathological image analysis predicts lung cancer prognosis. *J. Thorac. Oncol.* **2017**, *12*, 501–509. [CrossRef]
16. Coudray, N.; Ocampo, P.S.; Sakellaropoulos, T.; Narula, N.; Snuderl, M.; Fenyö, D.; Moreira, A.L.; Razavian, N.; Tsirigos, A. Classification and mutation prediction from non–small cell lung cancer histopathology images using deep learning. *Nat. Med.* **2018**, *24*, 1559–1567. [CrossRef]

17. Wei, J.W.; Tafe, L.J.; Linnik, Y.A.; Vaickus, L.J.; Tomita, N.; Hassanpour, S. Pathologist-level classification of histologic patterns on resected lung adenocarcinoma slides with deep neural networks. *Sci. Rep.* **2019**, *9*, 3358. [CrossRef]
18. Gertych, A.; Swiderska-Chadaj, Z.; Ma, Z.; Ing, N.; Markiewicz, T.; Cierniak, S.; Salemi, H.; Guzman, S.; Walts, A.E.; Knudsen, B.S. Convolutional neural networks can accurately distinguish four histologic growth patterns of lung adenocarcinoma in digital slides. *Sci. Rep.* **2019**, *9*, 1483. [CrossRef]
19. Bejnordi, B.E.; Veta, M.; Van Diest, P.J.; Van Ginneken, B.; Karssemeijer, N.; Litjens, G.; Van Der Laak, J.A.; Hermsen, M.; Manson, Q.F.; Balkenhol, M.; et al. Diagnostic assessment of deep learning algorithms for detection of lymph node metastases in women with breast cancer. *JAMA* **2017**, *318*, 2199–2210. [CrossRef]
20. Saltz, J.; Gupta, R.; Hou, L.; Kurc, T.; Singh, P.; Nguyen, V.; Samaras, D.; Shroyer, K.R.; Zhao, T.; Batiste, R.; et al. Spatial organization and molecular correlation of tumor-infiltrating lymphocytes using deep learning on pathology images. *Cell Rep.* **2018**, *23*, 181–193. [CrossRef]
21. Campanella, G.; Hanna, M.G.; Geneslaw, L.; Miraflor, A.; Silva, V.W.K.; Busam, K.J.; Brogi, E.; Reuter, V.E.; Klimstra, D.S.; Fuchs, T.J. Clinical-grade computational pathology using weakly supervised deep learning on whole slide images. *Nat. Med.* **2019**, *25*, 1301–1309. [CrossRef]
22. Iizuka, O.; Kanavati, F.; Kato, K.; Rambeau, M.; Arihiro, K.; Tsuneki, M. Deep learning models for histopathological classification of gastric and colonic epithelial tumours. *Sci. Rep.* **2020**, *10*, 1504. [CrossRef] [PubMed]
23. Lucas, M.; Jansen, I.; Savci-Heijink, C.D.; Meijer, S.L.; de Boer, O.J.; van Leeuwen, T.G.; de Bruin, D.M.; Marquering, H.A. Deep learning for automatic Gleason pattern classification for grade group determination of prostate biopsies. *Virchows Arch.* **2019**, *475*, 77–83. [CrossRef] [PubMed]
24. Xu, H.; Park, S.; Hwang, T.H. Computerized classification of prostate cancer gleason scores from whole slide images. *IEEE/ACM Trans. Comput. Biol. Bioinform.* **2019**, *17*, 1871–1882. [CrossRef] [PubMed]
25. Raciti, P.; Sue, J.; Ceballos, R.; Godrich, R.; Kunz, J.D.; Kapur, S.; Reuter, V.; Grady, L.; Kanan, C.; Klimstra, D.S.; et al. Novel artificial intelligence system increases the detection of prostate cancer in whole slide images of core needle biopsies. *Mod. Pathol.* **2020**, *33*, 2058–2066. [CrossRef]
26. Rana, A.; Lowe, A.; Lithgow, M.; Horback, K.; Janovitz, T.; Da Silva, A.; Tsai, H.; Shanmugam, V.; Bayat, A.; Shah, P. Use of deep learning to develop and analyze computational hematoxylin and eosin staining of prostate core biopsy images for tumor diagnosis. *JAMA Netw. Open* **2020**, *3*, e205111. [CrossRef]
27. Silva-Rodríguez, J.; Colomer, A.; Dolz, J.; Naranjo, V. Self-learning for weakly supervised gleason grading of local patterns. *IEEE J. Biomed. Health Inform.* **2021**, *25*, 3094–3104. [CrossRef]
28. da Silva, L.M.; Pereira, E.M.; Salles, P.G.; Godrich, R.; Ceballos, R.; Kunz, J.D.; Casson, A.; Viret, J.; Chandarlapaty, S.; Ferreira, C.G.; et al. Independent real-world application of a clinical-grade automated prostate cancer detection system. *J. Pathol.* **2021**, *254*, 147–158. [CrossRef]
29. Otálora, S.; Marini, N.; Müller, H.; Atzori, M. Combining weakly and strongly supervised learning improves strong supervision in Gleason pattern classification. *BMC Med. Imaging* **2021**, *21*, 1–14. [CrossRef]
30. Hammouda, K.; Khalifa, F.; El-Melegy, M.; Ghazal, M.; Darwish, H.E.; El-Ghar, M.A.; El-Baz, A. A Deep Learning Pipeline for Grade Groups Classification Using Digitized Prostate Biopsy Specimens. *Sensors* **2021**, *21*, 6708. [CrossRef]
31. Kanavati, F.; Toyokawa, G.; Momosaki, S.; Rambeau, M.; Kozuma, Y.; Shoji, F.; Yamazaki, K.; Takeo, S.; Iizuka, O.; Tsuneki, M. Weakly-supervised learning for lung carcinoma classification using deep learning. *Sci. Rep.* **2020**, *10*, 9297. [CrossRef]
32. Naito, Y.; Tsuneki, M.; Fukushima, N.; Koga, Y.; Higashi, M.; Notohara, K.; Aishima, S.; Ohike, N.; Tajiri, T.; Yamaguchi, H.; et al. A deep learning model to detect pancreatic ductal adenocarcinoma on endoscopic ultrasound-guided fine-needle biopsy. *Sci. Rep.* **2021**, *11*, 8454. [CrossRef] [PubMed]
33. Kanavati, F.; Ichihara, S.; Rambeau, M.; Iizuka, O.; Arihiro, K.; Tsuneki, M. Deep learning models for gastric signet ring cell carcinoma classification in whole slide images. *Technol. Cancer Res. Treat.* **2021**, *20*, 15330338211027901. [CrossRef] [PubMed]
34. Kanavati, F.; Tsuneki, M. A deep learning model for gastric diffuse-type adenocarcinoma classification in whole slide images. *arXiv* **2021**, arXiv:2104.12478
35. Kanavati, F.; Tsuneki, M. Breast invasive ductal carcinoma classification on whole slide images with weakly-supervised and transfer learning. *Cancers* **2021**, *13*, 5368. [CrossRef] [PubMed]
36. Tsuneki, M.; Kanavati, F. Deep learning models for poorly differentiated colorectal adenocarcinoma classification in whole slide images using transfer learning. *Diagnostics* **2021**, *11*, 2074. [CrossRef]
37. Kanavati, F.; Ichihara, S.; Tsuneki, M. A deep learning model for breast ductal carcinoma in situ classification in whole slide images. *Virchows Arch.* **2022**, 1–14. [CrossRef] [PubMed]
38. Kanavati, F.; Tsuneki, M. Partial transfusion: On the expressive influence of trainable batch norm parameters for transfer learning. *arXiv* **2021**, arXiv:2102.05543.
39. Tan, M.; Le, Q. Efficientnet: Rethinking model scaling for convolutional neural networks. In Proceedings of the International Conference on Machine Learning, PMLR, Long Beach, CA, USA, 9–15 June 2019; pp. 6105–6114.
40. Otsu, N. A threshold selection method from gray-level histograms. *IEEE Trans. Syst. Man Cybern.* **1979**, *9*, 62–66. [CrossRef]
41. Kingma, D.P.; Ba, J. Adam: A method for stochastic optimization. *arXiv* **2014**, arXiv:1412.6980.
42. Abadi, M.; Agarwal, A.; Barham, P.; Brevdo, E.; Chen, Z.; Citro, C.; Corrado, G.S.; Davis, A.; Dean, J.; Devin, M.; et al. TensorFlow: Large-Scale Machine Learning on Heterogeneous Systems. 2015. Available online: tensorflow.org (accessed on 1 March 2020).

43. Pedregosa, F.; Varoquaux, G.; Gramfort, A.; Michel, V.; Thirion, B.; Grisel, O.; Blondel, M.; Prettenhofer, P.; Weiss, R.; Dubourg, V.; et al. Scikit-learn: Machine Learning in Python. *J. Mach. Learn. Res.* **2011**, *12*, 2825–2830.
44. Hunter, J.D. Matplotlib: A 2D graphics environment. *Comput. Sci. Eng.* **2007**, *9*, 90–95. [CrossRef]
45. Efron, B.; Tibshirani, R.J. *An Introduction to the Bootstrap*; CRC Press: Boca Raton, FL, USA, 1994.
46. Epstein, J.I.; Egevad, L.; Amin, M.B.; Delahunt, B.; Srigley, J.R.; Humphrey, P.A. The 2014 International Society of Urological Pathology (ISUP) consensus conference on Gleason grading of prostatic carcinoma. *Am. J. Surg. Pathol.* **2016**, *40*, 244–252. [CrossRef] [PubMed]
47. Kweldam, C.; van Leenders, G.; van der Kwast, T. Grading of prostate cancer: A work in progress. *Histopathology* **2019**, *74*, 146–160. [CrossRef] [PubMed]
48. Gaudin, P.; Reuter, V. Benign mimics of prostatic adenocarcinoma on needle biopsy. *Anat. Pathol.* **1997**, *2*, 111–134. [PubMed]
49. Egan, A.M.; Lopez-Beltran, A.; Bostwick, D.G. Prostatic adenocarcinoma with atrophic features: Malignancy mimicking a benign process. *Am. J. Surg. Pathol.* **1997**, *21*, 931–935. [CrossRef]

*Review*

# Application of Artificial Intelligence in Pathology: Trends and Challenges

Inho Kim [1], Kyungmin Kang [1], Youngjae Song [1] and Tae-Jung Kim [2,*]

1. College of Medicine, The Catholic University of Korea, 222 Banpo-daero, Seocho-gu, Seoul 06591, Republic of Korea
2. Department of Hospital Pathology, Yeouido St. Mary's Hospital, College of Medicine, The Catholic University of Korea, 10, 63-ro, Yeongdeungpo-gu, Seoul 07345, Republic of Korea
* Correspondence: kimecho@catholic.ac.kr; Tel.: +82-2-3779-2157

**Abstract:** Given the recent success of artificial intelligence (AI) in computer vision applications, many pathologists anticipate that AI will be able to assist them in a variety of digital pathology tasks. Simultaneously, tremendous advancements in deep learning have enabled a synergy with artificial intelligence (AI), allowing for image-based diagnosis on the background of digital pathology. There are efforts for developing AI-based tools to save pathologists time and eliminate errors. Here, we describe the elements in the development of computational pathology (CPATH), its applicability to AI development, and the challenges it faces, such as algorithm validation and interpretability, computing systems, reimbursement, ethics, and regulations. Furthermore, we present an overview of novel AI-based approaches that could be integrated into pathology laboratory workflows.

**Keywords:** artificial intelligence; computational pathology; digital pathology; histopathology image analysis; deep learning

## 1. Introduction

Pathologists examine pathology slides under a microscope. To diagnose diseases with these glass slides, many traditional technologies, such as hematoxylin and eosin (H&E) staining and special staining, have been used. However, even for experienced pathologists, intra- and interobserver disagreement cannot be avoided through visual observation and subjective interpretation [1]. This limited agreement has resulted in the necessity of computational methods for pathological diagnosis [2–4]. Because automated approaches can achieve reliable results, digital imaging is the first step in computer-aided analysis [5]. When compared to traditional digital imaging technologies that process static images through cameras, whole-slide imaging (WSI) is a more advanced and widely used technology in pathology [6].

Digital pathology refers to the environment that includes tools and systems for digitizing pathology slides and associated metadata, in addition their storage, evaluation, and analysis, as well as supporting infrastructure. WSI has been proven in multiple studies to have an excellent correlation with traditional light microscopy diagnosis [7] and to be a reliable tool for routine surgical pathology diagnosis [8,9]. Indeed, WSI technology provides a number of advantages over traditional microscopy, including portability, ease of sharing and retrieving images, and task balance [10]. The establishment of the digital pathology environment contributed to the development of a new branch of pathology known as computational pathology (CPATH) [11]. Novel terminology and definitions have resulted from advances in computational pathology (Table 1) [12]. The computational analysis of pathology slide images has made direct disease investigation possible rather than relying on a pathologist analyzing images on a screen [13]. AI approaches aided by deep learning results are frequently used to combine information from digitized pathology images with their associated metadata. Using AI approaches that computationally evaluate

**Citation:** Kim, I.; Kang, K.; Song, Y.; Kim, T.-J. Application of Artificial Intelligence in Pathology: Trends and Challenges. *Diagnostics* **2022**, *12*, 2794. https://doi.org/10.3390/diagnostics12112794

Academic Editor: Masayuki Tsuneki

Received: 26 September 2022
Accepted: 11 November 2022
Published: 15 November 2022

**Publisher's Note:** MDPI stays neutral with regard to jurisdictional claims in published maps and institutional affiliations.

**Copyright:** © 2022 by the authors. Licensee MDPI, Basel, Switzerland. This article is an open access article distributed under the terms and conditions of the Creative Commons Attribution (CC BY) license (https://creativecommons.org/licenses/by/4.0/).

the entire slide image, researchers can detect features that are difficult to detect by eye alone, which is now the state-of-the-art in digital pathology [14].

Table 1. Computational pathology definitions.

| Terms | Definition |
|---|---|
| Artificial intelligence (AI) | The broadest definition of computer science dealing with the ability of a computer to simulate human intelligence and perform complicated tasks. |
| Computational pathology (CPATH) | A branch of pathology that involves computational analysis of a broad array of methods to analyze patient specimens for the study of disease. In this paper, we focus on the extraction of information from digitized pathology images in combination with their associated metadata, typically using AI methods such as deep learning. |
| Convolutional neural networks (CNN) | A form of deep neural networks with one or more convolutional layers and various different layers that can be trained using the backpropagation algorithm and which is suitable for learning 2D data such as images. |
| Deep learning | A subclassification of machine learning that imitates a logical structure similar to how people conclude using a layered algorithm structure called an artificial neural network. |
| Digital pathology | An environment in which traditional pathology analysis utilizing slides made of cells or tissues is converted to a digital environment using a high-resolution scanner. |
| End-to-end training | An opposite concept of feature-crafted methods in a machine learning model, a method which learns the ideal value simultaneously rather than sequentially using only one pipeline. It works smoothly when the dataset is large enough. |
| Ground truth | A concept of a dataset's 'true' category, quantity, or label that serves as direction to an algorithm in the training step. The ground truth varies from the patient- or slide-level to objects or areas within the picture, depending on the objective. |
| Image segmentation | A technique for classifying each region into a semantic category by decomposing an image to the pixel level. |
| Machine learning | An artificial intelligence that parses data, learns from it, and makes intelligent judgments based on what it has learned. |
| Metadata | A type of data that explains other data. A single histopathology slide image in CPATH may include patient disease, demographic information, previous treatment records and medical history, slide dyeing information, and scanner information as metadata. |
| Whole-slide image (WSI) | An whole histopathological glass slide digitized at microscopic resolution as a digital representation. Slide scanners are commonly used to create these complete slide scans. A slide scan viewing platform allows for image examination similar to that of a regular microscope. |

The conventional pathological digital image machine learning method requires particularly educated pathologists to manually categorize abnormal picture attributes before incorporating them into algorithms. Manually extracting and analyzing features from pathological images was a time-consuming, labor-intensive, and costly method that led to many disagreements among pathologists on whether features are typical [15]. Human-extracted visual characteristics must be translated into numerical forms for computer algorithms, but identifying patterns and expressing them with a finite number of feature markers was nearly impossible in some complex diseases. Diverse and popular studies to 'well' learn handmade features became the basis for a commercially available medical image analysis system. After all the algorithm development steps, its performance often had a high false-positive rate, and generalization in even typical pathological images was limited [16]. Deep learning, however, has enabled computers to automatically extract feature vectors from pathology image example data and learn to build optimal algorithms on their own [17,18], even outperforming physicians in some cases, and has now emerged as a cutting-edge machine learning method in medical clinical practice [19]. Diverse deep architectures trained with huge image datasets provide biological informatics discoveries and outstanding object recognition [20].

The purpose of this review is to enhance the understanding of the reader with an update on the implementation of artificial intelligence in the pathology department regarding requirements, work process and clinical application development.

## 2. Deveopment of AI Aided Computational Pathology

Integrating artificial intelligence into the workflow of the pathology department can perform quality control of the pre-analytic, analytic, and post-analytic phases of the pathology department's work process, allowing quality control of scan images and formalin-fixed paraffin-embedded tissue blocks, integrated diagnosis with joining clinical information, ordering necessary pathology studies including immunohistochemistry and molecular studies, automating repetitive tasks, on-demand consultation, and cloud server management (Figure 1), which, finally allow precision medicine by enabling us to use a wide range of patient data, including pathological images, to develop disease-preventive and treatment methods tailored to individual patient features. To achieve the above-mentioned goals, there are crucial elements required for CPATH. A simple summary of the required steps for the application of an AI with CPATH is demonstrated in Figure 2.

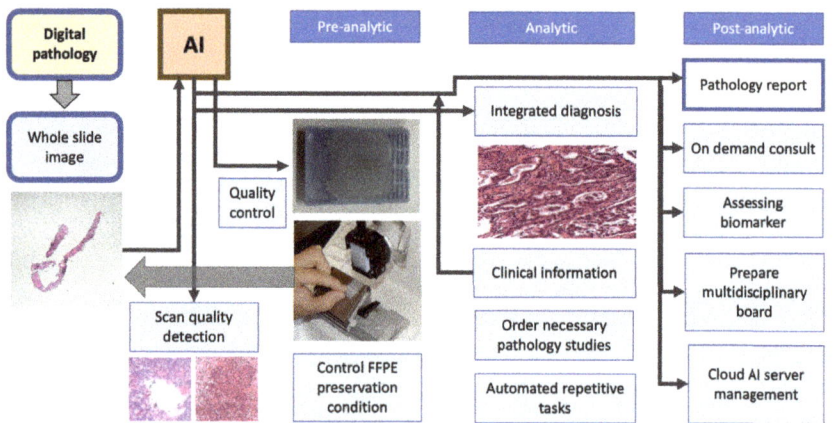

**Figure 1.** Embedding AI into pathology department workflow. The digital pathology supplies whole-slide images to artificial intelligence, which performs quality control of pre-analytic phase, analytic phase and post-analytic phase of pathology laboratory process.

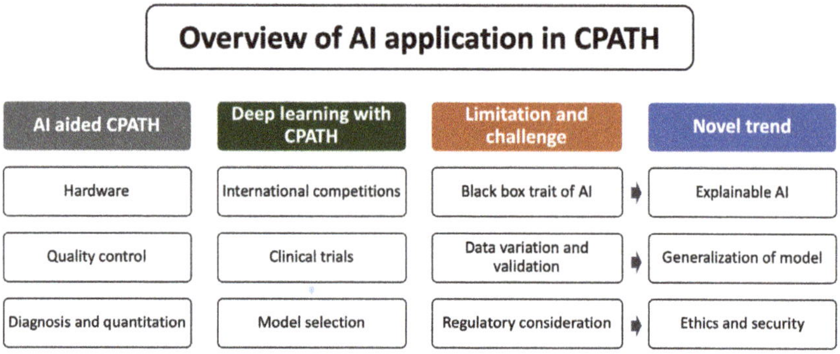

**Figure 2.** Requirement for clinical applications of artificial intelligence with CPATH.

*2.1. Equipment*

Transitioning from glass to digital workflows in AP requires new digital pathology equipment, image management systems, improved data management and storage capacities, and additional trained technicians [21]. While the use of advanced high-resolution hardware with multiple graphical processing units can speed up training, it can become prohibitively expensive. Pathologists must agree to changes to a century-old workflow. Given that change takes time, pathologist end-users should anticipate change-management challenges independent of technological and financial hurdles. AI deployment in the pathology department requires digital pathology. Digital pathology has many proven uses, including primary and secondary clinical diagnosis, telepathology, slide sharing, research data set development, and pathology education or teaching [22]. Digital pathology systems provide time- and cost-saving improvements over the traditional microscopy technique and improve inter-observer variation with adequate slide image management software, integrated reporting systems, improved scanning speeds, and high-quality images. Significant barriers include the introduction of technologies without regulatory-driven, evidence-based validation, the resistance of developers (academic and industrial), and the requirement for commercial integration and open-source data formats.

*2.2. Whole Slide Image*

In the field of radiology, picture archiving and communication systems (PACS) were successfully introduced owing to infrastructure such as stable servers and high-performance processing devices, and they are now widely used in deep learning sources [23,24]. Similarly, in the pathology field, a digital pathology system was developed that scans traditional glass slides using a slide scanner to produce a WSI; it then stores and transmits it to servers [13]. Because WSI which has an average of 1.6 billion pixels and occupies 4600 megabytes (MB) per unit, thus taking up much more space than a DICOM (digital imaging and communications in medicine) format, this technique took place later in pathology than in radiography [25]. However, in recent years, scanners, servers, and technology that can quickly process WSI have made this possible, allowing pathologists to inspect images on a PC screen [6].

*2.3. Quality Control Using Artificial Intelligence*

AI tools can be embedded within a pathology laboratory workflow before or after the diagnosis of the pathologist. Before cases are sent to pathologists for review, an AI tool can be used to triage them (for example, cancer priority or improper tissue section) or to help with screening for unexpected events (e.g., tissue contamination or microorganisms). After reviewing a case, pathologists can also use AI tools to execute certain tasks (e.g., counting mitotic figures for tumor grading or measuring nucleic acid quantification). AI software can also run in the background and execute tasks such as quality control and other tasks all the time (e.g., correlation with clinical or surgical information). The ability of AI, digital pathology, and laboratory information systems to work together is the key to making a successful AI workflow that fits the needs of a pathology department. Furthermore, pre-analytic AI implementation can affect the process of molecular pathology. Personalized medicine and accurate quantification of tumor and biomarker expression have emerged as critical components of cancer diagnostics. Quality control (QC) of clinical tissue samples is required to confirm the adequacy of tumor tissue to proceed with further molecular analysis [26]. The digitization of stained tissue slides provides a valuable way to archive, preserve, and retrieve important information when needed.

*2.4. Diagnosis and Quantitation*

A combination of deep learning methods in CPATH has been developed to excavate unique and remarkable biomarkers for clinical applications. Tumor-infiltrating lymphocytes (TILs) are a prime illustration, as their spatial distributions have been demonstrated to be useful for cancer diagnosis and prognosis in the field of oncology [27]. TILs are the principal activator of anticancer immunity in theory, and if TILs could be objectively measured across the tumor microenvironment (TME), they could be a reliable biomarker [20]. TILs have been shown to be associated with recurrence and genetic mutations in non-small cell lung cancer (NSCLC) [28], and lymphocytes, which have been actively made immune, have proved to have a better response, leading to a longer progression-free survival than the ones that did not show much immunity [29]. Because manual quantification necessitates a tremendous amount of work and is easily influenced by interobserver heterogeneity [30,31], many approaches are being tested in order to overcome these hurdles and determine a clinically meaningful TIL cutoff threshold [32]. Recently, a spatial molecular imaging technique obtaining spatial lymphocytic patterns linked to the rich genomic characterization of TCGA samples has exemplified one application of the TCGA image archives, providing insights into the tumor-immune microenvironment [20].

On a cellular level, spatial organization analysis of TME containing multiple cell types, rather than only TILs, has been explored, and it is expected to yield information on tumor progression, metastasis, and treatment outcomes [33]. Tissue segmentation is done using the comprehensive immunolabeling of specific cell types or spatial transcriptomics to identify a link between tissue content and clinical features, such as survival and recurrence [34,35]. In a similar approach, assessing image analysis on tissue components, particularly focusing on the relative amount of area of tumor and intratumoral stroma, such as the tumor-stroma ratio (TSR), is a widely studied prognostic factor in several cancers, including breast cancer [36,37], colorectal cancer [38,39], and lung cancer [40]. Other studies in CPATH include an attempt to predict the origin of a tumor in cancers of unknown primary source using only a histopathology image of the metastatic site [41].

One of the advantages of CPATH is that it allows the simultaneous inspection of histopathology images along with patient metadata, such as demographic, gene sequencing or expression data, and progression and treatment outcomes. Several attempts are being made to integrate patient pathological tissue images and one or more metadata to obtain novel information that may be used for diagnosis and prediction, as it was discovered that predicting survival using merely pathologic tissue images was challenging and inaccurate [42]. Mobadersany et al. used a Cox proportional hazards model integrated with a CNN to predict the overall survival of patients with gliomas using tissue biopsy images and genetic biomarkers such as chromosome deletion and gene mutation [43]. He et al. used H&E histopathology images and spatial transcriptomics, which analyzes RNA to assess gene activity and allocate cell types to their locations in histology sections to construct a deep learning algorithm to predict genomic expression in patients with breast cancer [44]. Furthermore, Wang et al. employed a technique known as 'transcriptome-wide expression-morphology' analysis, which allows for the prediction of mRNA expression and proliferation markers using conventional histopathology WSIs from patients with breast cancer [45]. It is also highly promising in that, as deep learning algorithms progress in CPATH, it can be a helpful tool for pathologists and doctors making decisions. Studies have been undertaken to see how significant an impact assisting diagnosis can have. Wang et al. showed that pathologists employing a predictive deep learning model to diagnose the metastasis of breast cancer from WSIs of sentinel lymph nodes reduced the human error rate by nearly 85% [46]. In a similar approach, Steiner et al. looked at the influence of AI in the histological evaluation of breast cancer with lymph node metastasis, comparing pathologist performance supported by AI with pathologist performance unassisted by AI to see whether supplementation may help. It was discovered that algorithm-assisted pathologists outperformed unassisted pathologists in terms of accuracy, sensitivity, and time effectiveness [47].

## 3. Deep Learning from Computational Pathology

### 3.1. International Competitions

The exponential development in scanner performance making producing WSI easier and faster than previously, along with sophisticated viewing devices, major advancements in both computer technology and AI, as well as the accordance to regulatory requirements of the complete infrastructure within the clinical context, have fueled CPATH's rapid growth in recent years [15]. Following the initial application of CNNs in histopathology at ICPR 2012 [48], several studies have been conducted to assess the performance of automated deep learning algorithms analyzing histopathology images in a variety of diseases, primarily cancer. CPATH challenges are being promoted in the same way that competitions and challenges are held in the field of computer engineering to develop technologies and discover talented rookies. CAMELYON16 was the first grand challenge ever held, with the goal of developing CPATH solutions for the detection of breast cancer metastases in H&E-stained slides of sentinel lymph nodes and to assess the accuracy of the deep learning algorithms developed by competition participants, medical students and experienced professional pathologists [49]. The dataset from the CAMELYON16 challenge, which took a great deal of work, was used in several other studies and provided motive for other challenges [50–52], attracting major machine learning companies such as Google to the medical artificial intelligence field [53], and is said to have influenced US government policy [54]. Since then, new challenges have been proposed in many more cancer areas using other deep learning architectures with greater datasets, providing the driving force behind the growth of CPATH (Table 2). Histopathology deep learning challenges can attract non-medical engineers and medical personnel, provide prospects for businesses, and make the competition's dataset publicly available, benefiting future studies. Stronger deep learning algorithms are expected to emerge, speeding the clinical use of new algorithms in digital image analysis. Traditional digital image analysis works on three major types of measures: image object localization, classification, and quantification [12], and deep learning in CPATH focuses on those metrics similarly. CPATH applications include tumor detection and classification, invasive or metastatic foci detection, primarily lymph nodes, image segmentation and analysis of spatial information, including ratio and density, cell and nuclei classification, mitosis counting, gene mutation prediction, and histological scoring. Two or more of these categories are often researched together, and deep learning architectures like convolutional neural networks (CNN) and recurrent neural networks are utilized for training and applications.

Table 2. Examples of grand challenges held in CPATH.

| Challenge | Year | Staining | Challenge Goal | Dataset |
| --- | --- | --- | --- | --- |
| GlaS challenge [55] | 2015 | H&E | Segmentation of colon glands of stage T3 and T4 colorectal adenocarcinoma | Private set—165 images from 16 WSIs |
| CAMELYON16 [56] | 2016 | H&E | Evaluation of new and current algorithms for automatic identification of metastases in WSIs from H&E-stained lymph node sections | Private set—221 images |
| TUPAC challenge [57] | 2016 | H&E | Prediction of tumor proliferation scores and gene expression of breast cancer using histopathology WSIs | 821 TCGA WSIs |
| BreastPathQ [58] | 2018 | H&E | Development of quantitative biomarkers to determinate cancer cellularity of breast cancer from H&E-stained WSIs | Private set—96 WSIs |
| BACH challenge [59] | 2018 | H&E | Classification of H&E-stained breast histopathology images and performing pixel-wise labeling of WSIs | Private set—40 WSIs and 500 images |
| LYON19 [60] | 2019 | IHC | Provision of a dataset as well as an evolution platform for current lymphocyte detection algorithms in IHC-stained images | LYON19 test set containing 441 ROIs |
| DigestPath [61] | 2019 | H&E | Evaluation of algorithms for detecting signet ring cells and screening colonoscopy tissue from histopathology images of the digestive system | Private set—127 WSIs |
| HEROHE ECDP [62] | 2020 | H&E | Evaluation of algorithms to discriminate HER2-positive breast cancer specimens from HER2-negative breast cancer specimens with high sensitivity and specificity only using H&E-stained slides | Private set—359 WSIs |
| MIDOG challenge [63] | 2021 | H&E | Detection of mitotic figures from breast cancer histopathology images scanned by different scanners to overcome the 'domain-shift' problem and improve generalization | Private set—200 cases |

Table 2. Cont.

| Challenge | Year | Staining | Challenge Goal | Dataset |
|---|---|---|---|---|
| CoNIC challenge [64] | 2022 | H&E | Evaluation of algorithms for nuclear segmentation and classification into six types, along with cellular composition prediction | 4981 patches |
| ACROBAT [65] | 2022 | H&E, IHC | Development of WSI registration algorithms that can align WSIs of IHC-stained breast cancer tissue sections with corresponding H&E-stained tissue regions | Private dataset—750 cases consisting of 1 H&E and 1–4 matched IHC |

## 3.2. Dataset and Deep Learning Model

Since public datasets for machine learning learning in CPATH, such as the Cancer Genome Atlas (TCGA), the Cancer Image Archive (TCIA), and public datasets created by several challenges, such as the CAMELYON16 challenge dataset, are freely accessible to anyone, researchers who do not have their own private data can conduct research and can also use the same dataset as a standard benchmark by several researchers comparing the performance of each algorithm [15]. Coudray et al. [66], Using the inception-v3 model as a deep learning architecture, assessed the performance of algorithms in classification and genomics mutation prediction of NSCLC histopathology pictures from TCGA and a portion of an independent private dataset, which was a noteworthy study that could detect genetic mutations using WSIs such as STK11 (AUC 0.85), KRAS (AUC 0.81), and EGFR (AUC 0.75). Guo et al. used the Inception-v3 model to classify the tumor region of a breast cancer [67]. Bulten et al. used 1243 WSIs of private prostate biopsies, segmenting individual glands to determine Gleason growth patterns using UNet, followed by cancer grading, and achieved performance comparable to pathologists [68]. Table 3 contains additional published examples utilizing various deep learning architectures and diverse datasets. A complete and extensive understanding of deep learning concepts and existing architectures can be found [17,69], while a specific application of deep learning in medical image analysis can be read [70–72]. To avoid bias in algorithm development, datasets should be truly representative, encompassing the range of data that would be expected in the real world [19], including both the expected range of tissue features (normal and pathological) and the expected variation in tissue and slide preparation between laboratories.

Table 3. Summary of recent convolutional neural network models in pathology image analysis.

| Publication | Deep Learning | Input | Training Goal | Dataset |
|---|---|---|---|---|
| Zhang et al. [73] | CNN | WSI | Diagnosis of bladder cancer | TCGA and private—913 WSIs |
| Shim et al. [74] | CNN | WSI | Prognosis of lung cancer | Private—393 WSIs |
| Im et al. [75] | CNN | WSI | Diagnosis of brain tumor subtype | private—468 WSIs |
| Mi et al. [76] | CNN | WSI | Diagnosis of breast cancer | private dataset—540 WSIs |
| Hu et al. [77] | CNN | WSI | Diagnosis of gastric cancer | private—921 WSIs |
| Pei et al. [78] | CNN | WSI | Diagnosis of brain tumor classification | TCGA—549 WSIs |
| Salvi et al. [79] | CNN | WSI | Segmentation of normal prostate gland | Private—150 WSIs |
| Lu et al. [80] | CNN | WSI | Genomic correlation of breast cancer | TCGA and private—1157 WSIs |
| Cheng et al. [81] | CNN | WSI | Screening of cervical cancer | Private—3545 WSIs |
| Kers et al. [82] | CNN | WSI | Classification of transplant kidney | Private—5844 WSIs |
| Zhou et al. [83] | CNN | WSI | Classification of colon cancer | TCGA—1346 WSIs |
| Hohn et al. [84] | CNN | WSI | Classification of skin cancer | Private—431 WSIs |
| Wang et al. [45] | CNN | WSI | Prognosis of gastric cancer | Private—700 WSIs |
| Shin et al. [85] | CNN, GAN | WSI | Diagnosis of ovarian cancer | TCGA—142 WSIs |

Abbreviation: CNN, convolutional neural network; WSI, whole-slide image; TCGA, The Cancer Genome Atlas.

CNNs are difficult to train end-to-end because gigapixel WSIs are too large to fit in GPU memory, unlike many natural pictures evaluated in computer vision applications. A single WSI requires over terabytes of memory, yet high-end GPUs only give tens of gigabytes. Researchers have suggested alternatives such as partitioning the WSI into small sections (Figure 3) using only a subset or the full WSI compressed with semantic information preserved. Breaking WSI into little patches and placing them all in the GPU to learn everything takes too long; thus, picking patches to represent WSI is critical. For these reasons, randodmizing paches [86], selecting patches from region of interests [42], and randomly selecting patches among image clustering [87] were proposed. The multi-instance learning (MIL) method is then mostly employed in the patch aggregation step, which involves collecting several patches from a single WSI and learning information about the WSI as a result. Traditional MILs treat a single WSI as a basket, assuming that all patches contained within it have the same WSI properties. All patches from a cancer WSI, for example, are considered cancer patches. This method appears to be very simple, yet it is quite beneficial for cancer detection, and representation can be ensured if the learning dataset is large enough [88], which also provides a reason why various large datasets should be produced. If the learning size is insufficient, predicted patch scores are averaged, or classes that account for the majority of patch class predictions are estimated and used to represent the WSI. A more typical way is to learn patch weights using a self-attention mechanism, which uses patch encoding to calculate weighed sum of patch embeddings [89], with a higher weight for the patch that is closest to the ideal patch for performing a certain task for each model. Techniques such as max or mean pooling and certainty pooling, which are commonly utilized in CNNs, are sometimes applied here. There is an advantage to giving interpretability to pathologists using the algorithm because approaches such as self-attention can be presented in the form of a heatmap on a WSI based on patch weights.

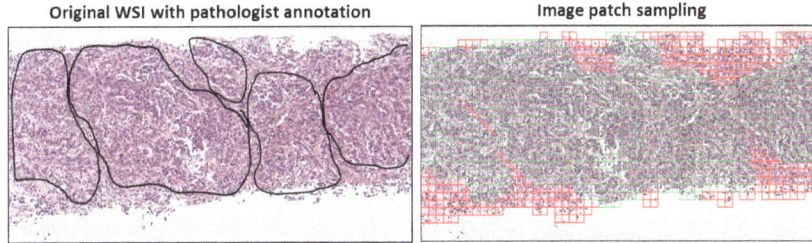

**Figure 3.** Images are divided into small patches obtained from tissue of WSI, which are subsequently prepared to have semantic features extracted from each patch. Green tiles indicate tumor region; red tiles indicate non-tumor region. Images from Yeouido St. Mary's hospital.

*3.3. Overview of Deep Learning Workflows*

WSIs are flooding out of clinical pathology facilities around the world as a result of the development of CPATH, including publicly available datasets, which can be considered a desirable cornerstone for the development of deep learning because it means more data are available for research. However, as shown in some of the previous studies, the accuracy of performance, such as classification and segmentation by algorithms commonly expressed in the area under the curve (AUC), must be compared to pathological images manually annotated by humans in order to calculate the accuracy of the performance. In this way, supervised learning is a machine learning model that uses labeled learning data for algorithm learning and learns functions based on it, and it is the machine learning model most utilized in CPATH so far. According to the amount and type of data, object and purpose (whether the target is cancer tissue or substrate tissue and calculating the number of lymphocytes), it can be divided into qualitative and distinct or quantitative and continuous representations, expressed as 'classification' [90] and 'regression' [91], respectively. Because the model is constructed by simulating learning data, labeled data are crucial, and the machine learning model's performance may vary. Unsupervised learning uses unlabeled images, unlike previous scenarios. This technology is closer to an AI since it helps humans collect information and build knowledge about the world. Except for the most basic learning, such as language character acquisition, we can identify commonalities by looking at applied situations and extending them to other objects. To teach young children to recognize dogs and cats, it is not required to exhibit all breeds. 'Unsupervised learning' can find and assess patterns in unlabeled data, divide them into groups, or perform data visualization in which specific qualities are compacted to two or three if there are multiple data characteristics or variables that are hard to see. A study built a complex tissue classifier for CNS tumours based on histopathologic patterns without manual annotation. It provided a framework comparable to the WHO [92], which was based on microscopic traits, molecular characteristics, and well-understood biology [93]. This study demonstrated that the computer can optimize and use some of the same histopathologic features used by pathologists to assist grouping on its own.

In CPATH, it is very important to figure out how accurate a newly made algorithm is, so there is still a lot of supervised learning. Unsupervised learning still makes it hard to keep up with user-defined tasks, but it has the benefit of being a very flexible way to build data patterns that are not predictable. It also lets us deal with changes we did not expect and allows us to learn more outside of the limits of traditional learning. It helps us understand histopathology images and acts as a guide for precision medicine [94].

Nonetheless, unsupervised learning is still underdeveloped in CPATH, and even after unsupervised learning, it is sometimes compared with labeled data to verify performance, making the purpose a little ambiguous. Bulten et al. classified prostate cancer and non-cancer pathology using clustering, but still had to verify the algorithm's ability using manually annotated images, for example [95].

Currently, efforts are made to make different learning datasets by combining the best parts of supervised and unsupervised learning. This is done by manually labeling large groups of pathological images. Instead of manually labeling images, such as in the 2016 TUPAC Challenge, which was an attempt to build standard references for mitosis detection [96], "weakly supervised learning" means figuring out only a small part of an image and then using machine learning to fill in the rest. Several studies have shown that combining sophisticated learning strategies with weakly supervised learning methods can produce results that are similar to those of a fully supervised model. Since then, many more studies have been done on the role of detection and segmentation in histopathology images. "NuClick", a CNN-based algorithm that won the LYON19 Challenge in 2019, showed that structures such as nuclei, cells, and glands in pathological images can be labeled quickly, consistently, and reliably [97], whereas 'CAMEL', developed in another study, only uses sparse image-level labels to produce pixel-level labels for creating datasets to train segmentation models for fully supervised learning [98].

## 4. Current Limitations and Challenges

Despite considerable technical advancements in CPATH in recent years, the deployment of deep learning algorithms in real clinical settings is still far from adequate. This is because, in order to be implemented into existing or future workflows, the CPATH algorithm must be scientifically validated, have considerable clinical benefit, and not cause harm or confuse people at the same time [99]. In this section, we will review the roadblocks to full clinical adoption of the CPATH algorithm, as well as what efforts are currently being made.

*4.1. Acquiring Quality Data*

It is critical that CPATH algorithms be trained with high-quality data so that they can deal with the diverse datasets encountered in real-world clinical practice. Even in deep learning, the ground truth should be manually incorporated into the dataset in order to train appropriate diagnostic contexts in supervised learning to classify, segment, and predict images based on it [100]. The ground truth can be derived from pathology reports grading patient outcomes or tumors, as well as scores assessed by molecular experiments, depending on the study's goals, which are still determined by human experts and need a significant amount of manual labor to obtain a 'correct' dataset [12]. Despite the fact that datasets created by professional pathologists are of excellent quality, vast quantities are difficult to obtain due to the time, cost, and repetitive and arduous tasks required. As a result, publicly available datasets have been continuously created, such as the ones from TCGA or grand challenges, with the help of weakly supervised learning. Alternative efforts have recently been made to gather massive scales of annotated images by crowdsourcing online. Hughes et al. used a crowdsourced image presentation platform to demonstrate deep learning performance comparable to that of a single professional pathologist [101], while López-Pérez et al. used a crowdsourced deep learning algorithm to help a group of doctors or medical students who were not pathologists make annotations comparable to an expert in breast cancer images [102]. Crowdsourcing may generate some noise, but it shows that non-professionals of various skill levels could assist with pathological annotation and dataset generation. Obtaining quality data entails more than just obtaining a sufficient raw pathological image slide of a single disease from a patient or hospital; it also includes preparing materials to analyze and process the image in order to extract useful data for deep learning model training. By using strategies such as selecting patches with cells while excluding patches without cells from raw pictures, as demonstrated in Figure 4, collecting quality data may be made easier.

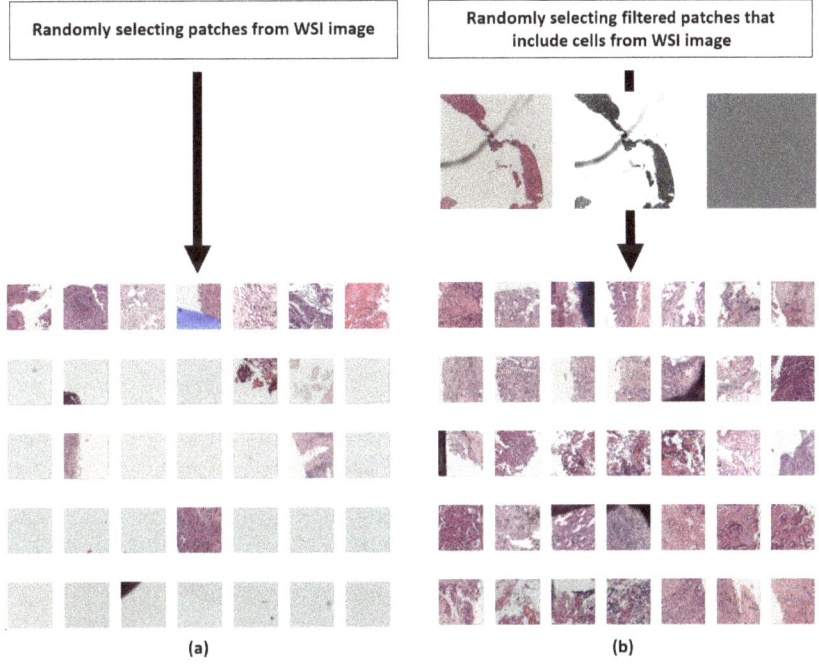

**Figure 4.** (**a**) Random sampling of 100 patches selected arbitrarily from an WSI image. (**b**) Random sampling of 100 patches after application of Laplace filter (which highlights areas with great changes) from WSI image. Images from Yeouido St. Mary's Hospital

### 4.2. Data Variation

Platform diversity, integration, and interoperability represent yet another significant hurdle for the creation and use of AI tools [103]. Recent findings show that current AI models, when trained on insufficient datasets, even when utilizing precise and pixel-by-pixel labelling, can exhibit a 20% decline in performance when evaluated on independent datasets [88]. Deep learning-based algorithms have produced outstanding outcomes in image analysis applications, including digitized slide analysis. Deep learning-based systems face several technological problems, including huge WSI data, picture heterogeneity, and feature complexity. To achieve successful generalization properties, the training data must include a diverse and representative sample of the disease's biological and morphological variability, as well as the technical variables introduced in the pre-analytical and analytical processes in the pathology department, as well as the image acquisition process [104]. A generic deep learning-based system for histopathology tissue analysis. The previously introduced framework is a series of strategies in the preprocessing-training-inference pipeline that showed improved efficiency and generalizability. Such strategies include an ensemble segmentation model, dividing the WSI into smaller overlapping patches, efficient inference algorithms, and a patch-based uncertainty estimation methodology [105,106]. Technical variability challenges can also be addressed by standardizing and preparing CPATH data to limit the effects of technical variability or to make the models robust to technical variability. Training the deep learning model on large and diverse datasets may lower the generalization error to some extent [107].

The amount and quality of input data determine the performance of the deep learning algorithm [108,109]. Although the size of datasets has been growing over the years with the development in CPATH, even if algorithms trained using learning datasets perform well on test sets, it is difficult to be certain that algorithms perform well on actual clinical encounters because clinical data come from significantly more diverse sources than studies. Similarly, when evaluating the performance of deep learning algorithms with a specific validation set for each grand challenge, it is also difficult to predict whether they will perform well in actual clinical practice. Color variation is a representative example of the variation of data. Color variation is caused by differences in raw materials, staining techniques used across different pathology labs, patient intervariability, and different slide scanners, which affect not just color but also overall data variation [110]. As a result, color standardization as an image preparation method has long been devised to overcome this problem in WSI. Because predefined template images were used for color normalization in the past, it was difficult to style transformation between different image datasets, but recent advances in generative adversarial networks (GAN) among deep learning artificial neural networks have allowed patches to be standardized without organizational changes. For example, using the cycle-GAN technique, Swiderska-Chadaj et al. reported an AUC of 0.98 and 0.97 for two different datasets constructed from prostate cancer WSIs [72,111]. While efforts are being made to reduce variation and create well-defined standardized data, such as color standardization and attempts to establish global standards for pathological tissue processing, staining, scanning, and digital image processing, data augmentation techniques are also being used to create learning datasets with as many variations as possible in order to learn the many variations encountered in real life. Not only the performance of the CPATH algorithm but also many considerations such as cost and explainability should be thoroughly addressed when deciding which is more effective for actual clinical introduction.

*4.3. Algorithm Validation*

Several steps of validation are conducted during the lengthy process of developing a CPATH algorithm in order to test its performance and safety. To train models and evaluate performance, CPATH studies on typical supervised algorithms separate annotated data into individual learning datasets and test datasets, the majority of which employ datasets with features fairly similar to those of learning datasets in the so-called 'internal verification' stage. Afterwards, through so-called 'external validation', which uses data for tests that have not been used for training, it is feasible to roughly evaluate if the algorithm performs well with the data it would encounter in real clinical practice [15]. However, simply because the CPATH algorithm performed well at this phase, it is hard to ascertain whether it will function equally well in practical practice [112]. While many studies on the CPATH algorithm are being conducted, most studies use autonomous standards due to a lack of established clinical verification standards and institutional validation. Even if deep learning algorithms perform well and are employed with provisional permission, it is difficult to confirm that their performance exhibits the same confirmed effect when the algorithm is upgraded in the subsequent operation process. Efforts are being made to comprehend and compare diverse algorithms regardless of research techniques, such as the construction of a complete and transparent information reporting system called TRIPOD-AI in the prediction model [113].

Finally, it should be noted that the developed algorithm does not result in a single performance but rather continues within the patient's disease progress and play an auxiliary role in decision-making; thus, relying solely on performance as a ratification metric is not ideal. This suggests that, in cases where quality measure for CPATH algorithm performance is generally deemed superior to or comparable to pathologists, it should be defined by examining the role of algorithms in the whole scope of disease progression in a patient in practice [114]. This is also linked to the solution of the gold-standard paradox [14]. This is a paradox which may ariase during the segmentation model's quality control, where pathologists are thought to be the most competent in pathological picture analysis, but algorithmic data are likely to be superior in accuracy and reproducibility. This paradox may alternatively be overcome by implementing the algorithm as part of a larger system that tracks the patient's progress and outcomes [12].

*4.4. Regulatory Considerations*

One of the most crucial aspects for deep learning algorithms to be approved by regulatory agencies in order to use AI in clinical practice is to understand how it works, as AI is sometimes referred to be a "black box" because it is difficult for humans to comprehend exactly what it does [114]. Given the difficulty of opening up deep learning artificial neural networks and their limited explainability due to the difficulty of understanding how countless parameters interact at the same time, more reliable and explainable models for complex and responsible behaviors for diagnosis and treatment decisions and prediction are required [115]. As a result, attempts have been made to turn deep learning algorithms into "glass boxes" by clarifying the input and calculating the output in a way that humans can understand and analyze [116–118].

The existing regulatory paradigm is less adequate for AI since it requires rather small infrastructure and little human interaction, and the level of progress or results are opaque to outsiders, so potential dangers are usually difficult to identify [119]. Thus far, the White House has issued a memorandum on high-level regulatory principles for AI in all fields in November 2020 [120], the European Commission issued a similar white paper in February 2020 [121], and UNESCO made a global guideline on AI ethics in November 2021 [122], but these documents unfortunately do not provide a very detailed method to operate artificial intelligence in the context of operations. Because artificial intelligence is generally developed in confined computer systems, progress has been made outside of regulatory environments thus far, and regulatory uncertainty can accelerate development while also fueling systemic dangers at the same time. Successful AI regulations, as with many new technologies, are expected to be continuously problematic in the future, as regulations and legal rules will still lag behind developing technological breakthroughs [123]. Self-regulation in industrial settings can be theoretically beneficial and is already in use [124], but it has limitations in practice because it is not enforced. Ultimately, a significant degree of regulatory innovation is required to develop a stable AI environment. The most crucial issue to consider in this regard is that, in domains such as health care, where even a slight change can have a serious influence, regulations of AI should be built with the consideration of the overall impact on humans rather than making arbitrary decisions alone.

## 5. Novel Trends in CPATH

*5.1. Explainable AI*

Because most AI algorithms have unclear properties due to their complexity and often lacking robustness, there are substantial issues with AI trust [125]. Furthermore, there is no agreement on how pathologists should include computational pathology systems into their workflow [126]. Building computational pathology systems with explainable artificial intelligence (xAI) methods is a strong substitute for opaque AI models to address these issues [127]. Four categories of needs exist for the usage of xAI techniques and their application possibilities [128]: (1) Model justification: to explain why a decision was made, particularly when a significant or unexpected decision is created, all with the goal of developing trust in the model's operation; (2) Model controlling and debugging: to avoid dangerous outcomes. A better understanding of the system raises the visibility of unknown defects and aids in the rapid identification and correction of problems; (3) Model improving: When a user understands why and how a system achieved a specific result, he can readily modify and improve it, making it wiser and possibly faster. Understanding the judgments created by the AI model, in addition to strengthening the explanation-generating model, can improve the overall work process; (4) Knowledge discovery: One can discover new rules by seeing the appearance of some invisible model results and understanding why and how they appeared. Furthermore, because AI entities are frequently smarter than humans, it is possible to learn new abilities by understanding their behavior.

Recent studies in breast pathology xAI quickly presented the important diagnostic areas in an interactive and understandable manner by automatically previewing tissue WSIs and identifying the regions of interest, which can serve pathologists as an interactive computational guide for computer-assisted primary diagnosis [127,129]. An ongoing study is being done to determine which explanations are best for artificial intelligence development, application, and quality control [130], which explanations are appropriate for situations with high stakes [115], and which explanations are true to the explained model [131].

With the increasing popularity of graph neural networks (GNNs), their application in a variety of disciplines requires explanations for scientific or ethical reasons in medicine [132]. This makes it difficult to define generalized explanation methods, which are further complicated by heterogeneous data domains and graphs. Most explanations are therefore model- and domain-specific. GNN models can be used for node labeling, link prediction, and graph classification [133]. While most models can be used for any of the above tasks, defining and generating explanations can affect how a GNN xAI model is structured. However, the power of these GNN models is limited by their complexity and the underlying data complexity, although most, if not all, of the models can be grouped under the augmented paradigm [134]. Popular deep learning algorithms and explainability techniques based on pixel-wise processing ignore biological elements, limiting pathologists' comprehension. Using biological entity-based graph processing and graph explainers, pathologists can now access explanations.

*5.2. Ethics and Security*

AI tool creation must take into account the requirement for research and ethics approval, which is typically necessary during the research and clinical trial stages. Developers must follow the ethics of using patient data for research and commercial advantages. Recognizing the usefulness of patient data for research and the difficulties in obtaining agreement for its use, the corresponding institution should establish a proper scheme to provide individual patients some influence over how their data are used [103]. Individual institutional review boards may have additional local protocols for permitting one to opt out of data use for research, and it is critical that all of these elements are understood and followed throughout the design stage of AI tool creation [104]. There are many parallels to be found with the AI development pipeline; while successful items will most likely transit through the full pathway, supported by various resources, many products will, however, fail at some point. Each stage of the pipeline, including the justification of the tool for review and being recommended for usage in clinical guidelines, can benefit from measurable outcomes of success in order to make informed judgments about which products should be promoted [135]. This usually calls for proof of cost or resource savings, quality improvements, and patient impact and is thus frequently challenging to demonstrate, especially when the solution entails major transformation and process redesign.

Whether one uses a cloud-based AI solution for pathology diagnostics depends on a number of things, such as the preferred workflow, frequency of instrument use, software and hardware costs, and whether or not the IT security risk group is willing to allow the use of cloud-based solutions. Cloud-based systems must include a business associate's agreement, end-to-end encryption, and unambiguous data-use agreements to prevent data breaches and inappropriate use of patient data [21].

## 6. Conclusions and Future Directions

AI currently has enormous potential to improve pathology practice by reducing errors, improving reproducibility, and facilitating expert communication, all of which were previously difficult with microscopic glass slides. Recent trends of AI applicaion should be affordable, practical, interoperable, explainable, generalizable, manageable, and reimbursable [21]. Many researchers are convinced that AI in general and deep learning in particular could help with many repetitive tasks using digital pathology because of recent successes in image recognition. However, there are currently only a few AI-driven software tools in this field. As a result, we believe pathologists should be involved from the start, even when developing algorithms, to ensure that these eagerly anticipated software packages are improved or even replaced by AI algorithms. Despite popular belief, AI will be difficult to implement in pathology. AI tools are likely to be approved by regulators such as the Food and Drug Administration.

The quantitative nature of CPATH has the potential to transform pathology laboratory and clinical practices. Case stratification, expedited review and annotation, and the output of meaningful models to guide treatment decisions and predict patterns in medical fields are all possibilities. The pathology community needs more research to develop safe and reliable AI. As clinical AI's requirements become clearer, this gap will close. AI in pathology is young and will continue to mature as researchers, doctors, industry, regulatory agencies, and patient advocacy groups innovate and bring new technology to health care practitioners. To accomplish its successful application, robust and standardized computational, clinical, and laboratory practices must be established concurrently and validated across multiple partnering sites.

**Author Contributions:** Conceptualization, T.-J.K.; data curation, K.K. and Y.S.; writing—original draft preparation, I.K.; writing—review and editing, I.K. and T.-J.K.; supervision, T.-J.K.; funding acquisition, T.-J.K. All authors have read and agreed to the published version of the manuscript.

**Funding:** This work was supported by the National Research Foundation of Korea (NRF) through a grant funded by the Korean government (MSIT) (grant number 2017R1E1A1A01078335 and 2022R1A2C1092956) and the Institute of Clinical Medicine Research in the Yeouido St. Mary's Hospital.

**Institutional Review Board Statement:** The study was conducted according to the guidelines of the Declaration of Helsinki and approved by the Institutional Review Board of Yeouido St. Mary's hospital (SC18RNSI0005 approved on 22 January 2018).

**Informed Consent Statement:** Not applicable.

**Data Availability Statement:** Data sharing is not applicable to this article.

**Conflicts of Interest:** The authors declare no conflict of interest.

## References

1. Gurcan, M.N.; Boucheron, L.E.; Can, A.; Madabhushi, A.; Rajpoot, N.M.; Yener, B. Histopathological image analysis: A review. *IEEE Rev. Biomed. Eng.* **2009**, *2*, 147–171. [CrossRef] [PubMed]
2. Wolberg, W.H.; Street, W.N.; Heisey, D.M.; Mangasarian, O.L. Computer-derived nuclear features distinguish malignant from benign breast cytology. *Hum. Pathol.* **1995**, *26*, 792–796. [CrossRef]
3. Choi, H.K.; Jarkrans, T.; Bengtsson, E.; Vasko, J.; Wester, K.; Malmström, P.U.; Busch, C. Image analysis based grading of bladder carcinoma. Comparison of object, texture and graph based methods and their reproducibility. *Anal. Cell. Pathol.* **1997**, *15*, 1–18. [CrossRef] [PubMed]

4. Keenan, S.J.; Diamond, J.; Glenn McCluggage, W.; Bharucha, H.; Thompson, D.; Bartels, P.H.; Hamilton, P.W. An automated machine vision system for the histological grading of cervical intraepithelial neoplasia (CIN). *J. Pathol.* **2000**, *192*, 351–362. [CrossRef]
5. Weinstein, R.S.; Graham, A.R.; Richter, L.C.; Barker, G.P.; Krupinski, E.A.; Lopez, A.M.; Erps, K.A.; Bhattacharyya, A.K.; Yagi, Y.; Gilbertson, J.R. Overview of telepathology, virtual microscopy, and whole slide imaging: Prospects for the future. *Hum. Pathol.* **2009**, *40*, 1057–1069. [CrossRef] [PubMed]
6. Farahani, N.; Parwani, A.V.; Pantanowitz, L. Whole slide imaging in pathology: Advantages, limitations, and emerging perspectives. *Pathol. Lab. Med. Int.* **2015**, *7*, 4321.
7. Saco, A.; Ramírez, J.; Rakislova, N.; Mira, A.; Ordi, J. Validation of whole-slide imaging for histolopathogical diagnosis: Current state. *Pathobiology* **2016**, *83*, 89–98. [CrossRef]
8. Al-Janabi, S.; Huisman, A.; Vink, A.; Leguit, R.J.; Offerhaus, G.J.A.; Ten Kate, F.J.; Van Diest, P.J. Whole slide images for primary diagnostics of gastrointestinal tract pathology: A feasibility study. *Hum. Pathol.* **2012**, *43*, 702–707. [CrossRef]
9. Snead, D.R.; Tsang, Y.W.; Meskiri, A.; Kimani, P.K.; Crossman, R.; Rajpoot, N.M.; Blessing, E.; Chen, K.; Gopalakrishnan, K.; Matthews, P.; et al. Validation of digital pathology imaging for primary histopathological diagnosis. *Histopathology* **2016**, *68*, 1063–1072. [CrossRef]
10. Williams, B.J.; Bottoms, D.; Treanor, D. Future-proofing pathology: The case for clinical adoption of digital pathology. *J. Clin. Pathol.* **2017**, *70*, 1010–1018. [CrossRef]
11. Astrachan, O.; Hambrusch, S.; Peckham, J.; Settle, A. The present and future of computational thinking. *ACM SIGCSE Bulletin.* **2009**, *41*, 549-550. [CrossRef]
12. Abels, E.; Pantanowitz, L.; Aeffner, F.; Zarella, M.D.; van der Laak, J.; Bui, M.M.; Vemuri, V.N.; Parwani, A.V.; Gibbs, J.; Agosto-Arroyo, E.; et al. Computational pathology definitions, best practices, and recommendations for regulatory guidance: A white paper from the Digital Pathology Association. *J. Pathol.* **2019**, *249*, 286–294. [CrossRef]
13. Zarella, M.D.; Bowman, D.; Aeffner, F.; Farahani, N.; Xthona, A.; Absar, S.F.; Parwani, A.; Bui, M.; Hartman, D.J. A practical guide to whole slide imaging: A white paper from the digital pathology association. *Arch. Pathol. Lab. Med.* **2019**, *143*, 222–234. [CrossRef] [PubMed]
14. Aeffner, F.; Wilson, K.; Martin, N.T.; Black, J.C.; Hendriks, C.L.L.; Bolon, B.; Rudmann, D.G.; Gianani, R.; Koegler, S.R.; Krueger, J.; et al. The gold standard paradox in digital image analysis: Manual versus automated scoring as ground truth. *Arch. Pathol. Lab. Med.* **2017**, *141*, 1267–1275. [CrossRef] [PubMed]
15. Van der Laak, J.; Litjens, G.; Ciompi, F. Deep learning in histopathology: The path to the clinic. *Nat. Med.* **2021**, *27*, 775–784. [CrossRef]
16. Chan, H.P.; Samala, R.K.; Hadjiiski, L.M.; Zhou, C. Deep learning in medical image analysis. *Annu. Rev. Biomed. Eng.* **2020**, *19*, 221–248.
17. LeCun, Y.; Bengio, Y.; Hinton, G. Deep learning. *Nature* **2015**, *521*, 436–444. [CrossRef]
18. Schmidhuber, J. Deep learning in neural networks: An overview. *Neural Netw.* **2015**, *61*, 85–117. [CrossRef]
19. Verma, P.; Tiwari, R.; Hong, W.C.; Upadhyay, S.; Yeh, Y.H. FETCH: A Deep Learning-Based Fog Computing and IoT Integrated Environment for Healthcare Monitoring and Diagnosis. *IEEE Access* **2022**, *10*, 12548–12563. [CrossRef]
20. Saltz, J.; Gupta, R.; Hou, L.; Kurc, T.; Singh, P.; Nguyen, V.; Samaras, D.; Shroyer, K.R.; Zhao, T.; Batiste, R.; et al. Spatial organization and molecular correlation of tumor-infiltrating lymphocytes using deep learning on pathology images. *Cell Rep.* **2018**, *23*, 181–193. [CrossRef]
21. Cheng, J.Y.; Abel, J.T.; Balis, U.G.; McClintock, D.S.; Pantanowitz, L. Challenges in the development, deployment, and regulation of artificial intelligence in anatomic pathology. *Am. J. Pathol.* **2021**, *191*, 1684–1692. [CrossRef] [PubMed]
22. Volynskaya, Z.; Evans, A.J.; Asa, S.L. Clinical applications of whole-slide imaging in anatomic pathology. *Adv. Anat. Pathol.* **2017**, *24*, 215–221. [CrossRef] [PubMed]
23. Mansoori, B.; Erhard, K.K.; Sunshine, J.L. Picture Archiving and Communication System (PACS) implementation, integration & benefits in an integrated health system. *Acad. Radiol.* **2012**, *19*, 229–235. [PubMed]
24. Lee, J.G.; Jun, S.; Cho, Y.W.; Lee, H.; Kim, G.B.; Seo, J.B.; Kim, N. Deep learning in medical imaging: General overview. *Korean J. Radiol.* **2017**, *18*, 570–584. [CrossRef] [PubMed]
25. Kohli, M.D.; Summers, R.M.; Geis, J.R. Medical image data and datasets in the era of machine learning—Whitepaper from the 2016 C-MIMI meeting dataset session. *J. Digit. Imaging* **2017**, *30*, 392–399. [CrossRef] [PubMed]
26. Chung, M.; Lin, W.; Dong, L.; Li, X. Tissue requirements and DNA quality control for clinical targeted next-generation sequencing of formalin-fixed, paraffin-embedded samples: A mini-review of practical issues. *J. Mol. Genet. Med.* **2017**, *11*, 1747–0862.
27. Salgado, R.; Denkert, C.; Demaria, S.; Sirtaine, N.; Klauschen, F.; Pruneri, G.; Wienert, S.; Van den Eynden, G.; Baehner, F.L.; Pénault-Llorca, F.; et al. The evaluation of tumor-infiltrating lymphocytes (TILs) in breast cancer: Recommendations by an International TILs Working Group 2014. *Ann. Oncol.* **2015**, *26*, 259–271. [CrossRef]
28. AbdulJabbar, K.; Raza, S.E.A.; Rosenthal, R.; Jamal-Hanjani, M.; Veeriah, S.; Akarca, A.; Lund, T.; Moore, D.A.; Salgado, R.; Al Bakir, M.; et al. Geospatial immune variability illuminates differential evolution of lung adenocarcinoma. *Nat. Med.* **2020**, *26*, 1054–1062. [CrossRef]

29. Park, S.; Ock, C.Y.; Kim, H.; Pereira, S.; Park, S.; Ma, M.; Choi, S.; Kim, S.; Shin, S.; Aum, B.J.; et al. Artificial Intelligence-Powered Spatial Analysis of Tumor-Infiltrating Lymphocytes as Complementary Biomarker for Immune Checkpoint Inhibition in Non-Small-Cell Lung Cancer. *J. Clin. Oncol.* **2022**, *40*, 1916–1928. [CrossRef]
30. Khoury, T.; Peng, X.; Yan, L.; Wang, D.; Nagrale, V. Tumor-infiltrating lymphocytes in breast cancer: Evaluating interobserver variability, heterogeneity, and fidelity of scoring core biopsies. *Am. J. Clin. Pathol.* **2018**, *150*, 441–450. [CrossRef]
31. Swisher, S.K.; Wu, Y.; Castaneda, C.A.; Lyons, G.R.; Yang, F.; Tapia, C.; Wang, X.; Casavilca, S.A.; Bassett, R.; Castillo, M.; et al. Interobserver agreement between pathologists assessing tumor-infiltrating lymphocytes (TILs) in breast cancer using methodology proposed by the International TILs Working Group. *Ann. Surg. Oncol.* **2016**, *23*, 2242–2248. [CrossRef] [PubMed]
32. Gao, G.; Wang, Z.; Qu, X.; Zhang, Z. Prognostic value of tumor-infiltrating lymphocytes in patients with triple-negative breast cancer: A systematic review and meta-analysis. *BMC Cancer* **2020**, *20*, 179. [CrossRef] [PubMed]
33. Lee, K.; Lockhart, J.H.; Xie, M.; Chaudhary, R.; Slebos, R.J.; Flores, E.R.; Chung, C.H.; Tan, A.C. Deep Learning of Histopathology Images at the Single Cell Level. *Front. Artif. Intell.* **2021**, *4*, 754641. [CrossRef] [PubMed]
34. Jiao, Y.; Li, J.; Qian, C.; Fei, S. Deep learning-based tumor microenvironment analysis in colon adenocarcinoma histopathological whole-slide images. *Comput. Methods Programs Biomed.* **2021**, *204*, 106047. [CrossRef]
35. Failmezger, H.; Muralidhar, S.; Rullan, A.; de Andrea, C.E.; Sahai, E.; Yuan, Y. Topological tumor graphs: A graph-based spatial model to infer stromal recruitment for immunosuppression in melanoma histology. *Cancer Res.* **2020**, *80*, 1199–1209. [CrossRef]
36. Moorman, A.; Vink, R.; Heijmans, H.; Van Der Palen, J.; Kouwenhoven, E. The prognostic value of tumour-stroma ratio in triple-negative breast cancer. *Eur. J. Surg. Oncol.* **2012**, *38*, 307–313. [CrossRef]
37. Roeke, T.; Sobral-Leite, M.; Dekker, T.J.; Wesseling, J.; Smit, V.T.; Tollenaar, R.A.; Schmidt, M.K.; Mesker, W.E. The prognostic value of the tumour-stroma ratio in primary operable invasive cancer of the breast: A validation study. *Breast Cancer Res. Treat.* **2017**, *166*, 435–445. [CrossRef]
38. Kather, J.N.; Krisam, J.; Charoentong, P.; Luedde, T.; Herpel, E.; Weis, C.A.; Gaiser, T.; Marx, A.; Valous, N.A.; Ferber, D.; et al. Predicting survival from colorectal cancer histology slides using deep learning: A retrospective multicenter study. *PLoS Med.* **2019**, *16*, e1002730. [CrossRef]
39. Geessink, O.G.; Baidoshvili, A.; Klaase, J.M.; Ehteshami Bejnordi, B.; Litjens, G.J.; van Pelt, G.W.; Mesker, W.E.; Nagtegaal, I.D.; Ciompi, F.; van der Laak, J.A. Computer aided quantification of intratumoral stroma yields an independent prognosticator in rectal cancer. *Cell. Oncol.* **2019**, *42*, 331–341. [CrossRef]
40. Zhang, T.; Xu, J.; Shen, H.; Dong, W.; Ni, Y.; Du, J. Tumor-stroma ratio is an independent predictor for survival in NSCLC. *Int. J. Clin. Exp. Pathol.* **2015**, *8*, 11348.
41. Lu, M.Y.; Chen, T.Y.; Williamson, D.F.; Zhao, M.; Shady, M.; Lipkova, J.; Mahmood, F. AI-based pathology predicts origins for cancers of unknown primary. *Nature* **2021**, *594*, 106–110. [CrossRef] [PubMed]
42. Zhu, X.; Yao, J.; Huang, J. Deep convolutional neural network for survival analysis with pathological images. In Proceedings of the 2016 IEEE International Conference on Bioinformatics and Biomedicine (BIBM), Shenzhen, China, 15–18 December 2016; pp. 544–547.
43. Mobadersany, P.; Yousefi, S.; Amgad, M.; Gutman, D.A.; Barnholtz-Sloan, J.S.; Vega, J.E.V.; Brat, D.J.; Cooper, L.A. Predicting cancer outcomes from histology and genomics using convolutional networks. *Proc. Natl. Acad. Sci. USA* **2018**, *115*, E2970–E2979. [CrossRef] [PubMed]
44. He, B.; Bergenståhle, L.; Stenbeck, L.; Abid, A.; Andersson, A.; Borg, Å.; Maaskola, J.; Lundeberg, J.; Zou, J. Integrating spatial gene expression and breast tumour morphology via deep learning. *Nat. Biomed. Eng.* **2020**, *4*, 827–834. [CrossRef]
45. Wang, Y.; Kartasalo, K.; Weitz, P.; Acs, B.; Valkonen, M.; Larsson, C.; Ruusuvuori, P.; Hartman, J.; Rantalainen, M. Predicting molecular phenotypes from histopathology images: A transcriptome-wide expression-morphology analysis in breast cancer. *Cancer Res.* **2021**, *81*, 5115–5126. [CrossRef] [PubMed]
46. Wang, D.; Khosla, A.; Gargeya, R.; Irshad, H.; Beck, A.H. Deep learning for identifying metastatic breast cancer. *arXiv* **2016**, arXiv:1606.05718.
47. Steiner, D.F.; MacDonald, R.; Liu, Y.; Truszkowski, P.; Hipp, J.D.; Gammage, C.; Thng, F.; Peng, L.; Stumpe, M.C. Impact of deep learning assistance on the histopathologic review of lymph nodes for metastatic breast cancer. *Am. J. Surg. Pathol.* **2018**, *42*, 1636. [CrossRef]
48. Roux, L.; Racoceanu, D.; Loménie, N.; Kulikova, M.; Irshad, H.; Klossa, J.; Capron, F.; Genestie, C.; Le Naour, G.; Gurcan, M.N. Mitosis detection in breast cancer histological images An ICPR 2012 contest. *J. Pathol. Inform.* **2013**, *4*, 8.
49. Bejnordi, B.E.; Veta, M.; Van Diest, P.J.; Van Ginneken, B.; Karssemeijer, N.; Litjens, G.; Van Der Laak, J.A.; Hermsen, M.; Manson, Q.F.; Balkenhol, M.; et al. Diagnostic assessment of deep learning algorithms for detection of lymph node metastases in women with breast cancer. *JAMA* **2017**, *318*, 2199–2210. [CrossRef]
50. Kong, B.; Wang, X.; Li, Z.; Song, Q.; Zhang, S. Cancer metastasis detection via spatially structured deep network. In *Information Processing in Medical Imaging. IPMI 2017*; Lecture Notes in Computer Science; Springer: Cham, Switzerland, 2017; pp. 236–248.
51. Li, Y.; Ping, W. Cancer metastasis detection with neural conditional random field. *arXiv* **2018**, arXiv:1806.07064.
52. Lin, H.; Chen, H.; Graham, S.; Dou, Q.; Rajpoot, N.; Heng, P.A. Fast scannet: Fast and dense analysis of multi-gigapixel whole-slide images for cancer metastasis detection. *IEEE Trans. Med. Imaging* **2019**, *38*, 1948–1958. [CrossRef]
53. Liu, Y.; Gadepalli, K.; Norouzi, M.; Dahl, G.E.; Kohlberger, T.; Boyko, A.; Venugopalan, S.; Timofeev, A.; Nelson, P.Q.; Corrado, G.S.; et al. Detecting cancer metastases on gigapixel pathology images. *arXiv* **2017**, arXiv:1703.02442.

54. Bundy, A. *Preparing for the Future of Artificial Intelligence*; Executive Office of the President National Science and Technology Council: Washington, DC, USA, 2017.
55. Sirinukunwattana, K.; Pluim, J.P.; Chen, H.; Qi, X.; Heng, P.A.; Guo, Y.B.; Wang, L.Y.; Matuszewski, B.J.; Bruni, E.; Sanchez, U.; et al. Gland segmentation in colon histology images: The glas challenge contest. *Med. Image Anal.* **2017**, *35*, 489–502. [CrossRef] [PubMed]
56. Fan, K.; Wen, S.; Deng, Z. Deep learning for detecting breast cancer metastases on WSI. In *Innovation in Medicine and Healthcare Systems, and Multimedia*; Springer: Berlin/Heidelberg, Germany, 2019; pp. 137–145.
57. Zerhouni, E.; Lányi, D.; Viana, M.; Gabrani, M. Wide residual networks for mitosis detection. In Proceedings of the 2017 IEEE 14th International Symposium on Biomedical Imaging (ISBI 2017), Melbourne, Australia, 18–21 April 2017; pp. 924–928.
58. Rakhlin, A.; Tiulpin, A.; Shvets, A.A.; Kalinin, A.A.; Iglovikov, V.I.; Nikolenko, S. Breast tumor cellularity assessment using deep neural networks. In Proceedings of the 2019 IEEE/CVF International Conference on Computer Vision Workshops, Seoul, Korea, 27–28 October 2019.
59. Aresta, G.; Araújo, T.; Kwok, S.; Chennamsetty, S.S.; Safwan, M.; Alex, V.; Marami, B.; Prastawa, M.; Chan, M.; Donovan, M.; et al. Bach: Grand challenge on breast cancer histology images. *Med. Image Anal.* **2019**, *56*, 122–139. [CrossRef] [PubMed]
60. Jahanifar, M.; Koohbanani, N.A.; Rajpoot, N. Nuclick: From clicks in the nuclei to nuclear boundaries. *arXiv* **2019**, arXiv:1909.03253.
61. Da, Q.; Huang, X.; Li, Z.; Zuo, Y.; Zhang, C.; Liu, J.; Chen, W.; Li, J.; Xu, D.; Hu, Z.; et al. DigestPath: A Benchmark Dataset with Challenge Review for the Pathological Detection and Segmentation of Digestive-System. *Med. Image Anal.* **2022**, *80*, 102485. [CrossRef] [PubMed]
62. Eloy, C.; Zerbe, N.; Fraggetta, F. Europe unites for the digital transformation of pathology: The role of the new ESDIP. *J. Pathol. Inform.* **2021**, *12*, 10. [CrossRef]
63. Aubreville, M.; Stathonikos, N.; Bertram, C.A.; Klopleisch, R.; ter Hoeve, N.; Ciompi, F.; Wilm, F.; Marzahl, C.; Donovan, T.A.; Maier, A.; et al. Mitosis domain generalization in histopathology images–The MIDOG challenge. *arXiv* **2022**, arXiv:2204.03742.
64. Graham, S.; Jahanifar, M.; Vu, Q.D.; Hadjigeorghiou, G.; Leech, T.; Snead, D.; Raza, S.E.A.; Minhas, F.; Rajpoot, N. Conic: Colon nuclei identification and counting challenge 2022. *arXiv* **2021**, arXiv:2111.14485.
65. Weitz, P.; Valkonen, M.; Solorzano, L.; Hartman, J.; Ruusuvuori, P.; Rantalainen, M. ACROBAT—Automatic Registration of Breast Cancer Tissue. In Proceedings of the 25th International Conference on Medical Image Computing and Computer Assisted Intervention (MICCAI 2022), Singapore, 18–22 September 2022.
66. Coudray, N.; Ocampo, P.S.; Sakellaropoulos, T.; Narula, N.; Snuderl, M.; Fenyö, D.; Moreira, A.L.; Razavian, N.; Tsirigos, A. Classification and mutation prediction from non–small cell lung cancer histopathology images using deep learning. *Nat. Med.* **2018**, *24*, 1559–1567. [CrossRef]
67. Guo, Z.; Liu, H.; Ni, H.; Wang, X.; Su, M.; Guo, W.; Wang, K.; Jiang, T.; Qian, Y. A fast and refined cancer regions segmentation framework in whole-slide breast pathological images. *Sci. Rep.* **2019**, *9*, 882. [CrossRef]
68. Bulten, W.; Pinckaers, H.; van Boven, H.; Vink, R.; de Bel, T.; van Ginneken, B.; van der Laak, J.; Hulsbergen-van de Kaa, C.; Litjens, G. Automated deep-learning system for Gleason grading of prostate cancer using biopsies: A diagnostic study. *Lancet Oncol.* **2020**, *21*, 233–241. [CrossRef]
69. Goodfellow, I.; Bengio, Y.; Courville, A. *Deep Learning*; MIT Press: Cambridge, MA, USA, 2016.
70. Litjens, G.; Kooi, T.; Bejnordi, B.E.; Setio, A.A.A.; Ciompi, F.; Ghafoorian, M.; Van Der Laak, J.A.; Van Ginneken, B.; Sánchez, C.I. A survey on deep learning in medical image analysis. *Med. Image Anal.* **2017**, *42*, 60–88. [CrossRef] [PubMed]
71. Shen, D.; Wu, G.; Suk, H.I. Deep learning in medical image analysis. *Annu. Rev. Biomed. Eng.* **2017**, *19*, 221–248. [CrossRef]
72. Yi, X.; Walia, E.; Babyn, P. Generative adversarial network in medical imaging: A review. *Med. Image Anal.* **2019**, *58*, 101552. [CrossRef] [PubMed]
73. Zhang, Z.; Chen, P.; McGough, M.; Xing, F.; Wang, C.; Bui, M.; Xie, Y.; Sapkota, M.; Cui, L.; Dhillon, J.; et al. Pathologist-level interpretable whole-slide cancer diagnosis with deep learning. *Nat. Mach. Intell.* **2019**, *1*, 236–245. [CrossRef]
74. Shim, W.S.; Yim, K.; Kim, T.J.; Sung, Y.E.; Lee, G.; Hong, J.H.; Chun, S.H.; Kim, S.; An, H.J.; Na, S.J.; et al. DeepRePath: Identifying the prognostic features of early-stage lung adenocarcinoma using multi-scale pathology images and deep convolutional neural networks. *Cancers* **2021**, *13*, 3308. [CrossRef]
75. Im, S.; Hyeon, J.; Rha, E.; Lee, J.; Choi, H.J.; Jung, Y.; Kim, T.J. Classification of diffuse glioma subtype from clinical-grade pathological images using deep transfer learning. *Sensors* **2021**, *21*, 3500. [CrossRef]
76. Mi, W.; Li, J.; Guo, Y.; Ren, X.; Liang, Z.; Zhang, T.; Zou, H. Deep learning-based multi-class classification of breast digital pathology images. *Cancer Manag. Res.* **2021**, *13*, 4605. [CrossRef]
77. Hu, Y.; Su, F.; Dong, K.; Wang, X.; Zhao, X.; Jiang, Y.; Li, J.; Ji, J.; Sun, Y. Deep learning system for lymph node quantification and metastatic cancer identification from whole-slide pathology images. *Gastric Cancer* **2021**, *24*, 868–877. [CrossRef]
78. Pei, L.; Jones, K.A.; Shboul, Z.A.; Chen, J.Y.; Iftekharuddin, K.M. Deep neural network analysis of pathology images with integrated molecular data for enhanced glioma classification and grading. *Front. Oncol.* **2021**, *11*, 2572. [CrossRef]
79. Salvi, M.; Bosco, M.; Molinaro, L.; Gambella, A.; Papotti, M.; Acharya, U.R.; Molinari, F. A hybrid deep learning approach for gland segmentation in prostate histopathological images. *Artif. Intell. Med.* **2021**, *115*, 102076. [CrossRef] [PubMed]

80. Lu, Z.; Zhan, X.; Wu, Y.; Cheng, J.; Shao, W.; Ni, D.; Han, Z.; Zhang, J.; Feng, Q.; Huang, K. BrcaSeg: A deep learning approach for tissue quantification and genomic correlations of histopathological images. *Genom. Proteom. Bioinform.* **2021**, *19*, 1032–1042. [CrossRef] [PubMed]
81. Cheng, S.; Liu, S.; Yu, J.; Rao, G.; Xiao, Y.; Han, W.; Zhu, W.; Lv, X.; Li, N.; Cai, J.; et al. Robust whole slide image analysis for cervical cancer screening using deep learning. *Nat. Commun.* **2021**, *12*, 5639. [CrossRef] [PubMed]
82. Kers, J.; Bülow, R.D.; Klinkhammer, B.M.; Breimer, G.E.; Fontana, F.; Abiola, A.A.; Hofstraat, R.; Corthals, G.L.; Peters-Sengers, H.; Djudjaj, S.; et al. Deep learning-based classification of kidney transplant pathology: A retrospective, multicentre, proof-of-concept study. *Lancet Digit. Health* **2022**, *4*, e18–e26. [CrossRef]
83. Zhou, C.; Jin, Y.; Chen, Y.; Huang, S.; Huang, R.; Wang, Y.; Zhao, Y.; Chen, Y.; Guo, L.; Liao, J. Histopathology classification and localization of colorectal cancer using global labels by weakly supervised deep learning. *Comput. Med. Imaging Graph.* **2021**, *88*, 101861. [CrossRef]
84. Höhn, J.; Krieghoff-Henning, E.; Jutzi, T.B.; von Kalle, C.; Utikal, J.S.; Meier, F.; Gellrich, F.F.; Hobelsberger, S.; Hauschild, A.; Schlager, J.G.; et al. Combining CNN-based histologic whole slide image analysis and patient data to improve skin cancer classification. *Eur. J. Cancer* **2021**, *149*, 94–101. [CrossRef]
85. Shin, S.J.; You, S.C.; Jeon, H.; Jung, J.W.; An, M.H.; Park, R.W.; Roh, J. Style transfer strategy for developing a generalizable deep learning application in digital pathology. *Comput. Methods Programs Biomed.* **2021**, *198*, 105815. [CrossRef]
86. Naik, N.; Madani, A.; Esteva, A.; Keskar, N.S.; Press, M.F.; Ruderman, D.; Agus, D.B.; Socher, R. Deep learning-enabled breast cancer hormonal receptor status determination from base-level H&E stains. *Nat. Commun.* **2020**, *11*, 5727.
87. Yao, J.; Zhu, X.; Jonnagaddala, J.; Hawkins, N.; Huang, J. Whole slide images based cancer survival prediction using attention guided deep multiple instance learning networks. *Med. Image Anal.* **2020**, *65*, 101789. [CrossRef]
88. Campanella, G.; Hanna, M.G.; Geneslaw, L.; Miraflor, A.; Werneck Krauss Silva, V.; Busam, K.J.; Brogi, E.; Reuter, V.E.; Klimstra, D.S.; Fuchs, T.J. Clinical-grade computational pathology using weakly supervised deep learning on whole slide images. *Nat. Med.* **2019**, *25*, 1301–1309. [CrossRef]
89. Lu, M.Y.; Williamson, D.F.; Chen, T.Y.; Chen, R.J.; Barbieri, M.; Mahmood, F. Data-efficient and weakly supervised computational pathology on whole-slide images. *Nat. Biomed. Eng.* **2021**, *5*, 555–570. [CrossRef] [PubMed]
90. He, K.; Zhang, X.; Ren, S.; Sun, J. Deep residual learning for image recognition. In Proceedings of the 2016 IEEE Conference on Computer Vision and Pattern Recognition, Las Vegas, NV, USA, 27–30 June 2016; pp. 770–778.
91. Long, J.; Shelhamer, E.; Darrell, T. Fully convolutional networks for semantic segmentation. In Proceedings of the 2015 IEEE Conference on Computer Vision and Pattern Recognition, Boston, MA, USA, 7–12 June 2015; pp. 3431–3440.
92. Louis, D.N.; Perry, A.; Reifenberger, G.; Von Deimling, A.; Figarella-Branger, D.; Cavenee, W.K.; Ohgaki, H.; Wiestler, O.D.; Kleihues, P.; Ellison, D.W. The 2016 World Health Organization classification of tumors of the central nervous system: A summary. *Acta Neuropathol.* **2016**, *131*, 803–820. [CrossRef] [PubMed]
93. Faust, K.; Bala, S.; Van Ommeren, R.; Portante, A.; Al Qawahmed, R.; Djuric, U.; Diamandis, P. Intelligent feature engineering and ontological mapping of brain tumour histomorphologies by deep learning. *Nat. Mach. Intell.* **2019**, *1*, 316–321. [CrossRef]
94. Roohi, A.; Faust, K.; Djuric, U.; Diamandis, P. Unsupervised machine learning in pathology: The next frontier. *Surg. Pathol. Clin.* **2020**, *13*, 349–358. [CrossRef] [PubMed]
95. Bulten, W.; Litjens, G. Unsupervised prostate cancer detection on H&E using convolutional adversarial autoencoders. *arXiv* **2018**, arXiv:1804.07098.
96. Veta, M.; Heng, Y.J.; Stathonikos, N.; Bejnordi, B.E.; Beca, F.; Wollmann, T.; Rohr, K.; Shah, M.A.; Wang, D.; Rousson, M.; et al. Predicting breast tumor proliferation from whole-slide images: The TUPAC16 challenge. *Med. Image Anal.* **2019**, *54*, 111–121. [CrossRef]
97. Koohbanani, N.A.; Jahanifar, M.; Tajadin, N.Z.; Rajpoot, N. NuClick: A deep learning framework for interactive segmentation of microscopic images. *Med. Image Anal.* **2020**, *65*, 101771. [CrossRef]
98. Xu, G.; Song, Z.; Sun, Z.; Ku, C.; Yang, Z.; Liu, C.; Wang, S.; Ma, J.; Xu, W. Camel: A weakly supervised learning framework for histopathology image segmentation. In Proceedings of the 2019 IEEE/CVF International Conference on Computer Vision, Seoul, Korea, 27 October–2 November 2019; pp. 10682–10691.
99. Huss, R.; Coupland, S.E. Software-assisted decision support in digital histopathology. *J. Pathol.* **2020**, *250*, 685–692. [CrossRef]
100. Madabhushi, A.; Lee, G. Image analysis and machine learning in digital pathology: Challenges and opportunities. *Med. Image Anal.* **2016**, *33*, 170–175. [CrossRef]
101. Hughes, A.J.; Mornin, J.D.; Biswas, S.K.; Beck, L.E.; Bauer, D.P.; Raj, A.; Bianco, S.; Gartner, Z.J. Quanti.us: A tool for rapid, flexible, crowd-based annotation of images. *Nat. Methods* **2018**, *15*, 587–590. [CrossRef]
102. López-Pérez, M.; Amgad, M.; Morales-Álvarez, P.; Ruiz, P.; Cooper, L.A.; Molina, R.; Katsaggelos, A.K. Learning from crowds in digital pathology using scalable variational Gaussian processes. *Sci. Rep.* **2021**, *11*, 11612. [CrossRef] [PubMed]
103. Colling, R.; Pitman, H.; Oien, K.; Rajpoot, N.; Macklin, P.; CM-Path AI in Histopathology Working Group; Bachtiar, V.; Booth, R.; Bryant, A.; Bull, J.; et al. Artificial intelligence in digital pathology: A roadmap to routine use in clinical practice. *J. Pathol.* **2019**, *249*, 143–150. [CrossRef] [PubMed]
104. Acs, B.; Rantalainen, M.; Hartman, J. Artificial intelligence as the next step towards precision pathology. *J. Intern. Med.* **2020**, *288*, 62–81. [CrossRef] [PubMed]

105. Khened, M.; Kori, A.; Rajkumar, H.; Krishnamurthi, G.; Srinivasan, B. A generalized deep learning framework for whole-slide image segmentation and analysis. *Sci. Rep.* **2021**, *11*, 11579. [CrossRef] [PubMed]
106. Pradhan, K.S.; Chawla, P.; Tiwari, R. HRDEL: High Ranking Deep Ensemble Learning-based Lung Cancer Diagnosis Model. *Expert Syst. Appl.* **2022**, *213*, 118956. [CrossRef]
107. Narla, A.; Kuprel, B.; Sarin, K.; Novoa, R.; Ko, J. Automated classification of skin lesions: From pixels to practice. *J. Investig. Dermatol.* **2018**, *138*, 2108–2110. [CrossRef]
108. Bera, K.; Schalper, K.A.; Rimm, D.L.; Velcheti, V.; Madabhushi, A. Artificial intelligence in digital pathology—New tools for diagnosis and precision oncology. *Nat. Rev. Clin. Oncol.* **2019**, *16*, 703–715. [CrossRef]
109. Niazi, M.K.K.; Parwani, A.V.; Gurcan, M.N. Digital pathology and artificial intelligence. *Lancet Oncol.* **2019**, *20*, e253–e261. [CrossRef]
110. Wu, Y.; Cheng, M.; Huang, S.; Pei, Z.; Zuo, Y.; Liu, J.; Yang, K.; Zhu, Q.; Zhang, J.; Hong, H.; et al. Recent Advances of Deep Learning for Computational Histopathology: Principles and Applications. *Cancers* **2022**, *14*, 1199. [CrossRef]
111. Swiderska-Chadaj, Z.; de Bel, T.; Blanchet, L.; Baidoshvili, A.; Vossen, D.; van der Laak, J.; Litjens, G. Impact of rescanning and normalization on convolutional neural network performance in multi-center, whole-slide classification of prostate cancer. *Sci. Rep.* **2020**, *10*, 14398. [CrossRef]
112. Kleppe, A.; Skrede, O.J.; De Raedt, S.; Liestøl, K.; Kerr, D.J.; Danielsen, H.E. Designing deep learning studies in cancer diagnostics. *Nat. Rev. Cancer* **2021**, *21*, 199–211. [CrossRef] [PubMed]
113. Collins, G.S.; Moons, K.G. Reporting of artificial intelligence prediction models. *Lancet* **2019**, *393*, 1577–1579. [CrossRef]
114. Kelly, C.J.; Karthikesalingam, A.; Suleyman, M.; Corrado, G.; King, D. Key challenges for delivering clinical impact with artificial intelligence. *BMC Med.* **2019**, *17*, 195. [CrossRef]
115. Rudin, C. Stop explaining black box machine learning models for high stakes decisions and use interpretable models instead. *Nat. Mach. Intell.* **2019**, *1*, 206–215. [CrossRef] [PubMed]
116. Shrikumar, A.; Greenside, P.; Kundaje, A. Learning important features through propagating activation differences. In Proceedings of the 34th International Conference on Machine Learning, Sydney, Australia, 6–11 August 2017; pp. 3145–3153.
117. Selvaraju, R.R.; Cogswell, M.; Das, A.; Vedantam, R.; Parikh, D.; Batra, D. Grad-CAM: Visual Explanations from Deep Networks via Gradient-Based Localization. In Proceedings of the 2017 IEEE International Conference on Computer Vision, Venice, Italy, 22–29 October 2017; pp. 618–626.
118. Guidotti, R.; Monreale, A.; Ruggieri, S.; Turini, F.; Giannotti, F.; Pedreschi, D. A survey of methods for explaining black box models. *ACM Comput. Surv.* **2018**, *51*, 93. [CrossRef]
119. Scherer, M.U. Regulating artificial intelligence systems: Risks, challenges, competencies, and strategies. *Harv. JL Tech.* **2015**, *29*, 353. [CrossRef]
120. House, W. Guidance for regulation of artificial intelligence applications. *Memo. Heads Exec. Dep. Agencies* **2020**.
121. Commission, E. *On Artificial Intelligence—A European Approach to Excellence and Trust*; European Commission Luxembourg: Luxembourg, 2020.
122. Pita, E.V. UNESCO and the Governance of Artificial Intelligence in a Globalized World. The Need for a New Legal Architecture. *Ann. Fac. Der. U. Extremad.* **2021**, *37*, 273.
123. Allen, T.C. Regulating Artificial Intelligence for a Successful Pathology Future. *Arch. Pathol. Lab. Med.* **2019**, *143*, 1175–1179. [CrossRef]
124. Guihot, M.; Matthew, A.F.; Suzor, N.P. Nudging robots: Innovative solutions to regulate artificial intelligence. *Vand. J. Ent. Tech. L.* **2017**, *20*, 385.
125. von Eschenbach, W.J. Transparency and the black box problem: Why we do not trust AI. *Philos. Technol.* **2021**, *34*, 1607–1622. [CrossRef]
126. Parwani, A.V. Next generation diagnostic pathology: Use of digital pathology and artificial intelligence tools to augment a pathological diagnosis. *Diagn. Pathol.* **2019**, *14*, 138. [CrossRef] [PubMed]
127. Tosun, A.B.; Pullara, F.; Becich, M.J.; Taylor, D.; Fine, J.L.; Chennubhotla, S.C. Explainable AI (xAI) for anatomic pathology. *Adv. Anat. Pathol.* **2020**, *27*, 241–250. [CrossRef] [PubMed]
128. Krajna, A.; Kovac, M.; Brcic, M.; Šarčević, A. Explainable Artificial Intelligence: An Updated Perspective. In Proceedings of the 2022 45th Jubilee International Convention on Information, Communication and Electronic Technology (MIPRO), Opatija, Croatia, 23–27 May 2022; pp. 859–864.
129. Binder, A.; Bockmayr, M.; Hägele, M.; Wienert, S.; Heim, D.; Hellweg, K.; Ishii, M.; Stenzinger, A.; Hocke, A.; Denkert, C.; et al. Morphological and molecular breast cancer profiling through explainable machine learning. *Nat. Mach. Intell.* **2021**, *3*, 355–366. [CrossRef]
130. Lage, I.; Chen, E.; He, J.; Narayanan, M.; Kim, B.; Gershman, S.; Doshi-Velez, F. An evaluation of the human-interpretability of explanation. *arXiv* **2019**, arXiv:1902.00006.
131. Sixt, L.; Granz, M.; Landgraf, T. When explanations lie: Why modified BP attribution fails. *arXiv* **2019**, arXiv:1912.09818.
132. Holzinger, A.; Malle, B.; Saranti, A.; Pfeifer, B. Towards multi-modal causability with graph neural networks enabling information fusion for explainable AI. *Inf. Fusion* **2021**, *71*, 28–37. [CrossRef]
133. Zhang, J.; Chen, J.; Xuan, Q. Link Prediction Based on Hyper-Substructure Network. In *Graph Data Mining*; Springer: Berlin/Heidelberg, Germany, 2021; pp. 29–48.

134. Adnan, M.; Kalra, S.; Tizhoosh, H.R. Representation learning of histopathology images using graph neural networks. In Proceedings of the 2020 IEEE/CVF Conference on Computer Vision and Pattern Recognition Workshops, Seattle, WA, USA, 14–19 June 2020; pp. 988–989.
135. Koromina, M.; Pandi, M.T.; Patrinos, G.P. Rethinking drug repositioning and development with artificial intelligence, machine learning, and omics. *OMICS J. Integr. Biol.* **2019**, *23*, 539–548. [CrossRef]